A Reference Grammar of Kotiria (Wanano)

STUDIES IN
THE NATIVE LANGUAGES
OF THE AMERICAS

Editors
Douglas R. Parks
Raymond J. DeMallie

Recipient of the Mary R. Haas Award
Presented by
The Society for the Study of the Indigenous Languages of the Americas

A REFERENCE GRAMMAR OF KOTIRIA (WANANO)

Kristine Stenzel

University of Nebraska Press
Lincoln and London

In cooperation with the American Indian Studies Research Institute, Indiana University, Bloomington

© 2013 by the Board of Regents of the University of Nebraska
All rights reserved
Manufactured in the United States of America

This book is published as part of the Recovering Languages and Literacies of the Americas initiative. Recovering Languages and Literacies is generously supported by the Andrew W. Mellon Foundation.

Library of Congress Control Number: 2013937811

For my husband Jorge
and my son Julian

Contents

List of tables	xiii
List of figures and maps	xv
Preface	xvi
Acknowledgments	xvii
Abbreviations used in glosses	xix
Abbreviations for example sources	xxi
Format of examples and texts	xxii
1 The Kotiria and their language	1
1.1 Linguistic diversity in Brazilian Amazonia	1
1.2 The Tukanoan language family	3
1.2.1 Research on Tukanoan languages	6
1.2.2 Research on the Kotiria language	8
1.3 The Kotiria: demographics and geographic location	8
1.4 A brief history of contact	13
1.5 Linguistic exogamy, multilingualism, and the Vaupés social system	15
1.6 The specter of language loss and the development of language maintenance programs	18
2 Phonology	22
2.1 Phonemic inventory	22
2.2 Consonants	23
2.2.1 Plosives: voiced, voiceless unaspirated, voiceless aspirated	24
2.2.2 The relation of [d] and [r]	30
2.2.3 The affricate /ʧ/	32
2.2.4 Allophones of oral consonants	34
2.3 Vowels and vowel harmony	36
2.4 The syllable	38
2.4.1 Shapes, constraints, and association rules	38
2.4.2 Moras in prosodic structure	39
2.5 Suprasegmental nasalization	42
2.5.1 Nasal allophones and derivations of [+nasal] morphemes	43
2.5.2 Spreading processes	45
2.6 Suprasegmental tone	48
2.6.1 Tone or pitch accent?	48
2.6.2 Derivations and spreading processes	50
2.6.3 Monomoraic roots and tonal melodies	55

2.7		Suprasegmental glottalization	59
	2.7.1	Segment or suprasegment?	60
	2.7.2	Association and derivations	65
	2.7.3	Glottalization and preaspiration	67
2.8		Cooccurrence of suprasegmentals	69
2.9		Other commonly occurring phonological processes	69
	2.9.1	Fusion of like vowels	69
	2.9.2	Vowel devoicing	71
2.10		The Kotiria practical orthography	72

3 Words — 76

3.1		Basic morphological processes	76
3.2		Roots: noun, verb, and particle	78
3.3		Verbal words	81
	3.3.1	Finite, simple nonfinite, and nominalized nonfinite verbs	81
	3.3.2	Derived verbs	83
3.4		Nominal words	86
	3.4.1	Simple nouns	86
	3.4.2	Derived nouns	86
3.5		Words expressing adjectival and adverbial notions	87
3.6		Properties of roots, suffixes, and clitics	89
3.7		Phonological and grammatical words	93
3.8		Some considerations on the orthographic word	96

4 Noun classes and noun formation — 98

4.1		Noun classes in Eastern Tukanoan languages	98
4.2		Animates	101
	4.2.1	Nouns with human referents: gender and number	102
	4.2.2	Nonhuman individual animates	107
	4.2.3	Inherently collective animates	112
	4.2.4	Linguistic coding and the hierarchy of animates	113
4.3		Inanimates	113
	4.3.1	Mass nouns	114
	4.3.2	Countable nouns: unsuffixed nouns and body part nouns with +*ro*	116
	4.3.3	Inanimates with classifiers	119
4.4		General properties of Kotiria noun classification	128
4.5		Derived nouns	130
	4.5.1	Nominals derived from verbal roots	130
	4.5.2	Nominals derived from particles	136
4.6		The negative nominal ~*de*	140
4.7		Pronouns	142
	4.7.1	Deictic forms: first and second person	142
	4.7.2	Anaphoric forms: third person	143
	4.7.3	Anaphoric forms for inanimates	145
4.8		Noun compounds	150

5 Nominal morphology — 152

5.1 Additional morphemes coding lexical information — 152
    5.1.1 Evaluatives: -~ka 'diminutive', -wɨ'rɨ 'augmentative' — 153
    5.1.2 Other qualifying morphemes: -khɨ 'additive', -dita 'solitary', and (-)waro 'emphatic' — 156

5.2 Morphemes coding grammatical information — 158
    5.2.1 Locatives +i, -pɨ — 159
    5.2.2 Object +re — 161
    5.2.3 Comitative-instrumental =~be're — 163

5.3 Morphemes coding discourse-level information — 164
    5.3.1 Referential =ta — 164
    5.3.2 Contrastive subject -se'e — 165
    5.3.3 Emphatic ~hi'da — 167
    5.3.4 Restrictions and interesting combinations — 167

5.4 Review of morphophonological processes — 169
    5.4.1 Nasalization, tone specification, and spreading — 169
    5.4.2 Status of morphemes — 171

6 Noun phrases — 173

6.1 Constituent order in noun phrases — 173
6.2 Determiners — 175
6.3 Quantifiers — 177
    6.3.1 Numbers — 177
    6.3.2 Other quantifiers — 183
6.4 Possession — 185
    6.4.1 Pronominal possession — 186
    6.4.2 Possession by a noun or NP — 187
    6.4.3 Locative possession: ~baka — 188
    6.4.4 The possessive root ya — 189
6.5 Interrogatives — 191
    6.5.1 Interrogative nominals — 191
    6.5.2 Interrogative modifiers — 193
6.6 Descriptive (adjectival) nominalizations — 194
6.7 Multiple modifiers — 195

7 Verbal semantics and serialization processes — 198

7.1 Stative verbs — 198
    7.1.1 Copula: hi — 199
    7.1.2 Nonexistence: ~badia — 202
    7.1.3 Stative possession: khɨa — 203
    7.1.4 Position — 204
    7.1.5 Adjectival statives — 206
7.2 Activity verbs — 206
7.3 Motion verbs — 209
    7.3.1 Basic motion verbs: wa'a 'go' and ta 'come' — 209

	7.3.2	Directional verbs	213
	7.3.3	Relational motion verbs	214
	7.3.4	Verbs of placement	215
7.4	Verbs of sensory perception and mental processes		216
7.5	Common verb serialization constructions		221
	7.5.1	Motion verbs coding direction or manner	223
	7.5.2	Aspectual functions of noninitial verbs	229
	7.5.3	Other noninitial roots coding aspect	234
	7.5.4	Modal functions of noninitial verbs	238
	7.5.5	Other types of serialized constructions	241
7.6	Verbs with incorporated nouns		242

8 Nonroot stem morphemes in the verb — 244

8.1	Overview of the morphology of finite verbs		244
8.2	Negation: *-era*		246
8.3	Intensification and emphasis: *-yʉ'dʉ*		250
8.4	Modality		251
	8.4.1	Dubitative: *-bo*	252
	8.4.2	Frustrative: *-~ba*	252
	8.4.3	Favoritive: *-pe*	253
	8.4.4	Other modal morphemes	254
8.5	Imperfective and perfective aspect		255
	8.5.1	Imperfective aspect: *-ati*	256
	8.5.2	Perfective aspect: *-wa'a*	258
	8.5.3	The function of the suffix *+a*	263
8.6	Order of verbal morphemes and degree of grammaticalization		264

9 Clause modality — 268

9.1	Evidentials: overview and previous analyses		269
9.2	A revised analysis of Kotiria evidentials		271
	9.2.1	Nonfirsthand evidence: hearsay	273
	9.2.2	Visual external firsthand evidence	274
	9.2.3	Nonvisual external firsthand evidence	282
	9.2.4	External firsthand evidence: inference	284
	9.2.5	Internal firsthand evidence: assertion	285
	9.2.6	Hierarchization of evidential categories and the notion of deixis	293
	9.2.7	Kotiria evidentials and epistemic values	295
	9.2.8	Further remarks on the evidential categories	297
9.3	Irrealis		298
	9.3.1	Prediction and intention	299
	9.3.2	Negative irrealis	301
9.4	Interrogatives		303
	9.4.1	Aspectual distinctions in questions	304
	9.4.2	Questions involving supposition or speculation	305
9.5	Directive modality		307

9.5.1		Imperative: +*ga*	307
9.5.2		Permissive: -~*ba*	308
9.5.3		Admonitive -*ri* and adversative -*kuru*	309
9.5.4		Exhortatives: (~*sa* . . .) ~(*hi'*)*da*	310
9.5.5		Reporting requests, demands, and warnings	311

10 Clause structure — 313

- 10.1 Subject agreement — 314
  - 10.1.1 Subject agreement morphology on realis finite verbs — 315
  - 10.1.2 Subject agreement morphology in other constructions — 316
  - 10.1.3 Adverbial clauses without subject agreement — 319
- 10.2 Intransitives — 321
- 10.3 Transitives — 321
  - 10.3.1 Objects with and without +*re* — 323
  - 10.3.2 More on the semantics of +*re* — 326
- 10.4 Ditransitives — 336
- 10.5 Verbs with locative arguments — 337
  - 10.5.1 Stative verbs with locative arguments — 337
  - 10.5.2 Motion verbs with locative arguments — 340
  - 10.5.3 Another verb with object and oblique arguments — 343
- 10.6 Valency-changing roots — 344
- 10.7 Adjuncts — 345
  - 10.7.1 Locative — 346
  - 10.7.2 Temporal expressions and adjuncts — 348
  - 10.7.3 Comitative — 353
  - 10.7.4 Instrumental — 354
  - 10.7.5 The status of =~*be're* — 355

11 Complex sentences — 357

- 11.1 Order of constituents in clauses — 357
- 11.2 Preverbal modification — 358
  - 11.2.1 Adverbials: quality and evaluation — 358
  - 11.2.2 Adverbials: manner — 359
  - 11.2.3 Adverbials: ~*hi'da* 'emphatic' — 361
  - 11.2.4 Adverbials: similarity, comparison, and contrast — 363
  - 11.2.5 Adverbials: interrogative — 366
- 11.3 Verbs with clausal complements — 368
  - 11.3.1 Modal with ~*kha'ba* — 368
  - 11.3.2 Progressive with ~*di* — 369
  - 11.3.3 Purposive with *wa'a* and *ta* — 371
- 11.4 Quoted speech constructions — 371
- 11.5 Perfective and causative constructions with *yoa* — 373
- 11.6 Other clauses with sequences of verbs — 376
- 11.7 A summary comparison of multiple-verb constructions — 379

Appendix 1: Texts	380
Oral narratives	380
Written texts from *Let's Study in Kotiria*	450
Appendix 2: Vocabulary	457
References	487
Index	499

List of tables

Table 1.1	Sorensen's classification of Eastern Tukanoan	5
Table 1.2	Classification of the Tukanoan family according to Waltz and Wheeler (1972) and Barnes (1999)	5
Table 1.3	Classification of Tukanoan according to Ramirez	5
Table 2.1	Kotiria consonant phonemes	22
Table 2.2	Kotiria vowel phonemes	23
Table 2.3	Cognates of Kotiria words with initial unaspirated voiceless plosives	28
Table 2.4	Disyllabic roots with word-initial voiceless plosives	29
Table 2.5	*CV* roots with word-initial voiceless plosives	29
Table 2.6	Kotiria aspiration from deletion of vowel before /h/	30
Table 2.7	Correspondences between Kotiria [tʃ] and Eastern Tukanoan [k]	33
Table 2.8	Further examples of loss of a left-edge syllable in Kotiria	41
Table 2.9	Kotiria *CV* roots with *CVV* cognates in Wa'ikhana	42
Table 2.10	Some minimal pairs for nasalization	43
Table 2.11	Kotiria [Ønasal] morphemes	46
Table 2.12	Monomoraic roots with initial L tone	59
Table 2.13	Minimal pairs for glottalization in *CVCV* roots	59
Table 2.14	Minimal pairs for glottalization in *CVV* roots	59
Table 2.15	Cognates of Kotiria words with glottal stop coda	61
Table 2.16	Words with LH or LHL melody and no glottal stop	64
Table 2.17	Contrast of glottal stop and preaspiration	67
Table 2.18	Contrasts of suprasegmentals within roots	68
Table 2.19	Characteristics of suprasegmentals	70
Table 3.1	Distribution of morphemes per word in two Kotiria texts	78
Table 3.2	Root shapes	79
Table 3.3	Properties of morphemes	90
Table 4.1	Animate nouns	102
Table 4.2	Inanimates	114
Table 4.3	Personal pronouns	142
Table 5.1	Phonological specification of nominal morphemes	172
Table 6.1	Possessive proclitics	186

Table 9.1	Clause modality	269
Table 9.2	Kotiria evidentials according to Waltz and Waltz	271
Table 9.3	Subject agreement suffixes for irrealis and nominalized verbs	300
Table 10.1	Arguments and adjuncts	314
Table 10.2	Subject agreement suffixes for irrealis and nominalized verbs	316
Table 10.3	Word order and argument coding in Eastern Tukanoan languages	334
Table 10.4	Marking of adjuncts	346
Table 11.1.	Properties of multiple-verb constructions	379

List of figures and maps

Figures

Figure 3.1	Relations between phonological word and grammatical word in the surface form of verbal words	95
Figure 3.2	Relations between phonological word and grammatical word in the surface form of nominal words	95
Figure 3.3	Relations between phonological word and grammatical word in the surface form of particle-root nominal words	96
Figure 4.1	Major features of Kotiria noun classes	101
Figure 4.2	Hierarchy of animates	113
Figure 4.3	The noun classification continuum	129
Figure 5.1	Nominal morphology	152
Figure 6.1	Morphology of number modifying constructions	182
Figure 6.2	Order of modifiers within the NP	196
Figure 8.1	Morphology of finite verbs	245
Figure 8.2	Relatively lexical vs. relatively grammatical properties of noninitial morphemes in the verb	265
Figure 9.1	Revised analysis of Kotiria evidentials	272
Figure 9.2	Alignment and mismatches of aspect in evidentials and events or states	280
Figure 9.3	Interrogative clause modality compared with statement clause modality	303
Figure 11.1	A sample form from a Kotiria linguistic census	359

Maps

Map 1.1 Location of ethnic-linguistic groups in the Vaupés region   9

Preface

This grammar is the result of ten years of ongoing study of the Kotiria language and practical work on language issues with the Kotiria people. It is a slightly expanded and substantially reorganized version of my dissertation, completed in 2004 at the University of Colorado, and is based on a corpus of primary data that includes an extensive lexical database and dozens of recorded narratives (seven of which are given with full interlinear analysis in appendix 1), elicited words and sentences, texts written by the Kotiria themselves (five of these are included in appendix 1), and observations during numerous field trips to Kotiria communities from 2000 on. The analysis both builds on previous research and suggests new hypotheses and avenues of investigation.

The portrait of the language offered here is not exhaustive; although I have tried to present an overview that is as comprehensive as possible, there are certainly many issues yet to be investigated. It is nevertheless my hope that this grammar will be a useful tool not only for researchers of Tukanoan and other Amazonian languages, but also for typologists in general, as well as theoretical linguists who look to descriptions of languages as an essential source of primary language data. With this in mind, I have adopted a basic functional-typological framework, and have tried to offer ample exemplification and argumentation for each hypothesis or affirmation presented.

Acknowledgments

This research would not have been possible without generous aid from a number of organizations and individuals in the United States and in Brazil whom I would like to gratefully acknowledge. First, I would like to reiterate my thanks to the University of Colorado department of linguistics and to Drs. Jule Gomez de Garcia, David Rood, Zygmunt Frajzyngier, and Barbara Fox for their guidance and support during the early years of my work on Kotiria. Thanks are also due to a number of other scholars whose generous exchange of ideas and encouragement over the years have greatly contributed to this work, in particular Elsa Gomez-Imbert, Patience Epps, Bruna Franchetto, Janet Chernela, Henri Ramirez, Alexandra Aikhenvald, Denny Moore, and Nathan and Carolyn Waltz. Additionally, heartfelt appreciation goes to Paul Kroeber for his excellent editorial guidance and to Renata Alves of the Instituto Socioambiental for her design of the map. Moreover, I am sincerely grateful to the Instituto Socioambiental, to the staff of their Rio Negro Program in São Gabriel da Cachoeira, and to my colleagues Marta Azevedo and Lúcia Alberta Andrade for their assistance and comradeship in the field.

I do not even know how to begin to thank the Kotiria people, who have not only shared their language with me, but have also welcomed me into their communities and taken care of me with great skill, sincere affection, and much good humor. I am particularly indebted to my primary consultants: Mateus Cabral, Agostinho Ferraz, Ricardo Cabral, Emília Cabral, and Domingos Cabral; professors and students of the Kotiria school: José Galves Trindade, Elizabete Teixeira, Fausto Ferraz, Mariano Gama Alvarez, Silvestre Galvão Trindade, and Ediberto Almeida Teixeira, among others; the residents of the Kotiria communities of Carurú Cachoeira, Arara Cachoeira, Matapí, Jutica, Ilha de Inambú, and Jacaré, as well as my Kotiria friends in Iauaretê—Engênio Trindade and his wife Elsa, Mario Figueiredo and his wife Leopoldina—for their goodwill and hospitality.

Finally, over the years, my research with the Kotiria has received essential financial, institutional, and logistic support from a number of different sources whom I sincerely thank: the University of Colorado Graduate School, the Endangered Languages Fund, the Wenner-Gren Foundation, the National Science Foundation and the National Endowment for the Humanities (dissertation grant 0211206 and DEL fellowship 52150-05), the Brazilian National Counsel for Scientific and Technological

Development, the Hans Rausing Endangered Languages Project (School of Oriental and African Studies, University of London, grant MDP-0155), the Instituto Socioambiental (in São Paulo and São Gabriel da Cachoeira), the Museu Paraense Emílio Goeldi, and the Graduate Program in Social Anthropology and the Department of Linguistics and Philology of the Federal University of Rio de Janeiro.

Abbreviations used in glosses

Section numbers (with §) indicate where the principal discussions of grammatical categories can be found (these are not necessarily the only places where a given category is discussed).

1/2/3	first/second/third person (pronouns, §4.7, §6.4.1; verb inflection, §9.2, §9.3.1, §10.1)
ADD	additive (§5.1.2)
ADMON	admonitive (§9.5.3)
ADVERS	adversative (§9.5.3)
AFFEC	affected (§8.5.3)
ALT	alternate (§4.5.2, §6.2)
ANPH	anaphoric (§§4.7.2–4.7.3, §6.2)
ASSERT	assertion (§9.2.5)
AUG	augmentative (§5.1.1)
[B]	word borrowed from Portuguese
BEN	benefactive (§10.6)
CLS	classifier (§4.3.3)
COLL	collective (§7.5.3)
COM	comitative (§5.2.3, §10.7)
COMPL	completive (§7.5.3)
COMP	comparative (§11.2.4)
CONTR	contrastive subject (§5.3.2, §11.2.4)
COP	copula (§7.1.1)
CQUANT	quantifier of count noun (§6.3.2, §6.5.2)
DEF	definite (§4.7.3)
DEIC	deictic (§4.5.2, §6.2)
DEM	demonstrative (§4.5.2, §6.2)
DESID	desiderative (§7.4, §7.5.4)
DIFF	diffuse (§9.2.1)
DIM	diminutive (§5.1.1)
DIST	distal (demonstrative or deictic, §4.5.2; aspect, §7.5.2)
DUB	dubitative (§8.4.1)
EMPATH	empathetic (§8.4.4)
EMPH	emphatic (§5.1.2, §5.3.3, §11.2.3)
EXC	exclusive (§4.7, §6.4.1)
EXRT	exhortative (§9.5.4)
FAV	favoritive (§8.4.1)
FEM	feminine (§4.2.1, §9.3, §10.1.2)
FRUS	frustrative (§8.4.2)
HSAY	hearsay (§9.2)
IMPER	imperative (§9.5.1)

IMPERF	imperfective (§8.5.1, §9.2, §9.4.1)
INC	inclusive (§4.7, §6.4.1)
IND	individualizer (§4.2.3)
INFER	inference (§9.2.4)
INST	instrumental (§5.2.3, §10.7)
INT	interrogative (verb inflection) (§9..4)
INTENS	intensifier (§8.3)
INTENT	intention (§9.3.1)
IRR	irrealis (§9.3.2)
LOC	locative (§5.2.1, §10.5, §10.7)
MASC	masculine (§4.2.1, §9.3, §10.1.2)
MOV	movement (motion verb) (§7.3, §7.5.1)
MQUANT	quantifier of mass noun (§6.5.2)
NEG	negative (nominal, §4.6; negation of verb, §8.2, §9.3.2)
NEG.ASSESS	negative assessment (§8.4.4)
NOM	nominalizer (§4.5.1)
NONVIS	nonvisual (§9.2.3)
OBJ	object (§5.2.2, §§10.3–10.5, §10.7.2)
PERF	perfective (§8.5.2, §9.2, §9.4.1)
PERMIS	permissive (§9.5.2)
PL	plural (§4.2, §4.3.2)
POSS	possessive (§6.4.1)
PREDICT	prediction (§9.3.1)
PROG	progressive (§11.3.2)
PROX	proximal (§4.5.2)
QUOT	quotative (§9.2)
RECIP	reciprocal (§10.6)
REF	referential (§5.3.1)
REM	remote (§4.5.2)
SG	singular (§4.2)
SOL	solitary (§5.1.2)
SUPP	supposition (§9.4.2)
SW.REF	switch reference (§10.1.3)
TERM	terminative (§8.4.4)
VBZ	verbalizer (§3.3.2)
VIS	visual (§9.2.2)
WH	interrogative word (§6.5, §11.2.5)

Abbreviations for example sources

Examples from the texts in appendix 1 are indicated by "A" followed by the text number and sentence number; thus "[A7.14]" indicates that the example comes from sentence 14 of text 7.

Examples from other texts not included in appendix 1 are identified by the abbreviated codes in the list below. (Sentence numbering is not given; some of these texts are not yet publicly available, and numbering could change before they appear.)

1. Oral narratives and conversations:

Manioc	"Foods Made From Manioc": an explanation of how manioc, a staple of the Kotiria diet, is processed and of the different foods made from it
Ancestors	"How Our Ancestors Got Women": a narrative recounting an unsuccessful "bride-napping" trip to a nearby village undertaken by a group of young men
Baskets	"A Conversation about Baskets": a conversation in which three women examine and comment on some baskets and other woven items

2. Written texts from the book *Let's Study in Kotiria: Kotiria Animal Stories* (see appendix 1 for a general description of this book and how it was written):

LSK: Agoutis
LSK: Anteaters
LSK: Armadillos
LSK: Bananas
LSK: Buriti
LSK: Cows
LSK: Deer
LSK: Dogs
LSK: Firewood
LSK: Fish
LSK: Frogs
LSK: Limes
LSK: Parrots
LSK: Snakes
LSK: Squirrels
LSK: Tails
LSK: Toucans
LSK: Turtles
LSK: Wasps

Format of examples and texts

Most examples follow the four-line format in (1). The first line gives the utterance using the orthography currently employed by the Kotiria with whom I have been working. (See §1.6 for information on the Kotiria school and the current state of discussions on orthography development, and §2.10 for an explanation of the practical orthography.) In the second line, words are divided into morphemes and are written in an orthography that is closer to the basic phonological form of morphemes and that also includes tone marking (with acute accent marking high tone). The third line gives morpheme-by-morpheme glosses of the Kotiria forms. The fourth line provides a free translation in English. (Portuguese words occasionally appear when no exact English equivalent for a Kotiria term is available.)

(1) *yɨ'ɨ Mo mahkariropɨ hiha*
    yɨ'ɨ ~bó ~bakánri+ro-pɨ hí-ha
    1SG Mõ village+NOM+SG-LOC COP-VIS.IMPERF.1
    'I am from Mõ (the village of Carurú Cachoeira).'

The texts in appendix 1 follow essentially the same format.

1 The Kotiria and their language

This chapter introduces the Kotiria[1] people, their language, and the sociolinguistic context in which it is spoken. An overview of linguistic diversity in Amazonia, of Kotiria's place within the Tukanoan language family,[2] and of the history of research is presented in §§1.1–1.2. Kotiria demography, location, and contact history are sketched in §§1.3–1.4. Section 1.5 outlines important features of the Vaupés social system, focusing on linguistic exogamy, multilingualism, and language contact, and §1.6 surveys current language maintenance and documentation efforts.

1.1 Linguistic diversity in Brazilian Amazonia

The Amazonian basin, covering parts of Peru, Bolivia, Ecuador, Venezuela, Colombia, and Brazil, is one of the world's most linguistically diverse regions (for details, see the articles in UNESCO 2006). Currently, it is within the Brazilian portion of the basin, known officially as "Amazônia Legal"[3] (henceforth "Brazilian Amazonia"), that

---

[1] During the eight years I have worked with this language community, there has been a change in their attitude towards the name "Wanano," by which the group is generally known to the outside world. There are, in fact, several versions of this name—Wanano, Guanano, and Uanano—that appear alternately in the literature; however, it is name that has no meaning in their own language, nor does anyone seem to know its origin or meaning in any other language. It is a name given by unknown outsiders and its use has been called into question by village leaders and the directors, teachers, and students of the indigenous school. In 2006, the group publicly adopted the policy of using exclusively their own traditional name *Kotiria* 'water people' to refer to themselves and to their language and have requested that the outsiders working with them do the same. Indeed, other groups throughout the region have made similar requests, among them the Wa'ikhana (also known in the region as Piratapuyo), with whom I also work. Such decisions alongside other expressions of pride and self-determination reflect the increasing empowerment of local groups and strengthening of long-repressed self-esteem.

[2] Both the terms "Tukano" and "Tukanoan" are used in the literature to refer to the language family. For clarity in this work, I use "Tukano" to refer to the language and "Tukanoan" to refer to the language family as a whole.

[3] "Legal Amazonia" includes all the states of Brazil's northern region: Acre, Amazonas, Amapá, Pará, Rondônia, Roraima, and Tocantins, as well as the central-west state of Mato Grosso, and the portion of the northeastern state of Maranhão lying west of the forty-fourth meridian. This macroregion shares borders with Bolivia, Peru, Colombia, Venezuela, Guyana, Surinam, and French Guiana, and covers

we find both the highest concentration of indigenous people and the greatest density of languages within this vast rainforest: over 140 languages, belonging to some forty different families (Moore 2006).[4] There are moreover, two creole languages, seven languages classified as isolates, and an estimated forty-five to sixty indigenous groups with whom there is still little or no contact, and about whose languages virtually nothing is known.

In the 2010 national census,[5] the total population of Brazil figures at slightly under 191,000,000, and the indigenous population is listed as approximately 818,000, an increase of 11.4 percent over the decade.[6] Nonetheless, although the indigenous population of Brazil has grown steadily over the past twenty-five years, it still represents only 4 percent of the total population.

Thus, Brazil's total indigenous population is proportionately quite small, and the sizes of individual indigenous groups vary greatly—Moore and Gabas (2006) estimate that only 15 percent of the groups have more than a thousand speakers. Ten percent have between 501 and 1,000, 18 percent have 251 to 500, 25 percent have 101 to 250, 8 percent have 51 to 100, and 24 percent have 50 or fewer. The average population size of indigenous groups in Brazil is less than two hundred speakers (Leite and Franchetto 2006). These statistics point to a serious state of endangerment for virtually all of the indigenous languages spoken in Brazilian Amazonia; indeed, it is predicted that, even with current growing efforts to protect indigenous languages and oral

approximately 5,217,423 km^2, corresponding to approximately 61 percent of Brazilian territory. Together, the states of Amazonas and Pará represent more than 55 percent of this total.

[4] Both numbers of groups and numbers of languages vary in different sources. The Instituto Socioambiental (Socioenvironmental Institute, ISA), the foremost source of information on Brazil's indigenous population, lists a total of 225 ethnic indigenous groups within Brazilian territory (Ricardo and Ricardo 2006), while the Conselho Indigenista Missionário (Indian Missionary Council) lists 241 groups on their website (http://www.cimi.org.br/). As for the total number of indigenous languages, the generally cited figure for all of Brazil is 170 to 180 (Rodrigues 2005). The slightly more conservative figure cited here corresponds to the more rigorous linguistic, rather than ethnic or political, criteria used as a basis for classification by Moore (2006).

[5] This information is from the website of the Instituto Brasileiro de Geografia e Estatística (Brazilian Institute of Geography and Statistics); see http://www.ibge.gov.br/censo2010/resultados_do_censo2010.php.

[6] Sources such as Franchetto (2005) and the ISA website, however, indicate the indigenous population to be in the 380,000–450,000 range. These differences are due to use of different classificatory criteria, the National Census figure being solely based on a question on the census form that calls for self-classification as to "Color/Race," the choices being "White," "Black," "Yellow," "Mixed [*Pardo*]," or "Indian," while the sources showing lower estimates base their count on mixed criteria including, among other factors, place of residence and use of indigenous languages.

traditions,[7] more than half of these languages will be silenced before the end of this century.

1.2 The Tukanoan language family

The languages of the Tukanoan family are spoken in northwestern Amazonia, including areas of Brazil, Colombia, Ecuador, and Peru. The Western branch consists of four language groups with a total population of around four thousand: the Colombian Koreguaje are the largest group (totaling 1,745); the Secoya and Siona, located in Colombia and Ecuador, have a combined population of approximately two thousand (the Colombian Siona being the larger group, numbering 1,675); and the Orejón in Peru number some four hundred.[8] Speakers of Western Tukanoan languages have little contact with speakers of Eastern Tukanoan languages, spoken in the Brazilian state of Amazonas and in the Colombian department of Vaupés. The Eastern branch is comprised of sixteen languages:[9] Bará (also known as Waimajã), Barasana, Desano, Karapana, Kotiria (also known as Wanano), Kubeo, Makuna, Pisamira, Siriano, Taiwano (also known as Eduuria), Tanimuka (also known as Retuarã), Tatuyo, Tukano, Tuyuka, Wa'ikhana (also known as Piratapuyo), and Yuruti.[10] Of these, only Desano, Koti-

---

[7] For a more thorough overview of current policies and initiatives, see Stenzel (2006).

[8] Population statistics for Colombia are from the 2005 General Census (www.dane.gov.co/censo/). Other resources consulted are Licht and Reinoso (2006), Mondragón (2006), and the Consolidación de la Amazonía website (http://www.coama.org.co/). The Colombian census also gathered information about language use, showing that Koreguaje is spoken by 80 percent of the ethnic population, while only 24 percent of the Siona population use their language.

[9] A review of the literature reveals a great deal of variation of spellings for these language names. We find, for example, Desana/Desano, Tuyuca/Tuyuka, Kubeo/Cubeo, Waimahã/Waimajã, among others. The forms adopted here reflect current tendencies in the region (e.g., a preference for use of *k* rather than *c*) and requests for self-determined denomination, as mentioned in n. 1.

[10] Classifications of Eastern Tukanoan languages vary. Sorensen's (1967) list of thirteen languages did not include Makuna, Pisamira, or Tanimuka/Retuarã. Waltz and Wheeler's (1972) classification did not include Tanimuka/Retuarã, Pisamira, Taiwano/Eduuria or Yuruti, but did include Papiwa. Malone's (1987) list included neither Taiwano/Eduuria nor Pisamira. The most recent classifications are those of Barnes (1999), which includes Tanimuka/Retuarã, Taiwano/Barasana, and Bará/Waimajã as a single language, Ramirez (1997a), which includes Waimahã as a separate language, but does not include Pisamira or Taiwano, and Gomez-Imbert and Kenstowicz (2000), the source for the sixteen languages listed here. The sixteenth edition of *Ethnologue* (Gordon and Grimes 2005) lists twenty-five languages in total. For the Eastern branch, they include Waimahã as a dialect of Bará, Pokanga as a dialect of Barasana, and Arapaso as a dialect of Tukano. They also list two extinct Eastern Tukanoan languages:

ria, Tukano, Tuyuka, Kubeo, and Wa'ikhana are spoken by populations divided between the two countries. The remainder are spoken almost exclusively in Colombia. The total population of the Eastern Tukanoan groups, in both Brazil and Colombia, is approximately twenty-six thousand (Federação das Organizações Indígenas do Rio Negro, Instituto Socioambiental 2006:42–48, and the 2005 Colombian census.). There is little reliable information as to actual numbers of speakers among the Eastern Tukanoan groups living in Brazil. However, information on language use gathered during the Colombian census of 2005 shows that among the Eastern Tukanoan populations living in Colombia, the Taiwano language is currently used by only 25 percent of the ethnic population (itself numbering only 166), and that Bará, Pisamira, and Tatuyo are spoken by less than half (42 to 45 percent) of their respective populations, while the remaining languages are used by 60 to 80 percent of their total populations. In Brazil, Tukano is undoubtedly the most widely spoken language, with over six thousand speakers. Moreover, a process of language shift to Tukano affecting the Eastern Tukanoan groups in the Vaupés subregion (most notably the Desano and Wa'ikhana) can currently be observed. This process, spurred by migration out of traditional territories and outside interference, has led to the breakdown of language transmission patterns and cultural practices among these populations (discussed further in Stenzel 2005).

Since scholarship on Tukanoan languages began, several subclassifications of Tukanoan languages have been proposed. Sorensen (1969) made no reference at all to the Western languages, but posited four subgroups of Eastern Tukanoan, as in table 1.1. (Sorensen did not label the subgroups; they are numbered in the table for convenience of reference.)

Barnes (1999), following Waltz and Wheeler (1972), proposes subgrouping for the entire family as in table 1.2. This classification, however, has been questioned by Franchetto and Gomez-Imbert, particularly in regard to the "Central" group (2003:233). They argue that there are no solid linguistic criteria to sustain a "Central" group that is, moreover, composed of the geographically southernmost (Tanimuka/ Retuarã) and northernmost (Kubeo) groups.

Based on a study of cognates (Huber and Reed 1992), Ramirez (1997a:17) establishes seven subgroups that he labels as "languages"; he refers to individual members of subgroups as "dialects" (table 1.3; the numbers correspond to his subgroups).

Yahuna, whose speakers have shifted to Makuna, and Miriti(tapuya), whose speakers have shifted to Tukano. Tanimuka is listed as a Western language.

The Kotiria and their language

TABLE 1.1. SORENSEN'S CLASSIFICATION OF EASTERN TUKANOAN

1	2	3	4
Tukano	Piratapuyo	Desano	Kubeo
Tuyuka	Wanano	Siriano	
Yuruti			
Paneroa (Barasana)			
Eduuria			
Karapana			
Tatuyo			
Barasana			

TABLE 1.2. CLASSIFICATION OF THE TUKANOAN FAMILY ACCORDING TO WALTZ AND WHEELER (1972) AND BARNES (1999)

WESTERN NORTH	WESTERN SOUTH	CENTRAL	EASTERN NORTH	EASTERN CENTRAL	EASTERN SOUTH
Orejón	Koreguaje	Kubeo	Piratapuyo	Bará/ Waimahã	Barasana/ Taiwano
	Secoya	Tanimuka/	Tukano	Tatuyo	Makuna
	Siona	Retuarã	Wanano	Karapana	
				Tuyuka	
				Desano	
				Yuruti	
				Siriano	

TABLE 1.3. CLASSIFICATION OF TUKANOAN ACCORDING TO RAMIREZ

WESTERN	CENTRAL	EASTERN				
1	2	3	4	5	6	7
Secoya	Kubeo	Tanimuka	Makuna Barasana	(a) Ye'pâ-masa/ Tukano	Desano Siriano	Wanano Piratapuyo
Koreguaje						
Orejón				(b) Waimahã		
Siona				Tuyuka		
				Bará		
				Yuruti		
				(c) Tatuyo		
				Karapana		

It is clear that more detailed descriptions of individual languages are needed before a definitive classification of the languages in the family can be established. However, the available literature does indicate that certain languages are indeed closely related, among them Kotiria and Wa'ikhana. Waltz (2002), for example, offers an analysis of some of the phonological and morphological similarities and differences between these closely related languages and the ways each has evolved from a reconstructed protolanguage.

1.2.1 Research on Tukanoan languages

Research on the languages of the Tukanoan family began to make its way into the linguistics literature in the late 1960s. Among the first analyses to appear were Sorensen's article focusing on the exogamic marriage system of the northwest Amazonian peoples and their resulting multilingualism (Sorensen 1967) and his dissertation on Tukano (Sorensen 1969). During this same period, several collections of phonological sketches of indigenous languages being studied by Summer Institute of Linguistics (SIL) linguists in Colombia were also published; among these were sketches of some of the Eastern Tukanoan languages, including Wanano/Kotiria[11] (Waltz and Waltz 1967) and Piratapuyo/Wa'ikhana, its closest sister language (Klumpp and Klumpp 1973). Shortly thereafter, pedagogical grammars of Guanano/Kotiria (Waltz 1976) and Tukano (West 1980) were published in Colombia.

Following a tradition of ethnographic observation beginning with Theodor Koch-Grünberg (1995 [originally published in 1909]) in the first decade of the twentieth century and consolidated in mid-century with works such as Goldman's (1963) study of the Kubeo, a number of excellent anthropological publications on Tukanoan groups were produced during the and 1970s and 1980s. Both Reichel-Dolmatoff (1971) and Buchillet (1983) worked with the Desano. There are superb studies of the Barasana (C. Hugh-Jones 1979; S. Hugh-Jones 1979) and the Makuna (Ärhem 1981), and an excellent analysis of linguistic exogamy in the region based on research with the Bará (Jackson 1983). During the same period, Chernela (e.g., 1983, 1989, 1993) published a number of interesting studies on aspects of Kotiria culture. In addition, Bruzzi (1977) offers insights on Vaupés culture from the Salesian missionary perspective and Ribeiro (1995) provides a fascinating overview of production and trade among all the groups. More recently, we find work on the Tuyuka (Cabalzar 2000), as well as studies focusing on the

---

[11] The Waltzes used the Spanish form of the group's name, "Guanano," in their publications up to the 1990s.

evolution of and changes in Tukanoan culture resulting from migration and interaction with outside cultures (Lasmar 2005; Andrello 2006).

The list of publications related to Tukanoan languages has grown and diversified steadily over the past two decades. There are extensive studies or reference grammars of the Eastern Tukanoan languages Barasana (Gomez-Imbert 1997a; Jones and Jones 1991), Desano (Miller 1999), Kubeo (Morse and Maxwell 1999), and Tukano (Sorensen 1969; Ramirez 1997a, 1997b), and two reconstructions of Proto-Tukanoan (Waltz and Wheeler 1972; Malone 1987). Additionally, there are articles that focus on phonological elements of particular languages (Kaye 1971; Barnes 1996; Gomez-Imbert 2001, 2005; Gomez-Imbert and Kenstowicz 2000; Stenzel 2007a) as well as studies relating to cross-linguistic typological issues such as switch-reference (Longacre 1983), noun classification (Gomez-Imbert 1982, 1996, 2007c; Barnes 1990; Derbyshire and Payne 1990; Aikhenvald 2000), evidential systems (Barnes 1984; Frajzyngier 1985; Willett 1988; Malone 1988; Gomez-Imbert 1997a, 1999a, 2003a, 2007; Aikhenvald and Dixon 1998; de Haan 1999, 2001a; Aikhenvald 2003a, 2004; Stenzel 2008), language contact phenomena (Aikhenvald 2002a; Stenzel and Gomez-Imbert 2009), and most recently, serial verb constructions (Aikhenvald 2006; Gomez-Imbert 2007a; Stenzel 2007b).

There have been several attempts to bring together some of the accumulated findings related to the Tukanoan language family, among them a chapter by Janet Barnes in Dixon and Aikhenvald's overview of Amazonian languages (1999). This chapter presents a very general overview that focuses on some of the common characteristics of languages in the family rather than on the features on which they differ. More detailed information on individual languages in the family can be found in the Instituto Caro y Cuervo's catalogue of linguistic data on the indigenous languages of Colombia (Gonzáles de Pérez and Rodríguez de Montes 2000). This immense publication includes a large section with grammatical sketches and wordlists from thirteen Eastern Tukanoan languages: Tatuyo, Karapana, Bará, Barasana, and Makuna (Gomez-Imbert and Hugh-Jones 2000), Kubeo (Ferguson et al. 2000), Pisamira (Gonzáles de Pérez 2000), Siriano (Criswell and Brandrup 2000), Tukano (Welch and West 2000), Tuyuka (Barnes and Malone 2000), Yuruti (Kinch and Kinch 2000), Wa'ikhana/Piratapuyo (Ardila 2000), and Kotiria/Wanano (Waltz and Waltz 2000). Though these sketches were actually written in the late 1980s and vary in size and detail, their publication in one volume represents an important source of cross-linguistic data on the family. Most recently, we find short overviews of the language family by Barnes (2006) and Gomez-Imbert (2011).

1.2.2 Research on the Kotiria language

The first known grammatical outline of Kotiria was written by the Salesian missionary Antônio Giacone (1967),[12] and was followed shortly thereafter by a great amount of work on the language by Nathan and Carolyn Waltz. The Waltzes worked with the Kotiria under the auspices of the Summer Institute of Linguistics in Colombia (known there as "Instituto Lingüístico de Verano") for over thirty years (1963–96). They lived for short periods in the communities of Santa Cruz and Villa Fátima, and then for twenty-six years in Jutica (*Ñapima*), where they conducted language studies and religious activities such as Bible study, hymn singing, and Bible video nights. They additionally organized courses on farming, animal husbandry, mechanics, guitar, carpentry (in a sawmill they set up), and writing. They moreover proposed an orthography and developed and distributed a number of teaching materials for use in village schools. Their publications include a translation of the New Testament (Waltz, Waltz, and Melo 1982), a pedagogical grammar (Waltz 1976a), several papers on aspects of Kotiria phonology and discourse structure (Waltz and Waltz 1967; Waltz 1976b; Waltz 1982), a volume containing a study of kinship terms, a grammatical sketch of the language, and a lengthy interlinearized text (Waltz and Waltz 1997), and the grammatical overview of the language found in the Caro y Cuervo collection (Waltz and Waltz 2000). Nathan Waltz also coauthored the only published reconstruction of Proto-Tukanoan (Waltz and Wheeler 1972). Before his death in 2005, he published an important comparative analysis of Kotiria and Wa'ikhana (Waltz 2002), and completed work on a bilingual (Wanano-Spanish) dictionary, posthumously published in Colombia (Waltz 2007).[13]

1.3 The Kotiria: demographics and geographic location

The Kotiria ethnic-linguistic group numbers some 2,000, approximately 65 percent of whom live in Colombia (1,300, according to the 2005 Colombian census) and 35 percent in Brazil (Federação das Organizações Indígenas do Rio Negro and Instituto Socioambiental 2006:43). The majority of the Kotiria population still lives in their traditional territory, covering most of the east-west stretch of the Vaupés River

---

[12] Giacone used the name "Uanano" for the language.
[13] I was very pleased to be able to help Carolyn Waltz with the distribution of the dictionary after it was published and to see how excited the Kotiria were to have access to this important resource. As they looked through the dictionary, many of the younger speakers were surprised to find examples of words and expressions that reflect differences between their speech and that of their Colombian relatives, or that have undergone change over time.

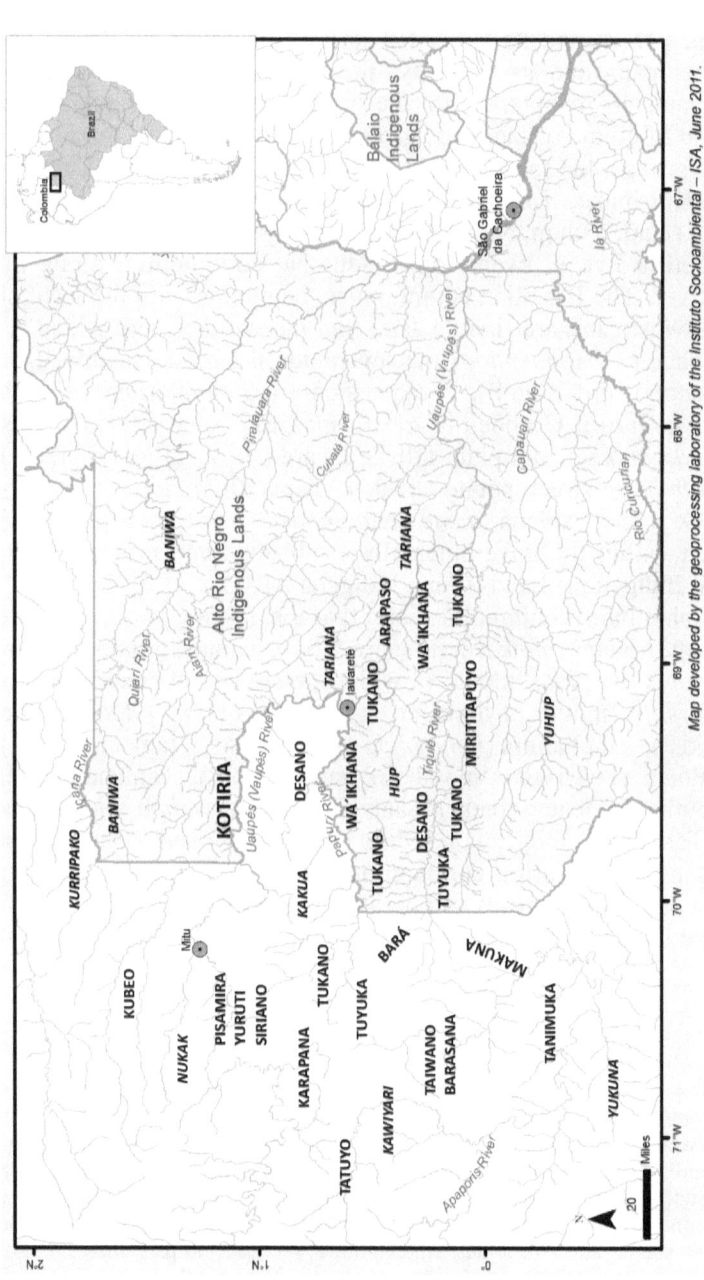

Map 1.1. Location of ethnic-linguistic groups in the Vaupés region. The shaded areas of the main map represent the Alto Rio Negro and Balaio Indigenous Lands. Names of Tukanoan groups are in roman capitals (e.g., KOTIRIA); names of non-Tukanoan groups are in italic capitals (e.g., *TARIANA*).

where it forms the border between Brazil and Colombia. Map 1.1 shows the region and locations of the major rivers—the Vaupés (Uaupés in Brazil) and its larger tributaries, including the Papurí and Tiquié; the Içana and its tributary, the Aiarí, to the north; and the Apaporis and its tributaries to the west—and the current spatial distribution of ethnic or language groups within it. Besides the Eastern Tukanoan groups, the map also shows the locations of Arawak groups (Baniwa, Kurripako, Tariana, Yukuna, Kawiyari) and groups in the Nadahup[14] (Hup, Yuhup, Nukak, Kakua) family.

The Kotiria live in twenty-one traditional communities along the Vaupés River. The Brazilian communities, beginning with the location furthest downstream, are Ilha de Japú (*mu nɨhko* 'japú bird island'),[15] Arara Cachoeira (*maha phoa* 'macaw rapids'), Ilha de Inambú (*kha nɨhko* 'inambú bird island'), Poraque Ponta (*sã'ama wahpa* 'electric eel rapids'), Carurú Cachoeira (*koama phoaye* 'noisy stream rapids/ falls' or *moa phoaye* 'salt plant falls'), Jacaré (*soma* 'alligator creek'), Jutica (*ñahpima* 'sweet potato creek'), Taína (*nihiphoto* 'mouth of boy's creek'), and Taracuá (*mene koana ñoaka* 'black ant rapids'). All are located within the governmentally established and protected Alto Rio Negro Indigenous Lands (Área Indígena ARN).

The Colombian communities are Ibacaba (*ñɨmɨ phoa*), furthest downstream, Matapí (*bɨhkakopa* 'snare falls'), Taína Colombia, Igarapé Paca (*sama nia phito* 'mouth of white spotted agouti creek'), Macuco (*phota phito* 'mouth of thorn creek'), Ananás (*sãne phoaka* 'pineapple rapids'), Vila Fátima (*boho phoa* or *wahte phoa* 'tapioca rapids'), Inambú Ponta (*kha phito* 'mouth of hawk creek'), Tamanduá (*mie phito* 'mouth of anteater creek'), Santa Cruz (*phoa wahpa* 'hairy stone rapids'), Tabatinga (*bohta phoa* 'white clay rapids') and Taiaçú (*yehse phoa* 'pig rapids'). Kotiria communities in Brazil range in size from those with only a few houses and perhaps fifteen to twenty-five inhabitants to the largest village, Carurú Cachoeira, currently with some 140

---

[14] I utilize the language family denomination suggested by Epps (2008:9) rather than the more common "Makú," which is considered to be offensive. It should be noted that while Kakua and Nukak are generally identified as belonging to this language family, their genetic relationship to other Nadahup languages—Hup, Yuhup, Dâw, and Nadëb, the latter two spoken to the south of the area shown in the map—has yet to be completely substantiated (Epps 2008:3–9).

[15] Kotiria names and translations, where known, are given in parentheses. For an explanation of the transcription of Kotiria, see chapter 2, especially §2.10. The names commonly used and that appear on maps are a mixture of Língua Geral (Nheengatú), Portuguese, or Spanish.

inhabitants.[16] The largest of the Colombian communities is Villa Fátima, with several hundred residents (primarily but not exclusively ethnic Kotiria); it is located upriver to the west in Colombia, close to the town of Mitú and within territory occupied primarily by the Kubeo.

According to two studies undertaken by the Instituto Socioambiental during the last decade, 140 Kotiria (approximately 19 percent of the total population in Brazil) reside in the mission town of Iauaretê (Andrello, Buchillet, and Azevedo 2002), and 101 Kotiria (14 percent) currently live in the city of São Gabriel da Cachoeira (Federação das Organizações Indígenas do Rio Negro and Instituto Socioambiental 2005:20). There are no statistics on the number of Kotiria residing in the town of Mitú, in Colombia.

Historical records analyzed by Wright (2005:80–81) confirm Kotiria occupation of this same territory in the 1740s, and the history of the region reconstructed through oral narratives and archeological evidence indicates a much older occupation pre-dating the Tariana migration to the Vaupés region approximately seven hundred years ago (Amorim1987; Neves 1998:158, 206; Wright 2005:13). We can see from the map that the geographic location of the Kotiria is somewhat removed from the core region occupied by other Eastern Tukanoan groups. This has kept them in close contact with two Arawak groups with whom they have formed long lasting "in-law" relations (see §1.5 below): the Tariana, whose territory on the Vaupés begins just downriver from the Kotiria (two of the three remaining Tariana-speaking communities are located there), and one of the Baniwa subgroups, who live on the Aiarí river but are easily reached via several relatively short overland trails (see Koch-Grünberg 1995, vol. 1:167–76; Neves 1988:116–17). The Kotirias' closest neighbors upriver on the Vaupés are the Eastern Tukanoan Kubeo, who have also had intense historical relations with the Baniwa (see Goldman 1963; Koch-Grünberg 1995, vol. 2:68; Gomez-Imbert 1996:446; Wright 2005:11). Interestingly, the Kubeo sib with whom the Kotiria maintain in-law relations, the *Yurémava*, is also the sib with the greatest Arawak linguistic influence; they are purported to be descendents of speakers of the Arawak language Inkacha who migrated to the Querarí river in Kubeo territory and assimilated into the local population.[17]

We can thus see that the Kotiria sociolinguistic context includes notable Arawak influence. The history of the relations between the

---

[16] The population of the village fluctuates somewhat because Carurú is the site of the Khumuno Wʉ'ʉ Kotiria Indigenous School and some families reside there only during the school year.

[17] According to Simón Valencia López, a Kubeo linguist and member of this sib (p.c. 2004). See also Valencia López (1994).

Kotiria, the Kubeo, and the Arawak Baniwa and Tariana is reflected in physical evidence, in oral and cultural traditions of many different types (Koch-Grünberg 1995, vol. 2:63; Wright 2005:89; Amorim 1987), and in a number of diffused linguistic traits (discussed in Stenzel and Gomez-Imbert 2009).

Indeed, according to one origin myth, the name *Kotiria* was given to the group's original ancestor by the Kubeo. This ancestor existed in spirit form and lived in a hollow tree. Once, this spirit took on the form of a handsome man and went to a Kubeo ceremony, where he enchanted the women and lured them back to his tree. The next day, the Kubeo men followed their trail to the tree and decided to burn it, but each time the fire was lit, water descended from the tree to douse the flames. The Kubeo thus concluded that the beings inside must be *Kotiria* 'water people'. Eventually, though, the fire took, and the spirit of the Kotiria left the tree and traveled to the great Ipanoré rapids (some two hundred kilometers downriver on the Vaupés), from which all the Tukanoan peoples are believed to originate. The great spirit *Ko'amakɨ* lived there, and he blew smoke on the spirit of the Kotiria, who then became human. After all the different groups had been created, there was a great celebration and dances were given to each group, but the Kotiria ancestor, *Muktiro*, claimed the most beautiful dances and traveled upriver to the great falls at what is now Carurú and stopped at the rock called *Khumuno Wɨ'ɨ* 'house of the shaman'. Muktiro claimed this rock and the surrounding area as home for his people.[18]

In keeping with Vaupés social norms (described in §1.5), to this day the alliances the Kotiria have maintained with the Kubeo, Tariana, and Baniwa are reflected in marriage practices. Approximately 50 percent of Kotiria men are currently married to women from one of these three groups,[19] and we can assume that all three languages historically figured in the repertoire of languages spoken by in-marrying wives in traditional Kotiria communities. Indeed, a small survey of self-evaluated language proficiency among a group of forty Kotiria men shows Baniwa and Kubeo to be among the languages most widely known, the other most commonly-spoken languages being Tukano, Desano, and Tuyuka (Stenzel 2005:20–21). It is not surprising that the Tariana lan-

---

[18] This myth was recounted by Jesuíno Trindade and was transcribed and translated by his son José Galves Trindade in November 2003. The name of the Kotiria Indigenous School, *Khumuno Wɨ'ɨ*, refers to this origin myth.

[19] Data on marriages in twelve communities was collected in September 2004 by the author and Lucia Alberta Andrade de Oliveira of the Instituto Socioambiental. Data on marriages of Kotiria men residing in Iauaretê are from Andrello, Buchillet, and Azevedo (2002). No information from the Kotiria communities upriver in Colombia is currently available.

guage no longer figures in the Kotirias' linguistic repertoire, despite the large number of marriages between Kotiria men and Tariana women (over 25 percent); it simply reflects the fact that over the past century and a half, nearly all ethnic Tariana have shifted to use of Tukano.

1.4 A brief history of contact

Although they live in a region that is extremely remote and even today difficult to reach, the indigenous peoples who live along the Upper Rio Negro and its tributaries have had various types of contact with outsiders for nearly five hundred years.[20] The first mention of the Vaupés (Uaupés) river is found in the records of the Philip von Hutten and Hernan Perez de Quesada expedition (1538–41), which followed the Orinoco river inland in search of El Dorado. The first reference to the river with "water black as ink" (the Rio Negro) is found in the 1542 records of the expedition headed by Francisco Orellana, traveling inland on the waterway now known as the Amazon. Neither of these records makes mention of the inhabitants of the region.

During the 1600s, occupation of the northern coastal areas of the continent by Europeans led to further exploration, and from the early part of the century, indigenous people from the upper Rio Negro region were captured by Carib groups invading from the north, who enslaved them and traded them to the Dutch. Throughout the 1700s, numerous Portuguese expeditions penetrated from the east, enslaving thousands of Indians and spreading diseases such as smallpox and measles, which all but wiped out entire populations.

The Jesuits arrived in the late 1700s and from their base in São Gabriel da Cachoeira established a mission at Ipanoré, midway between São Gabriel and Iauaretê, where nearly impassible rapids posed a natural impediment to further upriver exploration. Missionary activity expanded in the 1800s, first by the Capuchins, and later by other Franciscan orders, alongside official programs for the resettlement of Indians from the Içana, Vaupés, and Xié rivers to Ipanoré and other upriver missions. The practice of resettlement continued into the twentieth century, despite the Indians' resistance to policies dictating that they should leave behind their traditional lifestyle and social organization, adopt new agricultural methods, provide labor and forest products for colonists, defend territories claimed by the crown, and generally be educated in the ways of the dominant white Europeans.

---

[20] This brief summary is based on the detailed accounts of Chernela (1983) and (1993) as well as Federação das Organizações Indígenas do Rio Negro and Instituto Socioambiental (2006).

The Salesian presence in the Upper Rio Negro area dates to the second decade of the twentieth century. Between 1915 and 1945, they founded missions in São Gabriel da Cachoeira (on the Rio Negro), Taracuá and Iauaretê (both on the Vaupés), and Pari Cachoeira (on the Tiquié), strategic locations that became centers of religious, educational, and mercantile activities. They established primary schools (first to fourth grade) in smaller communities and three large boarding schools at the missions. The most promising students were sent to live at these schools from about the age of nine (fifth grade), and some went on to study at secondary or technical schools in São Gabriel. These schools still exist, though they stopped boarding students in the late 1980s. Besides their focus on education, the Salesian presence had profound effects on everyday life in Indian communities. Appointed "animators" mediated relations between the missionaries and local populations, while catechists performed weekly religious rituals in the communities and encouraged the Indians to abandon their traditional beliefs and practices, including the habit of dwelling in communal longhouses (Chernela 1993:40–41).

The first mention of the Kotiria people appears in the records of naturalist Alfred Wallace's 1852 expedition along the Uaupés. Of the ten communities he mentions, only half are presently inhabited, among them Carurú, famous for its enormous rapids, which he describes as

> greater than any we had yet seen—rushing amongst huge rocks down a descent of perhaps fifteen or twenty feet. The only way of passing this, was to pull the canoe over the dry rock, which rose considerably above the level of the water, and was rather rugged, being interrupted in places by breaks or steps two or three feet high. [Wallace 1969: 240]

In 1904–5, the German ethnologist Theodor Koch-Grünberg traveled in the region and spent several weeks among the Kotiria. He published a Kotiria wordlist (Koch-Grünberg 1913–16), and his account of his travels contains detailed descriptions of settlements such as Matapí and Carurú, whose population he then estimated at two hundred; information on the history and occupation of Kotiria territory; accounts of the relations between the Kotiria, Baniwa, and Kubeo; as well as observations of exchange ceremonies, dances, and burial practices. He made some of the first observations of the numerous petroglyphs that are found throughout the region (Koch-Grünberg 1995, vol. 2:55–67).

1.5 Linguistic exogamy, multilingualism, and the Vaupés social system

The Kotiria people participate in the well-known exogamic and multilingual Vaupés social system originally described by Sorensen (1967) and further documented in studies by linguists and anthropologists such as Chernela (1983, 1989, 1993), Jackson (1983), Gomez-Imbert (1991, 1996, 1999b), Aikhenvald (1999, 2002a), and Stenzel (2005). For the people who participate in this system, patrilineal descent and social identification with one's father's language group (whether or not this is accompanied by de facto language use, as in the case of the ethnic Tariana who have undergone a process of language shift to Tukano), form the foundation of social organization, establishing boundaries between groups and providing each individual with an unalterable identity that defines his or her relationships to all other individuals in the system.

The Vaupés social system is based on a classificatory distinction between agnates (members of one's own group, who identify equally with one's father's language and are understood to be one's "relatives") and affines (potential marriage partners, members of other linguistic-ethnic groups). Agnatic relations confer the status of classificatory sibling on all males and females of one's own generation; all males of one's father's generation are considered to be one's classificatory uncles, and so on, though the terms used to refer to kinship relations and the vocatives used in traditional address reflect complex distinctions of rank within more general categories.[21] Moreover, each group traditionally identifies certain other groups as agnates. In other words, for each group, there are other groups classified as belonging to the same phratry. Thus, even though they are speakers of different languages, members of such phratric groups are considered to be too closely related in historical and mythological terms to be eligible marriage partners. According to Chernela (1993:27–48), the Kotiria traditionally consider four groups to be "brother groups" and therefore unmarriageable: the Wa'ikhana, Arapaso, Siriano, and Tuyuka.

Outside affinal groups, on the other hand, are those with which one's group maintains ongoing marital exchanges; these groups are collectively classified as "in-laws." Marriage between agnates is expressly prohibited; the prescribed norm is marriage outside of one's own group, the principle of linguistic exogamy.[22] While this basic

---

[21] See, for example, Chernela's discussion of such terms in Kotiria (1993:60–71) and C. Hugh-Jones's discussion of Barasana (1979:287–90).

[22] There are, however, two Eastern Tukanoan groups, the Makuna and the Kubeo, who recognize exogamous units within the language or group. As a result, for members

principal might lead us to conclude that one can essentially marry anybody (as long as the person does not have agnate status), in fact one's potential pool of matrimonial candidates is constrained by several other fundamental elements of the system.

First of all, individuals not only attune to the norm of proscribed marriage between agnates, but also strive to fulfill a prescribed ideal: marriage to a cross-cousin (the offspring of one's mother's brother or of one's father's sister) that also completes a bilateral de facto or symbolic exchange of sisters (Jackson 1983:126; see also the models in Stenzel 2005). Secondly, the general norm in Vaupés society is that of virilocal residence. In other words, upon marriage, a bride is expected to reside with her husband's group, quite often in her husband's natal community. This is, even today, a very strong tendency, as evidenced in a recent study of marriages in the Vaupés region (Azevedo 2005).[23]

Virilocal residence itself reflects and reinforces another grounding tenet of the system: the fundamental relationship between each language group and an established geographic territory. Indeed, geographic location is an essential factor in determining which language groups maintain long-term contact through marriage exchanges. Studies such as those of Goldman (1963), C. Hugh-Jones (1979), Jackson (1983), Gomez-Imbert (1996), Cabalzar (2000), and Azevedo (2005) demonstrate that the "in-law" groups for any given community tend to be those that are geographically more accessible. The creation and maintenance of affinal relations with neighboring groups not only facilitates practical matters such as courtship visits by unmarried men to the communities of potential brides and exchanges of goods with, and travel after marriage to, in-law communities, but is also an important means of strengthening regional social, political, economic, and (in the past) defensive alliances.[24]

Vaupés social organization, based as it is on patrilineal language group affiliation, exogamic marriage norms (constrained by geographic location and the prescribed ideals of cross-cousin unions and sister exchange), and the practice of virilocality, has several important linguistic consequences. The first is multilingualism at intersecting regional, community, familial and individual levels. As is seen in the map above, the region is home to speakers of some twenty-five in-

of these groups, it is possible to marry a speaker of the same language. For additional information, see Chernela (1989) and Gomez-Imbert (1999b).

[23] The study is based on data from the Censo Indígena Autônoma do Rio Negro, which was carried out among 16,897 people in 314 indigenous communities as well as the city of São Gabriel da Cachoeira. The data are analyzed in relation to five geographic subregions: Iauaretê, Tiquié/Uaupés, Içana, Upper Rio Negro, and Lower Rio Negro.

[24] For a summary of the literature addressing this issue see Azevedo (2005:39–40).

digenous languages from three different language families. Among those groups who participate in the marriage system based on linguistic exogamy (basically the Eastern Tukanoan and Arawak groups), each local community is comprised of a group of men sharing the same ethnic identity and language and their multiethnic wives, who generally come from a circumscribed set of in-law groups. The children of the community identify ethnically and linguistically with their fathers, but are additionally exposed to and learn, to a greater or lesser extent, their mothers' languages and the languages spoken by the other in-marrying wives. Thus, each individual is raised in a bilingual household within a multilingual community and will acquire linguistic knowledge that reflects the local language repertoire. Additionally, all individuals are expected to master the national language (Portuguese or Spanish), as well as any locally employed lingua franca, such as Tukano, in the Vaupés subregion.

The second consequence of the Vaupés system is, of course, intense, ongoing linguistic contact. One of the general results of this long-term contact has been the widespread diffusion of linguistic features such as tone, nasalization, use of serialized verb roots, switch-reference marking, and evidential systems, leading researchers such as Dixon and Aikhenvald (1998:241) to describe the Vaupés as a distinct linguistic area (see also Epps 2005, and for a more detailed overview of Nadahup involvement, Epps 2007). Aikhenvald (2002a) further argues that the Vaupés linguistic area is rather unique in that there has been no historical dominance of any one group over the others; basically, the languages in contact share equal status, a situation that creates a type of convergence characterized by indirect, multilateral diffusion.[25] In contrast to many contact situations, there is very little borrowing of lexical forms, a restriction that helps preserve each language as separate. This is why evidence of convergence must be sought in grammatical structures rather than in the lexicons of specific languages (Aikhenvald 2002a:266–67).

Gomez-Imbert also contributes some important insights into the nature and results of linguistic contact among the groups of the Vaupés system. She characterizes the system as composed of the opposing yet

[25] However, it should be noted that historically, the egalitarian social conditions that permit such multilateral diffusion probably only existed internally, among the Eastern Tukanoan groups, and perhaps between intermarrying Eastern Tukanoan and Arawak groups (see Stenzel and Gomez-Imbert 2009). No such conditions have ever existed between Eastern Tukanoan and Nadahup groups and research has shown fairly unidirectional influence of Tukanoan languages on Nadahup languages (see Epps 2005, 2007). Moreover, over at least the past one hundred to 150 years, there has been massive Tukanoan influence on Tariana (Arawak), extensively documented by Aikhenvald (e.g., 2002a, 2003b).

complementary processes of convergence and divergence, fusion (in which features of diverse languages become more alike), and fission (in which distinctions between languages become more accentuated). The inevitable interference of a child's mother's language on the acquisition and use of the father's language is an impetus for convergence, inducing fusion in the long term. On the other hand, speakers make "conscious and explicit efforts" to emphasize the differences between languages so that the uniqueness of each group's identity (language) can be preserved. Such marked differentiation stimulates divergence, ensuring that groups remain distinct over long periods of time (Gomez-Imbert 1991:547).

1.6 The specter of language loss and the development of language maintenance programs

The sociolinguistic characteristics of the Vaupés system described above are still generally attested among the Kotiria who reside in traditional communities (for a more detailed overview, see Stenzel 2005). The majority of the Kotiria continue to live within their established territory and generally maintain longstanding marriage alliances with their closest geographic neighbors. The principles of virilocal residence and the norms regarding language use within Kotiria communities are also in force: in-marrying wives are still expected to learn their husbands' language and to use it in public settings, and children acquire and use Kotiria as their language of identity. Thus, in Kotiria community settings, the language remains quite robust and patterns of individual and community multilingualism of the type described earlier can still be found.

However, there is an observable decline in use of the language among the Kotiria who move away from traditional communities and come to reside in communities such as Iauaretê and São Gabriel da Cachoeira. Migration has been on the rise over the past several decades due to a number of different factors, the most important being the need for families to accompany children completing their secondary school education. Others migrate in search of employment opportunities, because of health care concerns, or due to irresolvable conflicts in their communities. Whatever the motives behind migration, Kotiria speakers outside of their traditional communities inevitably encounter new linguistic environments that require them to adopt languages other than Kotiria for daily use and make maintenance of their own native language extremely difficult. Language shift for some indigenous migrants occurs in stages, and may include an initial shift to Tukano. Parallel or subsequent to this shift to the local indigenous lingua franca, displaced Kotiria use the national language—necessary for school, access to public resources, and military service—more and more as the language of their daily lives.

It is nearly inevitable that Kotiria children raised in urban centers such as São Gabriel will become monolingual in Portuguese within two generations. I have observed that children of adults who were raised in the traditional communities have a good passive comprehension of the Kotiria still spoken by the older members of their family, but they usually do not speak it themselves. Current socioeconomic conditions that promote migration and consequent language shift thus exacerbate the threat of endangerment and make linguistic maintenance efforts all the more urgent. Luckily, such efforts are already underway.

The Kotiria display an acute awareness of the importance of language preservation and an eagerness to invest in projects to maintain and strengthen use of their language. They have observed the process of language loss among other groups in the region and among the migrant members of their own language community, and are very aware that although the language is still robust in traditional contexts, the situation, even there, could change quickly and drastically. Thus, they are working to develop strategies to reverse language shift tendencies and are steadfastly investing in projects that will protect and fortify their culture and language.

Over the past two decades, and particularly since the late 1990s, the Kotiria and other indigenous groups in the Upper Rio Negro region have been increasingly involved in political organization, founding local councils and sending representatives to meetings and workshops on everything from health care to fish farming, from the revitalization of traditional arts to the development of literacy materials for local schools. They have established local representative associations, entered the regionally powerful Federation of Indigenous Organizations of the Rio Negro (Federação das Organizações Indígenas do Rio Negro [FOIRN]), and established alliances with non-governmental organizations such as the Instituto Socioambiental (ISA).

Among a variety of projects, including research on and documentation of cultural practices, demographic and geographic mapping, studies of environmental issues, and pilot projects on sustainable food production, ISA has worked with state and municipal education authorities to promote a number of programs related to indigenous education. From 1997 to 2007, ISA's Rio Negro Indigenous Education Project invested in efforts such as the Magistério Indígena, a training program for indigenous primary school teachers, guidance and funding for the publishing of didactic materials in indigenous languages, and support for the founding and development of autonomous indigenous schools in the region (first with the Baniwa and the Tuyuka in 2000, and later with the Kotiria in 2002, the Tukano in 2003, and the Tariana in 2005).

Indeed, the opportunity to consolidate my study of the language with more extensive community work came about in 2001, when a group of teachers and community leaders who were completing the training course for indigenous teachers decided it was time to form a Kotiria school based on the newly developing national ideals for indigenous education—essentially, that it be bilingual, self-determined, and culturally appropriate (see Stenzel 2006). To aid the process, they requested outside organizational and pedagogical assistance from ISA and asked if I could help with issues such as orthography and materials development. The school was officially founded in 2002 during my first linguistic workshop with the community.

In the ensuing years, we have worked together (and in conjunction with education specialists and anthropologists) not only to analyze the language, establish a writing system, and create literacy and other pedagogic materials, but also to document Kotiria traditions, history, verbal arts, knowledge of plants, animals, horticulture, astronomy, etc. Indeed, as the school has developed and expanded, so too has the language community's awareness of the need for much more extensive linguistic and cultural documentation, so much so that activities related to the full-fledged linguistic documentation project for Kotiria and Wa'ikhana (funded by the Hans Rausing Endangered Languages Project at the School of Oriental and African Studies, University of London, 2007–10) were incorporated into the curriculum for the newly founded (2007) Kotiria secondary school. A team of four students and their teacher coordinator were trained in basic documentary methodology, use of audio and video recording equipment, and basic annotation of the data. Among the products resulting from the documentation project is an archive of over sixty audio and video recordings of natural language use by speakers of different ages and from different villages. The recordings exemplify a number of different speech genres, from traditional narratives to casual conversation, from personal interviews to public speeches; they also a register examples of many different cultural situations, activities and traditional knowledge. Materials collected through the project have also been integrated into teaching materials, books, a practical grammar, and a multimedia dictionary for use in the school.

It has been a privilege to work with people such as the Kotiria, who, despite many past and present hardships, are so thoroughly invested in and optimistic about the future of their language and culture, as these words from the introduction to *Wa'ikina Khiti* 'Animal Stories' (text

8 in appendix 1), the first primer written by the Kotiria, eloquently demonstrate:

> *A'rithu hira wa'ikina khiti yaya'urithu. Sã pho'na bu'eti hira. Ã yoana, sã kotiria ne bosi sã yahoare durukuare. A'ripa mahkaina, ba'aro mahkaina, hipitina. Wa'maropɨre, ñarana yare, bu'ena ñaro yɨ'dɨa thɨ'othui sã. Mipɨre sã yakotiria yare bu'ena phiro wahcheha. Yoaripa sã thɨ'oturi ba'aro a'rire sɨha. Ã yoana, a'ri thure hoaha sã kotiria. Setembro 2002 khɨ'ma hichɨ, yoarithu hira. Wa'ikina khiti kotiria ya me're.*

'This is our own Kotiria animal storybook. It is our animal storybook, for our children to study. This way, we Kotiria won't forget how to write and speak our language. For those here now, and for those who come later, for everybody. When we were young, it was really hard for us to understand school in the white people's language. Now we're very happy to have our own Kotiria learning (writing system or school). What we've been thinking about for a long time has arrived That's why we Kotiria are writing this book. It's September of the year 2002, and we're making this book. Animal stories in our own Kotiria language.'

2 Phonology

This chapter presents an overview of Kotiria phonology, including its phonemic inventory and allophonic variants (§§2.1–2.3), features of the syllable—basic shapes, restrictions, and derivations—the role of moras in prosodic structure (§2.4), and some commonly occurring phonological processes (§2.9). The complexity of the phonological system of the language resides in the interaction of the (relatively simple) segmental and (quite rich) suprasegmental levels; in the latter, features of nasalization, tone, and glottalization freely combine and, in the cases of nasalization and tone, engender spreading that creates diverse variation at the surface level (§§2.5–2.8).

2.1 Phonemic inventory

Kotiria has the largest phonemic inventory among the Eastern Tukanoan languages, with six vowels and fourteen consonants. Phonemes are shown in tables 2.1 and 2.2; segments are characterized by features following Clements and Hume (1996). All vowels, voiced obstruents, and approximants have nasal allophones (see §2.5.1).

TABLE 2.1. KOTIRIA CONSONANT PHONEMES

	LABIAL	CORONAL [+ant]	CORONAL [−ant]	VELAR	LARYNGEAL
[−continuant]					
[+voice]	b	d		g	
[−voice]	p	t		k	
[−voice] [spread glottis]	p^h	t^h		k^h	
[+continuant]		s			
[−continuant] [+continuant]			tʃ		
[+approximant]	w		j		
[spread glottis]					h

2.2 Consonants

TABLE 2.2. KOTIRIA VOWEL PHONEMES

	i	e	ɨ	u	o	a
[open 1]	−	−	−	−	−	+
[open 2]	−	+	−	−	+	+
[labial]				+	+	
[coronal]	+	+				
[dorsal]			+	+	+	+

2.2 Consonants

All consonants can occur as syllable onsets. The aspirated voiceless obstruents /p^h t^h k^h/ occur only word-initially and are fully contrastive with /b d p t k s ʧ w j h/ in this position (1).[1]

(1) ba   [báa]   'be rotten'
     da   [dáá]   'be small'
     pa   [pá]   'another' (particle root)
     ta   [táa]   'come'
     ka   [káa]   'monkey'
     pha   [p^háá] 'stomach'
     tha   [t^háá] 'grass'
     kha   [k^háá] 'hawk'
     ~sa   [sá̃ã́]   'be inside'
     cha   [ʧáá]   'cooked food; feast'
     wa   [wáá]   'give'
     ya   [jáa]   'bury'

The voiced obstruent /d/ has allophones [d] and [r] (strictly speaking, the latter is always realized as a flap, but I use the more convenient symbol [r]), in complementary distribution: [d] occurs word-initially and [r] occurs word-internally.[2] The voiced obstruent /g/ also occurs

---

[1] CV roots, except for particle roots such as *pa* 'another', are realized phonetically as [CVV], given that the minimal prosodic structure of roots is bimoraic; see also §2.4.2. High tone (H) in phonetic transcriptions is indicated by the acute accent marker, while low tone (L) is unmarked; for discussion of tone, see §2.6. Nasalization in Kotiria is morphemic and is indicated by ~ preceding the morpheme (see §2.5).

[2] In fact [d] also occurs word-internally at the beginning of nonsuffixal elements such as classifiers and serialized verbs (see §2.2.2 and §7.5). Hence I distinguish *d* from *r* in all examples and representations.

primarily in word-internal, morpheme-initial position, and contrasts with [r] and other suffix-initial segments such as /h/ (2).[3]

(2) a. +ra [ra] ~ [r̃ã] evidential suffix (VIS.IMPERF.2/3)
    b. +ga [ga] ~ [ŋã] imperative
    c. -ha [ha] evidential suffix (VIS.IMPERF.1)

2.2.1 Plosives: voiced, voiceless unaspirated, voiceless aspirated
The voiced and voiceless unaspirated plosives in Kotiria require few remarks other than the limited distribution of /g/, which rarely occurs word-initially, and the tendency for coronals /d t/ to be realized interdentally. What is unique to Kotiria is that it alone among Eastern Tukanoan languages has developed a three-way series of contrastive plosives. While all Eastern Tukanoan languages, including Kotiria, have contrastive voiced and voiceless series at three points of articulation,[4] Kotiria has also developed a contrastive voiceless aspirated series, as is seen in (1) above and in the minimal pairs in (3).

(3) p — p^h piri [pírí] 'three-sided basket'
            phi-ri [p^hírí] 'big one; being'
    t — t^h tua [túá] 'be strong'
            thua [t^húa] 'be near'
    k — k^h koa [kóá] 'perceive; taste'
            kho'a [k^hoʔá] 'return'

There are actually two kinds of aspiration associated with voiceless segments in Eastern Tukanoan languages: preaspiration, which is allophonic (see also §2.7.4), and postaspiration, which in Kotiria is phonemic. Postaspiration occurs coarticulated with word-initial voiceless plosives, as in (3) above. Preaspiration occurs morpheme-internally before voiceless consonants, as in the words in (4).

(4) dapu [da^{h}pú] 'head'
    dita [di^{h}tá] 'be alone'
    duka [dɨ^{h}ká] 'begin'

---

[3] See (20) below for a rare example of /g/ in word-initial position. Suffixes set off by + rather than a dash allow spreading of nasality from the stem; see §2.5.2.

[4] In general, the labial and coronal pairs are fully developed as contrastive segments while the velars are not. All Eastern Tukanoan languages have the frequently occurring voiceless /k/; however, besides Kotiria only Barasana, Makuna, Desano, Siriano, Wa'ikhana/Piratapuyo, and the Western Tukanoan language Siona have developed the voiced counterpart /g/ as a contrastive segment. In Yuruti, Pisamira, Karapana, Tuyuka, Tatuyo, Bará, and Tukano, /g/ occurs only as an allophone or with highly restricted distribution (Gomez-Imbert 2011).

duse [dɨʰsé] 'mouth'
dicha [diʰʧá] 'fruit'

Kotiria preaspiration occurs only within root morphemes and not across morpheme boundaries within multimorphemic words. To illustrate the difference, in a word such as *dia-pɨ* [díápɨ́] (river-LOC), there is no preaspiration of the suffix-initial /p/ of the locative morpheme, even though it occurs word-internally. Even when a suffix-initial voiceless consonant follows a monomoraic particle root, and therefore is in the onset of the second syllable of the word, it is not preaspirated; this can be seen in the realization of the suffix-initial /k/ of the feminine morpheme *-ko* in the third person feminine pronoun *ti-ko+ro* [tíkóró]. This shows that preaspiration applies only to (voiceless) C_2 of roots, as in *dapu* [daʰpú] 'head', and the other roots in (4), not to the onset of the second syllable of a word. In words with compounded roots, each containing noninitial voiceless consonants in C_2 position, preaspiration consistently occurs only in the leftmost root and is weaker or nonexistent in roots to the right, particularly in fast speech.

There are two different analyses of the underlying segments involved in the predictable, morpheme-internal preaspiration in Kotiria and Eastern Tukanoan languages spoken in the Vaupés region (Wa'ikhana/Piratapuyo, Tukano, Siriano, Desano, and Tuyuka). Nathan Waltz represents such aspiration in Kotiria as underlying geminate vowels, the second of which is devoiced before a voiceless consonant (2002:160). Thus a word such as *dapu* 'head' is represented as [daa̯pú]. Similar representations of preaspiration as a [VV̥] sequence before voiceless consonants are found in studies of Tuyuka (Barnes and Malone 2000) and Siriano (Criswell and Brandrup 2000).

Gomez-Imbert (2011), on the other hand, analyzes the Eastern Tukanoan languages in which no preaspiration occurs (the Eastern Tukanoan languages of the Piraparaná region: Karapana, Tatuyo, Barasana, Taiwano, Tanimuka/Retuarã, Bará, and Makuna), as having geminated morpheme-internal plosives derived from underlying simple Cs (5a). The process results in phonetic lengthening and association of the geminate C as a coda on the first syllable, although there is no underlying coda position (5b). (Example (5) is from Barasano [Gomez-Imbert 1997a:38].)

(5) a. Gemination

$$[-cont]$$
$$|$$
$$\sim y\ a\ b\ á$$
$$C\ V\ C\ V$$

  b. Resyllabification and surface lengthening

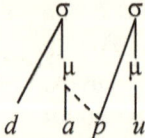

C V C   C V   [ñǎm:ǎ] 'deer'

This same analysis views the preaspiration in the Eastern Tukanoan languages of the Vaupés region (Yuruti, Tukano, Siriano, Desano, Tuyuka, Wa'ikhana/Piratapuyo, and Kotiria) as also deriving from gemination restricted to voiceless C_2 (6a), followed by debuccalization of the resyllabified coda C (6b) and a readjustment from [−voice] to the unmarked, default [spread glottis] value for laryngeals, realized as aspiration (6b–c).

(6) a. Gemination and resyllabification

d   a p u

  b. Recreation of features for geminate C and delinking

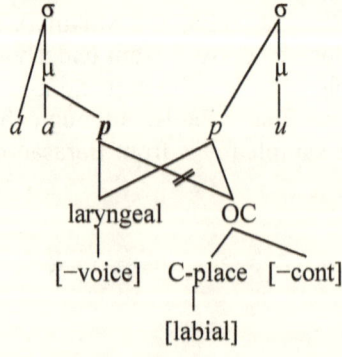

c. Debuccalization and readjustment

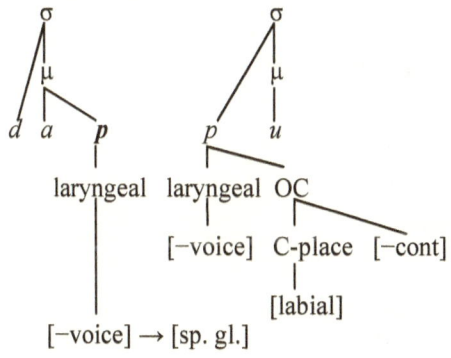

[daʰpú] 'head'

The Gomez-Imbert analysis offers two clear advantages. First, an analysis of derived geminate consonants preserves the basic bimoraic structure posited for the majority of roots (see §2.4.2). Second, it creates a unified underlying representation for all Eastern Tukanoan languages from which the different synchronic patterns of the Eastern Tukanoan languages in the two subregions can be derived.

The Eastern Tukanoan languages spoken in the Vaupés region all have the morpheme-internal preaspiration described above. Postaspiration also occurs to a certain extent in the same group of languages; however, it has only become phonemic in Kotiria. Instances of postaspiration in Desano, Tuyuka, Tukano, and Wa'ikhana/Piratapuyo are generally viewed as the result of the fast-speech tendency for vowels to delete morpheme-internally before /h/, as in (7).[5]

(7)   a.   *aarí pehè*   [aʔli pʰe]   'this time' (Wa'ikhana [N. Waltz 2002:162])

         b.   *pahi-gó*   [pà̰higó]   'big woman' (Tukano [Welch and West 2000:420])

Only in Kotiria has word-initial postaspiration developed into a contrastive feature. Nathan Waltz (2002) offers a diachronic analysis of the development of Kotiria postaspiration. He posits the series *p, *t, *k for Proto-Tukanoan and the later development of aspiration on all word-initial voiceless plosives in Kotiria (8a), possibly due to the long-standing contact between Kotiria and Arawak languages—Tariana and Baniwa—which have a full range of aspirated consonants, both voiced

---

[5] In (7), the authors' original phonetic transcriptions have been preserved.

and voiceless.[6] Over time, erosion of word-initial syllables in Kotiria left what were formerly morpheme-internal unaspirated voiceless consonants in word-initial position (8b). The result was a new set of morphemes with initial unaspirated plosives that contrast synchronically with the otherwise aspirated series (Waltz 2002:162).

(8)   a. General postaspiration:

$C_{[-voice]} \rightarrow C^h \: / \: \_\_ V(C)V$

       b. Historical deletion:

$(C)V \rightarrow \emptyset \: / \: \_\_ C_{[-voice, -aspirated]} V$

Cross-linguistic data from other Eastern Tukanoan languages[7] show that a process of left-edge erosion has indeed occurred in Kotiria and that the result appears to be as Waltz predicted. The Kotiria words in table 2.3 have word-initial unaspirated voiceless plosives while cognates from other Eastern Tukanoan languages are vowel-initial.

TABLE 2.3. COGNATES OF KOTIRIA WORDS WITH INITIAL UNASPIRATED VOICELESS PLOSIVES

YURUTI	TATUYO	TUKANO	WA'IKHANA	KOTIRIA		
oʰkó	*óko*	*akó*	*aʰkó*	*ko* [kóo]	'water'
waʰtí	*atí*	*aatá*	*aʰtá*	*ta* [táa]	'come'
oʰpí	*opí*	*upí*	*uʰpí*	*pi* [píi]	'tooth'
~iʰtá	*~itá*	*~itá*	*~iʰtá*	*~ta* [tã́ã]	'rock'

We should note that where syllable erosion has left former morpheme-internal voiceless Cs (which would have been preaspirated) in initial position, no traces of the preaspiration remain. This demonstrates a cross-linguistic tendency for preaspiration to occur only in medial and final positions (Ladefoged and Maddieson 1996:70).

Taking the Waltz analysis one step further, we should expect lexical data to reveal the following tendencies for roots in Kotiria: word-initial voiceless plosives in disyllabic roots should be aspirated (following the

---

[6] Both Tariana and Baniwa have three aspirated voiceless stops, /ph th kh/, as well as the aspirated voiced stop /dh/, aspirated nasals /mh nh and ñh/, and an aspirated bilabial glide /wh/ (Aikhenvald 2002a:38). If postaspiration developed in Kotiria under the influence of Arawak languages, it is as yet unclear why it developed only on voiceless Cs, though Gomez-Imbert (p.c. 2008) suggests that, being restricted to initial position, it could be the result of a tone/pitch accent effect.

[7] Wa'ikhana data is from Waltz (2002); Tatuyo data is from Gomez-Imbert and Hugh-Jones (2000) and Gomez-Imbert (p.c. 2003, 2008). Tukano data comes from Ramirez (1997b) and Yuruti data from Kinch and Kinch (2000). The original phonetic representations of these authors are preserved.

rule in (8a)), and unaspirated word-initial plosives should occur primarily in roots with *CV* shape (the result of the diachronic erosion formalized in (8b)). However, these tendencies are not altogether borne out in the data, as we see in table 2.4. In relation to the first tendency, an inspection of 152 *CVCV* and CV_1V_2 roots with initial voiceless plosives shows that while many such roots do have aspirated voiceless plosives, there are nearly as many that have unaspirated word-initial voiceless plosives.

TABLE 2.4. DISYLLABIC ROOTS WITH WORD-INITIAL VOICELESS PLOSIVES

ASPIRATED		UNASPIRATED	
p^h	38	p	12
t^h	11	t	25
k^h	37	k	29
TOTAL	86	TOTAL	66

As for simple *CV* roots, table 2.5 shows that the numbers of roots with aspirated and unaspirated initial voiceless plosives are essentially the same.

TABLE 2.5. *CV* ROOTS WITH WORD-INITIAL VOICELESS PLOSIVES

ASPIRATED		UNASPIRATED	
p^h	5	p	4
t^h	3	t	3
k^h	6	k	8
TOTAL	14	TOTAL	15

Waltz postulates that some *CV* roots with initial aspirated plosives may be the result of the lexicalization of the process exemplified in (7) above for Wa'ikhana and Tukano, whereby vowels are deleted before the glottal fricative /h/ (2002:164). Though there are only a few such examples, the Tukano and Wa'ikhana disyllabic cognates of these Kotiria terms (table 2.6) suggest that this may be a valid interpretation for certain cases. Clearly, though, a definitive conclusion as to the development of the aspirated plosives in Kotiria has yet to be reached.

TABLE 2.6. KOTIRIA ASPIRATION FROM DELETION OF VOWEL BEFORE /h/

TUKANO	WA'IKHANA	KOTIRIA		
	pehé	pha [pʰáá]	'time'	
di'pĩhi	pihĩ	~phi [pʰĩ́]	noun classifier used for bladelike objects	
pǎhĩ	pahí	phi [phíí]	'be big'	

2.2.2 The relation of [d] and [r]

In (1) we saw that all consonant phonemes occur in word-initial position. The consonants that regularly occur in word-internal, morpheme-initial position are exemplified in (9).

(9) a. *-bo* [bo] dubitative
    b. *-pʉ* [pʉ] locative
    c. *-ta* [ta] intention
    d. *-ka* [ka] evidential suffix (ASSERT.IMPERF)
    e. *-si* [si] negative irrealis
    f. *-ha* [ha] evidential suffix (VIS.IMPERF.1)
    g. *-chʉ* [tʃʉ] switch reference
    h. *-wʉ'rʉ* [wʉʔrʉ] augmentative
    i. *-ya* [ja] plural
    j. *+ra* [ra] evidential suffix (VIS.IMPERF.2/3)
    k. *+ga* [ga] imperative

Comparing (1) and (9), we see that the aspirated voiceless plosives /pʰ tʰ kʰ/ and the voiced plosive [d] are the only word-initial consonants that do not occur in word-internal position as well. The absence of the aspirated plosive series in word-internal position strengthens the hypothesis that contrastive postaspiration developed only in word-initial position, as outlined in the previous section. As for the voiced plosive [d], examination of the Kotiria lexicon shows that this segment occurs in complementary distribution with the flap [r], the former occurring word-initially and the latter word-internally (but see examples (10)–(13) and further considerations below). Given the basic *(C)V* syllable structure of Eastern Tukanoan languages, all word-internal plosives inevitably fall between two vowels, a typical environment for lenition, leading to the hypotheses that [r] results from a process of weakening of the voiced plosive word-internally. In a similar vein, Ramirez (1997a:31) classifies [r] as an allophone of /d/ in intervocalic position in oral morphemes in Tukano, and Gomez-Imbert (2011) affirms that this same distribution in Siriano, Yuruti, Pisamira, Tuyuka, Bará, Wa'ikhana/Piratapuyo, and Desano reflects a general tendency for lenition of coronals in Eastern Tukanoan languages; interestingly, [r] as an allophone of /d/ also occurs in the Western Tukanoan language Siona.

The two existing reconstructions of Proto-Tukanoan postulate different protosegments and paths of development for these voiced coronals. Waltz and Wheeler (1972) posit protosegments *r, *d, and *n, with subsequent merging of *d and *n to /d/ and suprasegmentalization of the nasal feature. This would have left an underlying distinction between oral segments /r/ and /d/, but does not explain why, if both were underlying, they occur as allophones or in synchronic complementary distribution in languages such as Kotiria. Malone (1987), on the other hand, identifies a single protosegment *d. This segment has remained in the Eastern Tukanoan phonemic inventory and occurs synchronically in all Eastern Tukanoan languages, with two allophones besides [d]: [n] in nasal contexts and, in a subgroup of Eastern Tukanoan languages, [r] in word-internal position.

The statement that the allophone [d] occurs only word-initially while [r] occurs only word-internally in Kotiria actually requires some qualification. Example (10) shows that grammatical suffixes consistently occur with word-internal, suffix-initial [r]. Examples (11)–(13), on the other hand, show that there are, in fact, many instances of word-internal phonetic [d] in Kotiria. Example (11) shows a series of nouns marked by the classifier -dᵾ, used to identify cylindrical, straight objects, while (12) and (13) are examples of multimorphemic verbal words with serialized roots, one of which in each case begins with [d].

(10) a. [híra]
          hi+ra
          COP+VIS.IMPERF.2/3
          'you/he/she/it/they are'

      b. [tíró]
          ti+ro
          ANPH+SG
          'he, it, that, the' (an animate, nonfeminine entity)

      c. [síri]
          si+ri
          be.hot+NOM
          'hot one (day)'

(11)   a. [hóádɨ]
            hoa-dɨ
            write-CLS:cylindrical.straight
            'pen, pencil'

        b. [nõʰsǎdɨ]
            ~yosa-dɨ
            force.into-CLS:cylindrical.straight
            'spear, arrow'

        c. [tuádɨ]
            tua-dɨ
            stick-CLS:cylindrical.straight
            'branch'

(12)   [ʧɨ́duatiga]
        chɨ-dua-ati+a
        eat-DESID-IMPERF+ASSERT.PERF
        '(She) was wanting to eat (fruit).'

(13)   [mŭmŭ́diha]
        ~bɨbɨ-diha
        go.quickly-go.down
        '(They) quickly got out of (their hammocks).'

The explanation for this distribution is clear if we look at each case from a morphological perspective. Word-internal instances of [d] occur when the morphemes in question are roots or classifiers (which are themselves often full roots or reduced roots—see §4.3.3). Their realization with phonetic [d] attests a different morphological status than that of suffixes, which are always bound and have none of the other phonological properties that characterize root morphemes (see §3.5). Thus, it is the status of a morpheme rather than just its overall linear position within a phonological word that determines the phonological distribution rule for [d] versus [r] as realizations of /d/. Phonological and morphological properties interact to mark the inherent status of morphemes.

2.2.3. The affricate /ʧ/

According to Barnes, all but two Tukanoan languages (Bará, Tatuyo) have the voiceless fricative /s/ in their phonemic inventories and only Kotiria has developed a contrastive voiceless alveopalatal affricate /ʧ/ (1999:211). Gomez-Imbert (2011) indicates a rather more complex picture, with Eastern Tukanoan languages having contrasting sets of voiced and voiceless coronals distinguished by the feature [±anterior]. All Eastern Tukanoan languages maintain the [+anterior] segments /t d/. Variation occurs in the [−anterior] category, further exemplifying a family-wide tendency she has observed for coronals to be lenited. In a number of Eastern Tukanoan languages, [−anterior] /c ɟ/ have developed into the continuants /s j/ (Tuyuka, Tanimuka/Retuarã, Desano, Siriano, Tukano, Wa'ikhana/Piratapuyo, and Kotiria), while the /c ɟ/ segments are retained in Kubeo, Yuruti, Pisamira, Karapana, Makuna, and Bará/Taiwano. Kotiria is unique among Eastern Tukanoan languages in that it has developed a four-way contrast of [+anterior] coronals: the plosive /t/, the aspirated plosive /tʰ/, the voiced plosive /d/ and the fricative /s/, as well as a contrasting [−anterior] set comprised of the affricate /tʃ/ and the voiced approximant /j/, of which the voiced affricate [dʒ] is an allophone (see §2.2.4 below).[8] Contrasts in the Kotiria coronals are exemplified in (14)–(15).

(14) [+anterior]
 -dʉ   [dʉ]   classifier for cylindrical straight objects
 ~sʉ   [sʉ̃ʉ̃]   'arrive'
 tʉ   [tʉ́ʉ]   'stick'
 thʉ   [tʰʉ́ʉ]   'push'

(15) [−anterior]
 yʉ   [jʉ]   'first person singular possessive'
 chʉ   [tʃʉ́ʉ]   'eat'

On the basis of a comparison with Wa'ikhana/Piratapuyo cognates, Nathan Waltz (2002) argues that Kotiria /tʃ/ has four different sources in the protolanguage: *s (word-initially), *k, *g, and *y (word-internally), and suggests that adjacency to front and/or high vowels at earlier stages of the language motivated the changes. While the examples in table 2.7 indicate a word-internal correspondence between Eastern Tukanoan [k] and Kotiria [tʃ], further cross-linguistic data from additional Eastern Tukanoan languages is required before we can affirm the

TABLE 2.7. CORRESPONDENCES BETWEEN KOTIRIA [tʃ] AND EASTERN TUKANOAN [k]

BARASANO	TUKANO	WA'IKHANA	KOTIRIA		
wekí	wekí	wekí	wachʉ [waʰtʃṹ]	'tapir'
~yikí	~yekági	~yekí	~yʉchʉ [jʉ̈ʰtʃṹ]	'leg'
riká	diká		dicha [diʰtʃá]	'fruit'
		dekó	dacho [daʰtʃó]	'day'

---

[8] It is interesting that the Western Tukanoan language Siona also has /t s tʃ/ as well as a voiced affricate /dʒ/ (Wheeler 1992:22).

other relationships Waltz suggests. (Stenzel and Gomez-Imbert [2009] argue that Kotiria /tʃ/, like aspiration, may have developed under areal influence of Arawak languages; the same possibility is mentioned, but not explored in any detail, by Waltz [2000:170].)

2.2.4 Allophones of oral consonants

Both the labial approximant /w/ and the coronal approximant /j/ have allophones in oral environments: /w/ is frequently realized as fricative [v] in word-initial position (16), while /j/ has the affricate allophone [dʒ] in both word-initial and word-internal position (17).

(16)   wese   [weʰsé] ~ [veʰsé]   'garden'
       wi'i   [wiʔí] ~ [viʔí]   'return'
       wɨpɨ   [wɨʰpú] ~ [vɨʰpú]   'spider'
       wa'a   [waʔá] ~ [vaʔá]   'go'

(17)   yoa   [joá] ~ [dʒoá]   'do/make'
       yɨkɨ   [jɨʰkú] ~ [dʒɨʰkú]   'tree'
       phayɨ   [pʰajú] ~ [pʰadʒú]   'many / a lot'

Variation between [j] and [dʒ] occurs only before dorsal (back) vowels; before coronal (front) vowels, only [j] occurs, as we see in (18). Variation between [j] and [dʒ] is the first example we have seen so far of allophonic variation conditioned by these subclasses of vowels (as outlined in §2.3 below).

(18)   yese   [jeʰsé]   'pig'
       waye   [wajé]   'cut open'

Another extremely common variation conditioned by subclasses of vowels is that associated with the flap [r], which alternates with [l] in word-internal position before coronal vowels /i e/. This variation can be seen in the sample of Kotiria writing in (19), in which the author's spontaneous writing clearly replicates speech patterns.[9] The top line of each sentence (in angle brackets < >) reproduces the author's original spelling. Subsequent lines give a standardized version with interlinear analysis. Words in which [r] is replaced by [l] before coronal vowels /i e/ can be seen in the author's spelling in sentences 1 and 5); many words can be seen throughout the example where the author writes <r>, because [r] precedes a dorsal vowel /a o u/. In line 4, one should

---

[9] In orthography development workshops with the Kotiria, we have analyzed a number of texts such as this one. Because many Kotiria still learn to read and write first in Spanish or Portuguese, which have contrastive /r/ and /l/ segments, they tend to write these sounds when they occur in their own language, preserving what they believe to be separate phonemic identities. It has been interesting to see their reaction to the discovery that these sounds in Kotiria are actually variants of a single phoneme with different realizations depending on context.

note the author's rendition of the Portuguese name Luis: <dui>. The rendition of this name with word-initial <d> conforms to two different phonological rules in Kotiria: first, that the allophone [l] does not precede a dorsal vowel, and second, that it is the allophone [d] and not [r] or [l] that occurs word-initially.

(19) *Goliro* 'The good fisherman', by Carmem Melo (Muniz 2001:149)

1 <aliro hira wai goholiro tiro>

   a'rí+ró   hí+ra   wa'í   gó+ri+ro
   DEM.PROX+SG COP+VIS.IMPERF.2/3 fish   be.skillful+NOM+SG

   tí+ró
   ANPH+SG

   'This guy is a good fisherman.'

2 <wahaãno waro moñoerara tiro>

   ~wahá+ro   wa'á+ro   ~boyo-éra+ra   tí+ró
   kill+SG   go+SG   fail-NEG+VIS.IMPERF.2/3 ANPH+SG

   'When he goes fishing, he never fails.'

3 <to wa'atsʉ ñuna tsunada ni masihã>

   to=wa'á-chʉ   ~yʉ́+rá   chʉ́-~dáká
   3SG.POSS=go-SW.REF see+VIS.IMPERF.2/3 eat-do.together

   ~dí-~basi-ha
   say-know-VIS.IMPERF.1

   'When we see him going (fishing), we can say, "Let's eat!"'

4 <to wa'ma õse hira, dui hira>

   to=~wabá   ~ó-sé   hí+ra
   3SG.POSS=name DEIC.PROX-be.like COP+VIS.IMPERF.2/3

   duí   hí+ra
   Luis COP+VIS.IMPERF.2/3

   'His name is like this: it's Luis.'

5 <tiro namotiliro hira>

   tí+ró   ~dabó-ti+ri+ro   hí+ra
   ANPH+SG wife-VBZ+NOM+SG COP+VIS.IMPERF.2/3

   'He is married.'

6 <pʉaro phonatira tiro>

   phʉá+ro   ~pho'dá-ti+ra   tí+ró
   two+SG   children-VBZ+VIS.IMPERF.2/3 ANPH+SG

   'He has two children.'

7   <tina wamatira idu>
    tí-~da   ~wabá-tí+rá   idú
    ANPH-PL   name-VBZ+VIS.IMPERF.2/3   Eduardo
    'They call one Eduardo.'

8   <pairo wamatira madú>
    pá-iro   ~wabá-tí+rá   madú
    other-NOM.SG name-VBZ+VIS.IMPERF.2/3 Manuel
    'The other is called Manuel.'

2.3   Vowels and vowel harmony

Kotiria shares with all Tukanoan languages except Tanimuka/Retuarã a basic system of six contrastive vowels, characterized in table 2.2 and exemplified in (20). In oral morphemes, the mid ([−open 1, +open 2]) vowels /e/ and /o/ are realized as [ɛ] and [ɔ], a noncontrastive variation not indicated in the phonetic transcriptions. In nasal morphemes, the allophones of these same vowels are [ẽ] and [õ] respectively (see §2.5.1 below). In the present work, the symbol [ʉ] is not used with its usual IPA value, but instead represents a high vowel most often phonetically realized as the high back unrounded [ɯ], varying noncontrastively in certain contexts with the more central [ɨ]. The Kotiria have opted to use <ʉ> in their orthography, judging it to be more easily recognizable than <ɨ> (which is used in the orthographies for some other Eastern Tukanoan languages but which the Kotiria find is too easily confused with <i> or even <t>, especially in handwritten texts) or <ɯ> (which is too easily mistaken for <w>, a symbol also used in their orthography). For the sake of simplicity, I use <ʉ> in all representations of Kotiria, including phonetic transcriptions.

(20) ka   [káa]   'monkey'
      khu   [kʰuú]   'turtle'
      ko   [koó]   'water / medicine'
      ~kʉ   [kʉ̃́]¹⁰   'one'
      ki   [kíí]   'mandi fish'
      ~ke   [kẽ́ẽ́]   'beak/nose'

The choice to characterize vowel features following Clements and Hume (1996), rather than using the high/low and front/central/back features found in Barnes (1999:210) and in most of the literature on Eastern Tukanoan languages, focuses attention on an important distinction between the class of coronal vowels /i e/ and the class of dorsal vowels /ʉ u o a/. We have seen that this distinction is key to

---

[10] The root ~kʉ 'one' behaves like a particle root; its vowel does not undergo lengthening.

understanding certain allophonic processes such as the variations [j ~ dʒ] and [r ~ l] outlined in §2.2.4.

The question of vowel harmony in Kotiria was addressed by Nathan Waltz (2002:178–91), who gives an overview of vowel shifts from "Proto-WP" (his term for the ancestor of Kotiria/Wanano and Wa'ikhana/Piratapuyo). The cross-linguistic synchronic data presented by Waltz and Wheeler (1972) also indicate that systematic variation indeed exists. However, the question of whether these variations constitute a system of regular assimilation—vowel harmony—or whether they are better analyzed as the result of reduction linked to other features such as stress has yet to be answered. In this section, I offer a summary of Waltz's analysis and point out some of the relevant as-yet unanswered questions.

Waltz and Waltz state that "in Kotiria, it is common for a vowel to assimilate to the position of the preceding vowel" (2000:456; my translation), and they cite an example in which the initial vowel of the nominalizing suffix -*iro* surfaces as [i] after a front vowel in the stem (21a) and as [ɨ] after a central vowel (21b).[11]

(21) a. [i] after front vowel [e]
dasé-iro
Tukano-MASC
'a Tukano man'

b. [ɨ] after central vowel [a]
di'i-~baka-ɨdo
clay-people-MASC
'a Tuyuka man'

This example suggests a system of vowel harmony with the following properties:

- it operates between roots (origin morpheme) and suffixes (target morpheme);
- it has left-to-right (perseverative) directionality;
- it affects only the first vowel of the suffix; and
- it has the harmonizing feature of place (front to front, central to central) but not of height.

---

[11] Waltz and Waltz (2000) and Waltz (2002) use the symbol <ɨ> to represent the same vowel for which I use the symbol <ʉ>. Waltz's dictionary (2007) also adopts <ʉ>.

The system displays the basic components of vowel harmony understood to be "agreement among vowels in successive syllables in respect of one or more features" (Matthews 1997:400). However, the fact that harmony affects just the first vowel of the suffix presents a problem, in that according to Kenstowicz, "typically all of the vowels of the language participate in the harmonic constraint. In addition, the harmony applies in an essentially unbounded fashion, affecting all the relevant vowels within the domain (typically the word)" (1994:347). Thus, it is characteristic of vowel harmony systems that all the vowels in the target morpheme be affected, a feature not attested in these Kotiria examples. Moreover, in Waltz and Wheeler's initial and more extensive presentation of vowel variations (1972), as well as in Nathan Waltz's later analyses of comparative data (2002), we find examples of harmony with respect to the feature of height rather than or in addition to place, as well as examples of right-to-left (anticipatory) directionality, sometimes between morphemes and sometimes within them. Thus, while it is possible that some harmonizing processes may be at work, the exact characteristics and defining features of a vowel harmony system, if there is indeed such a system at work in Kotiria, have yet to be fully demonstrated.

2.4 The syllable

2.4.1 Shapes, constraints, and association rules

Kotiria has basic *(C)V* syllable shape. Onsets of word-initial syllables may be any single oral consonant[12] with the exception of the flap [r]. We recall, furthermore, that while the voiced velar plosive /g/ can occur word-initially, as in *go+ri+ro* in sentence 1 of (18) above, it is extremely rare in this position. Onsets of word-internal syllables include [r], /g/, and [ʔ] in a subset of glottalized roots. There is no underlying coda position, but a glottal coda can be derived in roots with suprasegmental glottalization, described in §2.7.2 below. Basic derivations are given in (22), following two simple association rules (in accordance with the principles of syllabification given by Ewen and van der Hulst [2001]):

• Each *V* is identified as the vocalic nucleus.

• Any *C* to the left of the nucleus is associated as an onset.

A third association rule applies in derived syllables in glottalized roots only:

---

[12] I refer here only to the underlying inventory of oral phonemes. Nasal allophones of any permitted oral segment also surface as onsets, but are analyzed as the result of a suprasegmental feature (see §2.5).

Phonology

- Any *C* to the right of the nucleus (in Kotiria this can only be a glottal stop) is associated as rhyme (see derivations in (50)).

(22) a. *koa* [koá] 'taste, perceive'

$$
\begin{array}{c}
\sigma\ \sigma \\
|\ \ | \\
\text{CV V} \\
k\ o\ a
\end{array}
\rightarrow
\begin{array}{c}
\sigma\ \sigma \\
\wedge\ | \\
\text{C V.V} \\
k\ o\ a
\end{array}
$$

b. *buti* [bʉtí] 'be hard'

$$
\begin{array}{c}
\sigma\ \ \sigma \\
|\ \ \ | \\
\text{C V C V} \\
b\ ʉ\ t\ i
\end{array}
\rightarrow
\begin{array}{c}
\sigma\ \ \ \sigma \\
\wedge\ \ \wedge \\
\text{C V . C V} \\
b\ ʉ\ \ t\ i
\end{array}
$$

c. *phua+ro* [pʰʉáro] 'two'

$$
\begin{array}{c}
\sigma\ \ \sigma\ \ \sigma \\
|\ \ \ |\ \ \ | \\
\text{C V\ \ V\ CV} \\
p^h ʉ\ \ a\ \ r\ o
\end{array}
\rightarrow
\begin{array}{c}
\sigma\ \ \sigma\ \ \sigma \\
\wedge\ \ |\ \ \wedge \\
\text{C V . V . C V} \\
p^h ʉ\ \ a\ \ r\ o
\end{array}
$$

d. *~aga* [ãŋã́] 'poisonous snake'

$$
\begin{array}{c}
\sigma\ \ \sigma \\
|\ \ \ | \\
\text{V C V} \\
\sim a\ g\ a
\end{array}
\rightarrow
\begin{array}{c}
\sigma\ \ \sigma \\
|\ \ \wedge \\
\text{V . C V} \\
\sim a\ g\ a
\end{array}
$$

2.4.2 Moras in prosodic structure

Having discussed syllable types and rules of association, we can now look at other aspects of prosodic structure. In Kotiria syllables basic rhymes are simply *V*, and each vocalic nucleus is analyzed as associated with a single mora. Since onsets are viewed as extramoraic and directly linked to the syllable, since there are no long vowels, and since the derived glottal coda in a subset of glottalized roots has no effect on syllable weight, each of the allowed syllable shapes in Kotiria—basic underlying *(C)V* and the derived *(C)Vʔ*—is associated with a single mora (23).

(23)

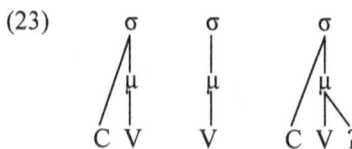

Though we have yet to examine the concept of "word" in Kotiria (the focus of chapter 3), we should be aware that most Kotiria words are built from nominal or verbal roots, the great majority of which are bimoraic, as we see in the small sample in (24).[13]

(24) a. ~khadɨ [kʰãnɨ̃] 'sugarcane'

  b. ~aga [ãŋá̃] 'poisonous snake'

  c. hoa [hóá] 'write'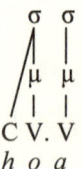

  d. dɨ'te [dɨʔté] 'chop'

While the overwhelming majority of roots correspond to one of the patterns in (24), Kotiria also has a reasonable number of noun and verb roots that I analyze as underlyingly monomoraic—for example, those in (1), table 2.3, (14)–(15), and (20). The comparative examples in table 2.3 as well as those in table 2.8 indicate that a great number of such monomoraic roots in Kotiria are the result of diachronic loss of a left-edge syllable and its associated mora.[14]

---

[13] Although Barnes (1999) makes no mention of moraic structure in her overview of Tukanoan languages, bimoraic structure is analyzed as basic in Tukano (Ramirez 1997a:53–56) and in Barasana (Gomez-Imbert 1997a:35–41; Gomez-Imbert 1997b).

[14] Waltz identifies some sixty such roots and attributes loss of initial syllables in Kotiria to the interaction between syllable stress (all dropped vowels are in unstressed syllables) and features of adjacent consonants (Waltz 2002:176–77).

TABLE 2.8. FURTHER EXAMPLES OF LOSS OF A LEFT-EDGE SYLLABLE IN KOTIRIA

WA'IKHANA	TUKANO	KOTIRIA	
aké	áké	ka [káa]	'monkey'
esá	éhá	~sɨ [sɨ̃ɨ̃́]	'arrive'
así	~así	si [síi]	'be hot'
~eke	~e'ke	~ke [kẽ́ẽ́]	'beak/nose'
~iki		ki [kíí]	'mandi fish'

Though these roots are underlyingly monomoraic, a rule of bimoraic prosodic minimality for words causes lengthening of the vowels of roots when the roots occur as independent words; this is illustrated in (25a–b) (and is reflected in phonetic transcriptions in examples).[15] Such roots revert to monomoraic status when they occur as constituents in multimorphemic words, where word-level prosodic minimality is satisfied by additional morphemes, as we see in (25c).

(25)   a. Lengthening in root pronounced as independent word:

chɨ [tʃɨ́ɨ] 'eat'

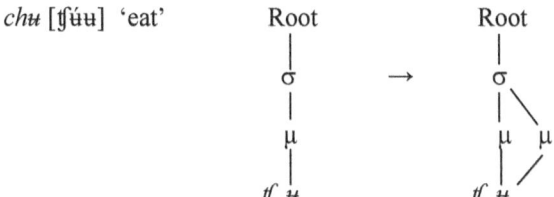

b. Association of tone to lengthened root:

---

[15] Gomez-Imbert's (1997a) analysis of Barasana was the first work to recognize the prosodic minimality condition for an Eastern Tukanoan language. More recently, Gomez-Imbert (2011) states that the two-mora prosodic template for words is the norm throughout the family.

c. Monomoraic realization of root in multimorphemic word and association of tone to suffix mora:

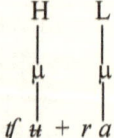

surface form of word: [ʧɨ́ra] '(they) eat'

Interestingly, some *CV* roots in Kotiria whose cognates in Wa'ikhana, the most closely related sister language within the family, have the shape *CVV* (where both vowels are the same) can alternate between [CVV] and [CV] realizations in multimorphemic words. One example in which this alternation occurs is ~*ba* 'stream', seen in table 2.9.[16] However, most *CV* roots with *CVV* cognates, such as the words for 'turtle' and 'grass' (also in table 2.9), are consistently shortened; they display the same phonological behavior observed in roots whose *CV* shape is the result of initial syllable loss, most likely as the result of analogy to the latter.[17] Thus we can see that the development of a class of monomoraic roots in Kotiria, whether the result of syllable loss or analogy, is clearly an innovation within the family.

TABLE 2.9. KOTIRIA *CV* ROOTS WITH *CVV* COGNATES IN WA'IKHANA

	WA'IKHANA (in all environments)	KOTIRIA as independent word	in multimorphemic words
'turtle'	kuu$_{LH}$ [kuú]	khu$_{LH}$ [kʰuú]	khu+ri [kʰúrí] 'turtles'
'grass'	taa$_{LH}$ [taá]	tha$_H$ [tʰáá]	tha+ro [tʰáró] 'field'
'stream'	~baa$_{LH}$ [mã̌ã́]	~ba$_H$ [mã́ã́]	~ba-pɨ [mã́ã̌pɨ́] ~ [mã̌pɨ́] 'in the stream'

2.5 Suprasegmental nasalization

Nasalization is a suprasegmental feature found in all Eastern Tukanoan languages (Barnes 1999:211).[18] It operates autonomously as a feature associated to the morpheme: each morpheme is lexically marked as inherently nasal [+nasal], inherently oral [−nasal], or is an unmarked

---

[16] Wa'ikhana forms in the table are from my own fieldwork on Wa'ikhana.

[17] Roots in which I have observed alternate [CVV] ~ [CV] pronunciation when the root is followed by another morpheme in the word are indicated in the vocabulary appendix with the second vowel in parentheses.

[18] Descriptions of suprasegmental nasalization processes in specific Eastern Tukanoan languages are provided by Kaye (1971) for Desano, Barnes (1996) for Tuyuka, Gomez-Imbert (1997a:400–493; 1998) for Barasana; and Ramirez (1997a: 53–91) for Tukano.

[Ønasal] "chameleon"[19] that will receive its [±nasal] feature value from the previous morpheme by means of spreading.

All vowels and consonants, except those specifically designated as [−voice], which are transparent to nasalization, have nasal allophones derived through the association of the suprasegmental nasal feature.

2.5.1 Nasal allophones and derivations of [+nasal] morphemes

Example (26) gives the phonemic inventory of Kotiria and the nasal allophones that are derived from oral phonemes via suprasegmental nasalization. Contrastive minimal pair examples are given in table 2.10.

(26) a. /p^h t^h k^h s ʧ p t k/
([−voice]; transparent to nasalization; no nasal allophones in [+nasal] contexts)

b. /h b d r g w j i ʉ u e a o/
allophonic variants in [+nasal] contexts:
[h̃ m n r̃ ŋ w̃ ɲ ĩ ʉ̃ ũ ẽ ã õ]

TABLE 2.10. SOME MINIMAL PAIRS FOR NASALIZATION

	[−nasal]			[+nasal]		
b/~b	bʉ'ʉ	[bʉʔʉ́]	'piranha'	~bʉ'ʉ	[mʉ̃ʔʉ̃́]	2.SG 'you'
d/~d	di	[díí]	'blood'	~di	[nĩĩ́]	'say'
w/~w	waha	[wahá]	'row, drag'	~waha	[w̃ãhã́]	'kill'
j/~j	yo	[jóó]	'corn'	~yo	[ɲṍṍ]	'show'
h/~h	hu	[húú]	'smoke'	~hu	[h̃ũũ]	'worm'

Derivation of the surface forms of roots requires placement of the [±nasal] feature on a separate tier linked directly to the syllables comprising the morpheme (Gomez-Imbert 2003a:174). Given that any [−nasal] morpheme is entirely composed of oral segments, its underlying and surface realizations will always be identical; no derivations for this type of morpheme are therefore required. The examples in (27) show how surface realizations of [+nasal] roots are derived from underlying oral forms.[20]

The key to correct derivation of surface nasalization is specification on the laryngeal tier. Examples (27a) and (27b) show roots in which all

---

[19] This term was first used by Jones and Jones (1991:14), and has since been adopted by other researchers. I adopt the [±nasal] notation used by Gomez-Imbert (1997a, 1998) and refer to morphemes that are lexically unmarked for [±nasal] values as [Ønasal].

[20] In (27) only, underlying [+nasal] forms are not identified by the tilde.

segments have either [+voice] or [spread glottis] specification on the laryngeal tier; nasalization is fully acquired by these segments and they are realized as the appropriate corresponding nasal allophones, as given in (26). Example (27c) shows that segments specified as [−voice]—all voiceless stops, the affricate [tʃ] and fricative [s]—are transparent: they are unaffected by the nasal suprasegmental and do not inhibit realization of the feature in adjacent segments.

(27) a. ~yabi [ɲãmĩ́] 'night'

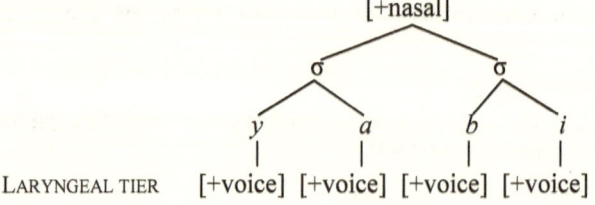

b. ~waha [w̃ãh̃ã́] 'kill'

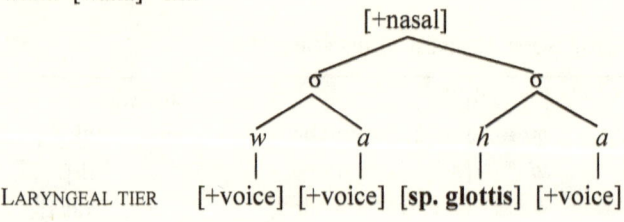

c. ~busu [mũʰsṹ] 'lesser anteater'

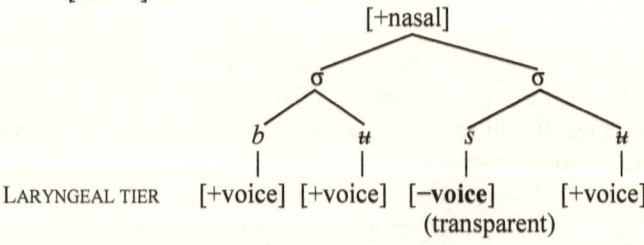

d. ~*waku* [w̃ãʰkũ] 'remember'

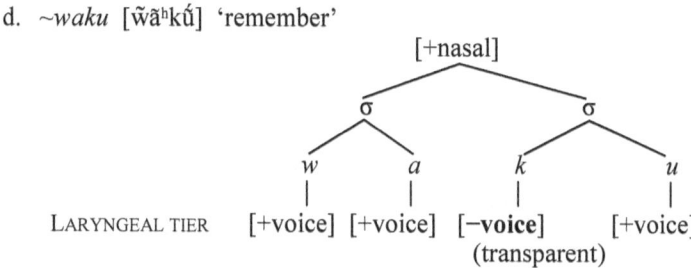

e. ~*bachɨ* [mãʰɟ̃ɨ̃] 'leafcutter ant'

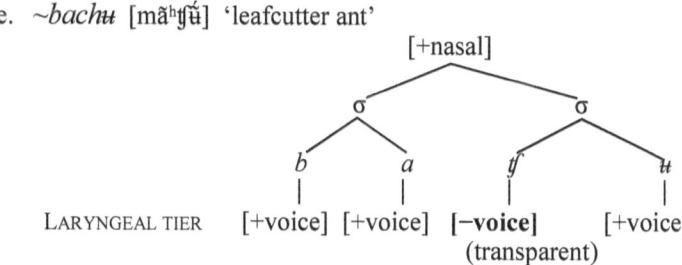

2.5.2 Spreading processes

In the previous section we saw that the [±nasal] feature is associated to the morpheme. We now turn to the spread of the nasal feature within the phonological word (discussed in detail in chapter 3). A phonological word is minimally composed of an independent root, but is more commonly composed of a root and one or more affixed morphemes, which may be compounded or serialized roots, nonroot stem morphemes, or suffixes. All roots and nonroot stem morphemes, and a subset of suffixes, are specified with unalterable [+nasal] or [−nasal] values; this leaves only unmarked [Ønasal] suffix morphemes as eligible targets for the spread of the [±nasal] feature. A complete list of [Ønasal] grammatical morphemes is given in table 2.11. Although only a small subset of suffixes are [Ønasal], they are among the most frequently occurring suffixes in the language, and include all suffixes composed of a single vowel. Among those with the shape *CV*, however, there is no way to predict, from frequency, meaning or morphological position, which ones will be [Ønasal]. For example, among the singular and plural suffixes, all of which occur frequently, the plural suffix for animates, -~*da*, is [+nasal], while both the animate singular suffix, +*ro*, and the plural suffix for inanimates, +*ri*, are [Ønasal]; the locative and objective case markers are about equally frequent, but locative -*pɨ* is [−nasal] and objective +*re* is [Ønasal]. All [Ønasal] morphemes are preceded by + (rather than a dash) in glosses and when cited in the text, to indicate their special phonological status.

TABLE 2.11. KOTIRIA [ØNASAL] MORPHEMES

+a	plural (animates)
+a	evidential (ASSERT.PERF)
+a	affectedness (AFFEC)
+ga	imperative
+i	locative
+i	evidential (VIS.PERF.1)
+o	feminine
+ɨ ~ +i	masculine
+ra	evidential (VIS.IMPERF.2/3)
+re	evidential (VIS.PERF.2/3)
+re	objective case marker (OBJ)
+ri	nominalizer
+ri	plural (inanimates)
+ro	singular (animates)

In (28), we see one such suffix, the unmarked [Ønasal] nominal suffix +ro (animate singular). This suffix has two surface forms—either nasal [r̃õ] as in (28a), or oral [ro], as in (28b)—depending on the [±nasal] specification of the preceding morpheme.

(28) a. [nãmṍr̃õ] 'a wife' [+nasal]

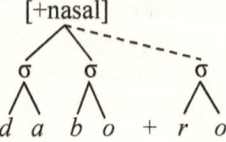

d a   b o + r o

b. [jaíró] 'a jaguar' [−nasal]

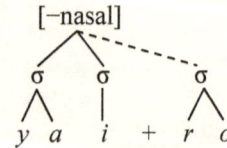

y a   i + r o

Any inherently marked morpheme—either [+nasal] or [−nasal]—blocks spread, and the process ceases at the boundary of the phonological word. We observe the spreading process in the surface realizations of unmarked suffixes such as +ro in (28) and (29b), +re in (30b) and (32), and the nominalizer +ri in (30a), in contrast to suffixes that are inherently marked with [±nasal] values, such as the [+nasal] diminutive -~ka (29a) and animate plural nominalizer -ida (31b) and the [−nasal] locative -pɨ (30b).

Phonology

The specific characteristics of association and spreading of the [±nasal] suprasegmental result in three types of phonological words: entirely nasal (29), entirely oral (30), and mixed (31)–(32).

(29) [+nasal words]

    a. all morphemes [+nasal]

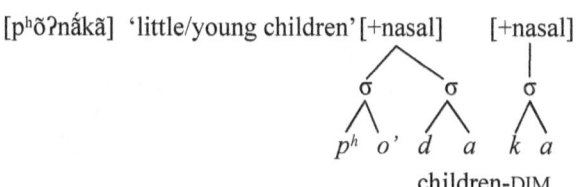

[pʰõʔnãkã] 'little/young children'

children-DIM

    b. compounded [+nasal] roots with spreading to [Ønasal] suffix +ro

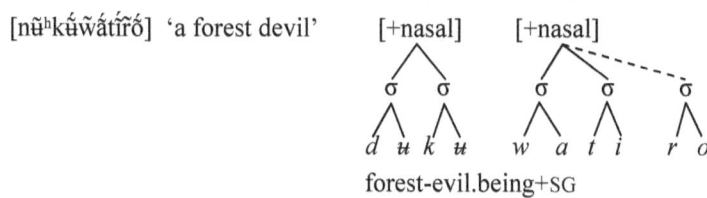

[nũʰkũ̃wã́tĩ̃rṍ] 'a forest devil'

forest-evil.being+SG

(30) [−nasal] words

    a. mixed [−nasal] and [Ønasal] morphemes

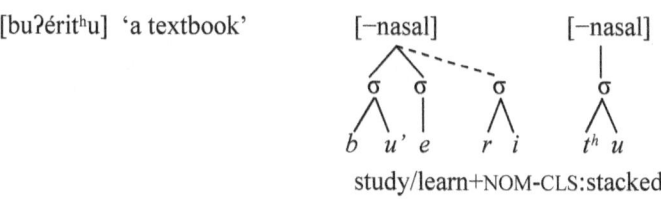

[buʔéritʰu] 'a textbook'

study/learn+NOM-CLS:stacked

    b. [−nasal] morphemes with spreading to [Ønasal] suffix +re

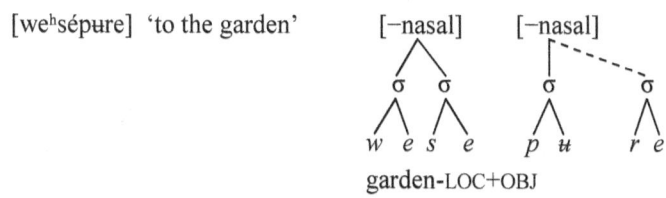

[weʰsépu̶re] 'to the garden'

garden-LOC+OBJ

Although [nasal] is argued to be a privative feature in much current phonological theory (e.g., Ewen and van der Hulst 2001), Eastern Tukanoan languages provide typological evidence that, while they may be rare, there are languages for which we must postulate both [+nasal] and [−nasal] values in order to fully understand spreading and blocking processes. Indeed, we can only derive Eastern Tukanoan surface forms correctly by assuming binary values, as we see when we look at spreading processes in words such as those in (31)–(32). In (31a) and (31b), the fact that all morphemes are underlyingly marked for [nasal] creates oral-nasal contours within each phonological word. Both (31b), in which all morphemes are marked for [nasal], and (32), with combinations of marked and unmarked morphemes, demonstrate that we need both [+nasal] and [−nasal] values to be able to account for the surface realizations of different kinds of nonnasalized morphemes. We must differentiate between [−nasal] and [Ønasal]; otherwise all nonnasalized morphemes would be potential targets for spreading, whereas in fact those that are inherently oral, in other words [−nasal], block spreading.

(31) words containing both [+nasal] and [−nasal] morphemes

a. [waʔáduanã] 'our wanting to go'

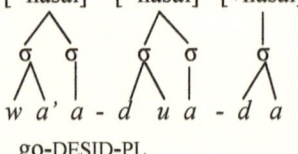

b. [mãsãjáʰkã́ĩnã́] 'kidnappers'

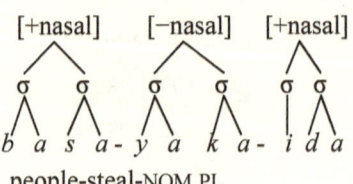

(32) words containing both [+nasal] and [−nasal] morphemes, with spreading to [Ønasal] suffixes

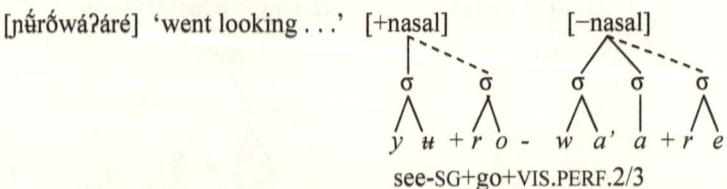

2.6 Suprasegmental tone

2.6.1 Tone or pitch accent?

The second suprasegmental process affecting the surface realization of words in Kotiria is pitch variation, a feature of all Eastern Tukanoan languages, though it is still a matter of debate whether this pitch variation should be typologically classified as tone or as pitch accent. In her overview of the Tukanoan language family, Barnes states that "[all] the Tucano languages have accent, or pitch-accent systems in which there is high pitch vs. low pitch .... High pitch is usually associated with accent" (1999:212). In her analysis of Tuyuka, she describes the language as having two autosegmental processes—nasalization and accent—the interaction of which results in three-way lexical contrasts (Barnes 1996).

Barnes's blanket characterization of all Eastern Tukanoan languages as pitch-accent languages unfortunately ignores evidence from important studies of tone in Eastern Tukanoan such as Gomez-Imbert's work on Tatuyo (Gomez-Imbert 1982) and Barasana (Gomez-Imbert 1997a, 2001; Gomez-Imbert and Kenstowicz 2000) and Ramirez's study of Tukano (Ramirez 1997a). Gomez-Imbert identifies H and HL tonal melodies for Barasana roots, both of which normally occur with an additional extrametrical left-edge L. Ramirez analyzes Tukano as having morphemes with H(igh), L(ow), and Rising tone melodies (1997a:92).

Waltz and Waltz (2000) also propose H and L tones, with accent associated to the first H-toned syllable, for Kotiria. They also state that if a phonological word contains secondary accented syllables with H tones, these will be automatically lowered, given that only there is only one H tone allowed in a phonological word. Such medial tones or contours are understood to be noncontrastive "adjusted" H tones. Primary accent associated with H tone is predictably located (with few exceptions) on the final syllable of roots (Waltz and Waltz 2000:455).

The Kotiria system as described by Waltz and Waltz (2000) is characterized by an association of H tone with a single accent peak. Such associations are found in prototypical pitch-accent systems combining distinctive tone with culminative accent (as outlined in Hyman 1978). In contrast, Gomez-Imbert argues that Barasana has more prototypical features of a tone language than of a stress or pitch-accent language, though she classifies Barasana as a "restricted tone" language given that only two tonal melodies—H and HL—are distinguished (2001:405). In my view, Kotiria tonal phenomena display a great many similarities to the tonal system of Barasana as described by Gomez-Imbert, and the summary that follows draws much from her analyses. There are four contrastive surface tonal patterns for roots in Kotiria. In a draft version of my in-progress lexical database, roots with the four patterns occurred with the following frequencies: LHL, 48 percent; LH, 21 percent; HL, 18 percent; H, 13 percent. As material is added to the database, the exact frequencies may change slightly, but the strong preponderance of the LHL pattern is clear.

If all instances of left-edge L are classified as extrametrical, these four tonal patterns can be condensed into two underlying contrastive tonal melodies: H and HL. Following Prince's (1999) work on extrametrical elements, I analyze the left-edge L tone as a peripheral unit, one that is never involved in spreading processes. Moreover, given that Eastern Tukanoan languages are polysynthetic and that roots are almost always the initial constituents of words, a left-edge L tone could function primarily as a phonological marker indicating a new prosodic unit.

2.6.2 Derivations and spreading processes

In Kotiria, the tonal melody of a root aligns to its left edge and each tonal element associates from left to right to an individual mora, the tone-bearing unit. Simple derivations and examples of tonal melody contrasts are given in (33)–(35).[21] Unassociated moras are targets for immediate tonal spread from the left, as we see in (34b) and (35a), but we should also note that in (33b) the final L tone of the bare root form remains unassociated because there is no root-internal tone-bearing unit available. Unlike tone languages in which multiple associations of tones to tone-bearing units result in contour tones (see cases in Kenstowicz 1994 and Goldsmith 1999), unassociated tones in Kotiria remain unrealized until morphological processes have provided additional tone-bearing units to which they can be assigned and thus be realized on the surface.[22]

(33) a. [sù?á] 'weave'

$$\begin{array}{cc} L & H \\ | & | \\ \mu & \mu \\ | & | \\ s\ u' & a \end{array}$$

b. [sù?á] 'go into the brush'

$$\begin{array}{ccc} L & H & L \\ | & | & \\ \mu & \mu & \\ | & | & \\ s\ u' & a & \end{array}$$

---

[21] In this section only, both H and L tones are overtly marked in the phonetic forms: the grave accent mark indicates L tone and the acute accent mark indicates H tone.

[22] In this respect, Kotiria contrasts with Barasana, in which there is an optional process whereby speakers lengthen the final mora of a LHL root in order to provide a tone-bearing unit for the realization of an unassociated L tone (Gomez-Imbert 2001:375).

(34) a. [kʰòá] 'return'

b. [kʰóá] 'half, part'

(35) a. [tóá] 'plant'

b. [tòá] '(do) again'

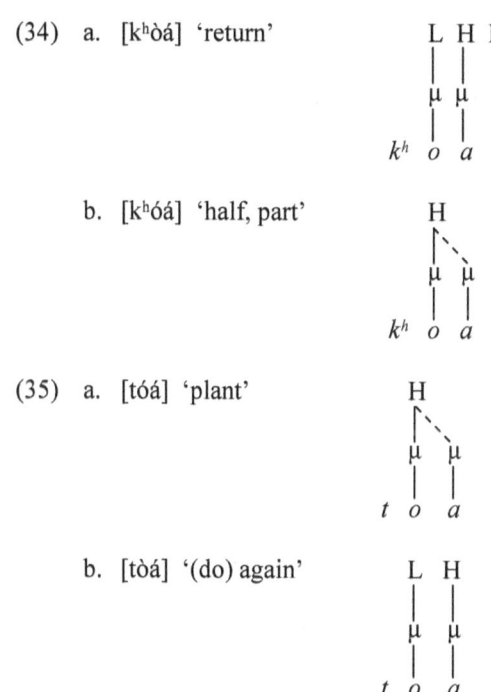

As was the case with the suprasegmental [±nasal] feature, only certain morpheme types are consistently marked for tone. Lexical roots always have associated tonal melodies, whereas most suffixes are unmarked for tone and thus are eligible targets for tonal spread. Spreading of tones to such unmarked morphemes is often the only means of determining whether or not the underlying melody of a root is actually LH or LHL. Being bimoraic, most bare root forms have only two available tone-bearing units and most roots begin with L tone; thus, both LH and LHL roots display a surface LH root melody, as in (33) above and (36).

(36) a. [dìé] 'dog'

b. [mã̀nṹ] 'husband'

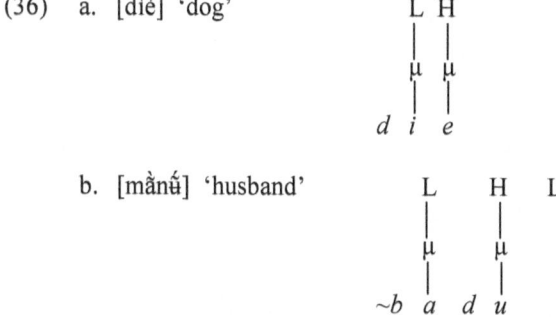

The tonal contrast of LH and LHL roots is only exposed when an additional morpheme, such as the unmarked animate singular +*ro*, is appended, allowing for the spread of either the H tone of a LH root (37a) or the association of the otherwise unassociated final L of a LHL root (37b).

(37) a. [dìéró] 'a dog'

b. [mã̀nṹrõ̀] 'a husband'

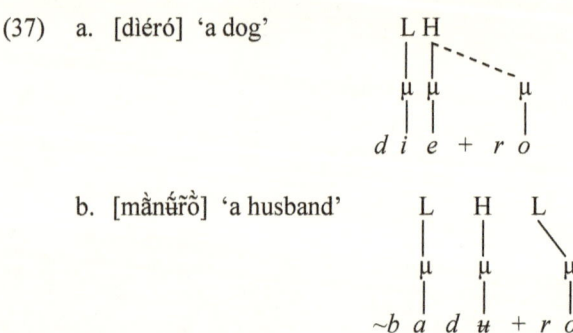

Suprasegmental tonal melodies, like suprasegmental [±nasal] values, are associated to the morpheme and the scope of spreading for both features is the phonological word. Similarly to nasalization, tonal spreading proceeds left to right from marked to unmarked morphemes, which surface with either a H or a L tone variant.

Suprasegmental tone and nasalization differ, however, in several significant ways. First, whereas the [±nasal] feature assigns a single value to an entire morpheme, marking it as either all oral or all nasal, each tone of a root's tonal melody is individually associated with a mora. However, some roots have more tones than they have moras; these roots have an underlying unassociated tone, one that can only surface when morphological processes provide an extra mora to which the tone can associate, as in (37b).

Tone and nasalization also contrast in the way in which they spread. Within a phonological word only unmarked morphemes are eligible for the spread of [±nasal] values, as any inherently marked morpheme blocks spread and retains its [±nasal] value. As a result, as we saw in (31)–(32) above, a phonological word may be composed of both oral and nasal morphemes. The general pattern of tonal spread operates differently: the tonal melody of the leftmost root morpheme, the tonological head, is replicated over the entire phonological word, spreading to unmarked affixed morphemes and overriding the inherent tonal melodies associated to morphemes such as noninitial roots in compounds or serializations. The only exception to this general pattern involves bound grammatical morphemes that have their own inherent tonal melodies, the single clear case being the negative suffix -*era*. The

HL melody of this morpheme neutralizes H tones in the immediately preceding root. Thus, a root such as the H-tone copula *hi* is realized with L tone when negated, allowing the negative suffix to retain its HL melody—that is, *hi-era* is pronounced [hiéra] (see §8.2 for additional examples and discussion).

In other words, there are two general interrelated tonal spreading processes: simple tonal spread from marked to unmarked morphemes (as in (35a)), and a process involving the delinking and substitution of the inherent tones of dependent roots in compounding or serializing constructions. Specifically, in multiple-root constructions, the tonal melodies associated with noninitial roots are delinked, and the melody of the leftmost root is associated with the entire sequence of roots. A new multimorphemic phonological root with a single tonal melody isthus derived according to the rule Gomez-Imbert represents as "[R_1 + R_2] → R_1" (2001:381). Once this rule has applied, spreading to unmarked suffixes takes place. The result of either tonal spread process—simple spread or the more complex process in words with multiple roots—is the formation of a phonological word with a single tonal melody established by the leftmost (tonological head) root.

In this respect, tonal melodies, while lexically assigned and contrastive in individual root forms, display a less stable lexical association than do [±nasal] feature values. Morphological processes determine whether or not the inherent tonal melody of a morpheme will prevail over the entire phonological word (the case of word-initial roots) or be delinked (the case of noninitial elements).

Examples (38)–(43) illustrate tonal spreading processes with the four types of root melodies—LHL, LH, HL, and H—in initial root position and give derivations of surface tonal patterns of phonological words.[23] In (38) we see a word whose initial root has the most common tonal melody, LHL. Given the canonical bimoraic structure of root morphemes, the final L of this melody is only revealed by additional morphology. Thus, in (38), the final L tone of the LHL verb root ~*yosa* 'force into' is associated to the unmarked nominal classifier for straight, cylindrical objects -*dɨ*. The resulting phonological word in has an overall LHL melody.

(38)   initial root: [ɲõʰsá] 'force into; stab'   L H L
                                                      | |
                                                ~y o s a

---

[23] The moraic tier is omitted in these examples.

54   Chapter 2

    association of tone with suffix:

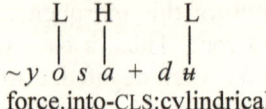

force.into-CLS:cylindrical

    surface form of word: [ɲǒʰsǎdù] 'a spear, arrow'

The roots in (39) and (40) have LH melodies. The final H of the LH noun root *bi'i* 'rat' in (39) spreads to the unmarked plural suffix +*a*, resulting in the LH word 'rats'. In (40) we see a serialization of a LH verbal root ~*waku* 'be aware' and a LHL root ~*basi* 'know'. This is our first example of the tone substitution process outlined above, in which the tonal melody of the leftmost root (the phonological head) prevails over the other roots in a multiple-root construction. The underlying tonal melody of the noninitial root is delinked and a new root unit with a single LH melody—that of the initial root—is derived. The resulting phonological words in both examples have overall LH melodies.

(39)   initial root: [bì?í] 'rat'

    spreading of tone to suffix:

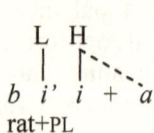

rat+PL

    surface form of word: [bì?íá] 'rats'

(40)   initial root: [w̃ǎʰkǔ] 'be aware'

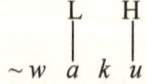

    delinking of tone on noninitial root:

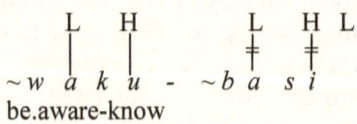

be.aware-know

    spreading of tone to noninitial root:

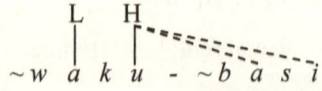

    surface form of word: [w̃ǎʰkǔmǎʰsî] '(you) should be careful'

The initial roots of the words in (41) and (42) have the less frequently occurring HL and H tonal melodies. Example (41) illustrates tonal spread in a serialization of two verbal roots: HL *phi'a* 'go out into' and LHL ~*su* 'arrive'. The derivation in (42) shows the delinking

Phonology

of the HL melody of the noninitial root ~su and association of the final L of the initial root to its available mora, the result being a derived phonological unit composed of two serialized roots but with a single HL melody. The final L of the derived multiple-root unit then spreads to the unmarked evidential suffix. The resulting phonological word has an overall HL melody.

(41) initial root: [pʰíʔà] 'go out into'

$$\begin{array}{cc} H & L \\ | & | \\ p^h \; i' & a \end{array}$$

delinking of tone on
noninitial root:

$$\begin{array}{cccc} H & L & & L\;H\;L \\ | & | & & \not{|} \\ p^h & i' & a \; - \; {\sim}s\;\textit{u} & + \; a \end{array}$$
go.out.into-arrive+ASSERT.PERF

spreading of tone to noninitial
root and suffix:

$$p^h \; i' \quad a \; - \; {\sim}s \; \textit{u} \quad + \quad a$$

surface form of word: [pʰíʔàsṳ̀à] '(he) went out into (a clearing)'

The initial root of the word in (42) has a H tonal melody, and in the derivation, we see spreading of the H tone of *toa* 'plant' to the affixed unmarked evidential suffix, resulting in a phonological word with overall H melody.

(42) initial root: [tóá] 'plant'

$$\begin{array}{c} H \\ \wedge \\ t \; o \; a \end{array}$$

spreading of tone to suffix:

$$\begin{array}{c} H \\ \wedge \quad \text{-----} \\ t \; o \; a \; + \; r \; a \end{array}$$
be.sharp+VIS.IMPERF.2/3

surface form of word: [tóárá] '(They) plant (sugarcane)'

2.6.3 Monomoraic roots and tonal melodies

It is interesting to note what happens with the tonal melodies of monomoraic roots. As with bimoraic roots, monomoraic roots occur with all four tonal melodies, as we can see in (43).

(43) a. Monomoraic roots with LH melodies

    ba   'swim'
    bo   'forget, lose'
    ~ba   'be small'

	~bi	'now'
	khu	'turtle'
	ta	'come'

b. Monomoraic roots with LHL melodies

	~da	'get'
	khʉ	'manioc root'
	~kha	'chop, cut, hit'
	ko	'water, medicine'
	~sa	'be inside'
	~sʉ	'arrive'
	ya	'possession'

c. Monomoraic roots with H melodies

	be	'inject, plant'
	bu	'agouti' (type of)
	bʉ	'edge of X, shore'
	~ba	'stream'
	~bi	'honey'
	~bʉ	'carry on one's back'
	cha	'prepared food, meal'
	da	'be small'
	di	'blood'
	~di	'which' (interrogative)
	~du	'buzz (noise)'
	ho	'banana'
	ho	'drawing, letter'
	hu	'smoke'
	ki	'mandi fish'
	kha	'hawk'
	~ke	'beak, nose'
	o	'acari fish'
	~o	'hang by a thread or stem'
	~pe	'breast'
	~pu	'suckle'
	~pʉ	'crab'
	pha	'stomach'
	~phu	'leaf'
	se	'cucura fruit'
	~ta	'rock'
	tha	'grass'
	thʉ	'push'
	wa	'give'
	yo	'corn'
	~yʉ	'see/look'

d. Monomoraic roots with HL melodies

ba	'decompose'
~bʉ	'man'
chʉ	'eat'
du	'speak, talk'
~di	'be' (progressive auxiliary)
~di	'say, warn, wonder'
go	'be skillful as a fisherman'
hi	'be' (copula)
~hu	'worm'
~hʉ	'burn'
ka	'black monkey'
ko	'relative (Kotiria)'
khe	'be fast'
pi	'tooth'
phi	'be big'
si	'be hot'
so	'be different'
tʉ	'stick'
wʉ	'fly'
ya	'bury'
~ya	'be bad/ugly/evil'
~yo	'show'

However, (43) shows that H and HL melodies occur much more frequently with monomoraic roots with than they do with bimoraic roots. This tendency is particularly obvious in roots that underwent loss of the left-edge mora (as discussed in §2.4.2), which indicates that loss of the left-edge mora has generally resulted in loss of the left-edge tonal element L associated to it as well. However, such loss is not attested for all monomoraic roots, given that we can still identify a number of monomoraic roots with associated LH or LHL melodies. For these roots, loss of the initial mora did not erase the left-edge L, but merely left it as an extra unassociated tonal element which is only realized when such roots occur as independent words and the rule of bimoraic prosodic minimality forces lengthening, as discussed in §2.4.2.

Indeed, what we observe in the surface forms of monomoraic roots within multimorphemic words is that they are consistently realized with H tone. The fact that all monomoraic roots are realized with H tone when there is only one mora available for tone follows from another rule determining that initial root morphemes, as heads of phonological words, must be realized with at least one H tone. Thus, the association of tonal melodies of monomoraic LH or LHL roots in multimorphemic words is necessarily adjusted: the left-edge, extramoraic

L is left as unrealized and association begins with the H tone of the underlying melody.

The tonal processes that affect a monomoraic root with underlying LHL melody are exemplified in (44). When such a root is an independent word, its vowel is lengthened (44a), and tones are associated to the moras of the lengthened vowel in the usual way—the initial L associates to the first mora and the H to the second mora, leaving the final L unassociated (44b). But when the root is followed by another morpheme in the word (44c), its vowel is not lengthened, and it is the initial (left-edge) L that is left unassociated; the H tone is associated with the single mora of the root, and the final L is associated with the next morpheme.

(44) root: $khɨ_{LHL}$ [kʰɨ́ɨ́] 'manioc root'

a. lengthening when root is an independent word:

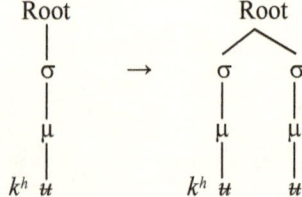

b. association of tone to lengthened root:

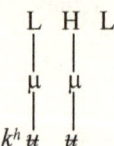

c. monomoraic realization of root in multimorphemic word, with unassociated left-edge L:

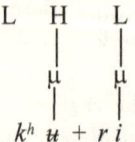

surface form of word: [kʰɨ́ri] 'manioc roots'

Further examples of monomoraic roots with LH and LHL melodies are shown in table 2.12. In the vocabulary (appendix 2), the tonal melodies of this subset of monomoraic roots are represented as (L)H or (L)HL as a reminder of this particular phonological behavior. When monomoraic roots are cited in the text, phonetic representations are given.

TABLE 2.12. MONOMORAIC ROOTS WITH INITIAL L TONE

ROOT	AS INDEPENDENT WORD (with lengthening and initial L realized)		IN MULTIMORPHEMIC WORD (with initial L unrealized, and final L associated to the following morpheme)		
ta_{LH}	[taá]	'come'	ta-tu'sʉ	[tátúʔsʉ́]	'just come'
bo_{LH}	[boó]	'forget'	bo-si	[bósí]	'will not forget'
~$sʉ_{LHL}$	[sʉ̃ʉ̃́]	'arrive'	~sʉ-~ida	[sʉ̃ĩnã]	'arriving ones'
ko_{LHL}	[koó]	'water'	ko-ti-ri-a	[kótiria]	'Kotiria, water people'

2.7 Suprasegmental glottalization

The third suprasegmental phonological feature in Kotiria is glottalization, which is formally characterized by the feature [constricted glottis] and occurs in approximately 23 percent of roots. The contrastive nature of this feature in Kotiria is shown in the minimal pairs of roots with shapes *CVCV* (table 2.13) and *CVV* (table 2.14).

TABLE 2.13. MINIMAL PAIRS FOR GLOTTALIZATION IN *CVCV* ROOTS

GLOTTALIZED			NONGLOTTALIZED		
~si'di	[sĩʔnĩ]	'drink'	~sidi	[sĩnĩ]	'ask for'
~da'ka	[nãʔká]	'miriti fruit'	~daka	[nã^hká]	'do/be together'
du'ti	[duʔtí]	'hide, escape'	duti	[du^htí]	'illness'
phu'ti	[pʰuʔtí]	'grated manioc'	phuti	[pʰu^htí]	'blow (a flute)'
~da'bo	[nãʔmṍ]	'rope'	~dabo	[nãmṍ]	'wife'

TABLE 2.14. MINIMAL PAIRS FOR GLOTTALIZATION IN *CVV* ROOTS

GLOTTALIZED			NONGLOTTALIZED		
khʉ'a	[kʰʉʔá]	'lice'	khʉa	[kʰʉá]	'have'
wʉ'ʉ	[wʉʔʉ́]	'house'	wʉ	[wʉ́ʉ]	'fly'
so'a	[soʔá]	'long-tailed fish'	soa	[sóá]	'grind'
su'a	[suʔá]	'weave'	sua	[suá]	'pick fruit'
wʉ'a	[wʉʔá]	'peel'	wʉa	[wʉá]	'pick up'

2.7.1 Segment or suprasegment?

Kotiria is not the only Eastern Tukanoan language in which glottal stops occur in roots. Waltz and Wheeler (1972) classify Kotiria, Wa'ikhana/Piratapuyo, and Tukano as a related subgroup within the family based, in part, on the fact that glottal stop occurs contrastively in roots in these languages,[24] and Gomez-Imbert (2011) points out that glottal stops occur (though less frequently) in two other Eastern Tukanoan languages of the Vaupés region—Desano and Siriano—as well as in Tanimuka/Retuarã and in the Western Tukanoan language Siona. They do not occur in the languages of the Piraparaná, an indication of their development as an areal feature.

Early works on Eastern Tukanoan languages analyzed glottal stop as a feature of a subset of vowel phonemes in Tukano (Sorensen 1969:19–23) or as an element of a "glottalized syllable" in Desano (Kaye 1970), but in most of the more recent literature on Eastern Tukanoan, glottal stops are analyzed as consonant segments. Thus we find glottal stops included in the phonemic inventories of Wa'ikhana/ Piratapuyo (Klumpp and Klumpp 1973:109; Ardila 2000:493), Desano (Miller 1999:9), Tukano (Welch and West 2000:420), and Kotiria (Waltz and Waltz 2000:453).

However, we find that the distribution of glottal stops is quite different from that of all other consonants, for glottal stops occur neither word-initially nor morpheme-initially. They only occur as onsets of noninitial syllables in roots syllabified as *CV.ʔV*, as in the Kotiria data in (45), or as codas of initial syllables in roots syllabified as *CVʔ.CV* (table 2.15). Indeed, glottal stops are the only allowed codas in these Eastern Tukanoan languages, whose syllable structure otherwise strictly prohibits codas.

(45) ba'a   [baʔá]   'bass (fish)'
      po'a   [poʔá]   'clean/break open'
      bi'i   [biʔí]   'rat'
      bi'a   [biʔá]   'close'
      bu'e   [buʔé]   'study'
      wɨ'a   [wɨʔá]   'peel'
      do'a   [doʔá]   'cook'
      sɨ'o   [sɨʔó]   'sift'

---

[24] For a discussion of other noncontrastive glottal-stop-like sounds in Kotiria, see Stenzel 2007a.

monomoraic roots are cited in the text, phonetic representations are given.

TABLE 2.12. MONOMORAIC ROOTS WITH INITIAL L TONE

ROOT	AS INDEPENDENT WORD (with lengthening and initial L realized)		IN MULTIMORPHEMIC WORD (with initial L unrealized, and final L associated to the following morpheme)		
ta_{LH}	[taá]	'come'	ta-tu'sʉ	[tátúʔsʉ́]	'just come'
bo_{LH}	[boó]	'forget'	bo-si	[bósí]	'will not forget'
~$sʉ_{LHL}$	[sʉ̃ʉ̃́]	'arrive'	~sʉ-~ida	[sʉ̃́ĩnã]	'arriving ones'
ko_{LHL}	[koó]	'water'	ko-ti-ri-a	[kótiria]	'Kotiria, water people'

2.7 Suprasegmental glottalization

The third suprasegmental phonological feature in Kotiria is glottalization, which is formally characterized by the feature [constricted glottis] and occurs in approximately 23 percent of roots. The contrastive nature of this feature in Kotiria is shown in the minimal pairs of roots with shapes *CVCV* (table 2.13) and *CVV* (table 2.14).

TABLE 2.13. MINIMAL PAIRS FOR GLOTTALIZATION IN *CVCV* ROOTS

GLOTTALIZED			NONGLOTTALIZED		
~si'di	[sĩʔnĩ́]	'drink'	~sidi	[sĩnĩ́]	'ask for'
~da'ka	[nãʔkã́]	'miriti fruit'	~daka	[nãʰkã́]	'do/be together'
du'ti	[duʔtí]	'hide, escape'	duti	[duʰtí]	'illness'
phu'ti	[pʰuʔtí]	'grated manioc'	phuti	[pʰuʰtí]	'blow (a flute)'
~da'bo	[nãʔmṍ]	'rope'	~dabo	[nãmṍ]	'wife'

TABLE 2.14. MINIMAL PAIRS FOR GLOTTALIZATION IN *CVV* ROOTS

GLOTTALIZED			NONGLOTTALIZED		
khʉ'a	[kʰʉʔá]	'lice'	khʉa	[kʰʉá]	'have'
wʉ'ʉ	[wʉʔʉ́]	'house'	wʉ	[wʉ́ʉ]	'fly'
so'a	[soʔá]	'long-tailed fish'	soa	[sóá]	'grind'
su'a	[suʔá]	'weave'	sua	[suá]	'pick fruit'
wʉ'a	[wʉʔá]	'peel'	wʉa	[wʉá]	'pick up'

2.7.1 Segment or suprasegment?
Kotiria is not the only Eastern Tukanoan language in which glottal stops occur in roots. Waltz and Wheeler (1972) classify Kotiria, Wa'ikhana/Piratapuyo, and Tukano as a related subgroup within the family based, in part, on the fact that glottal stop occurs contrastively in roots in these languages,[24] and Gomez-Imbert (2011) points out that glottal stops occur (though less frequently) in two other Eastern Tukanoan languages of the Vaupés region—Desano and Siriano—as well as in Tanimuka/Retuarã and in the Western Tukanoan language Siona. They do not occur in the languages of the Piraparaná, an indication of their development as an areal feature.

Early works on Eastern Tukanoan languages analyzed glottal stop as a feature of a subset of vowel phonemes in Tukano (Sorensen 1969:19–23) or as an element of a "glottalized syllable" in Desano (Kaye 1970), but in most of the more recent literature on Eastern Tukanoan, glottal stops are analyzed as consonant segments. Thus we find glottal stops included in the phonemic inventories of Wa'ikhana/Piratapuyo (Klumpp and Klumpp 1973:109; Ardila 2000:493), Desano (Miller 1999:9), Tukano (Welch and West 2000:420), and Kotiria (Waltz and Waltz 2000:453).

However, we find that the distribution of glottal stops is quite different from that of all other consonants, for glottal stops occur neither word-initially nor morpheme-initially. They only occur as onsets of noninitial syllables in roots syllabified as *CV.ʔV*, as in the Kotiria data in (45), or as codas of initial syllables in roots syllabified as *CVʔ.CV* (table 2.15). Indeed, glottal stops are the only allowed codas in these Eastern Tukanoan languages, whose syllable structure otherwise strictly prohibits codas.

(45)   ba'a   [baʔá]   'bass (fish)'
      po'a   [poʔá]   'clean/break open'
      bi'i   [biʔí]   'rat'
      bi'a   [biʔá]   'close'
      bu'e   [buʔé]   'study'
      wʉ'a   [wʉʔá]   'peel'
      do'a   [doʔá]   'cook'
      sʉ'o   [sʉʔó]   'sift'

---

[24] For a discussion of other noncontrastive glottal-stop-like sounds in Kotiria, see Stenzel 2007a.

Phonology

TABLE 2.15. COGNATES OF KOTIRIA WORDS WITH GLOTTAL STOP CODA

KOTIRIA	WA'IKHANA/ PIRATAPUYO	TUKANO	
da'po [daʔpó]	*da'po* [daʔpó]	*da'po* [daʔpó]	'foot'
po'ka [poʔká]	*po'ka* [poʔká]	*po'ka* [poʔká]	'manioc flour'
~wa'ba [w̃ãʔmã́]	*~wa'ba* [w̃ãʔmã́]	*~wa'ba* [w̃ãʔmã́]	'new'
ya'pi [jaʔpí]	*ya'pi* [jaʔpí]	*ya'pi* [jaʔpí]	'smooth'
~bʉ'do [mʉ̃ʔnṍ]	*~bʉ'do* [mʉ̃ʔnṍ]	*~bʉ'do* [mʉ̃ʔnṍ]	'tobacco'
~ye'be [ɲẽʔmẽ́]	*~ye'be* [ɲẽʔmẽ́]	*~ya'ba* [ɲãʔmã́]	'tongue'

There have been several analyses of the origin of the glottal stop in these positions. Waltz and Wheeler (1972) postulate that a Proto-Tukanoan segment *ʔ was fully retained in Kotiria, Wa'ikhana/Piratapuyo, and Tukano, and partially retained in Desano and Siona. In all these languages, *CV.ʔV* morphemes are taken to have preserved from the Proto-Tukanoan forms both basic *CV* syllable structure and the glottal segment as a consonant in onset position, while synchronic occurrences of the glottal stop in coda position are viewed as the result of diachronic vowel loss in *CVʔV* roots with an unstressed second syllable (46a), followed by fusion of the resulting eroded *CVʔ* root with a *CV* suffix and resyllabification of the newly formed morpheme (46b–c). In most, but not all, cases the glottal segment was later lost (46d), resulting in a final reconstitution of *CVCV* structure, the predominant synchronic pattern overall (Waltz and Wheeler 1972:133).

(46)   a.   vowel loss: V → Ø / CV.ʔ__-[CV]$_{suffix}$
       b.   morpheme fusion: *CV.ʔ-[CV]* → *CVʔCV*
       c.   resyllabification: *CVʔCV* → *CVʔ.CV*
       d.   glottal loss: ʔ → Ø / CV__CV

Unfortunately, Waltz and Wheeler's study provides few examples of *CVʔCV* roots that reconstruct as either a combination of a *CVʔV* root with a *CV* suffix or, alternatively, as a trisyllabic root with a parallel *CVʔVCV* shape. Rather, a number of the protolanguage forms given in this work are reconstructed as containing ʔC clusters, e.g., *aʔti 'come', *buʔsa 'cotton', and *diʔpó 'foot', among others (Waltz and Wheeler 1972:137–49). There is also little evidence to support the hypothesis that trisyllabic roots might once have been more common, although the study does reconstruct *toʔatu 'drum' and *wiʔdia 'forehead'. Were such roots commonplace in the protolanguage, we would expect to find relics in Kotiria and other languages, but in fact, Ramirez (1997a:53) states that 97 percent of Tukano morphemes are monosyllabic or disyllabic, and that the few cases of trisyllabic lexemes are either borrowed words or lexemes with unanalyzable suffixes. Gomez-Imbert (1997a:76–85) also identifies bimoraic root shape as basic in Barasana and lists only a small number of trimoraic lexemes, some of which clearly have onomatopoeic origins. In short, there is no regular cross-linguistic synchronic evidence to indicate an earlier pattern of commonplace trisyllabic roots in Eastern Tukanoan languages, and a firm explanation for the development of the glottal in coda position is still lacking.

As for the glottal onset, Malone (1987, sections 4 and 6) postulates a suprasegment *ʔ in the protolanguage that surfaced in sequences of like vowels in *CVV* morphemes in order to reinforce the *CV* structure of the second syllable. This glottal suprasegment was later lost in most Eastern Tukanoan languages, and in the few languages in which it was retained (Kotiria, Wa'ikhana/Piratapuyo, Tukano, and Siriano), it developed into a contrastive segment occurring most frequently in word-internal position.

Gomez-Imbert (2011) proposes a hypothesis that requires neither a glottal segment nor a glottal suprasegmental in the protolanguage. She argues that Tukanoan languages can be subgrouped according to their basic types of allowed syllable structures. Most Eastern Tukanoan languages (Kubeo, Yuruti, Pisamira, Karapana, Tatuyo, Barasana, Makuna, Bará, and Tuyuka) regularly allow *(C)V(V)* syllables and do not have a glottal segment. Other languages, Kotiria among them, allow some *(C)V(V)* syllables but favor more strict *(C)V* structure; these are the languages in which the glottal stop tends to occur in *VV* sequences (its occurrence being phonemic in Kotiria, Wa'ikhana/Piratapuyo, and Tukano, phonetic in Siriano and Desano). She analyzes the C_2 glottal stop in *CV.CV* roots as having developed, when L tone occurred on V_1, as the default consonant filling a vacant onset spot in an otherwise unfavored *(C)V* syllable: *CV.V* → *CV.ʔV*.

We know that restrictions on onsetless syllables can motivate consonant insertion in an effort to reestablish *CV* syllable structure, and we moreover know that a simple glottal segment might well be the default consonant of choice in such a process, especially if stimulated by other phonetic properties such as laryngealization or low tone. However, if there is a process of *CV* syllable reconstitution in Kotiria, we should note that it applies asymmetrically. First, there is morphological asymmetry, as only root morphemes appear to be targets. Single-*V* affix morphemes such as the evidential suffixes +*a* (ASSERT.PERF) and +*i* (VIS.PERF.1) (among others) are not systematically preceded by glottal stops, contrary to what one might expect were reconstitution of *CV* structure with a glottal stop applicable to all syllables regardless of their morphological status. Secondly, there is asymmetry even within the class of root morphemes, given the synchronic frequency of plain (nonglottalized) *CVV* roots such as those in the second column of table 2.14 above. Finally, there is syllable-position asymmetry in *CV* reconstruction: only internal *V*-shaped syllables of root morphemes, not initial syllables, appear to be regular candidates for glottal epenthesis.[25]

Nathan Waltz explores a hypothesis whereby glottal stop development is linked to tone (2002). He focuses on roots with two types of underlying structures—*CV̀V̀CV́* and *CV̀V́*—both of which contain long vowels[26] (represented as *VV*) and L pitch/tone. In roots of the first type (47), the occurrence of L pitch across the *VV* sequence leads to laryngealization of the second segment, which is subsequently dropped, leaving only the surface realization of a glottal stop. In roots of the second type (48), a glottal stop surfaces between like vowels in a LH pitch sequence and serves a demarcative function: "The second vowel is not dropped but is simply *separated* from the previous geminate vowel by the glottal stop" (Waltz 2002:159; emphasis added).

(47)   *CV̀V̀CV́*   *waatá*   [waʔtá]   'to sand'

(48)   *CV̀V́*   *bii*   [biʔí]   'rat'

What is problematic is that this analysis posits regularly occurring roots that are trimoraic and contain a sequence of two L tones, as in (47); this structure is highly divergent from the characteristic structure identified for roots in Kotiria and other Eastern Tukanoan languages (see §3.2, as well as Ramirez 1997a:53–56 and Gomez-Imbert and Hugh-Jones 2000:421). It moreover suggests that occurrence of the glottal stop is a product of long vowels in *CVV* roots such as (48), but it has nothing to say about the occurrence of the glottal stop in *CVV* roots with sequences of different vowels, as in most of the roots in the first column of table 2.14 above. Indeed, approximately one third of the glottalized roots in Kotiria have the shape CV_1V_2.

It is unclear whether Waltz presumes laryngealization of all low-pitched vowels or just of long vowels. He does not discuss laryngealization in *CV̀V́* or *CV̀ʔV́*, and in my own Kotiria data there is no evidence of consistent laryngealization of single L-toned vowels in LH

---

[25] According to Malone (1987), glottal stops regularly occur in vowel-initial words in the Eastern Tukanoan languages Tukano, Tuyuka, Siriano, and the Western Tukanoan languages Siona, Orejón, and Koreguaje. Criswell and Brandrup (2000:397) confirm this tendency in Siriano, and Gomez-Imbert (1982:15) observes that glottal stops optionally occur before vowel-initial words in Tatuyo. None of these studies argue phonemic status for the glottal stop in word-initial position.

[26] Called "geminate vowel clusters" by Waltz.

contexts. Indeed, all the morphophonological evidence points to laryngealization being conditioned by repeated L tone occurrence in contexts of L tone spread (see (49)).

As for the "demarcative" function Waltz proposes for the glottal stop in LH sequences, accepting it would entail a reevaluation of the idea that glottal epenthesis occurs only in the context of long vowels, and leave us to wonder whether the development of the glottal stop is to be attributed mainly to long vowels or to the occurrence of a tonal boundary. Moreover, if we accept the notion that the glottal stop has an essentially demarcative function, we must then explain why so many lexical roots in Kotiria—both *CVV* and *CVCV*, as we see in table 2.16—have a LH tonal sequence with no glottal stop at the tonal boundary. Indeed, over two-thirds of the root morphemes in my database have LHL or LH melodies (meaning they contain a LH rise, the target context for "demarcation") but only about a fourth of these are glottalized.

TABLE 2.16. WORDS WITH LH OR LHL MELODY AND NO GLOTTAL STOP

CV̀V́		*CV̀CV́*	
~bie [mĩẽ́]	'anteater'	*bʉhʉ* [bʉhʉ́]	'laugh'
bia [biá]	'pepper'	*~sayo* [sãɲṍ]	'scream'
die [dié]	'dog'	*wihi* [wihí]	'go outside'
phoa [pʰoá]	'hair / feather'	*chowe* [ʧowé]	'vomit'
sua [suá]	'pick (fruit)'	*sipa* [siʰpá]	'be shiny'

We are also left with no explanation for roots such as those in table 2.15 and in (49) below, which have LH tonal sequences on the first two moras and the more unusual *CVʔCV* shape. The occurrence of the glottal stop in such roots cannot be attributed to a need for LH tone sequence demarcation, since, if we assume such roots to be originally simple *CVCV*, what motivated their differentiation from *CVCV* roots that have no glottal stop at the tonal boundary, such as those in the second column of table 2.16?

(49) *dʉ'te* [dʉʔté] 'tie up/off (i.e. the edge of a basket'
~wa'ka [w̃ãʔkã́] 'wake up'
~da'bo [nãʔmṍ] 'rope'
~kʉ'ba [kʉ̃ʔmã́] 'year'
sa'wi [saʔwí] 'bump (on one's body)'

In sum, the demarcation hypothesis is as yet not confirmed by the data.

2.7.2 Association and derivations

I analyze glottalization as a third suprasegmental associated with root morphemes. It is formally represented by the feature [constricted glottis] and differs from suprasegmental nasalization and tone in three significant ways. First, whereas the [±nasal] and tonal melody suprasegmentals are part of the lexical specification for all roots, [constricted glottis] is marked on only a subset of root morphemes (approximately one fourth). Additionally, while examples of affixes marked as [±nasal] are fairly common and there are also examples of affixes with associated tonal melodies, I have identified no affixes marked as [constricted glottis]. Third, in contrast to nasalization and tone, there is no evidence that the [constricted glottis] feature spreads.

Like tone, the [constricted glottis] feature attaches to a mora, but unlike tone, it is mora-edge sensitive and occurs only once in a root: it associates to the right edge of the first mora only. This association guarantees that the [constricted glottis] feature will always manifest itself in intermoraic position, just once, as a single glottal gesture perceived as a glottal stop after the first vowel of the root morpheme.[27] Once the feature is manifest in the root, syllabification associates the glottal gesture either as a coda in *CVCV* roots or as an onset in *CVV* roots, as we see in the derivations in (50a) and (50b), respectively. ("UR" in these examples stands for "underlying representation.")

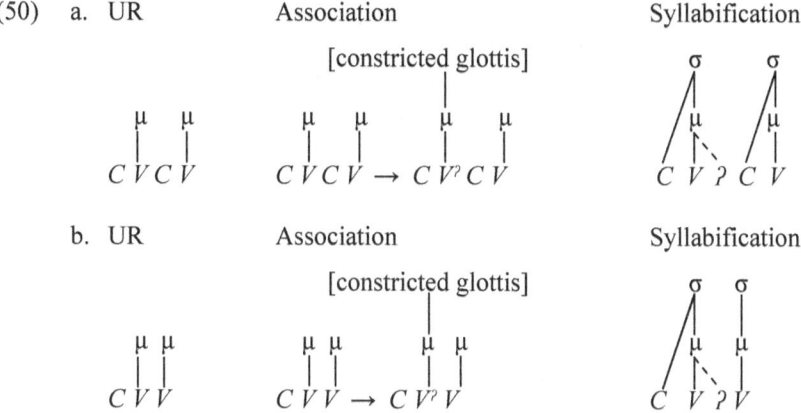

---

[27] According to Malone (1987), in the Western Tukanoan language Orejón, the glottal may also surface in word-final position. It is nevertheless not unusual for a language to restrict manifestation of a feature to a single instance within a unit. For example, like Kotiria, Yucatec Mayan allows only one glottalized segment per stem (Kenstowicz 1994). Ongoing acoustic studies by myself and Didier Demolin indicate that glottalization in both Kotiria and Wa'ikhana is phonetically realized as several different kinds of glottal gestures, not only true glottal stops.

This analysis is in some ways similar to Ramirez's analysis of "laryngealized" tone in Tukano. For Ramirez, laryngealization is an independent suprasegmental feature that attaches to the final part of the first-syllable vocalic segment. It interacts with L tone to produce "super low pitch," which is realized in fast speech as a slightly "stiff-voice" quality and in more formal or slow speech as a glottal stop. When the laryngealized vowel has an associated H tone, there is little or no change of voice quality (Ramirez 1997a:66).[28]

However, my analysis differs from Ramirez's in that I assert that suprasegmental glottalization and tone in Kotiria operate independently. Evidence for this assertion is found, first of all, in the fact that even though in Kotiria (as in Tukano) there is a tendency for glottalization and L tone to cooccur, we find examples of glottalized roots in Kotiria, given in (51) below, that have H tone on the first mora, and in such roots the glottal stop is consistently realized (in contrast to H-toned roots in Tukano). Though not abundant (they comprise a mere 2 percent of the [constricted glottis] set), glottalized roots with an initial H tone point to the synchronic independence of the two features. Second, not only is glottalization realized in Kotiria in H-toned contexts such as the roots in (51), but Kotiria seems to further contrast with Tukano in that glottal stops can be consistently perceived, and not just in formal speech.

(51) ~hi'da   [hĩ?nã]   'be the same'
      pe'ri   [pé?ri]   'all'
      phi'a   [pʰĩ?a]   'move out into an open area'

Finally, the most compelling evidence that the [constricted glottis] feature is independent from tone comes from examples such as (52), in which a glottalized root (~pha'a 'move across') occurs as the noninitial root in a serialized root construction with a H tone initial root (ba 'swim'). In §2.6.2, we saw that in serializations the tonal melody of the noninitial root is supplanted by that of the initial root. In (52), this process results in a LH melody for the entire phonological word. Were we to postulate that the glottal stop is only realized in the presence of L tone (as it appears to be in Tukano), we would predict that glottalization should not be fully realized in the (derived) H-tone dependent root ~pha'a. However, as the phonetic transcription of the serialized verb indicates, glottalization is preserved in the surface realization of the noninitial root, even though it has H tone.

---

[28] According to Criswell and Brandrup (2000:398), the same alternation of the glottal with laryngealization of the vowel in careful vs. fast speech also occurs in Siriano.

(52) ~bɨ'ɨ ba-~pha'a+re
      2.SG   swim-MOV.across+VIS.PERF.2/3
      'You swam across (a river).'

      [baá] (LH) - [pʰã̌ʔã̌] (LHL) → [baápʰã̌ʔãr̃ẽ̌]

2.7.3 Glottalization and preaspiration

Finally, it is important that we understand the relationship of glottalization with preaspiration. In §2.2.1, we saw that in Kotiria and the other Eastern Tukanoan languages of the Vaupés region, there is regular preaspiration of voiceless consonants in root-internal position, the exact same position in which the glottal stop occurs in *CVCV* roots. We also find that roots with these two laryngeal qualities occur in complementary distribution, which might tempt us to postulate some sort of shared underlying laryngeal feature that surfaces as a glottal stop before voiced consonants and as preaspiration before voiceless ones. Such an orderly solution would be nice, but is unfortunately not borne out by the data, for in tables 2.13 and 2.15 above and in table 2.17 below, we see that glottal stops can occur before voiced and voiceless C_2 segments in *CVCV* roots. Indeed, there is no way to predict the occurrence of the glottal stop in terms of consonant adjacency.

TABLE 2.17. CONTRAST OF GLOTTAL STOP AND PREASPIRATION

CVCV WITH GLOTTAL STOP		*CVCV* WITH PREASPIRATION	
~*da'ka* [nã̌ʔkã́]	'miriti fruit'	~*daka* [nã̌ʰkã́]	'do together, be together'
da'po [daʔpó]	'foot'	*dapo* [daʰpó]	'allow'
phu'ti [pʰuʔtí]	'manioc meal'	*phuti* [pʰuʰtí]	'blow (a flute)'
sa'se [saʔsé]	'be alone'	*sase* [saʰsé]	'be gluttonous'
ya'pi [jaʔpí]	'be smooth'	*yapi* [jaʰpí]	'be full'

Preaspiration, on the other hand, is completely predictable, occurring consistently and inevitably before voiceless segments in nonglottalized roots, as we see in the second column of table 2.17 and as is formalized in (53) below. Moreover, in contrast to the glottal stop, no lexical contrasts are created by the occurrence or absence of preaspiration;[29] it merely creates a set of preaspirated voiceless consonants that are allophones of their unaspirated counterparts.

---

[29] Indeed, there are no known languages in which preaspiration constitutes a contrastive feature (Ladefoged and Maddieson 1996).

TABLE 2.18. CONTRASTS OF SUPRASEGMENTALS WITHIN ROOTS

	UNDERLYING SEGMENTAL FORM		UNGLOTTALIZED	[constricted glottis]
(a)	da	[−nasal]	da_H [dáá] 'be small'	
		[+nasal]	~da_{LHL} [nãã̌] 'carry'	~$da'a_{LH}$ [nã̌ʔá̌] 'buriti fruit'
	doa	[−nasal]	doa_{LHL} [doá] 'envy'	$do'a_{LH}$ [doʔá] 'cook'
		[+nasal]	~doa_H [nṍá̌] 'be good, be beautiful'	
	wa	[−nasal]	wa_{HL} [wáa] 'give'	$wa'a_{LHL}$ [waʔá] 'go'
		[+nasal]		~$wa'a_{LHL}$ [w̃ãʔá̌] 'be leaning'
(b)	sa	[−nasal]	sa_H [sáá] 'let's X'	$sa'a_{LH}$ [saʔá] 'dig'
		[+nasal]	~sa_{LHL} [sã̌ã̌] 'be inside'	~$sa'a_{LH}$ [sã̌ʔá̌] 'electric eel'
	soa	[−nasal]	soa_H [sóá] 'grind'	$so'a_{LH}$ [soʔá] 'sarapo fish'
			soa_{LHL} [soá] 'rest'	
		[+nasal]		~$so'a_{LHL}$ [sõʔá̌] 'be red, ripen'
(c)	bʉ	[−nasal]	$bʉ_H$ [bʉ́ʉ́] 'edge, shore'	$bʉ'ʉ_{LH}$ [bʉʔʉ́] 'piranha'
		[+nasal]	~$bʉ_{HL}$ [mʉ̃́ʉ̃] 'person, man'	~$bʉ'ʉ_{LH}$ [mʉ̃ʔʉ́] 'you'
			~$bʉ_H$ [mʉ̃́ʉ̃́] 'carry on back'	
	khoa	[−nasal]	$khoa_H$ [kʰóá] 'half/part of something'	$kho'a_{LHL}$ [kʰoʔá] 'return'
				$kho'a_{LHL}$ [kʰoʔá] 'sweep'
		[+nasal]	~$khoa_H$ [kʰṍá̌] 'throw'	~$kho'a_{LHL}$ [kʰõʔá̌] 'bone'
(d)	ba	[−nasal]	ba_{HL} [báa] 'decompose'	$ba'a_{LH}$ [baʔá] 'bass'
			ba_{LH} [baá] 'swim'	
		[+nasal]	~ba_H [mã́á̌] 'river'	~$ba'a_{LH}$ [mãʔá̌] 'be small'
				~$ba'a_{LHL}$ [mãʔá̌] 'path'

Phonology 69

(53) Glottalization: C V ʔ C V   C V ʔ C V
                            | |
                        [+voice]   [−voice]

   Preaspiration: C V C V   *C V h C V   C V h C V   *C V C V
                     | | | |
                  [+voice]   [+voice]   [−voice]   [−voice]

Such an analysis presupposes that previous association of the laryngeal feature [constricted glottis] to the target slot in the root (see (50) above) effectively blocks association of any subsequent laryngeal features, such as the [spread glottis] of preaspiration, to the same position. This prediction is borne out by the data and provides an explanation for the mixed root shapes in tables 2.13 and 2.17.

2.8 Cooccurrence of suprasegmentals

Under the suprasegmental interpretation of glottalization, the underlying forms of all Kotiria roots are *(C)V(C)V* or *(C)V*. The three types of suprasegmental feature—tone, nasality, and glottalization—can combine freely within a root, creating a range of surface realizations. The examples of multiply-contrasting lexical items (based on the same *CVV* or *CV* forms) in table 2.18 demonstrate the application of this analysis. Three-way contrasts are given in part (a) of the table, four-way contrasts in part (b), two five-way contrasts in part (c), and a six-way contrast in part (d). Glottalized roots are given in the rightmost column of the table; [+nasal] rows are ordered below [−nasal] rows. Tonal melodies are specified after each root.

Table 2.19 summarizes the individual properties of suprasegmentals in Kotiria. We can see that although all suprasegmentals are features of root morphemes, each associates in unique ways to different prosodic elements, interacts with various phonological properties, such as voicing and manner, and displays unique behavior in morphological processes.

2.9 Other commonly occurring phonological processes

2.9.1 Fusion of like vowels

Among the most commonly occurring phonological phenomena in Kotiria are the fusion of like vowels across morphological boundaries and vowel devoicing in the context of voiceless consonants. The fusion of like vowels occurs regularly in multimorphemic words, for example, in verbal words containing the morpheme coding imperfective aspect,

TABLE 2.19. CHARACTERISTICS OF SUPRASEGMENTALS

	NASALIZATION	TONE	GLOTTALIZATION
Feature of:	all root morphemes, some suffix morphemes	all root morphemes, some suffix morphemes	subset of root morphemes only
Associates to:	syllables, with manifestation in all eligible segments (segmental tier)	individual moras (prosodic tier)	right edge of first mora (prosodic tier)
Interacts with or is sensitive to properties of:	voicing; manner	prosodic structure	prosodic structure
Behavior in morphological processes:	spreads (only to unmarked morphemes)	spreads (to noninitial roots and unmarked morphemes)	does not spread

-*ati*. When the preceding root ends in a vowel other than /a/, all segments of -*ati* are fully pronounced, as in the verbal word in (54a), *hi-ati-a* [híatiʔa] (the glottal stop before the final vowel is a phonetic byproduct of L-tone spread). If however, the preceding morpheme ends in /a/, the encounter of like vowels across morpheme boundaries, as in (54b), results in fusion, so that the verbal word *chʉ-dua-ati-a* is pronounced [ʧʉ́duatia].

(54) a. *phanopʉre hiatiga mahsayahkaina*
 ~*phadó-pʉ+re*   *hí-ati+a*[30]
 long.ago-LOC+TMP COP-IMPERF+ASSERT.PERF
 ~*basá-yáká-~ídá*
 people-steal-NOM.PL
 'In the olden days therewere people-stealers.' [A4.1]

---

[30] For this speaker of the narrative from which this sentence is taken, pronunciation of the perfective assertion suffix varies between +*a* and +*ga*. He is the only speaker I worked with who presented this variation, which has been preserved in the first lines of examples. The morphemically analyzed line, however, reflects the common underlying form +*a*.

b. *tikoro, to namono, chɨduaatiga wahsore*
   tí-kó+ró   *to=~dabó+ro*   *chɨ́-dua-ati+a*
   ANPH-FEM+SG   3SG.POSS=wife+SG   eat-DESID-IMPERF+ASSERT.PERF
   wasó+ré
   siringa.fruit+OBJ
   'The woman, his wife, wanted to eat siringa fruit.' [A5.3]

2.9.2 Vowel devoicing

A second frequently occurring process is the devoicing and reduction of vowels before the glottal fricative /h/, even across word boundaries, to the point that the vowel is virtually eliminated and an aspirated segment is the result. This process occurs in commonplace expressions such as the one meaning 'that's it' or 'that's all (there is)'. The full expression is given in (55). Note that in fast speech the two words are fused into a single phonological word (with appropriate adjustment of the tonal melody); the vowel is no longer acoustically present and the glottal fricative is realized as aspiration on the preceding voiceless plosive. Recall that Nathan Waltz (2002:163) suggests that some cases of lexical postaspiration in Kotiria developed in this way, as exemplified in table 2.6.

(55) *tó-pɨ+ro=ta*   *hí+ra*
      DEF-LOC+SG=REF   COP+VIS.IMPERF.2/3
      'That's it.' / 'That's all.'

      Careful pronunciation: [tópɨrota híra]
      Fast speech pronunciation: [tópɨrotʰíra]

Low-toned vowels are also regularly devoiced between or before voiceless consonants, as we see in the examples in (56). What appear to be initial consonant clusters—[sʰt] and [rʰk]—are the acoustic result of this highly productive process.[31]

(56) *sito*   [si̥ʰtó], [sʰtó]   'move in a circular fashion'
      situ   [si̥ʰtú], [sʰtú]   'clay pot'
      sopaka   [so̥ʰpáka], [sʰpáka]   'outside; door'
      roka   [ro̥ʰka], [rʰka]   'throw, do/be at a distance; distal aspect'
      rɨka   [rɨ̥ʰka]   'begin'
      ruku   [rṵʰku], [rʰku]   'stand; continuous/durative aspect'

---

[31] The aspectual markers *roka, rɨka,* and *ruku* in (56) occur as noninitial serialized roots in the word, and therefore are shown with word-internal *r* instead of underlying /d/.

2.10 The Kotiria practical orthography

Since I began work with the Kotiria, one of our primary goals has been to develop a practical orthography for the language. Alhough Nathan and Carolyn Waltz proposed an orthography during their years among the Kotiria, one that is still used by a number of Kotiria in Colombia who still have access to materials the Waltzes developed, there is no unified writing system among the population as a whole. My language workshops have been conducted with the Kotiria in Brazil (though with participation of some Colombian Kotiria), and we began by having individuals write using whichever system they were familiar or most comfortable with in order to avoid attaching evaluative labels to any particular system and thereby possibly discouraging those who were experimenting with the act of writing their own language for the first time. As people became more comfortable with the practice of writing, questions naturally arose about different options and we began, together, to analyze the structural elements of the language related to these questions—for the most part, these were issues having to do with phonology—and aid them in formulating proposals. This is still an ongoing process, but step by step, the Kotiria are developing an orthography that is informed by linguistic analysis and developed in practice as a useful and comfortable tool.

Over the years, a number of decisions have been made and certain conventions have been established and are currently in use; these are represented in the first lines of examples with interlinear analysis in subsequent chapters as well as in the texts in appendix 1. The most important features of the practical orthography can be illustrated by looking at a few lines from texts in appendix 1.

While we have seen that all three suprasegmental features—tone, nasalization and glottalization—are distinctive in the language, the Kotiria have decided not to mark them all in their orthography. Of the three features, tone is considered to have the lowest functional load and is not marked at all. The Kotiria have no problem identifying words in context without tone marking; moreover, when we experimented with tone marking, they found it to be cumbersome and somewhat confusing. Glottalization is represented very simply in the orthography by an apostrophe in the glottalized morpheme, as in the words *ña'a*, *wa'ire*, *do'a*, *tu'sʉ* and *ba'a* in (57) as well as *wa'a* in (59).

The representation of nasalization, which is viewed by the Kotiria as the most important of the three features, has also been the most complex issue to deal with, and currently, the Kotiria orthography reflects decisions involving a combination of phonetic and phonological information. The Kotiria understand that, phonologically, nasalization affects entire morphemes and that all eligible segments are affected; thus they recognize that it is both redundant and troublesome to overtly mark each individual segment within a nasalized morpheme. Nevertheless, [+nasal] morphemes need to be identified in some way, and the simplest solution has been to represent [+nasal] morphemes by one of two means. Morphemes that contain an underlying /b/, /d/, or /j/ are written using the corresponding orthographic symbols <m, n, ñ>, which reflect the surface (phonetic) realizations of these segments in nasal environments and are symbols familiar to the Kotiria from their contact with written Portuguese and Spanish. Any morpheme containing <m, n, ñ> is automatically recognized as [+nasal] and no further marking by means of diacritics is necessary, as we see in the words *numiase'e*, *ña'a*, and *tina* in (57). In the case of [+nasal] morphemes that do not contain /b/, /d/, or /j/, the first vowel of the morpheme is marked by a tilde, identifying the whole morpheme as [+nasal], as we see in the case of the dimutive suffix ~*ka* in the word *pakorokãre* in (58) and in *sũ* and *khãra* in (59).[32] There is still no true consensus among the Kotiria regarding how [Ønasal] morphemes that take on the value [+nasal] through spreading should be represented, and in their writing we can observe a certain amount of variation. Generally, such morphemes tend not to be overtly marked as nasalized, as we see in the case of the suffixes +*re* and +*a* in the two words in (58) and +*ra* in *khãra* in (59). However, words composed of a [+nasal] root and the morpheme +*ro* are more often than not written with the surface realization of the underlying /d/ as <n>, as in *namono* 'wife'.

(57) *numiase'e ña'a wa'ire do'a, ti tu'sʉriba'aro tina chʉ yoara*
 ~*dubí+a-se'e*   ~*ya'á*   *wa'í+ré do'á*
 woman+PL-CONTR get.with.hand fish+OBJ cook

 ti=tu'sʉ́+ri-ba'a+ro   *tí-~da chʉ́*
 ANPH=finish+NOM-do/be.after+SG ANPH-PL eat

 yoá+ra
 do/make+VIS.IMPERF.2/3

 'The women take the fish and cook (it and) afterwards, they eat.' [A1.22]

(58) *pakorokãre tuinakaa*
 pá-ko+ro-~ka+re   *tuí-~daka+a*
 ALT-FEM+SG-DIM+OBJ put.in.front-do/be.together+ASSERT.PERF

 'She clasped her (other) little girl to the front (of her body).' [A5.21]

---

[32] In order to be able to tell how far nasalization spreads, one of course needs to know where a morpheme written with <m, n, ñ> or a tilde begins and ends, but this is not a problem for native speakers of the language.

(59)   *tina wehsepɨre sɨ̃, yɨhkɨrire khãra*
       tí-~da   wesé-pɨ+re   ~sɨ́   yɨkɨ́+ri+re
       ANPH-PL   garden-LOC+OBJ   arrive   tree+PL+OBJ
       ~khá+ra
       chop/cut+VIS.IMPERF.2/3
       'When they (the men) arrive at the garden, they chop down trees.'
       [A1.16]

Example (59) also shows that the Kotiria have opted to represent in their orthography not only contrastive postaspiration, as in the word *khãra*, but also the allophonic preaspiration that occurs in the words *wehsepɨre* and *yɨhkɨrire*. They understand that preaspiration is predictable in root-internal position and would therefore not need to be represented in the orthography (in the orthography of closely-related Tukano, preaspiration is conventionally not represented). Nonetheless, after a period of experimentation, they decided they felt more comfortable marking preaspiration, arguing, first of all, that it helped them recognize root morphemes, and secondly, that it was such a salient feature of their pronunciation that the words just looked wrong without it. They did, however, decide that in (not uncommon) cases where words have both postaspiration and preaspiration, such as ~*phicho+ro* [pʰĩʰtʃõnó] 'tail' and *khiti* [kʰiʰtí] 'story', only postaspiration should be marked (yielding the orthographic forms <phĩchono> and <khiti>), their view being that too many instances of <h> in a single word look confusing. In fact, in such words, the combination of postaspiration and preaspiration conditions devoicing of the vowel that occurs between them, so that the two aspirations fuse to a certain extent in the actual pronunciation; thus, marking aspiration only once in such words again reflects a good deal of the phonetic reality.

The examples above also show the basic orthographic conventions related to word division. A multimorphemic word such as *tu'sɨriba'aro* (57), though relatively long, is recognized as forming a single semantic unit and is written as a single word. The cliticized particle *ti* that precedes this word in (57), however, is generally written as a separate word (see further discussion of grammatical, phonological and orthographic words in §3.7 and §3.8).

The orthographic representations in the first lines of examples and text sentences in the present book were generally not produced directly in written form by the Kotiria. They are my own attempt to offer, as much as possible, a standardized representation that reflects both my analysis of the language and the decisions regarding their orthography that have been progressively made by the language community. Consequently, these lines have been modified over time and may contain some inconsistencies reflecting still unclarified issues. The first lines of those texts in appendix 1 that are specifically identified as written texts, on the other hand, were originally written by Kotiria in our orthography workshops, but these have also been standardized in accordance with established conventions, at the Kotiria's request.

3 Words

Words in Kotiria are composed according to a basic morphological template that demonstrates Kotiria to be a typologically polysynthetic, agglutinating, and canonically suffixing language. Word formation processes in Kotiria involve several types of morphemes: roots (noun, verb, and particle), nonroot stem morphemes, a restricted set of proclitics and enclitics, and suffixes; each type is defined by phonological and syntactic properties, and the types can be thought of as forming a continuum (§3.2, §3.6). From these, the two basic classes of words—verbal and nominal—are built. Each class contains specific subtypes: verbal words may be finite, simple nonfinite, nominalized, or derived from noun roots, or may contain incorporated nouns (§3.3). Nominal words fall into both closed and open classes: the closed class includes sets of pronouns and interrogative nominals while the open class includes simple nominals and nominals derived from particle or verb roots (§3.4). Adjectival semantic notions are expressed by stative verb roots that are frequently nominalized, while adverbial notions are expressed in a variety of ways, in both nominal and verbal words (§3.5). While phonological and grammatical words generally coincide in Kotiria, some mismatching occurs in the case of words with proclitics or enclitics (§ 3.7).

3.1 Basic morphological processes

The minimal structural requirements of an independently occurring word in Kotiria are bimoraic prosody and inherent specification for the suprasegmental features of nasalization, tone, and glottalization. Among the classes of morphemes that meet these requirements and can occur as independent words in Kotiria are lexical noun and verb roots (1)–(2), pronouns (3), and various types of modifiers (4)–(6).

(1) a'riro hira ba'a
 a'rí+ró   hí+ra   ba'á
 DEM.PROX+SG COP+VIS.IMPERF.2/3   bass
 'This is a bass.'[1]

---

[1] From a short text that appears as example (118) in chapter 4.

(2) wɨha soa wihpe yoara
wɨhá sóá wipé yoá+ra
peel grate sieve do/make+VIS.IMPERF.2/3
'(Women) peel, grate, and squeeze/sieve (manioc).' [A1.12]

(3) sã yoaropɨ, yɨ phɨkɨ me're thɨ'oi
~**sá** yoá+ro-pɨ **yɨ**=phɨk+ɨ́=~be're
1PL.EXC be.far+SG-LOC 1SG=parent+MASC=COM/INST
thɨ'ó+i
hear+VIS.PERF.1
'We, from far away, (I) with my father, heard (the sounds).' [A2.9]

(4) a'ri khiti
a'rí khití
DEM.PROX story
'this story'

(5) phayɨ wãhtia
phayɨ́ ~watí+á
many evil.being+PL
'many evil creatures; many devils'

(6) phɨa khɨ'ma
phɨá ~khɨ'bá
two year
'two years'

Monomorphemic words constitute from 25 to 30 percent of an average text, and approximately one-third of these are simple noun or verb roots. The rest are typically personal or possessive pronouns, negative or interrogative nouns, quantifiers, determiners, or discourse marking expressions. Multimorphemic words are composed of a root and one or more affixed morphemes, which may be other roots, suffixes, or clitics. Approximately 70 percent of all words are composed of two to four morphemes, while fewer than 5 percent are composed of five or more morphemes, as we see in a sample count from two narratives (table 3.1; full texts appear in appendix 1).

In multimorphemic words, the head root occurs as the leftmost constituent and all other affixed morphemes attach to its right, the canonical template being that in (7).

(7)   ROOT + [[ROOT(S)] [NONROOT STEM MORPHEME(S)] [SUFFIX(ES)]]

TABLE 3.1. DISTRIBUTION OF MORPHEMES PER WORD IN TWO KOTIRIA TEXTS

MORPHEMES PER WORD	A Hunter and His Dogs (appendix 1, text 6)		In the Olden Days There Were People-Stealers (appendix 1, text 4)	
	OCCURRENCES	%	OCCURRENCES	%
1	82	23	112	32
2	147	41	137	39
3	84	23	74	21
4	31	9	25	7
5 +	13	4	3	1
TOTALS	357	100	351	100

Categories of affixes on noun roots include those coding gender, class, number, quality, grammatical role, and discourse-level information (see chapter 5). Categories of affixes on verb roots code different types of adverbial, aspectual, and modal information as well as negation and emphasis (see chapters 7 and 8). Morphophonological processes, in particular the realization of suprasegmental nasalization, tone, and glottalization, regularly affect the surface realizations of morphemes within multimorphemic words. Such processes, however, do not generally affect the shape of affixed morphemes. So, as is the case in all Eastern Tukanoan languages, once the effects of such processes are discerned, individual morphemes in Kotiria words are fairly easy to identify.

3.2   Roots: noun, verb, and particle

The great majority of words in Kotiria are formed from nominal or verbal roots, which share the basic phonological characteristics of surface-level bimoraic prosody and lexical specification for the suprasegmental features of nasalization, glottalization, and tone. Roots of both classes may have *V*, *CV*, *CVV*, or *CVCV* shapes (table 3.2), the latter two predominating.

Both nominal and verbal roots can occur as independent words, as we saw in (1)–(2). Syntactically, a noun root can represent a complete noun phrase and a verb root can represent a complete, albeit nonfinite, verb phrase. Morphologically, such roots can also be the head morphemes of multimorphemic nominal (8)–(9) or verbal (10)–(11) words.

TABLE 3.2. ROOT SHAPES

	NOUN		VERB	
V	o	[óó] 'acari fish'	~o	[ǫ́ǫ́] 'hang by a thread or stem'
CV	ho	[hóó] 'banana'	~hɨ	[hɨ̃́ɨ̃́] 'burn'
CVV	~bie	[mĩẽ́] 'anteater'	yoa	[joá] 'do, make'
	bi'i	[biʔí] 'rat'	wa'a	[waʔá] 'go'
CVCV	kopa	[koʰpá] 'hole'	phuti	[pʰuʰtí] 'blow (play a flute)'
	~da'bo	[nã̃ʔmṍ] 'flute'	~kha'ba	[kʰã̃ʔmã́] 'want, need'

(8) yɨhkɨkɨkãre
    yɨkɨ́-kɨ-~ka+re
    tree-CLS:tree-DIM+OBJ
    'little stick'

(9) khumuwɨ'rɨpɨre
    ~**khubú**-wɨ'rɨ-pɨ+re
    log-AUG-LOC+OBJ
    'inside the big log'

(10) chɨduaatika
    chɨ́-dua-ati-ka
    eat-DESID-IMPERF-ASSERT.IMPERF
    'was wanting to eat'

(11) si'nikhã'ayɨ'dɨwa'aa
    ~**si'dí**-~kha'a-yɨ'dɨ-wa'a+a
    drink-dream-INTENS-go+ASSERT.PERF
    'became very drunk'

Particle roots are analyzed as a subclass of noun roots. Like noun roots, some can occur as phonologically independent words, as is the case with *a'ri* 'this' in (4); more commonly, however, they occur as the initial morphemes in multimorphemic nominal words. Particle roots take only nominal morphology, and it can be of all types. For instance, the nominal words in (12)–(15) are all formed from particle roots and morphemes that occur exclusively on nouns: -*ko* 'feminine', +*ro* 'singular', ~*ka* 'diminutive', ~*phi* 'long, bladelike' (classifier), -*pɨ* 'locative', +*re* 'object' (case marker), and =~*be're* 'comitative-instrumental' (case marker).

(12) a'riphĭme're
 a'rí-~phí=~be're
 DEM.PROX-CLS:bladelike=COM/INST
 'with this knife'

(13) pakorokãre
 pá-ko+ro-~ka+re
 ALT-FEM+SG-DIM+OBJ
 'the other little girl'

(14) tikorore
 tí-kó+ró+ré
 ANPH-FEM+SG+OBJ
 'her'

(15) ŏpᵻre
 ~ó-pᵻ+ré
 DEIC.PROX-LOC+OBJ
 'here'

However, particle roots differ from lexical noun roots in one very important way: particle roots by themselves (that is, without additional morphology) cannot function as noun phrases. Particle roots with no additional morphology can be modifiers in noun phrases that also contain an overt associated noun, as in (4). But when there is no overt modified noun, the particle root requires additional morphology in order to function as a noun phrase, as in (12)–(15). Particle roots thus can be considered syntactically bound. (For types of particle roots, see §4.5.2). Examples (16)–(17) demonstrate this distinction. In (16), we see the full sentence from which (12) was taken. The derived nominal word *a'ri-~phi* 'this knife' is a syntactically independent, phonologically fused noun phrase, marked by the final, cliticized morpheme =~be're as the instrument used to accomplish the verbal action. In (17), the same particle root *a'ri* is the phonologically independent modifier of *khiti* 'story' in the full noun phrase *a'ri khiti* 'this story'; the particle word is not syntactically independent because its status is that of modifier.

(16) a'riphĭ me're narokha'mare
 a'rí-~phí=~be're
 DEM.PROX-CLS:bladelike=COM/INST
 ~dá+ro=~kha'ba+re
 get+(3)SG=want/need+VIS.PERF.2/3
 'You have to take/get it (your heart) out with this knife.' [A7.76]

(17) *a'ri khiti õita phitira*
 a'rí khití ~ó+í=ta phití+ra
 DEM.PROX story DEIC.PROX-LOC=REF end+VIS.IMPERF.2/3
 'Here's where this story ends.' [A6.70]

While most particle roots have a single, consistently realized associated tonal melody, such as the H melody of *si* 'distal demonstrative', the HL melody of *pa* 'alternate', and the LH melody of *a'ri* 'proximal demonstrative', interesting tonal variations occur with the particle root *ti* 'anaphoric'. When this root is the initial morpheme in pronominal forms such as the third singular masculine *ti+ro* and feminine *ti-ko+ro*, or in pronominals formed with nominal classifiers, such as *ti-~phi* 'that knife', it imposes a H melody over the phonological word, these forms being pronounced respectively as [tíró], [tíkóró] and [típʰí]. It would thus appear that *ti* has an associated H melody. However, we find that the third plural pronominal form *ti-~ida* has a HL melody, being consistently pronounced [tínã]. Moreover, when *ti* occurs as an independent modifier of a noun phrase, while it is sometimes pronounced with H tone, it much more often behaves as a clitic, attaching to the lefthand margin of the word and realized with L tone, as in *ti kopapɨ* 'into the/that hole' [tikoʰpápɨ́]. (For more discussion of clitics, see §§3.6–3.7 and also §4.7.3.)

Because there are only three types of root morphemes—verb, noun, and particle (the last being a subtype of nominal root)—there are only two basic types of words in Kotiria: verbal and nominal. In general, verbal and nominal words are easily distinguished by the fairly distinct sets of morphemes that regularly occur as verbal or nominal affixes. Yet when it comes to affixes, there is not always an absolute relationship between form and meaning. Pairs of homophonous suffixes from different sets do exist, such as the nominal objective case marker *+re* and the verbal visual evidential marker *+re*, and the nominal third person plural marker *+a* and the verbal assertion evidential marker *+a*. Additionally, morphological crossover occurs for specific functions; for instance, noun class suffixes on verbal words function as nominalizers (see §10.1.2.). In most cases, however, nominal and verbal words are distinguishable by their morphology.

3.3 Verbal words

3.3.1 Finite, simple nonfinite, and nominalized nonfinite verbs

The three most common types of verbal words are finite, simple nonfinite, and nominalized nonfinite. Only finite verbal words are fully inflected, having clause modality morphology (marking the sentence as a statement, question, command, etc.) as their final morphological constituent (see chapter 9). Quite often, the finite verbal word is the final constituent of the sentence, though ultimately, it is morphology rather than sentential word order that indicates which verbal word is finite.

All other verbal words in a sentence are nonfinite, and occur either as simple uninflected roots, as in the sequence of verbs in (2), or as nominalizations. Simple nonfinite verbal words occur in chaining constructions, in which a single grammatical subject performs a series of separate, sequential actions (see §§11.5–6). Nominalized verbal words occur either as complements within particular types of verbal constructions (see §11.3), or to indicate the dependent status of an entire clause.

Examples (18)–(23) demonstrate these three types of verbal words, all composed with the same verb root *wa'a* 'go'. The verbal words containing *wa'a* in (18) and (19) are finite; this is evidenced by the verb-final morphology with the evidential suffix +*a* in (18), indicating that the sentence is a perfective realis statement, and the combination of the dubitative suffix -*bo* and evidential suffix -*ka* in (19), which code the sentence as a speculation (see §9.2.5).

(18) *pase'epɨ wa'aa*
 pá-se'e-pɨ   *wa'á+a*
 ALT-CONTR-LOC go+ASSERT.PERF
 '(He) went off somewhere.' [A7.15]

(19) *da'rana wa'aboka*
 da'rá-~da   *wa'á-bo-ka*
 work-(1/2)PL go-DUB-ASSERT.IMPERF
 'We might go to work.'

There are two verbal words containing *wa'a* in (20): the first is a simple nonfinite verbal word—an uninflected verb root in a chaining construction—and the second is a finite verbal word in which *wa'a* codes change of state (see §8.5.2).

(20) *wa'a sɨhka khãriawa'aa*
 wa'á súka   *~kharí+a=wa'a+a*
 go   lie.down sleep+AFFEC=go+ASSERT.PERF
 '. . . he went, lay down, and went to sleep.' [A7.98]

Examples (21)–(23) show *wa'a* in nominalized verbal words that are complements in constructions coding inferential and nonvisual evidence. In (21) *wa'a* is nominalized by the suffix +*ri* as a complement to the finite verb *hi* 'be' in the construction coding inference (see §9.2.4), while in (22) *wa'a* is nominalized by the noun class suffix +*ro* (showing third person subject agreement) as a complement to *koa* 'to perceive' in the construction coding non-visual sensory (in this case auditory) evidence (see §9.2.3). The same noun suffix *+ro* is used to nominalize the entire dependent clause *~waha+ro wa'a+ro* 'when Luis goes fishing' in (23).

(21) *yʉ'ʉ khãriyʉ'dʉa wa'ari hika*
      yʉ'ʉ ~kharí-yʉ'dʉ+a   wa'á+ri   hi-ka
      1SG sleep-INTENS+AFFEC go+NOM(INFER) COP-ASSERT.IMPERF
      'I've been asleep a long time.' [A7.128]

(22) *borasʉka'a wa'aro koataa*
      borá-~sʉ-ka'a   wa'á+ro koá-ta+a
      fall-arrive-do.moving go+(3)SG NONVIS-come+ASSERT.PERF
      '(The man heard) he fell right down.' [A7.86]

(23) *wãharo wa'aro moñoerara tiro*
      ~wahá+ro wa'á+ro ~boyo-éra+ra   tí+ró
      kill+SG   go+SG   fail-NEG+VIS.IMPERF.2/3 ANPH+SG
      'When (Luis) goes fishing (killing), he never fails.'[2]

3.3.2 Derived verbs

There are three ways in which new, or more semantically refined, verbs can be derived in Kotiria. The most productive process involves verb root serialization, discussed in detail in §7.5, §8.3, and §8.5.2. The second process, somewhat less productive but by no means uncommon, involves use of the verbalizing morpheme *-ti*. This morpheme occurs in (24) on the noun root *~pho'da* 'children, offspring', resulting in the verb *~pho'dati* [pʰõʔnãti] 'reproduce, have babies', and in (25) on the noun root *ko* 'water, medicine' to derive the verb *koti* [kótí] 'take medicine' (see also (39) below). It can also indicate that one has a specific attribute, as in *phoa+ri-~yai-ti+ri+ro* (hair+PL-be.bad/ugly-VBZ+NOM+SG) 'one who has horrible hair, is horribly hairy' or *~dabo-ti+ri+ro* (wife-VBZ+NOM+SG) 'be married; one who has a wife'.

Once derived, a new verb takes typical verbal morphology, such as the evidential suffixes *+ra* in (24) and *+a* in the first occurrence in (25). A derived verb can also be nominalized; we see this in the second occurrence in (25), where the derived verb *koti* is then nominalized by the morpheme *+ro*, resulting in the nominal word 'medicine-taking'.

---

[2] From the short text that appears as example (19) in chapter 2.

(24) tina ba'ro phayɨ pho'natira.
 tí-~da=ba'ro phayɨ́ ~pho'dá-ti+ra
 ANPH-PL=kind many/a.lot offspring-VBZ+VIS.IMPERF.2/3
 'This kind (of animal, the anteater) has a lot of offspring.' [A11.8]

(25) kotimaa, kotirose'e, ne tirore thɨoeraa.
 kó-ti-~ba+a   kó-ti+ro-se'e
 medicine-VBZ-FRUS+ASSERT.PERF medicine-VBZ+SG-CONTR
 ~dé tí+ró+ré   thɨo-éra+a
 NEG ANPH+SG+OBJ be.successful-NEG+ASSERT.PERF
 'He took medicine, however it (the medicine-taking) didn't cure him.' [A7.165]

The third derivational process is noun incorporation, the most common type being that in which a transitive verb and an associated nonreferential noun object (one that is unmarked for definiteness or number; see also §7.6 and §10.3.2) combine to create a more semantically specific but syntactically intransitive verb stem (for incorporation of nouns in temporal adverbial expressions, see §10.7.2). The resulting intransitive predicate denotes a single concept that is usually a habitual or ritualized action, prototypical of Mithun's Type I noun incorporation (1984:848). Three typical instances of verbs with incorporated nouns are *die-~ku* [diékũ] 'egg-lay' (26),[3] *~daho-~sa* [nãhõsã] 'flatbread-make' (lit., 'flatbread-spread'; it refers to baking in a wide flat oven) (27), and *wa'i-~kida-~waha* [waʔíkĩnáwãhá] 'animal(s)-kill'[4] (i.e., 'hunt') (28). Once they have been derived, regular morphological processes apply to noun-incorporating verbs. For example, in (26b) and (27), the incorporating verbs are nominalized, by *-~ida* and *+ri* respectively. In (28) the incorporating verb is serialized with two additional verb roots *-sito-ta* and then takes the verb-final suffix *+ga*.

(26) a. yɨhkɨkɨ kohpapɨ diekũ pho'natira tiro
  yɨkú-kɨ   kopá-pɨ́   **dié-~ku**   ~pho'dá-ti+ra
  tree-CLS:tree hole-LOC egg-lay offspring-VBZ+VIS.IMPERF.2/3
  tí+ró
  ANPH+SG
  '(A toucan) reproduces by laying eggs in a hollow tree.' [LSK: Toucans]

---

[3] Some speakers use verb ~sa 'be inside' in an alternate construction for 'egg-lay'.
[4] Both cross-linguistically and in Kotiria itself, it is uncommon for a plural marker to occur in an incorporated noun, as it does in *wa'i-~**kida**-~waha*. I have found no other similar forms in the language.

b. *diekũina tiroba'ro*
   ***dié-~ku-**~ida   tí+ró=ba'ro*
   egg-lay-NOM.PL ANPH+SG=kind
   'This kind (of fish, bass) are egg-layers.'[5]

(27) *nahosãri hika*
   *~**dahó-~sa**+ri   hí-ka*
   flatbread-lay+NOM(INFER) COP-ASSERT.IMPERF
   '(Somebody) is making (baking) flatbread.'

(28) *tʉ me're mʉ'ʉ wa'ikinawãha sihtotaga*
   *tʉ́=~be're   ~bʉ'ʉ̌ **wa'í-~kídá-~wáhá***
   stick=COM/INST 2SG   animal-PL-kill
   sitó-ta+ga
   MOV.circular-come+IMPER
   'With this stick, you go around hunting.' [A7.131]

While most noun incorporation in Kotiria results in derived intransitive stems such as those in (26)–(28), we also run across occasional occurrences of Mithun's (1984:863) Type IV incorporation, which results in a syntactically transitive verb stem that can take an independent noun phrase as its object. This is the case in (29), where the verb *~dabo-da're* [nãmõda?re] 'wife-make' has *ti-~da+re* 'them' as its case-marked object. The pronoun *ti-~da+re* is identified in an explanatory phrase at the end of the sentence as 'young women from many different groups'; the latter phrase is shown to be an object by the final suffix +*re* on *~pho'da- ~dubi+a* 'young women'.

(29) *tinare namoda'reataa, phayʉ mahsakurua pho'nanumiare*
   tí-~da+re   ~dabó-da're+a-ta+a
   ANPH-PL+OBJ wife-make+AFFEC-REF+ASSERT.PERF
   phayʉ́ ~basá-kʉ́rʉ́+á   ~pho'dá-~dubi+a+re
   many   people-group+PL children-female+PL+OBJ
   '(They) married them, young women from many different groups (tribes).' [Ancestors]

The fact that a verb with an incorporated noun can occur in this type of syntactically transitive construction suggests that various types of incorporation may have once been more commonly employed in Kotiria (assuming Mithun's implicational hierarchy). Synchronically, only Type I noun incorporation is productive.

---

[5] From the short text that appears as example (118) in chapter 4.

3.4 Nominal words

In addition to the open classes of simple and derived nouns discussed below, there are several closed sets of nominal words with special functions that are presented elsewhere in this grammar. Among these are the negative nominal ~*de* (§4.6), interrogative nominals (§6.5.1), and pronouns (§4.7).

3.4.1 Simple nouns

The most common nominal words are simple nouns, built from a noun root that may occur in uninflected (30)–(31) or inflected (32)–(33) form, depending on the class of the noun and its grammatical role in the sentence. Simple nominals can function as complements of the copula (30) or as arguments of verbs (31)–(33).

(30) *a'riro ñama phiriro hira*
 a'rí+ró ~*yabá phí+ri+ro hi+ra*
 DEM.PROX+SG deer be.big+NOM+SG COP+VIS.IMPERF.2/3
 'This is a big deer.' [LSK: Deer]

(31) *tirore topɨ khiti ya'uga*
 tí+ró+ré tó-pɨ **khití** *ya'ú+a*
 ANPH+SG+OBJ REM-LOC story tell+ASSERT.PERF
 'There they told him the story.' [A4.50]

(32) *wĩhsoa chɨka bɨhtiaditare*
 ~*wiso+a chú-ka butí+a-dita+re*
 squirrel+PL eat-ASSERT.IMPERF be.hard+PL-SOL+OBJ
 'Squirrels eat hard things only.' [LSK: Squirrels]

(33) *yɨ'ɨ wahsore chɨduamaka*
 yɨ'ɨ **wasó+ré** *chú-dua-~ba-ka*
 1SG siringa.fruit+OBJ eat-DESID-FRUS-ASSERT.IMPERF
 ~*dí+a*
 say+ASSERT.PERF
 'I wish I had some siringa fruit to eat.' [A5.4]

3.4.2 Derived nouns

While many nominal words are built on noun roots, nominal words that are derived from other types of roots (particle and verbal) occur equally frequently in the data. Nominal words derived from particle roots have pronounlike status (see §4.5.2) and frequently function as arguments. For example, the nominal word in (12) above is marked as an instrument, while those in (13)–(14) are marked as objects. Nominal words derived from verb roots can also function as arguments: as subject in (34), as object in (35), and as complement of the copular construction in (36).

(34) *phiriro khõaa*
 phí+ri+ro   ~**khoá+a**
 be.big+NOM+SG   be.lying+ASSERT.PERF
 'The big one (guy) was lying there.' [A7.96]

(35) *mia wa'i dainakãre chɨka tiro*
 ~**bí-a**   **wa'í**   **dá-~ídá-~ká+ré**   **chú-ka**
 sardine+PL fish   be.small-NOM.PL-DIM+OBJ eat-ASSERT.IMPERF
 tí+ró
 ANPH+SG
 'It (a bass) eats sardines and small fish.' [6]

(36) *phadopɨre hiatiga mahsayahkaina*
 ~**phadó-pɨ+re**   **hí-ati+a**
 do/be.before-LOC+OBJ   COP-IMPERF+ASSERT.PERF
 ~**basá-yáká-~ídá**
 people-steal-NOM.PL
 'In the olden days there were people-stealers.' [A4.1]

3.5 Words expressing adjectival and adverbial notions

In Kotiria, there are no lexical categories "adjective" or "adverb." Adjectival notions referring to things such as the physical attributes or qualities of an object or entity are indicated, for the most part, by stative verbs such as *phi* 'be big', *da* 'be small', *phia* 'be sour', ~*doa* 'be good/beautiful', ~*ya* 'be bad/ugly', ~*so'a* 'be red', and so forth. Two types of evidence clearly demonstrate the underlying verbal status of these roots. First, like other types of verb roots, stative roots with adjectival meanings require nominalizing morphology to derive nominal words (see also §6.6). If we compare, for example, the nominals *da-~ida-~ka* 'little ones' (35), derived from an stative verb, and ~*basa-yaka-~ida* 'people-stealers' (36), derived from a noun-verb compound, we see that they are both nominalized by the same animate plural nominalizing morpheme -~*ida*. Secondly, though stative verb roots with adjectival meanings are very frequently nominalized, (37)–(38) show they can also occur as simple inflected verbs.

---

[6] From the short text that appears as example (118) in chapter 4.

(37)   tinare wãha tiro wahcheawa'aa.

   tí-~da+re   ~wahá   tí+ró   waché+a=wa'a+a
   ANPH-PL+OBJ kill   ANPH+SG be.happy+AFFEC=go+ASSERT.PERF
   'He killed them (some monkeys, and) he became happy.' [A7.11]

(38)   tire thɨ'o, tiro suataa te ti ka'apɨ.

   tí+ré   thɨ'ó   tí+ró   suá-ta+a   té
   ANPH+OBJ hear   ANPH+SG be.angry-come+ASSERT.PERF   all.the.way

   ti=ka'á-pɨ
   ANPH=near-LOC

   'When he (the father) heard that, he raged off until he was there by (the log).' [A4.54]

While nearly all adjectival notions are expressed in nominal words derived from stative verb roots, there are also a very few cases of roots, such as *bɨkɨ*, which can take either verbal or nominal morphology directly. As a verb root, *bɨkɨ* means 'grow' or 'mature' (39). As a noun root (marked for gender when the referent is human; see §4.2.1) it has the related meaning of an 'elder' or 'mature' person or entity (40), evidence that an inherently qualitative noun root can develop from a verbal concept.

(39)   bɨhkɨaka to ba'aro dihchatika

   bɨkɨ́+a-ka   to   ba'á+ró   dichá-tí-ká
   grow+(3)PL-PREDICT   REM   do/be.after+SG fruit-VBZ-PREDICT

   '(After the seeds are planted, bananas) will grow and later produce fruit.' [LSK: Bananas]

(40)   tiro bɨhkɨro

   tí+ró   **bɨk+ɨ́+ro**
   ANPH+SG elder+MASC+SG

   'The old man ...'

Adverbial notions are expressed in a number of different ways in Kotiria, including verb root serialization (§7.5.1) and independent nominal words (§11.2). Some adverbial nominals are built on noun roots, such as the temporal adverbs in (41)–(42). Others, such as (43)–(44), are derived from verb roots by the nominalizing morpheme +*ro*, followed by other types of nominal morphology, including the objective case suffix +*re*, which also occurs on temporals (§10.7.2).

(41)   mihchare

   ~bichá+ré
   today+OBJ

   'today'

(42) mihchakãkãre
 ~bichá-~ká-~ká+ré
 today-DIM-DIM+OBJ
 'right now'

(43) wã'maropɨre
 ~wa'bá+ro-pɨ+re
 be.young/new+SG-LOC+OBJ
 'in the beginning'

(44) ti bo'reka'arore
 ti=bo'ré-ka'a+ro+re
 ANPH=be.light-do.moving+SG+OBJ
 'in the morning'

Adverbial nominal words expressing quality (45)–(46) and manner (47)–(48) are also derived from verb roots by the same nominalizing morpheme +ro.

(45) mari noaro irimoare wi'bomahsika
 ~barí   ~dóá+ró   ~iríboa+re   wi'bó-~básí-ká
 1PL.INC be.good+SG lime+OBJ   store-know-ASSERT.IMPERF
 'We should store limes well.' [LSK: Limes]

(46) ñaro wihkĩrika tina wimia
 ~yá+ro   ~wikí-ri-ka   tí-~da   ~wibí+a
 be.bad+SG itch-ADMON-ASSERT.IMPERF ANPH-PL   suck+PL
 'It itches badly when they (horseflies) bite.' [A9.4]

(47) kherokã chɨa
 khé-ro-~ka   chú+a
 be.fast-SG-DIM   eat+ASSERT.PERF
 'eat very quickly'

(48) phirokã yoaka
 phí+ro-~ka   yoá-ka
 be.slow+SG-DIM   do/make-ASSERT.IMPERF
 'do very slowly'

3.6 Properties of roots, suffixes, and clitics

Table 3.3 summarizes the phonological and syntactic properties that distinguish morpheme types. Defining properties are listed on the left-hand side. Five of these are phonological, indicating whether morphemes in a particular class are inherently marked for the suprasegmental features of nasalization, glottalization, and tone, whether or not they tend to have underlying bimoraic structure, and whether or not they can occur as phonologically independent words. The sixth property is syntactic, indicating whether a morpheme can occur as a syntactically free element. This final distinction serves to differentiate independent roots, which can occur as phonologically independent and syntactically free words—as with *ba'a* 'bass' in (1)—from particle roots, which are syntactically bound (serving as modifiers of the kind illustrated in (4)) even when they are phonologically independent words (see discussion in §3.2). Five morpheme types are distinguished in the table—three types of roots (independent noun or verb [R_{indep}], particle [$R_{particle}$], and dependent noun or verb [R_{dep}]), nonroot stem morphemes (NSM), and suffixes. (The distinction between dependent roots and nonroot stem morphemes is somewhat fuzzy, however, as is discussed later in this section.)

TABLE 3.3. PROPERTIES OF MORPHEMES

PROPERTIES:		R_{indep}	$R_{particle}$	R_{dep}	NSM	suffix
phonological:	[±nasal]	+	+	+	+	(−)
	tone	+	+	−	(−)	(−)
	glottalized	+	(−)	+	(−)	−
	bimoraic	(+)	(−)	(+)	(+)	−
	independent	+	+	−	(−)	−
syntactic:	free	+	−	−	−	−

Symbols in parentheses indicate tendencies rather than absolutes. For example, the indication "(−)" for bimoraic structure of particle roots means that while particle roots tend not to have bimoraic structure, there are a few exceptions, such as the deictic demonstrative *a'ri*. The marking of independent roots as "(+)" for the same property indicates that while most independent roots are underlyingly bimoraic, a small subset of them are not (see §2.4.2). The indication of suprasegmental features of nasalization and tone as "(−)" for suffixes means that though most suffixes are unmarked for these features, a handful of suffixes, such as the nasalized plural *-~da* and the HL-tone negative *-era*, are marked. Nonroot stem morphemes show the greatest variation of features: they generally have marked [±nasal] specification but are usually unmarked for tone; some still have bimoraic structure while others do not; none are syntactically free. In general, nonroot stem morphemes are not phonologically independent, but different types of such morphemes are phonologically affected in different ways that are further discussed below.

The left-to-right order of the morpheme types on the chart can be understood as reflecting an internal hierarchy, with independent roots at the highest level and suffixes at the lowest. The differences between these extremes are notable. Independent roots generally have bimoraic structure, are always marked for suprasegmental features, and can occur as both phonologically and syntactically free words. Suffixes, on the other hand, are monomoraic, are rarely marked for suprasegmental features, and are always bound, both phonologically and syntactically.

In between these two extremes are morphemes that display varying degrees of grammaticalization, this being evident both from the loss of independent phonological features and, in some cases, from semantic generalization (see §4.4 and §8.6 for more on the status of nominal and verbal morphemes). Many of the noninitial morphemes in morphologically complex nouns and verbs are most likely former roots that are undergoing grammaticalization and whose status is now that of bound morphemes. They display varying degrees of semantic recoverability and loss of the phonological features that characterize independent roots. Those that are further along in the grammaticalization process have either lost their bimoraic structure or show evidence of segmental erosion; nearly all have lost independent tone specification (a notable exception being the negative -*era*, §8.2) but most retain inherent specification for the [±nasal] feature. Nonroot stem morphemes occur in medial position and are followed by suffixes. We should note, however, that the intermediate columns in table 3.3 represent positions on a continuum rather than discrete, rigid categories in the hierarchy.

Stem formation varies in terms of complexity. A simple stem is composed of a single independent root, while a complex stem can be composed of a single root or sequence of compounded roots (see §4.8 and §7.6) along with dependent roots and other nonroot stem morphemes.

Besides the types of morphemes in table 3.3, Kotiria also has one set of developing proclitics and several enclitics. The proclitics are possessive pronominals, which, with the exception of the third person singular possessive, are derived from the full pronominal forms: *yʉ* (1SG.POSS) 'my', ~*sa* (1PL.EXC.POSS) and ~*badi* (1PL.INC.POSS) 'our', ~*bʉ* (2SG.POSS) and ~*bʉsa* (2PL.POSS) 'your', *to* (3SG.POSS) 'her/his', and *ti* (3PL.POSS) 'their'. All possessive markers, even those with bimoraic structure, show phonological reduction to a consistent L tone, and four of the seven show reduction to monomoraic structure as well. Thus, unlike the full personal pronouns from which they are derived, possessive pronominal markers no longer meet the criteria for independent word status (see also §6.4.1).

One of the most frequently occurring enclitics is the morpheme =~*be're*, which, when it occurs as the final marker of a nominal word, marks it as having a comitative or instrumental role (see also §5.2.3 and §§10.7.3–10.7.5). This morpheme retains some of the properties of a root morpheme—it is bimoraic and has [+nasal] specification—yet in its function as a grammatical marker it consistently occurs with L tone, rather than having the tone of the initial root spread to it. Certain other roots also behave as clitics, such as =*ba'ro*, which indicates a 'type' or 'kind' of entity (as in line 6 of example (118) in chapter 4), as well as =*wa'a* 'go' in a construction coding perfectivity (§8.5.2) and =~*kha'ba* 'want', in a construction indicating deontic modality (§11.3.1). The consistent shift to L tone of the proclitics and these enclitics indicates processes of grammaticalization from full root to suffix by way of cliticization. While nonroot stem morphemes can easily participate in regular tonal spreading processes due to their medial position, proclitics and enclitics, because of their positioning at the outer margins of words, resist full incorporation into the larger phonological word. Yet, in themselves, they no longer constitute independent phonological words; synchronically, they are L-tone dependents.

Table 3.3 above summarizes the phonological and syntactic properties of morphemes in initial and noninitial positions. From the lack of tone specification and syntactic independence for dependent roots, we can deduce that only independent and particle roots can occur in initial position in nominal or verbal words. The table also suggests somewhat fuzzy boundaries between dependent roots and nonroot stem morphemes and between these and suffixes, whose features vary only in terms of the kinds of tendencies mentioned earlier. Such differences reflect differing degrees of grammaticalization, and we find that while many roots can appear in either initial or noninitial position, others occur only in noninitial position (many examples can be found in §7.5). The latter represent the first phase in the grammaticalization process, displaying all the phonological criteria of independent roots except for inherent tonal melody, which is lost as the roots became both phonologically and syntactically bound. Over time, such noninitial roots may show further signs of reduction such as loss of initial segments or of syllables (and hence mora), and perhaps suprasegmental specification, becoming increasingly more like suffixes.

3.7 Phonological and grammatical words

A phonological word is a phonological unit with defining properties related to segmental and prosodic features as well as to the application of basic phonological rules (Dixon and Aikhenvald 2002:13). In Kotiria, there are three minimal segmental and prosodic criteria for the phonological word:

- it is bimoraic;
- it has at least one H tone (most often occurring on the second mora);
- in terms of phonological rule application, it is the domain of spreading of the suprasegmental features of tone and nasalization (as discussed in chapter 2).

Moreover, the phonological word is the unit after which pauses in speech occur, and is the unit most often identified by speakers as a "word." The most notable exceptions to this statement occur, not surprisingly, with the possessive proclitics and the comitative-instrumental enclitic described in the previous section. There are also a few other left-edge or right-edge morphemes that display similar cliticlike behavior, among them the particle roots *ti* and *to* in certain contexts (described in §3.2 and §4.7.3) and the discourse-marking morphemes ~*a*= 'so' or 'then' (also in proclitic position) and the referential =*ta* (§5.3.1), an enclitic. Speakers rather consistently classify the proclitic possessives as separate words, despite the fact that no other monomoraic or L-tone units are ever identified as words. This phenomenon may be attributable to the fact that these proclitics are developing in a language that is canonically suffixing. Because there is really no template for prefixal morphemes in a Kotiria speaker's internal grammar, speakers conceive of such atypical forms as separate words despite their deficient phonological form. It should be noted, moreover, that speakers sometimes use the full pronoun forms rather than the cliticized forms in possessive constructions, following the general tendency for use of full pronouns in possessive constructions in most Eastern Tukanoan languages (Barnes 1999:218). It is likely that the cliticized possessive forms in Kotiria have developed under the influence of neighboring Arawak languages but that this development is, at the same time, constantly being resisted through ongoing contact with Tukanoan languages (Waltz 2002; Aikhenvald 2003b; Stenzel and Gomez-Imbert 2009).

There is no consensus among Kotiria speakers as to whether or not the enclitic =~*be're* is a separate word or a morpheme attached to the preceding noun. This ambiguous view of =~*be're* is reflected in spontaneous writing, where examples of both treatments can be found. This morpheme is most certainly a root which has been coopted and cliticized as a grammatical marker. It may be a reflection of the recentness of this process that some speakers attune more to the phonological properties of the morpheme while others focus on its semantics. In any case, the suffixlike position in which it occurs is certainly more in keeping with the internal grammatical template of speakers of an essentially suffixing language.

A grammatical word is a unit within which grammatical morphemes occur in a fixed order and which has conventionalized coherence and meaning (this definition is adapted from Dixon and Aikhenvald 2002:19). Thus, all the types of words outlined earlier in this chapter, from independently occurring noun or verb roots to multimorphemic composites, meet the criteria for grammatical word in Kotiria. A Kotiria grammatical word begins with an independent root, which may occur as the sole root, forming a simple stem, or may be serialized with another root or multiple roots to form a complex stem, which in most, but not all, cases takes one or more affixed morphemes. While both noun and verb roots can occur in isolation, more often they take affixes, and for each type of root there is a conventionalized set of morphemes that occur in relatively fixed order (see chapters 5 and 8).

Recalling the basic patterns of morphological word-building, we see that for verbal words, the phonological word and grammatical word coincide (figure 3.1). Dependent roots are stem-building morphemes and nonroot stem morphemes are affixes within the morphological template; neither type of morpheme constitutes an internal grammatical word. For verbs with incorporated nouns (§3.3.2, §7.6), the noun+verb root combination can be thought of as jointly occupying the "VR_{indep}" position of figure 3.1.

As for nominal words, those that are built from noun or particle roots show patterns similar to that given above for verbal words. However, because nominal words can also be marked by proclitics such as the possessives or the particle root *ti* or by enclitics such as the comitative-instrumental =~*be're* or referential =*ta*, there can be a kind of mismatch between the phonological word and grammatical word, since these two types of clitics do not participate in the phonological word in the same way that stem morphemes and suffixes do. They are not affected by the tonal spreading processes that have the phonological word as their domain, but attach to the fringes of the phonological word as dependent L-tone elements. Moreover, because certain clitics are so closely related to and recently derived from roots, they can be viewed as still retaining at least partial grammatical-word

Words

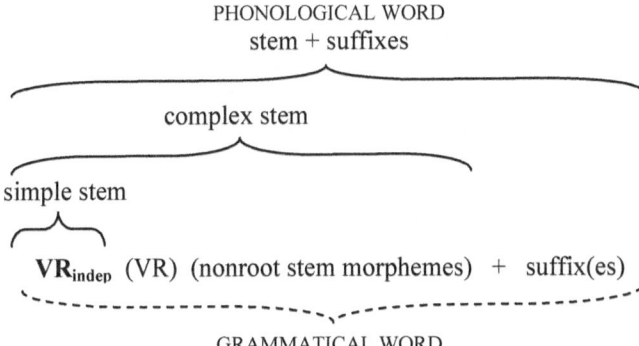

Figure 3.1. Relations between phonological word and grammatical word in the surface form of verbal words. Phonological word and grammatical word coincide. VR = verb root (independent or dependent); VR_{indep} = independent verbal root.

status, though their status as independent lexical entities is clearly eroding. In short, such clitics are marginal in several respects.

Thus, in the nominal word, phonological word and grammatical word coincide unless one of these two types of clitics is present (figure 3.2). As with verbal words, compounded roots and other types of bound nonroot stem morphemes are not considered to be internal grammatical words within nominal words.

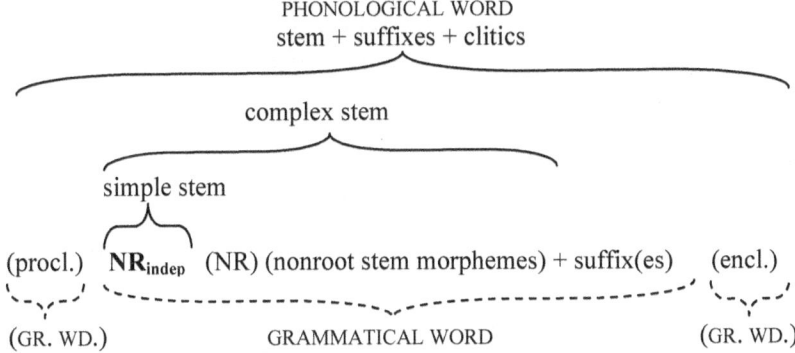

Figure 3.2. Relations between phonological word and grammatical word in the surface form of nominal words. A phonological word may consist of more than one grammatical word. Encl. = enclitic; gr.wd. = grammatical word; NR = nominal root (independent or dependent); NR_{indep} = independent nominal root; procl. = proclitic.

Finally, like nominals built from noun roots, the phonological word and grammatical word will coincide in a nominal built from a particle root unless it is marked by an enclitic such as the comitative-instrumental. Otherwise, the particle root and its accompanying suffixes form a single grammatical word (figure 3.3).

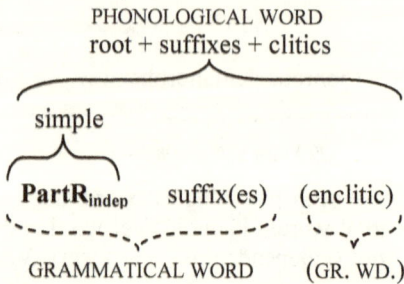

Figure 3.3. Relations between phonological word and grammatical word in the surface form of particle-root nominal words. A phonological word may consist of more than one grammatical word. Gr.wd. = grammatical word; PartR$_{indep}$ = independent particle root.

3.8   Some considerations on the orthographic word

The general conventions relating to how phonological features of the language are represented in the practical orthography were discussed in §2.10. We can now briefly consider the relevance of the concept of "word" to decisions on what constitutes an orthographic word.

Because phonological and grammatical words generally coincide, there is usually little controversy as to where words begin and end. Pauses tend to occur between phonological words, even those that include the proclitics or enclitics mentioned above, suggesting that speakers are primarily sensitive to phonological criteria. Yet when they write, speakers differ in their representation of proclitics and enclitics. Occasionally, these proclitics or enclitics are written together with their phonological host, but more often than not (and more often with proclitics than with enclitics), they are written as separate words, even though they are not truly phonologically independent. This shows that speakers are also sensitive to grammatical information, and that the mismatch between phonological words and grammatical words is still a tricky issue.

Speakers also occasionally find it strange that their words, in particular verbal words, are often so much longer than corresponding words in Portuguese or Spanish. When such issues have arisen, we have examined the morphological processes of the language in order to help speakers understand that each language has its own word-building processes and that these can and should be reflected in writing.

4 Noun classes and noun formation

Kotiria, like other Eastern Tukanoan languages (see the comparative overview in §4.1), has a very rich system of noun formation and noun classification expressed by both noun class morphology and noun classifiers. The base of the noun classification system is the division of nouns into two classes: animates and inanimates. These are subcategorized in a number of different ways according to features such as gender and number for animates, and countability and number, as well as shape, function, type, and other identifying traits for inanimates. Differing degrees of linguistic marking reveal a hierarchy of animates with humans and humanlike entities at the highest levels and collective animates and animates coded by inanimate shape classifiers at the lowest (§4.2). This latter group are, in a sense, demoted to the status of inanimates, and constitute an overlapping class of animates coded as inanimates, a linguistic hybrid of the two major classes. Within the class of inanimates (§4.3), classifiers are often used to derive different kinds of nouns from a single root. There are classifiers of various types, some of which are more highly grammaticalized than others. Taken all together, noun class morphology and classifiers form a continuum of noun classification resources (§4.4): The major class suffixes coding gender and number are the most grammaticalized classification morphemes and the least grammaticalized forms are independent noun roots that can be the classifier constituents in compounds.

Nouns can be based on lexical noun roots, or derived from verb or particle roots through very productive derivational processes (§4.5). Classifier constructions can be regarded as a subtype of noun compounding (§4.8). More grammaticalized types of nominals include the negative nominal ~*de* (§4.6), and several sorts of nominal constructions that can function as pronouns (§4.7). For animates, first and second person forms have a deictic origin, while third person forms are derived from the anaphoric particle in most situations, though deictic forms are also possible in special contexts. Pronouns with inanimate referents are also derived from the anaphoric particle and the appropriate coreferential nominal morphology.

4.1 Noun classes in Eastern Tukanoan languages

Like other Eastern Tukanoan languages, Kotiria has an elaborate system of noun classification—a system of morphemes whose semantics denote "some salient perceived or imputed characteristic of the entity to which an associated noun refers" (Allan 1977:285). As is outlined by Derbyshire and Payne (1990), the noun classification systems of Eastern Tukanoan languages challenge Dixon's (1986) typological categorization of languages as having either grammatical noun class or lexical noun classifier systems systems as well as the tripartite typology of numeral, concordial, and verb-incorporated classifier systems. Derbyshire and Payne rightly point out that many Amazonian languages, among them Tukanoan languages, display interesting mixtures of elements from two or more of these systems. Eastern Tukanoan languages, for example, have both extensive systems of bound noun classifier morphemes and modified versions of numerical classifiers; they code gender as an integrated element of their systems, show class agreement in numerical constructions through affixation instead of independent lexical items, and use the same set of classifier morphemes (with the exception of gender-coding morphemes) in more than one system and for both inflectional and derivational functions (Derbyshire and Payne 1990:245–46; Barnes 1990:273–74; Aikhenvald 2000:10, 220–21).

In much of the literature on individual Eastern Tukanoan languages, noun classification is analyzed according to a basic structural formula [noun root + classificatory suffix], the combination forming a single phonological word. Most analyses group classifier suffixes into broad and specific semantic categories. Broad categories code animate-inanimate, masculine-feminine, and singular-plural distinctions, while specific categories code inanimate items according to criteria such as shape, arrangement, origin, and function. Animate suffixes are generally identified as 'masculine singular', 'feminine singular', and 'plural', while lists of inanimate classifiers include dozens of morphemes: ninety-two in Tuyuka (Barnes 1990:273–74), 112 in Desano (Miller 1999:35–42), 137 in Barasana (Jones and Jones 1991:35–43), and 150 in Kubeo, including a set of independent nouns which may themselves serve as classifiers to other nouns (Morse and Maxwell 1999:73). Morse and Maxwell propose a continuum of classifier categories with varying degrees of semantic specificity ranging from semantically general "one-syllable bound morphemes" to "multisyllable nonbound morphemes, which have independent stress" and more specific reference. They also note that certain animates in Kubeo are suffixed by shape classifiers or take the feminine suffix in their generic form (Morse and Maxwell 1999:73–79).

The occurrence of inanimate classifiers on animate nouns and the use of feminine in generic forms are a notable departure from the Eastern Tukanoan norm, and are analyzed by Gomez-Imbert (1996) as attributable to extensive contact between Kubeo speakers and speakers of Baniwa (Arawak) and integration of Arawak categories into the preexisting Kubeo nominal classification system. Indeed, both the Kubeo and the Kotiria have historically interacted with and frequently marry speakers of Baniwa, and it is likely that the less extensive, though parallel, use of shape-denoting classifiers on some animates in Kotiria can be traced to the same sociocultural source (see Stenzel and Gomez-Imbert 2009).

Analyses of the classification system in Tukano (Sorensen 1969; West 1980; Ramirez 1997a) all identify a primary animate-inanimate distinction, but offer differing analyses of the features that establish further levels of subcategorization. West focuses on number and gender distinctions for animates and identifies a limited set of shape or function classifier suffixes (1980:111–19). For Sorensen (1969:193–98), the feature of gender establishes four categories: 'masculine', 'feminine', 'common' (animate plural, in which gender is neutralized), and 'neuter' (inanimates, unmarked for gender). His list of some fifty classifiers includes one-syllable suffixes as well as "reduplicative" classifiers: noun roots that can also function as classifiers (these are identified as "repeater" classifiers in Aikhenvald's typology [2000: 222]). Ramirez adds a feature [± countable] for inanimates that determines singular and plural forms, and identifies six shape classifier suffixes whose main function is to derive countable or pluralizable forms from uncountable nouns (1997a:211). In contrast to most of the literature on Eastern Tukanoan languages, Ramirez does not consider rootlike "reduplicative" or "repeater" classifiers to be suffixes; he analyzes them as dependent nouns in a modifier-head relationship (1997a: 235).

Gomez-Imbert's detailed analysis of noun classification in Tatuyo distinguishes noun "classes" from noun "classifiers". Noun classes, in her terms, are obligatorily coded, express inherent properties of nouns, and show agreement on predicates, while noun classifiers are not obligatory and do not show inherent properties of nouns, but rather qualify a noun in some way, such as function or physical manifestation. A hierarchy of the features [±animate], [±singular], and [±feminine] establishes four noun classes—'masculine singular', 'feminine singular', 'animate plural', and a generic class into which most inanimates fall; these latter may be further qualified through use of classifiers from a set of nearly one hundred (1982:76–81). Gomez-Imbert was the first to analyze the noun classification system as a continuum of forms, from highly grammaticalized bound, one-syllable class suffixes with no underlying phonological specification for suprasegmental features, to classifiers, which display varying degrees of grammaticalization. Some are bound forms with more generalized semantics and monosyllabic configuration, while others are free, generally disyllabic morphemes with more specific semantics. Unlike suffixes, classifiers often retain underlying specifications for suprasegmental features (Gomez-Imbert 1982:110–16).

Waltz and Waltz (1997:33–34) analyze singular-plural distinctions as basic to the Kotiria system, with animate-inanimate as a secondary feature. They also identify nine primarily shape-denoting classifiers. In another work, on the other hand (Waltz and Waltz 2000:458–60), they speak of two nominal classes: independent roots (animate or inanimate) and classifier roots (denoting shape, arrangement, or function) that may function as free morphemes or bound suffixes.[1]

4.2 Animates

Figure 4.1 gives an alternate view of the system in a binary feature tree representation of Kotiria noun classes. The two major classes are animate and inanimate, with subcategorization according to the features of gender and number for animates, and of countability and number for inanimates. Note that within this basic system, the morpheme $+ro$ occurs both as a singulative with animates (shown in the figure as $+ro_{SING}$), and as a partitive with inanimates (shown in the figure as $+ro_{PART}$).

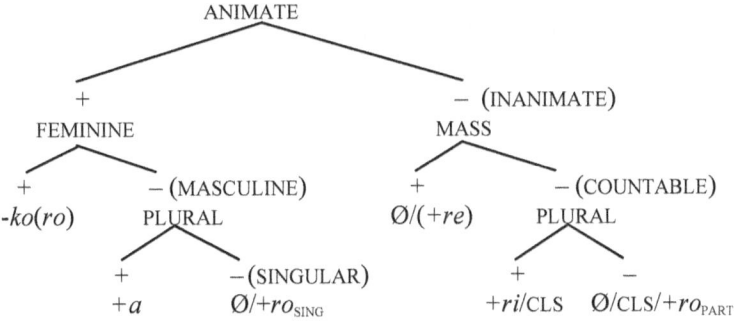

Figure 4.1. Major features of Kotiria noun classes.

Like all Eastern Tukanoan languages, Kotiria codes a major class distinction between animate and inanimate nouns. Table 4.1 shows a

---

[1] Like the other articles in the same volume, Waltz and Waltz's 2000 article was actually written nearly a decade earlier. For this reason, their 1997 analysis is taken to be the most contemporary.

further subdivision of animates into human and nonhuman categories. The nonhuman category then distinguishes between higher-level and lower-level animates. The highest nonhuman category is labeled as "individual" because each entity is conceived of as constituting a separate being, having some specific property that gives it salience to humans; animals such as jaguars, monkeys, snakes, or parrots fall within this category. The "individual" category contrasts with that of "collective" animates, which are conceived of and linguistically coded as gregarious—they are entities that live and move in groups; bees, termites, and minnows are examples of beings in this category.

TABLE 4.1. ANIMATE NOUNS

ROOT	GENDER		NUMBER	
	masculine	feminine	singular	plural
HUMAN				
With inherent gender	root ends in *ɨ*	root ends in *o*	+*ro* (oblig.)	+*a*/-~*da*
Other human nouns	-Ø/+*ɨ*	-*ko*/+*o*		
NONHUMAN				
Individual				
higher	Ø	-*koro* (opt.)	+*ro* (oblig.)	+*a*/-~*da*
lower	Ø	Ø	Ø	(-*ya*)
Collective (root is inherently plural, ending in +*a*/-~*da*)	Ø	Ø	-*kiro*	

4.2.1 Nouns with human referents: gender and number

There are a number of subclasses of animate nouns in Kotiria, the first major division being that between animate nouns with human referents and animate nouns with nonhuman referents. The morphological property that establishes human nouns as a distinct class is gender marking. Although gender marking often leads to a labeling of the entire system as a "gender" system, gender in Kotiria is coded as a secondary feature of only certain subsets of nouns, generally those with human referents. The unmarked value for most noun roots with human referents is masculine; feminine is generally marked by overt morphophonological means, athough a few roots, such as ~*dubi* 'woman' or 'female' (9a), which does not end in [o], can be considered inherently feminine, thus requiring no additional morphological marking.

The roots of the words given in (1)–(7) (feminine words in the (a) examples, corresponding masculine words in the (b) examples) come from a subset of nouns in which the gender-coding suffixes -*ko* (feminine) or -*kʉ* (masculine) have undergone phonological reduction to *o* or *ʉ* and are synchronically incorporated into the bimoraic template for roots as V_2.[2] The root ~*wami* 'older sibling' in (4) is an exception, as it retains full bimoraic structure with a final [i] onto which the feminine +*o* is affixed (4a). The masculine form in (4b), which ends in [i], probably represents a lexification that took place during the period of vowel shift from [ʉ] to [i] (Waltz 2002:180). Nearly all such roots with "incorporated" gender marking are Kotiria kinship terms that can function both as referent nouns and as vocatives[3] and are evidence of a process of ongoing grammaticalization of major class suffixes (see Gomez-Imbert 1982:113). Note that while the full gender morpheme forms appear to be present in (5)–(7), preaspiration of the voiceless plosive *k* in these words is evidence that this segment constitutes part of the root rather than the gender suffix, since aspiration of this sort does not generally occur across morpheme boundaries (see §2.1.1).

(1) a. *ñʉhchono*
~*yʉch+ó+ró*
grandparent+FEM+SG
'grandmother'

b. *ñʉhchono*
~*yʉch+ʉ́+ró*
grandparent+MASC+SG
'grandfather'

---

[2] We might expect some masculine nouns to have the unreduced suffix -*kʉ*, analogous to the feminine suffix -*ko* (as in (10a) and (11a)). In fact, no regular lexical masculine nouns have unreduced -*kʉ* (see additional comments in §4.2.2), but this suffix does occur regularly in nominalizations (§10.1.2), where it is clearly the counterpart to -*ko* within the paradigm. In my text collection, it also occurs in a single noun obviously derived from such a nominalization (namely ~*wahá-kʉ+ri+ro+re* 'the one (curupira that I) killed' [A7.112]).

[3] The complexity of the kinship term system reflects the cultural significance of kinship relationships (both real and conceptual) in defining and reinforcing relations of rank and responsibility within Kotiria society. The frequent use of these terms as vocatives in everyday speech may explain their higher degree of grammaticalization. Analyses and lists of Kotiria kinship terms are provided by Chernela (1993:60–71) and Waltz and Waltz (1997:15–24).

(2) a. tañono
    ~tay+ó+ró
    cousin+FEM+SG
    'marriageable female cross-cousin'[4]

b. tañᵾno
    ~tay+ᵾ+ró
    cousin+MASC+SG
    'marriageable male cross-cousin'

(3) a. ba'oro
    ba'+ó+ró
    younger.sibling+FEM+SG
    'younger sister'

b. ba'ᵾro
    ba'+ᵾ+ró
    younger.sibling+MASC+SG
    'younger brother'

(4) a. wãmiono
    ~wabí+ó+ró
    older.sibling+FEM+SG
    'older sister'

b. wãmino
    ~wabí+ró
    older.sibling+SG
    'older brother'

(5) a. phᵾkoro
    phᵾk+ó+ró
    parent+FEM+SG
    'mother'

b. phᵾkᵾro
    phᵾk+ᵾ+ró
    parent+MASC+SG
    'father'

(6) a. mahkono
    ~bak+ó+ró
    child+FEM+SG
    'daughter'

b. mahkᵾno
    ~bak+ᵾ+ró
    child+MASC+SG
    'son'

(7) a. bᵾhkoro
    bᵾk+ó+ro
    elder+FEM+SG
    'old woman'
    (also 'wife')

b. bᵾhkᵾro
    bᵾk+ᵾ+ro
    elder+MASC+SG
    'old man'
    (also 'husband')

The grammaticalization of the gender suffixes is fully evident in terms such as those for 'husband' and 'wife' for which the feminine and masculine roots are unrelated (8), though, as noted above, the generic root for 'female' or 'woman', ~dubi, does not end in *o* (9a).

(8) a. namono
    ~dabó+ro
    wife+SG
    'wife'

b. manᵾno
    ~badᵾ+ro
    husband+SG
    'husband'

---

[4] The distinction between types of cousins—cross-cousins, or those whom one may marry, and cousins who are one's classificatory siblings—is linguistically coded in Tukanoan languages, reflecting its importance to their system of linguistic exogamy.

(9) a. *numino*   b. *mɨno*
        ~dubí+ró   ~bɨ́+ro
        woman+SG   man+SG
        'female; woman'   'male; man'

Illustrating the general gender-marking pattern for nouns with human referents, we can see in the following derived nouns that these take the suffix *-ko* in their singular forms if the referent is female, and are interpreted as masculine when that suffix is absent.

(10) a. *yo'garikoro*   b. *yo'gariro*
        yo'gá+ri-ko+ro   yo'gá+ri+ro
        fish+NOM-FEM+SG   fish+NOM+SG
        'fisherwoman'   'fisherman'

(11) a. *a'rikoro*   b. *a'riro*
        a'rí-kó+ró   a'rí+ró
        DEM.PROX-FEM+SG   DEM.PROX+SG
        'this woman'   'this man'

The second defining feature of nouns with human referents is that they are obligatorily marked for number. The default marker of singular human nouns is the suffix *+ro*, as seen in (1)–(11). Plural is marked on human nouns in several different ways. The animate plural suffix *+a* is used to pluralize a small set of nouns with human referents (or humanlike referents as in (19c) and (20c) below), such as those in (12).

(12) a. *numia*   b. *mɨa*   c. *phɨtoa*
        ~dubí+a   ~bɨ́+a   phɨtó+á
        female+PL   male+PL   leader+PL
        'females; women' 'males; men'   'leaders; supervisors'

For the plurals of female kin, a cliticized construction *~sa ~dubia*, literally 'our (excl.) women', is used (the (a) examples in (13)–(16)), and there is a special plural suffix *-~sɨba* (the (b) examples in (13)–(16)) that pluralizes terms for any group of humans for whom one should show added respect, such as husbands, "older" siblings (in fact referring to classificatory siblings who are from higher-ranked sibs), or ancestors. The term for 'ancestors', though grammatically marked by default as masculine, may be used inclusively for both males and females. For other kin, the alternate form of the animate plural suffix *-~da* is used (17).

(13) a. *ñᵾhcho sã numia*
 ~yᵾch+ó=~sa-~dubi+a
 grandparent+FEM=1EXC.POSS-woman+PL
 'grandmothers'

 b. *ñᵾhchᵾsᵾma*
 ~yᵾch+ᵾ́-~sᵾba
 grandparent+MASC-PL
 'grandfathers; ancestors'

(14) a. *ñamo sã numia*
 ~dabó=~sa-~dubi+a
 wife=1EXC.POSS-woman+PL
 'wives'

 b. *manᵾsᵾma*
 ~badᵾ́-~sᵾba
 husband-PL
 'husbands'

(15) a. *phᵾko sã numia*
 phᵾk+ó=~sa-~dubi+a
 parent+FEM=1EXC.POSS-woman+PL
 'mothers'

 b. *phᵾkᵾsᵾma*
 phᵾk+ᵾ́-~sᵾ́bá
 parent+MASC-PL
 'fathers'

(16) a. *wamio sã numia*
 ~wabí+ó=~sa-~dubi+a
 older.sibling+FEM=1EXC.POSS-woman+PL
 'older sisters'

 b. *wamisᵾma*
 ~wabí-~sᵾ́bá
 older.sibling-PL
 'older brothers'

(17) a. *ba'ana numia*
 ba'á-~dá ~dubí+a
 younger.sibling-PL woman+PL
 'younger sisters'

b. *ba'ana*
   ba'á-~dá
   younger.sibling-PL
   'younger brothers'

The two forms of the plural suffix, *+a* and *-~da*, are most likely diachronically linked, with *-~da*, the older form, gradually undergoing reduction (including loss of inherent nasalization) and grammaticalization as *+a*. The plural nominalizing construction *+ri-~da* is also undergoing reduction to two different forms, *-~i-da* or *+ri+a*; the latter is seen in the name the Kotiria use for themselves, *ko-ti+ri+a* 'water people'. Further evidence of a reduction in progress comes from lexicalized plurals with *-~da*, such as *~pho'da* 'children, offspring', forms that have resisted reduction and can be interpreted as relics of the complete original form. Cross-linguistic evidence also indicates that the original form of the plural suffix was *-~da*. This continues to be the basic animate plural marker in Kubeo and Tuyuka, whereas Desano and Siriana have *-a* as the basic form. Like Kotiria, Tukano, Barasana, Bará, Pisamira, and Yuruti have an *-a/-~da* alternation, with some tendency toward semantic specialization whereby *-~da* is only used for animates with human referents, while *-a* is the plural marker for other animates.

Examples (12)–(17) also show that gender is neutralized in plurals marked by the *+a/-~da* suffixes; plurals of human nouns are by default masculine, and groups of females are identified by the construction *~sa ~dubia* following the head noun. An exception to this general rule for pluralization is the kinship terms for 'younger sibling', *ba'a* (17), where the full root (cf. singular forms with gender incorporation in (3) above) is independently pluralized by *-~da*.

4.2.2 Nonhuman individual animates

The second category of animate nouns includes those whose referents are nonhuman, but are cognitively recognized and linguistically coded as individual entities rather than as members of collectives. Gomez-Imbert introduces the notion of "cognitive saliency" as the basis for this linguistic differentiation, stating that

> Some animals are "closer" to human beings than others. This closeness makes them perceptually salient, and this is reflected at the linguistic level by unmarked forms. Salient properties should be related with physical appearance, behavior, or the sort of relation humans entertain with animals in everyday experience. . . . This fits the general pattern of Tukanoan languages, where nouns referring to non-gregarious

(salient) vs. gregarious (non-salient) animals are morphologically different. [Gomez-Imbert 1996:456]

Within the general class of nonhuman individual animates, there is a small subset of entities that can be analyzed as being even closer to humans than the rest of the higher-level animates. These nouns, like nouns with human referents, are obligatorily suffixed by +*ro* in their singular forms, as seen in the (a) examples in (18)–(22). Nouns in this small subset can be optionally coded for gender in their singular forms; as in the case of humans, female is the marked category, characterized by means of the fused suffix -*koro* in addition to the singular marker +*ro* (the (b) examples in (19)–(22)). The plural forms of these nouns (the (c) examples in (18)–(22)) generally follow the pattern for humans; the unmarked plural suffix +*a* codes masculine, while the plural for females involves use of the cliticized ~*dubia* 'women', so that 'female dogs' would have the form *dieya-~dubia*, literally 'dogs-females'.

(18) a. *phinono* b. —— c. *phinoa*
         ~*phidó+ró*   ~*phidó+á*
         snake+SG   snake+PL
         'snake'   'snakes'

(19) a. *boraro* b. *borarokoro* c. *boraroa*
         borá+ro   *borá+ro-koro*   *borá-ro+a*
         curupira+SG   curupira+SG-FEM   curupira+SG+PL
         'curupira'[5] 'female curupira' 'curupiras'

(20) a. *wãhtiro* b. *wãhtirokoro* c. *wãhtia*
         ~*watí+ró*   ~*watí+ró-kóró*   ~*watí+á*
         evil.being+SG   evil.being+SG-FEM   evil.being+PL
         'evil being;   'evil female being; 'evil beings;
         devil'   she-devil'   devils'

---

[5] The term "curupira" is a borrowing from Língua Geral (Nheengatú) and is used throughout Amazonia to refer to jungle-dwelling creatures who are generally malicious and can cause serious harm people who have the misfortune to encounter them. Stories involving curupiras are very common (texts 5 and 7 in appendix 1 are two examples), and it is often the case in such tales that curupiras take on humanlike form so that people will not immediately recognize them. However humanlike curupiras may appear at first, their strange ways usually reveal them for what they are; not being as clever as humans, they can sometimes be tricked into harming themselves or fooled long enough to allow humans to escape.

(21) a. *yairo*   b. *yairokoro*   c. *yaiya*
   yaí+ró   *yaí+ró-kóró*   *yaí-yá*
   jaguar+SG   jaguar+SG-FEM   jaguar-PL
   'jaguar'   'female jaguar'   'jaguars'

(22) a. *diero*   b. *dierokoro*   c. *dieya*
   dié+ró   *dié+ró-kóró*   *dié-yá*
   dog+SG   dog+SG-FEM   dog-PL
   'dog'   'female dog'   'dogs'

What seems to be double marking of singular in the exceptional and highly marked terms in the (b) examples in (19)–(22) is most likely evidence of an older system of gender and number coding. Both Kotiria and closely related Wa'ikhana must once have utilized to a greater extent the singular gender markers *-kʉ/-ko* (or *-gʉ/-go*) that are found in other Eastern Tukanoan languages. However, this subgroup of Eastern Tukanoan languages underwent a vowel shift $ʉ \rightarrow i$ that resulted in adjustments to the system and an intermediate stage with the forms *-kiro/-koro/-~kida*, which are still used synchronically in Wa'ikhana (see §4.7). Over time, consistent overt marking of masculine eroded in Kotiria, resulting in the synchronic pattern with the (unmarked masculine) form *+ro*, and the marked feminine *-ko+ro*. The highly marked feminine forms with *-koro* in the (b) examples, the singulative *-kiro* for collectives (see §4.2.3.), and the irregular singular and plural forms of certain lexical items such as 'animal'—singular *wa'i-kiro*, plural *wa'i-~kida*—are relics from the intermediate stage and may imply semantic notions in addition to gender and number.[6]

Following Gomez-Imbert's analysis, the explanation for the parallel linguistic coding of humans and the creatures in (18)–(22) can be found in a combination of salient traits that go beyond qualities such as physical size or domestication. Jaguars, armadillo, deer, and anteaters are all large, forest-dwelling beasts, but only jaguars fall into this marked category of nonhuman animates. Dogs, cows, and chickens are all domesticated animals, but only dogs are linguistically differentiated. Saliency, in these cases, is cultural in origin. Dogs, for instance, play an extremely important role in Kotiria daily life both as pets and as hunting partners, making them the most important animal in Kotiria communities and the one with which humans develop the closest

---

[6] The suffix *-koro*, for example, can also be used to imply that a female entity is exceptionally large, old, powerful, or dangerous. When affixed to a proper name, it is used to show respect; for example, I am generally called by my Kotiria nickname 'Kiri' by the adults with whom I work, whereas the school children respectfully call me *Kirikoro*, a term equivalent to "Dona Kiri" in Portuguese or "Doña Kiri" in Spanish.

relationships (as shown in "The Hunting Dog Story," text 2 in appendix 1). The prominence of jaguars, on the other hand, can be attributed to the mythical and linguistic association between jaguars and shamans that is common to all Tukanoan groups (Jackson 1983:197). As in most Eastern Tukanoan languages, the same word, *yairo*, is used for both, and all things associated with jaguars (such as their teeth and pelts) are highly esteemed.

Snakes, and in particular the anaconda, are also extremely important in Kotiria mythology. According to the Kotiria origin myth, the ancestors of the current Kotiria groups emerged from the body of a sacred anaconda-canoe. The anaconda, with prehuman beings inside, swam from its origins in the mythical Milk Lake (nowadays considered to be Rio de Janeiro's Guanabara Bay) into the ocean and up to the mouth of the Amazon and from there upstream to the Negro and Vaupés Rivers. Along the way, the prehuman beings acquired human qualities, knowledge, and form. When the anaconda-canoe reached the headwaters, it turned around, stretching its body along the river. At each place where its curving body rose to the surface, the ancestor of one of the patrilineal Kotiria kin groups established his territory and lineage; internally, descent groups from ancestors emerging closer to the head are higher-ranked than those of ancestors emerging closer to the tail (Chernela 1993:5). Finally, the fact that magical beings such as curupiras and ~*watia* 'devils, spirits' are given linguistic coding parallel to that of humans is due to the fact that such beings often take on human form and have many humanlike characteristics.

Other individual animates—and most animates fall into this class—are only marked for gender in very exceptional cases in which gender is both known and relevant to discourse. These animates differ from the subgroup in the previous section in that they are not overtly marked as singular entities; the bare root form functions as both the unmarked singular and in situations of generic reference, where the characteristic properties of typical individuals of the species are being described. We can see clear examples of unmarked animate nouns used in this way in texts 9, 10, and 11 in appendix 1, from the "Kotiria Animal Stories" collection, as well as the short text given in full as (118) below (see also the discussion in §4.3.2). Plural is the marked category, coded by the suffix +*a*. A sample of nouns in this class are shown in (23)–(32). Example (32b), like (21c) and (22c) above, comes from a small subset of animate nouns that have the irregular plural -*ya*.[7]

The the plural forms in (29)–(31), in which the final root vowel *a* is replaced by *e*, are analyzed by Waltz (2002:190) as relic forms of

---

[7] Another frequently used noun in this subset is the word *ko-ya* 'relatives'.

Nouns and noun classes 111

Proto-Kotiria-Wa'ikhana (Waltz's "Proto-WP") noun roots with front vowels. Though a major vowel shift affected all vowels in the singular forms, the plural forms still show alternation of the final vowel. By analogy, certain roots which ended in *a* in Proto-Kotiria-Wa'ikhana, such as *~baha* 'macaw' (31), now also display this alternation.

(23) a. *mie*
~*bié*
'anteater'
b. *miea*
~*bié+a*
'anteaters'

(24) a. *phamo*
~*phabó*
'armadillo'
b. *phamoa*
~*phabó+á*
'armadillos'

(25) a. *khu* [kʰuú]
khú
'turtle'
b. *khua*
khú+á
'turtles'

(26) a. *mohko*
~*bóko*
'catfish'
b. *mohkoa*
~*bóko+a*
'catfish' (pl.)

(27) a. *yehse*
yesé
'pig'
b. *yehsea*
yesé+a
'pigs'

(28) a. *ñama*
~*yabá*
'deer'
b. *ñamaa*
~*yabá+á*
'deer' (pl.)

(29) a. *dahsa*
dasá
'toucan'
b. *dahsea*
dasé+á
'toucans'

(30) a. *ba'a*
ba'á
'bass'
b. *ba'ea*
ba'é+á
'bass' (pl.)

(31) a. *maha*
~*bahá*
'macaw'
b. *mahea*
~*bahé+á*
'macaws'

(32) a. *ka* [káa]
ká
'monkey'
b. *kaya*
ká-ya
'monkeys'

4.2.3 Inherently collective animates

The final category of animate nouns refers to gregarious creatures, such as most types of insects, worms, and some types of fish—in other words, creatures that live and move as collectives, exemplified in (33)–(37). In contrast to roots for "individual" animates, nearly all roots for nouns in this class can be analyzed as inherently plural. Most roots referring to collective animates end in *a* or *~da* (the root for 'leafcutter ants' (33) is one of the few that do not); these endings appear to be etymologically the same as the plural markers used with individual inanimates. Some such collective inanimate roots have an unusual three-mora shape, such as the roots for 'flies' (34) and 'maggots' (36); these may represent an intermediate stage in a grammaticalization process that will eventually fuse the plural markers into a two-mora root.

For collective animates, 'plural' is the unmarked value for number and 'singular' the marked value. Reference to an individual member of a collective requires the addition of an individualizing suffix *-kiro* on the plural stem, although some stems lose their final *a* when *-kiro* is attached (e.g., (36b)). The function of *-kiro* for collective animates is similar to the partitive function *+ro* performs for mass nouns (see §4.3.1 below): it is a tool for specifying or singling out an individual referent from a collective. Synchronically, there is evidence that the initial consonant of the suffix *-kiro* is lost in some words, especially among younger speakers, as seen in (36b) and (37b).

(33) a. *mahchɨ*
~*bachɨ́*
'leafcutter ants'

b. *mahchɨkiro*
~*bachɨ́-kiro*
leafcutter.ants-IND
'a leafcutter ant'

(34) a. *khomana*
~*khobáda*
'flies'

b. *khomanakiro*
~*khobáda-kiro*
flies-IND
'a fly'

(35) a. *mia*
~*bía*
'sardines'

b. *miakiro*
~*bía-kiro*
sardines-IND
'a sardine'

(36) a. *dahchoa*
dachóá
'maggots'

b. *dahcho(k)iro*
dachó-(k)iró
maggots-IND
'a maggot'

(37) a. hũa   b. hũ(k)iro
       ~húa   ~húa-(k)iro
       'worms'   worms-IND
                     'a worm'

4.2.4 Linguistic coding and the hierarchy of animates

Gender and number marking reveal a hierarchy of animates, shown in table 4.2. Entities with greater hierarchical status are coded for the greatest number of features. Human nouns, for example, are obligatorily coded for both gender and number, whereas gender is only optionally marked for lower animates and is nonexistent for collectives.

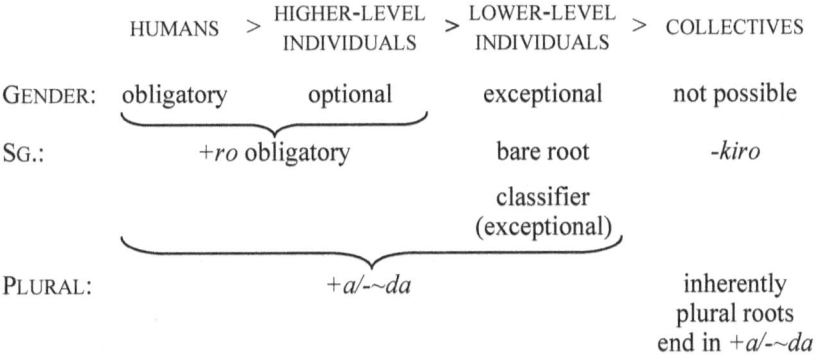

Figure 4.2. Hierarchy of animates.

4.3 Inanimates

The second major noun class is that of inanimates, which can be subcategorized according to a mass-count distinction (similar analyses have been proposed for Tukano [Ramirez 1997a:201] and for Siriano [Criswell and Brandrup 2000:405]). Further subcategorization is revealed in the coding of number for count nouns. Some count nouns have zero marking in their singular forms and are pluralized by +ri (§4.3.2). Other count nouns are singularized by suffixlike classifiers or the partitive +ro (§§4.3.2–4.3.3). These are generally pluralized by +ri, which replaces the classifier or +ro to indicate multiple entities, though for some cases we find that special plural classifiers are used. In still other cases, when nouns with reduced or full noun classifiers such as ~phu 'leaf of X' are pluralized, the classifier remains and is itself suffixed by +ri. These patterns are summarized in table 4.2.[8]

---

[8] Nominalizations with and without the suffix +ri are discussed in §4.5.1.

4.3.1 Mass nouns

Mass nouns are morphologically distinguished by the fact that they have no plural forms. The bare root identifies not a singular, but an uncountable referent.

TABLE 4.2. INANIMATES

ROOT TYPE	NUMBER MARKING	
	SINGULAR	PLURAL
MASS	$\emptyset$ (uncountable)	(no plural)
COUNT		
count noun derived from mass noun or verb root	$+ro_{PART}$	varied strategies
without classifier	$\emptyset$	$+ri$
body parts	$+ro_{PART}$ / classifier	$+ri$
with suffixlike classifier	classifier	$+ri$ "plural" classifier
with reduced or full noun classifier	classifier	classifier+ri
nominalizations without +ri	classifier / $+ro_{PART}$	varied strategies
nominalizations with +ri	classifier	varied strategies

NOTE: $+ro_{PART}$ = partitive +ro.

(38) *phu'ti*
    phu'ti
    'grated manioc'

(39) *mi* [mĩĩ]
    ~bí
    'honey'

(40) *chipe*
    ~chípe
    'sap'

(41) *ya'pa*
    ya'pá
    'ground'

The addition of the suffix +ro to a mass noun (42)–(44) or to a verb root (45)–(48) can derive a count noun that denotes a semantically

Nouns and noun classes 115

related singular entity or instance—a sort of partitive function. There is no single strategy for pluralization of derived nouns; indeed, speakers could not readily think of forms corresponding to the notions of pluralized 'fields' (44c) or 'roofs' (46c) at all. For other derived nouns, the closest pluralized notion requires additional morphology, such as the compound construction in (42c) referring to a 'rainy season' (a series of rainstorms or rainy days), or the use of the bare form of the noun with a phonologically independent pluralizer (43c). Interestingly, other derived nouns are pluralized by the suffix +*a* substituting the "partitive" +*ro* (45c) and (47c), while the same +*a* occurs in conjunction with +*ro* in (48c). An in-depth investigation of number marking is currently underway, and further discussion of these observed patterns will have to await conclusions from this study.

(42) a. *ko* [koó] b. *koro* c. *kodahchori*
       kó   *kó+ró*   *kó-dáchó+rí*
       'water'   'rainstorm'   water-day+PL
                                    'rainy days/season'

(43) a. *mʉ'ro* b. *mʉ'roro* c. *mʉ'ro pe'ri*
       ~*bʉ'ró*   ~*bʉ'ró+ró*   ~*bʉ'ró pé'ri*
       'tobacco'   'cigar;   tobacco many
                    cigarette'   'cigars; cigarettes'

(44) a. *tha* [tʰáá] b. *tharo* c. ——
       thá   *thá+ró*
       'grass'   'field'

(45) a. *ño* [ɲõ̂õ] b. *ñono* c. *ñoa*
       ~*yó*   ~*yó+ró*   ~*yó+a*
       'show'   'mirror'   'mirrors'

(46) a. *mʉa* b. *mʉaro* c. ——
       ~*bʉ́á*   ~*bʉ́á+ró*
       'be high' 'sky; roof'

(47) a. *kha'ti* b. *kha'tiro* c. *kha'tia*
       kha'tí   *kha'tí+ró*   *kha'tí+á*
       'live'   'life'   'lives'

(48) a. *khua* b. *khuaro* c. *khuaro*
       khuá   *khuá+ró*   *khuá+ró+á*
       'be afraid' 'danger'   'dangers'

Mass nouns can themselves be derived by the addition of the plural suffix +*a* to another mass noun, e.g., ~*phudi*+*a* (pain+PL) 'poison', or to a verb (49)–(50).

(49) a. *si'ni* b. *si'nia*
 ~*si'dí*   ~*si'dí*+*a*
 'drink'   'caxiri beer; fermented liquid'

(50) a. *chʉ* [tʃʉ́ʉ] b. *chʉa*
 chʉ́   *chʉ́*+*a*
 'eat'   'food'

These examples show that the morphemes +*ro* and +*a* have semantically related yet distinct functions when suffixed to different classes of noun roots. The suffix +*ro* functions as a singularizer with animates and as a derivational partitive with inanimate mass nouns (see also Ramirez 1997a:209–11). It is glossed throughout as "SG" to reflect a common semantic feature as a denotator of singular entities. The suffix +*a* functions as a pluralizer of animates and a subset of derived inanimate nouns and is also employed to derive mass nouns. It is glossed throughout as "PL" to reflect a common semantic feature as a denotator of plural (or at least nonindividualized) entities.

4.3.2 Countable nouns: unsuffixed nouns and body part nouns with +*ro*

In general, countable inanimates are pluralized by the suffix +*ri*. There are, however, a few irregular plural suffixes, such as -*pori*, used to pluralize ~*dako* 'island' (51), -*se(ri)*, used to pluralize *wʉ'ʉ* 'house' (52) and *phʉ'ʉ* 'basket'. The full form of the latter irregular plural also occurs in Tukano (Ramirez 1997a:209), while Kotiria speakers vary between use of the full and the reduced forms, indicating that a process of phonological erosion and leveling leading toward a synchronic general plural suffix +*ri* is underway. Another irregular plural that occurs more frequently is -*phoka*, which occurs as a plural classifier on nouns that take the classifier -*ka*, for rounded objects, in their singular forms, an example being *waso* 'siringa fruit' (53). All these irregular plural markers suggest that the language formerly had a larger paradigm of plural markers coding shape or function as well as number, and that some relic forms persist synchronically alongside the more general plural suffix +*ri*.

(51) a. *nɨhko* b. *nɨhkopori*
    ~*dɨkó*   ~*dɨkó-pórí*
    'island'   'islands'

(52) a. *wɨ'ɨ*   b. *wɨ'ɨse(ri)*
    wɨ'ɨ́   *wɨ'ɨ́-sé(rí)*
    'house'   'houses'

(53) a. *wahsoka* b. *wahsophoka*
    wasó-ka   *wasó-phoka*
    'siringa fruit' 'siringa fruits'

Subcategories of inanimates are identified by the means employed to denote a singular entity. Some inanimate roots, like the "individual" animates discussed in §4.2.2, are free morphemes; the unsuffixed root functions as the unmarked singular. Many of the nouns in this subset are manufactured items, such as axes, or objects such as islands, gardens, and houses, which are not marked as having a fixed shape.

(54) a. *wehse*   b. *wehseri*
    wesé   *wesé+ri*
    'garden'   'gardens'

(55) a. *khoma*   b. *khomari*
    ~*khobá*   ~*khobá+ri*
    'ax'   'axes'

It should be noted, however, that most nouns (body part nouns are an exception), regardless of whether or they occur marked or unmarked in their singular forms, can occur unmarked when they are used in situations of generic reference—for example, in sentences describing the characteristic properties or uses of typical examples of the objects or species in question. Thus, in (56)–(57), ~*bisi* 'vine', *wɨ'ɨ* 'house', and ~*wipi* 'açaí fruit' are all unmarked, yet only *wɨ'ɨ* belongs to the subset of nouns that have unmarked singular forms. For singular reference to a particular vine or açaí fruit in a nongeneric situation, the classifier -*da*, for threadlike objects, would occur on ~*bisi* and the classifier -*ka*, for rounded objects, would occur on ~*wipi*. Unmarked generic forms of nouns also occur in situations in which the reference is to an actual, though nonspecific, entity, such as the syntactically unmarked "generic" nouns discussed in §10.3.2.

(56) *mihsi me're wɨ'ɨ dɨ'teka*
~*bisí*=~*be're*   *wɨ'ɨ*   *dɨ'té-ká*
vine=COM/INST house tie.up-ASSERT.IMPERF
'Houses are tied together with vine.'

(57) *wĩhpi hika mahsa ti toaa*
~*wipí*   *hí-ka*   ~*basá*   *ti=tóá+á*
açaí.fruit COP-ASSERT.IMPERF people 3PL.POSS=plant+PL
'Açaí is (a plant) people cultivate.'

A second subset of inanimate noun roots, those denoting body parts, obligatorily take either the suffix +*ro* (the most common marker) or a shape classifier (more rarely, but see (69a) and (70c) below) in their singular forms and pluralize with the suffix +*ri* (58)–(63), according to the pattern for inanimates. Thus, following Ramirez's (1997a) analysis of the cognate morpheme in Tukano, we should recognize +*ro* as having a secondary derivational function. In this case, it derives an inanimate part from an animate whole—a parallel to its partitive function on mass nouns, where it derives a pluralizable count noun from an unpluralizable mass noun. In situations of generic reference to body parts, the singular form with +*ro* is used, as we see in (64).

(58) a. *da'poro*   b. *da'pori*
       da'pó+ró   *da'pó+rí*
       'foot'   'feet'

(59) a. *kha'moro*   b. *kha'mori*
       ~*kha'bó+ró*   ~*kha'bó+rí*
       'ear'   'ears'

(60) a. *pĕro*   b. *pĕri*
       ~*pé+ró*   ~*pé+rí*
       'breast'   'breasts'

(61) a. *phichono*   b. *phichori*
       ~*phichó+ró*   ~*phichó+rí*
       'tail'   'tails'

(62) a. *kĕro*   b. *kĕri*
       ~*ké+ró*   ~*ké+rí*
       'nose; beak'   'noses; beaks'

(63) a. *dihsero* b. *dihseri*
    disé+ró   *disé+rí*
    'mouth'   'mouths'

(64) *da'poro tuaerara diero*
    da'pó+ró *tu(a)-éra+ra*   *dié+ró*
    foot+SG   be.strong-NEG+VIS.IMPERF.2/3   dog+SG
    'Dogs have weak (fragile) paws.'

4.3.3 Inanimates with classifiers

The third subset of countable inanimate nouns are those whose unmarked form indicates reference to the basic edible part of a particular type of plant, as in (65a), (66a), and (67), while singular or individual reference to a particular part of the plant or to a product made from it is accomplished by use of classifiers; this reveals individuation to be one of the primary functions of classifiers (Craig 1992:295). Some classifiers denote shape or configuration features such as 'rounded', 'flat', or 'cylindrical and curved' (66b); others refer to more specific forms or qualities such as 'tree bearing X' (65d), 'palm bearing X' (66d), 'leaf of X', as in (65e) and (66e), or 'product made from X', as in (65c) and (66c). Many noun roots, such as those for plants, can thus be individuated by a number of different classifiers denoting specific properties or parts, depending on which feature the speaker wishes to call attention to. Nouns identified by a classifier denoting a specific part, such as 'tree or palm bearing X' or 'leaf of X', are then pluralized by +*ri*, as in (65d), (65e), (66d) and (66e); another example appears in (84) below. It is interesting that when pluralized, the classifier for 'tree' appears in its full noun form *y̶u̶k̶u̶* (65d).

(65) a. *se*
       sé [séé]
       'cucura fruit' (generic)

    b. *seka*
       sé-ká
       cucura-CLS:round
       'a (single) cucura fruit'

    c. *seko*
       sé-kó
       cucura-CLS:liquid
       'cucura juice'

d. *seku*
sé-kʉ
cucura-CLS:tree
'a cucura tree'

seyʉhkuri
sé-yʉkʉ+ri
cucura- tree+PL
'cucura trees'

e. *sephũ*
sé-~phú
cucura-leaf
'leaf of a cucura plant'

sephũ
sé-~phú+ri
cucura-leaf+PL
'leaves of a cucura plant'

(66) a. *ho*
hó [hóó]
'banana fruit' (generic)

b. *hoparo*
hó-pároó
banana-CLS:cylindrical, curved
'a banana'

c. *hoko*
hó-kó
banana-CLS:liquid
'banana juice; mashed bananas'

d. *hoño*
hó-~yó
banana-CLS:palm
'banana tree'

hoñori
hó-~yó+ri
banana-CLS:palm+PL
'banana trees'

e. *hophũ*
hó-~phú
banana-leaf
'leaf of a banana tree'

hophũri
hó-~phú+ri
banana-leaf+PL
'leaves of a banana tree'

(67) *bu hiape chʉka: khʉ, ñamʉ*
bú   hi+a-pe   khʉ   ~nabʉ́
agouti COP+SG-CQUANT manioc.root cará.tuber
'The things agoutis eat are: manioc (roots and) cará (tubers).' [LSK: Agoutis]

There are basically three types of classifiers in Kotiria. Suffixlike classifiers have very generalized semantics and appear on many different types of noun roots. They tend to have one-syllable shapes, and the source roots from which they have evolved are no longer recognizable or recoverable. Reduced-root classifiers are recognizable reductions of full noun roots. Finally, full-root classifiers are noun roots that can almost always also stand alone as free morphemes, and can be noninitial roots in compounding constructions.

In (68)–(76), examples are given of general suffixlike shape or type classifiers whose original source roots are no longer recoverable and whose grammatical status is somewhat undefined. They are neither fully grammaticalized suffixes nor are they fully or partially recognizable roots functioning as modifiers to other roots; thus they are somewhat like clitics, in that they "occupy an intermediate position between a full-fledged phonological word and an affix" (Aikhenvald 2002b:43). Indeed, these classifying morphemes display phonological and morphological behavior that is neither completely like an affix nor completely like a lexical root. For example, some classifiers appear to have undergone reduction to a more suffixlike monomoraic form while others retain rootlike bimoraic structure. Like lexical roots, all classifiers retain inherent specification for suprasegmental [±nasal] values, and, as is true of lexical roots in multimorphemic words, initial /d/ of a classifier can occur word-internally realized as [d] rather than as the suffix-initial [r] (as discussed in §2.2.2). On the other hand, classifiers lose inherent tone associations, thus forming a single phonological word with the preceding root, and they show different degrees of potential grammatical independence.

A close examination of the words in (68)–(77) shows that classifiers have several different functions. First, classifiers serve to qualify nouns, calling attention to some salient feature such as shape, as in (68)–(74), quality, such as 'sharpness' in (75), or configuration, as in (76)–(77). Secondly, as mentioned earlier in this section, classifiers (like the "partitive" +ro) denote singular entities (compare (68c) and (68d)); to indicate multiple entities, the classifier (or +ro) is generally either replaced by the suffix +ri, as in (68e) and (69c), or by a special plural classifier (coding both shape and number, as discussed in §4.3.2 above), as in (71b). Thirdly, classifiers are also used to derive nouns from verbs—animate, as in (68a), or inanimate, as in (68b), (70a), (70b), (70c), (75a), (75b), (76b)—or from determiners, as in (76a) (see also §4.5). In (68a), the animate *phirida* 'a long ropelike being' (referring to a snake) is derived from a nominalized verbal root *phi* 'be big' and the classifier for ropelike or threadlike objects, -*da*. In (68b), the same classifier for threadlike objects is used to derive 'fishing line' from the nominalized verbal root *yo'ga* 'to fish'. In (76a), the classifier for stacked objects is used with the demonstrative to derive *a'ri-thu* 'this book'. Finally, we also see that more than one classifier can qualify a root, each addition serving to further specify the noun, as in (75c), in which the root *yʉkʉ* 'tree' takes both the singularizing classifier for 'tree' as well as the classifier for 'bladelike' objects, resulting in the noun *yuku-ku-~phi* 'wooden knife'.

(68) *-da* 'filiform, ropelike, threadlike'

    a. *phirida*
       phí+ri-da
       be.big+NOM-CLS:ropelike
       'a long ropelike one' (used to describe a dead snake)

    b. *yo'garida*
       yo'gá+ri-da
       fish+NOM-CLS:ropelike
       'fishing line'

    c. *phoada*
       phoá-dá
       hair-CLS:threadlike
       'strand of hair'

    d. *phoaro*
       phoá+ró
       hair+SG
       'feather'

    e. *phoari*
       phoá+rí
       hair+PL
       'hair' or 'feathers'

(69) *-ku* 'tree, shaftlike'

    a. *ñuhchuku*
       ~yuchú-ku
       leg-CLS:tree/shaft
       'leg'

    b. *yuhkuku*
       yukú-ku
       tree-CLS:tree/shaft
       'tree'

    c. *yuhkuri*
       yuhku+ri
       tree+PL
       'trees'

(70) -dɨ 'cylindrical and straight'
    a. *tuadɨ*
       tuá-dɨ
       be.strong-CLS:cylindrical.straight
       'branch'

    b. *hoadɨ*
       hóá-dɨ
       write-CLS:cylindrical.straight
       'pen, pencil'

    c. *ñohsadɨ*
       ~yosá-dɨ
       force.into-CLS:cylindrical.straight
       'spear, arrow'

(71) -*ka* 'round'
    a. *tãka*
       ~tá-ká
       rock-CLS:round
       'stone'

    b. *tãphoka*
       ~tá-phóká
       rock-CLS:round
       'stones'

    c. *wãmoka*
       ~wabó-ká
       hand-CLS:round
       'hand'

    d. *sũ'ika*
       ~su'í-ká
       snail-CLS:round
       'snail'

    e. *pũka*
       ~pú-ká
       crab-CLS:round
       'crab'

(72) -to/-ro 'concave'[9]

   a. *biato*
      biá-tó
      pepper-CLS:concave
      'cooking pot' (also 'fish-pepper stew', a daily staple)

   b. *phɨ'ɨro*
      phɨ'ɨ́-ró
      basket-CLS:concave
      'basket'

   c. *khumuno*
      ~*khubú-ro*
      sitting.object-CLS:concave
      'bench' (of the traditional type, with a slightly concave top)

(73) -*paro* 'cylindrical and curved'

   a. *hoparo*
      hó-páró
      banana-CLS:cylindrical.curved
      'banana'

   b. *wɨhpoparo*
      wɨpó-páró
      hairy.caterpillar-CLS:cylindrical.curved
      'caterpillar'

   c. *meneparo*
      ~*bedé-paro*
      inga.fruit-CLS:cylindrical.curved
      'inga fruit'

(74) -*phata* 'flat'

   khumuphata
   ~*khubú-phata*
   sitting.object-CLS:flat
   'bench' (made of boards)

---

[9] I am grateful to Elsa Gomez-Imbert for pointing out the allomorphy of the classifier -*to*/-*ro* 'concave'. (For more on the allomorphy and development of this classifier, see Gomez-Imbert 1982:103–8.)

(75) -~phi 'bladelike'
   a. *yoariphĩ*
      yoa+ri-~phi
      be.long+NOM-CLS:bladelike
      'machete'
   b. *sioriphĩ*
      sió+rí-~phí
      be.sharp+NOM-CLS:bladelike
      'knife'
   c. *yɨhkɨkɨphĩ*
      yɨkɨ́-kɨ-~phí
      tree-CLS:tree-CLS:bladelike
      'wooden knife'
   d. *sĩ'ariphĩ*
      ~si'á+ri-~phi
      ignite+NOM-CLS:bladelike
      'torch'

(76) -*thu* 'stacked'
   a. *a'rithu*
      a'rí-thú
      DEM:PROX-CLS:stacked
      'this book'
   b. *bu'erithu*
      bu'é+ri-thu
      study/learn+NOM-CLS:stacked
      'textbook'

(77) -~*ki* 'bunch'
   hokĩ
   hó-~kí
   banana-CLS:bunch
   'bunch of bananas'

It is noteworthy that shape classifiers occur on the animates in (68a), (71d), (71e) and (73b); such classifiers do not generally occur on animate nouns in Eastern Tukanoan languages. The exceptions are Kubeo, in which a number of higher-level and lower-level animates are coded by shape or as inherently feminine, and Kotiria, where shape classifiers are only used with certain lower-level animates as a means of singularizing them. To understand the use of shape classifiers on animates, we should recall that members of the lower levels in the hierarchy of animates (figure 4.2) have few salient distinguishing features. Thus, the use of shape classifiers on certain kinds of fauna (animates) results from the fact that they cannot be otherwise individuated. According to Gomez-Imbert,

> This additional faunal categorization [the use of shape classifiers on animates] is a generalization from a linguistically marked category with inanimate referents (natural objects and artifacts) to a category of animate non-human referents ... as if they [the animates] were submitted to a perceptive rank demotion. In other words, some morphological borrowing from the much wider field of inanimate coding takes place in order to facilitate identification and reference to these animates. [1996:457]

The classifiers in (78)–(80) show different kinds of reduction of root to classifier. In (78), the *CV* root undergoes phonological reduction from two moras to one mora when it functions as a classifier. The roots in (79)–(80) are also morphologically reduced as classifiers, though the pattern of reduction varies. In (79), the second syllable of the full root *yɨkɨ* 'tree' becomes the generic classifier for trees -*kɨ*, while in (80) it is the first syllable of the full root *phɨ'ɨ* 'basket' that becomes the generic classifier for baskets, -*pɨ*. This classifier is usually also phonologically reduced, losing the initial postaspiration of the voiceless plosive, always realized in the full root form.

(78)   full root: ~*ba* [máá] 'river; stream'; reduced form: -~*ba*

   pihtama
   pitá-~ba
   port-CLS:river
   'river port'

(79)   full root: *yɨkɨ* 'tree'; reduced form: -*kɨ*
   a. *phichakɨ*
      phichá-kɨ
      shoot-CLS:tree/shaft
      'shotgun'
   b. *mɨ'rokɨ*
      ~*bɨ'ró-kɨ*
      tobacco-CLS:tree/shaft
      'a fat cigar'

(80) full root: in *phɨ'ɨ-ro* (basket-CLS:concave) 'basket'; reduced form: *-pɨ*
   kɨ̃pɨ
   ~*kɨ́-pɨ́*
   one-CLS:basket
   'one basket'

All classifiers retain their underlying specification for suprasegmental nasality but lose specification for tonal melody; they are always open to tonal melody spread from the initial noun root. In (78), for example, the full root ~*ba* has underlying H tone and is [+nasal]. As a classifier on *pita* 'port', which has underlying LHL tone and is [−nasal], ~*ba* retains its specification for nasality (even though *pita* is an oral morpheme), but loses its H tone, since as a bound classifier it becomes a target for spread of the final L tone of the LHL initial root.

A small sample of full-root classifiers is shown in (81)–(85).

(81) a. *khãnɨkahpa*
   ~*khadɨ́-kápá*
   sugarcane-shoot/seedling
   'sugarcane shoot'

   b. *sãrekahpa*
   ~*saré-kápá*
   pineapple-shoot/seedling
   'pineapple shoot'

(82) a. *phiriwɨ'ɨ*
   phí+ri-wɨ'ɨ
   be.big+NOM-house
   'longhouse' (traditional construction for communal dwelling)

   b. *bu'eriwɨ'ɨ*
   bu'é+ri-wɨ'ɨ
   study+NOM-house
   'school'

(83) *ñɨmɨphũri*
   ~*yɨbɨ́-~phú+rí*
   bacaba.fruit-leaf+PL
   'leaves of the bacaba fruit tree'

(84) *na'año*
   ~*da'á-~yó*
   buriti.fruit-palm
   'buriti palm'

(85) yʉhkʉkohpa
 yʉkʉ́-kopa
 tree-hole
 'knothole'

I regard combinations of noun with full-root classifier as a type of noun compounding (see §4.8). In fact, it is rather hard to draw a line between noun+classifier combinations and other noun+noun compounds—both have the form noun+noun, with the two roots forming the stem of a single phonological word. Indeed, it is the fusion of the two roots into a single phonological word that distinguishes compounds in general from other types of constructions composed of sequences of nouns, such as possessive modification of one noun by another (see §6.4.2).

In classifier compounds, noun roots in noninitial position are not morphologically reduced; however, like the classifiers in (78)–(80), they do undergo phonological changes that attest their dependent status: they retain underlying specification for nasality but, like all other classifiers, lose specification for tone, the tonal melody of the independent root predominating. The fact that full-root classifiers retain some underlying phonological specifications while losing others is evidence that their grammatical status differs from that of the most suffixlike classifiers. The latter, for the most part, are one-syllable, monomoraic affixes that have generally lost underlying specification for nasality and display segmental restrictions, such as those governing the distribution of [d] and [r] in word-initial or word-internal position.

4.4 General properties of Kotiria noun classification

Figure 4.3 shows the Kotiria noun classification system as a continuum of all the varied types shown in the previous sections (drawing from Sorensen 1969; Gomez-Imbert 1982; and Ramirez 1997a). On the righthand side are the fully grammaticalized suffixes with generalized semantics denoting noun class and the features of animacy, gender, and number. Moving toward the center we find different subsets of classifiers, with more specific semantics and with variable one- or two-syllable shapes. These may have more or less recognizable or recoverable root sources depending on the degree of grammaticalization, and indeed, those in the leftmost column can also function as independent lexical roots. Yet even these roots undergo a kind of phonological reduction when they are used as classifiers, inasmuch as they lose their

Nouns and noun classes

inherent tonal melody when the melody of the initial root spreads over the entire phonological word.

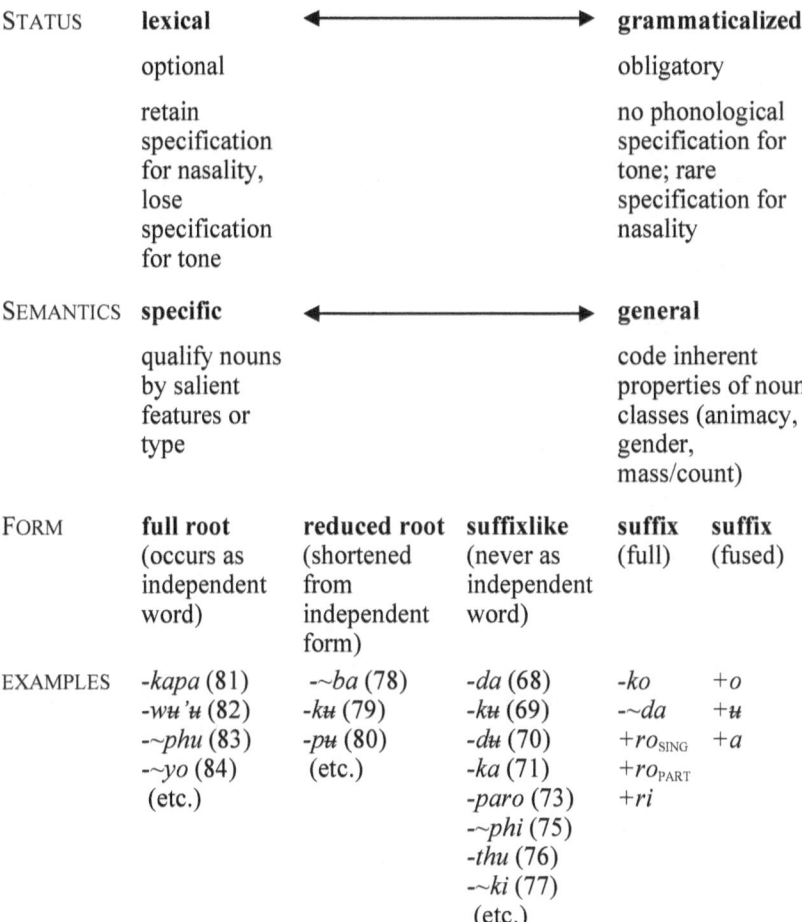

Figure 4.3. The noun classification continuum.

Comparing the Kotiria system with the systems of other Tukanoan languages, we find that it presents some important innovations. Though it shares with other Eastern Tukanoan languages a major class distinction between animates and inanimates and extensive means of classification, there is a significant difference in the coding of animates. Kotiria does not employ the fused gender-number morphemes *-(k)ʉ/-(k)o* for singular human animates that are found in most other Eastern Tukanoan languages; rather, it has developed separate marked coding of 'female', *-ko*, and an overall marker for singular animates, *+ro* (not to be confused with the homophonous *-ro* that occurs on inanimates as a shape classifier for concave objects, where it displays the alternation *-ro/-to*, as in (72)).

The latter development creates an interesting case of polysemy for the morpheme *+ro* within the domain of noun classification. For animates, *+ro* has a singulative function: it is the marker for singular animate entities. For inanimates it has a related function as a partitive: it can derive a singular countable entity from a mass noun or verbal root or designate a part-whole relationship, as with body parts.

4.5 Derived nouns

4.5.1 Nominals derived from verbal roots

Derivation of animate nominals from verbal roots is a two-step process (86). First the verb root is nominalized by the suffix *+ri*, forming a derived nominal stem. This nominal stem can then take appropriate noun classification morphology.

(86) verb root — nominalizer — noun classification morphology:
  +ro (masculine singular)
  -ko+ro (feminine singular)
  -~da (plural)

This extremely productive process is exemplified in (87), showing the singular masculine (87a), singular feminine (87b), and plural (87c) forms of animate nouns derived from the verb *yo'ga* 'to fish'. In all three forms, the root is first nominalized by *+ri*, and then appropriate noun class morphology is affixed: *+ro* (singular and, by default, masculine), *-ko+ro* (feminine singular), and *-~da* (plural). Three singular noun forms for 'hunter' are shown in (88)–(89), each derived from a different verbal root or combination of roots, and additional animate nouns derived from a variety of verb roots appear in (90)–(92).

(87)   a. *yo'gariro*
           yo'gá+ri+ro
           fish+NOM+SG
           'fisherman'

       b. *yo'garikoro*
           yo'gá+ri-ko+ro
           fish+NOM-FEM+SG
           'fisherwoman'

Nouns and noun classes 131

      c. *yo'garina*
        yo'gá+ri-~da
        fish+NOM-PL
        'fishermen, fisherwomen'

(88) *tiniriro*
      ~tidí+rí+ró
      wander.around+NOM+SG
      'hunter; person walking/wandering around'

(89) a. *wa'ikina wãhariro*
        wa'í-~kídá ~wahá+ri+ro
        animal-PL   kill+NOM+SG
        'hunter'

      b. *wa'ikina ko'tariro*
        wa'í-~kídá ko'tá+ri+ro
        animal-PL   wait+NOM+SG
        'hunter'

(90) a. *bu'eriro*
        bu'é+ri+ro
        study/learn+NOM+SG
        'teacher; student'

      b. *hoariro*
        hoá+rí+ró
        write+NOM+SG
        'writer'

      c. *hoarikoro*
        hoá+rí-kó+ró
        write+NOM-FEM+SG
        'female writer'

(91) a. *do'atiriro*
        do'á-tí+rí+ró
        illness-VBZ+NOM+SG
        'sick person'

      b. *do'ariro*
        do'á+rí+ró
        cook+NOM+SG
        'cook'

(92) hũriro
~hú+rí+ró
smoke+NOM+SG
'smoker'

Descriptive nominals are derived from stative (adjectival) verb roots. The speaker in (93) was referring to a cranky child, (94) is part of a description of a dead snake, (95) and (96) are both taken from a description of an evil jungle being whose body was covered with a gluey substance, and (97) is from a text about a macaw.

(93) phũmeriro
~phubé+ri+ro
be.tired+NOM+SG
'tired one'

(94) phirida
phí+ri-da
be.big+NOM-CLS:ropelike
'long ropelike one'

(95) ñariro
~yá+ri+ro
be.bad+NOM+SG
'evil/ugly one'

(96) sṹ'ariro
~sʉ'á+ri+ro
be.sticky+NOM+SG
'sticky one'

(97) sõ'ariro
~so'á+ri+ro
be.red+NOM+SG
'red one'

The suffix +ro is polysemous, performing various distinct, though related, functions within the single domain of noun classification. The inanimate plural suffix +ri and the nominalizer +ri are better seen as homophonous, but this homophony in no way creates confusion for Kotiria speakers, as the two morphemes +ri code elements in different functional domains. Additionally, there is a significant morphological difference between the two forms: only the plural suffix +ri can appear in word-final position, whereas the nominalizer +ri always follows a verb root and must itself be followed by a suffix coding number in the case of a plural referent (except when it is used as the nominalizer of complements in the 'inference' evidential construction; see §9.2.4).

Synchronically, there is widespread alternation between the fully realized forms +ri+ro (singular) and +ri-~da (plural) exemplified in (93)–(97) and the phonologically reduced or fused forms -iro/-~ida in (92)–(94). While some sorts of reduction occur in fast speech, these alternations occur regularly in both fast and careful speech and suggest a process whereby fused forms coding singular and plural animate nominalizations are becoming grammaticalized. Indeed, movement toward morphophonological fusion is the expected tendency for affixes, such as these highly productive nominalizers, that are of high semantic relevance to their stems (Bybee 1985).

(98) koiro
kó-iro
relative-NOM.SG
'relative; fellow Kotiria"

(99) moaphoa mahkaina
~bóá-phóá ~baká-~ida
salt.plant-falls village-NOM.PL
'Moaphoa (Carurú Cachoeira) villagers'

(100) mahsayakhaina
~basá-yáká-~ídá
people-steal-NOM.PL
'kidnappers'

Inanimate nouns can also be derived from verbal roots. However, while all derived animates require that the verb root be nominalized by the suffix +ri, this morpheme is not obligatory in the derivation of inanimates. More often, verb stems are nominalized directly through suffixation of nominal classification morphemes (often by +ro, with its partitive function), the template being that in (101).

(101) verb root — (nominalizer) — noun classification morphology:
+ro/classifier (singular)
varied strategies for pluralization

The forms in (102)–(105), several of them repeated from §4.3.3, show the two variants of derivation by means of classifiers: with the nominalizing suffix +ri (102)–(103) and without it (104)–(105). The source of this variation is unclear and we have yet to discover whether there are older patterns of noun derivation that would shed some light on the issue. While it is possible that use of +ri is being gradually extended from the derivation of animates to include that of inanimates, given the general pattern for direct derivation of inanimates without +*ri*, it is also possible that the direction of change is just the opposite, that a once-general nominalizer +*ri* is undergoing reanalysis and grammaticalization as a deriver of animates only.[10] We can see from (104b) and (105b) that the strategies for pluralization of inanimates derived without +*ri* vary, as we saw in §4.3.1; as noted there, we must wait for more complete analysis of the interaction of number and classifier marking in order to fully understand the patterns.

(102) *sioriphĩ*
 sió+rí-~phí
 be.sharp+NOM-CLS:bladelike
 'knife'

(103) *bu'erithu*
 bu'é+ri-thu
 study/learn+NOM-CLS:stacked
 'textbook'

(104) a. *phichayahpa*   b. *phichayahpari*
 phichá-yápá   *phichá-yápá+rí*
 shoot-seed   shoot-seed+PL
 'bullet'   'bullets'

(105) a. *hoadɨ*   b. *hoaayɨhkɨ*
 hóá-dɨ   *hóá+á-yɨkɨ*
 write-CLS:cylindrical.straight   write+PL-tree
 'pen'   'pens'

The derivation of abstract inanimate nouns is also accomplished without the morpheme +*ri*. Such derivation occurs through suffixation of +*ro* (again performing a partitive-like function) directly to the verb root, as in (106)–(109). (The roots in (106)–(109) are all verbs: 'to answer', 'to scream', etc.)

(106) *yɨ'tiro*
 yɨ'tí+ro
 answer+SG
 'an answer'

---

[10] Interestingly, in Tukano, +*ri* is used in the derivation of inanimates only (Ramirez 1997a:248).

(107) *pihsuro*
  pisú+ró
  call+SG
  'a scream'

(108) *khã'aro*
  ~kha'á+ro
  dream+SG
  'a dream'

(109) *bo'rero*
  bo're+ro
  be.light+SG
  'morning, dawn'

Examples (110)–(111) provide a final illustration of how productively noun classification morphology is used in the derivation of nouns from verb roots. In each example, animate, inanimate generic, and inanimate specific forms are derived from the same verb root—*phi* 'be big' (110) and *khua* 'be dangerous' (111)—by means of different classifiers. The animate nominals in (110a) and (111a) are derived through suffixation of the nominalizer *+ri* and singulative *+ro*. Generic reference to a 'thing, situation, or event' with the property denoted by the root is accomplished by direct suffixation of partitive *+ro* to the verb, in (110b) and (111b). Derivation of a nominal with a specific referent, 'a big X', requires the nominalizer *+ri* and a specific classifier, as in (110c) and (111c).

(110) a. animate *phiriro*
    phí+ri+ro
    be.big+NOM+SG
    'a big one' (being)

  b. inanimate generic *phiro*
    phí+ro
    be.big+SG
    'a big thing/situation/event'

  c. inanimate specific *phirima*
    phí+ri-~ba
    be.big+NOM-CLS:river
    'a wide river'

(111) a. animate   *khuariro*
khuá+ri+ro
be.dangerous+NOM+SG
'a dangerous one (being)'

b. inanimate generic   *khuaro*
khuá+ro
be.dangerous+SG
'danger; a dangerous thing/situation/event'

c. inanimate specific   *khurarima*
khuá+ri-~ba
be.dangerous+NOM-CLS:river
'a dangerous river'

4.5.2 Nominals derived from particles

Examples (112)–(117) show animate and inanimate nominals derived from different kinds of particles and even combinations of particles (115b–c), including those coding deixis, anaphora, and alternation. Such nominals are concordial elements, and most often accompany a referent head noun in a modifying function (see chapter 6). However, if the referent is clear, they can also serve as pronominals, standing in for a noun (discussed further in §4.7.3). The identifying qualities of derived nominals of this type are provided by noun class morphology indicating gender, number, shape, etc. The generic classifier suffix *+re* is used to derive generic or mass nouns such as *a'ri+re* 'this thing' (112f) or *si+re* 'that thing' (113d), while combinations involving the 'alternate' particle root *pa* express nonspecific temporal and spatial notions *pa-te* 'sometimes' (114d) and *pa-se'e-pʉ* 'somewhere' (114e). (See also example (42) in chapter 9 for use of *pa-te* 'if' in the protasis of a conditional sentence.)

(112) *a'ri* 'proximal demonstrative'

     a. *a'riro*
a'rí+ró
DEM.PROX+SG
'this man; this one' (animate)

     b. *a'rikoro*
a'rí-kó+ró
DEM.PROX-FEM+SG
'this woman'

Nouns and noun classes

  c. *a'rina*
   a'rí-~da
   DEM.PROX-PL
   'these ones' (animate)

  d. *a'rithu*
   a'rí-thú
   DEM.PROX-CLS:stacked
   'this book'

  e. *a'riphĩ*
   a'rí-~phí
   DEM.PROX-CLS:bladelike
   'this knife'

  f. *a'rire*
   a'rí-ré
   DEM.PROX-CLS:generic
   'this thing' (generic or mass noun)

(113) *si* 'distal demonstrative'

  a. *siro*
   sí+ró
   DEM.DIST+SG
   'that man; that one' (animate)

  b. *sikoro*
   sí-kó+ró
   DEM.DIST-FEM+SG
   'that woman'

  c. *sina*
   sí-~da
   DEM.DIST-PL
   'those ones' (animate)

  d. *sire*
   sí-ré
   DEM.DIST-CLS:generic
   'that thing' (generic or mass noun)

  e. *siphãre*
   sí-~pháré
   DEM.DIST-side
   'that side' (of a table or other object)

(114) *pa* 'alternate, other'
- a. *pairo*
  pá-iro
  ALT-NOM.SG
  '(an)other one' (animate)
- b. *paina*
  pá-~ida
  ALT-NOM.PL
  'others' (animate)
- c. *panɨmɨ*
  pá-~dɨbɨ
  ALT-day
  'the next day'
- d. *pate*
  pá-te
  ALT-CLS:time
  'sometimes'
- e. *pase'epɨ*
  pá-se'e-pɨ
  ALT-CONTR-LOC
  'somewhere'

(115) *~o* 'proximal deictic'
- a. *õi*
  ~ó+í
  DEIC.PROX+LOC
  'here'
- b. *õpadɨ*
  ~ó-pá-dɨ́
  DEIC.PROX-ALT-CLS:cylindrical.straight
  'a stick like this, a stick this big'
- c. *õparithu*
  ~ó-pá+rí-thú
  DEIC.PROX-ALT+NOM-CLS:stacked
  'a pile like this, a pile this big'

(116) ~so'o 'distal deictic'

    sõ'opɨ

    ~so'ó-pɨ́
    DEIC.DIST-LOC
    'there'

(117) *to* 'remote deictic; anaphoric; definite'

    topɨ

    tó-pɨ
    REM-LOC
    'there, the' (see §4.7.3)

The descriptive text in (118) serves well to illustrate many of the different kinds of nouns and nominal constructions discussed so far.[11]

(118) 1 *a'riro hira ba'a*

    a'rí+ró   *hí+ra*   **ba'á**
    DEM.PROX+SG COP+VIS.IMPERF.2/3 bass
    'This (one, species of fish) is a bass.'

    2 *tiro diapɨ hika*

    tí+ró   **diá-pɨ́**   *hí-ka*
    ANPH+SG river-LOC COP-ASSERT.IMPERF
    'It lives in the river.'

    3 *mia wa'i dainakãre chɨka tiro*

    ~bí+a   **wa'í** **dá-~ídá-~ká+ré**   *chɨ́-ka*
    sardine+PL fish be.small-NOM.PL-DIM+OBJ eat-ASSERT.IMPERF

    tí+ró
    ANPH+SG
    'It eats sardines (and) small fish.'

    4 *bɨhɨina dainakã ba'aa hika*

    bɨhɨ́-~ida   **dá-~ídá-~ká**   **ba'á+á**
    be.large-NOM.PL be.small-NOM.PL-DIM bass+PL
    hí-ka
    COP-ASSERT.IMPERF
    'There are large (and) small ones.'

---

[11] This text is from the *Let's Study in Kotiria: Kotiria Animal Stories* collection, but is not included in appendix 1.

5 nuhturi khuaina hira tina
   ~dutú+rí khuá-~ida   hí+ra   tí-~da
   scale+PL hold/have-NOM.PL COP+VIS.IMPERF.2/3 ANPH-PL
   'They have scales.' (lit., 'they're scaly ones, ones with scales')

6 wi'o diekũina tiro ba'ro
   wi'ó   dié-~ku-~ida   tí+ró=ba'ro   wi'ó
   CONTR egg-lay-NOM.PL   ANPH+SG=kind   CONTR
   'This type (of fish) are egg-layers.'

7 pho'natiro phayu pho'natira
   ~pho'dá-ti+ro   phayú   ~pho'dá-ti+ra
   offspring-VBZ+(3)SG   many   offspring-VBZ+VIS.IMPERF.2/3
   'When it reproduces, there are many (offspring).'

Sentence 1 begins with a demonstrative nominal: the particle *a'ri* 'this' is nominalized by the third-person marker +*ro*, showing agreement with the predicate noun *ba'a* 'bass'. In both sentence 1 and sentence 2 we find examples of noun roots that are unmarked for number or shape: the animate *ba'a* 'bass', unmarked for number, functions as generic predicative noun identifying a species of fish in 1, and in sentence 2, the inanimate *dia* 'river' belongs to the subgroup of roots that take no shape classifiers. Singular (generic) reference for 'bass' continues until sentence 4, where the plural form *ba'a+a* occurs; the context is a description of the varying sizes of bass, indicated by the derived nominals *buhu-~ida* 'large ones' and *da-~ida-~ka* 'small ones'. In sentence 3 we find a second example of an animate noun pluralized by -*a*: ~*bi+a* 'sardines'. We know that 'bass' continues as a plural referent in sentences 5 and 6 because, among other things, the nouns describing bass as ~*dutu-ri khua-~ida* 'scaly ones' and *die-~ku-~ida* 'egg-layers' have the derivational morphology indicating plural, -~*ida*. In sentence 5 we also see that ~*dutu* 'scale' (within 'ones that have scales', a combination of noun plus derived noun) has the inanimate plural suffix +*ri*. Finally, in sentence 6, the nominalization *die-~ku-~ida* is an example of a verb with an incorporated noun (*die-~ku* 'egg-lay').

4.6   The negative nominal ~*de*

Kotiria has an uninflected, inherently negative nominal ~*de* [néé] that always occurs preverbally. It can be glossed as 'nothing', as in sentence 1 of (119) and in (121); 'nobody, no one', as in (122) and (123); 'none of X, no X', as in sentence 2 of (119) and in (120); or 'never', as in (124) and (125). Verbs in clauses which have ~de are always marked as negative by the morpheme -era (see also §8.2).

(119) 1   *tiro bʉhkʉro ne maniaa. ne bohkeraa*

       tí+ró   *bʉk+ʉ́+ro*   *~dé*   *~badía+a*
       ANPH+SG elder+MASC+SG NEG not.exist+ASSERT.PERF

       ~dé *bok(a)-éra+a*
       NEG find-NEG+ASSERT.PERF

       'The old man (was too late and) there was nothing, (he) didn't find anything.'

    2 *ne maniaa tina paina dieyakã*

       ~dé *~badía+a*   *tí-~da*   *pá-~ida*   *dié-yá-~ká*
       NEG not.exist+ASSERT.PERF ANPH-PL ALT-NOM.PL dog-PL-DIM

       'There were no little dogs there.' [A6.11–12]

(120) *ne mania to namono*

     ~dé *~badía+a*   *to=~dabó+ro*
     NEG not.exist+ASSERT.PERF 3SG.POSS=wife+SG

     'His wife wasn't there.' [A4.56]

(121) *ne bahuera*

     ~dé *bahu-éra+a*
     NEG be.visible-NEG+ASSERT.PERF

     'There was no trace of it.' (or 'Nothing was there.') [A7.120]

(122) *ne noare ya'ukʉ ninobʉ,*

     ~dé *~doá+re* *ya'ú-kʉ*   *~dí-~dobʉ*
     NEG WH+OBJ tell-(1/2)MASC be.PROG-IMP.EMPH

     'Tell no one.' [A7.152]

(123) *ne ahika nieraa topʉ*

     ~dé *ahí-kʉ*   *~di-éra+a*   *tó-pʉ*
     NEG be.concerned-(1/2)MASC be.PROG-NEG+ASSERT.PERF REM-LOC

     'He was there, concerned about nothing.' (or '. . . about no one.') [A4.17]

(124) *kotimaa, kotirose'e, ne tirore thʉoeraa*

     kó-ti-~ba+a   *kó-ti+ro-se'e*
     medicine-VBZ-FRUS+ASSERT.PERF medicine-VBZ+SG-CONTR

     ~dé *tí+ró+ré*   *thʉo-éra+a*
     NEG ANPH+SG+OBJ be.successful-NEG+ASSERT.PERF

     'He took medicine, but it (the medicine-taking) never cured him.' [A7.165]

(125) *ne mahsi to mahsieratiga*
 ~dé ~basi to=~basi-era-ati+a
 NEG know 3SG.POSS=know-NEG-IMPERF+ASSERT.PERF
 'We never knew what had happened to them.' [A4.7]

4.7 Pronouns

Kotiria personal pronouns form a single paradigm composed of two types of morphemes: those rooted in personal deixis, which require no nominal antecedent, and those derived from anaphoric particles (following Gomez-Imbert 1982:224). Subject forms are given in table 4.3, and any of these forms can be coded as a grammatical object by adding the suffix +*re* (see §5.2.2 and §§10.3–10.4). The forms of possessive pronominals are given in §6.4.1, where possessive modifiers in noun phrases are discussed.

TABLE 4.3. PERSONAL PRONOUNS

	SINGULAR	PLURAL	
DEICTIC			
1st person	*yʉ'ʉ* [jʉʔʉ́]	~*bari* [mã́rĩ́] (inclusive)	~*sa* [sã́ã́] (exclusive)
2nd person	~*bʉ'ʉ* [mã̃ʔʉ̃́]	~*bʉsa* [mʉʰsã́]	
ANAPHORIC			
3rd person (masculine)	*ti+ro* [tíró]	*ti-~da* [tína]	
3rd person (feminine)	*ti-ko+ro* [tíkóró]	*ti ~dubia* [tínũmĩã́]	

4.7.1 Deictic forms: first and second person

The deictic pronominals are *yʉ'ʉ* (first person singular) and ~*bʉ'ʉ* (second person singular). These forms have nearly exact cognates in all Eastern Tukanoan languages. As for the plurals of these deictic pronominals, comparison with other Tukanoan languages indicates that they were historically composed of the initial syllable of the first or second person forms plus an associative or plural morpheme (synchronically realized as ~*ha*/~*sa*/~*a*), yielding meanings along the lines of 'I and those with me', 'you and those with you.' Gomez-Imbert (1982:225) points out that the second person plural in Tatuyo is clearly analyzable as a composite, and the same is true for Kotiria. However, further cross-linguistic comparison suggests that the first person plural exclusives were most likely composites as well. While the initial morpheme has apparently been lost in the first person plural exclusive in Kotiria, synchronically ~sa, it has been partially or fully retained in the cognate forms in a number of other Eastern Tukanoan languages: Kubeo *jɨxa*, Tukano and Yuruti *ĩsã*, Tuyuka *ĩs'ã*, Barasana *yiá*, Macuna *giá*, and Desano and Siriano *gɨa*.

4.7.2 Anaphoric forms: third person

The most interesting differences between Kotiria pronouns and those used in most of the other Eastern Tukanoan languages in the family are found in the third person forms. Bimoraic forms paralleling nominal class markers—*ii/~ii/~kii/~igi* (masculine singular), *oo/~oo/koo/igo/soo* (feminine singular), and *~ida/~kida/~da/~a* (animate plural)—function as personal pronouns in most Eastern Tukanoan languages. Though not overtly marked as such, they are anaphoric elements in this function. In Kotiria, on the other hand, the forms that function as third person pronouns are overtly derived from the anaphoric particle root *ti* plus the appropriate concordial noun class marker for the antecedent: *+ro* (masculine and general animate singular), *-ko+ro* (feminine singular), or *-~da* (animate plural) (see table 4.3; discourse examples of *ti* can be seen in sentences 2, 3, 5, and 6 of (118) above). There is no suffix coding feminine plural on animate noun roots, and the same applies to the anaphoric pronominal constructions: reference to women is accomplished through compounding with the word *~dubia* 'women, females'. The difference between Kotiria third person pronouns and those in other Eastern Tukanoan languages is clearly exemplified in (126).

(126) a. Tukano (West 1980:178)[12]

    cɨ̃   yoarópɨ wa'á-mi
    3SM   far   go-3SM
    'He went far away.'

b. Kotiria

    tí+ró   yoá+ró-pɨ́   wa'á+ra
    ANPH+SG be.long+SG-LOC go+VIS.PERF.2/3
    'He went far away.'

The only other Eastern Tukanoan language that has pronoun forms parallel to those found in Kotiria is Wa'ikhana (Piratapuyo), where we find cognate forms *ti-kɨdo/-kido* (masculine singular), *ti-kodo* (feminine singular), and *ti-~kɨda/~-kida* (plural). Constructions with *ti* also

---

[12] West's original Tukano spelling has been preserved; I have translated the interlinear elements and free translation from the West's Spanish. In this example, "3SM" is 'third person singular masculine', following the usage of the source.

exist in closely related languages such as Tukano (Ramirez 1997a: 322), but these forms have an anaphoric function only and do not serve as personal pronouns. In Kotiria (and Wa'ikhana), the same forms constructed from the particle *ti* serve both functions.

In fact, the same forms based on *ti* that can function as pronouns in Kotiria often cooccur with full referent nouns, and in this case they have a third function: they code the definiteness of an already mentioned protagonist, as we see in (119), repeated as (127). At this point in the text, a man's little dog has run off into the forest chasing an animal and has disappeared. In the preceding sentence, the man and his sons are searching for the dog together. In sentence 1 of (127), however, the sole referent is the man; it is he who does not find anything, who realizes there are no dogs in the place he is searching. Thus, in this utterance we see *ti+ro*, literally 'that one' (animate), followed by the full noun referent *bʉk-ʉ+ro* 'old one', establishing the referentiality or definiteness of 'the old man' as the previously mentioned main protagonist of the text. In sentence 2, the anaphoric construction *ti-~da*, literally 'those ones' (animate plural), followed by the noun phrase *pa-~ida die-ya-~ka* (other.ones little.dogs), indicates the plural referent to be the previously mentioned dogs and not any other animate plural possibility, such as the sons, mentioned in the sentence just before.

(127) 1 *tiro bʉhkʉro ne maniaa. ne bohkeraa*

tí+ró   *bʉk+ʉ́+ro*   ~dé   ~badía+a
ANPH+SG elder+MASC+SG NEG not.exist+ASSERT.PERF

~dé bok(a)-éra+a
NEG find-NEG+ASSERT.PERF

'The old man (was too late and) there was nothing, (he) didn't find anything.'

2 *ne maniaa tina paina dieyakã*

~dé ~badía+a   *tí-~da*   *pá-~ida*   dié-yá-~ká
NEG not.exist+ASSERT.PERF ANPH-PL ALT-NOM.PL dog-PL-DIM

'There were no little dogs there.' [A6.11–12]

When reference is clear, however, anaphoric constructions function as pronouns, fulfilling the same grammatical roles as their full noun antecedents, as we see in (128), from a little later in the same story. The man and his sons have now found the little dog; it is being eaten by an evil snakelike creature, and the man decides to take action. In (128a), the anaphoric *ti+ro* (whose antecedent is obviously the man because, speakers explain, only humans have shotguns) functions as a pronoun in the grammatical role of subject. In sentence 1 of (128b), the anaphoric *ti+ro* again functions as a pronoun, this time marked as the grammatical object by the case-marking suffix *+re*. The antecedent for this pronoun and for the possessor *to* in *to dapu* 'his head' in sentence 3 is the evil snake.

(128) a. ã yo tiro phichakɨ khɨaa
  ~a=yó **tí+ró** phichá-kɨ́ khɨá+a
  so=do ANPH+SG shoot-CLS:tree hold/have+ASSERT.PERF
  'So, he (the old man) had (was holding) a shotgun.' [A6.30]

  b. 1 sɨ̃ tirore phichaba'a yoaa
   ~sɨ́ **tí+ró+ré** phichá-bá'á yoá+a
   arrive ANPH+SG+OBJ shoot-do/be.after do/make+ASSERT.PERF
   'He went right over to it (the snake) and shot (it).'

   2 to dahpuwaroi phichawa'arokaa
   to=dapú-waro+i phichá-wá'á-róká+á
   3SG.POSS=head-EMPH+LOC shoot-go-DIST+ASSERT.PERF
   'Its (the snake's) head exploded (when it was shot).' [A6.34–35]

Anaphoric constructions predominate in the pronominal function; however, occasionally other types of nominal constructions also function as pronouns. In the following interesting example from a narrative, a man lost in the forest has encountered a humanlike creature, and, after a strange conversation in which the creature asks the man to give him his heart, the man realizes that the creature means him harm (129). The deictic construction *a'ri+ro* 'this one', referring to the creature, functions as a pronominal in the role of grammatical subject. In his quoted speech or thought, the man uses a deictic rather than an anaphoric element as a pronoun because the referent is physically present at the scene.

(129) yɨ'ɨre a'riro chɨduaro nika nithɨ'othua
  yɨ'ɨ́+ré **a'rí+ró** chú-dua+ro ~dí-ka
  1SG+OBJ DEM.PROX+SG eat-DESID+(3)SG be.PROG-ASSERT.IMPERF
  ~dí-thɨ'o-thu+a
  say-hear-think+ASSERT.PERF
  '"This thing (the curupira) wants to eat me," he said to himself.' [A7.53]

4.7.3 Anaphoric forms for inanimates

Anaphoric forms for inanimates follow the pattern for other nominal elements derived from particles described in §4.5 and the personal pronoun anaphors described in §4.7.2. Anaphoric or definite reference can be made to inanimates in forms constructed from the particle *ti* and any of the three types of classifier morphemes mentioned in §4.3.3. Though anaphoric constructions with full noun roots are the most common type (130)–(133), *ti* can also be combined with classifiers, as in (134)–(136). As discussed in §3.2, the phonological behavior of *ti* varies somewhat. When *ti* is combined with a full noun root, it more often than not behaves like a proclitic—it has L tone and forms a single phonological word with the noun it modifies, which maintains its own inherent tonal melody. When *ti* occurs with a classifier, it forms a single phonological word with HL melody.

(130) *ti phŭri*
   ti=~phú+rí
   ANPH=leaf+PL
   'those/the leaves'

(131) *ti nʉma*
   ti=~dʉ́bá
   ANPH=day
   'that/the day'

(132) *ti kohpa*
   ti=kopá
   ANPH= hole
   'that/the hole'

(133) *ti ku'tu*
   ti=ku'tú
   ANPH=clearing
   'that/the clearing'

(134) *tire*
   tí-re
   ANPH-CLS:generic
   'that/the object, situation, event' (generic reference)

(135) *tipʉ*
   tí-pʉ
   ANPH-CLS:basket
   'that/the basket'

(136) *tiphĩ*
   tí-~phi
   ANPH-CLS:bladelike
   'that/the knife'

grammatical object by the case-marking suffix +*re*. The antecedent for this pronoun and for the possessor *to* in *to dapu* 'his head' in sentence 3 is the evil snake.

(128) a. *ã yo tiro phichakɨ khɨaa*
~*a*=*yó* ***tí+ró*** *phichá-kɨ́* *khɨá+a*
so=do ANPH+SG shoot-CLS:tree hold/have+ASSERT.PERF
'So, he (the old man) had (was holding) a shotgun.' [A6.30]

b. 1 *sɨ̃ tirore phichaba'a yoaa*
~*sɨ́* ***tí+ró***+*ré* *phichá-bá'á* *yoá+a*
arrive ANPH+SG+OBJ shoot-do/be.after do/make+ASSERT.PERF
'He went right over to it (the snake) and shot (it).'

2 *to dahpuwaroi phichawa'arokaa*
to=dapú-waro+*i* *phichá-wá'á-róká+á*
3SG.POSS=head-EMPH+LOC shoot-go-DIST+ASSERT.PERF
'Its (the snake's) head exploded (when it was shot).' [A6.34–35]

Anaphoric constructions predominate in the pronominal function; however, occasionally other types of nominal constructions also function as pronouns. In the following interesting example from a narrative, a man lost in the forest has encountered a humanlike creature, and, after a strange conversation in which the creature asks the man to give him his heart, the man realizes that the creature means him harm (129). The deictic construction *a'ri+ro* 'this one', referring to the creature, functions as a pronominal in the role of grammatical subject. In his quoted speech or thought, the man uses a deictic rather than an anaphoric element as a pronoun because the referent is physically present at the scene.

(129) *yɨ'ɨre a'riro chɨduaro nika nithɨ'othua*
yɨ'ɨ́+ré ***a'rí+ró*** *chú-dua+ro* ~*dí-ka*
1SG+OBJ DEM.PROX+SG eat-DESID+(3)SG be.PROG-ASSERT.IMPERF
~*dí-thɨ'o-thu+a*
say-hear-think+ASSERT.PERF
'"This thing (the curupira) wants to eat me," he said to himself.' [A7.53]

4.7.3 Anaphoric forms for inanimates

Anaphoric forms for inanimates follow the pattern for other nominal elements derived from particles described in §4.5 and the personal pronoun anaphors described in §4.7.2. Anaphoric or definite reference can be made to inanimates in forms constructed from the particle *ti* and any of the three types of classifier morphemes mentioned in §4.3.3. Though anaphoric constructions with full noun roots are the most common type (130)–(133), *ti* can also be combined with classifiers, as in (134)–(136). As discussed in §3.2, the phonological behavior of *ti* varies somewhat. When *ti* is combined with a full noun root, it more often than not behaves like a proclitic—it has L tone and forms a single phonological word with the noun it modifies, which maintains its own inherent tonal melody. When *ti* occurs with a classifier, it forms a single phonological word with HL melody.

(130) *ti phŭri*
 ti=~phú+rí
 ANPH=leaf+PL
 'those/the leaves'

(131) *ti nʉma*
 ti=~dʉ́bá
 ANPH=day
 'that/the day'

(132) *ti kohpa*
 ti=kopá
 ANPH= hole
 'that/the hole'

(133) *ti ku'tu*
 ti=ku'tú
 ANPH=clearing
 'that/the clearing'

(134) *tire*
 tí-re
 ANPH-CLS:generic
 'that/the object, situation, event' (generic reference)

(135) *tipʉ*
 tí-pʉ
 ANPH-CLS:basket
 'that/the basket'

(136) *tiphĩ*
 tí-~phi
 ANPH-CLS:bladelike
 'that/the knife'

Anaphoric constructions such as these can function as pronouns if reference has been clearly established. For semantic reasons, inanimates are less likely to occur in subject or agent roles, and thus, pronouns with inanimate referents will usually be marked as objects or instruments. In example (137), from a point a little later on in the same narrative from which (129) comes, the man is now offering his knife to the evil creature, which he has tricked into attempting to cut out its own heart. The demonstrative *a'ri-~phi* 'this knife' (marked as an instrument by *-~be're*), and its full noun referent *yʉ'so+ri-~phi* 'knife' (marked as a grammatical object by *+re*) occur in sentence 1 of this excerpt. The anaphoric construction *ti-~phi+re*, functioning as a pronoun and marked as the grammatical object, occurs in sentence 2.

(137) 1   *a'riphĩ me're narokha'mare, ni, yʉ'soriphĩre ñui wĩoa tirore*
        a'ri-~phi=~be're
        DEM.PROX-CLS:bladelike=COM/INST
        ~dá+ro=~kha'ba+re   ~di
        get+(3)SG=want/need+VIS.PERF.2/3 say
        ***yʉ'só+ri-~phi**+re*   ~yuí-~wio+a
        cut+NOM-CLS:bladelike+OBJ offer-MOV.outward+ASSERT.PERF
        tí+ró+ré
        ANPH+SG+OBJ

    '"(You) have to take it out with this knife," he (the man) said (and) offered it out to him (the curupira).'

   2   *ti phĩre tiro hi'na ña'a to yahiripho'nare phirokã beñʉa*
        ***tí-~phi**+re*   *tí+ró*   ~hí'da ~ya'á
        ANPH-CLS:bladelike+OBJ ANPH+SG EMPH grab
        to=yahiri~pho'da+re *phí+ró-~ká*
        3SG.POSS=heart+OBJ be.slow+SG-DIM
        bé-~yʉ+a
        inject/insert-try+ASSERT.PERF

    'He (the curupira) immediately grabbed the knife (and) slowly tried to cut out his heart.' [A7.76–77]

Parallel to constructions with *ti* for animates, anaphoric or definite reference to times, places, or events is established in constructions involving the remote deictic particle *to*. The constructions with *to* in (138)–(140) indicate previously established temporal or spatial referents. These examples also show that, like *ti*, the phonological behavior of *to* varies: it can occur as an independent modifying element with H tone, as in its first occurrence in (138), but more often occurs either as the head root of phonological word with an overall HL tone, as we see in *topɨ* 'that place' (138) and *tokakai* 'there' (139), or cliticized to a full root, as in *to phanopɨre* 'long ago' (140).

(138) *to khĩ'ori ora karaka duripa, topɨ pihsutaa ñami kɨta karaka duripa*
   tó   ~khi'ó+rí   óra   káráká dú+ri-pa
   DEF be.arranged+NOM hour[B] rooster speak+NOM-CLS:time
   tó-pɨ   pisú-ta+a   ~yabí ~kɨ́=ta káráká
   REM-LOC call-come+ASSERT.PERF night one=REF rooster
   dú+ri-pa
   speak+NOM-CLS:time
   '**At the appointed cock-crowing hour**, (from) **that place** came a call, at the first nighttime crowing hour.' [A4.19]

(139) *tokakai tiro khãrikhõaa*
   tó-kaka+i   tí+ró   ~khari-~khoa+a
   DEF-EMPH+LOC ANPH+SG sleep-be.lying+ASSERT.PERF
   '**There** he lay down and went to sleep.' [A7.26]

(140) *ã hiatiga diamini to phanopɨre*
   ~a=hí-ati+a   diá-~bídí
   SO=COP-IMPERF+ASSERT.PERF river-high.water
   to=~phadó-pɨ+re
   DEF=do/be.before-LOC+OBJ
   'That's how it used to be **long ago**, before the flood.' [A4.70]

The same particle *to* also occurs very frequently in subordinate adverbial clauses that link events in discourse, as in the sequence in (141) and in the (nearly adjacent) sentences in (142).

(141) 1 *mari khõaãwa'achɨ, khuãyɨ'dɨra*
       ~barí   ~khóá-wá'á-chɨ   khuá-yɨ'dɨ+ra
       1PL.INC throw-go-SW.REF be.dangerous-INTENS+VIS.IMPERF.2/3
       'When we take off (in an airplane), it's very dangerous.'

     2 *to wahkɨnoka wã'kachɨ, mari khapari bɨhkɨawa'ara, mari kɨachɨ*
       to=~wakú-~dóká   ~wa'ká-chɨ   ~bari=khapá+rí
       DEF=be.aware-COMPL get.up-SW.REF 1PL.INC.POSS=eye+PL
       bɨkú+a=wa'a+ra   ~barí   kɨá-chɨ
       grow+AFFEC=go+VIS.IMPERF.2/3 1PL.INC be.afraid-SW.REF
       'When we realize **that** (the airplane is going up), our eyes grow big, because we're afraid.' [A12.4–5]

(142) 1   yɨ'ɨ chɨduaka, nia . . .
         yɨ'ɨ   chú-dua-ka   ~dí+a
         1SG   eat-DESID-ASSERT.IMPERF say+ASSERT.PERF
         '"I want to eat it (your heart)," (the curupira) said. . . .'

      2   to ã nichɨ, tiro mahsɨnose'e tirore nia
         to=~á=~dí-chɨ   tí+ró   ~basɨ+ro-se'e   tí+ró+ré
         DEF=so=say-SW.REF   ANPH+SG   man+SG-CONTR   ANPH+SG+OBJ
         ~dí+a
         say+ASSERT.PERF
         'When (the curupira) said **that**, the man responded . . .' [A7.44–46]

Finally, *to* occurs in the common expression meaning 'that's it' or 'that's all', which speakers commonly use to close a story or any kind of public address (143).

(143) topɨrota hira yairo khiti
       tó-pɨ+ro=ta   hí+ra   yaí+ró   khiti
       DEF-LOC+SG=REF   COP+VIS.IMPERF.2/3   jaguar+SG   story
       '**That's all** there is to the jaguar story.' [A10.5]

The occurrence of *to* with animates in (144) and (145) is unusual. I analyze these instances of *to* as reductions of the sequence *ti+ro*, which we saw in §4.7.2 to be regularly used for definite reference to animates. The difference in the observed tonal behavior of *to* in these two examples can also be easily understood as the result of fast speech reduction.

(144) to yairo chɨto phanore tiro bohso wãha yoare
       tó   **yaí+ró**   chú   to=~phadó+re   tí+ró   bosó
       DEF   jaguar+SG   eat   REM=do/be.before+OBJ ANPH+SG   agouti
       ~wahá   yoá+re
       kill   do/make+VIS.PERF.2/3
       'Before **the jaguar** ate (him), (the dog had) hunted down an agouti.' [A2.7]

(145) to wa'ikiro wãhariroditare sã nathuai wɨ'ɨpɨre
       to=wa'í-kíró   ~wahá+ri+ro-dita+re   ~sá
       DEF=animal+SG   kill+NOM+SG-SOL+OBJ   1PL:EXC
       ~dá-thúá+í   wɨ'ɨ-pɨ+ré
       get-return+VIS.PERF.1   house-LOC+OBJ
       'We took home only **the dead animal** (that the dog had hunted).' [A2.13]

4.8 Noun compounds

We can loosely identify two subtypes of noun compounds. The first are compound constructions composed of a noun and a full-root noun classifier, which occurs in noninitial position, and the second are compounds that result in a new lexical item identifying a specific entity. In both types of compounds, the noninitial noun is the semantic head, while the initial noun can be interpreted as further qualifying it in some way. For many lexical compounds, though certainly not all, the qualification is semantically transparent. For example, in the lexical noun compound in (146) we understand the semantic head to be ~*pabo* 'armadillo', qualified as to its size by the noun *wachɨ* 'tapir, bull'. The result of the compound is a new lexical term for an armadillo of the 'tapir'-like or, as we would say, the 'giant' type, while in (148) the compound describes a particular type of evil creature, specifically one that dwells in the 'jungle'. Such compounding constructions are particularly productive in names for species of animals, fish, and birds, while verb-noun compounds are extremely common in names of new inanimate lexical terms—e.g., *phi+ri-wɨ'ɨ*, in which the verb 'be big' is nominalized and then compounded with the word for 'house' to form 'longhouse'.

(146)   *wahchɨphamo*
        wachɨ́-~phábó
        tapir-armadillo
        'giant armadillo'

(147)   *nɨhkɨwãhtiro*
        ~dɨkɨ́-~wátí+ró
        jungle-devil+SG
        'jungle devil'

Similarly, as we saw in §4.3.3, classifying compounds such as ~*kadɨkapa* 'sugarcane **shoot**' (81a), or *bu'eriwɨ'ɨ* 'school **house**' (82b), the noninitial nouns 'shoot' and 'house' are the semantic heads of the compounds, while the roots or derived nominals to their left indicate the type of shoot or house (building) in question. The basis for claiming that noninitial nouns denoting types of shoots, buildings, leaves (83), palms (84), or holes (85) are more classifier-like than simple nouns such as 'armadillo' (146) or 'devil' (147) in compounds really comes down to the fact that the former tend to occur in a greater numbers of combinations, in "productive, paradigm-like sets," as Epps characterizes similar constructions in Hup (2008:217).

In fact, whether the noninitial noun is considered a full-root classifier or a simple noun, the noun compounding construction is structurally the same, and the two nouns involved are subject to the same phonological processes (described in §4.3.3). In sum, noun compounding—lexical or classifying—is an extremely productive process by which any noun can receive more detailed semantic specification or by which new nominal concepts can be created.

5 Nominal morphology

Kotiria has a complex template of nominal morphology coding lexical, grammatical, and discourse-level information, summarized in figure 5.1. Among the morphemes coding lexical information, which occur closest to the root, those relating to nominalization, gender, and number (positions 1 through 3 in the figure) were discussed in chapter 4. The semantics and the phonological and grammatical status of the morphemes that appear in positions 4 through 7 are discussed in this chapter. Position 4, immediately following the suffixes coding gender and number information, is where evaluative and other qualifying markers occur: the diminutive, augmentative, additive, solitary, and emphatic suffixes; these are discussed in §5.1. Next, morphemes shown in positions 5 and 6 of the figure (discussed in §5.2) code syntactic relations: locative, objective, and comitative-instrumental. Morphemes coding discourse-level information occur word-finally (position 7 of the figure, discussed in §5.3). Section 5.4 reviews the phonological status of the different kinds of nominal morphology, and assesses the degree to which morphemes are grammaticalized.

STEM	\multicolumn{4}{c}{LEXICAL}	\multicolumn{2}{c}{SYNTACTIC}	DISCOURSE
	1	2	3	4	5	6	7
VR	+*ri* (NOM)	gender -*ko*/+*o*	number +*ro*	eval./qual. -~*ka* (DIM)	loc. +*i*	+*re* (OBJ) =~*be're* (COM/INST)	-*se'e* (CONTR) =*ta* (REF)
particle root (+ root)		Ø/+*ʉ*	-*kiro* (IND) -CLS +*a*/-~*da* +*ri*	-*wʉ'rʉ* (AUG) -*khʉ* (ADD) -*dita* (SOL) (-)*waro* (EMPH)	-*pʉ*		

Figure 5.1. Nominal morphology. Eval. = evaluative; loc. = locative; qual. = qualifying; VR = verb root.

5.1 Additional morphemes coding lexical information

Chapter 4 described and exemplified noun root types, derived nominals with and without the nominalizer +*ri*, and the ways in which major

Nominal morphology 153

animate and inanimate noun classes in Kotiria are distinguished by morphology coding class, gender, and number. This noun-defining morphology is shown in the first four columns in figure 5.1 (stem and lexical positions 1 to 3). Together, these form the basic lexical identity of a noun. Further lexical specification is possible, however, by use of additional evaluative and other qualifying suffixes.

5.1.1   Evaluatives: *-~ka* 'diminutive', *-wɨ'rɨ* 'augmentative'

The Kotiria diminutive *-~ka* has cognates throughout the family, the common variants being *-~ka/-~ga/-aka/-~aka/-~aga*. As in other Eastern Tukanoan languages, the diminutive occurs far more frequently in Kotiria than the augmentative, and it is used in a variety of ways. First, it is used in the most semantically transparent sense to indicate the relative size of both inanimates (1)–(6) and animates (7)–(13). (In the noun phrase in (13), the diminutive morpheme appears on both the modifier and head constituents.)

(1)   *khitikã*
      khití-~ka
      story-DIM
      'little story'

(2)   *wɨ'ɨkã*
      wɨ'ɨ-~ká
      house-DIM
      'little house'

(3)   *tɨkã*
      tɨ́-~ka
      stick-DIM
      'little stick'

(4)   *phɨ'ɨsekã*
      phɨ'ɨ-sé-~ká
      basket-PL-DIM
      'little baskets'

(5)   *hirikumukã*
      hí+ri-~kubu-~ka
      COP+NOM-tree.trunk-DIM
      'little log-like thing'

(6) *noapʉkã*
    ~*dóá-pʉ́-~ká*
    be.beautiful-CLS:basket-DIM
    'beautiful little basket'

(7) *numinokã*
    ~*dubí+ro-~ka*
    woman+SG-DIM
    'little girl'

(8) *mahkʉnokã*
    ~*bak-ʉ́+ró-~ká*
    child-MASC+SG-DIM
    'little son'

(9) *numia pho'nakã*
    ~*dubí+a   ~pho'dá-~ka*
    woman+PL children-DIM
    'women's little girls'

(10) *tinakã*
     tí-~da-~ka
     ANPH-PL-DIM
     'little ones' (referring to some children)

(11) *dierokã*
     dié+ró-~ká
     dog+SG-DIM
     'little dog'

(12) *dieyakã*
     dié-yá-~ká
     dog-PL-DIM
     'little dogs'

(13) *kũirokã marirokã*
     ~*kʉ́-iró-~ká   ~bá+rí+ró-~ká*
     one-NOM.SG-DIM be.small+NOM+SG-DIM
     'one little one' (referring to a dog)

The diminutive morpheme is also frequently used in adverbially-employed nominal constructions (§3.5), where it augments a quality (14) or attenuates it (15) (see also (62)–(63) below and §11.2), depending on the context. For its use as an indefinite quantifier in noun phrases, see §6.3.2.

(14) a. *kherokã*
   khé+ro-~ka
   be.fast+SG-DIM
   'very quickly'

   b. *ñakã*
   ~yá-~ka
   be.bad-DIM
   'really evil'

   c. *to ka'aikã*
   to=ka'á+i-~ka
   3SG.POSS=side+LOC-DIM
   'right beside'

(15) *phirokã*
   phí+ro-~ka
   be.slow+SG-DIM
   'rather slowly'

Unlike the diminutive, the augmentative in Kotiria diverges from the pattern found in the other Eastern Tukanoan languages, where a number of variants contain an element *-ro*: *-roho* (Tukano), *-Vro* (Tatuyo, Barasana), and *-ro* (Desano). As in other Eastern Tukanoan languages, the augmentative in Kotiria occurs far less frequently than the diminutive.

(16) *phinonowɨ'rɨ*
   ~phidó+ró-wɨ'rɨ
   snake+SG-AUG
   'big snake'

(17) *phiridawɨ'rɨ*
   phí+ri-da-wɨ'rɨ
   be.big+NOM-CLS:ropelike-AUG
   'long ropelike one' (in reference to the same snake as in (16))

(18) *borarowɨ'rɨ*
   borá+ro-wɨ'rɨ
   curupira+SG-AUG
   'huge curupira'

(19) õpadɨwɨ'rɨ
~ó-pá-dɨ́-wɨ́'rɨ́
DEIC.PROX-ALT-CLS:cylindrical.straight-AUG
'a big cigar like this'

(20) korowɨ'rɨ
kó+ro-wɨ'rɨ
water+SG-AUG
'big rainstorm'

(21) phoari ñatirirowɨ'rɨ
phoá+rí ~yá-ti+ri+ro-wɨ'rɨ
hair+PL be.bad-ATTRIB+NOM+SG-AUG

'a large, horribly hairy being' (in reference to the same being as in (18))

5.1.2 Other qualifying morphemes: -khɨ 'additive', -dita 'solitary', and (-)waro 'emphatic'

There are several additional morphemes that can also occur after the initial lexical morphology marking gender and number to further qualify the noun within a specific context. The most frequent of these is the additive -khɨ, which yields the meaning 'also, too, as well'. Examples with this marker are shown in (22)–(24) and also (43) below.

(22) tiro wa'ikirore bohãa, tirokhɨ hi'na
tí+ró wa'í-kíró+ré bó-~ha+a
ANPH+SG animal+SG+OBJ lose-be.unexpected+ASSERT.PERF
tí+ró-khɨ́ ~hí'da
ANPH+SG-ADD EMPH

'He (the little dog) lost the animal he was hunting (and) **he too** suddenly got lost.' [A6.9]

(23) mɨ'ɨkhɨ yɨ'ɨre mɨ'ɨ yahiripho'nare waga koiro
~bɨ'ɨ́-khɨ yɨ'ɨ́+ré ~bɨ'ɨ=yahíri~pho'da+re[1] wá+gá
2SG-ADD 1SG+OBJ 2SG(POSS)=heart+OBJ give+IMPER
kó-iro
relative-NOM.SG

'Now **you too** give me your heart, relative.' [A7.73]

(24) bahsakoriti hu yoaa, phutiphayo, to pho'nakhɨre phutiphayo
basá-kó+ri-tí hú yoá+a
sing/dance-bless+NOM-VBZ smoke do/make+ASSERT.PERF

---

[1] The annotation "2SG(POSS)" indicates irregular use of a full pronominal form in a possessive construction. See §6.4.1.

phutí-pháyó   ***to=~pho'dá-khɨ+re***   *phutí-pháyó*
blow-spread.out 3SG.POSS=children-ADD+OBJ blow/play-spread.out
'He blessed himself, blowing smoke (on himself and) on **his sons too**.'
[A6.53]

A noun can also be qualified by the morpheme *-dita*, yielding a reading of 'only X' (25)–(26), or 'X alone, X by itself' (27). Note that in (27), two position 4 morphemes cooccur, the diminutive *-~ka* preceding the solitary *-dita*.

(25)   1   *dierore chɨbɨroropɨ nia*

         dié+ró+ré   *chɨ-bɨró+ró-pɨ*   *~dí+a*
         dog+SG+OBJ eat-go.down+(3)SG-EMPATH be.PROG+ASSERT.PERF

         'It (a huge snake-like creature) was already swallowing down the poor dog.'

   2   *õ to dahpudita bahua chɨbɨrochɨ*

         ~ó   ***to=dapú-dita***   *bahú+a*
         DEIC.PROX 3SG.POSS=head-SOL be.visible+ASSERT.PERF

         chɨ-bɨró-chɨ
         eat-go.down-SW.REF

         '**Only the (dog's) head** was still showing as it (the snake) swallowed.' [A6.17–18]

(26)   *to wa'ikiro wãhariroditare sã nathuai wɨ'ɨpɨre*

         to=wa'í-kiró   ***~wahá+ri+ro-dita+re***   *~sá*
         DEF=animal+SG kill+NOM+SG-SOL+OBJ 1PL.EXC

         ~dá-thúá+í   *wɨ'ɨ-pɨ+ré*
         get-return+VIS.PERF.1 house-LOC+OBJ

         'We took home **only the dead animal** (that the dog had hunted).' [A2.13]

(27)   *kɨ̃irokã marirokãdita hia nɨnɨsihtota*

         ~kɨ́-író-~ká   ***~bá+rí+ró-~ká-dítá***   *hí+a*
         one/a+ NOM.SG-DIM be.small+NOM+SG-DIM-SOL COP+ASSERT.PERF

         ~dɨdɨ́-sito-ta
         chase-MOV.circular-come

         '(And) there was **a little one (dog)** chasing around **alone (by itself)**.' [A6.8]

Finally, a noun can be marked by the 'emphatic' morpheme *(-)waro*. I group this morpheme with other qualifying morphemes because of its semantics and optional occurrence in the fourth position of the noun template, but should point out that it is not as completely grammaticalized as the other qualifying markers. While it can occur as a phonologically incorporated stem morpheme in a nominal word, as in (28)–(29), it can also occur as a phonologically independent emphatic modifier following the noun and taking its own grammatical suffixation, as in (30)–(31). The most frequent, though not exclusive, use of (-)waro is in nominal expressions marked as locatives, to emphasize identification of a specific time or place, 'right there' or 'right then', as we see in (29)–(31).

(28) yʉ'ʉse'e phayʉwarore ti bahsaba'rore, karisu phutiabarore mahsierai
yʉ'ʉ-se'e   phayú-**wáró**+ré   ti=basá=ba'ro+re
1SG-CONTR many/a.lot-EMPH+OBJ ANPH=sing/dance=kind+OBJ
karísu phutí+a=ba'ro+re   ~basi-éra+i
flute blow/play+PL=kind+OBJ know-NEG+VIS.PERF.1
'(Unlike the others) I didn't know hardly any of those kinds of dances (and) flute-playing.' [A3.19]

(29) to dahpuwaroi phichawa'arokaa
to=dapú-**waro**+i   phichá-wá'á-róká+á
3SG.POSS=head-EMPH+LOC shoot-go-DIST+ASSERT.PERF
'Its head exploded.' [A6.35]

(30) sõ'o waroi hikʉ, pihsukʉka na'inokai
~so'ó   **wáró**+í   hí-kʉ   pisú-kʉ-ká
DEIC:DIST EMPH+LOC COP-(1/2)MASC call-(1/2)MASC-PREDICT
~da'í-~doka+i
be.dark-COMPL+LOC
'"When I'm right over there, I'll call in the dark."' [A4.12]

(31) ba'aro hi'na ñamidahchomahka'i waroi, yoaropʉ kʉiro taro koataa sõ'oba'ropʉ
ba'á+ro   ~hí'da ~yabí-dáchó-~báká+í **wáró**+í
do/be.after+SG EMPH night-middle-origin-LOC EMPH+LOC
yoá+ró-pʉ   ~kʉ-író   tá+ro
be.far+SG-LOC one/a-NOM:SG come+(3)SG
koá-ta+a   ~so'ó-bá'á+ró-pʉ
NONVIS-come+ASSERT.PERF DEIC:DIST-do/be.after+SG-LOC
'Later, right in the middle of the night, in the distance (he heard) someone approaching.' [A7.27]

5.2 Morphemes coding grammatical information

Morphology marking the grammatical role of a noun in a clause occurs to the right of morphology coding lexical information that establishes the identity of the noun as a specific entity or thing. The morphemes that code such grammatical information appear in the fifth and sixth suffixal positions in figure 5.1. (For more on argument coding, see chapter 10.)

5.2.1 Locatives +i, -pʉ

Nouns that refer to a location are coded by the visual locative +i (deictically proximate or known) or nonvisual -pʉ (anaphoric, deictically distal or unknown) (see also §10.7). Nominals coded as locatives can be derived from any type of root: particle (32)–(37), verbal (38)–(39), or nominal (40)–(42).

(32) õi hire

~ó+í   hí+re
DEIC.PROX-LOC COP+VIS.PERF.2/3
'Here she is.' [A4.58]

(33) a'ri khiti õita phitira

a'rí   khití   ~ó+í=ta   phití+ra
DEM.PROX story   DEIC.PROX+LOC=REF end+VIS.IMPERF.2/3
'Here's where this story ends.' [A6.70]

(34) yʉ'ʉ sõ'opʉ tinikʉ wa'aha koyaka'apʉ

yʉ'ʉ   ~so'ó-pʉ́   ~tidí-kʉ   wa'á-ha
1SG   DEIC.DIST-LOC   visit-(1/2)MASC go-VIS.IMPERF.1
kó-ya-ka'a-pʉ
relative-PL-near-LOC
'I'm going (there) to visit (our) relatives' (village).' [A4.10]

(35) tiro dierore wahawa'aka'a sõ'oba'aropʉ ñarikohpa sa'a, yakhõ'anokaa

tí+ró   dié+ró+ré   wahá-wa'a-ka'a
ANPH+SG   dog+SG+OBJ   pull-go-do.moving

~so'ó-bá'á+ró-pʉ́   ~yá+ri-kopa   sa'á
DEIC.DIST-be.after+SG-LOC be.bad+NOM-hole   dig

yá-~kho'a-~doka+a
bury-lie-COMPL+ASSERT.PERF

'He dragged the dog a little way away, dug a rough hole (and) buried (it).' [A6.49]

(36) topʉ sʉ, wa'ikinare mahkasihtotaa

tó-pʉ   ~sʉ   wa'í-~kídá+ré
REM-LOC   arrive   animal-PL+OBJ

~baká-sito-ta+a
look/search.for-MOV.circular-come+ASSERT.PERF
'Arriving there, he went around in search of animals.' [A7.9]

(37) ne topɨre tipɨre tinieraha ninokaa
~dé tó-pɨ+re **tí-pɨ+re** ~tidi-éra-ha
NEG REM-LOC+OBJ ANPH-LOC+OBJ wander-NEG-VIS.IMPERF.1
~dí-~doka+a
say-COMPL+ASSERT.PERF
'I never go hunting there in that place.' [A6.60]

(38) tu'sɨ, ti ñamire hi'na khã'aropɨre tirore ya'ua
tú'sɨ ti=~yabí+re ~hí'da **~kha'á+ro-pɨ+re** tí+ró+ré
finish ANPH=night+OBJ EMPH dream+SG-LOC+OBJ ANPH+SG+OBJ
ya'ú+a
warn+ASSERT.PERF
'When he was done, that very night he was warned in a dream.' [A6.54]

(39) sõ'o waroi hikɨ, pihsukɨka na'inokai
~so'ó wáró+í hí-kɨ pisú-kɨ-ká
DEIC.DIST EMPH+LOC COP-(1/2)MASC call-(1/2)MASC-PREDICT
~da'í-~doka+i
be.dark-COMPL+LOC
'"When I'm right over there, I'll call in the dark."' [A4.12]

(40) no'oi hiri, nia
~do'ó+í hí-ri
WH+LOC COP-INT
'Where is she?' [A4.57]

(41) wa'mamahare, boraa ti kohpapɨ
~wa'bá-~báhá-ré borá+a
wrap.around-MOV.up/down-CLS:generic fall+ASSERT.PERF
ti=kopá-pɨ
ANPH=hole-LOC
'(The snake) wrapping around (the dog), retreated down into the hole.' [A6.22]

(42) to saño dɨ'tamaniaboraachɨ, pɨ diabu'ipɨ pairo sañoro koataa
to=~sayó dɨ'tá-~badia-bora+a-chɨ
3SG.POSS=yell/scream make.noise-not.exist-fall+PL-SW.REF
pɨ **diá-bu'i-pɨ** pá-iro ~sayó+ró
LOC river-top-LOC ALT-NOM.SG yell/scream+SG

koá-ta+a
NONVIS-come+ASSERT.PERF

'Just as (the snake's) scream died away, from far away upriver, another one (snake) screamed (they heard it).' [A6.39]

5.2.2 Object +*re*

There is no overt marking of the grammatical subject in Kotiria, but nouns functioning as objects of transitive (43)–(44) or ditransitive (45) verbs, as well as temporal adjuncts, are coded by the objective case suffix +*re* (see also §§10.3–10.4 and §10.7.2), shown in the sixth suffixal position of figure 5.1.

(43) *thʉ'o to koyare wã'ko, ti phʉkorore wã'koa*

    thʉ'ó   to=kó-ya+re   ~wa'kó
    hear   3SG.POSS=relative-PL+OBJ   wake

    ti=phʉk+ó+ró+ré   *~wa'kó+a*
    3PL.POSS=parent+FEM+SG+OBJ   wake+ASSERT.PERF

    'He heard (his father's call), woke **his brothers** (and) **their mother**.' [A4.21]

(44) *ti phʉkʉrore ya'ua wa'aga*

    ti=phʉk+ʉ́+ró+ré   *ya'ʉ́+a   wa'á+a*
    3PL.POSS=parent+MASC+SG+OBJ   tell+(3)PL   go+ASSERT.PERF

    'They went to tell **their father**.' [A4.41]

(45) *mʉ'ʉ yahiripho'nare yʉ'ʉre waga, nia*

    ~bu'ʉ=yahíri~pho'da+re[2]   *yʉ'ʉ́+ré   wá+gá*
    2SG(POSS)=heart+OBJ   1SG+OBJ   give+IMPER

    'Give me **your heart**.' [A7.51]

Locative nominals are coded as arguments (generally goals) of motion verbs by the suffix sequence -*pʉ+re*, but only when they have already been established in discourse as referential, as in (46)–(47) (see §10.5).

(46) *topʉre tiro wiha wa'aa*

    tó-pʉ+re   *tí+ró*   *wihá*   *wa'á+a*
    REM-LOC+OBJ   ANPH+SG   MOV.outward   go+ASSERT.PERF

    'He left **that place** (a previously mentioned shelter in the forest).' [A7.104]

(47) *mʉase'e tina bo'reka'arore, biato chʉ tu'sʉ tinakhʉ wehsepʉre wa'ara*

    ~bʉ́+a-se'e   tí-~da   bo'ré-ka'a+ro+re
    man+PL-CONTR   ANPH-PL   be.light-do.moving+SG+OBJ

---

[2] The annotation "2SG(POSS)" indicates irregular use of a full pronominal form in a possessive construction. See §6.4.1.

>   biátó   chɨ́ tu'sɨ́   tí-~da-khɨ
>   pepper/fish.stew eat finish   ANPH-PL-ADD
>   **wesé-pɨ+re**   wa'á+ra
>   garden-LOC+OBJ   go+VIS.IMPERF.2/3
>
> 'The men, as soon as they've eaten breakfast, they also go (there) **to the garden**.' [A1.15]

Example (48) clearly shows the difference between coding of a locative as an adjunct—in other words, a locative that represents the setting of an event—with no object suffix, and coding of a locative as an established referential goal of a motion verb (with the object suffix *+re*). In sentence 1, *~o-pɨ* 'here' is coded as the goal of the motion verb *ta* 'come', while in sentence 2 the same element functions as an adjunct and is coded only as a locative by *-pɨ* (see also §10.5 and §10.7.1, as well as Stenzel 2008b).

> (48) 1 *ã yoai, yɨ'ɨ ŏpɨre ta*
>   ~a=yoá+i   yɨ'ɨ   ~ó-pɨ+ré
>   so/then=do/make+(1/2)MASC   1SG   DEIC.PROX-LOC+OBJ
>   tá
>   come
>   'Then I came **here** (to the United States) . . .'
>
>   2 *mipɨre ŏpɨ yɨ'ɨ hiha*
>   ~bí-pɨ+ré   ~ó-pɨ   yɨ'ɨ   hí-ha
>   now-LOC+OBJ   DEIC.PROX-LOC   1SG   COP-VIS.IMPERF.1
>   '. . . and now **here** I am.' [A1.3]

Temporal expressions, which establish the referential temporal grounding of events in discourse, can also be coded by *+re* (49)–(51) (see also §10.7.2).

> (49) *tipare tina ne kɨ̆koro bokaera ã ta moñonokaa*
>   **tí-pa+re**   tí-~da   ~dé   ~kɨ́-kó+ró   bok(a)-éra
>   ANPH-time+OBJ   ANPH-PL   NEG   one-FEM+SG   find-NEG
>   ~a=tá   ~boyó~doka+a
>   so=REF   fail-COMPL+ASSERT.PERF
>   '**That time** they didn't get (kidnap) any women; so they failed completely.' [Ancestors]
>
> (50) *yɨ'ɨ mihchare wa'ikinawahai wa'aika*
>   yɨ'ɨ   **~bichá+ré**   wa'í-~kidá-~wáhá+í   wa'á+i-ka
>   1SG   today+OBJ   animal-PL-kill+(1/2)MASC   go+(1/2)MASC-PREDICT
>   '**Today**, I'm going hunting.' [A7.4]

(51) yɨ soanɨmarire yɨ'ɨ hiropɨre
   yɨ=soá-~dɨba+ri+re   yɨ'ɨ=hí+ro-pɨ+re
   1SG.POSS=rest-day+PL+OBJ   1SG(POSS)=COP+SG-LOC+OBJ
   '**On my special (resting) days**, where I lived . . .' [A3.2]

5.2.3 Comitative-instrumental =~be're

A third grammatical marker codes relations between two nouns: either a comitative relationship between two nouns (52)–(53) or the instrumental use of one noun (usually, though not necessarily inanimate) by another (54)–(55). These two functions are both coded by the cliticized (always L tone) morpheme =~be're (see also §§10.7.3–10.7.5). This is the final morpheme shown, along with the suffix +re, in the sixth position in figure 5.1; however, unlike the object marker +re, =~be're does not cooccur with either of the locative markers +i or -pɨ.

(52) tina khãria ñamichawa'achɨ, ti sa'sero, ti phɨkoro khãri, tiro ti phɨkuro topɨ wa'a to koya me're
   tí-~da   ~kharí+a   ~yabícha-wa'a-chɨ   ti=sa'sé+ró
   ANPH-PL   sleep+(3)PL   night-go-SW.REF   ANPH=be.alone+SG
   ti=phɨk+ó+ró   ~kharí tí+ró
   3PL.POSS=parent+FEM+SG   sleep ANPH+SG
   ti=phɨk+ú+ró   tó-pɨ   wa'á
   3PL.POSS=parent+MASC+SG   REM-LOC   go
   to=kó-ya=~be're
   3SG.POSS=relative-PL=COM/INST
   'Going to sleep when night came, alone with their mother, their father went off **with his relatives** . . .' [A4.15]

(53) sã yoaropɨ, yɨphɨkɨ me're thɨ'oi
   ~sá   yoá+ro-pɨ   **yɨ=phɨk+ú=~be're**
   1PL.EXC be.far+SG-LOC   1SG=parent+MASC=COM/INST
   thɨ'ó+i
   hear+VIS.PERF.1
   'We, from far away, **(I) with my father**, heard (the sounds).' [A2.9]

(54) a'riphĩ me're narokha'mare
   a'rí-~phĩ=~be're
   DEM.PROX-CLS:bladelike=COM/INST
   ~dá+ro=~kha'ba+re
   get+(3)SG=want/need+VIS.PERF.2/3
   '(You) have to take it (your heart) out **with this knife** . . .' [A7.76]

(55) tɨ me're mɨ'ɨ wa'ikinawãha sihtotaga
 tɨ́=~be're ~bɨ'ɨ wa'i-~kidá-~wáhá sitó-ta+ga
 stick=COM/INST 2SG animal-PL-kill MOV.circular-come+IMPER
 '**With this stick**, you'll go around hunting (animal-killing).' [A7.131]

5.3 Morphemes coding discourse-level information

The final position in table 5.1 shows morphemes that code discourse-level information. These morphemes appear as the final constituents in nominal constructions, following all morphemes that code lexical and syntactic information. The three most frequently occurring discourse markers are the referential clitic *=ta*, the contrastive suffix *-se'e*, and an additional independent emphatic marker *~hi'da*.

5.3.1 Referential *=ta*

The morpheme *=ta*, which, like *=~be're*, is always realized with L tone due to its enclitic status, is an extremely frequent discourse marker that can appear on a variety of word types, the most frequent being nominal words. Though its exact meaning in any given sentence is heavily context-dependent, its basic function when suffixed to a noun is to emphasize cross-reference to a previously mentioned or reactivated topical noun, yielding a meaning akin to 'that very X' or 'that same X'. We see this in (56) (several sentences from a single narrative, "The Curupira Story").

(56) a. 1 phirirota khõaro khõa yariawa'ari hia
 phɨ́+ri+ro=ta ~khoá+ro ~khoa
 be.big+NOM+SG=REF be.lying+SG be.lying
 yarí+á wa'á+ri hí+a
 die+AFFEC go+NOM(INFER) COP+ASSERT.PERF
 '**The big guy** (the curupira) was lying there, (apparently) lying there dead.'

 2 yɨ'soriphĩ to yahiripho'napɨta duhkua
 yɨ'só+ri-~phi to=yahíri~pho'da-pɨ=ta
 cut+NOM-CLS:bladelike 3SG.POSS=heart-LOC=REF
 dukú+a
 stand+ASSERT.PERF
 'The knife was sticking (lit., 'standing') **right in his heart**.' [A7.96–97]

 b. tirota, yɨ'ɨ boraro yɨ'ɨ wãhakɨrirore ñɨsibɨ
 tí+ró=ta yɨ'ɨ borá+ro yɨ'ɨ
 ANPH+SG=REF 1SG curupira+SG 1SG

~wahá-kɨ+ri+ro+re   ~yú-síbú
kill-MASC+NOM+SG+OBJ   see/look-INTENT
'I'm going there to see **him**, the curupira I killed.' [A7.112]

Before (56a) in the narrative, the man had tricked the evil creature into stabbing itself with a knife, and now, in the morning light, the man sees the creature flat out on the ground, to all appearances dead. The nominal referring to the creature is *phi+ri+ro=ta* 'big one' in sentence 1 of (56a), marked by *=ta* to emphasize that this was indeed the same creature with whom the man had had his disturbing encounter in the darkness. Because this noun is the grammatical subject, it requires only core lexical morphology (see §10.2 for more on subjects). In sentence 2 of (56a), the man sees the knife he offered to the creature stuck 'right in its heart', with 'heart' marked by *-pɨ* as a locative and then emphasized by *=ta*. Finally, in (56b), from a little later in the same narrative, some years have passed and the man has decided to go back to the place where he had the encounter with the creature. The creature is identified by the third person pronominal *ti+ro* marked by *=ta* to emphasize that this is the same creature from earlier in the story. The nominalization *~waha-~kɨ+ri+ro+re*, which functions as a relative clause 'the one I killed', is coded as the grammatical object of *~yɨ-* 'see'. We see, then, that *=ta* can mark nouns in a variety of grammatical roles (see also (62) below).

5.3.2 Contrastive subject *-se'e*

The morpheme *-se'e* occurs as a discourse marker much less frequently than *=ta*, and appears only on some subject nominals. It functions to indicate a contrast between subject nouns in adjacent sentences, much the same as the switch-reference marker *-chɨ* indicates a contrast in subjects between adverbial and main clauses within a sentence (see §10.1.2). Frequently, though not exclusively, *-se'e* is used when the subjects involved are both pronouns and the speaker wishes to avoid ambiguity. The use of *-se'e* on a noun can mean 'but/however X', 'the other X', 'X, though', or 'X, on the other hand', as we see in (57), again from "The Curupira Story."[3]

In the darkness of night, the man is first approached by the creature, and it greets him (sentence 1). The creature is identified in this clause

---

[3] The same morpheme, usually in reduced, monomoraic form, occurs in a lexicalized construction with the alternate particle root: *pa-se('e)-pɨ* 'somewhere'. This is the only instance in my data in which *-se'e* does not occur in final position, the slot for discourse markers. The fact that it can occur as a nonfinal stem morpheme followed by a grammatical suffix suggests that it was formerly a root which has grammaticalized as a discourse marker.

by the pronominal *ti+ro*. The same pronominal is marked with *-se'e* as a contrastive subject in sentence 2 because the referent is now the man.

(57) 1 *ne koiro, nia tiro*
~~dé   kó-iro   ~dí+a   **tí+ró**
hello relative-NOM.SG say+ASSERT.PERF ANPH+SG
'"How's it going, relative," **he** (the creature) said.'[4]

2 *yɨ'tieraa tirose'e koiro*
yɨ'ti-éra+a   **tí+ró-sé'é**   *kó-iro*
answer-NEG+ASSERT.PERF ANPH+SG-CONTR relative-NOM.SG
'But **he (the man)** didn't answer.' [A7.34–35]

The lines in (58) occur much later in the story, after the curupira has given the man a magic stick that makes him a spectacularly successful hunter. The contrastive *-se'e* marks the noun phrase *to ko-ya-se'e* 'his (the man's) relatives' (sentence 2), who find the man's success suspicious, and question it (sentence 3).

(58) 1 *wa'ikinawãharo wa'aro, tɨre nawa'aka'a, wa'ikina phayɨ wãhaatia*
wa'i-~kídá-~wáhá+ró wa'á+ro tú+re   ~dá-wa'a-ka'a
animal-PL-kill+(3)SG go+(3)SG stick+OBJ get-go-do.moving
wa'í-~kídá phayɨ   ~wahá-ati+a
animal-PL many/a.lot kill-IMPERF+ASSERT.PERF
'When he went hunting, he took the stick along and would always kill lots of animals.'

2 *ã ta yoa to koyase'e tirore sinituaatimaa*
*~á=ta yoá **to=kó-ya-se'e**   tí+ró+ré*
so=REF do 3SG.POSS=relative-PL-CONTR ANPH+SG+OBJ
~sidítu+a-ati-~ba+a
ask+PL-IMPERF-FRUS+ASSERT.PERF
'**His relatives, though,** were always demanding to know (unsuccessfully):'

3 *mɨ'ɨ do'se yoa wãhahari*
~bɨ'ɨ   do'sé yoá   ~wahá-hari
2SG   WH   do/make kill-INT.IMPERF
'"How do you kill (hunt so many animals)?"' [A7.155–57]

---

[4] Indians throughout the Amazon define and address each other as 'relative'. White people and spirits fall into other categories of beings, so when the creature addresses the man as 'relative', he is clearly trying to trick him.

Later, the man has been bitten by a poisonous snake and is dying (59). He takes medicine, but to no avail, and subsequently dies. The contrastive morpheme marks the nominalized verb *ko-ti+ro* 'the medicine-taking' in sentence 2.

(59) 1 *kotimaa*
kó-ti-~ba+a
medicine-VBZ-FRUS+ASSERT.PERF
'He took medicine,'

2 *kotirose'e ne tirore thɨoeraa*
kó-ti+ro-se'e   *~dé   tí+ró+ré*
medicine-VBZ+SG-CONTR NEG   ANPH+SG+OBJ
thɨo-éra+a
be.successful-NEG+ASSERT.PERF
'**however, it (the medicine-taking)** didn't cure him.' [A7.165]

5.3.3 Emphatic *~hi'da*

Like *=ta*, the discourse marker *~hi'da* is used in both nominal and verbal constructions, but *~hi'da* is not a bound morpheme (see also §11.3). It is phonologically independent, has a HL tonal melody, and is never inflected, properties that indicate it to be a root that has taken on the function of emphasis in various contexts. It cooccurs with nouns in a similar way to *=ta*, resulting in the meaning 'the same X', or 'that very X'.

(60) *ba'aro mahsɨno hi'na topɨrota hi'na*...
ba'á+ro   ~basɨ́+ro ~hí'da tó-pɨ+ro=ta   ~hí'da
do/be.after+SG man+SG EMPH   DEF-LOC+SG=REF   EMPH
'The **same guy, right then** ...' [A7.54]

(61) *ã yo tiro hi'na bɨhkɨro mɨmɨ busũ ñɨ*...
~a=yó tí+ró   ~hí'da bɨk+ɨ́+ró   ~bɨbɨ́ bɨ́-~sɨ
so=do   ANPH+SG EMPH   elder+MASC+SG   run   shore-arrive
~yɨ́
see/look
'Then **the same old man** ran to the shore, looked...' [A6.24]

5.3.4 Restrictions and interesting combinations

The order of elements in Kotiria noun morphology, as seen in figure 5.1 at the beginning of this chapter, corresponds well to that predicted by Bybee's claim that "there is a strong correspondence between the content of a linguistic unit and the mode of expression it takes" (1985:7). The farther a suffix is from the stem, the wider the context to which the suffix makes reference. Suffixes that are closest to the stem tend to be lexical, more closely linked to the core meaning of the word; suffixes that are farther from the stem mark the word for its role in the clause, and then for its role in discourse. In Kotiria, the stem root occurs to the left, followed by morphology that establishes its basic lexical identity. This core unit can then be marked as to its role in ever-wider contexts—the clause and discourse.

While the relative ordering of morphemes follows the scheme in figure 5.1, not all combinations of the morphemes listed there are possible. Some restrictions apply; for example, within the sphere of lexical coding, gender is marked only on animates, and the individualizer -*kiro* can be used only with collective animates. In the sphere of syntactic coding, a noun can be marked as both locative and object by the combination -*pɨ*+*re*, but we find no cases in which a noun is marked with both the locative and the comitative-instrumental morpheme =~*be're*. As for discourse marking morphemes, we have seen that restrictions related to the grammatical role of the noun apply: the referential =*ta* can be used on nouns in any grammatical role, while contrastive -*se'e* occurs on subjects only.

Although not every possible combination of morphemes is exemplified in the textual data, many are. A few examples of multi-morphemic nouns are shown in (62)–(68); relevant contextual information is provided in parentheses. Examples (62)–(63) have nominal roots, (64)–(66) are derived from verb roots, and (67)–(68) are derived from particle roots.

(62) *numia phonakãreta*
      ~*dubí* +*a*   ~*pho'dá*-~*ka* +*re* =*ta*
      woman +PL children -DIM +OBJ =REF
      N   3   N   4   6   7
      '(These are good) for little girls (to play with).' [Baskets]

(63) *yɨhkukukãre*
      yɨkú-*kɨ*   -~*ka* +*re*
      tree -CLS:tree -DIM +OBJ
      N   3   4   6
      '(He made) the little stick (appear).' [A7.33]

Example (64) is composed of three roots, two of them nominal and one verbal. The initial noun root, *karaka* 'chicken, rooster' is compounded with the verb root *du* 'speak, talk'; this stem is nominalized by +*ri* and then further takes the noun classifier -*pa* 'time', yielding the noun for 'cock-crowing hour'.

(64) karaka duripa
 káráká dú +ri -pa
 rooster speak +NOM -CLS:time
 N V 1 3
 'the cock-crowing hour' [A4.11]

(65) yɨ'soriphĩkãpɨ
 yɨ'só +ri -~phi -~ka -pɨ
 cut +NOM -CLS:bladelike -DIM -LOC
 V 1 3 4 5
 '(He put the monkey heart) on the tip of the little knife.' [A7.55]

The nominal in (66) functions as a temporal adverbial (see §10.7.2). The initial verb root ~ba'a 'do after, be after' is first nominalized by +ro. This stem is then marked by the diminutive -~ka (whose emphasizing and attenuating functions were discussed in §5.1.1). The final morpheme is the referential =ta, resulting in a nominal meaning 'just after'.

(66) ba'arokãta
 ba'á +ro -~ka =ta
 do/be.after +SG -DIM =REF
 V 3 4 7
 'just after' [A7.68]

(67) õ ba'arokãi
 ~ó -ba'á +ro -~ka +i
 DEIC.PROX -do/be.after +SG -DIM +LOC
 P V 3 4 5
 '(just going) a little way' [A7.163]

(68) pakorokãre
 pá -ko +ro -~ka +re
 ALT -FEM +SG -DIM +OBJ
 P 2 3 4 6
 '(She took) the other little girl . . .' [A5.21]

5.4 Review of morphophonological processes

5.4.1 Nasalization, tone specification, and spreading

Examples (62)–(68) can also serve to review and demonstrate the main phonological processes that govern Kotiria word formation:

- All roots are lexically specified for the suprasegmental features of nasalization, tonal melody, and glottalization.

- Nasalization and tone features of the root spread left to right to all unmarked morphemes.

- Dependent roots retain specification for nasality/orality and glottalization, but relinquish specification for tone, as the melody of the phonological head (the leftmost root) will predominate and spread.

The morphophonological processes that result in the surface realizations of (63) and (65) are displayed in (69) and (70), respectively.

The word in (69) is composed of an oral root *yʉkʉ* with a LHL melody, followed by an oral classifier morpheme *-kʉ*. The first two tones of the root associate to the root moras and the final, unassigned, L tone associates to the mora of the classifier affix. The diminutive *-~ka* is inherently nasal but has no tonal specification, so the final L tone of the root spreads to it as well. The object marker *+re* is unmarked for nasality or tone; it becomes nasalized due to spread of the [+nasal] specification of the diminutive, and gets L tone from the root.

(69)   *yʉkʉ-kʉ-~ka+re* [jʉʰkúkʉkãr̃ẽ] (= (63))

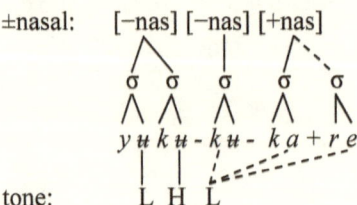

In (70), the oral, glottalized root *yʉ'so* also has a LHL melody. (In the representation, "[cg]" abbreviates "constricted glottis.") It is followed by the nominalizer *+ri*, which is unspecified for nasality; the [−nasal] value of the root spreads to *+ri*. Its first two tones associate to the root moras and the final L tone associates to the mora of the first affix and then spreads to all successive constituents. Each of the final three morphemes—the classifier *-~phi*, the diminutive *-~ka*, and the locative *-pʉ*—retains its underlying specification for nasality; thus, no spreading of this feature occurs after the initial stem formation.

Nominal morphology

(70) yʉ'so+ri-~phi-~ka-pʉ [jʉʔsóripʰĩkãpʉ] (= (65))

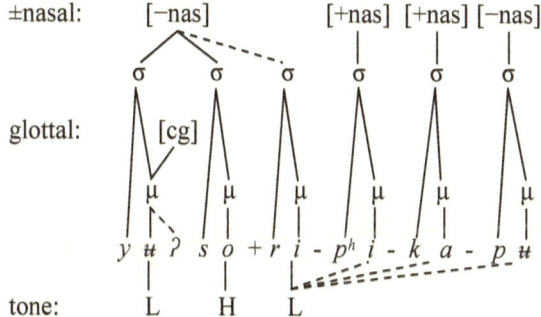

5.4.2 Status of morphemes

The phonological properties of the morphemes discussed in this chapter, as well as those of the morphemes in suffixal positions 1 through 3 that were discussed in chapter 4, indicate that these morphemes are grammaticalized to varying degrees. Specifically:

- All monomoraic suffixes that are unmarked for nasality (i.e., [Ønasal]) or tone, and are thus open to spreading of [±nasal] and tone from the left, can be considered fully grammaticalized suffixes.

- Other suffixes—a few monomoraic ones, and all bimoraic suffixes—retain inherent specification for nasality, and in rare cases for tone as well (and block the spreading of the properties for which they are specified). These suffixes can be considered to be grammaticalized to a lesser degree.

These properties are summarized in table 5.1.

It is evident that the more frequently-occurring morphemes coding information in the syntactic and discourse spheres (locative, object, and referential) are more suffixlike in shape and behavior, and are further along in the grammaticalization process, than morphemes such as the comitative =~be're, the contrastive -se'e or the solitary -di'ta, all of which are used less frequently.

TABLE 5.1. PHONOLOGICAL SPECIFICATION OF NOMINAL MORPHEMES

			NASALITY	TONE
LEXICAL	1 (nominalizer)	+*ri*	[Ønasal]	
	2 (gender)	-*ko*/+*o*	[−nasal]/[Ønasal]	
		Ø/+*ʉ*	[Ønasal]	
	3 (number)	-*kiro* IND	[−nasal]	
		+*ro*	[Ønasal]	
		-*a*/-~*da*	[Ønasal]/[+nasal]	
		-CLS	[±nasal]	
		+*ri*	[Ønasal]	
	4 (evaluative)	-~*ka* DIM	[+nasal]	
		-*wʉ'rʉ* AUG	[−nasal]	
	(qualifying)	-*khʉ* ADD	[-nasal]	
		-*dita* SOL	[−nasal]	
		-*waro* EMPH	[−nasal]	
SYNTACTIC	5 (locative)	+*i*	[Ønasal]	
		-*pʉ*	[−nasal]	
	6 (nonlocative)	+*re* OBJ	[Ønasal]	
		=~*be're* COM/INST	[+nasal]	L
DISCOURSE	7	-*se'e* CONTR	[−nasal]	
		=*ta* REF	[−nasal]	L

6 Noun phrases

This chapter describes the internal syntax of noun phrases (NPs) in Kotiria. Noun phrase structure follows a basic template in which most types of modifiers generally precede the head noun (§6.1). The basic types of modifiers include determiner and quantifying expressions (§§6.2–6.3), possessive and interrogative modification (§§6.4–6.5), and adjective-like descriptive nominalizations (§6.6); the ordering and use of multiple modifiers within NPs is discussed in §6.7. The lexical noun classification morphology described in chapter 4 occurs on most types of modifiers (determiners, number quantifiers, interrogatives, and descriptives), establishing a kind of semantic agreement between the head noun and the modifier.

Several features of Kotiria NPs contrast with those found in other Eastern Tukanoan languages and are presumably innovative. One such feature is the deployment of plural marking in number modification: in Kotiria, both number modifier roots and head nouns show patterns of pluralization that differ depending on noun class. Innovations also have taken place in the expression of possession: Kotiria has developed a system of personal possessive proclitics (reduced forms of personal pronouns) that form a single phonological unit with the possessed noun; moreover, the possessive morpheme *ya*, analyzed as a genitive prefix or suffix in much of the literature on Eastern Tukanoan, displays all the properties of a root morpheme in Kotiria.

6.1 Constituent order in noun phrases

Like other Eastern Tukanoan languages (see §10.4.3), Kotiria has basic object-verb clausal word order and displays the typologically correlated internal NP structure in which modifiers precede head nouns (Givón 2001, vol. 1:242). This basic structure occurs in most modifying constructions, with the exception of those involving the quantifier *pe'ri* and descriptives.

The basic categories of modifiers found in noun phrases include different types of determiners (1)–(3), quantifiers (4)–(5), possessives (6), interrogatives (7), and descriptives (8).

(1) deictic
a'ri khiti
a'rí   khití
DEM.PROX story
'this story'

(2) anaphoric
tiphĩ yɨ'soriphĩ
ti-~phí   yɨ'só+ri-~phi
ANPH-CLS:bladelike cut+NOM-CLS:bladelike
'this knife'

(3) alternate
pairo ka yahiripho'na
pá-iro   ká   yahíri~pho'da
ALT-NOM.SG monkey heart
'another monkey heart'

(4) number
kũiro mɨno
~kú-író   ~bú+ro
one-NOM.SG man+SG
'one man'

(5) quantity
phayɨ wãhtia
phayú ~watí+á
many devil+PL
'many devils'

(6) possessive
to dieya
to=dié-yá
3SG.POSS=dog-PL
'his dogs'

(7) interrogative
do'se a'riro mahsɨro
do'sé a'rí+ró   ~basú+ro
WH   DEM.PROX+SG being+SG
'what kind of being?'

(8) descriptive (adjectival) nominalization
buhɨina dainakã ba'aa
buhú-~ida   dá-~ídá-~ká   ba'á+á
be.large-NOM.PL   be.small-NOM.PL-DIM   bass+PL
'large and small bass'

The examples above indicate that some kinds of modifiers (specifically demonstratives, quantifiers, the "alternate," interrogatives, and descriptives) can take classifying morphology corresponding to the overtly marked or understood features of the head noun; how this works is one of the things that is presented in more detail in the following sections.

6.2 Determiners

The deictic particles *a'ri*, *si*, *~o*, *~so'o*, and *to*, the anaphoric particle *ti*, and the alternate particle *pa* can all be used either as pronominals (independent NPs) or as modifiers within an NP (see §3.2, §4.5.2, and §4.7); I label them determiners when they are used as modifiers. Determiners precede head nouns and form separate phonological words. They occur with obligatory nominal morphology showing agreement with the nouns they modify. The most frequently occurring determiners are the demonstrative *a'ri* 'this', the anaphorics *ti* and *to* 'that, there, the', and the alternate *pa* 'other, another'. Their primary function is to introduce new participants or, in the case of the anaphorics, to link reference to a previously mentioned participant.

The inherent classificatory features of the head noun (whether overtly coded or merely implicit) are morphologically marked on the determiner when the noun is first introduced. In subsequent mentions of the entity, the head noun does not need to appear; a deictic, anaphoric, or alternate particle with the same classifying morphology, which is obligatory, can be used as a pronoun referring to it.[1] In the discourse in (9), for example, the inherent feminine, singular, and animate features of the referent of the proper noun 'Kristine' are coded on the demonstrative *a'ri* 'this' by the suffixes *-ko* (feminine) and *+ro* (singular, animate) in sentence 1; these also occur on the pronominal form in sentence 2. In (10), the noun *dasa* 'toucan' is inherently animate and singular, features coded by the suffix *+ro* on the demonstrative (sentence 1) and subsequently in the anaphoric pronominal (sentence 2).

---

[1] The general claim that reference is initially established by using a noun holds true for all text data. However, conversational data shows that referents for pronouns can be established through gestural deixis. Once, for example, a head gesture in the direction of a neighbor's house was sufficient to establish a referent for the pronoun 'he'.

(9) 1 *yʉ'ʉ topʉre a'rikorore kristinare ya'uika yʉ'ʉse'e*
      yʉ'ʉ   tó-pʉ+re   a'rí-kó+ró+ré
      1SG   REM-LOC+OBJ   DEM.PROX-FEM+SG+OBJ
      kristína+re   ya'ʉ́+i-ka   yʉ'ʉ́-se'e
      Kristine+OBJ   tell+(1/2)MASC-PREDICT   1SG-CONTR
      'I'm going to tell **this woman** Kristine (how it is) there.'

   2 *mari hiropʉre*
      ~bari=hí+ro-pʉ+re
      1PL.INC.POSS=COP+SG-LOC+OBJ
      'Our way of being/living there.' [A1.4–5]

   3 *ã yoai tikorore ya'uika yʉ'ʉse'e*
      ~a=yoá+i   *tí-kó+ró+ré*
      so/then=do/make+(1/2)MASC   ANPH-FEM+SG+OBJ
      ya'ʉ́+i-ka   *yʉ'ʉ́-se'e*
      tell+(1/2)MASC-PREDICT   1SG-CONTR
      'So, I'm going to tell **her**.' [A1.6]

(10) 1 *ã yochʉ ñʉ, tida do'se yoamahsi mari, a'ria ñarire . . .*
      do'sé   yoá-~basi
      WH   do/make-know
      ~barí   a'rí+á   ~yá+ri+re
      1PL.INC DEM.PROX+PL   be.bad+NOM+OBJ
      '"What can we do about **these evil ones**?" . . .'

   2 *tinare wĩha phayʉ hʉ̃ga tipare tina wãhtia*
      tí-~da+re   *~wihá   phayʉ   ~hʉ́+a*
      ANPH-PL+OBJ   set.afire   many   burn+ASSERT.PERF
      tí-pá+ré   *tí-~da*   *~watí+á*
      ANPH-CLS:time+OBJ   ANPH-PL   devil+PL
      'They set fire to **them** (and) burned many of **those devils** that day.'
      [A4.61–63]

Noun phrases with modifiers formed from the alternate *pa* or anaphoric *ti* are extremely common. Like the deictic *a'ri*, the alternate modifier also introduces a new entity, albeit another entity of the same type as one that has already been mentioned, such as the 'monkey heart' in (11).

(11) *yʉ'ʉre wanamoata payahiripho'nare*
     yʉ'ʉ́+ré   wá-~dábó+gá=ta   pá-yahiri~pho'da+re
     1SG+OBJ   give-repeat+IMPER=REF   ALT-heart+OBJ

     'Give me **another heart**.' [A7.62]

Noun phrases 177

Noun phrases with anaphoric determiners reestablish reference to a previously mentioned entity, marking the NP as definite. The anaphoric NP construction *ti+ro bora+ro ~ya-~ka* 'the evil curupira' in (12), for example, appears after a number of lines of narrative in which only simple pronouns were used.

(12) *to ã nichɨ, thɨ'oro tiro boraro ñakã yɨ'tia*
 to=~á=~dí-chɨ   *thɨ'ó+ro*   *tí+ró*   *borá+ro*   *~yá-~ka*
 DEF=so=say-SW.REF   hear+SG   ANPH+SG   curupira+SG   be.bad-DIM
 yɨ'tí+a
 answer+ASSERT.PERF

'Hearing what (the man) said, **the** evil **curupira** responded . . .' [A7.74]

6.3 Quantifiers

6.3.1 Numbers

Number modifiers also precede head nouns, form separate phonological units, and—unlike other quantity modifiers—display some classifying morphology. Like other Eastern Tukanoan languages, Kotiria has only three simple number roots: *~kɨ* 'one', *phɨa* 'two', and *tia* 'three'; these and the internally complex number *phititia* 'four' are the only quantity modifiers that are marked with classifying morphology. (This pattern exemplifies a well-known cross-linguistic tendency, noted by Aikhenvald [2000:41], for agreement markers to occur only on smaller numbers). Only a limited range of classifying morphology appears on numbers—a subset of the morphology that marks singular nouns, even though most of the numbers mark quantities greater than one.

When it modifies an animate noun, *~kɨ* 'one' obligatorily occurs with the nominalizer *-iro*, whereas other numbers that modify animate nouns obligatorily take the suffix *+ro*. The partitive, rather than singulative, function of *+ro* is evident in this construction, indicating 'a certain exact number of X'.

In the case of inanimates, in my data so far, I have found that the only shape classifier that occurs on number modifiers in Kotiria is *-ria* 'round (and usually somewhat elongated)', seen in (13c), (14a), and (15c) (this classifier is also seen in a few nouns, e.g., *wɨ-ria* 'airplane', *phuti-ria* 'tubular flute'). Waltz (2002:189) analyzes *-ria* as a general classifier indicating 'paucal, few'. However, I have found its use on numbers to be restricted to those that modify inanimate nouns that have a rounded shape, such as airplanes, flutes, canoes, oranges, coconuts, stones, and hats. What is interesting is that even if the noun itself takes the more common shape classifier for round objects, *-ka*, it is *-ria* that occurs on its number modifier. The origin of the discrepancy between use of *-ria* on numbers (and in the interrogative construction in (63) below) and *-ka* on the nouns themselves is still unknown. It may that *-ria* is a relic from a set of paucal classifiers used for different types of inanimates; however, it is clearly not an all-purpose synchronic marker meaning 'paucal', since inanimates that never take shape classifiers, even when numerically paucal, do not allow a modifying number to take *-ria*, as is seen in (13a), (13b), (14b), and (15b).

(13) ~*kʉ* 'one'

    a. *kʉ̃ khitikã*

       ~*kʉ́ khití-~ka*
       one story-DIM

       'one little story; a little story'

    b. *kʉ̃ ku'tukã*

       ~*kʉ́ ku'tú-~ka*
       one clearing-DIM

       'one little clearing; a little clearing'

    c. *kʉ̃ria bʉhsoka*

       ~*kʉ́-ríá   bʉsó-ka*
       one-CLS:round canoe-CLS:round

       'one canoe; a canoe'

    d. *kʉ̃iro mʉno*

       ~*kʉ́-iró   ~bʉ́+ro*
       one-NOM.SG man+SG

       'one man; a man'

    e. *kʉ̃iro dierokã*

       ~*kʉ́-iró   dié+ró-~ká*
       one-NOM.SG dog+SG-DIM

       'one little dog; a little dog'

(14) *phʉa* 'two'

    a. *phʉaria bʉhsoka*

       phʉá-ria   bʉsó-ka
       two-CLS:round canoe-CLS:round

       'two canoes'

Noun phrases

    b. *phɨa khɨ'ma*
       phɨá ~khɨ'bá
       two   year
       'two years'

    c. *phɨaro dieya*
       phɨá+ro dié-yá
       two+SG dog-PL
       'two dogs'

(15) *tia* 'three'

    a. *tia khɨ'ma*
       tiá   ~khɨ'bá
       three year
       'three years'

    b. *tia ñono*
       tiá   ~yo+ro
       three show+SG
       'three mirrors'

    c. *tiaria bɨhso*
       tiá-ríá   bɨsó
       three-CLS:round canoe
       'three canoes'

    d. *tia wɨ'ɨse*
       tiá   wɨ'ɨ́-sé
       three house-PL
       'three houses'

    e. *tiaro kaya*
       tiá+ró   ká-ya
       three+SG monkey-PL
       'three monkeys'

    f. *tiaro numia*
       tiá+ró   ~dubí+a
       three+SG woman+PL
       'three women'

    g. *tiaro dieya*
       tiá+ró   dié-yá
       three+SG dog-PL
       'three dogs'

As is obvious from the above examples, the morphology of the head noun is also of interest in constructions with numbers. Waltz (2002:190) states that in Kotiria and six other Eastern Tukanoan languages, head nouns modified by number words pluralize only at 'four', indicating that semantically and syntactically, quantities from 'one' to 'three' group together as paucals. Ramirez (1997a:333) affirms this same pattern of pluralization in Tukano, and Barnes (1999:221) claims it to be the norm throughout the family.

In fact, the Kotiria system reveals itself to be rather more complex, with systematic differences in pluralization according to the class of noun being quantified. Animate head nouns pluralize not at 'four', but at 'two', as we see from *phɨa+ro die-ya* 'two dogs' (14c), *tia+ro ka-ya* 'three monkeys' (15e), *tia+ro ~dubi+a* 'three women' (15f), and *tia+ro die-ya* 'three dogs' (15g).

As for inanimates, the subset of 'rounded' inanimates (those for which the modifying number takes the classifier *-ria*) is marked differently from inanimates for which the modifying number does not take *-ria*. This is exemplified in the forms for 'one', 'two', and 'three canoes', in (13c) (14a) and (15c): both the modifier and the head noun are marked by classifiers for the quantity 'two', while in the case of 'three', the modifier continues to be marked by the classifier, but the head noun itself reverts to the zero-marked plural form. Further investigation is needed to confirm whether this pattern applies to all 'rounded' inanimates in exactly the same way.[2]

Two different patterns are followed by non-'rounded' inanimates. In (14b) 'two years', (15a) 'three years', and (15b) 'three mirrors', we see that neither the modifier nor the head noun have any additional morphology. The modifiers are uninflected and the head nouns are in their singular forms. On the other hand, in (15d) 'three houses', the head noun is pluralized. Thus, at the number 'three', some inanimates pluralize while others do not; as yet, there are no identifiable semantic criteria for which inanimates do which.

The quantities 'four' and 'five' are indicated by more complex expressions. The quantity 'four' is indicated by a compound *phititia*, the morphological analysis of which is as yet not clear, though the root certainly indicates a collective or an undetermined quantity and is the same root used in words such as *hi-phiti+ro* 'everything' or *hi-phiti-~da* 'everyone' (in both these forms postaspiration of *ph* is often

---

[2] According to some speakers, the final vowel is lengthened to indicate plural, though this not consistently attested.

suppressed, since it is in noninitial position).³ Like 'two' and 'three', 'four' is marked by +*ro* before animates (16d), and by -*ria* before rounded objects (16b). All nouns modified by 'four', however, whether animate or inanimate, have plural (or generic) forms, as we see throughout (16).

(16)   *phititia* 'four'

 a. *phititia kɨ'mari*
  phitítia ~kɨ'bá+ri
  four year+PL
  'four years'

 b. *phititiaria bɨhso*
  phitítia-ria bɨsó
  four-CLS:round canoe
  'four canoes'

 c. *phititia wɨ'ɨse*
  phitítia wɨ'ɨ́-sé
  four house-PL
  'four houses'

 d. *phititiaro dieya*
  phitítia+ro dié-yá
  four+SG dog-PL
  'four dogs'

The quantity 'five' is a phrasal construction ~*kɨ* ~*waboka* 'one hand' plus *phiti+a* (*phiti* is the same element that appears in 'four', and it occurs with the plural morpheme +*a*, to derive the notion of 'quantity'). The entire expression indicates the quantity 'five'—literally, 'a hand's worth/amount/quantity'. It is interesting, too, that unlike all the number modifiers examined thus far, the construction for 'five' takes no additional morphology for rounded inanimate objects (compare (16b) with (17b)), and takes the plural morpheme ~*da* (instead of partitive +*ro*) before plural animates (compare (16d) with (17c)).

(17)   *kũ wamoka phitia* 'five'

 a. *kũ wamoka phitia kɨ'mari*
  ~*kɨ* ~*wabóka phití+a* ~*kɨ'bá+ri*
  one hand COLL+PL year+PL
  'five years'

---

³ The Kotiria word for 'four' is thus not a clear cognate of the construction for 'four' in languages such as Tatuyo: *bàpà-Vri* (pair-PL), in other words 'two pairs' (Gomez-Imbert 1982:232).

b. *kũ wamoka phitia bʉhso*
   ~kũ ~wabóka phití+a   bʉsó
   one hand   COLL+PL   canoe
   'five canoes'

c. *kũ wamoka phitiana dieya*
   ~kũ ~wabóka phití+a-~da   die-ya
   one hand   COLL+PL-PL   dog-PL
   'five dogs'

The features of the number modifier system from 'one' to 'five' are summarized in figure 6.1. Far from being a simple system in which nouns pluralize at 'four', the Kotiria system displays systematic morphological differentiation on both number modifiers and on heads, according to classes of animate and inanimate nouns. This complexity represents a significant departure from other Eastern Tukanoan languages.

	Morphology on Number Modifier			Morphology on Head Noun		
	Inan.	Inan. rd.	Animate	Inan.	Inan. rd.	Animate
~kũ 'one'	Ø	-ria (CLS)	-iro (NOM.SG)	Ø or CLS	-ka (CLS)	+ro (SG)
phua 'two'	Ø	-ria (CLS)	+ro (SG)	Ø		+a/~da/-ya (PL)
tia 'three'	Ø	-ria (CLS)	+ro (SG)	Ø	Ø (PL)	+a/~da/-ya (PL)
phititia 'four'	Ø	-ria (CLS)	+a/~da/-ya (PL)	Ø or +ri (PL)	Ø (PL)	+a/~da/-ya (PL)
~kũ ~waboka phitia 'five'		Ø	+a/~da/-ya (PL)	Ø or +ri (PL)	Ø (PL)	+a/~da/-ya (PL)

Figure 6.1. Morphology of number modifying constructions. Inan. = inanimate; rd. = round.

The expression of numbers higher than five can be accomplished through combinations of 'hands' (indicating groups of five) and individual smaller numbers; however, such expressions rarely occur in natural speech. Synchronically, when a Kotiria speaker needs to express exact numbers above five, borrowed terms from Portuguese or Spanish are used. Cross-linguistic information indicates that this is the pattern throughout the region (Aikhenvald 2003b:104; Epps 2008:312).

One final observation should be made about number modifiers. By far the most frequently occurring number root modifier is ~kʉ 'one', suggesting that it has an extended semantic function beyond that of indicating a singular quantity. Indeed, like NPs with deictic modifiers, NP constructions of the type 'one X' nearly always introduce new participants in discourse, as in (18)–(20). Thus, coding of indefinite reference is understood to be a second function of such constructions. This is not a surprising conclusion given cross-linguistic evidence that the numeral 'one'—a quantifier implying existence—tends to develop into a marker of referentiality implying genericity (Givón 1981). Once a participant has been introduced by means of a construction with ~kʉ, anaphoric constructions with *ti*, which are inherently definite, can be employed.

(18) *kʉ̃ta hia kʉ̃iro mʉno to namonore õse nia*
~*kʉ́=ta*   *hí+a*   ~*kʉ́-író*   ~*bʉ́+ro*   *to*=~*dabó+ro+re*
one/a=REF COP+PL one/a-NOM.SG man+SG 3SG.POSS=wife+SG+OBJ
~*ó-sé*   ~*dí+a*
DEIC.PROX-be.like say+ASSERT.PERF
'Once **a man** said this to his wife . . .' [A7.3]

(19) *ã ta yoa ñamichapʉ hi'na, kʉ̃ ku'tukãpʉ, õpari ku'tukãpʉre phi'asʉ̃a*
~*a=tá*   *yoá*   ~*yabícha-pʉ*   ~*hí'da*   ~*kʉ̃*   *ku'tú-~ka-pʉ*
so=REF do/make night-LOC EMPH one/a clearing-DIM-LOC
~*ó-pá+rí*   *ku'tú-~ka-pʉ+re*
DEIC.PROX-ALT+NOM clearing-DIM-LOC+OBJ
phi'a-~sʉ+a
MOV.out.into-arrive+ASSERT.PERF
'As night was falling, he went out into **a little clearing**, a little clearing like this.' [A7.18]

(20) *thuwa'a to'i kʉ̃iro khatama'a bohkasʉ̃a toi*
thuá-wa'a tó+i   ~*kʉ́-író*   *khatá~bá'á*
return-go REM+LOC one/a-NOM.SG jacú.bird
boká-~sʉ+a   *tó+i*
find-arrive+ASSERT.PERF REM+LOC
'(The man) going back, came upon **a jacú bird**.' [A7.18]

6.3.2 Other quantifiers

Kotiria speakers can also talk about unspecified small or large quantities of objects or beings. In natural speech this is accomplished by the use of the indefinite quantifiers ~*ka* [kãã́] 'some; a little; a few', *phayʉ* 'many; a lot of', and *pe'ri* 'many; all of'. As a rule, ~*ka* (21) and *phayʉ* (22a)–(22c) precede the head noun, though *phayʉ* also occurs (less frequently) in posthead position (22d)–(22e). On the other hand, *pe'ri* is a rare case of a modifier that consistently occurs in posthead position (23). None of these modifiers take any classifying morphology; with all of them, head nouns have plural forms.

(21) ~ka 'a few; some'

  kã sõ'akã phoari
  ~ká ~so'á-~ka phoá+rí
  a.few be.red-DIM feathers+PL
  'a few red feathers; some red feathers'

(22) phayʉ 'many'

  a. phayʉ wãtia
     phayʉ́ ~watí+á
     many evil.being+PL
     'many devils'

  b. phayʉ yahkaina
     phayʉ́ yaká-~ida
     many steal-NOM.PL
     'many thieves/kidnappers'

  c. phayʉ mahsakurua
     phayʉ́ ~basá-kúrú+á
     many people-group+PL
     'many groups' (i.e. language or ethnic groups)

  d. wa'ikina phayʉ
     wa'í-~kídá phayʉ́
     animal-PL many
     'many animals'

  e. wa'mayapia phayʉ
     ~wa'báyapi+a   phayʉ́
     young.adult.relative+PL many
     'many young relatives'

(23) pe'ri 'all; many'

  a. topeina pe'ri
     tó-pe-~ida   pé'ri
     DEF-CQUANT-NOM.PL many
     'that many'

  b. tida pe'ri
     tí-~da   pé'ri
     ANPH-PL many
     'all of them'

c. *numiaña'arimahsa pe'ri*
   ~dubí+a-~ya'a+ri~basa   *pé'ri*
   woman+PL-catch+NOM-people   many
   'all the woman-stealers/kidnappers'

Besides its function as a modifier, *phayʉ* can also occur without an overt head noun, as an independent quantifying expression meaning 'many; a lot; lots', as long as whatever there is 'a lot of' can be understood from the context. In (24a), cultural knowledge about the many ways manioc liquid is used in cooking allows us to understand *phayʉ* to refer to a variety of different foodstuffs, whereas in (24b), we understand from the derived verb *~pho'dati* 'to reproduce' that *phayʉ* refers to a lot of babies or offspring.

(24) a. *ti ñohkare phayʉ yoahata*
        ti=~yoká+ré   ***phayú***   *yoá-ha=ta*
        ANPH= manioc.liquid+OBJ   many   do/make-VIS.IMPERF.1=REF
        'We make **a lot** (of different things to eat) with the manioc liquid.' [Manioc]

   b. *tina ba'ro phayʉ pho'natira*
       tí-~da=ba'ro   ***phayú***   *~pho'dá-ti+ra*
       ANPH-PL=kind   many/a.lot   offspring-VBZ+VIS.IMPERF.2/3
       'These (armadillos) have **a lot** of offspring.' [A11.8]

6.4 Possession

The third type of modification is that which expresses a possessive or belonging relationship between two entities. Such relationships are coded by several different means in Kotiria.

In general, the coding of possession in Eastern Tukanoan languages involves three elements that combine in the canonical order for modifiers in NPs: a possessor, which may be an independent noun, a full NP, or the full or reduced form of a personal pronoun; a genitive-type marker *ya/ye* (for plural possessed nouns); and the possessed noun.

However, interesting variation in the use of these elements occurs from language to language. For example, Wa'ikhana/Piratapuyo (Waltz 2002:189), Tukano (Ramirez 1997a:324), Barasana (Gomez-Imbert 1997a:183, 197–201), and Desano (Miller 1999:48) use full subject pronouns in possessive constructions, while other languages, such as Tatuyo (Gomez-Imbert 1982:249), Kubeo (Morse and Maxwell 1999:125), and Kotiria, have some reduced pronominal forms. Use and analysis of the genitive marker, too, varies greatly. It is alternately analyzed as a suffix (Barnes 1999:218), a prefix (Ramirez 1997a:324), or a noun root (Gomez-Imbert 2011); it is said to be obligatory in some languages, absent in others, and optional in still others. We turn now to the specifics of how possession is coded in Kotiria.

6.4.1 Pronominal possession

Table 6.1 displays the Kotiria pronominal possessive markers, which are quite obviously derived from full personal pronouns (cf. table 4.3).

TABLE 6.1. POSSESSIVE PROCLITICS

	SINGULAR	PLURAL
1ST PERSON	*yʉ* [jʉ]	INC ~*bari* [mãrĩ]
		EXC ~*sa* [sã]
2ND PERSON	~*bʉ* [mũ]	~*bʉsa* [mũʰsã]
3RD PERSON	*to* [to]	*ti* [ti]

With the exception of the first and second person plural forms, possessive pronominal markers undergo both morphological and phonological reductions, becoming monomoraic and losing the second syllable high tone of the independent personal forms; first and second person plural forms undergo phonological reduction (loss of high tone) only (see also §3.6). This phonological reduction entails a loss of independent phonological word status (as discussed in §3.7), since in terms of tone, these markers become part of the phonological word containing the possessed noun. However, they retain a degree of grammatical word status in that nasalization of a possessive pronominal marker does not spread to the possessed root (26). Given such properties, these morphemes are analyzed as having synchronic proclitic status (see also Waltz 2002:188). They are separated by spaces in the first lines of examples, in keeping with the Kotirias' own perception of their status as separate words.

(25) *yʉ phʉkʉ*
    yʉ=phʉk+ʉ́
    1SG.POSS= parent+MASC
    'my father'

(26) *mʉ yaro*
    ~*bʉ=yá+ro*
    2SG.POSS=possession+SG
    'your stuff/things'

(27) to pho'na
     to=~pho'dá
     3SG.POSS=children
     'his/her children'

(28) ti wa'i wãhaina
     ti=wa'í   ~wahá-~ida
     3PL.POSS=fish kill-NOM.PL
     'their catch (of fish)'

We should note, however, that while speakers consistently use the reduced forms in elicited possessive NPs, reduced forms are not always used in natural speech, especially for the first and second person singular forms. Indeed, in the majority of textual occurrences of first or second person possessive constructions, the full pronominal forms *yu'u* and *~bu'u* are used.[4] However, when the same speakers are asked about use of the full or reduced forms, they insist that the reduced forms are correct. As for the three forms that are not morphological reductions, Waltz (2002:189) finds that they too undergo systematic loss of stress, though this is another area in which variation occurs in my data. These variations may indicate dialectal differences or synchronic overlap of paradigms due to an incomplete process of grammaticalization.

6.4.2 Possession by a noun or NP

The modifier in a possessive or noun-noun relationship can also be another noun (29) or a full NP (30)–(31), juxtaposed to the possessed noun. Like most modifiers, noun or NP possessors precede the possessed head nouns, although, unlike pronominal possessive markers, noun or NP possessors retain phonological independence. Indeed, it is the phonological independence of each constituent in noun-noun possessive constructions that differentiates them from noun compounds (§4.8), which form a single phonological unit.

(29) ka yahiripho'na
     ká   yahíri~pho'da
     monkey   heart
     'a monkey's heart'

---

[4] In examples where this is the case (e.g., (23), (45), and (51) in chapter 5), the full form appears in the glossed line, and the possessive function is indicated in parentheses in the glosses: "1SG(POSS)," "2SG(POSS)."

(30) yɨ mahko manuno
   yɨ=~bak+ó   ~badú+ro
   1SG.POSS=child+FEM husband+SG
   'my daughter's husband'

(31) mɨ mahko to hiro
   ~bɨ=~ba-kó   to=hí+ro
   2SG.POSS=child-FEM 3SG.POSS=COP+SG
   'your daughter's village' (lit., 'your daughter her place/village')

6.4.3 Locative possession: ~baka

In Kotiria, there is a special noun-noun possessive construction that expresses relationships between beings and their places of origin or the places with which they are identified. The head noun is a nominalization (by means of noun class morphology) of the root ~*baka* 'place of origin' (33) or, when the referent is human, 'village', as in ~*baka+ri+ro-pɨ* 'one who is from X, one who belongs to X'. The modifier is the specific place to which the entity is associated, for example *Mõ*, *Mahaphoa*, and *Khanako* in (32), the forest in (33), and the flooded forest in (34). The same root compounded with the distal *-roka* (see §7.5.2) has also been lexicalized as a noun meaning 'jungle', literally 'a far-off origin' (see example (124e) in chapter 7). In (34) we can assume nominalization of ~*baka* by the zero marker of generic or mass nouns such as ~*da'a* 'buriti fruit'. As in constructions involving independent nouns or NPs, the constituents of a locative possession construction are phonologically independent.

(32) a. yɨ'ɨ Mo mahkariropɨ hiha
   yɨ'ɨ ~bó ~baká+ri+ro-pɨ   hí-ha
   1SG   Mõ   village+NOM+SG-LOC   COP-VIS.IMPERF.1
   'I am **from Mõ**.' [A1.2]

   b. pabɨ'se dohkare hira mahaphoa mahkaina khanako mahkaina
   pá-bɨ'se   doká+ré   hí+ra
   ALT-side   below+CLS:generic COP+VIS.IMPERF.2/3
   ~bahápóá   ~baká-~ídá   ~khádákó ~baká-~ídá
   Mahaphoa   village-NOM.PL   Khanako   village-NOM.PL
   'The downriver ones (friends) are **Mahaphoa (Arara Cachoeira) (and) Khanako (Ilha de Inambú) villagers**.' [A3.5]

(33) yɨhkɨkɨ mahkaina yehsea
   yukɨ-kɨ   ~baká-~ídá   yesé+a
   tree-CLS:tree origin-NOM.PL   pig+PL
   'wild pigs' (lit., 'pigs **from the forest**')

(34) na'a wahtoromahka hira
 ~da'á **wató+ró** ~**baká** hí+ra
 buriti.fruit flooded.forest+SG origin COP+VIS.IMPERF.2/3
 'Buriti fruit are **from (grow in) the flooded forest**.' [LSK: Buriti]

6.4.4 The possessive root *ya*

Unlike some Eastern Tukanoan languages, which require the possessive marker *ya* in possessive NPs involving alienable possession (Barnes 1999:218), in Kotiria, any noun can be directly possessed by a pronominal proclitic, another noun, or an NP. Direct possessive modification occurs with all types of head nouns, from kin (35) and body parts (36)–(37) to objects (38)–(39) and abstract nouns (40), with no overt distinction as to alienability.

(35) to namono
 to=~dabó+ro
 3SG.POSS=wife+SG
 'his wife'

(36) to piri
 to=píri
 3SG.POSS=teeth
 'his teeth'

(37) to yahiripho'na
 to=yahíri~pho'da
 3SG.POSS= heart
 'his heart'

(38) to puhka
 to=púka
 3SG.POSS-blowgun
 'his blowgun'

(39) to yʉ'soriphĩkã
 to=yʉ'só+ri-~phi-~ka
 3SG.POSS=cut+NOM-CLS:bladelike-DIM
 'his little knife'

(40) to ma'a
 to=~ba'á
 3SG.POSS=path/river
 'his way (home)'

Nevertheless, Kotiria has a morpheme *ya* [jaá] that occurs in certain possessive-like constructions. There is both phonological and morphological evidence for an analysis of this morpheme not as prefix or suffix, but as a root meaning 'possession' or 'belonging'. First, *ya* has an underlying [−nasal] specification and LHL tone, phonological properties associated with roots but not with suffixes. Secondly, as in compounding constructions but unlike the procliticized possessive pronouns discussed above, *ya* spreads its final L tone over a following root. This is seen in *to ya-wɨ'ɨ-pɨ* [tojáwɨʔɨpɨ] 'his/her/its own house'. Third, *ya* can be the root morpheme in derivations such as those in (41)–(44), (46), and (61)–(63). In other words, though arguably it may have suffix or prefix status in other Eastern Tukanoan languages, *ya* in Kotiria displays all the defining properties of a root morpheme (for analyses of *ya* as a "relational possessive" root morpheme also in Tatuyo and Barasana, see Gomez-Imbert 1982, 1997a).

(41) *to yaro*
 to=yá+ro
 3SG.POSS=possession+SG
 'his/her stuff/things'

(42) *to yahiro*
 to= yá-hi+ro
 3SG.POSS-possession-COP+SG
 'place for his/her personal things'

(43) *kotiria yamahkari*
 kó-ti+ri+a   yá-~baka+ri
 water-VBZ+NOM+PL possession-village+PL
 'Kotiria villages'

(44) *kotiria yame're bu'e hi'na*
 kó-ti+ri+a   *yá=~be're*   *bu'é*   *~hí'da*
 water-VBZ+NOM+PL possession=COM/INST study/learn EXRT
 'Let's study with **our own Kotiria** (language).' (title of the Kotiria children's story book)

Used in a compound with a noun, *ya* emphasizes or reinforces reference within the possessive relationship, yielding the meaning 'possessor's own X' (see also Waltz and Waltz 1997:34). Constructions with *ya* typically occur in situations in which more than one possible referent for the possessed noun could be understood from discourse.

This is seen in (45)–(46), from a narrative. There are two houses mentioned in this text. The first is a little house the protagonist builds for himself out of leaves when he realizes he has become lost in the forest and needs a shelter in which to spend the night (45). The second is his own house, where he lives with his wife. In the story, he builds the little house one day and returns to his own house the next day, after a strange encounter with an evil forest creature during the night. The compound with *ya* in (46) differentiates the second house mentioned—the man's own (permanent) one—from the temporary one he built in the forest.

(45) 1 *to'i dɨ'tesihtotaa. nataa*
 tó+í dɨ'té-sító-tá+á
 REM+LOC chop-MOV.circular-come+ASSERT.PERF
 ~dá-ta+a
 get-come+ASSERT.PERF
 'He went around cutting (leaves). He brought them back.'

 2 *õpari wɨ'ɨkã yoaa*
 ~ó-pá+rí wɨ'ɨ-~ká yoá+a
 DEIC.PROX-ALT+NOM house-DIM do/make+ASSERT.PERF
 'He made a little house, this big (like this).' [A7.21–22]

(46) ... *thuaa te to yawɨ'ɨpɨ*
 thuá+a té to=yá-wɨ'ɨ-pɨ
 return+ASSERT.PERF all.the.way 3SG.POSS=POSS-house-LOC
 '(He grabbed the monkeys, yanked out his knife), (and) went all the way back **home**.' [A7.105]

6.5 Interrogatives

6.5.1 Interrogative nominals

There are three *wh*-interrogative nominals in Kotiria used in questions about people, places, and things: *~doa* [nõã́] 'who', *~do'o-pɨ/~do'o-i* [nõʔṍpɨ́, nõʔṍĩ́] 'where', and *yaba* [jabá] 'what'. Questions about time, 'when', reasons, 'why', and processes, 'how', are verbal constructions described in §11.2.5.

Referents for *~doa* are necessarily human (or humanlike, as evil creatures often are).

(47) *noa hihari tikoro*
 ~doá hí-hari tí-kó+ró
 WH INT.IMPERF ANPH-FEM+SG
 '**Who** is she?'

(48) *noa mɨ'ɨre ya'uri*
~*doá* ~*bɨ'ɨ+ré* *ya'í-ri*
WH   2SG+OBJ   tell-INT
'**Who** told you (something)?'

To ask about a location, Kotiria speakers use the interrogative ~*do'o* with a locative suffix +*i* or -*pɨ*.

(49) *no'oi hihari mɨ'ɨ*
~*do'ó+í*   *hí-hari*   ~*bɨ'ɨ*
WH+LOC   INT.IMPERF   2SG
'**Where** are you from?'

(50) *no'oi hiri nia*
~*do'ó+í*   *hí-ri*   ~*di+a*
WH+LOC   COP-INT   say+ASSERT.PERF
'"**Where** is she?" he asked.' [A4.57]

(51) *no'opɨ sɨri mɨ'ɨ*
~*do'ó-pú*   ~*sɨ-ri*   ~*bɨ'ɨ*
WH-LOC   arrive-INT   2SG
'**Where** did you go?' (lit., 'Where did you arrive [get to]?')

Finally, the interrogative *yaba* 'what' can be used alone to pose a question about an inanimate object (52) or with appropriate nominal morphology to ask about an unspecified animate being, as in (53), where the speaker is speculating about what kind of being(s)—human or otherwise—could be making the strange noise that he hears in the night. In everyday speech, *yaba* also functions as a filler word used when the speaker has momentarily forgotten a word or needs to pause for a moment during speech but plans to continue, much like the English *um*.

(52) *yaba hihari a'ri*
yabá   *hí-hari*   *a'rí*
WH   COP-INT.IMPERF   DEM.PROX
'**What**'s this?'

(53) *yabariro hikari hi'na ni tiro*
yabá+rí+ró   *hí-ka-ri*   ~*hi'da*
WH+NOM+SG   COP-SUPP-INT   EMPH
'**Who/what** (in the world!) could that be?' [A7.28]

6.5.2 Interrogative modifiers

There are also three interrogative modifiers in Kotiria. The first, ~*di* [nĩĩ] 'which', can be the root of derived nominals (54)–(55). It can also function as an independent modifier preceding the head noun (56)–(57). As an independent modifier, like anaphoric and deictic modifiers, ~*di* is morphologically marked for features cross-referencing it to the head noun, such as the animate singular +*ro* in (57). Note that in (54)–(56), ~*di* cooccurs with the root =*ba'ro* 'kind, type'; this implies that the speaker has a specific group of referents in mind, in essence asking 'which of these X?' (56).

(54) *niroba'ro*
 ~*dí+ró=ba'ro*
 WH+SG=kind
 'Which man (of these men) . . . ?'

(55) *nikoroba'ro*
 ~*dí-kó+ró=ba'ro*
 WH-FEM+SG=kind
 'Which woman (of these women) . . . ?'

(56) *niba'ro khiti hoari mɨ'ɨ*
 ~***dí=ba'ro*** *khití hóá-rí* ~*bɨ'ɨ*
 WH=kind story write-INT 2SG
 '**Which** of these stories did you write?'

(57) *nino wiarirore mɨ'ɨ ko wari*
 ~***dí+ró*** *wiá+rí+ró+ré* ~*bɨ'ɨ kó wá-ri*
 WH+SG be.young+NOM+SG+OBJ 2SG water give-INT
 '**Which** child did you give water to?'

To question quantities in Kotiria, one uses modifiers composed of the *wh*-interrogative ~*do'o* and the suffixes -*pe*, indicating a countable quantity, or -*puru*, indicating an uncountable or mass quantity. Thus, the forms ~*do'o-pe* [nõʔṍpe] (58) and ~*do'o-pe-~da* [nõʔṍpenã] (59) are used respectively to inquire about quantities of countable inanimate and animate nouns, while ~*do'o-puro* [nõʔṍpuro] 'how much' is used to inquire about mass quantities (60).

(58) *no'ope bɨhso mɨ'ɨ khɨahari*
 ~***do'ó-pé*** *bɨsó* ~*bɨ'ɨ khɨá-hari*
 WH-CQUANT canoe 2SG hold/have-INT.IMPERF
 '**How many** canoes do you have?'

(59) no'opena mɨ pho'na hihari

   ~do'ó-pé-~dá   ~bɨ=~pho'dá   hí-hari
   WH-CQUANT-PL   2SG.POSS=children   COP-INT.IMPERF

   'How many children do you have?' (lit., 'How many of your children are there?')

(60) no'opuro phayuru mɨ'ɨ yoari

   ~do'ó-púró   phayúrú   ~bɨ'ɨ   yoá-ri
   WH-MQUANT   caixiri.beer   2SG   make/do-INT

   'How much caixiri beer did you make?'

Finally, to ask about the possessor of an object, one uses a expression consisting of the independent interrogative nominal ~doa and the possessive root ya, which can be compounded with a full noun root (61), or take appropriate animate classification morphology (62) or inanimate classifiers (63). Note that the classifier -ria in this interrogative construction is the same one used for rounded objects on numbers.

(61) noa yakhiti hihari

   ~doá yá-khiti   hí-hari
   WH   possession-story   COP-INT.IMPERF

   'Whose story is this?'

(62) noa yairo diero hihari

   ~doá yá-iro   dié+ró   hí-hari
   WH   possession-NOM.SG   dog+SG   COP-INT.IMPERF

   'Whose dog is this?'

(63) noa yaria a'ria bɨhsoka hihari

   ~doá yá-ria   a'rí-(rí)á
   WH   possession-CLS:round   DEM.PROX-CLS:round

   bɨsó-ka   hí-hari
   canoe-CLS:round   COP-INT.IMPERF

   'Whose canoe is this?'

6.6 Descriptive (adjectival) nominalizations

The fifth type of NP modification is that in which nominals derived from stative-adjectival verb roots (§4.5.1) function as descriptive modifiers of other nouns. Unlike the other types of modification addressed so far, the order of constituents in this type of noun-noun modification varies. Adjectival modifiers can precede their heads (64), but more frequently follow (65)–(67).

(64) noapɨkakã phɨ'ɨsekã
 ~dóá-pú-ká~-ká phɨ'ú-sé-~ká
 be.beautiful-CLS:basket-CLS:round-DIM basket-PL-DIM
 '(These are) **beautiful little** baskets.' [Baskets]

(65) mia wa'i dainakãre chɨka tiro
 ~bí+a wa'i dá-~ídá-~ká+ré chú-ka
 sardine+PL fish be.small-NOM.PL-DIM+OBJ eat-ASSERT.IMPERF
 tí+ró
 ANPH+SG
 'It (a bass) eats sardines (and) **small** fish.'[5]

(66) kẽro yoariro hika dahsa
 ~ké+ró yoá+rí+ró hí-ka dasá
 beak+SG be.long+NOM+SG COP-ASSERT.IMPERF toucan
 'Toucans have **long** beaks.' [LSK: Toucans]

(67) tiro chɨka phũri wĩaphũrire
 tí+ró chú-ka ~phú+rí ~wiá-~phú+rí+ré
 ANPH+SG eat-ASSERT.IMPERF leaf+PL be.young-leaf+PL+OBJ
 'It (a howler monkey) eats **green** (lit., 'young') leaves.'[6]

6.7 Multiple modifiers

Kotiria NPs do not commonly contain multiple modifiers. This is not surprising, considering that evaluative and other qualifying elements, such as the diminutive, augmentative, or additive, are coded on the noun itself, and that often the head of an NP will itself be derived from one of the otherwise modifying elements. Furthermore, some combinations would be semantically impossible, such as the cooccurrence of both an exact number and a general quantity marker. Finally, the postnominal position of descriptive (adjectival) modifiers partly resolves what might be a more complicated issue if all types of modifiers preceded the head noun. However, from examples given throughout this chapter, it is clear that number, determiner, quantity (specifically *phayɨ* and *~ka*), and interrogative modifiers all tend to precede the noun within the NP. A few other naturally occurring text examples with multiple modifiers indicate the relative ordering of modifiers shown in figure 6.2. The cooccurrence of determiner and number modifiers in (68) show the ordering of these two types, while (69) and (70) indicate that interrogatives tend to procede other types of modifiers. In (71)–(73) we find pronominally possessed constituents preceded by determiner or num-

---

[5] From the short text that appears as example (118) in chapter 4.
[6] From the short text that appears as example (43) in chapter 9.

ber modification. Recalling that pronominal possession is accomplished by proclitics that form a single phonological unit with the head noun, it is not surprising that this type of possessive construction would form a core unit and that other modifiers would have to occur on the margin. Similarly, although the noun-noun possessive construction in (74) does not form a single phonological word, the juxtaposition of the two nouns in such constructions forms an uninterruptable core semantic unit whose modifiers also occur on its margins.

interrogative	determiners (ANPH/DEIC/ALT)	number; quantity (*phayɨ, ~ka*)	possessor (pronoun/ noun/NP)	NOUN	descriptive; quantity (*pe'ri*)

Figure 6.2. Order of modifiers within the NP.

(68) *tina phɨaro wahchoa*

    tí-~da   *phɨá+ro*   *wachó+a*
    ANPH-PL   two+SG   parrot+PL
    determiner number   N

    'The two (adult) parrots (bring food to their offspring).' [LSK: Parrots]

(69) *do'se a'riro mahsɨro*

    do'sé   *a'rí+ró*   *~basɨ+ro*
    WH   DEM.PROX+SG being+SG
    interrogative determiner   N

    'What kind of being?' [A7.37]

(70) *noa yairo diero hihari*

    ~doá   *yá-iro*   *dié+ró* *hí-hari*
    WH   possession-NOM.SG dog+SG COP-INT.IMPERF
    interrogative possession   N

    'Whose dog is this?'

(71) *tiro to pahkɨpɨ*

    tí+ró   *to=páku-pɨ*
    ANPH+SG 3SG.POSS=body-LOC
    determiner POSS=N

    '(that) his body' [A4.43]

(72) *tiaro to pho'na*
 tiá+ró   to=~pho'dá
 three+SG 3SG.POSS=children
 number   POSS=N
 'her three sons (children)' [A4.41]

(73) *kũiro to mahkuno*
 ~kũ-iró   to=~bak+ũ+ró
 one-NOM.SG   3SG.POSS=child+MASC+SG
 number   POSS=N
 'one of his sons' [A4.20]

(74) *pairo ka yahiripho'nare*
 pá-iro   ká   yahíri~pho'da+re
 ALT-NOM.SG   monkey   heart+OBJ
 determiner   N(possessor) N(possessed)
 'another monkey heart' [A7.64]

7 Verbal semantics and serialization processes

This chapter presents the major semantic classes of verbs in Kotiria. The stative class (§7.1) includes a copula, a verb indicating nonexistence, and verbs expressing possessive, locational, and descriptive or adjectival states, while the nonstative class (§§7.2–7.4) encompasses activity verbs, verbs of motion (including subclasses of directional, relational, and placement verbs), and verbs of perception and mental processes. Two productive processes involving combinations of roots are examined: serialized verb constructions (§7.5), which are commonly used to express adverbial, aspectual, and modal distinctions, and verbs with incorporated nouns (§7.6). Verbs from different semantic classes and subclasses show different behavior in serialized constructions.

7.1 Stative verbs

The division of verbs into stative and nonstative classes can be justified from morphosyntactic evidence. The internal morphology of stative verbal words is generally less complex than that of nonstative verbal words. Moreover, while it is not unheard of for a stative verb root to occur as the initial root in the serialized verb constructions discussed in §7.5, such combinations are rather rare; thus, stative and nonstative verbs tend to have distinct morphological templates (discussed in §8.1).[1]

The stative verbs discussed in this section are the copula *hi* [híí] 'be, exist'; the 'nonexistential' *~badia*; the stative possessive *khɨa* 'hold, have'; locative or positional statives; and finally, adjectival statives. Verbs in this category are prototypically intransitive, requiring only a subject argument (see §10.5.1 for exceptional cases of stative verbs that occur with marked oblique locative arguments).

---

[1] Only a few studies of Eastern Tukanoan languages propose classes of verbs. Morse and Maxwell distinguish between "stative" and "dynamic" verbs in Kubeo (1999:15), and Sorensen (1969:132–34) refers to classes of "stative" and "active" verbs in Tukano. Both these studies justify the distinctions based on morphological templates. In Ramirez's study of Tukano, he identifies the semantic classes of "stative," "position" (stative), "adjectival" (also stative), "active," and "process" verbs, although he later states that the only real distinction occurs in the morphological behavior of stative verbs in auxiliary verb constructions (1997a:95, 152).

7.1.1 Copula: *hi*

The Kotiria copula *hi* has as its closest cognate form the Wa'ikhana copula *ihi*, while in a number of Eastern Tukanoan languages we find variants of ~*(a)di* (Tukano, Tuyuka, Desano, Tatuyo) with both nasality and, like the Wa'ikhana form, an initial *V* syllable.[2] However, a form cognate with the latter, ~*di* [nḭ̃], has been retained in the Kotiria complement construction indicating progressive aspect (see §11.3.2).

The Kotiria copula *hi* is used, first of all, in sentences referring to the permanent states or attributes of concrete or abstract entities (such as the weather in (4)). Copula constructions take nominal predicates, either lexical nouns (1), nouns derived from other nouns (2)–(3), or nominalizations of verbs (4)–(7). In (6) and (7), we find nominals that are first verbalized by -*ti*, and then renominalized by +*ri*, creating nouns meaning 'one who has X'.

(1) *a'riro hira ba'a*
   a'rí+ró   *hí+rá*   *ba'á*
   DEM.PROX+SG COP+VIS.IMPERF.2/3 bass
   'This (one, species of fish) is a bass.'[3]

(2) *yɨ'ɨkhɨ hiha koiro*
   yɨ'ɨ-khɨ   *hí-ha*   *kó-iro*
   1SG-ADD   COP-VIS.IMPERF.1   relative-NOM.SG
   'I am your/a relative.' [A7.39]

(3) *nɨhkɨwãhtiro hia*
   ~*dɨkɨ́-~watí+ró*   *hí+a*
   forest-devil+SG   COP+ASSERT.PERF
   '(He) was a forest devil.' [A7.57]

(4) *siri dahcho hira*
   sí+ri   *dachó*   *hí+ra*
   be.hot+NOM   day   COP+VIS.IMPERF.2/3
   'It's hot.' (lit., 'The day is a hot one.')

(5) *kẽro yoariro hika dahsa*
   ~*ké+ró*   *yóá+rí+ró*   *hí-ka*   *dasá*
   beak+SG   be.long+NOM+SG   COP-ASSERT.IMPERF   toucan
   'Toucans have long beaks.' (lit., 'A toucan is a long-beaked one.')
   [LSK: Toucans]

---

[2] Other languages show even more distinct forms such as ~*ya* (Barasana, Yuruti), *ba/kɨ* (Kubeo), and ~*ara* (Siriano).

[3] Example (1) is from the short text that appears as example (118) in chapter 4.

(6) phoari ñatirirowɨ'rɨ hia tiro
    phoá+rí   ~yá-ti+ri+ro-wɨ'rɨ   hí+a
    hair+PL   be.bad+ATTRIB+NOM+SG-AUG   COP+ASSERT.PERF
    tí+ró
    ANPH+SG
    'He was a large horribly hairy being.' [A7.103]

(7) tiro namotiriro hira
    tí+ró   ~dabó-ti+ri+ro   hí+ra
    ANPH+SG   wife-VBZ+NOM+SG   COP+VIS.IMPERF.2/3
    'He is married.' (lit., 'He is one who has a wife.')

The copula also occurs in sentences referring to permanent (8)–(9) or temporary (10) states of being in a specific spatial or temporal location.

(8) tiro diapɨ hika
    tí+ró   diá-pɨ́   hí-ka
    ANPH+SG   river-LOC COP-ASSERT.IMPERF
    'It (a bass) lives in the river (rather than in streams or in the flooded forest).'[4]

(9) yɨ'ɨ Mo mahkariropɨ hiha
    yɨ'ɨ́   ~bó   ~baká+ri+ro-pɨ   hí-ha
    1SG   Mõ   village+NOM+SG-LOC   COP-VIS.IMPERF.1
    'I am from Mõ.' (lit., 'I am a Mõ-villager.') [A1.2]

(10) tina ti wɨ'ɨ phiriwɨ'ɨpɨ hira
    ti-~da   ti=wɨ'ɨ́   phí+ri-wɨ'ɨ-pɨ
    ANPH-PL   3PL.POSS=house be.big+NOM-house-LOC
    hí+ra
    COP+VIS.IMPERF.2/3
    'They (some women) were in their house, in the longhouse.' [Ancestors]

The copula occurs as the head of the nominalization referring to a village ('place of being') in (11) and as the head of the indefinite temporal hi+a 'once' in (12).

(11) mɨ mahko to hiropɨre
    ~bɨ=~bak+ó   to=hí+ro-pɨ+re
    2SG.POSS=child+FEM   3SG.POSS=COP+SG-LOC+OBJ
    'in your daughter's village' [Baskets]

---

[4] Example (8) is from the short text that appears as example (118) in chapter 4.

(12)   kṹta hia kṹiro mʉno to namonore õse nia
       ~kṹ=ta   **hí**+a   ~kṹ-író   ~bʉ́+ro   to=~dabó+ro+re
       one/a=REF   COP+PL   one/a-NOM.SG   man+SG   3SG.POSS=wife+SG+OBJ
       ~ó-sé   ~dí+a
       DEIC.PROX-be.like   say+ASSERT.PERF
       'Once a man said this to his wife: ....' [A7.3]

Finally, (13)–(15) show that the copula can indicate simple existence.

(13)   tiaro numia hira
       tía+ro   ~dubía   **hí**+ra
       three+SG   women   COP+VIS.IMPERF.2/3
       'There were three women (in the longhouse).' [Ancestors]

(14)   bʉhʉina dainakã ba'aa hika
       bʉhú-~ida   dá-~ídá-~ká   ba'á+á   **hí**-ka
       be.large-NOM.PL   be.small-NOM.PL-DIM   bass+PL   COP-ASSERT.IMPERF
       'There are large and small bass.'[5]

(15)   phanopʉre hiatiga mahsayahkaina
       ~phadó-pʉ+re   **hí**-ati+a
       do/be.before-LOC+OBJ   COP-IMPERF+ASSERT.PERF
       ~basá-yáká-~ídá
       people-steal-NOM.PL
       'In the olden days there were people-stealers.' [A4.1]

Besides occurring in nominalizations referring to spatial or temporal locations, the copula is used in nominalizations referring to beings, for example, the 'one who did X' in (16) or the 'ones who have the property X' in (17), or objects identified by noun classifiers, such as the 'cylindrical thing' in (18). It is also the root for nominalizations with indefinite reference: *hi-phiti+ro* 'everything' (19) and *hi-phiti-~da* 'everyone' (20).

(16)   mʉ'ʉ hikʉ yʉ'ʉre wã'kora
       ~bʉ'ʉ   **hí-kʉ**   yʉ'ʉ́+ré   ~wa'kó+ra
       2SG   COP-(1/2)MASC   1SG+OBJ   wake+VIS.IMPERF.2/3
       'You're **the one** who woke me up.' [A7.129]

(17)   paritʉri hina hira: mahkoa dihsia bʉ'ʉa
       parí-tʉ+ri   **hí-~ida**   hí+ra   ~bakó+a
       shape-CLS:disk+NOM   COP-NOM.PL   COP+VIS.IMPERF.2/3   paku.fish+PL
       disí+á   bʉ'ʉ́+á
       disi.fish+PL   piranha+PL

---

[5] Example (14) is from the short text that appears as example (118) in chapter 4.

'The rounded **ones** (species of fish) are: paku, disi, piranhas . . .' [LSK: Fish]

(18) õpadɨ hidɨ mɨ'ɨre waita
     ~ó-pá-dɨ   **hí-dɨ**
     DEIC.PROX-ALT-CLS:cylindrical.straight   COP-CLS:cylindrical.straight
     ~bɨ'ɨ+ré   wá+i-ta
     2SG+OBJ   give+(1/2)MASC-INTENT
     'I'm going to give you **one** (a previously mentioned magic hunting stick) like this (i.e., this big).' [A7.130]

(19) kɨ̃iro hiatiga to pho'na, namono, hiphitiro
     ~kɨ-író   hí-ati+a   to=~pho'dá   ~dabó+ro
     one/a-NOM.SG COP-IMPERF+ASSERT.PERF 3SG.POSS=children wife+SG
     hí-phiti+ro
     COP-COLL+SG
     'Once there was a man (with) children, a wife, **everything**.' [A5.2]

(20) to namonore hiphitina ya'ua
     to=~dabó+ro+re   **hí-phiti-~da**   ya'ú+a
     3SG.POSS=wife+SG+OBJ COP-COLL-PL tell+ASSERT.PERF
     '(The man) told his wife (and) **everyone** . . .' [A4.9]

7.1.2 Nonexistence: ~*badia*

A common feature of Eastern Tukanoan languages is that they have at least one inherently negative stative verb indicating 'nonexistence' or 'not having'. In Kotiria this verb is ~*badia*, which has nearly exact cognates throughout the family. Cognates are labeled and glossed in different ways in the literature: the Desano cognate *bãra* is glossed as 'not be' (Miller 1999:110), the Tuyuka cognate *bãdĩ* is interpreted as 'not have' (Barnes 1999:220), and the two negative stative verbs in Tukano, *mãrí* and *moó*, are glossed respectively as 'not be/exist' and 'not have/possess' (Ramirez 1997a:154). Example (21), from a conversation between two women, and (22)–(23), from texts, demonstrate uses of this verb in Kotiria.

(21) A: mɨ mahko to hiropure mahchɨ maniari
     ~bɨ=~bak+ó   to=hí+ro-pɨ+re   ~bachú
     2SG.POSS=child+FEM 3SG.POSS=COP+SG-LOC+OBJ leafcutter.ant
     ~badía-ri
     not.exist-INT
     'Aren't there any (edible) ants in your daughter's village?'

B: *ne maniare*
   ~*dé* ~***badía****+re*
   NEG not.exist+VIS.PERF.2/3
   'No, there are none.' [Baskets]

(22) *marire chɨa maniara*
   ~*barí+ré* *chɨa* ~***badía****+ra*
   1PL.INC+OBJ food not.exist+VIS.IMPERF.2/3
   'There isn't any food for us.' [A7.5]

(23) *ne mania to namono*
   ~*dé* ~***badía****+a* *to=~dabó+ro*
   NEG not.exist+ASSERT.PERF 3SG.POSS=wife+SG
   'His wife wasn't there.' [A4.56]

7.1.3 Stative possession: *khɨa*

The verb *khɨa* 'have' codes the state of possession, and is also used, though less frequently, in the semantically related nonstative sense 'hold' (e.g., in (27) below), in accordance with a cross-linguistic tendency for possessive 'have'-type verbs to develop from transitive 'hold'-type verbs. In present-day Kotiria, the same verb can be used to express both meanings, though it is much more frequently used with stative semantics, as in (24)–(26). In (24) and (26) *khɨa* occurs in nominalized constructions.

(24) *naboroa ti sĩ'ari khɨarire*
   ~*dá-boro+a* *ti=~si'á+rí* ***khɨá****+ri+re*
   get-lower+ASSERT.PERF ANPH=torch+PL hold/have+NOM+OBJ
   '(They) took down (from a storage place overhead) the torches they had.' [A4.25]

(25) *ã yoa õse hiare khɨari a'rina*
   ~*a=yoá* ~*ó-sé* *hí+a+re* ***khɨá****-ri*
   so=do/make DEIC.PROX-be.like COP+PL-CLS:generic hold/have-INT
   a'rí-~dá
   DEM.PROX-PL
   'So! These people have ones (baskets) like this?' [Baskets]

(26) *phũria khɨariro hira tiro*
   ~*phurí+a* ***khɨá****+ri+ro* *hí+ra* *tí+ró*
   poison+PL hold/have+NOM+SG COP+VIS.IMPERF.2/3 ANPH+SG
   'It (a pit viper) is extremely poisonous.' (lit., 'It is one having a lot of poison.') [LSK: Snakes]

(27) tiro phichakɨ khɨaa
 tí+ró   phichá-kú   **khɨá**+a
 ANPH+SG shoot-CLS:tree/shaft hold/have+ASSERT.PERF
 'He (the father) had/was holding a shotgun.' [A6.30]

7.1.4 Position

An interesting subset of stative verbs in Kotiria are those that indicate the position of an entity (see also Stenzel forthcoming). The complete set of position verbs is given in (28). Note that 'sit', 'stand', 'lie', and 'be/move inside' can be used both as statives (being in a seated, standing, or lying position; being inside a place) and as nonstatives (assuming a seated, standing, or lying position; moving into a place). The other position verbs are used only statively.

(28)
	~khoa	'be lying, lie'	stative/nonstative
	duhi	'be sitting, sit'	stative/nonstative
	duku	'be standing, stand'	stative/nonstative
	pisa	'be on' (supported on top or horizontal surface)	stative only
	~wa'a	'be leaning' (attached to or supported on a nonhorizontal surface)	stative only
	yosa	'be hanging' (vertically attached)	stative only
	~sa [sãã́]	'be/move inside'	stative/nonstative

The position verbs are exemplified in (29)–(35). They most often occur as the sole inflected verb of a finite clause, but can also occur in nominalized forms (31) and in serializations (34) and (35c). The position verb *duku* 'stand' in serializations such as those in (30) and (32b)—where we see its allomorphic form *-ruku*—codes 'continuous' aspect (see §7.5.2).

(29) diero parisabapɨ khõara
   dié+ró   parí-saba-pɨ   **~khoá**+ra
   dog+SG   form-mud-LOC   be.lying+VIS.IMPERF.2/3
   'The dog is lying in the mud.'

(30) chɨ tu'sɨ tina duhisɨ̃ durukuduhi
   chɨ́ tu'sɨ́   tí-~da   **duhí**-~sɨ   dú-rúkú-dúhi
   eat finish ANPH-PL   sit-arrive   speak-stand-be.sitting
   'As soon as they're done eating, they sit around conversing . . .'
   [A3.14]

(31) dukuriro
dukú+ri+ro
be.standing+NOM+SG
'(some)one standing up'

(32) a. tiro topɨ pihsaga
tí+ró   tó-pɨ   **pisá**+á
ANPH+SG REM-LOC be.on+ASSERT.PERF
'He (a disobedient boy) just stayed up there (on the roof).' [A5.31]

b. to ka'sarore õbaroi pihsarukuga
to=ka'sá+ro+re   ~ó-bá'á+ró+i
3SG.POSS=skin+SG+OBJ DEIC.PROX-do/be.after+SG+LOC
pisá-rúkú+á
be.on-stand+ASSERT.PERF
'His skin (that of a child devoured by evil beings) was there draped (over a windowsill).' [A5.42]

(33) ti hori tãkapɨ wã'ana
ti=hó+rí   ~tá-ká-pɨ   ~**wa'á**+rá
ANPH=drawing+PL rock-CLS:round-LOC be.leaning+VIS.IMPERF.2/3
'The drawings (petroglyphs) are leaning on (carved into the surface of) the rock.'

(34) bahsarɨkata namo thɨ'othuyohsaa
basá-rɨka=ta   ~dabo   thɨ'ó-thu-**yosa**+a
bless-begin=REF repeat hear-think-be.hanging+ASSERT.PERF
'He blessed himself again (and) hung (lying in his hammock) contemplating.' [A6.65]

(35) a. sãtamahari mɨhsa
~sá-tá-~báhá-rí   ~bɨsá
MOV.inside-come-PERMIS-INT 2PL
'Welcome!' (lit., 'Would you like to come in?')

b. topɨ dohparoa yoarose nure sãga tina pe'ri
tó-pɨ   dopá+ró+á   yoá+ró-sé   ~dú-re
REM-LOC bee+SG+PL   do/make+SG-be.like buzz-CLS:generic
~**sá**+a   tí-~da   pé'ri
be.inside+ASSERT.PERF ANPH-PL all
'There inside all of them (evil beings) were buzzing like bees.' [A4.60]

c. *tina nasã chuare chu yoara*

tí-~da	*~dá-~sá*[6]	*chúa+re*	*chú*
ANPH-PL	get-MOV.inside	food+OBJ	eat

yoá+ra
do/make+VIS.IMPERF.2/3

'They take the food inside and eat.' [A3.13]

7.1.5 Adjectival statives

We have seen that Kotiria has no lexical class of adjectives; rather, adjectival notions are expressed by stative verbs of the type 'be green', 'be large', 'be angry', and so on. Such verbs are frequently, though not always, nominalized and occur with the copula, as in (4)–(6) and (14). However, they can also function as inflected finite verbs, as we see in (36)–(37) (see also §3.5 and the examples there).

(36) *mipure sã yakotiria yare bu'ena phiro wahcheha*

~bí-pú+ré	*~sa=yá-ko-ti+ri+a*		*yá-re*
now-LOC+OBJ	1PL.EXC.POSS=POSS-water-VBZ+NOM+PL		POSS-CLS:generic

bu'é-~da	*phí+ro*	**waché-*ha***
study-(1/2)PL	be.big+SG	be.happy-VIS.IMPERF.1

'Now we're very happy to have our own Kotiria learning (writing system or school).' [A8.6]

(37) *tiro kuayu'duawa'aa*

tí+ró	***kuá-yu'du*+*a=wa'a+a***
ANPH+SG	be.frightened-INTENS+AFFEC=go+ASSERT.PERF

'He became very frightened.' [A7.31]

7.2 Activity verbs

Nonstative verbs group into subclasses—activity verbs, verbs of motion, and verbs of sensory perception and mental processes. Each of these groups of verbs performs specific functions in serialized verb constructions (see §7.5).

There is a large, open class of verbs in Kotiria that refer to activities—events or actions such as *~waha* 'kill', *soa* 'grind', *da'ra* 'work', and *chowe* 'vomit'. Activity verbs may be syntactically intransitive (38)–(42), transitive (43)–(48), or ditransitive (49)–(52), and prototypically have agentive subjects (see §§10.2–10.3). In the examples below, the subject of the clause, whatever its transitivity, is marked S, and objects are marked O; for ditransitives, a patient object

---

[6] This verb can also be realized as [sãʔã̀] in noninitial position, with phonetic insertion of a glottal gesture when low tone has spread from the initial root.

(O(pat)) is distinguished from a recipient object (O(rec)). For transitive activity verbs in noninitial position in serialized verb constructions, see §7.5.5.

INTRANSITIVE

(38) 1 khãdɨre yɨ'ɨ da'rai
       ~khadú+ré   [yɨ'ɨ]ₛ   da'rá+i
       yesterday+OBJ 1SG   work+VIS.PERF.1
       'Yesterday I worked.'

    2 tirose'e dahchopuro khãrire
       [tí+ró-sé'é]ₛ   dachó-púró ~kharí+re
       ANPH+SG-CONTR day-MQUANT sleep+VIS.PERF.2/3
       'He, on the other hand, slept all day.'

(39) mɨ'ɨ ba'aphã'are
    [~bɨ'ɨ]ₛ   ba'á-~pha'a+re
    2SG   swim-MOV.across+VIS.PERF.2/3
    'You swam across (a river).'

(40) phirota sañoa masaro yoarose phinonowɨ'rɨ
    phí+ró=ta   ~sayó+a   ~basú+ro
    be.big+SG=REF scream+ASSERT.PERF person+SG
    yoá+ro-se   [~phidó+ro-wɨ'rɨ]ₛ
    do/make+SG-be.like snake+SG-AUG
    'The big [-wɨ'rɨ] snake screamed loudly [phirota] like a person.' [A6.38]

(41) wehsere phi'a chɨka tiro
    wesé+re   phi'á   chú-ka   [tí+ró]ₛ
    garden+OBJ MOV.out.into eat-ASSERT.IMPERF ANPH+SG
    'He (the agouti) goes out into the garden and eats.' [LSK: Agoutis]

(42) mahkɨnakã sohpakapɨ pahpera
    [~bak+ ɨ-~dá-~ká]ₛ sopáka-pɨ papé+rá
    child+MASC-PL-DIM door-LOC   play+VIS.IMPERF.2/3
    'Little children play outside.'

TRANSITIVE

(43) tiro tiaro kayare wãhaa
    [tí+ró]ₛ   [tía+ro   ká-ya+re]ₒ   ~wahá+a
    ANPH+SG three+SG black.monkey-PL+OBJ kill+ASSERT.PERF
    'He killed three monkeys.' [A7.10]

(44) topɨre nuhkɨpɨ hiro wa'ikinare chɨra tiro yairo
[tó-pɨ+re ~dukú-pú hí+ro
REM-LOC+OBJ jungle-LOC COP+SG
wa'í-~kídá+ré]ₒ chú+ra   [tí+ró   yaí+ró]ₛ
animal-PL+OBJ   eat+VIS.IMPERF.2/3 ANPH+SG jaguar+SG
'The jaguar eats animals living there in the jungle.' [A10.3]

(45) phinonowɨ'rɨ tirore chowerɨkaa
[~phiró+ró-wɨ́'rɨ́]ₛ [tí+ró+ré]ₒ   chówe-rɨka+a
snake+SG-AUG   ANPH+SG+OBJ vomit-begin+ASSERT.PERF
'The big snake began to vomit him (the dog) up.' [A6.36]

(46) a'rithure hoaha sã kotiria
[a'rí-thú+ré]ₒ   hoá-ha   [~sá
DEM.PROX-CLS:stacked+OBJ write-VIS.IMPERF.1 1PL.EXC
kó-ti+ri+a]ₛ
water-VBZ+NOM+PL
'We Kotiria are writing this book.' [A8.8]

(47) wihsoa chɨka bɨhtiaditare
[~wisó+á]ₛ   chú-ka   [bɨtí+a-dita+re]ₒ
squirrel+PL   eat-ASSERT.IMPERF be.hard+PL-SOL+OBJ
'Squirrels eat hard things only.' [LSK: Squirrels]

(48) tiro ba'ro mahsare wa'ikinare wa'a sɨ wimika
[tí+ró=ba'ro]ₛ [~basá+ré   wa'í-kídá+ré]ₒ wa'á-~sɨ
ANPH+SG=kind   people+OBJ animal-PL+OBJ   go-arrive
~wibí-ka
suck-ASSERT.IMPERF
'This kind (of insect) lands on people and animals and sucks (their blood).' [A9.2]

DITRANSITIVE

(49) mɨ'ɨ yahiripho'nare yɨ'ɨre waga
[~bɨ'ɨ=yahíri~pho'da+re]ₒ₍pat₎ [yɨ'ɨ+ré]ₒ₍rec₎ wá+gá
2SG(POSS)=heart+OBJ   1SG+OBJ   give+IMPER
'Give me your heart.' [A7.43]

(50) tirore tɨre waa
[tí+ró+ré]ₒ₍rec₎ [tɨ́+re]ₒ₍pat₎ wá+a
ANPH+SG+OBJ   stick+OBJ   give+ASSERT.PERF
'He gave him the stick.' [A7.138]

(51) yɨ'ɨ wa'ire do'abosaita mɨ'ɨre
[yɨ'ú]s [wa'í+ré]O(pat) do'á-bósá+i-tá [~bɨ'ú+ré]O(rec)
1SG fish+OBJ cook-BEN+(1/2)MASC-INTENT 2SG+OBJ
'I'm going to cook the fish for you.'

(52) tirore topɨ khiti ya'ua
[tí+ró+ré]O(rec) [tó-pɨ]O(pat) khití ya'ú+a
ANPH+SG+OBJ REM-LOC story tell+ASSERT.PERF
'There (they) told him the story.' [A4.50]

7.3 Motion verbs

There are many verbs in Kotiria that express different kinds of physical motion. Besides the most basic subset, one subset includes verbs expressing inherently directional movement in relation to topographical features: 'uphill', 'upriver', 'downhill', or 'downriver'. Another subset of verbs indicates relational movement such as 'out of', 'into', 'across', or 'toward' a referential spatial point, while another is composed of verbs that indicate different types of placement or positioning. The semantic functions of motion verbs in serial verb constructions are discussed in §§7.5.1–7.5.2 below.

7.3.1. Basic motion verbs: *wa'a* 'go' and *ta* 'come'

The most basic and most frequently occuring motion verbs are *wa'a* 'go', and *ta* [taá][7] 'come', which code translocative motion (away from the speaker or reference point) and cislocative motion (toward the speaker or reference point) (Mithun 1999:139).[8] Examples of these verbs used as the initial roots in verbal words are seen in (53)–(55) for *wa'a* and in (56)–(59) for *ta*. Frequently *wa'a* is reduplicated as *wa'a-wa'a* to mean 'go far away'; in the context of (55) we can understand it to mean 'escape'.

(53) su'aropɨre wa'aeraatiga
su'á+ro-pɨ+re wa'a-éra-ati+ga
go.into.woods+SG-LOC+OBJ go-NEG-IMPERF+IMPER
'Don't be going into the woods.' [LSK: Snakes]

---

[7] This verb can also be realized as [tàʔà] in noninitial position, with phonetic insertion of a glottal gesture where there is spread of low tone from the initial root.

[8] In some of the literature on Eastern Tukanoan languages (e.g., Ramirez 1997a), such verbs are also labeled as "centrifugal" and "centripetal" respectively.

(54)　*to manɨno pasepɨ wa'aa*
　　to=~badɨ́+ro　　　　*pá=se'e-pɨ*　　*wa'á+a*
　　3SG.POSS=husband+SG　ALT=CONTR-LOC　go+ASSERT.PERF
　　'Her husband went off someplace.' [A5.5]

(55)　*sa nimaa wa'awa'a hi'na, ñaina hira*
　　sá　　*~di-~ba+a*　　　　　*wa'á-wa'a*　*~hi'da*
　　EXRT　say-FRUST+ASSERT.PERF　go-go　　　EXRT
　　~yá-~ida　　*hí+ra*
　　be.bad-NOM.PL　COP+VIS.IMPERF.2/3
　　'She urged (in vain), "Let's get out of here! These are evil beings."'
　　[A5.28–29]

(56)　*kɨ̃iro taro koataa sõ'oba'ropɨ*
　　~kɨ́-író　　*tá+ro*　　*koá-ta+a*
　　one-NOM.SG　come+(3)SG　NONVIS-come+ASSERT.PERF
　　~so'ó-bá'á+ró-pɨ
　　DEIC.DIST-do/be.after+SG-LOC
　　'(From somewhere in the distance) someone was approaching (he
　　　heard it).' [A7.27]

(57)　*koro tachɨ dura*
　　kó+ro　　*tá-chɨ*　　　　*dú+ra*
　　water+SG　come-SW.REF　talk+VIS.IMPERF.2/3
　　'(Frogs) croak when it rains.' [LSK: Frogs]

(58)　*numia ña'aina taa nia koatara*
　　~dubí+a　　*~ya'á-~ida*　*tá+á*　　*~dí+a*
　　woman+PL　catch-NOM.PL　come+(3)PL　be.PROG+(3)PL
　　koá-ta+ra
　　NONVIS-come+VIS.IMPERF.2/3
　　'Women-kidnappers are coming.' (the speaker hears them) [Ancestors]

(59)　*yɨ'ɨ tirore wãhakha'mai tai niha*
　　yɨ'ɨ　*tí+ró+ré*　　*~wahá-~kha'ba+i*　　*tá+i*
　　1SG　ANPH+SG+OBJ　kill-want+(1/2)MASC　come+(1/2)MASC
　　~di-ha
　　be.PROG-VIS.IMPERF.1
　　'I'm coming here to avenge him.' [A6.61]

After 'go' and 'come', the most frequently used motion verbs are those that refer to types of generic movements that occur in many different contexts, for instance, *~bɨ(bɨ)* [mɨ̆mɨ̃]~[mɨ̃] 'run, go quickly' (60)–(62), *~tidi* 'wander, walk, move around' (as when people hunt or when animals move from place to place) (63)–(65), *~dɨnɨ* 'follow, chase' (66)–(67), and *sito* 'circular movement, go around doing something, do something here and there' (68)–(69).

(60) *mɨmɨdihawa'a yarokã du'tibɨ wihaa*
~***bubú***-*diha-wa'a*   *yá+ro-~ka*   *du'tí-~bɨ*
run-MOV.downward-go POSS+SG-DIM escape-run
wihá+a
MOV.outward+ASSERT.PERF
'They quickly got down (from their own hammocks and) ran outside to escape.' [Ancestors]

(61) *kũiro dierokã paritarore mɨmɨbɨ'asũ thutia*
~*kú-író*   *dié+ró-~ká*   *parí-taro+re*
one-NOM.SG dog+SG-DIM lake-CLS:lake+OBJ
~***bubú***-*bu'a-~sɨ*   *thutí+a*
run-MOV.downward-arrive bark+ASSERT.PERF
'A little dog ran down to the shore of a lake (and) barked.' [A6.13]

(62) *tina mɨrɨkawa'aka'a sũ ñɨa*
tí-~da   ~***bú***-*rɨka-wa'a-ka'a*   ~*sɨ*   ~*yɨ+á*
ANPH-PL run-begin-go-do.moving arrive see/look+ASSERT.PERF
'They (the sons) went running over (to where their mother was being held captive), got there, (and) looked.' [A4.27]

(63) *dahchore tinika tiro mahkachɨro*
dachó+re ~***tidí***-*ká*   *tí+ró*
day+OBJ wander-ASSERT.IMPERF ANPH+SG
~*baká-chɨ+ro*
look/search.for-eat+(3)SG
'During the day, it (the anteater) goes around searching for food.' [LSK: Anteaters]

(64) *tiro tinika yɨhkɨri bu'ipɨ*
tí+ró   ~***tidí***-*ká*   *yɨkú+ri bu'í-pɨ*
ANPH+SG wander-ASSERT.IMPERF tree+PL top-LOC
'It (a squirrel) moves around up in the treetops.' [LSK: Squirrels]

(65) *ne topɨre tipɨre tinieraha*
~*dé tó-pɨ+re*   *tí-pɨ+re*   ~***tidí***-*éra-ha*
NEG REM-LOC+OBJ ANPH-LOC+OBJ wander-NEG-VIS.IMPERF.1
'I never go hunting there in that place.' [A6.60]

(66) *ti phɨkorore khã'i nɨnɨatiga te topɨ*
ti=phɨk+ó+ró+ré   ~*kha'í* ~***dudú***-*átí+á*
3PL.POSS=parent+FEM+SG+OBJ love follow-IMPERF+ASSERT.PERF

  té   *tó-pɨ*
  all.the.way REM-LOC

 'They loved their mother (and) followed after (her) all the way there (to the place the devil had taken her).' [A4.45]

(67) *diero nɨnɨwa'aka*
  dié+ró ~dɨdɨ́-wa'a-ka
  dog+SG follow/chase-go-ASSERT.IMPERF

  'Dogs chase (them, agoutis).' [LSK: Agoutis]

(68) *ñɨsemahari sihtotaa ti(na). yoaripa nɨnɨsihtotaa*
  ~yɨ́-sé-~báhá+rí
  see/look-be.like-MOV.up/down+NOM

  ***sitó**-ta+a*   *tí-(~da)*
  MOV.circular-come+ASSERT.PERF ANPH-PL

  yoá+rí-pá *~**dɨdɨ́**-sito-ta+a*
  be.long+NOM-time follow/chase-MOV.circular-come+ASSERT.PERF

  'They (the dogs) looked around like this. They chased around for a long time.' [A6.5–6]

(69) *tɨme're mɨ'ɨ wa'ikinawãha sihtotaga*
  tɨ́=~be're *~bɨ'ɨ́* *wa'í-~kídá-~wáhá* ***sitó**-ta+ga*
  stick=COM/INST 2SG animal-PL-kill MOV.circular-come+IMPER

  'With this stick, you go around hunting.' [A7.131]

  Less frequently used motion verbs, such as *~sio* 'slide', *wɨ* [wɨ́ɨ] 'fly', and *ba'a* 'swim' (70)–(72), are more contextually dependent.

(70) *a'riase sĩomɨ wihatanokaa*
  a'rí+á-sé *~sió-~bɨ́*
  DEM.PROX+PL-be.like slide-run

  wihá-ta-~doka+a
  MOV.outward-come-COMPL+ASSERT.PERF

  'It (the snake) came sliding out (of its hiding place) like this.' [A6.37]

(71) *a'ria wɨria wɨka minichakã yoarose*
  a'rí+á *wɨ́-ria*   *wɨ́-ka*
  DEM.PROX+PL fly-CLS:round.elongated fly-ASSERT.IMPERF

  ~bidícha-~ka yoá+ro-se
  bird-DIM do/make+SG-be.like

  'These planes fly like birds.' [A12.2]

(72) *thɨbaamɨ wihawa'aa diapɨ kotĩaropɨ*
  thɨ́-báá-~bɨ́ *wihá-wa'a+a*   *diá-pɨ*
  push-swim-run MOV.outward-go+ASSERT.PERF river-LOC

Verbal semantics and serialization processes 213

kó-~tia+ro-pɨ
water-current+SG-LOC

'She pushed off and quickly swam out into the river current.' [A5.35]

7.3.2 Directional verbs

A small subset of motion verbs in Kotiria indicate movement in a specific direction in relation to topographical features in the landscape, having, in a sense, an inherent goal. These are *~baha* 'go uphill', *yoha* 'go upriver', and *bu'a* 'go downhill or downriver'. These verbs express spatial orientations that are essential in the day-to-day life of the Kotiria. Extensive travel is only possible via waterways, and the Kotiria, like other groups in the Vaupés social system, travel frequently to spend time working gardens or fishing away from their villages, to visit in-laws, to participate in festivals, or to take care of business in larger communities. Part of each community's identity derives from its position on the riverway and in relation to other communities. When travelers pass by on the river or visitors arrive at a community, it is normal for the villagers to immediately identify in what direction on the river they are traveling or the direction from which they arrived; these specifications can imply a wealth of important information.

The origin of the land-based 'up' and 'down' directional verbs lies in the fact that the rivers in the region where the Kotiria live have water levels that fluctuate greatly from season to season—as much as six to seven meters in the annual cycle that includes two periods of flooding and draining (Chernela 1993:88). Hence, communities are strategically established on hills or on land elevated enough so as not to be flooded during the high water season. Furthermore, an essential requirement of an adequate community location is that there be at least one accessible river port nearby. One or more paths from the community lead to the port or ports, and these paths are used continuously throughout the day, as much of the business of daily life, such as washing and bathing, as well as all arrivals and departures, occurs at or near the port. Thus, when a speaker uses verbs such as *~baha* 'go uphill' or *bu'a* 'go down(hill)', one automatically understands the movement to be between the river port and a dwelling, and these need not be explicitly mentioned. Such is the case in (73), from a story (narrative 5 in appendix 1). Evil people-eating beings have arrived at a house in human form, but the woman living there realizes that they are not really human and probably intend to eat her and her children, so she devises a plan to escape. Making up an excuse that she needs to fetch some water with which to wash the fruit they have brought her, she heads to the port with her children and a big basin to use as a raft.

(73) 1 *bu'aa*
       bu'á+á
       go.downhill+ASSERT.PERF
       'She went down (to the port).'

   2 *bu'asɨ̃ tinakãre topɨ pohsaa*
      bu'á-~sɨ́   tí-~da-~ka+re   tó-pɨ
      go.downhill-arrive ANPH-PL-DIM+OBJ   REM-LOC
      posá+a
      fill+ASSERT.PERF
      'When she got down (to the port), she put the little ones in (the basin).' [A5.33–34]

In (74), from another story ("How Our Ancestors Got Women," not included in appendix 1), some men have arrived in a distant village in the middle of the night on a wife-kidnapping mission. From inside the longhouse (always located on higher ground), a woman hears them approaching (from the port downhill).

(74) *kɨ̃koro ti mahatachɨ thɨ'orokaa*
     ~kɨ́-kó+ró   ti=~**bahá**-tá-chɨ́
     one/a-FEM+SG   3PL.POSS=go.uphill-come-SW.REF
     thɨ'ó-róká+á
     hear-DIST+ASSERT.PERF
     '(From inside the longhouse) one woman heard them coming closer.'
     [Ancestors]

7.3.3 Relational motion verbs

There is also a subset of motion verbs indicating movement in relation to a contextually-established reference point. A few examples of such verbs are *phi'a* 'move out into' (75), *~sa* [sãã́] 'move inside' (76)–(77), *wiha* 'move outward' (physical movement by a person) (78)–(79), *~wio* 'move outward from an enclosed space', referring to the man's gaze in (80), and *~pha'a* 'move across' (in (39) above and (120c) below).

(75) *ku'tukãpɨre phi'asɨ̃a*
     ku'tú-~ka-pɨ+re   **phi'a**-~sɨ+a
     clearing-DIM-LOC+OBJ   MOV.out.into-arrive+ASSERT.PERF
     'He went out (of the forest) into a little clearing.' [A7.18]

(76) *ti numiare ña'a toarome're bɨrukuta'a sã ña'aatia*
     ti=~dubí+a+re   ~ya'á toá+ro=~be're
     ANPH=woman+PL+OBJ   catch be.fast+SG=COM/INST

~bú-ruku-ta   ~sá   ~ya'á-ati+a
run-stand-come MOV.inside catch-IMPERF+ASSERT.PERF

'(Men) would kidnap women quickly by surrounding (their longhouse) and then running (inside) to catch them.' [Ancestors]

(77) wʉ'ʉdu'tuka'ai sãma'nota

wʉ'ʉ́-du'tu-ka'a+i   ~sá-~ba'do=ta
house-around-side+LOC MOV.inside-penetrate=REF

'(He) was going a little way into (the brush) around his house . . .' [A7.163]

(78) yoatapʉ wihatu'sʉri hira

yóá-tá-pʉ́   **wihá**-tu'sʉ+ri
be.far-REF-LOC MOV.outward-finish+NOM(INFER)

hí+ra
COP+VIS.IMPERF.2/3

'They've just escaped (from inside the longhouse into the surrounding forest).' [Ancestors]

(79) ti bahtopʉ tikoro wihataga hi'na

ti=bató-pʉ   tí-kó+ró   **wihá**-ta+a
ANPH=be.last-LOC   ANPH-FEM+SG   MOV.outward-come+ASSERT.PERF

~hí'da
EMPH

'Right at the end, the woman finally came out (of the hollow log where she was held prisoner).' [A4.65]

(80) phorerokã wĩoñʉrokaa

phoré+ró-~ká   ~**wió**-~yʉ-roka+a
make.hole+SG-DIM   MOV.outward-see/look-DIST+ASSERT.PERF

'(He made a hole from inside a small shelter with leaf walls), and peered out.' [A7.75]

7.3.4 Verbs of placement

Verbs of placement are a subset of motion verbs that indicate the deliberate placement or (re)positioning of an object or entity, and in this sense can be distinguished from position verbs, which express stative notions. Examples of placement verbs include *boro* 'take down, lower' in (24) above, *dura* 'put over, cover' in (81), *phayo* 'spread out' in (81) and (83), *thua* 'place' in (82), *~daba* 'turn over' in (83), *tui* 'hold in front of, place in front of' in (84), and *~rapo* 'put on (the tip)' in (85).

(81) õba'aroi tirore fantasma duraphayoga
~ó-ba'a+ro+i   tí+ró+ré   fantasma
DEIC.PROX-do/be.after+SG+LOC ANPH+SG+OBJ ghost[B]
durá-**phayo**+a
put.over-spread.out+ASSERT.PERF
'They had spread (a layer of fruit) over the curupira (inside).' [A5.15]

(82) ti kaye thuara poaye wahtopɨ
ti=káyé   **thuá**+rá   poá-yé   wató-pɨ
ANPH=fishtrap place+VIS.IMPERF.2/3   rapids-PL   middle-LOC
'The big fishtrap is built/placed in the middle of the rapids.'

(83) khataro wĩha sɨ'aphayo, ba'aro namahã're phayo yoaha
khatá+ró   ~wihá   sɨ'á-**phayo**   ba'á+ro
flatbread.oven+SG set.afire sift-spread.out   do/be.after+SG
~dabá-~ha-re   **phayó**   yoá-ha
turn.over-TERM-CLS:generic   spread.out   do/make-VIS.IMPERF.1
'We light the (fire under the) oven (and) spread out (the sifted manioc meal used to make) the flatbread, (and) after one has been turned over (finished baking), we spread out (another).' [Manioc]

(84) pakorokãre tuinakaa
pá-ko+ro-~ka+re   **tuí**-~daka+a
ALT-FEM+SG-DIM+OBJ   put.in.front-do/be.together+ASSERT.PERF
'She clasped her little girl to the front (of her body and together they escaped).' [A5.21]

(85) yɨ'soriphĩkã so'towai sĩ'ophĩrãpo ñuiwĩoa
yɨ'só+ri-~phi-~ka   so'tó-wa+i   ~si'ó-~phi-~**rapo**
cut+NOM-CLS:bladelike-DIM   end-go+LOC   pierce-CLS:bladelike-put.on
~yuí-~wio+a
offer-MOV.outward+ASSERT.PERF
'He stuck it (a monkey heart) on the end of his knife (and) offered it out (of the hole).' [A7.65]

7.4 Verbs of sensory perception and mental processes

Like verbs of motion, Kotiria verbs of sensory perception and mental processes form a subclass of nonstative verbs identifiable primarily by the specific functions they perform in serial verb constructions. In this section, we consider the semantics of these verbs as word-initial roots and look at instances of semantic overlap; discussion of their functions in serializations is left for §7.5.4.

The Kotiria verbs of sensory and cognitive perception are listed in (86) and are exemplified in (87)–(95).

(86) ~yʉ   'see, look; realize'
      thʉ'o   'hear, feel'
      thʉ'o-thu 'smell; understand' (lit., 'feel-think')
      koa   'taste, perceive'

(The verb *koa* 'taste, perceive' is also the base of the nonvisual perception evidential *koa-ta*; see below and §9.2.3.)

The most semantically specific perception verb is ~yʉ, denoting visual perception (and also, by extension, to mentally 'see' or 'realize' something). It is generally used transitively, with objects taking the objective case marker +*re* (87)–(88), but we see it used intransitively in its first occurrence in (89).

(87) *ñʉa tirore. phiriro khõaa*
     ~yʉ́+á   tí+ró+ré
     see/look+ASSERT.PERF   ANPH+SG+OBJ
     phí+ri+ro   ~khoá+a
     be.big+NOM+SG   be.lying+ASSERT.PERF
     'He saw him (the curupira). The big guy was lying there.' [A7.101]

(88) *wa'a ñʉa ti khumuwʉ'rʉpʉre*
     wa'á ~yʉ́+á   ti=~khubú-wʉ'rʉ-pʉ+re
     go   see/look+ASSERT.PERF ANPH=log-AUG-LOC+OBJ
     'They went (and) looked at the big log.' [A4.59]

(89) *ñʉbu'aa. ñʉbohkaa*
     ~yʉ́-bú'á+á   ~yʉ́-bóká+á
     see/look-MOV.downward+ASSERT.PERF see/look-find+ASSERT.PERF
     'He looked down. He spotted (it).' [A6.15]

When used on its own, the root *thʉ'o* most commonly denotes auditory perception (90); however, it can also be semantically generalized to other kinds of nonvisual sensory perception such as touch, as in line 2 of (91), and in the serialization *thʉ'o-thu* 'feel-think', it is used to refer to the sense of smell (92).

(90) *kʉ̃koro ti mahatachʉ thʉ'orokaa*
     ~kʉ́-kó+ró   ti=~bahá-tá-chʉ́
     one/a-FEM+SG   3PL.POSS=go.uphill-come-SW.REF

thʉ'ó*-*róká*+*á
hear-DIST+ASSERT.PERF

'(From inside the longhouse) one woman heard them coming closer.' (= (74)) [Ancestors]

(91) 1 *topʉ wãhkuro to duraphayochʉ, tiro kʉamʉa*
    tó-pʉ   ~*wakú*+*ro*   *to*=*durá-phayo-chʉ*
    REM-LOC be.aware+SG 3SG.POSS=put.over-spread.out-SW.REF
    tí+*ró*   *kʉá-*~*bʉ*+*a*
    ANPH+SG be.surprised-run+ASSERT.PERF

'When (the creature hiding in the basket) felt the woman reaching (into the layer of fruit covering him up), he started.'

  2 *tikorokhʉ̃ thʉ'omahsimʉa*
    tí-kó+*ró-*~*khʉ́*   ***thʉ'ó-*~*basi-*~*bʉ*+*a***
    ANPH-FEM+SG-ADD feel-know-run+ASSERT.PERF

'She too could feel it right away.' [A5.16–17]

(92) *wa'iʉrina thʉ'othuha*
    wa'í-~*ʉ́rí-*~*dá*   ***thʉ'ó-thu-ha***
    fish-be.smelly-PL feel-think-VIS.IMPERF.1

'I smell rotten fish.'

Taste is indicated by the root *koa* (93)–(94).

(93) *koiro mʉ'ʉ yahiripho'na noaphitiaro koaka*
    kó-iro   ~*bʉ'ʉ*=*yahíri*~*pho'da*   ~*dóá-phítí*+*á*+*ró*
    relative-NOM.SG 2SG(POSS)=heart be.good-COLL+AFFECT+(3)SG
    koá-ka
    taste-ASSERT.IMPERF

'Relative, your heart tastes really good.' [A7.61]

(94) *to di'i noaro koaka*
    to=*di'í*   ~*dóá*+*ró*   ***koá-ka***
    3SG.POSS=meat be.good+SG taste-ASSERT.IMPERF

'Its (a cow's) meat tastes good.' [LSK: Cows]

This is also the initial root of the evidential marker *koa-ta* that appears in all statements based on direct nonvisual sensory perception (95).

(95) *numia ña'aina taa nia koatara*
    ~*dubí*+*a*   ~*ya'á-*~*ida*   *tá*+*á*   ~*dí*+*a*
    woman+PL catch-NOM.PL come+(3)PL be.PROG+(3)PL

koá-ta+ra
NONVIS-come+VIS.IMPERF.2/3

'Women-kidnappers are coming.' (the speaker hears them) (= (58))
[Ancestors]

Though there is a semantic connection, there is also a major functional difference between the verbs in (86) and the evidential marker *koa-ta*. The four verbs in (86) code the direct perceptions of the subject, while *koa-ta*, as is expected for an evidential, indicates the source of information upon which a speaker bases a statement (see §9.2.3).

Some verbs denoting emotional and cognitive processes include 'love' (96), 'hurt' (97), 'know' (sentence 1 of (98) and (99)), 'forget' (sentence 2 of (98)), 'remember, be aware' (100), 'be concerned, worry about' (101), 'want' (desiderative) (102), and 'wish' (103). Like verbs of sensory perception, most of these can be used both intransitively and transitively; intransitive uses are seen in (97) and (99), and transitive uses in (96), (98), (102), and (103).

(96) ti phᵾkorore khã'i nᵾnᵾti'aga te topᵾ

   ti=phᵾk+ó+ró+ré   ~kha'i   ~dᵾdᵾ-áti+á
   3PL.POSS=parent+FEM+SG+OBJ love   follow-IMPERF+ASSERT.PERF

   té   tó-pᵾ
   all.the.way   REM-LOC

   'They loved their mother (and) followed after (her) all the way there (to the place the devil had taken her).' (= (66)) [A4.45]

(97) phũriyᵾ'dᵾaka

   ~**phurí**-yᵾ'dᵾ+a-ka
   hurt-INTENS+AFFEC-ASSERT.IMPERF

   'It hurt a lot.' [A7.78]

(98) 1 mahsieraha yᵾ'ᵾ

      ~**basi**-éra-ha   yᵾ'ᵾ
      know-NEG-VIS.IMPERF.1   1SG

      'I don't know (any kinds of traditional Kotiria songs and dances).'

   2 boerakᵾrᵾ tire

      bo-éra-kᵾrᵾ   tí+re
      forget-NEG-ADVERS   ANPH+OBJ

      'I've forgotten them (unfortunately).' [A3.19–20]

(99) ne yᵾ'ᵾ mahsierako niha

   ~dé   yᵾ'ᵾ   ~**basi**-éra-ko   ~dí-ha
   NEG   1SG   know-NEG-(1/2)FEM   say-VIS.IMPERF.1

   'I don't know anything to say.' (female speaker) [Baskets]

(100) *ahiriro hiri hire. wahkũmahsiga tore*
   ahí+ri+ro   hí+ri   hí+re
   worry+NOM+SG COP+NOM(INFER) COP+VIS.PERF.2/3
   ~wakú-~bási+gá   tó-re
   be.aware-know+IMPER REM-CLS:generic
   '(It seems) there's a dangerous (worrisome) being in that place. (You should) be careful [*~waku*] there.' [A6.67–68]

(101) *ne ahikɨ nieraa topɨ*
   *~dé **ahí-kɨ**   ~di-éra+a   tó-pɨ*
   NEG be.concerned-(1/2)MASC be.PROG-NEG+ASSERT.PERF REM-LOC
   'He was there, concerned about nothing.' (or '... concerned about no one.') [A4.17]

(102) *tikoro, to namono, chɨduaatiga wahsore*
   *tí-kó+ró   to=~dabó+ro   chú-**dua**-ati+a*
   ANPH-FEM+SG 3SG.POSS=wife+SG eat-DESID-IMPERF+ASSERT.PERF
   wasó+ré
   siringa.fruit+OBJ
   'The woman, his wife, wanted to eat (had a craving for) siringa fruit.' [A5.3]

(103) *yɨ'ɨ wahsore chɨduamaka*
   *yɨ'ɨ   wasó+ré   chú-**dua**-~ba-ka*
   1SG siringa.fruit+OBJ eat-DESID-FRUS-ASSERT.IMPERF
   'I wish I had some siringa fruit to eat.' [A5.4]

The semantic overlap between verbs of perception and mental processes is clear in the use of *~yɨ* 'see' in the sense of 'realize' (104) and *thɨ'o* 'hear' in the sense of 'understand' (105).

(104) *bo'reka'achɨ ñɨ hi'na tiro wihaa*
   *bo'ré-ka'a-chɨ   ~**yɨ**   ~hí'da tí+ró*
   be.light-do.moving-SW.REF realize EMPH ANPH+SG
   wihá+a
   MOV.outward+ASSERT.PERF
   'When he realized it was morning, he went out (of his shelter).' [A7.100]

(105) *mari thɨ'oera*
   *~barí   **thɨ'o**-éra*
   1PL.INC hear-NEG
   '(If she speaks in another language), we won't hear (understand) ...' [Baskets]

7.5 Common verb serialization constructions

Serialized verb constructions (SVCs)—also referred to in some of the literature on Eastern Tukanoan languages as "independent-dependent" or "nuclear-satellite" root compounding—are a common and widely recognized feature of all Eastern Tukanoan languages (Sorensen 1969; Kaye 1970; Gomez-Imbert 1988, 2007a; Miller 1999; Ramirez 1997a; Stenzel 2007b). Most of the discussion about verb compounding or SVCs in Eastern Tukanoan languages has revolved around the semantic relations between verbs in SVCs and the resulting readings of such constructions. Kaye's analysis of Desano (1970:75–76), for example, points out that a serialization with the desiderative *dia* such as *waa-dia* (go-want) should be understood as 'want to go', with the second verb functioning as the semantic head. Miller's analysis of the same language (1999:100), on the other hand, argues that the leftmost root in a compound is always both the phonological and the semantic head, so a combination such as *ãĩ-bũhũ* (carry-cause.to.ascend), should be read as 'carry up'. Ramirez (1997a:182) claims exactly the opposite analysis for Tukano; he views each root in a serialization as complementing the root to its right. In a two-root combination, the leftmost, "independent," root (in Ramirez's terminology), though the phonological head of the combination, is the semantic complement to the noninitial "dependent" root, so that a serialization such as *oho-mií* (dive-take.out) should be read as 'take out (by) diving.' Ramirez does point out, however, that serializations involving motion or position verbs in noninitial position should be interpreted as simultaneous, so that a combination such as *ba'â-siha* (eat-walk) can be understood to express either 'to eat (while) walking' or 'to walk (while) eating'.

Gomez-Imbert's (1988) analysis of multiple verb constructions in Tatuyo and Barasana was the first to recognize that the semantic interpretation of SVCs in Eastern Tukanoan languages depends on both the syntactic properties of the verbs involved and the linear sequence of roots. Certain types of verb serializations—typically those involving transitive verb roots—express iconic cause-effect relationships in which the sequential order of roots corresponds to the referential chronology, as in Tatuyo *páá-wáá* (hit-divide.in.half), interpreted as 'to hit something round, dividing it in two'. Readings of simultaneous relationships result from serializations involving intransitive motion verbs, as in Barasana *yí-~tíbá* (do-be.fast), understood as 'do quickly'. Finally, in some serializations involving intransitive activity or postural verbs, the sequential order of the elements appears to express an inverse chronological order, so that Tatuyo *wéé+atí* (paddle-come), should be understood as 'to come (by) paddling.'

These different readings are determined by the transitivity of the roots and whether they are oriented to the subject or object of the clause. Direct or iconic relationships obtain when (in Gomez-Imbert's terminology) both the "nuclear" (initial) and "satellite" (noninitial) roots are transitive and oriented to the object. Simultaneous relationships obtain when the noninitial root is intransitive (thus having no effect on the valency of the initial transitive or intransitive root) and unoriented, meaning that the noninitial root merely indicates some spatial, aspectual, or adverbial modification of the initial root. Inverse relationships obtain in two kinds of serializations. First, inverse readings result from serializations involving intransitive 'go' and 'come' motion verbs; these verbs are oriented to the subject of transitive or intransitive initial verbs and have no effect on valency. Second, inverse readings obtain in serializations with transitive modal 'know' and 'order' verbs: serializations with 'know' leave the valency of the initial verb unaffected, while serializations with 'order' can modify it. Serializations with modal 'know' and 'order' verbs share an orientation to the subject of the initial verb (Gomez-Imbert 1988:100–106).

The types of relationships that Gomez-Imbert identifies in Tatuyo and Barasana fall within the parameters proposed in recent typologies of verb-serializing languages. Gomez-Imbert (2007a) concludes that SVCs in Eastern Tukanoan languages can be typologically classified as syntactically "nuclear" (a marked tendency in verb-final serializing languages, according to Foley and Olson [1985:45]), linearly "contiguous" and phonologically "incorporating" (in the terms outlined by Durie [1997:202–3]), and having the possibility of both "symmetric" and "assymetric" formulations (as defined by Aikhenvald [2006:21–37]).

Serialization is a highly productive component of Kotiria verbal morphology and is worthy of detailed examination. The most common serializations, discussed in the following sections, involve combinations of activity verbs and motion or postural verbs expressing adverbial, aspectual, and modal information. Serializations coding intensification and change of state are discussed respectively in §8.3 and §8.5.2.

The principal identifying syntactic and phonological features of Kotiria SVCs are the following (drawing on the discussions of Foley and Olson 1985; Durie 1997; Aikhenvald 2006; and Gomez-Imbert 2007a):

- SVCs contain two or more contiguous verb roots occurring with a single set of grammatical markers (e.g., of person, aspect, polarity, evidentiality or other clause modality) and forming a single phonological word, the domain of suprasegmental spreading processes.

Verbal semantics and serialization processes 223

- SVCs are monoclausal, packaging information so that it is presented as a single conceptual event; as such, there is a single, shared set of core arguments.

- SVCs contrast with other multiple verb constructions such as verb sequences or verbs requiring nominalized or other types of clausal complements (see §11.6).

- Though highly productive, many frequently occurring SVCs show signs of lexicalization and grammaticalization.

Most serializations in Kotiria involve two roots, though serializations of three or more roots—most often involving motion verbs—are not uncommon. In the present discussion, the terms "initial" and "noninitial" are used to refer to the linear positions of roots involved in serializations. The initial root occurs in leftmost position; as such it becomes the phonological head of the word and all other serialized roots are integrated into the domain of tonal spread from the phonological head root (the negator is an exception; see §8.2). Roots occurring in noninitial position in SVCs may belong to the class of "independent roots" (those that can occur as initial roots), or to the class of "dependent roots" (which only occur in noninitial position). In either case, the semantic interpretation of the multiple constituents of a SVC is combinatory, with each root contributing to the construction of a new semantic amalgam. The information that roots in noninitial position bring to SVCs may be a fairly transparent reflection or extension of their semantics as independently occurring roots, but this is not necessarily the case. The underlying semantics of noninitial roots are often partially bleached, so that the semantic result of the combination cannot be easily surmised, as the following sections will demonstrate.

7.5.1 Motion verbs coding direction or manner

As is the case in many languages with serializing constructions (Foley and Olson 1985:41; Aikhenvald 2006:22), in Kotiria we find that motion verbs are among the most common constituents. An intransitive motion verb can combine with virtually any nonstative transitive or intransitive root without affecting its underlying argument structure. The primary function of motion verbs in serializations is to code information about the manner in which the event expressed by the initial root occurs or the direction that it follows.

The most frequently occurring serializations of this type in Kotiria involve the motion verbs *wa'a* 'go' and *ta* 'come'. As noninitial verbs in SVCs, *wa'a* in (106) and *ta* in (107) indicate that the action of the initial root was accomplished while physically moving away from (translocative motion) or toward (cislocative motion) the speaker or other fixed reference point (for other functions of *wa'a* in serializations with stative verb roots, see §8.5.2).

(106)   *pihtamapʉ bu'awa'aga*

   pitá-~ba-pʉ   bu'á-wa'a+a
   port-river-LOC go.downhill-go+ASSERT.PERF

   'They headed down to the river port (from their house).' [A5.22]

(107)   *ti bahtopʉ tikoro wihataga hi'na*

   ti=bató-pʉ   tí-kó+ró   wihá-ta+a
   ANPH=be.last-LOC ANPH-FEM+SG MOV.outward-come+ASSERT.PERF

   ~hí'da
   EMPH

   'Right at the end, the woman finally came out (of the hollow log).' (= (79)) [A4.65]

Another extremely common serialization involving either *wa'a* or *ta* has as its initial verb *~da* [nã́ã́] 'get' or 'carry' (essentially, taking or having something in one's hands). Such serializations result in the notions 'bring' (108)–(109) and 'take' (110)–(111).

(108)   *mʉ'ʉ chʉduare natai*

   ~bʉ'ʉ=chʉ́-dua+re   ~dá-ta+i
   2SG(POSS)=eat-DESID+OBJ   get-come+VIS.PERF.1

   '(We) brought what you wanted to eat.' [A5.10]

(109)   *to'i dʉ'tesihtotaa. nataa*

   tó+i   dʉ'té-sító-tá+á
   REM-LOC chop-MOV.circular-come+ASSERT.PERF

   ~dá-ta+a
   get-come+ASSERT.PERF

   'He went around cutting (leaves). He brought them back.' [A7.21]

(110)   *familiare wehsewa'ainare no'oi wa'ainare yahka, nawa'aka'aa te mahkarokapʉre*

   familia+re   wesé-wa'a-~ida+re   ~do'ó+i   wa'á-~ida+re
   family₍ᵦ₎+OBJ garden-go-NOM.PL+OBJ   WH+LOC   go-NOM.PL+OBJ

   yaká ~dá-wa'a-ka'a+a   té
   steal get-go-do.moving+ASSERT.PERF all.the.way

   ~baká-róká-pʉ́+ré
   origin-DIST-LOC+OBJ

   'They would steal (kidnap) families going to their gardens (or) people going anywhere (and) carry them off into the jungle.' [A4.4]

(111) wa'ikinawãharo wa'aro, ture nawa'aka'a
 wa'í-~kídá-~wáhá+ró   wa'á+ro   tú+re   ~dá-wa'a-ka'a
 animal-PL-kill+(3)SG   go+(3)SG   stick+OBJ   get-go-do.moving
 'When he went hunting, he took the (magic) stick along . . .' [A7.155]

However, these same 'go' and 'come' motion verbs can be productively serialized with any number of verb roots—including an occasional adjectival stative root, such as 'be angry' in (114)—to indicate the spatial direction or orientation of the action (see also (106) above).

(112) tiro dierore wahawa'aka'a sõ'oba'aropu
 tí+ró   dié+ró+ré   wahá-wa'a-ka'a
 ANPH+SG   dog+SG+OBJ   pull-go-do.moving
 ~so'ó-bá'á+ró-pú
 DEIC.DIST-be.after+SG-LOC
 'He dragged the dog off a little way . . .' [A6.49]

(113) ñamire pihsuga nichu, ti orare wãhtiro pihsutaga
 ~yabí+ré   pisú+gá   ~dí-chu   ti=ora+re   ~watí+ró
 night+OBJ   call+IMPER   say-SW.REF   ANPH=hour[B]+OBJ   devil+SG
 pisú-ta+a
 call-come+ASSERT.PERF
 'If you told (someone) to call at night, a devil called (instead) at that hour.' [A4.69]

(114) tire thu'o, tiro suataa te ti ka'apu
 tí+ré   thu'ó   tí+ró   suá-ta+a
 ANPH+OBJ   hear   ANPH+SG   be.angry-come+ASSERT.PERF
 té   ti=ka'á-pu
 all.the.way   ANPH=near-LOC
 'When (the man) heard that, he raged off (into the forest) until he was there beside it (the log where his wife was being held captive).' [A4.54]

A 'go' or 'come' root can also be serialized with another motion verb root, as in *~baha-ta* 'come uphill' (74), *wiha-ta* 'come out of something' (79), and *~dudu-wa'a* 'go chasing after something' (115).

(115) nunuwa'aka'a tina
 ~dudú-wa'a-ka'a   tí-~da
 follow/chase-go-do.moving   ANPH-PL
 'They (the dogs) went chasing after it (an animal).' [A6.4]

Unlike *wa'a* and *ta*, independent roots that can also occur in non-initial position, there are motion verbs used in serializations to add adverbial-type information that only occur in noninitial position. One such verb is -*ka'a*, indicating that the action is done 'while moving continuously'. It frequently occurs as the final constituent in three-root serializations that include a motion verb, such as those in (110), (111), (112) and (115) above and (125a) below. When -*ka'a* is serialized with a nonmotion verb, it adds the more temporal notion of an action done 'immediately', as in (116) and in (131) below.

(116)   *chɨroka'aro koataa*

   chɨ+ro-ka'a+ro   *koá-ta+a*
   eat+SG-do.immediately+(3)SG   NONVIS-come+ASSERT.PERF

   '(The man could hear) the curupira eating it right away.' [A7.59]

Other commonly serialized motion verbs, for instance, *sito* and ~*bɨbɨ*, have slightly altered semantics when they occur in noninitial position in SVCs. For instance, as an independent verb, *sito* means 'move in a circular fashion' or 'run around' (68)–(69); in noninitial position in a serialization, it functions as a distributive, indicating that the action of the initial verb is repeated 'here and there' or that the subject 'goes around doing X'. (For the sake of consistency and to maintain morpheme identity, all roots are glossed according to their underlying or basic meaning. Alternate or additional semantics of verbs in noninitial position are included in the vocabulary list in appendix 2.)

(117)   *ñɨsemahari sihtotaa ti(na). yoaripa nɨnɨsitotaa*

   ~*yɨ-sé-~báhá+rí*
   see/look-be.like-MOV.up/down+NOM

   sitó-ta+a   *tí(-~da)*
   MOV.circular-come+ASSERT.PERF   ANPH-PL

   yoá+rí-pá   ~*dɨdɨ-sito-ta+a*
   be.long+NOM-time   follow/chase-MOV.circular-come+ASSERT.PERF

   'They (the dogs) looked around like this. They chased around for a long time.' (= (68)) [A6.5–6]

(118)   *to'i dɨ'tesihtotaa*

   tó+i   *dɨ'té-sitó-tá+á*
   REM-LOC   chop-MOV.circular-come+ASSERT.PERF

   'He went around cutting (leaves).' (from (109)) [A7.21]

As an independent verb, ~*bɨbɨ* means 'run; go quickly', but when it occurs in noninitial position, it has the more general meaning 'do X quickly'. It is also often phonologically reduced in form to ~*bɨ*, as we see in (119). In this sentence, ~*bɨbɨ* occurs first as a fully formed independent root and later as a reduced form -~*bɨ* in noninitial position.

(119) *mɨmɨdihawa'a yarokã du'tibɨ wihaa*
    ~***bɨbɨ***-*diha-wa'a*   *yá+ro-~ka*   *du'tí-~**bɨ***
    run- MOV.downward -go POSS+SG-DIM escape-run
    wihá+a
    MOV.outward+ASSERT.PERF
    'They quickly got down (from their own hammocks) and ran outside to escape.' (= (60)) [Ancestors]

A sample of relational motion verbs that exemplifies their manner-type semantics when used in SVCs is given in (120).

(120) a. *-~ba'do* 'move into, penetrate'
      sãma'no
      ~sá-~ba'do
      be.inside-MOV.into
      'reaching into (something)'

    b. *-diha* 'move down from, get down from'
      mɨmɨdiha
      ~bɨbɨ-diha
      run-MOV.downward
      'quickly getting down (from something like a hammock)'

    c. *-~pha'a* 'move across'
      mɨmɨphã'a
      ~bɨbɨ-~pha'a
      run-MOV.across
      'run crossing'

    d. *-~sa/-~sa'a* 'move inside'
      mɨmɨsã'a
      ~bɨbɨ-~sa'a
      run-MOV.inside
      'run entering'

    e. *-bu'a* 'move downward'
      ñɨbu'a
      ~yɨ́-bɨ́'á
      see/look-MOV.downward
      'looking down'

f. -~tidi 'do repeatedly'
ñutini
~yɨ́-~tídí
see/look-wander
'go visiting'

g. -~wio 'move outward'
ñuwĩo
~yɨ́-~wíó
look-MOV.outward
'looking out'

Finally, like other motion verbs discussed so far, position verbs and verbs of placement can be used in SVCs to express the manner in which an action was accomplished. In (121), the action of getting the torches involves 'lowering', indicated by the serialized verb *boro*. (122) describes one step in the process of 'flatbread-making', which involves distributing sifted manioc meal evenly onto a large flatbread "oven" (actually more like a huge metal skillet). When done in the proper manner, this sifted manioc meal should be 'evenly spread out', as the verb *phayo* in the serialization indicates. Finally, in (123), the manner in which the woman gets her child is by raising him up to carry him, as indicated by the serialization with the verb *wɨa*.

(121) *naboroa ti sĩ'ari khɨarire*

~dá-**boro**+a   ti=~si'á+rí   khɨá+ri+re
get-lower+ASSERT.PERF   ANPH=torch+PL hold/have+NOM+OBJ

'(They) took down (from a storage place overhead) the torches they had.' (= (24)) [A4.25]

(122) *khataro wĩha sɨ'aphayo, ba'aro namahã're phayo yoaha*

khatá+ró   ~wihá   sɨ'á-**phayo**   ba'á+ro
flatbread.oven+SG   set.afire sift-spread.out do/be.after+SG

~dabá-~ha-re   phayó   yoá-ha
turn.over-TERM-CLS:generic spread.out do/make-VIS.IMPERF.1

'We light the (fire under the) oven (and) spread out (the sifted manioc meal used to make) the flatbread, (and) after one has been turned over (finished baking), we spread out (another).' (= (83)) [Manioc]

(123) *to mahkɨrokãre nawɨarɨkaga*

to=~bak+ɨ+ró-~ká+ré   ~dá-**wɨá**-rɨká+á
3SG.POSS=child+MASC+SG-DIM+OBJ get-carry-begin+ASSERT.PERF

'She picked up (grabbed) her little boy.' [A5.20]

The examples in this section show that various types of verbs of motion in serializations attach a specification of direction or manner to the action of the initial verb. In serializations of two (or more) motion verbs, the result is a refined fusion of the separately-specified motions into a single, more detailed action.

7.5.2 Aspectual functions of noninitial verbs

A second major function of SVCs in general is to code an internal aspectual quality of an action or state: its inception, completion, repeated or durative realization, or its direct relation to a temporal reference point. Noninitial verbs coding aspectual distinctions often, though not invariably, come from the semantic classes of motion and stative position verbs.

The most commonly occurring noninitial roots with aspectual functions are listed and exemplified in (124)–(128). The first three roots, -*ruku* (the word-internal allomorph of *duku*), -*rʉka*, and -*roka*, all undergo an interesting phonological reduction in noninitial position: there is nearly complete devoicing of the vowel before the voiceless /k/, resulting in what sounds like a consonant cluster [rʰk].[9] This regular phonological reduction and the fact that these roots in their noninitial, aspectual uses begin with [r] rather than [d] are indications of grammaticalization.[10] As these roots grammaticalize further, it is likely that the first-syllable vowels will be completely lost and, given the restrictions on consonant clusters in Kotiria, that the initial [r] will also eventually erode. Synchronically, some Kotiria speakers can no longer identify the first vowel in these roots, nor do they indicate a vowel in their writing. However, in closely related Wa'ikhana we find *doke* (cognate to Kotiria *roka*) and *duku* (cognate to Kotiria *duku/ruku*) with fully realized vowels, further indications of the underlying forms that are undergoing synchronic modification in Kotiria.

The first verb in this group, -*ruku*—the word-internal form of *duku* 'stand, be standing'—adds a durative aspectual dimension to the semantics of the initial verb. If this is an activity verb, serialization with -*ruku* indicates that the action is repeated, while serialization of -*ruku* with an initial stative verb indicates an ongoing state. In (124a) the

---

[9] Because the initial vowels are devoiced and the final vowels are similar, it is often quite difficult to identify which of these verbs is actually being used, though context and residual lip movement can be useful indications. I am grateful to Nathan Waltz for pointing out some of the semantic differences between these similar forms and for his indication (p.c. 2002) of the underlying forms.

[10] The fact that aspectual -*ruku*, -*rʉka*, and -*roka* are regularly realized with initial [r] indicates that speakers have reinterpreted these morphemes in SVCs as having grammatical, rather than lexical, status and are thus applying the appropriate phonological restrictions governing the distribution of [d] vs. [r].

serialization of the root 'speak' with *-ruku* indicates that the two protagonists began to have an extended conversation; in (124b) *-ruku* indicates the repeated movement involved in the act of surrounding. In (124c), on the other hand, *-ruku* is used with a stative verb of placement and indicates that the object was put on display in a specific place or position. Examples (124b), (124c) and (127) below clearly show that *-ruku* in noninitial position no longer implies 'standing' position; this is another indication that it has grammaticalized as an aspectual marker when used as a noninitial root in a serialization.

(124) *-ruku* (allomorph of *duku* 'stand, be standing') 'durative aspect'

    a. *ãta yoa, tirome're durukua yoaa*
        ~a=tá   yoá   tí+ró=~be're   dú-**rúkú**+á
        so=REF do/make ANPH+SG=COM/INST speak-stand+(3)PL
        yoá+a
        do/make+ASSERT.PERF

       'So, (the man) started a conversation with him (the curupira).' [A7.41]

    b. *ti numiare ña'a toarome're burukuta'a sã ña'aatia*
        ti=~dubí+a+re   ~ya'á toá+ro=~be're
        ANPH=woman+PL+OBJ catch be.fast+SG=COM/INST
        ~bú-**ruku**-ta   ~sá   ~ya'á-ati+a
        run-stand-come MOV.inside catch-IMPERF+ASSERT.PERF

       '(Men) would kidnap women quickly by surrounding (their longhouse and) then running (inside) to catch them.' (= (76)) [Ancestors]

    c. *to ka'sarore õbaroi pihsarukuga*
        to=ka'sá+ro+re   ~ó-bá'á+ró+í
        3SG.POSS=skin+SG+OBJ DEIC.PROX-do/be.after+SG+LOC
        pisá-**rúkú**+á
        be.on-stand+ASSERT.PERF

       'His skin (that of a child devoured by evil beings) was there draped (over a windowsill).' (= (32b)) [A5.42]

The verb *-ruka*—the word-internal allomorph of *duka* 'begin'—is one of the roots coding aspect that is not a motion or position verb. It codes the beginning or inception of an action. However, speakers also affirm that it usually indicates an action beginning quickly, as in (125c), suggesting that its original semantics may have included a 'movement' component.

(125) *-ruka* (allomorph of *duka* 'begin') 'inceptive aspect'
    a. *tina murukawa'aka'a sũ ñua*
        *tí-~da ~bú-**ruka**-wa'a-ka'a ~sú ~yú+á*
        ANPH-PL run-begin-go-do.moving arrive see/look+ASSERT.PERF
        'They (the sons) went running over (to where their mother was being held captive), got there, (and) looked.' (= (62)) [A4.27]
    b. *phinonowu'ru tirore chowerukaa*
        *~phiró+ró-wú'rú tí+ró+ré   chówe-**ruka**+a*
        snake+SG-AUG   ANPH+SG+OBJ vomit-begin+ASSERT.PERF
        'The big snake began to vomit him (the dog) up.' (= (45)) [A6.36]
    c. *to makurokãre nawuarukaga*
        *to=~bak+ú+ró-~ká+ré   ~dá-wúá-**rúká**+á*
        3SG.POSS=child+MASC+SG-DIM+OBJ get-carry-begin+ASSERT.PERF
        'She picked up (grabbed) her little boy.' (= (123)) [A5.20]

The semantics of the third verb in this group, *-roka*, the word-internal allomorph of *doka* 'throw, project', involves motion as well as a deictic relation. This second notion is most salient in the synchronic use of *-roka* as a noninitial verb in SVCs, where it indicates that the action or state takes place with reference to a distant location. In (126a), it implies an outwardly-expanding motion from a fixed starting point, an explosion out into the distance; in (126b) and (126c), it implies things literally thrown or gotten rid of far off somewhere; in (126d), it denotes that the action of the verb has taken place in a far-off and unknown place; and in (126e), it is used in a nominalization indicating a distant place 'out, off, in the middle of the forest'.

(126) *-roka* (allomorph of *doka* 'project') 'do/be at a distance; distal aspect'
    a. *to dahpuwaroi phichawa'arokaa*
        *to=dapú-waro+i   phichá-wá'á-**róká**+á*
        3SG.POSS=head-EMPH+LOC shoot-go-DIST+ASSERT.PERF
        '(The snake's) head exploded (when it was shot).' [A6.35]
    b. *du'teta khõarokaa*
        *du'té-ta   ~khóá-**róká**+á*
        chop-separate throw-DIST+ASSERT.PERF
        '(He) cut it (the dead snake) into pieces (and) threw them apart.' [A6.48]

c. wãha, wãhaina khõarokaa
~wahá ~wahá-~ida ~khoá-**roka**+a
kill kill-NOM.PL lie-DIST+ASSERT.PERF
'The murderers killed (them and left them) lying off somewhere.'
[A4.5]

d. yɨ mahkɨre wãharokari hire
yɨ=~bak+ɨ+ré ~wahá-**roka**+ri hí+re
1SG.POSS=child+MASC+OBJ kill-DIST+NOM(INFER) COP+VIS.PERF.2/3
'My son's been killed (off somewhere).' [A6.58]

e. tina hira diapɨ mahkarokapɨ mahkaina
tí-~da hí+ra diá-pɨ ~baká-**roka**-pɨ
ANPH-PL COP+VIS.IMPERF.2/3 river-LOC origin-DIST-LOC
~baká-~ida
origin-NOM.PL
'Some (turtles) live in the river, and some are jungle-dwellers.'
[LSK: Turtles]

In contrast to the postural verb *duku* 'stand, be standing', whose use in noninitial position in SVCs codes durative aspect, the postural verbs *duhi* 'sit, be sitting', *yosa* 'hang, be hanging' (in (33) above), and *~khoa* 'lie, be lying' more straightforwardly indicate the positional orientation for the action of the initial verb. In (127), *duhi* occurs first as an independent predicate and then later in noninitial position in the serialization *du-ruku-duhi*. The utterance is part of a description of a Kotiria festival, which typically begins in the late afternoon when people arrive for a collective meal. They then take seats on benches that line the inside perimeter of the longhouse according to traditional etiquette for the spatial distribution of participants, and the ceremony continues throughout the night, with people drinking caxiri beer, conversing, and playing instruments while they sit in their appointed spots, a fact emphasized by the use of *duhi* in the serialization.

(127) chɨ tu'sɨ tina duhisɨ̃ durukuduhi
chɨ tu'sɨ tí-~da duhi-~sɨ dú-rúkú-**dúhí**
eat finish ANPH-PL sit-arrive speak-stand-sit
'As soon as they're done eating, they sit around conversing ...'
[A3.14]

Earlier in this chapter we saw that Kotiria codes a distinction between translocative movement (movement away from) and cislocative movement (movement toward) by means of the motion verbs *wa'a* 'go' and *ta* 'come'. It also codes the distinction between translocative and cislocative arrival by use of the motion verbs *~sɨ* 'arrive there' (at a place away from the speaker or a fixed reference point) (128a), and *wi'i* 'return/arrive here' (indicating arrival back to the speaker's location or a fixed reference point) (129a). When these verbs occur in non-initial position in SVCs, ~*sɨ* (128b) and *wi'i* (129b–c) contribute two semantic notions, one adverbial and the other aspectual: they indicate the (adverbial) directionality of the action of the independent verb as well as its (aspectual) complete accomplishment.

(128) a. *topɨ sũ ñɨ mahkamaa*

    tó-pɨ   ~*sũ*   ~*yú*   ~*baká-~ba+a*
    REM-LOC arrive see/look look/search.for-FRUS+ASSERT.PERF
    'He got there (and) looked, searching to no avail.' [A7.117]

  b. *borasɨka'a wa'aro koataa*

    borá-~sɨ-ka'a   *wa'á+ro*   *koá-ta+a*
    fall-arrive-do.moving go+(3)SG NONVIS-come+ASSERT.PERF
    'He fell right down (the man heard).' [A7.86]

(129) a. *tiro ti phɨkoropɨre wi'i sũ'aga*

    tí+ró   *ti=phɨk+ó+ró-pú+ré*   ***wi'i***
    ANPH+SG 3PL.POSS=parent+FEM+SG-LOC+OBJ arrive
    ~*sɨ'á+a*
    stick.onto+ASSERT.PERF
    'He (an evil creature) came up to (and) stuck onto their mother.' [A4.31]

  b. *ãyo õpɨre yɨ'ɨ kho'awi'ikɨka*

    ~*a=yó*   ~*ó-pú+ré*   *yɨ'ɨ*   *kho'á-**wi'i**-kɨ-ka*
    so=do DEIC.PROX-LOC+OBJ 1SG return-arrive-(1/2)MASC-PREDICT
    ~*dí+a*
    say+ASSERT.PERF
    'That's how I'll get back here.' [A4.14]

  c. *ti(na) numia wa'ariba'aropɨ numiaña'arimahsa peri mɨmɨ sãwi'ia*

    tí(-~da)   ~*dubí+a*   *wa'á+ri-ba'a+ro-pɨ*
    ANPH(-PL) woman+PL go+NOM-do/be.after+SG-LOC
    ~*dubí+a-~ya'a+ri-~basa*   *pé'ri*   ~*bɨbú*
    woman+PL-catch+NOM-people all   run
    ~*sá-**wi'i**+a*
    MOV.inside-arrive+ASSERT.PERF
    'Just after the women's escape, all the bride-nappers came quickly into (the longhouse).' [Ancestors]

7.5.3 Other noninitial roots coding aspect

Although aspectual distinctions are often coded by motion and postural verbs in SVCs, there are a number of other roots that contribute aspectual information when they occur in noninitial position. Some of these belong to the class of independent verb roots, though most are dependent roots. One frequently occuring root of this type is *-~doka*, which indicates that the action or state is completed (130). The root *-pha'yo* (131) also appears to confer a notion of completedness, though exactly how it contrasts with *-~doka* is a question that remains for future analysis.

(130) *-~doka* 'do/be completely; completive aspect'

a. *sṹnokaa tiro*

   ~sṹ-~doka+a   *tí+ró*
   arrive-COMPL+ASSERT.PERF ANPH+SG

   'He got back (home).' [A7.106]

b. *mɨmɨsã'a wi'inokaa*

   ~bɨbɨ́-~sa'a   *wi'í-~doka+a*
   run-MOV.inside arrive-COMPL+ASSERT.PERF

   '(They) all rushed inside.' [Ancestors]

c. *patena tina moñonokaatia*

   pá-te-~da   *tí-~da*   *~boyó-~doka-ati+a*
   ALT-time-PL ANPH-PL fail-COMPL-IMPERF+ASSERT.PERF

   'But sometimes they would be totally unsuccessful.' [Ancestors]

d. *butinokaa tina*

   butí-~doka+a   *tí-~da*
   disappear-COMPL+ASSERT.PERF ANPH-PL

   'They had completely disappeared.' [Ancestors]

e. *tiro borarowɨ'rɨ wã'karuku sɨ̃ bahuanokaa*

   tí+ró   *borá+ro-wɨ'rɨ*   *~wa'ká-ruku*   *~sɨ*
   ANPH+SG curupira+SG-AUG wake.up-stand arrive

   bahú+a-~doka+a
   be.visible+AFFEC-COMPL+ASSERT.PERF

   'The big Curupira revived and appeared whole before him.' [A7.125]

f. *mɨ'ɨre chɨnokaboka nia*

   ~bɨ'ɨ́+ré   *chɨ́-~doka-bo-ka*   *~dí+a*
   2SG+OBJ eat-COMPL-DUB-ASSERT.IMPERF say+ASSERT.PERF

   '"(We) would have eaten you up" (they) said.' [A5.38]

(131) kherokã me're chupha'yoroka'aro koataa
khé+ro-~ka=~be're   chú-**pha'yo**+ro-ka'a+ro
be.fast+SG-DIM=COM/INST eat-COMPL+SG-do.immediately+(3)SG
koá-ta+a
NONVIS-come+ASSERT.PERF
'(He heard) the curupira gobble it up completely.' [A7.60]

Another root that occurs exclusively in noninitial position in SVCs is -~*daka*. It indicates that an object or entity is integrated into the action performed by the subject but does not have a comitative or instrument role (for these Kotiria employs a syntactic marker =~*be're*; see §10.7.3).

(132) -~*daka* 'do/be together'

   a. *tirore nana'kaa. tiro thuaa*
      tí+ró+ré   ~dá-~**daka**+a   tí+ró
      ANPH+SG+OBJ   get-do/be.together+ASSERT.PERF   ANPH+SG
      thuá+a
      return+ASSERT.PERF
      '(The man) took it (the bird) with him. He went back home.' [A7.147]

   b. *pakorokãre tuinakaa*
      pá-ko+ro-~ka+re   tuí-~**daka**+a
      ALT-FEM+SG-DIM+OBJ   put.in.front-do/be.together+ASSERT.PERF
      'She clasped her little girl to the front (of her body and together they escaped).' (= (84)) [A5.21]

The root -*phiti*, which occurs as the initial root in the number word *phititia* 'four' (§6.3.1) and compounded in the derived nominals *hi-phiti*+*ro* 'everything' and *hi-phiti-~da* 'everyone' (in (19)–(20) above), can also occur in noninitial position in a serialization to indicate an action done collectively (133).

(133) *ã yoa tina kha'maphitibohka chu ñobo'e wa'a yoara*
      ~a=yoá   tí-~da   ~kha'bá-**phítí**-bóká   chú   ~yó-bo'e   wa'á
      so=do/make   ANPH-PL   do.RECIP-COLL-meet   eat   show-pray   go
      yoá+ra
      do+VIS.IMPERF.2/3
      'They get together to eat (and) pray.' [A3.9]

When speakers wish to indicate that a specific action is being repeated, the initial root is serialized with ~*dabo* 'repeat', as in (134). It is unclear why both -~*dabo* and -*toa*, which also indicates an action done 'again', cooccur in (134). The nuances of aspectual and other distinctions coded by SVCs is undoubtedly a prime topic for continued investigation.

(134) ~dabo 'repeat'
    a. *to hiriro a'riro soro hira ni, tirore topɨrota phichanamoatoa*
        tó   hí+ri+ro   a'rí+ró   só+ró
        REM COP+NOM+SG DEM:PROX+SG different+SG
        hí+ra   ~dí tí+ró+ré   tó-pɨ́+ró=ta
        COP+VIS.IMPERF.2/3 say ANPH+SG+OBJ DEF-LOC+SG=REF
        *phichá-~**dábó**+á-tóá*
        shoot-repeat+AFFEC-do.again
        '"And over there is another different one," he said, (and) he shot it (the snake) again.' [A6.46]

    b. *yɨ'ɨre wanamoata payahiripho'nare, nia*
        *yɨ'ɨ́+ré   wá-~**dábó**+gá=ta   pá-yahiri~pho'da+re*
        1SG+OBJ give-repeat+IMPER=REF ALT-heart+OBJ
        ~dí+a
        say+ASSERT.PERF
        '"Give me another heart," (he) said.' [A7.62]

The dependent verb *-~sidi* adds yet another kind of aspectual information: it relates the action of the initial verb to a specific referential time. In (135a), the reference time is the moment of speech, while in (135b), the action, 'passing out', takes place exactly following and as a result of the protagonists' previous act of running into each other head on. In (135c) and (135d), the reference is a more generalized current time 'now, nowadays'.

(135) *-~sidi* 'do then/now; do yet/still'
    a. *yɨ'ɨ õi kɨ̃ khiti ya'usinitai niha*
        yɨ'ɨ́   ~ó+i   ~kɨ́   khiti
        1SG DEIC.PROX+LOC one/a story
        *ya'ú-~**sidi**=ta+i   ~dí-ha*
        tell-do.now=REF+(1/2)MASC be.PROG-VIS.IMPERF.1
        'I'm going to tell a little story right now.' [A7.2]

    b. *yu'dɨka wa'asinia tina*
        *yu'dɨ́-ka   wa'á-~**sidi**+a   tí-~da*
        pass.out-ASSERT.IMPERF go-do.then+ASSERT.PERF ANPH-PL
        'They passed out right then.' [Ancestors]

c. *tire yɨ'ɨ mipɨre ne boerasinika*
   tí+re   yɨ'ɨ   ~bí-pú+ré   ~dé
   ANPH+OBJ   1SG   now-LOC+OBJ   NEG
   bo-éra-~sidi-ka
   forget-NEG-do.yet/still-ASSERT.IMPERF
   'That I have never forgotten.' [A3.16]

d. *mipɨkãre yoasinira. tina kha'maphitibohka chɨ ñobo'e wa'a yoara*
   ~bí-pú-~ká+ré   yoá-~sidi+ra
   now-LOC-DIM+OBJ   do/make-do.yet/still+VIS.IMPERF.2/3
   tí-~da   ~kha'bá-phíti-bóká   chú   ~yó-bo'e   wa'á
   ANPH-PL   do.RECIP-COLL-meet   eat   show-pray   go
   yoá+ra
   do+VIS.IMPERF.2/3
   'Nowadays, they still do that. They get together to eat (and) pray.' [A3.8–9]

Finally, the verb *tu'sɨ* 'finish' in noninitial position in SVCs indicates that the action of the initial verb has recently or just now been completed.

(136) *tu'sɨ* 'finish'
   a. *ã yo tirore wãhatu'sɨ chɨropɨ nia*
      ~a=yo   tí+ró+ré   ~wahá-**tu'sɨ**   chú+ro-pɨ
      so=do   ANPH+SG+OBJ   kill-finish   eat+(3)SG-EMPATH
      ~dí+a
      be.PROG+ASSERT.PERF
      'He (the snake) had just killed the poor dog (and) was already eating it.' [A6.23]

   b. *mari phɨkɨ tatu'sɨro koataka*
      ~bari=phɨk+ɨ   tá-**tú'sú**+ró
      1PL.INC.POSS=parent+MASC   come-finish+(3)SG
      koá-ta-ka
      NONVIS-come-ASSERT.IMPERF
      '(I heard) our father's just come (to the meeting place).' [A4.22]

   c. *mipɨre yɨ'ɨ chɨa bohkatu'sɨha. thuai niha*
      ~bí-pú+ré   yɨ'ɨ   chúa   boká-**tu'sɨ**-ha
      now-LOC+OBJ   1SG   food   find-finish-VIS.IMPERF.1
      thuá+i   ~dí-ha
      return+(1/2)MASC   be.PROG-VIS.IMPERF.1
      'I've found food now (and so) I'm going home.' [A7.12]

d. *yoatapɨ wihatu'sɨri hira*
   *yóá-tá-pɨ́   wihá-**tu'sɨ**+ri*
   be.far+REF-LOC MOV.outward-finish+NOM(INFER)
   hi+ra
   COP+VIS.IMPERF.2/3
   'They've just escaped (from inside the longhouse into the surrounding forest).' (= (78)) [Ancestors]

7.5.4 Modal functions of noninitial verbs

In Kotiria, deontic, or "agent-oriented," modality is coded by serializations in which verbs from the subset of verbs of mental processes occupy noninitial position. Agent-oriented modality is understood as the coding of "internal and external conditions on an agent with respect to the completion of the action expressed in the main predicate" (Bybee, Perkins, and Pagliuca 1994:177). The related notions of obligation, necessity, desire, and ability are included in this type of modality, but they are often coded by multiple means within the same language. This is certainly the case in Kotiria, which employs the mental process verb ~*basi* 'know' and the desiderative *-dua* (a grammaticalized dependent root), as means of coding agent-oriented modal functions in SVCs, and has also developed a construction with the verb ~*kha'ba* 'want' and a clausal complement as a means of coding necessity or obligation (discussed in §11.3.1).

The first of the deontic or agent-oriented modality verbs, ~*basi* 'know', occurs as an independent verb in (137).

(137) *mahsieraha. yɨ'ɨ boerakɨrɨ tire*
       ~***basi**-éra-ha*   *yɨ'ɨ* *bo-éra-kɨrɨ*   *tí+re*
       know-NEG-VIS.IMPERF.1 1SG   forget-NEG-ADVERS   ANPH+OBJ
       'I don't know (traditional Kotiria songs and dances). I've forgotten them (unfortunately).' (= (97)) [A3.19–20]

The extension of 'know'-type verbs to the expression of deontic modality is not surprising; such verbs are "[t]he most commonly documented lexical source for ability" (Bybee, Perkins, and Pagliuca 1994: 190). In Kotiria, when ~*basi* 'know' occurs in noninitial position in an SVC, it can have three different modal meanings—'ability to perform an action' (138)–(139), 'possibility' (140), and 'advisability' or 'suggestion' (141)–(142).

(138) *yɨ'ɨ yahiripho'nare wamahsieraka*
       *yɨ'ɨ=yahíri~pho'da+re wá-~**basi**-éra-ka*
       1SG(POSS)=heart+OBJ   give-know-NEG-ASSERT.IMPERF
       'I can't give you my heart.' [A7.47]

(139) 1 *tirore diero bohkamahsira yʉhkʉkohpapʉ kohpapʉ*
       tí+ró+ré   dié+ró   boká-~basi+ra
       ANPH+SG+OBJ dog+SG find-know+VIS.IMPERF.2/3
       yʉkú-kopa-pʉ kopá-pʉ́
       tree-hole-LOC hole-LOC
       'Dogs can find them (armadillos) in holes in trees or holes (in the ground).'

   2 *ã yoana sã nʉnʉwa'aka'a wãhamahsiha*
       ~a=yoá-~da   ~sá   ~dʉdʉ́-~wa'a-ka'a
       so=do/make-(1/2)PL 1PL.EXC follow/chase-go-do.moving
       ~wahá-~basi-ha
       kill-know-VIS.IMPERF.1
       'That's how we go after them and are able to kill them.' [LSK: Armadillos]

(140) 1 *wãharo wa'aro moñoerara tiro*
       wahá+ro   wa'á+ro   ~boyo-éra+ra   tí+ró
       kill+(3)SG go+(3)SG fail-NEG+VIS.IMPERF.2/3 ANPH+SG
       'When (Luis) goes fishing, he never fails'.

   2 *to wa'achʉ ñʉra chʉnaka nimahsiha*
       to=wa'á-chʉ   ~yʉ́+rá   chʉ́-~dáká
       3SG.POSS=go-SW.REF see+VIS.IMPERF.2/3 eat-do.together
       ~dí-~basi-ha
       say-know-VIS.IMPERF.1
       'When we see him going off (fishing), we can say, "Let's eat!"'[11]

(141) *irimoare mari mahsa do'atira mahkamahsika*
       ~iribóa+re ~barí   ~basá   do'á-tí+rá
       lime+OBJ   1PL.INC man   sickness-VBZ+VIS.IMPERF.2/3
       ~baká-~basi-ka
       look.for-know-ASSERT.IMPERF
       'When we're sick, we should look for (get) limes.' [LSK: Limes]

(142) *noaro wahkʉ̃mahsi duhimahsiha*
       ~dóá+ró   ~wakú-~básí   duhí-~basi-ha
       be.good+SG be.aware-know sit-know-VIS.IMPERF.1
       '(In airplanes we) should pay close attention and sit still.' [A12.6]

The dependent root *-dua* functions as a desiderative in serializations, indicating the subject's desire to perform the action indicated by the initial root. Although *-dua* does not occur in initial position, it

---

[11] From the short text that appears as example (19) in chapter 2.

displays root properties such as bimoraic structure and an initial [d] (which only occurs in morphemes that still retain a certain degree of lexical status), indicating an intermediate state of grammaticalization.

(143) yɨ'ɨ chɨduaka
    yɨ'ɨ chɨ-**dua**-ka
    1SG eat-DESID-ASSERT.IMPERF
    'I want to eat it.' [A7.44]

(144) yabaina mɨ'ɨ wãhaduainare wãhaga
    yabá-~ídá ~bɨ'ɨ ~wahá-**dua**-~ida+re ~wahá+ga
    WH-NOM.PL 2SG kill-DESID-NOM.PL+OBJ kill+IMPER
    'Go kill (hunt) whatever you want.' (lit., 'Go kill ones you want to kill.') [A7.136]

(145) mari kherokã wa'aduana wa'aka wɨriame're
    ~barí khé+ro-~ka wa'á-**dua**-~da wa'á-ka
    1PL.INC be.fast+SG-DIM go-DESID-(1/2)PL go-ASSERT.IMPERF
    wɨ-ria=~be're
    fly+round.elongated=COM/INST
    'When we want to go (somewhere) quickly, we go by plane.' [A12.3]

Two additional verbs can be tentatively classed as noninitial roots that express types of "agent-oriented" modality in SVCs. These are the rarely occurring -~yɨ 'attempt; try (unsuccessfully)' (146) and -sibɨ 'intend to' (147) (see also §9.3.1 for discussion of the clause modality intention marker and §11.3.3 for the purposive construction). It is likely that there are even more modal distinctions coded by SVCs in Kotiria than just the ones noted here; this is a topic that will receive additional attention in future studies.

(146) tiphĩre tiro hi'na ña'a to yahiripho'nare phirokã beñɨa
    tí-~phi+re tí+ró ~hí'da ~ya'á
    ANPH-CLS:bladelike+OBJ ANPH+SG EMPH grab
    to=yahíri~pho'da+re phí+ró-~ká bé-~yɨ+a
    3SG.POSS=heart+OBJ be.slow+SG-DIM inject/insert-try+ASSERT.PERF
    'He (the curupira) immediately grabbed the knife (and) slowly tried to cut out his heart.' [A7.77]

(147) tirota, yɨ'ɨ boraro yɨ'ɨ wãhakɨrirore ñɨsibɨ nia
    tí+ró=ta yɨ'ɨ borá+ro yɨ'ɨ ~wahá-kɨ+ri+ro+re
    ANPH+SG=REF 1SG curupira+SG 1SG kill-MASC+NOM+SG+OBJ

~yú-síbú   ~dí+a
see/look-intend say+ASSERT.PERF

'The same guy (said) "I'm going there to see that curupira that I killed," he said.' [A7.112]

7.5.5 Other types of serialized constructions

As was noted at the beginning of §7.1, it is not common for stative verbs to appear in serializations or with modality suffixes. However, they may do so in certain combinations, as in (148), where a stative positional verb is serialized with a root indicating durative aspect, and (149), where the copula occurs in a serialization that includes both an aspectual marker and the dubitative modality marker -*bo*.

(148) *to ka'sarore õbaroi pihsarukuga*
  to=ka'sá+ro+re   ~*ó-bá'á+ró+í*
  3SG.POSS=skin+SG+OBJ DEIC.PROX-do/be.after+SG-LOC
  pisá-rúkú*+á*
  be.on-stand+ASSERT.PERF
  'His skin (that of a child devoured by evil beings) was there draped (over a windowsill).' (= (32b)) [A5.42]

(149) *cho! õita hinokaboka ni*
  chó ~*ó+í=ta*   ***hí-~doka-bo****-ka*
  oh   DEIC.PROX+LOC=REF   COP-COMPL-DUB-PREDICT
  'Oh, maybe he's here.' [A6.14]

In §§7.5.1–7.5.2, we also saw that serializations expressing manner and aspectual distinctions generally have intransitive roots in noninitial position. However, although it is certainly not as common, serializations may also be composed of more than one transitive root, the noninitial root coming from the classes of transitive activity or placement verbs. Such constructions indicate cause-effect relations, with the initial verb coding the cause, as in *sɨ'a-phayo* (sift-spread.out) in (83) or ~*yɨ-boka* (look-find) in (89) above, as well as *dɨ'te-ta* (chop-separate) in (150).

(150) *dɨ'teta khõarokaa*
  dɨ'té-ta   ~*khóá-róká+á*
  chop-separate   throw-DIST+ASSERT.PERF
  'He cut it into pieces (and) threw them apart.' [A6.48]

7.6 Verbs with incorporated nouns

Verbs with incorporated nouns were discussed in §3.3.2 as special type of derived verb stem in which a transitive verb and its nonreferential noun object are compounded to form a syntactically intransitive verb stem with greater semantic specificity. Incorporation of this type is productive in Kotiria, and, as is typologically common, such verbs with incorporated nouns generally denote habitual or ritualized actions such as *die-~ku* 'egg-laying' and *~daho-~sa* 'flatbread-making (or spreading)'. Once a noun has been compounded with a verb in this way, the derived stem takes regular morphological marking for verbs, or can be nominalized through common derivational processes. It was also noted that although most noun incorporation in Kotiria produces intransitive stems, there are also rare cases of incorporation that result in a syntactically transitive stem; this is the case for *~dabo-da're* 'wife-make' in (151), which has the independent noun phrase *ti-~da+re* 'them' as its (syntactically marked) object. (See also §10.7 for examples of incorporated nouns in temporal adverbial expressions.)

(151) tinare namoda'reataa, phayɨ mahsakurua pho'nanumiare
   tí-~da+re   **~dabó-da're**+a-ta+a
   ANPH-PL+OBJ   wife-make+AFFEC-REF+ASSERT.PERF

   phayɨ ~basá-kúrú+á   ~pho'dá-~dubi+a+re
   many   people-group+PL   children-female+PL+OBJ

   '(They) married them, young women from many different groups (tribes).' [Ancestors]

As with noun-noun compounding (discussed in §4.8), in noun incorporation (or noun-verb compounding), the noun and verb roots fuse into a single phonological word with the initial root as the phonological head. The semantic relation between the roots is the opposite of their phonological relation: the noninitial root is the semantic head, while specification is provided by the initial root. We observe both relations in *wa'i-~kida-~waha*, commonly used for 'hunt', as in (152). The LH tonal melody of the entire word is that of the initial root *wa'i*, which spreads over the entire phonological word (following the process described in §2.6.2). The semantic head of the compound, however, is *~waha* 'kill', here specifically qualified as 'animal-killing' or 'hunting'.

(152) tɨ me're mɨ'ɨ wa'ikinawãha sihtotaga
   tɨ́=~be're   ~bɨ'ɨ   **wa'í-~kídá-~wáhá**
   stick=COM/INST   2SG   animal-PL-kill

sitó-ta+ga
MOV.circular-come+IMPER
'With this stick, you go around hunting (animal-killing).' (= (69))
[A7.131]

Full noun incorporation of this type is semantically similar to noun-verb constructions in which a transitive verb occurs with an immediately preceding object noun that is not case-marked by the case suffix +*re* 'objective' (see §§10.3.1–10.3.2). Like incorporated nouns, the unmarked noun in such constructions, for example, *chʉa* 'food' in (153), is always generic or unspecific. Moreover, the activities expressed by such constructions are of the same commonplace nature as those indicated by verbs with incorporated nouns. The main difference between these constructions seems to come down to whether or not the object noun is phonologically independent or fused. While it is possible that there is some as yet unrecognized semantic criterion for when the two different constructions are used, it may just come down to a question of frequency: the more frequent combinations grammaticalize to the point of full phonological fusion of the noun, while in less frequent combinations, the noun remains phonologically independent.

(153) *mipʉre yʉ'ʉ chʉa bohkatu'sʉha. thuai niha*
~*bí-pʉ́+ré*   *yʉ'ʉ* *chʉa* *boká-tu'sʉ-ha*
now-LOC+OBJ 1SG   food   find-finish-VIS.IMPERF.1
thuá+i   ~*di-ha*
return+(1/2)MASC be.PROG-VIS.IMPERF.1
'Now I've found food (and/so) I'm going home.' (= (136c)) [A7.12]

Mithun, in fact, discusses the possibility that juxtaposed noun-plus-verb constructions in which the constituents retain phonological independence might be a subtype of incorporation (1984:849). Indeed, certain analyses of Eastern Tukanoan languages refer to all unmarked generic nouns that occur directly before the verb as incorporated (Barnes 1999:220; Morse and Maxwell 1999:70–71); these studies, however do not mention the phonological properties of such combinations. For the time being, I view the two constructions in Kotiria as closely related, but reserve use of the term noun incorporation to refer only to what seems to be the most complete manifestation, in which a single phonological word is formed (see §10.3.2 for further discussion).

8 Nonroot stem morphemes in the verb

This chapter continues the description of the complex morphology of finite verbs in Kotiria, focusing on morphemes that are more grammaticalized than those examined in chapter 7 and that occur farther from the initial root. After showing the basic morphological template of verbs (§8.1), it goes on to discuss the specific grammatical categories of negation, intensification, modal distinctions, and imperfective and perfective aspect (§§8.2–8.5). (Analysis of word-final clause modality morphology is left for chapter 9.) A summary of the grammatical, semantic, and phonological properties of verbal morphemes (§8.6) reveals a continuum of degrees of grammaticalization much like that found for nominal morphemes.

8.1 Overview of the morphology of finite verbs

Figure 8.1 presents the template of finite verbal words and basic categories of verbal morphemes, with the obligatory constituents of any finite verbal word—the verb root at the beginning, and a final suffix coding clause modality—shown in bold type. The leftmost constituent (the initial verb root) is the phonological head of the verbal word. In noun incorporation constructions (§7.6), the incorporated noun plus the verb root can be thought of as jointly occupying the Root position in figure 8.1. Positions 1 through 3 after the root represent the categories of noninitial verb roots that most commonly occur in serialized verb constructions with initial nonstative verb roots; these positions are discussed in §7.5. All noninitial roots lose their own tonal melody and are integrated into the phonological word that is the domain of tonal spread from the initial root, though each root retains its underlying specification for nasality and glottalization. Many, though not all, independent roots can also occur in noninitial position in serializations and may or may not retain their bimoraic structure in this position. Roots such as ~bʉbʉ/~bʉ 'run; do quickly', for example, vary between phonologically full and reduced forms. The stem includes all morphology from the root through position 5; the lexical stem includes all morphology through position 3. A simple lexical stem consists of just a single verbal root, while a complex lexical stem may contain additional roots in a serialized construction (positions 1 through 3). Nonroot stem morphemes occur in positions 4 and 5.

Nonroot stem morphemes in the verb 245

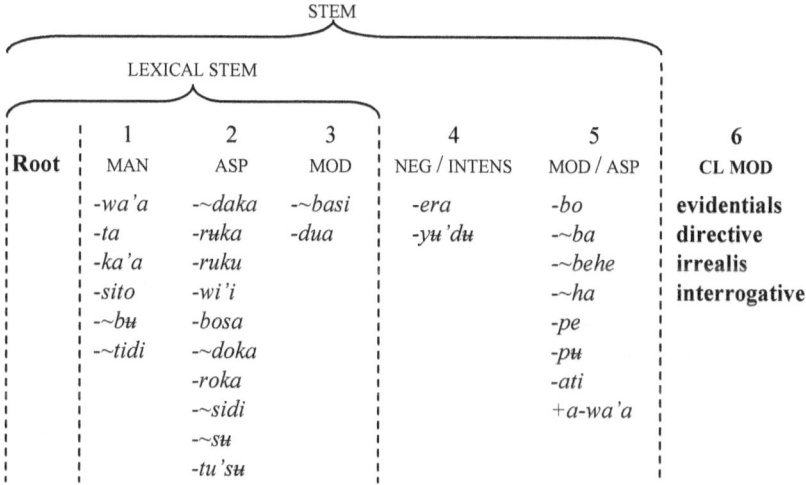

Figure 8.1. Morphology of finite verbs. ASP = aspect; CL MOD = clause modality; INTENS = intensification; MAN = manner; MOD = modality; NEG = negation.

The optional nonroot stem morphemes coding negation, emphasis, aspect, and various kinds of modality that follow the lexical stem are the topic of the present chapter. In general, these morphemes display higher degrees of grammaticalization, evidenced by greater phonological reductions and the fact that most of the morphemes in positions 4 and 5 cannot occur independently, in contrast to many of the noninitial roots in positions 1 through 3. Finally, position 6 is occupied by markers of four categories of clause modality; these are described in detail in chapter 9.

The morphology of stative verbal words is typically less complex than that of nonstative verbal words; as noted in §7.5.5, it is relatively rare for a stative verb root to occur with morphemes of positions 1 to 3 or with morphemes coding modality (cf. §7.1). In general, a stative verb root stands alone as the head of the verbal word and additional morphology includes only (optional) aspectual and (obligatory) clause modality markers, as in (1) and the examples in §7.1.1.

(1) a. *phanopɨre hiatiga mahsayahkaina*
         ~phadó-pɨ+re   ***hí-ati+a***
         do/be.before-LOC+OBJ COP-IMPERF+ASSERT.PERF
         ~basá-yáká-~idá
         people-steal-NOM.PL
         'In the olden days there were people-stealers.' [A4.1]

b. *yʉ'ʉ Mo mahkariropʉ hiha*
   yʉ'ʉ   ~bó   ~baká+ri+ro-pʉ   hí-ha
   1SG   Mõ   village+NOM+SG-LOC   COP-VIS.IMPERF.1
   'I am from Mõ.' [A1.2]

8.2   Negation: *-era*

All verbs in Kotiria, with the exception of the inherently negative verb *~badia* coding nonexistence (see §7.1.2), are negated by the morpheme *-era*, which generally immediately follows the lexical stem (in morphological position 4 in figure 8.1). Given its inherent phonological properties (HL tonal melody and [−nasal] specification), it is likely that *-era* was once an independent root that has undergone grammaticalization as a generic negative marker. Indeed, grammaticalization of negation-marking morphemes from inherently negative verbs is a widely attested process (Givón 2001, vol. 1:267), and we find that Tukano, for example, employs a dependent verb *we'e* (which may or may not be a cognate to Kotiria *-era*) as one of the two means by which verbs can be negated (Ramirez 1997a:152–53). Semantically, *-era* may have derived from an inherently negative verb root—its phonological effects on the verbal word, considered below, certainly indicate root status—but it no longer functions synchronically as an independent root and its semantic function is highly generalized and paradigmatic.

Examples (2)–(13) show that *-era* negates all semantic classes of verbs: stative (2)–(4); activity (5); motion (9); perception and mental processes (10)–(11); and speech (12). It negates transitive verbs, as in (5), (6), (9), intransitive verbs, as in (7)–(8), and nominalized verbs, as in (13).

(2)   *ne mari phʉkʉ hierara*
      ~dé   ~bari=phʉk+ʉ   hi-éra+ra
      NEG   1PL.INC.POSS=parent+MASC   COP-NEG+VIS.IMPERF.2/3
      'This isn't our father.' [A4.35]

(3)   *ne bahueraa*
      ~dé   bahu-éra+a
      NEG   be.visible-NEG+ASSERT.PERF
      'There was no trace of it.' [A7.120]

(4)   *õ wʉ̃hpoma'noerara*
      ~o   ~wʉpó-~ba'do-éra+ra
      DEIC.PROX   tie.off-MOV.into-NEG+VIS.IMPERF.2/3
      'It (the edge of a basket where the ends of the fibers were sticking out) isn't finished here.' [Baskets]

(5) mahsa chɨeraka dierore
~basá chɨ-**éra**-ka   dié+ró+ré
people eat-NEG-ASSERT.IMPERF dog+SG+OBJ
'People don't eat dogs.' [LSK: Dogs]

(6) yɨ'ɨ yahiripho'nare wamahsieraka
yɨ'ɨ=yahíri~pho'da+re   wa-~basi-**éra**-ka
1SG(POSS)=heart+OBJ   give-know-NEG-ASSERT.IMPERF
'I can't give you my heart.' [A7.47]

(7) ti phichõnome're boreraka
ti=~phichó+ro=~be're   bor(a)-**éra**-ka
3PL.POSS=tail+SG=COM/INST   fall-NEG-ASSERT.IMPERF
'Because of their tails, (monkeys) never fall.' [LSK: Tails]

(8) wãharo wa'aro moñoerara tiro
~wahá+ro   wa'á+ro   ~boyo-**éra**+ra   tí+ró
kill+(3)SG go+(3)SG   fail-NEG+VIS.IMPERF.2/3   ANPH+SG
'When (Luis) goes fishing, he never fails.'[1]

(9) ne topɨre tipɨre tinieraha
~dé tó-pɨ+re   tí-pɨ+re   ~tidi-**éra**-ha
NEG REM-LOC+OBJ   ANPH-LOC+OBJ   wander.around-NEG-VIS.IMPERF.1
'I never go hunting there in that place.' [A6.60]

(10) mari thɨ'oera
~barí   thɨ'o-**éra**
1PL.INC hear-NEG
'(If she speaks in another language), we won't hear (understand)...'
[Baskets]

(11) ñɨera ti mahsieraka yɨ'ɨ
~yɨ-**éra** tí   ~basi-**éra**-ka   yɨ'ɨ
see-NEG   ANPH   know-NEG-ASSERT.IMPERF   1SG
'I didn't see (anything), I know nothing (about it).' [A6.59]

(12) yɨ'tieraa tirose'e koiro
yɨ'ti-**éra**+a   tí+ró-sé'é   kó-iro
answer-NEG+ASSERT.PERF   ANPH+SG-CONTR   relative-NOM.SG
'But he (the man; lit., 'the other relative') didn't answer.' [A7.35]

---

[1] From the short text that appears as example (19) in chapter 2.

(13) *pairo diero wese wa'erariro hika*
   *pá-iro   dié+ró   wesé   wa'(a)-**éra**+ri+ro   hí-ka*
   ALT-NOM.SG dog+SG garden go-NEG+NOM+SG COP-ASSERT.IMPERF
   'Some dogs are lazy.' (lit., 'Some dogs are ones who don't want to go to the garden.') [LSK: Dogs]

It is notable that the negative *-era* is one of the few morphemes to display a systematic phonological effect on the root it modifies. The atypical directionality of this influence contrasts to the systematic left-to-right pattern of most phonological processes in Kotiria. The negative morpheme provokes two different phonological changes: tonal shift in all roots, and assimilation and deletion of the final *a* or *e* of a preceding root.

Unlike almost all other bound morphemes and noninitial roots in serialized verb constructions, *-era* has a fully realized inherent HL melody; it is also inherently [−nasal]. In order to allow full realization of the HL melody of the negative morpheme, all H tones inherent to the immediately preceding root morpheme are neutralized to L. The copula *hi*, for instance, whose inherent HL melody surfaces in words such as *hí-ra* (COP-VIS.IMPERF.2/3) or *hí-ro-pɨ* 'place of being; village', is realized with L tone when negated: *hi-éra*. The same is true for all roots in the negated words in (2)–(13) above and in (14) below.

(14) *hi-éra*   'not be'   (hi_{HL})
      bo-éra   'not forget'   (bo_{LH})
      chɨ-éra   'not eat'   ($chɨ_{HL}$)
      bahu-éra   'not be visible; not appear' ($bahu_{LHL}$)
      ~basi-éra   'not know'   (~$basi_{LHL}$)
      ~boyo-éra   'not fail'   (~$boyo_{LHL}$)
      ~di-éra   'not say'   (~di_{HL})
      ~yɨ-éra   'not see'   (~$yɨ_{H}$)

Additionally, roots ending in *a* undergo a second change, in which the final vowel of the root is deleted before the initial front vowel *e* of the negative morpheme, as seen in the forms in (15).

(15) *boa-éra*   [boéra]   'not pray'
      basa-éra   [baʰséra]   'not bless'
      wa'a-éra   [waʔéra]   'not go'
      khɨa-éra   [khɨéra]   'not have/hold'
      tua-éra   [tuéra]   'not be strong'

~kha'bé-era [khã?méra] 'not need'
~da-éra [néra] 'not get'

Although the observed change can be simply described as one in which there is deletion of [−high, −round] vowel *a* before the negative morpheme, there is some evidence to suggest that the change may in fact involve two steps: assimilation and degemination. First, my data shows that in at least one Kotiria *CaCa* root there is assimilation of both *a* vowels: underlying ~*waha-era* (kill-NEG) becomes [w̃ẽhéra] (Nathan Waltz (2002) gives additional examples of more general assimilation of *a* to *e*). Moreover, my field data from Kotiria's sister language Wa'ikhana show a parallel process of assimilation of root-final *a* to *e*, and in Barasana, both generalized assimilation of root-final vowels to monomoraic *V* suffixes and degemination occur (Gomez-Imbert 1997a:104–7). Finally, we also observe that when negated, roots ending in *e*, such as *pape* 'play', also undergo degemination (16).

(16) *pape-era* [papéra] 'not play'

Thus, although the forms in (15) give the simple impression of "final vowel deletion", they are preferably analyzed as resulting from a two-step phonological process. First the final back vowel *a* assimilates to the initial front vowel *e* of the negative morpheme; then the newly derived sequence *ee* reduces (degeminates) to *e*. The derivations in (17) illustrate the processes by which the surface realizations *bokera* 'not find' and *yoera* 'not do/make' are produced.

(17)   *boka-era* 'not find'   *yoa-era* 'not do'
   Assimilation of *a* to *e*:   ↓   ↓
   $a \rightarrow e$ / __]$_{Root}$ [$_{Neg}$ e *boke-era*   *yoe-era*

   Degemination of *ee*:   ↓   ↓
   $e \rightarrow \emptyset$ / __]$_{Root}$ [$_{Neg}$ e [bo^{h}kéra]   [yoéra]

In contrast, the negated verbs in (14), which have root-final vowels *i ʉ u o*, do not undergo assimilation and degemination; both the final vowel of the root and the initial vowel of the negative morpheme are phonologically realized. In careful speech, tonal shift occurs; the preceding root is pronounced with L tone, while H tone is clearly realized on the initial mora (the vowel *e*) of the negative morpheme. In fast speech, however, the root-final vowel and the initial vowel of the negative morpheme are often realized as a single mora, a kind of derived diphthong realized with H tone. This same process of diphthong-like realization of H-toned *VV* clusters (formed as the result of spreading) is common in fast speech; thus, for example, words such as ~*ó-pé-~ídá* 'these (animate beings), *tó+í* 'there', and *butúá* 'termites' are often heard with monomoraic *éí*, *óí*, and *úá*, respectively. In contrast, L-toned *VV* clusters are often realized with an intervening glottal stop–like sound (see Stenzel 2007a).

The negative construction is a clear exception to the normal Kotiria processes of morpheme agglutination with little phonological modification across morpheme boundaries and with left-to-right tonal spread. It is likely that these atypical phonological features, which result in a shift of phonological saliency to this morpheme, developed as a means of underscoring the importance of negation to the semantics of a proposition.

8.3   Intensification and emphasis: -*yɨ'dɨ*

Intensification of or emphasis on the state or action of a verb root is coded by -*yɨ'dɨ*, also shown in position 4 of figure 8.1. It occasionally occurs as an independent root whose semantics refers to the ongoing passage of time (18), but it is much more frequently used as an intensifier 'do/be X a lot'. In this function, *yɨ'dɨ* is usually serialized directly with a verbal root, preceding aspectual and clause modality markers (20)–(24), although in (19) it is compounded with a nominalized form having an adverbial function. In (20)–(22) -*yɨ'dɨ* emphasizes specific activities or feelings. In (23)–(24) it emphasizes adjectival states; such statements, in an appropriate context, can express the notion of superlative: 'the most X'.

(18)   ba'aro hi'na yoaa. phititia khɨ'mari yɨ'dɨri
       ba'á+ro   ~hí'da   yoá+a
       do/be.after+SG   EMPH   do/make+ASSERT.PERF

       phitítia-~khɨ'ba+ri   **yɨ'dɨ**+ri
       four-year+PL   time.pass+NOM
       'A long time passed, a period of four years.' [A7.111]

(19)   wa'maropɨre, ñarana yare, bu'ena ñaro yɨ'dɨa thɨ'othui sã
       ~wa'bá+ro-pɨ+re   ~yará-~da   yá-re
       be.young+SG-LOC+OBJ   white.people-PL POSS-CLS:generic

       bu'é-~da   ~yá+ro-**yɨ'dɨ**+a
       study/learn-(1/2)PL   be.bad+SG-INTENS+AFFEC

       thɨ'ó-thɨ+i   ~sá
       hear-think+VIS.PERF.1 1PL.EXC
       'When we were young, it was really hard for us to understand school in the white people's language.' [A8.5]

(20) mɨyɨ'dɨwa'aa
~bɨ́-yɨ'dɨ-wa'a+a
run-INTENS-go+ASSERT.PERF
'(The father snake) ran off.' [A6.63]

(21) phũriyɨ'dɨaka
~phurí-yɨ'dɨ+a-ka
hurt-INTENS+AFFEC-ASSERT.IMPERF
'It hurt a lot.' [A7.78]

(22) yɨ'ɨ khãriyɨ'dɨa wa'ari hi'ka
yɨ'ɨ́ ~kharí-yɨ'dɨ+a wa'á+ri hi-ka
1SG sleep-INTENS+AFFEC go+NOM(INFER) COP-ASSERT.IMPERF
'I've been asleep a long time!' [A7.128]

(23) tiro tuayɨ'dɨriro hira
tí+ró tuá-yɨ'dɨ+ri+ro hí+ra
ANPH+SG be.strong-INTENS+NOM+SG COP+VIS.IMPERF.2/3
'He's very strong.' / 'He's the strongest (one).'

(24) noayɨ'dɨria hira wi'o
~dóá-yɨ́'dɨ́+rí+á hí+ra wi'ó
be.beautiful-INTENS+NOM+PL COP+VIS.IMPERF.2/3 CONTR
'But they (some other baskets) are very beautiful.' (or '... the most beautiful.') [Baskets]

8.4 Modality

Certain modal notions are coded by serialization of roots in position 3, as seen in §7.5.4. In morphological position 5 of figure 8.1, we find a number of additional morphemes coding information related to the speaker's attitude toward the action or event, or assessment of how it will affect one of the participants in the discourse. Among such modal attitudes are 'doubt', and 'favorable, negative, or unexpected affectedness or results'. Modal morphemes of position 5 can cooccur with modal serializations (roots from position 3), as in (33), with the negative (from position 4), as in (28), and with aspectual markers (also shown in position 5), as in (39)–(40) below. However, I have no examples in which two or more of the modal morphemes from position 5 occur in the same word. The relative flexibility of the positioning of these morphemes within the verbal construction is noted in §8.4.3 below.

8.4.1 Dubitative: -*bo*

The dubitative morpheme -*bo* indicates that as far as the speaker is concerned, the event expressed by the verb is either less than completely certain to occur or is not completely true (see also §9.2.5). In (25) -*bo* is used to refer to plans that might or might not occur; in (26) it indicates the event that would have happened if an unexpected change had not occurred; in (27) it is used in a hypothetical construction; and in (28) -*bo* indicates that the speakers are doubtful that their father stuck to his original plan.

(25)   *da'rana wa'aboka*
       *da'rá-~da   wa'á-**bo**-ka*
       work-(1/2)PL go-DUB-ASSERT.IMPERF
       'We might go to work.'

(26)   *mɨ'ɨre chɨnokaboka nia*
       *~bɨ'ɨ+ré   chɨ́-~doka-**bo**-ka   ~dí+a*
       2SG+OBJ   eat-COMPL-DUB-ASSERT.IMPERF   say+ASSERT.PERF
       'We would have eaten you up.' [A5.38]

(27)   *pate ni yɨ'ɨ thuakɨ, yɨ'ɨkhɨ yɨ'ɨ bu'eboka*
       pá-te   ~di yɨ'ɨ   thuá+kɨ   yɨ'ɨ-khɨ   yɨ'ɨ
       ALT-CLS:time say 1SG   return+(1/2)MASC 1SG-ADD 1SG
       *bu'é-**bo**-ka*
       study/learn-DUB-ASSERT.IMPERF
       'If I ever went back, I would also learn (traditional songs and dances).' [A3.24]

(28)   *mɨ'ɨ ã nierabori hira sãre*
       *~bɨ'ɨ   ~a=~di-éra-**bo**+ri   hí+ra*
       2SG   so=say-NEG-DUB+NOM(INFER) COP+VIS.IMPERF.2/3
       ~sá+re
       1PL.EXC+OBJ
       'You didn't call us (but something else did).' [A4.53]

8.4.2 Frustrative: -~*ba*

The frustrative morpheme -~*ba* indicates the speaker's assessment that an expected state is no longer true, or that an action did not or cannot produce the desired outcome. In (29) and (30), the frustrative indicates that although spoken demands were made, they were not obeyed; in (31) it implies that the woman's gesture for her son to come down from the roof was in vain; in (32) it shows that the man's efforts of looking all over did not result in his finding anything; and in (33) it indicates a desire as yet unfulfilled.

(29) yɨ'ɨre khero mɨ'ɨ yahiripho'nare yɨ'ɨre waga nimaa
      yɨ'ɨ+ré khé+ro   ~bɨ'ɨ=yahíri~pho'da+re yɨ'ɨ+ré   wá+gá
      1SG+OBJ be.fast+SG 2SG(POSS)=heart+OBJ   1SG+OBJ   give+IMPER
      ~dí-~**ba**+a
      say-FRUS+ASSERT.PERF
      '"Give me your heart right now," he demanded (to no avail).' [A7.91]

(30) sa nimaa wa'awa'a hi'na
      sá   ~dí-~**ba**+a   wa'á-wa'a ~hí'da
      EXRT say-FRUS+ASSERT.PERF go-go   EXRT
      'She urged (in vain) "Let's get out of here!"' [A5.28]

(31) tiro pahpero minichakãre bɨepero nia. bɨaphimaa
      tí+ró   papé+ró   ~bidícha-~ka+re   bɨé-pe+ro
      ANPH+SG   play+(3)SG bird-DIM+OBJ   hunt.with.arrows-FAV+(3)SG
      ~dí+a   bɨáphi-~**ba**+a
      be.PROG+ASSERT.PERF   motion-FRUS+ASSERT.PERF
      'He was (on top of the house) playing at hunting birds. She motioned
      (to him, to no avail).' [A5.27]

(32) topɨ sũ ñɨ mahkamaa
      tó-pɨ   ~sũ   ~yɨ   ~baká-~**ba**+a
      REM-LOC   arrive see/look   look/search.for-FRUS+ASSERT.PERF
      'He got there and looked, searching to no avail.' [A7.117]

(33) yɨ'ɨ wahsore chɨduamaka
      yɨ'ɨ   wasó+ré   chú-dua-~**ba**-ka
      1SG   siringa.fruit+OBJ   eat-DESID-FRUS-ASSERT.IMPERF
      'I wish I had some siringa fruit to eat.' [A5.4]

8.4.3 Favoritive: -*pe*

The favoritive morpheme -*pe* (which occurs much less frequently than other markers of speaker attitude) indicates that the speaker judges the action of the verb to be favorable or enjoyable to one of the participants, as in (31) above, where the woman gestures to her son, who is 'happily' or 'enjoyably' playing at hunting up on the roof. In (34), the speaker's use of the favoritive indicates that he is pleased to be telling the story. The position of the favoritive marker appears to be more flexible than that of the dubitative or frustrative markers: in (34), -*pe* directly follows the first verb root in the three-root serialization rather than occurring after the final aspectual serialized root ~*sidi*, the more expected position for morphemes coding modal distinctions. I have grouped the favoritive together with other modal markers in position 5 because of its attitudinal semantics, but in fact its linear position within the verbal word is probably not fixed. (See additional remarks on sequencing in §8.6.)

(34) yɨ'ɨ mihchakãkãre a'ri numiakinare kɨro khitikã ya'uperɨkasinitai niha

yɨ'ɨ ~bichá-~ká-~ká+ré a'rí ~dubí+a-~kida+re ~kɨ+ró
1SG today-DIM-DIM+OBJ DEM.PROX woman+PL-PL+OBJ one/a+SG

khití-~ka ya'ú-**pe**-rɨka-~sidi-ta+i
story-DIM tell-FAV-begin-do.then/now-INTENT+(1/2)MASC

~dí-ha
be.PROG-VIS.IMPERF.1

'I'm happy to be telling these women a little story right now.' [A6.2]

8.4.4 Other modal morphemes

There are a few additional morphemes that occur much less frequently in the data and that, for now, I group in this position class of markers expressing aspectual and modal notions. The first of these is the terminative marker -~ha, which appears to indicate the speaker's assessment of the boundary point between significant episodes in discourse. In (35), it marks a father and son's return home after their dog has been tragically killed by a jaguar, a traumatic turn of events after which the family became and remained 'dogless' for a good period of time, while in (36) it marks the boundary between the prelude of a story—a woman telling her husband that she has a craving for a particular kind of fruit—and the consequences her declaration provokes: while her husband is away, evil beings arrive with a basket of that very fruit so that they can gain entry to the house and devour the woman and her children.

(35) ã yoana sã diero me'reraina thuahãkɨrɨ yoaripa

~a=yoá-~da ~sá dié+ró=~be'r(e)-éra-~ida
so/then=do/make-(1/2)PL 1PL:EXC dog+SG=COM/INST-NEG-NOM:PL

thuá-~**ha**-kɨrɨ yoá+rí-pá
return-TERM-ADVERS be.long+NOM-CLS:time

'Then we sadly remained dogless for a long time.' [A2.12]

(36) to a'rire du'timari nihachɨ, to manɨno pase'epɨ wa'aa

to=a'rí+ré du'tí-~bá+rí ~dí-~**ha**-chɨ
DEF=DEM:PROX+OBJ tell/request-FRUS+NOM say-TERM-SW.REF

to=~badɨ+ro pá=se'e-pɨ wa'á+a
3SG.POSS=husband+SG ALT=CONTR-LOC go+ASSERT.PERF

'Just after she said that, her husband went off someplace.' [A5.5]

A second marker, *-pɨ*, seems to indicate the speaker's empathy for a given protagonist in some unfortunate situation: in (37), it is a dog being swallowed by a huge snakelike creature, and in (38), it is a woman who has become attached to an evil forest devil that is literally sucking the life out of her; while *-~behe* (also in (38)) appears to indicate the speaker's intense negative assessment of the situation. Having only rare examples of these morphemes, though, my interpretation of them is still tentative. Investigation of these and other markers expressing speaker attitudes toward events should prove an interesting topic for future analysis.

(37) *dierore chuburoropɨ nia*
 dié+ró+ré   chú-búró+ró-pú   ~dí+a
 dog+SG+OBJ eat-go.down+(3)SG-EMPATH be.PROG+ASSERT.PERF
 'It was already swallowing down the poor dog.' 6.17

(38) *wi'omeheta yariaropɨ nia*
 *wi'ó-~**behe**=ta   yarí+á+ro-**pɨ***
 CONTR-NEG.ASSESS=REF die+AFFEC+(3)SG-EMPATH
 ~dí+a
 be.PROG+ASSERT.PERF
 'But poor thing, she was already (at the point of) death/dying.' [A4.66]

8.5 Imperfective and perfective aspect

In position 5 of figure 8.1—the final stem position—we also find morphemes that code imperfective or perfective grammatical aspect. Although it is not common for a verbal word to include both modal and aspectual markers from position 5, examples (39) and (40) show that they can cooccur, and when they do, aspectual markers precede modal markers.

(39) *ã ta yoa to koyase'e tirore sinituaatimaa*
 ~á=ta yoá to=kó-ya-se'e   tí+ró+ré
 so=REF do 3SG.POSS=relative-PL-CONTR ANPH+SG+OBJ
 *~sidítu+a-**ati**-~**ba**+a*
 ask+PL-IMPERF-FRUS+ASSERT.PERF
 'His relatives, though, were always demanding to know (unsuccessfully): . . .' [A7.156]

(40) *yɨ phɨkɨ mɨ'nohuriro hiatimare*
 yɨ=phɨk+ɨ́   ~bɨ'dó-hu+ri+ro
 1SG.POSS=parent+MASC tobacco-smoke+NOM+SG

hí-ati-~ba+re
COP-IMPERF-FRUS+VIS.PERF.2/3
'My father used to be a smoker.'

The distinction between perfective and imperfective aspects is understood to be one of perspective focus "on termination and boundedness" for the perfective, and "away from termination and boundedness" for the imperfective, which includes progressive or durative processes as well as habitual or repetitive events (Givón 2001, vol. 1:288–89). Position 5 is not the only place in Kotiria verb structure where aspectual distinctions are coded, however. A perfective-imperfective distinction is also coded in the visual evidential suffixes in position 6 (see §9.2.2), though it relates more to the evidence rather than the event itself. Below, some attention is given to the effects of combining categories in position 5 both with particular classes of roots and with particular categories in position 6.

8.5.1 Imperfective aspect: *-ati*

Grammatical imperfectivity in Kotiria is coded by the morpheme *-ati*. The interaction of this morpheme and the inherent properties of stative or nonstative verbs results in a variety of semantic distinctions. The combination of the imperfective *-ati* with a perfective clause-modality suffix on a stative verb or a verb of mental process yields readings of bounded yet durative or repeated states of being—situations that 'used to be', as in (40) above, (41), and (42), or mental states that go on or repeat over a period of time (43)–(44).

(41) *phanopɨre hiatiga mahsayahkaina*
~*phadó-pɨ+re*   *hí-ati+a*
do/be.before-LOC+OBJ   COP-IMPERF+ASSERT.PERF
~*basá-yáká-~ídá*
people-steal-NOM.PL
'In the olden days there were people-stealers.' [A4.1]

(42) *õ wɨ'ɨ yoarose phiri khumu, ti khumupɨ, tina phosaatiga*
~*ó*   *wɨ'ɨ*   *yoá+ro-se*   *phí+ri*   ~*khubú*
DEIC:PROX house be.long+SG-be.like be.big+NOM log
ti=~khubú-pɨ *tí-~da*   *phosá-ati+a*
ANPH=log-LOC ANPH-PL fill-IMPERF+ASSERT.PERF
'It was like a longhouse, the log, (and) they filled it (they were all living inside it).' [A4.38]

(43)   *tikoro, to namono, chɨduaatiga wasore*
tí-kó+ró   *to=~dabó+ro*   *chɨ́-dua-**ati**+a*
ANPH-FEM+SG   3SG.POSS=wife+SG   eat-DESID-IMPERF+ASSERT.PERF
wasó+ré
siringa.fruit+OBJ
'The woman, his wife, wanted to eat (had a craving for) siringa fruit.' [A5.3]

(44)   *tire, yɨ'ɨ patere wãkuatii*
tí+re   *yɨ'ɨ*   *pá-te+re*   *~wakú-**atí**+í*
ANPH+OBJ   1SG   ALT-CLS:time+OBJ   remember-IMPERF+VIS.PERF.1
'That, I remember (think about) sometimes.' [A3.17]

The combination of the imperfective *-ati* and a perfective clause-modality suffix on an activity verb also yields a reading of habituality or repetition, as in (45) and the two (nonadjacent) sentences from the narrative "How Our Ancestors Got Women" in (46).

(45)   *yɨ'ɨse'e bu'ewa'a yoatii hi'na*
yɨ'ɨ́-se'e   *bu'é-wa'a*   *yoá-**ati**+i*   *~hí'da*
1SG-CONTR   study/learn-go   do/make-IMPERF+VIS.PERF.1   EMPH
'(But) I was always going away to study.' [A3.18]

(46) a. *patena tina moñonokaatia*
      pá-te-~da   *tí-~da*   *~boyó-~doka-**ati**+a*
      ALT-CLS:time-PL   ANPH-PL   fail-COMPL-IMPERF+ASSERT.PERF
      'But sometimes they would be totally unsuccessful.' [Ancestors]

    b. *ti numiare ña'a toaro me're bɨrukuta'a sã ña'aatia*
      ti=~dubí+a+re   *~ya'á toá+ro=~be're*
      ANPH=woman+PL+OBJ   catch   be.fast+SG=COM/INST
      ~bɨ́-ruku-ta   *~sa*   *~ya'á-**ati**+a*
      run-stand-come   MOV.inside   catch-IMPERF+ASSERT.PERF
      '(Men) would kidnap women quickly by surrounding (their longhouse) and then running (inside) to catch them.' [Ancestors]

In clauses with motion or position verbs and plural subjects, the use of the imperfective often results in a distributive reading. In (47), for instance, it indicates the same location or position for each individual in the collective (see also (42) above); in (48) it shows that all three boys were doing the chasing; and in (49) the imperative is addressed to the second person plural—the admonition is equally distributed to all addressees.

(47) ti khumu phʉ'ichapʉ tina hiatiga
      ti=~khubú   phʉ'ichá-pʉ   tí-~da   hí-**ati**+a
      ANPH=log   inside-LOC   ANPH-PL   COP-IMPERF+ASSERT.PERF
      'They (a bunch of evil spirit-beings) were all there inside the log.'
      [A4.40]

(48) tina nʉnʉatiga: kʉ̃iro wa'mʉatariro, do'kai, pairo, tiaro to pho'na hia
      tí-~da   ~dʉdʉ́-**ati**+a
      ANPH-PL   follow/chase-IMPERF+ASSERT.PERF

      ~kʉ́-író   ~wa'bʉátá+rí+ró   do'kái   pá-iro
      one-NOM.SG   adolescent.boy+NOM+SG   young.boy   ALT-NOM.SG

      tiá+ró   to=~pho'dá   hí+a
      three+SG   3SG.POSS=children   COP+ASSERT.PERF

      'They chased (after their mother): one adolescent, a younger boy (and) another one; her three sons.' [A4.41]

(49) su'aropʉre wa'eraatiga
      su'á+ro-pʉ+re   wa'(a)-éra-**ati**+ga
      go.into.the.woods+NOM-LOC+OBJ   go-NEG-IMPERF+IMPER
      'Don't (any of you) be going into the woods.' [LSK: Snakes]

8.5.2 Perfective aspect: -wa'a

Grammatical perfectivity in Kotiria is coded in two ways. The first is a serial verb construction involving the verb wa'a 'go' and the second is a verb sequencing construction involving the verb yoa 'do', discussed in §11.4.

The verb wa'a 'go' has several functions in Kotiria. As an independent verb, it codes simple translocative motion (§7.3.1), and in non-initial position in a serialized verb construction with a nonstative verb, it indicates the directionality of an associated action (§7.5.1). In serializations with stative verbs, on the other hand, wa'a codes a particular type of perfectivity: a completed change to a new state, one in which the patient (subject or object) is totally affected (50)–(51). A clear instance in which wa'a is used in this sense is seen when we compare the two sentences in (51), which occur sequentially in a narrative (text 4 in appendix 1). In (51a), the narrator uses neither +a 'affected' nor perfective =wa'a (see observations below on the cliticlike phonological behavior of =wa'a) with the verb ~sʉ'a 'stick onto'. In the next sentence (51b), however, he then qualifies how complete the 'sticking onto' was, first comparing the action to an embrace, and then adding the perfective =wa'a, implying that the evil being and the women have essentially bonded together. A similar contrast is shown in (52), between the man who just gets (regularly) drunk (52a) and the one who gets 'really' or 'completely' drunk (52b),[2] the latter coded by the perfective =wa'a. The perfective construction with =wa'a also frequently occurs with yʉ'dʉ to express a change of state with an intensified outcome (52b) and (53). (For discussion of the element +a 'affected' that precedes wa'a in many of these examples, see §8.5.3.)

(50) tinare wãha tiro wahcheawa'aa
      tí-~da+re   ~wahá   tí+ró   waché+a-**wa'a**+a
      ANPH-PL+OBJ kill   ANPH+SG be.happy+AFFEC-go+ASSERT.PERF
      'He killed them (some monkeys, and) became happy.' [A7.11]

(51) a. tiro ti phʉkoropʉre wi'i sʉ̃'aga
        tí+ró   ti=phʉk+ó+ró-pʉ́+ré   wi'í
        ANPH+SG   3PL.POSS=parent+FEM+SG-LOC+OBJ arrive
        ~sʉ'á+a
        stick.onto+ASSERT.PERF
        'He (an evil being) came up to (and) stuck onto their mother.' [A4.31]

     b. tikorore kʉ̃ su'sʉ̃roseta yoamʉa, tikorore sʉ'ãawa'aga
        tí-kó+ró+ré   ~kʉ́   su'sú+ro-se=ta
        ANPH-FEM+SG+OBJ one/a embrace+SG-be.like=REF
        yoá-~bʉ+a   tí-kó+ró+ré
        do/make-run+ASSERT.PERF ANPH-FEM+SG+OBJ
        ~sʉ'á-**wa'a**+a
        stick.on-go+ASSERT.PERF
        'Quickly, as if he were embracing her, he stuck onto her.' [A4.32]

(52) a. si'nia bohkasʉ̃, si'nikhã'aa
        ~si'día   boká-~sʉ   ~si'dí-~kha'a+a
        caxiri.beer find-arrive drink-dream+ASSERT.PERF
        'He found caxiri beer there (and) got drunk.' [A4.16]

     b. ãta yoa kʉ̃ta hi'na tiro phayuru si'nikhã'ayʉ'dʉawa'aa
        ~á=ta   yoá ~kʉ́=ta ~hí'da tí+ró   phayúrú
        so=REF do   one=REF EMPH   ANPH+SG caxiri.beer
        ~si'dí-~kha'a-**yʉ'dʉ-wa'a**+a
        drink-dream-INTENS-go+ASSERT.PERF
        'Then, one day he got really drunk on caxiri beer.' [A7.160]

---

[2] Whenever caxiri beer is available, people are expected to drink liberally and allow for effects of the alcohol to manifest themselves. However, as in any social drinking situation, things can easily get out of hand, and people recognize the difference between drinking that leads to a nice buzz and drinking to the point of becoming completely intoxicated. This is the distinction indicated these examples.

(53) *tiro kɨayɨ'dɨawa'aa*
 tí+ró   kɨá-yɨ'dɨ+a-wa'a+a
 ANPH+SG be.afraid-INTENS+AFFEC-go+ASSERT.PERF
 'He became very frightened.' [A7.31]

As a noninitial verb, =*wa'a* also codes perfective aspect in serialized verb constructions with certain classes of nonstative verbs, as we see in (54)–(55). (Again, see §8.5.3 for the morpheme +*a* 'affected' that precedes *wa'a* in these examples.) The parallel between the perfectives of statives in (50)–(53) and the perfectives of nonstatives below is that for both, the grammatical subject is a semantic patient or experiencer rather than an agent. In most cases, the semantics of the nonstative verb itself entails that the subject is nonagentive (55)–(56). When the verb has an agentive subject, the addition of *(+a)=wa'a* results in a passivelike reading, as is the case in (54). Generally, though, marking perfectivity of a verb with an agentive subject is accomplished by a different construction: that involving the verb *yoa*, discussed in §11.5.

The perfective, change-of-state reading of =*wa'a* is again clear when we compare the sentences in (56). The first, without =*wa'a*, refers to a man who is just thinking about going to sleep (56a), while the second is talking about one who has actually fallen into slumber (56b). In the latter, the verb ~*khari* 'sleep' is marked by +*a*=*wa'a*.

(54) *ãga khõ'oawa'aa*
 ~*agá*   ~*kho'ó+a=wa'a+a*
 poisonous.snake bite+AFFEC=go+ASSERT.PERF
 '(The next day, the man was just going into the brush around his house and) he was bitten by a poisonous snake.' [A7.163]

(55) *kɨ̃iro diero, phirirowɨ'rɨ hirirowɨ'rɨ butiawa'aa*
 ~*kɨ-iró*   *dié+ró*   *phí+ri+ro-wɨ'rɨ*   *hí+ri+ro-wɨ'rɨ*
 one/a-NOM.SG dog+SG be.big+NOM+SG-AUG COP+NOM+SG-AUG
 butí+a=wa'a+a
 disappear+AFFEC=go+ASSERT.PERF
 'One dog, the biggest of all, disappeared.' [A6.7]

(56) a. *ti ku'tupɨ phi'asɨ, õita yɨ'ɨ khãriita, nia*
    ti=ku'tú-pɨ   *phi'á-~sɨ*   ~*ó+í=ta*
    ANPH=clearing-LOC MOV.out.into-arrive DEIC.PROX+LOC=REF
    yɨ'ɨ ~*kharí+i-ta*   ~*dí+a*
    1SG sleep-+(1/2)MASC-INTENT say+ASSERT.PERF
    'Emerging into the clearing, he said/thought, "I'll sleep here."'
    [A7.19]

b. *wa'a sɨhka khãriawa'aa*
   wa'á sɨka   ~kharí+a=**wa'a**+a
   go   lie.down sleep+AFFEC=go+ASSERT.PERF
   '... he lay down and went to sleep.' [A7.98]

In this perfective, change-of-state construction, *wa'a* contrasts with *wa'a* in other constructions in that it behaves phonologically like a clitic, realized with L tone. This is not clear from (54), (55), or (56a), in which the tone melody of the root is LHL and in which the L tone of *wa'a* might conceivably be produced by spreading. However, in (57), we see that the final H of the LH melody of *yari* 'die' spreads only to the 'affected' marker +*a*, while *wa'a* and the morphology following it are realized with L tone, a pattern not predicted from normal spreading processes. It is clear from words whose roots have H or LH tone that it is not spreading that causes L tone realization on *wa'a*, but cliticization.

(57) *toita yariawa'aa*
    tó+i=ta   yarí+á=wa'a+a
    REM+LOC=REF die+AFFEC=go+ASSERT.PERF
    'He died right there.' [A7.88]

However, *wa'a* does not behave like a clitic in constructions such as those in (58)–(60) below; there, even though *wa'a* has the same perfective semantic function, it occurs as a different kind of syntactic constituent and exhibits different phonological behavior. These three sentences are examples of the expression of information based on inferential (58)–(59) or nonvisual (60) sources of evidence (two of the verb-final categories of clause modality described in detail in chapter 9). The point about these two evidential categories that is important here is that they are coded by verbal constructions whose final element is a finite verb—the copula *hi* for the 'inference' category, and the perception verb *koa* for the 'nonvisual' category—which takes a nominalized verb as its complement. The suffix +*ri* is the nominalizing morpheme used in the 'inference' construction (§9.2.4), while nominalization in the 'nonvisual' construction is accomplished by subject agreement morphology (§10.1.2), such as the suffix +*ro* in (56).

(58) *yɨ'ɨ khãriyɨ'dɨa wa'ari hi'ka*
    yɨ'ɨ ~kharí-yɨ'dɨ+a   **wa'á+ri**   hí-ka
    1SG sleep-INTENS+AFFEC go+NOM(INFER) COP-ASSERT.IMPERF
    'I've been asleep a long time!' (= (22)) [A7.128]

(59) 1 bayʉ'dʉkã wa'ari hia
bá-yʉ'dʉ-~ka   **wa'á+ri**   hí+a
decompose-INTENS-DIM go+NOM(INFER) COP+ASSERT.PERF
'It (the curupira's body) had (apparently) decomposed completely.'

2 ne bahueraa
~dé bahu-éra+a
NEG be.visible-NEG+ASSERT.PERF
'There was no trace of it.' [A7.119–20]

(60) borasʉka'a wa'aro koataa
borá-~sʉ-ka'a   **wa'á+ro** koá-ta+a
fall-arrive-do.moving go+(3)SG NONVIS-come+ASSERT.PERF
'He fell right down (the man heard it).' [A7.86]

When *wa'a* occurs as the nominalized constituent in either of these constructions, it no longer behaves like a clitic, but instead constitutes the initial root of a word that is phonologically independent from the elements preceding it, occurring with its original LHL tonal melody. Thus, the verbal construct in (58) begins with the LHL root *~khari* 'sleep', followed by the intensifier morpheme *-yʉ'dʉ* and the morpheme *+a* 'affected', together pronounced as a single phonological word [kʰãrĩjʉʔdʉa]. These are followed by *wa'a*, which has its perfective function, but, being the nominalized constituent of the construction coding inference, constitutes an independent phonological word, separate from the preceding and following verbal constituents. It is realized with its own underlying LHL specification for tone, and the final L tone spreads to the nominalizing suffix *+ri*, resulting in [waʔári]. The finite copula closing the full verbal construction forms yet another independent phonological word. My hypothesis about why this different phonological behavior occurs is that historically, in the perfective construction, *wa'a* was a phonologically independent word (parallel to the still observed phonological independence of *yoa* in the perfective construction described in §11.5), and that its current cliticlike behavior indicates incipient grammaticalization. However, when the perfective *wa'a* occurs within one of these evidential constructions as a nominalized complement, it retains its historically independent status. It should be noted that *+ri* in other inference constructions freely nominalizes multimorphemic or serialized verb expressions (see (28) above and also the examples in §9.2.4). Thus, it is clearly not the case that *+ri* can only occur suffixed to a single root or that that addition of *+ri* requires a root to become an independent phonological word. Rather, it suggests that the explanation lies in synchronic variation involving *wa'a* itself: in certain contexts *wa'a* is a cliticized constituent while in others, though having exactly the same semantic function, it is a phonologically independent stem.

8.5.3 The function of the suffix +*a*

Perfective (=)*wa'a* is frequently preceded by the morpheme +*a*. The function of this morpheme in Kotiria is still not completely clear, though a review of the literature reveals a number of different analyses for its counterparts in other Tukanoan languages. For instance, the suffix -*ka*, presumed to be related to +*a*, was analyzed by Sorensen for Tukano as an indicator of "changed status (whether openly expressed, or implied) in the object of the verb ... or in the verb itself as its own object, as a result of the activity or state expressed in the verb" (1969:165–66).

Hypotheses as to the function of the more frequently occurring cognate morpheme +*a* include Kaye's analysis that it is a marker of 'nonpresent time or space' in Desano (1970:47), while Miller lists it as an aspectual suffix coding 'perfect' (1999:77). Ramirez categorically states that he is uncertain of its function in Tukano, saying only that it acts like a suffix and is phonologically fused with the preceding root (Ramirez 1997a:194). In Sorensen's analysis of Tukano, +*a* is described as a morpheme that "closes" a verb and prepares it to be followed by the auxiliary verb *wa* 'go', to which all further inflectional morphology is transferred. He adds that when +*a* occurs on a verb that is not followed by *wa*, it functionally resembles an infinitive marker (1969:85–186).

Waltz and Waltz suggest two functions for +*a* in Kotiria: that it can mark 'emphatic aspect' or that it codes the completed nature of a verb (as Miller suggests for Desano), though they add that it "seems to occur at the end of an episode or the end of a series of actions" (1997:42–46; my translation). What Sorensen recognizes for Tukano but Miller and the Waltzes do not mention in their analyses of Desano and Kotiria is that this morpheme is most often, though not exclusively, observed as a constituent in a particular type of verbal construction with a specific semantic function. In the case of Kotiria, +*a* most frequently occurs in the perfective contruction with (=)*wa'a*, suggesting that we can find clues to the semantic function of this morpheme by looking at its use in this construction. Recalling that the perfective construction with (=)*wa'a* includes notions of 'completeness' and 'change of state', it would appear that the addition of +*a* adds a further, related semantic indication of 'total affectedness' that occurs in such situations. This same notion of 'total affectedness' seems equally appropriate in situations that do not involve a change of state, where (=)*wa'a* does not appear, such as that of the intense pain expressed in

(61). Hence +*a* is glossed as "AFFEC" to reflect the notion of "total affectedness" that is central to the contexts in which it occurs.[3]

(61) phŭriyʉ'dʉaka
~phuri-yʉ'dʉ+a-ka
hurt-INTENS+AFFEC-ASSERT.IMPERF
'It hurt a lot.' (=(21) [A7.78]

8.6 Order of verbal morphemes and degree of grammaticalization

Although there are only two required constituents of a finite verbal word—a lexical root and morphology coding clause modality—the morphological template of verbal words in Kotiria, as seen in figure 8.1 at the beginning of this chapter, is quite complex. It allows stems to be composed of serialized roots, and to take a series of medial affixed morphemes coding negation, intensification, different types of speaker-oriented modality, and imperfective vs. perfective aspect.

While the verbal template is complex, some generalizations can be perceived in its ordering. Overall, it can be viewed as composed of a continuum of morpheme types with varying degrees of semantic and phonological independence. Morphemes occurring closer to the beginning of the word on the whole display more features of semantic and phonological independence than do morphemes occurring closer to the end of the verbal word; the most phonologically independent components are full roots occurring singly or as the initial roots in serializations, while the most grammaticalized components are completely bound and phonologically reduced suffixes. (The most notable exception is the negative morpheme -*era*.)

As with noun morphology (§4.4, §5.4.2), the order of noninitial morphemes in the verb roughly corresponds to a continuum of grammaticalization. Properties implying more lexical status vs. more grammaticalized status are summarized in figure 8.2.

The verb-final morphemes of position 6, discussed in chapter 9, are clearly highly grammaticalized on these parameters: they are obligatory, are nearly always monomoraic and unspecified for tone and nasality, and code semantic categories, such as evidentiality and illocutionary modality, that relate the clause to the speaker's knowledge or evaluation or to other features of the speech situation.

On the other hand, noninitial roots coding adverbial (manner) information and those with modal functions (positions 1 and 3 of figure

---

[3] Another example in which +*a* is not followed by *(=)wa'a* is seen in (19) above.

	lexical ←		→ grammaticalized
Distribution:	can occur as initial root, with same form and meaning	related in form and meaning to an initial root	cannot occur in initial position
	not obligatory in a verb		obligatory in a verb
Semantics:	modifies lexical meaning of verb root		relates described event to speaker or speech situation
Phonology:	usually two moras	one or two moras	one mora
	independently specified for tone, [± nasal], and glottalization	not specified for tone, but specified for [± nasal], and glottalization	unspecified for tone, [± nasal], and glottalization

Figure 8.2. Relatively lexical vs. relatively grammatical properties of noninitial morphemes in the verb.

8.1) are clearly the least grammaticalized constituents; many can function as either initial or noninitial roots with closely related, if not virtually identical, semantics. Such roots retain full bimoraic structure and underlying specification for nasality and glottalization, losing only tonal specification when in noninitial position. Serialized roots coding aspectual information (position 2) show a slightly higher degree of grammaticalization in that most no longer, or at best rarely, occur in initial position and their original meanings have become more generalized. Still, the fact that they retain bimoraic structure and inherent specification for nasality and glottalization attests to their status as verbal roots.

In positions 4–5, in the middle of figure 8.1, we find categories of verbal morphemes such as the negative, the intensifier (both analyzed as having grammaticalized root status), and several types of modal and aspectual morphemes. Because many of these intermediate morphemes are specified for the [±nasal] feature (arguably the most deeply rooted phonological feature linked to lexical identity), it is likely that they derive from verb roots; however, unlike the clearly recognizable roots further to the left, on the whole they display other types of phonological reduction that indicate greater degrees of grammaticalization. The notable exception is the negative morpheme *-era*: although it does not occur as an initial root, uniquely among the noninitial morphemes of Kotiria it retains its own specification for tone, while neutralizing the tone of the preceding root or roots to L. Negative *-era* also displays another phonological property that is unusual for Kotiria, inducing regular assimilation and deletion of final *a* of a preceding root.

With the exception of the leftmost, initial verb root and the rightmost final suffix coding clause modality, the organization of figure 8.1 is not intended to represent absolutely fixed positions for the different categories of verbal morphemes. It does, however, represent observed tendencies such as the fact that noninitial roots in serialized verb constructions occur contiguous to the initial root and are marked as a single lexical unit by subsequent morphology terminating with markers of clause modality; the fact that the negative marker occurs directly after the lexical stem (simple or complex) defining the event or state; and the fact that coding of perfective and imperfective and attitudinal modality close the morphological characterization of the event or state and occur just before markers of clause modality.

Some linear flexibility is possible, though, as noted in §8.4.3; while the modal morphemes generally tend to occur late in a verbal construct, the favoritive -*pe* appears to occur closer to the initial root, presumably for pragmatic reasons. Also, while there are clear tendencies for manner-type noninitial roots to occur before those coding aspectual information in serialized verb constructions, as in (62), it is possible for an aspectual root to occur between two different motion verbs, as in (63)–(64). Thus, the positions of constituents in figure 8.1 should be understood to represent tendencies rather than absolutes, given that speakers quite clearly can manipulate the order of some categories of morphemes for pragmatic purposes.

(62) *to mahkṹnokãre nawᵾarᵾkaga*
  to=~bak+ᵾ+ró-~ká+ré   *~dá-wᵾá-rᵾká+á*
  3SG.POSS=child+MASC+SG-DIM+OBJ get-carry-begin+ASSERT.PERF
  'She picked up (grabbed) her little boy.' [A5.20]

(63) *tina mᵾrᵾkawa'aka'a sᵾ̃ ñᵾa*
  tí-~da *~bᵾ́-rᵾka-wa'a-ka'a* *~sᵾ́* *~yᵾ́+á*
  ANPH-PL run-begin-go-do.moving arrive see/look+ASSERT.PERF
  'They (the sons) went off running over there (to the log where their mother was held captive) and looked.' [A4.27]

(64) *ti numiare ña'a toaro me're mᵾrᵾkuta'a sã̌ ña'aatia*
  ti=~dubí+a+re   *~ya'á toá+ro=~be're*
  ANPH=woman+PL+OBJ catch be.fast+SG=COM/INST
  ~bᵾ́-rᵾku-ta *~sá* *~ya'á-ati+a*
  run-stand-come MOV.inside catch-IMPERF+ASSERT.PERF
  '(Men) would kidnap women quickly by surrounding (their longhouse) and then running (inside) to catch them.' (= (46b)) [Ancestors]

Examples (65)–(67) further demonstrate the relative flexibility of order of the morphemes shown in figure 8.1. In (65), we see that morphemes of the same position class (in this example, two manner roots from position 2) can sometimes cooccur in a serialization. (Morphemes that fall into the same broad semantic class, but belong to different position classes, are also allowed to cooccur: the two aspectual morphemes in (66) and two markers of modality in (67).) Indeed, only cases where the use of one morpheme would logically exclude the other, such as the simultaneous coding of cislocative and translocative motion, or of perfective and imperfective aspect, seem to be absolutely ruled out. This reinforces the notion that the order classes of figure 8.1 are a representation of tendencies rather than a rigid template.

(65) *to'i dʉ'tesihtotaa. nataa*
  *tó+í   dʉ'té-**sitó-tá**+á*
  REM+LOC chop-MOV.circular-come+ASSERT.PERF
  ~dá-ta+a
  get-come+ASSERT.PERF
  'He went around cutting leaves. He brought them back.' [A7.21]

(66) *patena tina moñonokaatia*
  *pá-te-~da   ti-~da   ~boyó-~**doka-ati**+a*
  ALT- CLS:time-PL ANPH-PL fail-COMPL-IMPERF+ASSERT.PERF
  'But sometimes they would be totally unsuccessful.' (= (46a)) [Ancestors]

(67) *yʉ'ʉ wahsore chʉduamaka*
  *yʉ'ʉ   wasó+ré   chʉ-**dua-~ba**-ka*
  1SG   siringa.fruit+OBJ eat-DESID-FRUS-ASSERT.IMPERF
  'I wish I had some siringa fruit to eat.' (= (33)) [A5.4]

9 Clause modality

This chapter completes the description of Kotiria verbal morphology with an examination of clause modality, the only semantic category obligatorily coded on all finite verbal words. The four major categories of clause modality—realis (evidential), irrealis, interrogative, and directive—correspond to three primary sentence types—statements, interrogatives, and directive utterances such as imperatives. Markers in these categories are mutually exclusive and form a single paradigm. The discussion begins with a brief overview of the general syntactic and semantic characteristics of grammaticalized evidentials and a comparison of the present analysis with previous analyses of the Kotiria evidential system (§9.1). The coding of realis statements by evidential markers is the topic of §9.2, which outlines the core and extended semantics of the five evidential categories, their relation to aspectual distinctions, and their inherent epistemic values. Marking of irrealis statements is described in §9.3, followed by a discussion of the semantic links between the interrogative, evidential, and irrealis categories in §9.4. Directive modality and the morphemes coding, among others, imperative, exhortative, and admonitive utterances are the focus of §9.5.

Table 9.1 below expands position 6 of table 8.1—the set of verbal morphemes that appear in word-final position. Categories of morphemes discussed in the previous two chapters (positions 1 through 5 of table 8.1—the stem morphemes), which include deontic and attitudinal modal notions, code information related to the event itself. In contrast, the clause modality morphemes occurring in the final position of a finite verb, the subject of this chapter, indicate the speaker's relationship to the event or state expressed by the verb.

Clause modality morphemes form a single paradigm and are mutually exclusive, each subcategory of markers corresponding to one of three specific types of sentences—statements, questions, and directives. A sentence is marked either as a realis statement by one of the evidential categories, as an irrealis statement (predictive or speculative) by one of the irrealis statement markers, as a question by one of the interrogative morphemes, or as a command, warning, admonition, or request for permission by one of the directive morphemes. Evidentials function within this larger paradigm to give information about the speaker's cognitive relationship to or perspective on the event or state,

TABLE 9.1. CLAUSE MODALITY

STATEMENTS			
	REALIS (EVIDENTIAL)	hearsay	*-yu'ka, -yu'ti*
		visual	*+i, -ha, +re, +ra*
		nonvisual	*-koa (-ta)-*
		inference	*+ri hi-*
		assertion	*+a, -ka*
	IRREALIS	prediction	*-ka*
		intention-*ta*	
		negative	*-si*
INTERROGATIVES			
	REALIS	imperfective	*-hari*
		perfective	*-ri*
		supposition	*-ka-ri*
	IRREALIS	speculation	*-bo-ri*
DIRECTIVES		imperative	*+ga*
		permissive	*-~ba*
		admonitive	*-ri*
		adversative	*-kʉru*
		exhortative	*(~)sa...~(hi')da*

via the source of information upon which a statement is based. Evidentials are obligatory on all realis statements, the Kotiria equivalent of the basic declarative sentence.

The sorting of clause modality morphemes into "realis" and "irrealis" sets in the table and in the organization of sections in this chapter is partly a matter of convenience. In fact, it is better to conceptualize realis and irrealis as endpoints of a continuum. The "assertion" category, in particular, should be seen as occupying a sort of transitional zone between realis and irrealis. For discussion of these issues, see §§9.2.5–9.2.7 and §9.3.

9.1 Evidentials: overview and previous analyses

The present analysis assumes a basic distinction between evidentiality—a broad semantic category available in some form in every language, for instance the words in bold in the English sentences in (1)—and sets of syntactically and semantically constrained grammatical markers known as evidentials, exemplified in the elements in bold in the Kotiria sentences in (2).

(1) a. **I heard** the eight o'clock bus go by.
    b. **People say** that Karen is dating someone from the office.

(2) a. *numia ña'aina taa nia koatara*
       ~dubí+a ~ya'á-~ida tá+á   ~dí+a
       woman+PL catch-NOM.PL come+(3)PL be.PROG+(3)PL
       koá-ta+ra
       NONVIS-come+VIS.IMPERF.2/3
       'Women-kidnappers are coming.' (the speaker hears them) [Ancestors]

    b. *yɨ koiro kɨ̃iro yariawa'ayu'ti*
       yɨ=kó-iro   ~kú-iro   yarí+á=wa'a-**yu'ti**
       1SG.POSS=relative-NOM.SG   one-NOM.SG   die+AFFEC=go-HSAY.DIFF
       'One of my relatives died.' (the speaker learned from others)

The examples of Kotiria evidentials given in (2) and throughout this chapter conform to the general formal criteria for grammaticalized evidentials outlined by Anderson (1986) and Willett (1988) (but see discussion in Aikhenvald 2003a, 2004). First, their basic semantics indicates the speaker's source of information for a given statement; second, they are grammaticalized on the main predicate of the clause primarily (but not exclusively) as inflectional suffixes that conflate with distinctions of person, aspect, or referentiality; and finally, they show agreement with the grammatical subject of the clause.

The Kotiria evidential system was previously analyzed by Waltz and Waltz as composed of four categories, each conflated with tense (present vs. past) and person (first vs. nonfirst) distinctions. Table 9.2 summarizes their analysis (based on Waltz and Waltz 1997:38; 2000:456).[1]

Waltz and Waltz's analysis identifies two important features of the Kotiria system. First, it shows that the inference (Waltz and Waltz's "indicated")[2] evidential marker is morphologically composed of a nominalizing particle +*ri* followed by the auxiliary verb *hi* and a visual evidential suffix (Waltz and Waltz 2000:457). It also shows that the Kotiria system follows a pattern of distinguishing between first person

---

[1] Phonetic representations of the glottal stop vary slightly in the two sources. Here, *h* is used to represent the voiceless glottal fricative and the phonetic symbol ʔ is used for the glottal stop.

[2] A number of different labels are used for evidential categories in the literature on Eastern Tukanoan languages. To help the reader track category reference throughout this analysis, I have noted in parentheses labels that differ from mine.

TABLE 9.2. KOTIRIA EVIDENTIALS ACCORDING TO WALTZ AND WALTZ

	VISUAL	NONVISUAL	INDICATED	INFORMED (SECONDHAND)
PRESENT				
1st person	-ha			
2nd/3rd person	-ra	-ka	-ri hi-ra	-yuʔka
PAST				
1st person	-(ʔ)i			
2nd/3rd person	-(ʔ)re	-ʔa	-ri hi-re	-yuʔti

vs. nonfirst person; while other Eastern Tukanoan languages code person, gender and number of the grammatical subject in a pattern that distinguishes third person from nonthird person, Kotiria and its sister language Wa'ikhana diverge from this pattern.[3] In the Kotiria (and Wa'ikhana) paradigms, gender and number distinctions have undergone leveling and there has been a shift to a split between first person and nonfirst person, innovations that constitute a significant departure within the family. We should note, however, that these innovations are restricted to matrix clauses; both Kotiria and Wa'ikhana still employ subject agreement morphology that distinguishes between third person and nonthird person (and additionally marks gender for third person singular) in nominalizations and in certain types of irrealis constructions such as those expressing predictions, intentions, or hypothetical situations (see §10.1.2, and for Wa'ikhana, Waltz 2002:186–87).

9.2 A revised analysis of Kotiria evidentials

Figure 9.1 presents a revised view of the Kotiria evidential system. The righthand side of the table presents the forms of the evidentials and the five categories in the Kotiria evidential paradigm; on the left is a matrix of features that characterize the categories, beginning with a distinction between firsthand and nonfirsthand evidence.

---

[3] More information on the paradigms in other Eastern Tukanoan languages can be found in the following sources: Tuyuka is described by Barnes (1984:258), Barnes and Malone (2000:441), and Malone (1988:123); Desano by Miller (1999:64). Kubeo by Ferguson et al. (2000:363–34) and Morse and Maxwell (1999:39–40); Siriano by Criswell and Brandrup (2000:400); Yuruti by Kinch and Kinch (2000:479); Tukano by Welch and West (2000:424) and Ramirez (1997a:119–20); Barasana by Jones and Jones (1991:73) and Gomez-Imbert (1997a); Bará and Makuna by Malone (1988:133); and Tatuyo by Gomez-Imbert (2003b, 2007b).

Features						Forms	Categories
nonfirsthand	quotative					-yu'ka	hearsay
	diffuse					-yu'ti	
firsthand	external	direct	visual	1st	perf.	+i	visual
					imperf.	-ha	
				non1st	perf.	+re	
					imperf.	+ra	
			nonvisual			koa(-ta)-	nonvisual
		indirect				+ri hi-	inference
	internal				perf.	+a	assertion
					imperf.	-ka	

Figure 9.1. Revised analysis of Kotiria evidentials. 1st = first person subject; imperf. = imperfective; non1st = second or third person subject; perf. = perfective.

This revised view differs in two fundamental ways from Waltz and Waltz's analysis.[4] First, it includes an additional category coding nonvisual sensory evidence. It is important that we not equate this new nonvisual category with the category that Waltz and Waltz label as nonvisual. In terms of its semantic functions, Waltz and Waltz's nonvisual category corresponds to the category labeled as "assertion" in figure 9.1. The other four categories—visual, inference, hearsay, and assertion—correspond to categories proposed by Waltz and Waltz (their "visual," "indicated," "informed," and "nonvisual," respectively), although, as is noted in §9.2.3, the "visual" evidentials in the revised analysis are not necessarily restricted to coding literally visual evidence.

Second, while Waltz and Waltz identify tense distinctions for all evidential categories, the revised system does not recognize these. (This contrasts as well with much of the literature on Eastern Tukanoan languages, which includes tense distinctions for the evidential categories coding direct sensory evidence, visual or nonvisual.) The subdivisions of the hearsay category are argued below to refer to the source of

---

[4] Barnes (1984) and Malone (1988) also identify the firsthand vs. nonfirsthand feature as primary in the organization of the evidential systems in other Eastern Tukanoan languages. However, their discussions of other defining features and presentation of the final resulting categories differ significantly from the present analysis. Indeed, alternate feature organizations differ in interesting ways. For instance, in Gomez-Imbert's analysis of Tatuyo and Barasana (1997a, 2003b, 2007b), the direct-indirect distinction occupies the highest level of the feature matrix, creating an initial separation of the sensory categories from the inferential and hearsay categories. This analysis produces results that mirror Willett's (1988) typological framework.

information. In the visual and assertion categories, the perfective-imperfective distinction relates to the speaker's access to and acquisition of information, rather than to the reported event itself; it thus differs from tense in the normal sense, which relates the time of the reported event and the moment of speech.

9.2.1 Nonfirsthand evidence: hearsay

Placing firsthand vs. nonfirsthand as the highest-order opposition in the feature matrix in figure 9.1 above establishes an initial dichotomy between types of information to which the speaker has some kind of firsthand access—external or internal—and information that originates from others. This dichotomy is sufficient to characterize the hearsay category as information obtained through third parties. The two distinct forms of this evidential in Kotiria are shown in (3).

(3) a. *tiro wʉ'ʉpʉ wa'ayu'ka*

    *tí+ró   wʉ'ʉ́-pʉ́   wa'á-**yu'ka***
    ANPH+SG house-LOC go-HSAY.QUOT

    (Someone told me that) 'He went home.'

b. *tiro wʉ'ʉpʉ wa'ayu'ti*

    *tí+ró   wʉ'ʉ́-pʉ́   wa'á-**yu'ti***
    ANPH+SG house-LOC go-HSAY.DIFF

    (They say that) 'He went home.'

I analyze these two forms as coding not tense (as Waltz and Waltz suggest),[5] but distinctions between source referents (see Floyd 1999: 130–40). The form *-yu'ka* has a near-quotative function that evokes, but does not specifically identify, a particular referent as the original source of the information. It would be used by a speaker relating something he or she had just heard or been told, most likely by a person directly involved in the event. Use of *-yu'ti*,[6] on the other hand, indicates a diffuse or unidentifiable referent as the source of the information. This is the marker that would be used for rumor or for news coming from afar.

The fact is, though, that sentences with hearsay evidentials rarely occur in everyday speech. It is much more common for speakers to

---

[5] A tense distinction for this category would set Kotiria apart from the vast majority of Eastern Tukanoan languages. Only in the Morse and Maxwell analysis of Kubeo do we find an evidential marker of secondhand information cooccurring with a present tense marker (1999:36). None of the remaining languages have present-tense forms in the category of secondhand information, as evidentials of this type are fairly consistently analyzed as coding past or bounded situations.

[6] We should note that a very similar form *yʉ'ti* used as an independent root means 'answer', as in (59).

simply quote information from others directly. The motivation for this alternate strategy is unclear, but Aikhenvald notes the same restricted use of hearsay evidentials cross-linguistically throughout the Vaupés region and suggests that preference for direct speech complements is pragmatically motivated: it allows the speaker to "avoid making the choice of an evidential for another person and run the risk of undesired implications concerning 'validation' of the other person's evidence" (2002a:190).

It is also worth noting that the morpheme -*yu* of the Kotiria hearsay evidential surfaces throughout the family in forms belonging to several different evidential categories. It occurs, for example, in the past forms of the hearsay category (Tuyuka, Siriano), in the assertion (Barnes's "assumed") category (Tuyuka, Siriano, Desano, Yuruti), and in the inference (Barnes's "apparent") category (Makuna, Bará, Tatuyo, Karapana, Siriano, Desano, Yuruti) (Malone 1988:128, 133–34). Such similarities suggest that -*yu* may derive historically from a general marker of indirect evidence, and indeed it has been so analyzed in Bará, Tatuyo and Karapana by Gomez-Imbert (1986, 2003b, 2007b), and Gomez-Imbert and Hugh-Jones 2000).

9.2.2 Visual external firsthand evidence

There are four evidential categories characterized as firsthand in the feature matrix in figure 9.1 and three of these, are additionally qualified as indicating information coming from external sources (visual, nonvisual, and inference). These external categories are further distinguished by a dichotomy between direct and indirect sources of information. The direct categories are those involving visual and nonvisual sources of information, both of which indicate that the speaker has knowledge of the event or state expressed by the predicate through some kind of direct sensory evidence.

In daily speech, the majority of sentences are marked by the visual evidential category. The core semantics of this category indicates that the speaker is relating something he or she has experienced or has observed directly. Structurally, the visual category is the most complex; it has four forms that code distinctions of person (first person subject vs. nonfirst person subject) and aspect (imperfective vs. perfective). The first person imperfective suffix -*ha* is exemplified in (4)–(5) and the perfective form +*i* in (6)–(7). Examples (8) and (9) show the nonfirst person (second or third person) forms: imperfective +*ra* and perfective +*re*.

(4) yɨ'ɨkhɨ hiha koiro
 yɨ'ɨ-khɨ́ yɨ'ɨ́ hí-**ha**   kó-iro
 1SG-ADD 1SG COP-VIS.IMPERF.1 relative-NOM.SG
 'I too am your/a relative.' [A7.39]

(5) mipɨre sã yakotiria yare bu'ena phiro wahcheha
 ~bí-pɨ́+ré   ~sa=yá-ko-ti+ri+a   yá-re
 now-LOC+OBJ 1PL.EXC.POSS=POSS-water-VBZ+NOM+PL POSS-CLS:generic
 bu'é-~da   phí+ro   waché-**ha**
 study-(1/2)PL be.big+SG be.happy-VIS.IMPERF.1
 'Now we're very happy to have our own Kotiria learning (writing system or school).' [A8.6]

(6) yɨ'ɨse'e bu'ewa'a yoatii
 yɨ'ɨ́-se'e   bu'é-wa'a   yoá-ati+**i**
 1SG-CONTR study/learn-go do/make-IMPERF+VIS.PERF.1
 '(But) I was always going away to study.' [A3.18]

(7) to wa'ikiro wãhariroditare sã nathuai wɨ'ɨpɨre
 to=wa'í-kíró   ~wahá+ri+ro-dita+re ~sá
 DEF=animal+SG kill+NOM+SG-SOL+OBJ 1PL.EXC
 ~dá-thúá+**i**   wɨ'ɨ́-pɨ́+ré
 get-return+VIS.PERF.1 house-LOC+OBJ
 'We took home only the dead animal (that the dog had hunted).' [A2.13]

(8) õpɨ hira yɨ pho'na
 ~ó-pɨ́   hí+**ra**   yɨ=~pho'dá
 DEIC.PROX-LOC COP+VIS.IMPERF.2/3 1SG.POSS=children
 'Here he (a missing dog) is, my sons.' [A6.24]

(9) marire sõ'oi sĩ'a phitiboka du'tire
 ~barí+ré   ~so'ó+í   ~si'á phití-boka du'tí+**ré**
 1PL.INC+OBJ DEIC.DIST+LOC torch COLL-meet request+VIS.PERF.2/3
 '(Our father) told/asked us to meet (him) there with torches.' [A4.23]

PERFECTIVE AND IMPERFECTIVE. Tense has been proposed as a defining feature of the evidential system in Waltz and Waltz's analysis of Kotiria, as well as in many descriptions of Eastern Tukanoan languages. The term "tense," however, always requires considerable qualification in discussions of the evidential systems of Eastern Tukanoan languages, because the traditional definition of tense as coding events as past, present, or future in relation to a time-of-speech reference point (Givón 2001, vol. 1:285–86) does not quite match their semantics. The temporal information coded in these evidential systems (at least for the most commonly occurring categories) gives information about the speaker's access to the source of information, rather than supplying temporal information about the reported event itself. In many contexts, to be sure, the time of speaker's access to information and the time of the event itself align, but when they do not, it is clear that coding orients to the former.

Linguists analyzing some Tukanoan languages interpret distinctions within categories in the evidential systems as marking different kinds of tense oriented to different features. Barnes, for instance, states that in Tuyuka, tense distinctions for the inference (Barnes's "apparent") and assertion (Barnes's "assumed") evidential categories code "when the related event took place" (more or less matching the traditional definition of tense), while tense distinctions for visual, nonvisual, and hearsay (Barnes's "secondhand") evidential categories code "when the speaker obtained the information" (1984:265). We find other such qualified definitions of tense throughout much of the literature on Eastern Tukanoan languages, though curiously not in Waltz and Waltz's analysis of Kotiria. Ramirez (1997a), for example, analyzes Tukano as having a four-way evidential system with three-way tense distinctions: present, recent past, and distant past. For the visual, nonvisual (Ramirez's "perceived"), and hearsay categories, tense distinctions refer to both the occurrence of the event and when the speaker obtained the evidence, though there are no present tense forms for the hearsay category. For the inference category (Ramirez's "deduction"), tense refers only to the situation denoted by the verb stem: "I deduce *now* that X is doing/did something recently or remotely" (Ramirez 1997a:123 [my translation; emphasis in the original]).

Other Eastern Tukanoan languages—Tatuyo and Barasana (Gomez-Imbert 2007b), Kubeo (Morse and Maxwell 1999; Ferguson et al. 2000) and Kotiria (Stenzel 2008a, and in this description)—are analyzed as coding aspectual rather than temporal distinctions within the visual evidential category. These aspectual distinctions qualify the speaker's relationship to the event via source of information, rather than qualifying the event itself. Assuming that perfective markers indicate the boundedness or termination of states or events and that imperfective markers indicate states or events of an ongoing or unbounded nature, clauses marked by imperfective evidentials imply that from the speaker's perspective, there is ongoing or unbounded cognitive access to the source of information; clauses with perfective forms, on the other hand, imply that the source of information is no longer accessible or has ceased.

Clearly, distinguishing between tense and aspect is not always an easy task, particularly in the case of past tense and perfective aspect, which are often strongly associated, though I will assume that Kotiria perfective and imperfective are aspectual. More crucial is the fact that the Kotiria perfective and imperfective categories do not characterize the time of the reported event, but instead characterize the time at which the speaker acquires information about the event and whether or not that information is still accessible. Often, to be sure, the two times coincide, as in (6), (7), and (9) above, where the speaker's access to information about the event occurs at the same time as the event. In such cases, it is difficult to tell whether the past-or-perfective marking of the verb relates to the reported event or to the speaker's access to information. We can only recognize which distinction is actually being coded (event vs. access to information) by looking at some of the rare but revealing examples with visual evidentials in which such alignment does not occur, in other words, when the referential reported event and the speaker's access to information have different temporal properties.

The lines in (10), from dialogue in a narrative, occur after an evil being has attached himself to a woman and has carried her away to his dwelling place in a hollow log in the forest. The woman's sons, who witnessed her abduction, have run to tell their father and have led him back to the log. When the man arrives, he asks where the woman is (10a), and the sons reply that she is in the log (10b).

(10) a. *no'oi hiri*
      ~do'ó+i hí+ri
      WH+LOC COP+INT
      'Where is she?' [A4.57]

      b. *õi hire*
      ~ó+i   hí+**re**
      DEIC.PROX+LOC COP+VIS.PERF.2/3
      'Here she is.' [A4.58]

Note the perfective form of the evidential used in the sons' response. Since the boys saw the evil creature take their mother into the log and are affirming that she is still in there, an analysis assuming that the tense-or-aspect category of the inflectional ending relates to the time of the reported event itself would lead us to predict the use of an imperfective (or present tense) form for the evidential, but this is not the case. This use of the perfective form reveals that even though the mother's state of being in the log is ongoing, what is being coded in the evidential is the boundedness (or pastness) of the sons' visual access to that information.

Another revealing example is (11), from a different story. A group of evil beings in humanlike form (curupiras) have arrived at a house offering a basket of ripe siringa to a woman who had earlier that day expressed a craving for that very fruit. Their underlying plan, though, is to gain entry to the house and eat the inhabitants, a woman and her children. The woman invites them in, but soon becomes suspicious and makes up an excuse to go down to the river with her children before the evil beings can carry out their plan. She swims away with two of her children to safety just as one of the creatures runs down to the water's edge and utters the lines in (11). Note that although the woman has in fact already escaped (as the evil being readily admits), it is not the perfective (or past tense) form that is used in sentence 1 of (11). The explanation for the choice of the imperfective form comes from the fact that the evil creature's statement is based on evidence or information still before his eyes—he can see the woman in the river.

(11) 1 wãkumasiko mʉ'ʉ ñakã du'tira
 ~wakú-~basi-ko ~bʉ'ʉ́ ~yá-~ka du'tí+*ra*
 be.aware-know-FEM 2SG be.bad-DIM escape+VIS.IMPERF.2/3
 "'You escaped, evil clever woman.'"

 2 mʉ'ʉre chʉnokaboka nia
 ~bʉ'ʉ́+ré chʉ́-~doka-bo-ka ~dí+a
 2SG+OBJ eat-COMPL-DUB-ASSERT.IMPERF say+ASSERT.PERF
 "'(We) would have eaten you up" (they) said.' [A5.37–38]

The statements in (12), too, clearly illustrate that the distinctions coded by different visual evidential forms in Kotiria relate to properties of the acquisition and access to evidence, not the temporal properties of the reported event coded by the verb stem. These remarks occurred during an elicitation session in which a consultant was providing different forms of demonstratives; in the process, he ended up offering a pair of contrasting evidential forms as well. In (12a), he was referring to the small sitting room we were working in at the time, and he used the (expected) visual imperfective form. In (12b), however, he used the (unexpected) perfective form to refer to the sitting room in his neighbor's house. It is unlikely that the room in his neighbor's house had changed size since my consultant had last seen it, so how can we explain his use of the perfective form of the visual evidential? What we must conclude is that while the state of 'being narrow' was certainly ongoing, the fact that the actual visual evidence was not accessible to the speaker at that moment determined his choice of form.

(12) a. *a'ri tatia bi'sa nira*
 *a'rí   tatía   bi'sá   ~dí+**ra***
 DEM.PROX room be.narrow be.PROG+VIS.IMPERF.2/3
 'This room is narrow.'

 b. *si wᵾ'ᵾpᵾkã tatia bi'sa nire*
 sí   wᵾ'ᵾ-pᵾ-~ká   tatía   bi'sá
 DEM.DIST house-LOC-DIM room be.narrow
 *~dí+**re***
 be.PROG+VIS.PERF.2/3
 'The room in that little house is narrow.'

Examples such as these show that aspect in evidentials does not refer to the internal nature of the event or state expressed by the verb; rather, it codes information about the nature of the speaker's access to the evidence itself. Visual evidentials in their imperfective forms indicate the speaker's ongoing or unbounded cognitive access to the event or state via evidence currently available, because the speaker either is involved in the action or state, as in (13)–(14), or is a direct witness to it, as in (15).

(13) *yᵾ'ᵾ mihchakãkãre a'ri numiakinare kᵾro khitikã ya'uperᵾkasinitai niha*
 yᵾ'ᵾ ~bichá-~ká-~ká+ré a'rí   ~dubí+a-~kida+re ~kᵾ+ró
 1SG today-DIM-DIM+OBJ DEM.PROX woman+PL-PL+OBJ one/a+SG
 khití-~ka   ya'ú-pe-rᵾka-~sidi-ta+i
 story-DIM tell-FAV-begin-do.then/now-INTENT+(1/2)MASC
 *~dí-**ha***
 be.PROG-VIS.IMPERF.1
 'I'm happy to be telling these women a little story right now.' [A6.2]

(14) *ã yoakᵾ yᵾ'ᵾ tirore wãhakha'mai tai niha*
 ~a=yoá-kᵾ   yᵾ'ᵾ tí+ró+ré   ~wahá-~kha'ba+i
 so/then=do-(1/2)MASC 1SG ANPH+SG+OBJ kill-want+(1/2)MASC
 *tá+i   ~dí-**ha***
 come+(1/2)MASC be.PROG-VIS.IMPERF.1
 'So, I'm coming here to avenge him (my dead son).' [A6.61]

(15) 1 *wãhanokari hira mari dierore*
 *~wahá-~doka+ri   hí+**ra***
 kill-COMPL+NOM(INFER) COP+VIS.IMPERF.2/3
 ~bari=dié+ró+ré
 1PL.INC.POSS=dog+SG+OBJ
 'Our dog has just been killed.'

2   *phinonowɨ'rɨ hira*
~*phidó+ró-wú'rɨ   hí+ra*
snake+SG-AUG   COP+VIS.IMPERF.2/3
'(By) a big snake.' [A6.25–26]

Perfective forms, on the other hand, indicate that the speaker's cognitive access to the event or state is blocked because the evidence is bounded in time or space and is currently inaccessible, as in (10) and (12). Figure 9.2 represents the speaker (S) in three possible situations, with shaded areas representing the speaker's cognitive relationship, via evidence, to an event or state. Part A of the figure represents cases in which the boundedness or unboundedness of the event or state and of the speaker's access to evidence align. Part B represents situations such as (11), where the speaker's use of an imperfective evidential form indicates ongoing (unbounded) access to evidence that does not coincide with an already bounded event. Part C represents situations such as (10) and (12), in which the use of a perfective evidential form indicates bounded access to evidence, even when the event or state is itself unbounded.

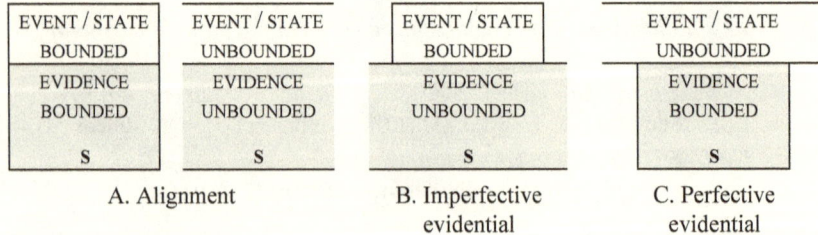

Figure 9.2. Alignment and mismatches of aspect in evidentials and events or states.

Still, the fact that alignment occurs so frequently, as in (4)–(9) above, suggests that the synchronic forms may both derive from and subsume what were formerly tense or aspectual distinctions that related to the reported event or state, rather than to the accessibility of evidence (see Bybee, Perkins, and Pagliuca 1994; de Haan 1999:96; de Haan 2001a). Tense distinctions relating to the reported event or state appear to be a salient feature of many Eastern Tukanoan languages and they are likely a historical feature of all of them. Diachronically, in Kotiria, however, the salient feature of evidential semantics—which I view as an aspectual distinction—relates to the accessibility of evidence. Synchronically, aspectual distinctions surface in all four first-hand evidential categories.

SEMANTIC EXTENSIONS OF VISUAL EVIDENTIALS. Although evidentials from the visual category are used with both active and stative verbs, the combination of imperfective forms of the visual category with certain classes of verbs can result in specific types of semantic readings. In examples (16)–(18), we see that the copula *hi*, suffixed by the imperfective form of a visual evidential, can be used to make statements of general fact. When imperfective forms of the visual evidential are suffixed to activity verbs, on the other hand, the resulting reading is generally that of habituality (19)–(21). These kinds of extended semantic interpretations are typical of languages with multiple evidential markers, such as Kotiria (Aikhenvald 2003a:13).

(16) *a'riro hira ba'a*
 a'rí+ró **hí+ra** *ba'á*
 DEM.PROX+SG COP+VIS.IMPERF.2/3 bass
 'This is a bass.'[7]

(17) *mihsime're ti yoaria hira*
 ~bisí=~be're ti=yoá+ri+a **hí+ra**
 fiber=COM/INST ANPH=do/make+NOM+PL COP+VIS.IMPERF.2/3
 'These (baskets) are made with fibers.' [Baskets]

(18) *phũria khʉariro hira tiro*
 ~phurí+a khʉá+ri+ro **hí+ra** *tí+ró*
 poison+PL hold/have+NOM+SG COP+VIS.IMPERF.2/3 ANPH+SG
 'It (a viper) is extremely poisonous.' [LSK: Snakes]

(19) *ne topʉre tipʉre tinieraha*
 *~dé tó-pʉ+re **tí-pʉ+re** ~tidi-éra-ha*
 NEG REM-LOC+OBJ ANPH-LOC+OBJ wander-NEG-VIS.IMPERF.1
 'I never go hunting there in that place.' [A6.60]

(20) *numia, tina chʉare yoara*
 *~dubí+a tí-~da chʉ́+a+re **yoá+ra***
 woman+PL ANPH-PL eat+PL+OBJ do/make+VIS.IMPERF.2/3
 '(Kotiria) women, they make the food.' [A1.7]

(21) *ã yoa, tina mʉase'e yo'gaa wa'ara*
 ~a=yóá tí-~da ~bʉ́+a-se'e yo'gá+a
 so/then=do/make ANPH-PL man+PL-CONTR fish+(3)PL
 wa'á+ra
 go+VIS.IMPERF.2/3
 '(And the Kotiria) men go fishing.' [A1.8]

---

[7] Example (16) is from the short text that appears as (118) in chapter 4.

9.2.3 Nonvisual external firsthand evidence

The second EXTERNAL and DIRECT evidential category codes NONVISUAL sources of information—essentially, evidence from sensory sources other than sight. In my data, use of the nonvisual evidentials generally indicates auditory evidence, as in (22), where a woman hears a group of men approaching, and in (23), where a man hears the thud (and, speakers indicate, may also feel the vibration) that a curupira (an evil, humanlike being) he has tricked into stabbing itself makes as it falls over.

(22) *numia ña'aina taa nia koatara*
~*dubí+a* ~*ya'á-~ida* *tá+á* ~*dí+a*
woman+PL catch-NOM.PL come+(3)PL be.PROG+(3)PL
koá-ta+ra
NONVIS-come+VIS.IMPERF.2/3
'Women-kidnappers are coming.' (the speaker hears them) (= (2a)) [Ancestors]

(23) *borasŭka'a wa'aro koataa*
borá-~sɨ-ka'a *wa'á+ro* *koá-ta+a*
fall-arrive-do.moving go+(3)SG NONVIS-come+ASSERT.PERF
'He (the curupira) fell right down.' (the speaker heard or otherwise perceived his falling down) [A7.86]

In Kotiria, nonvisual evidence is coded not by a single suffix, as was the case with the visual category, but by a construction involving the lexical verb root *koa* and a nominalized complement. By itself, *koa* is currently used to indicate 'taste' (as in (24) below), but historically, it was apparently used in the sense of 'make noise', as evidenced by the first word of the traditional Kotiria name for the village of Carurú Cachoeira (*koa-ma phoaye* [noisy-stream rapids/waterfalls]). When used to refer to auditory and other types of perceived evidence, *koa* is serialized with the motion verb *ta* 'come', indicating the cislocative directionality of the information: that the sound or feeling comes to the speaker from an external origin. The simple or serialized verbal stem then takes an evidential suffix from one of the two major categories of firsthand evidence: visual or assertion. Visual is the default category (and the most commonly used in everyday speech) indicating direct evidence: +*re* (perfective) or +*ra* (imperfective), as in (22). The perfective assertion suffix is used in narratives (23). The internal sensory perception of taste is coded by *koa* without *ta*, with the imperfective assertion suffix -*ka* (24), the same suffix used to mark sentences expressing other types of internal sensations (§9.2.5). (I have no examples indicating that *koa* without *ta* functions in an evidential sense to indicate other types of internal perception as the basis for a statement.)

(24) *to di'i noaro koaka*
 to=di'í   ~dóá+ró   koá-ka
 3SG.POSS=meat be.good+SG taste-ASSERT.IMPERF
 'Its (a cow's) meat tastes good.' [LSK: Cows]

As with other verbs that take clausal complements (see §11.3), the verb preceding the nonvisual evidential construction is nominalized by a suffix cross-referenced to the subject: in (22) it is +*a*, indicating a third person plural subject, and in (23)–(24) it is +*ro*, indicating a singular or generic third person subject.

Though not previously identified as a separate evidential category, the *koa* construction has clearly been grammaticalized and is consistently used to indicate nonvisual, albeit generally auditory, sources of sensory evidence. Within the evidential paradigm, the nonvisual category contrasts with the visual category, and in terms of frequency and formal coding, situations involving nonvisual evidence are undoubtedly the marked case. This justifies inclusion of the nonvisual as a fifth category within the Kotiria evidential system.

Returning briefly to the structure of the nonvisual construction, it may seem contradictory to find visual evidential suffixes marking a verb root specifically connoting nonvisual evidence. We should not let the labels confuse us, though. As the sole markers on a verb, visual suffixes indicate, by default, visual evidence, the essence of their core semantics. Within the general domain of direct sensory evidence, however, visual should be analyzed as the general, unmarked category. As constituents in evidential constructions such as the marked nonvisual category, visual evidential suffixes simply code general direct sensory evidence: their literally visual base is bleached, but their imperfective or perfective semantics remain.

Given that markers of the visual category occur as constituents in the nonvisual and (as we will see) inference evidential constructions and have semantic extensions in the expression of facts and habitual actions, we should explore whether the visual category might be more appropriately interpreted as an "unmarked" evidential category. Indeed, this is exactly what Gomez-Imbert (2007b) has suggested for Tatuyo and Barasana (see also the discussions of visual evidentials in Tariana [Arawak] and Hup [Nadahup], languages spoken in the same geographic region, by Aikhenvald [2003b:293–96] and Epps [2005: 623–25]). In light of its default semantics, I retain the label "visual," but the reader should bear in mind that the literally visual meaning is actually somewhat bleached when visual suffixes occur in other evidential constructions.

9.2.4 External firsthand evidence: inference

The third firsthand category in the Kotiria evidential paradigm is inference, used to express the speaker's conclusion about an event or state based on some type of observed results. Inference is distinguished from the visual and the nonvisual categories by the feature "indirect"; the speaker observes results rather than the actual event causing the results. Example (25) is from a conversation in which the speaker was examining a set of baskets that had been stored for a long period of time in an overstuffed closet. One of the baskets had been damaged, pushed in on one side, prompting one of the women to comment:

(25) ãyo tihpa wa'ari hira
 ~a=yó tipá wa'á+ri hí+ra
 so=do be.flat go+NOM(INFER) COP+VIS.IMPERF.2/3
 'So! This one's (been) flattened.' [Baskets]

In the narrative from which (26) comes, some men have gone to a distant longhouse to capture women for brides. Unfortunately for the men, the women hear them approaching (see (22)) and flee into the forest. The men, arriving to find only empty hammocks, draw the conclusion in (26).

(26) yoatapɨ wihatu'sɨri hira
 yóá=ta-pɨ wihá-tu'sɨ+ri
 be.far=REF-LOC MOV.outward-finish+NOM(INFER)
 hí+ra
 COP+VIS.IMPERF.2/3
 'They've just escaped.' [Ancestors]

Finally, in (27), from another story, the evil snake-being whose son went off to hunt but never returned draws a conclusion from this absence.

(27) yɨ mahkɨre wãharokari hire
 yɨ=~bak+ɨ+ré ~wahá-roka+ri hí+re
 1SG.POSS=child+MASC+OBJ kill-DIST+NOM(INFER) COP+VIS.PERF.2/3
 'My son's been killed.' [A6.58]

Like the nonvisual category, the inference category is coded by construction with a verb and a clausal complement. The main verb root, or set of serialized roots, as in (25)–(27) above, is nominalized by +ri. The use of this generic nominalizer rather than the subject agreement morphemes used in most clausal nominalizations (see §10.1.2) is consistent with the semantics of the inference category, in which focus is on a resultant state or on the results of an action performed by an unidentifiable or unrecoverable agent (resulting in a passive-like reading); I call attention to the fact that +*ri* has a special function in this specific construction by glossing it as "NOM(INFER)." The nominalized complement precedes the copula *hi*, marked by an evidential suffix from one of the two major categories of firsthand evidence: visual or assertion. As with the nonvisual construction, inference constructions in everyday speech are usually marked with suffixes from the visual category. The imperfective suffix +*ra* indicates evidence—in this case results—still readily accessible to the speaker, such as the actual basket in (25) or the empty hammocks before the men's eyes in (26), while the perfective suffix +*re* indicates currently inaccessible or distanced results, such as the son's unexpected absence in (27).

The perfective form of the assertion category is the default marker for the narrator's speech in myths and nonpersonal narratives, as we see in (28). A man has returned, after four years, to the place where he tricked a curupira into killing itself (see (23)), but he can now find no traces of its body. The narrator states the obvious conclusion:

(28) *bayʉ'dʉkã wa'ari hia*
 bá-yʉ'dʉ-~ka *wa'á+ri* ***hí+a***
 decompose-INTENS-DIM go+NOM(INFER) COP+ASSERT.PERF
 '(The body) had decomposed completely.' [A7.119]

9.2.5 Internal firsthand evidence: assertion

The final evidential category is assertion, used to mark statements the speaker makes based on internal or internalized evidence. This evidence can be founded on the speaker's own previous experience, resulting in reasoned suppositions, or on his or her cultural, historical, or physical knowledge of the world, resulting in statements of fact. Like the visual category, assertion has both perfective and imperfective forms, but person distinctions are neutralized.

The perfective form of the assertion category, +*a*, is the default evidential marker in myths and traditional narratives.[8] It occurs regularly as the verb-final marker of all sentences in which the speaker is in the role of narrator, as in (28) above, as well as (29) and (30), introductory lines to two different narratives. In (30), there are also examples of

---

[8] I worked with one speaker for whom pronunciation of the perfective assertion suffix varied between +*a* and +*ga*. His pronunciation is preserved in the first lines of examples, but the common underlying form +*a* appears in the morphemically analyzed line.

the quoted speech of one of the protagonists; like everyday speech, this can be marked by any category of clause modality appropriate to the situation. In line 2 of (30) the main protagonist uses an irrealis suffix indicating his own future plan (see §9.3.1), and in line 3 he uses a visual evidential.

(29) kɨ̃ta hia, kɨ̃iro mɨno to pho'name're wa'ikina ko'taro wa'aa mahkarokapɨ

~kɨ́=ta   hí+a   ~kɨ́-iró   ~bɨ́+ro
one/a=REF   COP+SG   one/a-NOM.SG   man+SG

to=~pho'dá=~be're   wa'í-~kídá   ko'tá+ro
3SG.POSS=children=COM/INST   animal-PL   wait+(3)SG

wa'á+a   ~baká-róká-pɨ́
go+ASSERT.PERF   origin-DIST-LOC

'Once a man went hunting with his children in the forest.' [A6.3]

(30) 1 kɨ̃ta hia kɨ̃iro mɨno to namonore õse nia

~kɨ́=ta   hí+a   ~kɨ́-iró   ~bɨ́+ro   to=~dabó+ro+re
one/a=REF   COP+PL   one/a-NOM.SG   man+SG   3SG.POSS=wife+SG+OBJ

~ó-sé   ~dí+a
DEIC.PROX-be.like   say+ASSERT.PERF

'Once a man said this to his wife:'

2 yɨ'ɨ mihchare wa'ikinawahai wa'aika

yɨ'ɨ   ~bichá+ré   wa'í-~kídá-~wáhá+í
1SG   today+OBJ   animal-PL-kill+(1/2)MASC

wa'á+i-ka
go+(1/2)MASC-PREDICT

'"Today I'm going hunting.'

3 marire chɨa maniara nia

~barí+ré   chɨ́a   ~badía+ra   ~dí+a
1PL.INC+OBJ   food   not.exist+VIS.IMPERF.2/3   say+ASSERT.PERF

'"There isn't any food for us," (he) said.' [A7.3–5]

In contrast to the perfective, which occurs primarily to mark traditional oral literature, the imperfective form of the assertion evidential is multifunctional. Speakers use it in a number of situations involving affirmations based on different types of internal or internalized evidence.

The first function of the imperfective form of the assertion evidential category, -ka, is to mark sentences that express the speaker's own emotions (31), bodily sensations (32)–(33), cognitive processes (34)–(35), and abilities (36). In other words, -ka is used to express the speaker's internal experiences and feelings—affirmations made in the absence of external evidence.

(31) *yɨ'ɨ bɨhawitiawa'aka*
yɨ'ɨ bɨháwítí+á-wá'á-ká
1SG be.sad+AFFEC-go-ASSERT.IMPERF
'It makes me sad.'

(32) *yɨ'ɨ phumeyɨ'dɨaka*
yɨ'ɨ ~phubé-yɨ'dɨ+a-ka
1SG be.tired-INTENS+AFFEC-ASSERT.IMPERF
'I'm tired.'

(33) *phũriyɨ'dɨaka*
~phurí-yɨ'dɨ+a-ka
hurt-INTENS+AFFEC-ASSERT.IMPERF
'It hurts a lot.' [A7.80]

(34) *yɨ'ɨ chɨduaka*
yɨ'ɨ chɨ́-dua-ka
1SG eat-DESID-ASSERT.IMPERF
'I want to eat (it).' [A7.44]

(35) *yɨ'ɨ mopɨ hiduamaka*
yɨ'ɨ ~bó-pɨ hí-dua-~ba-ka
1SG Mõ-LOC COP-DESID-FRUS-ASSERT.IMPERF
'I wish I were in Mõ.'

(36) 1 *yɨ'ɨ yahiripho'nare wamahsieraka...*
yɨ'ɨ=yahíri~pho'da+re wa-~basi-éra-ka
1SG(POSS)=heart+OBJ give-know-NEG-ASSERT.IMPERF
'I can't give you my heart. . . .'

2 *na to mahsieraka*
~dá tó ~basi-éra-ka
get DEF know-NEG-ASSERT.IMPERF
'I don't know (how to) take it out.' [A7.47–48]

The second function of *-ka* is to code the speaker's reasoned suppositions regarding the states or actions of others. The speaker's familiarity with the people in question, previous experience with similar situations, or knowledge of the world in general is sufficient base for such statements and no direct external source of information is required. In (37), for instance, we can assume that it is the speaker's personal knowledge of his mother's moods and behavior that allows him to speculate on her emotional state.

(37) yʉ phʉko wahcheka mihchare
      yʉ=phʉk+ó   waché-**ka**   ~bichá+re
      1SG.POSS=parent+FEM   be.happy-ASSERT.IMPERF   today+OBJ
      'My mother is happy today.'

In (38), both experience and general knowledge come into play. The utterance, from a narrative, occurs just after a curupira has politely asked a man to give him his heart (see (36) for the man's response). The man knows all about curupiras and their pernicious ways, though, and he can thus deduce the being's true intentions:

(38) yʉ'ʉre a'riro chʉduaro nika
      yʉ'ʉ+ré   a'rí+ró   chú-dua+ro   ~dí-**ka**
      1SG+OBJ   DEM.PROX+SG   eat-DESID+(3)SG   be.PROG-ASSERT.IMPERF
      'This thing (the curupira) wants (lit., 'is wanting') to eat me.' [A7.53]

Finally, the short conversation in (39) is a good example of the *-ka* evidential used in a reasoned supposition about others. The conversation occurred as I was arriving with a friend at his brother Eugenio's house at around one in the afternoon, a time when his brother was usually at home for lunch. Just before we got there, we ran into Eugenio's neighbor and this short conversation took place. Though the neighbor had not seen Eugenio that day, he knew enough about Eugenio's habits to affirm that he was home.

(39) My friend: *Eugenio hihari*
                   Eugenio hí-hari
                   Eugenio COP-INT.IMPERF
                   'Is Eugenio home?'

      The neighbor: *hika*
                    hí-**ka**
                    COP-ASSERT.IMPERF
                    'He is (because he is always home at this time).'

While use of *-ka* alone can indicate a reasoned supposition based on internalized evidence, speculations—or suppositions about which the speaker has doubts, or to which the speaker is less committed—are morphologically coded by the combination of the dubitative *-bo* plus *-ka* (40)–(41). By extension, this combination of morphemes is also used for hypothetical situations and in the apodosis of a conditional sentence such as (42). Thus, while some uses of *-ka* can be considered realis, the semantics of *-bo-ka* covers some situations that seem more reasonably classed as irrealis. This indicates that *-ka* falls in a kind of transitional area between realis and irrealis that is further discussed at the end of this section (see also the combination of realis statement and irrealis negative marking in (49)–(50) below).

(40) *cho! õita hinokaboka*
 *chó ~ó+í=ta   hí-~doka-bo-**ka***
 oh! DEIC.PROX+LOC=REF COP-COMPL-DUB-ASSERT.IMPERF
 'Oh, maybe he (a missing dog) is in here.' [A6.14]

(41) *da'rana wa'aboka*
 *da'rá-~da   wa'á-bo-**ka***
 work-(1/2)PL go-DUB-ASSERT.IMPERF
 'We might go to work.'

(42) *pate ni yɨ'ɨ thuakɨ, yɨ'ɨkhɨ yɨ'ɨ bu'eboka*
 pá-te   dí   yɨ'ɨ thuá-kɨ   yɨ'ɨ-khɨ yɨ'ɨ
 ALT- CLS:time say 1SG return-(1/2)MASC 1SG-ADD 1SG
 *bu'é-bo-**ka***
 study/learn-DUB-ASSERT.IMPERF
 'If I ever went back (to my village), I would also learn (traditional songs and dances).' [A3.24]

The third function of *-ka* is undoubtedly the most typologically interesting: it occurs in statements that reflect speakers' internalized knowledge about the world, knowledge acquired as part of their cultural and historical heritage. In other words, *-ka* marks statements that affirm culturally internalized generic facts or truths.

To a certain extent, this use overlaps with that of the imperfective visual evidential in the expression of facts, as we see in (43), a text written by a Kotiria schoolteacher. The text, about red howler monkeys, is accompanied by a drawing, and the first line deictically introduces the animal. The imperfective visual suffix *+ra* is used on the copula in this introductory line because the reader can "see" the monkey in the drawing. Indeed, Kotiria speakers use visual evidentials even when the objects or situations they are talking about are not physically present, as in the case of the drawing. Thus, visual evidentials are used to refer to things "seen" in drawings, photographs, videos, etc. In the ensuing lines of the text, however, the imperfective assertion suffix *-ka* is used to mark each statement of generic fact concerning the monkey's habits—facts the writer of the text need not have witnessed in order to affirm, since all Kotiria acquire general knowledge about the habits of forest animals.

(43) 1 emo hira
       ~ebó   hɨ+ra
       howler.monkey COP+VIS.IMPERF.2/3
       'This is a howler monkey.'

   2 tiro chɨka phɨ̃ri wĩaphɨ̃rire
      tí+ró   chɨ́-ka   ~phɨ́+rí ~wiá-~phɨ́+rí+ré
      ANPH+SG   eat-ASSERT.IMPERF leaf+PL   be.young-leaf+PL+OBJ
      'It eats (young) green leaves.'

   3 chɨka tha me're wamɨthare do'se to bohkare
      chɨ́-ka   thá=~be're   ~wabɨ́-thá+re
      eat-ASSERT.IMPERF grass=COM/INST   mature-grass+OBJ
      do'sé tó   boká+re
      WH   DEF find+OBJ
      'It eats grass, any mature grass that it can find.'

   4 yɨhkɨri bu'ipɨ tinika tiro
      yɨkɨ́+ri   bu'í-pɨ   ~tidí-ká   tí+ró
      tree+PL   top-LOC   wander-ASSERT.IMPERF   ANPH+SG
      'It moves around in the treetops.'

   5 ã̄yoaro tiro emo wamatika
      ~a=yoá+ro   tí+ró   ~ebó
      so=do+(3)SG   ANPH+SG howler.monkey
      ~wabá-tí-ká
      name-VBZ-ASSERT.IMPERF
      'So it's called a howler monkey.'

The final example in this section is an interesting case in which evidentials from different categories are combined in a unique way in a single clause to code a specific extended semantic function. The sentence in (44) has two markers of evidentiality, both the inference construction +ri hi- and the imperfective assertion suffix -ka. In §9.2.4 we saw that the inference construction typically combines with visual evidentials in everyday speech, while in traditional narratives it occurs with perfective assertion marker +a. How, then, are we to interpret the combination of the inference construction with the imperfective assertion marker? We should first consider some contextual information. The sentence comes from late in "The Curupira Story," when the man returns to the place where the creature had fallen (23) and its body decomposed (28). He digs into the ground there and this action somehow revives the curupira, releasing it from a deathlike sleep. When it arises and finds itself awake again, it utters the sentence in (44).

(44) yɨ'ɨ khãriyɨ'dɨa wa'ari hi'ka
    yɨ'ɨ ~khari-yɨ'dɨ+a   wa'á+ri   **hí-ka**
    1SG sleep-INTENS+AFFEC go+NOM(INFER)   COP-ASSERT.IMPERF
    'I've been asleep a long time!' [A7.128]

The final -ka in this sentence can be analyzed as expressing one of the core evidential functions of the imperfective assertion suffix, to mark statements of the speaker's feelings—in this case, the sense of having been "asleep." The inferential construction in this case may, on the one hand, be open to straightforward inferential interpretation: the being, regaining consciousness, infers that some length of time must have passed.[9] But this unusual construction may also have an alternate function coding mirativity, or unexpected information. Although mirativity is a semantic realm distinct from evidentiality per se, some languages use evidential markers to express mirativity as one of their extended semantic functions. Frequently, the markers used for this alternate function are inference or hearsay evidentials—which is not surprising, as these categories often group together as indicators of indirect evidence (see the typological framework in Willett 1988). The use of markers from categories indicating such indirect or external evidence in situations involving the internal sensation of surprise clearly captures the notion of something "which is new to the speaker, not yet integrated into his overall picture of the world" (DeLancey 1997:36). The curupira in the text is, in fact, expressing just this kind of surprise when it suddenly finds itself awake and restored after having been asleep (dead) for such a long time.

CATEGORY OVERLAP. Not all Eastern Tukanoan languages have evidential systems parallel to the five-way system of Kotiria, systems that include a category akin to assertion[10] and also differentiate between visual and nonvisual sensory evidence. A number of Eastern Tukanoan languages only have four evidential categories, one of which, though frequently labeled "nonvisual," also includes the semantic functions covered by the assertion category in Kotiria. This is the case in Kaye's analysis of Desano, in which he identifies the evidential categories "observed," "reported/inferred," and "nonvisible," which "covers cases which by their nature or location, the speaker cannot see" (1970: 28).

---

[9] I thank Patience Epps (p.c. 2008) for pointing out that this more straightforward reading is indeed possible.

[10] This category is frequently labeled "assumed" in the literature on Eastern Tukanoan, following Barnes's (1984) analysis of Tuyuka.

What is interesting from a cross-linguistic perspective is that in the languages that do have five-way systems, we find functional parallels for the hearsay, visual, and inference categories, but differences in the use of markers from the assertion and nonvisual categories. In general, markers from the assertion category (Barnes's "assumed" category) are used in statements that express either the speaker's general knowledge about things for which there is no external evidence or the physical sensations, emotions, and cognitive processes of others. However, there is a notable difference when it comes to statements referring to the physical sensations, emotions, and cognitive processes of the speaker. In Kotiria, the use of assertion category markers is extended to statements with first person referents, whereas in other Eastern Tukanoan languages, nonvisual markers are employed (see, for example, Malone [1988:131] for Tuyuka). Thus, we find that within the family, there are areas of semantic overlap between the nonvisual and assertion categories and that the Kotiria system indicates innovative semantic specification.

THE EVIDENTIAL NATURE OF ASSERTION. The category of assertion is certainly the most controversial category in the Eastern Tukanoan languages; indeed, its very existence raises some interesting theoretical questions. First, though generally labeled as an evidential, this category is sometimes conceived of as a kind of nonevidential, a catch-all category used in statements for which the speaker actually has no evidence whatsoever. However, we may also view the assertion category not as one whose essential semantics codes lack of evidence, but as one whose semantics represents a qualified type of inference, inference based on internalized knowledge that allows the speaker to make very strong claims about the world.

While it may be rare for a language to distinguish between and grammatically code different types of inference, both Givón (1982) and Willett (1988) discuss such subdivisions. Besides inferential conclusions based on observed results, Givón argues that languages may code inference by abduction or conclusions based on associations that can include such things as collective experience, recurring patterns of behavior, or cultural knowledge (1982:44–45). Willett, too, discusses languages that code inferential conclusions resulting from reasoning, based on "logic, intuition, previous experience in a similar situation, or even a dream" (1988:61), and he points to the "assumed" category of Tuyuka (as presented by Barnes [1984]) as an example of just this kind of inference. More recently, Aikhenvald (2003b:294) analyzes two of the evidential categories in Tariana as expressing 'specific' inference (from directly observed results) and 'generic' inference (from reasoning or common sense, without direct experience).

Gomez-Imbert (2007b:79–80) offers yet another analysis. While recognizing the existence of a category that marks what are apparently nonevidential situations, she claims that its basic semantics removes it from the domain of realis and places it within the domain of irrealis, alongside other markers of unreal situations such as futures, hypotheticals, and speculations. A parallel analysis is actually quite tempting for Kotiria, given the use of the imperfective *-ka* in speculations and in conditional constructions and the fact that a homophonous, and perhaps historically related, *-ka* morpheme occurs in irrealis constructions, as is seen in §9.3.

Assertion may well be a transitional category, occupying a gray area between realis and irrealis where some semantic overlap occurs. Does such overlap indicate movement toward future convergence of categories? Is it just an example of the fact that semantic categories are not always as discrete as our theoretical frameworks would have them be? For now, these remain open questions. Distinct linguistic forms may not necessarily represent sharply defined semantic territories, if, as Givón suggests, the semantics of evidential categories is internally scalar (1982:24–26). Conceiving of the semantics of evidentiality as a continuum of meanings, with each discrete evidential form actually including a range of possible meanings, allows us to easily envision semantic gray areas along the borders of categories.

9.2.6 Hierarchization of evidential categories and the notion of deixis

A scalar view of the semantics of evidentials is also important to the discussion of the hierarchical organization of evidential systems. Cross-linguistic studies show that evidential systems display internal orientation to different types of hierarchies: personal, in which the highest orientation is to the speaker; sensory, in which sight takes precedence over hearing and all other senses; directness, in which knowledge through the senses is higher than knowledge through inference; and proximity, where nearness to a scene is coded higher than distance from it (Givón 1982:44). Such hierarchies indicate that evidentials essentially express different types of deixis, a fundamental concept in analyses of the cognitive bases of evidentials, such as Floyd's research on Wanka Quechua (1999) and de Haan's work on the origins of visual evidentials (2001a).

In regard to Eastern Tukanoan languages, Barnes (1984) takes the hierarchy of categories within the Tuyuka evidential system to be visual > nonvisual > inference (Barnes's "apparent") > hearsay (Barnes's "secondhand") > assertion (Barnes's "assumed"), an order that implies overall speaker orientation to a combination of Givón's "sensory" and "directness" parameters. Ramirez's analysis of the hierarchy in Tukano inverts the categories of inference (Ramirez's "deduction") and hearsay, the latter viewed as grouping together with the visual and nonvisual (Ramirez's "perceived") categories of sensory evidence (Ramirez 1997a:121). Both analyses indicate, though, that speakers consistently mark their utterances with the highest level of evidence available from the hierarchy and attune, above all, to "the importance of indicating, by one's choice of an evidential, whether or not any visual evidence was observed" (Barnes 1984:262).

The Kotiria data suggest a hierarchy parallel to that of Tuyuka for the firsthand external categories—visual > nonvisual > inference—and, overall, that firsthand categories rank above hearsay categories. The status of the assertion category, however, deserves further discussion. We could argue, on the one hand, that the assertion category must necessarily be low in the hierarchy (as it is indicated to be in the Tuyuka system) because the internalized evidence it reflects cannot claim any higher-ranking deictic value related to either the sensory or the directness parameters that are clearly fundamental to Eastern Tukanoan evidential systems. On the other hand, the use of assertion markers in Kotiria oral literature and other types of cultural and historical material suggests that besides deixis of these two types, Kotiria has also developed a heightened orientation to personal deixis. This orientation may indeed be at the heart of the reorganization of the Kotiria system that led to the development of the first person vs. nonfirst person paradigm for visual evidentials and the general leveling of the forms of the other firsthand categories. In terms of semantics, increased orientation to the salience of the speaker may have effectively redefined the status of evidence internalized by the speaker and modified the ranking of the assertion category within the Kotiria evidential hierarchy.

Such an analysis would explain the somewhat overlapping use of visual and assertion markers in Kotiria in the expression of facts (as in (40)), and suggests that these two categories have parallel hierarchical status, at least for some functions. There is morphological evidence for such an analysis as well. Both the visual and the assertion categories are major evidential categories that can occupy the final position in a basic verbal template or appear as the final constituent in either of the two analytic firsthand categories, nonvisual and inference. In everyday situations, the visual suffixes for nonfirst person, +*ra* and +*re*, are the final morphological constituents in these constructions. There is a shift, though, when a speaker wishes to express general truths or suppositions. These are marked in conversation by the imperfective form -*ka* and in narratives by the perfective form +*a*, which replaces all three firsthand external category forms.

9.2.7 Kotiria evidentials and epistemic values

There are two remaining issues concerning the relationship between evidentiality and epistemic modality in Kotiria that need to be clarified. First, although distinctions of truth value are clearly not the semantic core of evidential categories, we will see that one of the extended semantic functions of evidentials clearly is to express degrees of speaker commitment to a proposition. Moreover, not all Kotiria evidential categories indicate equal levels of commitment, and the expression of differentiated epistemic values is directly related to the speaker's awareness of category hierarchization.

The epistemic implications of the visual, nonvisual, and inference (firsthand, external) categories are partly linked to the deictic nature of evidential (information source) coding and in part to the obligatory nature of evidential use. Each of the categories of firsthand evidence indicates a degree of speaker involvement or proximity to an event, and epistemic values accrue directly from these different relationships of directness and proximity (Floyd 1999:41–55). Essentially, although evidence is what is coded, what is understood or construed, by extension, is truth value. That such construal is intended and actually happens is clear from the fact that in Eastern Tukanoan languages one cannot use markers of doubt with any of the firsthand, external categories. To imply truth and at the same time overtly deny it is both nonsensical and ungrammatical.

The assertion category (firsthand, internal), on the other hand, indicates evidence established by conceptual contract and internalized by an individual or a community of speakers who share like experiences and culture. Assertion markers are used in the expression of the most unquestionable knowledge one can acquire: that which one's own body, culture, ancestors, and surrounding physical world provide. Such absolute and incontestable knowledge parallels, if not supersedes, in terms of epistemic value, that marked by the visual category.

However, the multiple semantic functions of the assertion category, especially the contexts in which its imperfective form is used, raise some doubts as to whether clauses with assertion markers are always intended to be true. We therefore need to consider some important morphological evidence. While there is no overt marker of truth in Kotiria,[11] we should recall that Kotiria does have a dubitative mor-

---

[11] Interestingly, though, Gomez-Imbert describes overt coding of truth in Tatuyo and Barasana. In Tatuyo, there is a prefix *ka-* that can be used with visual, inferential, and reported evidential categories to indicate that a statement is the "definitive version

pheme -*bo* used in sentences expressing speculation, doubt, or suspicion of untruth. In Kotiria, this morpheme cannot occur with direct evidential categories; speakers judge sentences in which -*bo* occurs with a visual or nonvisual evidential to be ungrammatical. For example, **ti+ro ko-iro hi-**bo**+ra* [ANPH+SG relative-NOM:SG COP-DUB+VIS.IMPERF.2/3] is unacceptable as a sentence expressing the idea 'he might be a relative (I'm not sure)' because the visual evidential +*ra* implies a known or observed fact: 'he *is* a relative'. The dubitative -*bo* is most frequently used with assertion evidentials (see also §8.4.1 and the examples there), and indeed speakers readily accept use of -*bo* in the above sentence if the final suffix is changed to -*ka*. There are cognate dubitative morphemes in most Eastern Tukanoan languages, and we find that the restrictions governing their cooccurrence with direct evidential categories are alike across the family. In Kotiria, and throughout Eastern Tukanoan, use of a morpheme indicating doubt with any of the direct evidential categories results in an ungrammatical sentence, comparable to the oddity of English **He left (I witnessed this myself) but I doubt it.*

The existence of a dubitative marker and the restrictions on its use shed light on the question of the epistemic value of evidentials: essentially, they indicate that statements without the dubitative marker have a default value of 'true' (see discussion in Frajzyngier 1985). Kotiria direct evidential categories—visual and nonvisual—cannot be marked for doubt due to the deictic nature and cognitive salience of the types of evidence that are at their core. Statements in which these categories are used are thus inherently nondubitative and imply truth. As for the categories of inference and assertion, statements containing the morpheme -*bo* can be analyzed as the marked case. This means that statements with assertion or inference evidentials but without the optional expression of doubt represent the unmarked value 'true' and thus also indicate speaker commitment to the veracity of the proposition (recall the use of assertion markers in myths and in generic statements of fact).

The obligatory nature of evidential coding also supports such an analysis. If a speaker must mark every statement with an evidential, and mark doubt, if present, by separate morphology, then we can assume all unmarked statements not to be devoid of truth value but to have a default value 'true'. And if one can lie using evidentials, it is not

of the situation in question," that the speaker has "sufficient elements to attribute a value of truth to the proposition" (2003b:124–25). In Barasana, the same epistemic value is coded by a tonal prefix, but cannot cooccur with a reported evidential (1997a: 287–89).

because they are unmarked for truth, but because a value of 'true' is implicit unless the statement is otherwise explicitly marked.

As for the relationship between the firsthand categories as a whole (with their assumed inherent epistemic extensions) and the secondhand category of hearsay, it is likely that hearsay is itself a marked category, though whether the marked value indicates diminished speaker commitment or neutrality to commitment distinctions has yet to be determined. We recall that speakers generally prefer to quote other speakers directly rather than repeat their statements with hearsay evidentials. On the one hand, this practice might indicate epistemic neutrality, in which case we can presume that speakers prefer to pass on another speaker's fully marked statement rather than blanch it of epistemic value by using a neutral marker. On the other hand, the lack of any kind of deictic relationship to the event (indicated by one of the firsthand categories) might automatically imply diminished commitment. These questions remain for further investigation.

Finally, we should consider what light the attested hierarchy of evidential categories can shed on the discussion of epistemic values. If all categories code commitment, should that commitment be viewed as equal across the board? Again, both Givón's (1982) notion of the scalar nature of categories within systems and Floyd's (1999) idea that differences of directness and proximity can result in variations of a scalar nature can prove insightful. These notions suggest that, within the firsthand categories, both the visual and the assertion categories can indicate complete speaker commitment to the proposition, though the origin of speaker certainty varies as to whether it is based on external or internal evidence. The two analytic categories, nonvisual and inference, would also imply commitment; however, it is a commitment naturally attenuated by the lesser values of directness and proximity associated with the sources of evidence these categories invoke.[12]

9.2.8 Further remarks on the evidential categories

Evidentials are by far the most complex and typologically interesting category of clause modality in Kotiria, with five evidential categories—hearsay, visual, nonvisual, inference, and assertion—that are conflated with distinctions of person, reference, and aspect. The typologically rare category of assertion is used in a variety of seemingly unrelated proposition types, from statements of absolute facts to rea-

---

[12] In more recent work, Michael (2008) proposes that evidentials can also either assign personal responsibility for events or mitigate it—functions typically overlooked in the literature on evidentials. Discussion of the status, functions, and semantics of evidentials is ongoing, and further analyses of languages with such systems promise interesting insights in the years to come.

soned speculations, all semantically linked by involving internalized sources of information. The Kotiria evidential categories are not completely discrete semantically: their core semantics, based on source of information, can be extended to other functions such as the coding of mirativity, and there are areas of overlap between categories. In particular, the semantics of the assertion category can overlap with that of the visual category in certain contexts.

The relationship between evidentials and epistemic values has been the subject of some discussion. Kotiria demonstrates that categorical statements of the either-or type—either evidentials are inherently modal and express epistemic meanings (Willet 1988:52; Palmer 1986:54; Chafe and Nichols 1986:vii; Bybee, Perkins, and Pagliuca 1994:180) or they are an independent category and are thus neutrally positioned in terms of epistemic values (de Haan 1999:94; Aikhenvald 2003a:1)—are impractical. Indeed, categorical claims are often attenuated in the same sources, for example Aikhenvald's statements to the effect that "[e]vidential markers may gain additional meanings and extensions such as the probability of an event or the reliability of information (often called 'epistemic' meanings)" (2003a:2) and that "[i]n systems of three terms or more, the visual evidential indicates events perceived through seeing and may be extended to cover direct observation, participation, control, generally known and observable facts, and also *certainty*" (2003a:13; emphasis added). In other words, though their core semantics may relate to the source of evidence, evidential systems often do participate in the coding of epistemic values and may indeed become the primary coding means. Furthermore, the observation that in some languages "evidentiality markers occupy the mood and modality slot in a verbal word, and are thus mutually exclusive with conditional, imperative, interrogative markers and so on" (Aikhenvald 2003a:11) indicates that evidentials in some languages can and should be analyzed as a modal category, as will be further demonstrated for Kotiria. In the following sections, we will see that expression of speaker commitment is not limited to realis statements. Kotiria markers of irrealis statements and interrogatives, though distinguishing fewer features than evidential categories do, nevertheless, also display sensitivity to scalar values of speaker commitment.

9.3   Irrealis

In the present analysis, I assume that realis and irrealis represent areas on a continuum that allow the speaker and hearer to communicate gradients of certainty based on available evidence. Constructions denoting lesser commitment on the part of the speaker fall within the domain of irrealis, while those more strongly asserted by the speaker belong to that of realis (Givón 1982, 2001; Bybee 1998). Thus, the fundamental difference between realis and irrealis statements is the nature of the supporting evidence evoked by the speaker and the possibility of challenge on the part of the addressee.

Statements with evidential markers fall toward the realis end of the continuum and prototypically correspond to events or states that have existed or still exist. Speakers can evoke different kinds of supporting evidence when referring to these events, and given that certain types of evidence are more salient than others, it is not surprising that we find a greater number of grammaticalized distinctions in the category of evidentials and that these distinctions reflect scalar differences. Statements for which a speaker is unwilling or unable to indicate evidence and that are open to challenge by the hearer fall toward the opposite end of the continuum, the domain of irrealis. Such statements are typically speculations, predictions, or hypotheses about events or states for which evidence is unavailable.

Scalar differentiation, however, does not end at the realis-irrealis frontier—differences as to the likelihood or probability of the event or state coming to pass are grammatically coded within the irrealis domain as well, as we will see in the following sections.

9.3.1 Prediction and intention

While statements with evidential marking can be regarded as realis, another set of clause modality markers codes irrealis statements. There is no future tense per se in Kotiria, but speakers can talk about actions or events yet to be realized in a number of different ways, using irrealis suffixes that express varying degrees of certainty. The first, and most common, of these irrealis suffixes, *-ka*,[13] marks a statement as a prediction (45)–(46).

(45) ãyo õpɨre yɨ'ɨ kho'awi'ikɨka
~a=yó ~ó-pɨ́+ré yɨ'ɨ́ kho'á-wi'i-**kɨ-ka**
so=do DEIC.PROX-LOC+OBJ 1SG return-arrive-(1/2)MASC-PREDICT
'That's how I'll get back here.' [A4.14]

---

[13] In the analyses of Waltz and Waltz (1997, 2000) and Waltz (2007), the difference between the evidential NONVISUAL (ASSERTION) suffix *-ka* and the future suffix *-ʔka* (here analyzed as a marker of IRREALIS) is marked by a glottal stop. Since I have not found the glottal stop to occur consistently in my data, I analyze ʔ not as an intrinsic constituent of the morpheme, but as a phonetic result of low tone spread throughout the verbal word (see Stenzel 2007a).

(46) yɨ'ɨ topɨre a'rikorore kristinare ya'uika yɨ'ɨse'e
　　　yɨ'ɨ tó-pɨ+re　　　 a'ri-kó+ró+ré
　　　1SG REM-LOC+OBJ DEM.PROX-FEM+SG+OBJ
　　　kristína+re　　ya'ú+**i-ka**　　　　yɨ'ú-se'e
　　　Kristine+OBJ tell+(1/2)MASC-PREDICT 1SG-CONTR
　　　'I'm going to tell this woman Kristine (how it is) there.' [A1.4]

The structure of irrealis verbs differs from that of realis verbs in that a subject agreement morpheme from the paradigm in table 9.3 precedes the irrealis suffix (whereas in realis verbs, either the realis morpheme itself is differentiated for subject person (first vs. nonfirst for the visual category) or else subject is not marked at all). This paradigm of subject agreement marking I take to be a relic of what was likely a full-scale paradigm of third person vs. nonthird person coding in all finite verbs in Kotiria, parallel to that found synchronically in other Eastern Tukanoan languages (except for Wa'ikhana, which shares the innovation to a first vs. nonfirst person paradigm).

TABLE 9.3. SUBJECT AGREEMENT SUFFIXES FOR IRREALIS AND NOMINALIZED VERBS

	SINGULAR	PLURAL
FIRST/SECOND PERSON	-ko (fem.) -kɨ / +i (masc.)	-~da
THIRD PERSON	+ro	+a

Looking at the Kotiria prediction construction, it is impossible not to note the similarity of the forms of the irrealis suffix -ka and the imperfective assertion evidential -ka discussed in §9.2.5; recall that the latter occurs in irrealis-like speculations (specifically, sentences with the morphological combination -bo-ka). It seems entirely plausible to assume a common origin for the two morphemes, which occur in statements that fall somewhere in the transition zone between realis and irrealis. Nevertheless, the two morphemes occur in what are clearly different constructions: the irrealis prediction -ka is preceded by an agreement suffix, while the imperfective assertion evidential is not.

In (45) and (46) above, agreement is marked by the nonthird person (first or second person, "1/2") masculine morphemes -kɨ and +i. Although both forms are used synchronically, I consider -kɨ to be the older form; it is more similar to the markers found in Wa'ikhana and a number of other sister languages. The +i form is certainly the more innovative, and is in line with other instances of shift from ɨ to i in the language (Waltz 2002:180). As observed for nominalized constructions

(§10.1.2), use of the two forms in irrealis constructions varies somewhat from speaker to speaker, though I observe two very general tendencies in my data. Certain older speakers (such as Agostinho Ferraz, narrator of texts 4 and 5 in appendix 1) prefer the *-kʉ* form in both irrealis constructions and in nominalizations. For speakers who use both *-kʉ* and *+i*, there is tendency toward use of *-kʉ* for second-person referents (as in (55) below) while *+i* is more frequently (though still not exclusively) used in constructions that have first-person referents.

The paradigm of agreement morphology in table 9.3 also appears in nominalized dependent clauses (e.g., the protasis in (42)) and in verbal elements in other types of complement constructions (e.g., the auxiliary verb construction in (38); see also §10.1.2).

The second irrealis suffix used in Kotiria is *-ta*, which codes the event as the speaker's own intention. Statements of intent with *-ta* are grammatically restricted to first person subjects, and, as mentioned above, the preferred first person morpheme *+i* occurs in the verbal words in (47) and (48), preceding the clause modality marker (so far in my data, I have not found the alternative first person form *-kʉ* used before *-ta*).

(47) *yʉ'ʉ wa'ire do'abosaita mʉ'ʉre*
 yʉ'ʉ   wa'í+re   do'á-bósá+í-tá   ~bʉ'ʉ+ré
 1SG   fish+OBJ   cook-BEN+(1/2)MASC-INTENT   2SG+OBJ
 'I'm going to cook the fish for you.'

(48) *õita yʉ'ʉ khãriita*
 ~ó+i=ta   yʉ'ʉ   ~kharí+í-ta
 DEIC.PROX+LOC=REF   1SG   sleep-+(1/2)MASC-INTENT
 'I'll sleep here.' [A7.19]

The distinction between predictions about events, marked by *-ka*, and statements of the speaker's own intentions, marked by *-ta*, can be viewed as a scale of the likelihood or probability of the event or state coming to pass. Thus, the statements that indicate the highest degree of certainty within irrealis are those coded as intentions by the suffix *-ta*; the speaker is indicating with absolute certainty that he or she will actually perform the action.

9.3.2 Negative irrealis

In Kotiria, while verbs in statements about realis situations are negated by the morpheme *-era*, irrealis statements are negated by the verb-final morpheme *-si*, with no preceding subject agreement marker.[14] Exam-

---

[14] Interestingly, no cognates for this morpheme have to date been identified in other Eastern Tukanoan languages (Elsa Gomez-Imbert, p.c. 2008).

ples (49)–(50) are from a conversation, at a point where two women were encouraging another older woman to say something in her first language (Kubeo) for my video camera. The older woman, embarrassed, made the statement in (49)—marked as a speculation—and two other women replied with the statements in (50).

(49) õpɨre yoa parithuari ñɨboka tina
~ó-pɨ+ré   yoá parí-thua+ri   ~yɨ́-bó-ká
DEIC.PROX-LOC+OBJ do time-return+PL see-DUB-ASSERT.IMPERF
tí-~da
ANPH-PL
'They'll probably watch (the video) over and over.' [Baskets]

(50) a. ñɨsi tina hi'na
~yɨ́-sí   ti-~da   ~hí'da
see/look-NEG.IRR ANPH-PL EMPH
'No, they won't!' [Baskets]

b. ñɨsi tina kɨ̃ta hira
~yɨ́-sí   ti-~da   ~kɨ́=ta   hí+ra
see/look-NEG.IRR ANPH-PL one/a=REF COP+VIS.IMPERF.2/3
'They won't. (They'll watch just) once.' [Baskets]

Another example of the use of -si is found in line 3 of (51), from the introduction to the storybook written by the Kotiria for use in village schools.

(51) 1 a'rithu hira wa'ikina khiti yaya'ɨrithu
a'rí-thú   hí+ra   wa'i-~kídá khiti
DEM.PROX-CLS:stacked COP+VIS.IMPERF.2/3 animal-PL story
yá-ya'u+ri-thu
POSS-tell+NOM-CLS:stacked
'This is our own (Kotiria) animal storybook.'

2 sã pho'na bu'eti hira
~sa=~pho'dá   bu'é-ti   hí+ra
1PL.EXC.POSS=children study/learn-VBZ COP+VIS.IMPERF.2/3
'It is for our children to study.'

3 ã yoana, sã kotiria ne bosi sã yahoare durukuare
~a=yoá-~da   ~sá   kó-ti+ri+a   ~dé
so=do-(1/2)PL 1PL.EXC water-VBZ+NOM+PL NEG

Clause modality 303

bó-sí	*~sa=yá-hoa+re*	*dú-ruku+a+re*
forget-NEG.IRR	1PL.EXC.POSS=POSS-write+OBJ	talk-stand+PL+OBJ

'This way, we Kotiria won't forget how to write and speak.' (or 'our writing and our language') [A12.1–3]

This section has shown that within the domain of irrealis, internal categorial distinctions code differences in the speaker's point of view and degree of commitment to an as-yet-unrealized proposition. The next section shows that parallel differences are also coded in questions.

9.4 Interrogatives

The third category of clause modality is comprised of morphemes that mark questions. This set of interrogative morphemes shares some semantic categories with those of statements. Figure 9.3 clarifies semantic relations among the interrogative section of table 9.1, comparing the placement of these categories along a continuum from realis to irrealis and indicating comparable categories for statements.

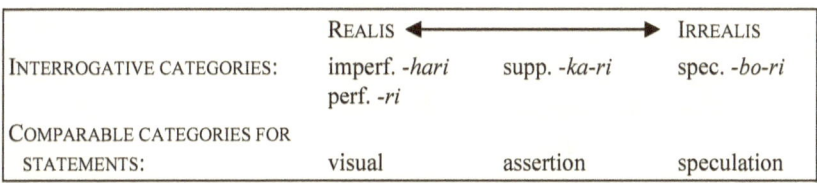

	REALIS		IRREALIS
INTERROGATIVE CATEGORIES:	imperf. *-hari* perf. *-ri*	supp. *-ka-ri*	spec. *-bo-ri*
COMPARABLE CATEGORIES FOR STATEMENTS:	visual	assertion	speculation

Figure 9.3. Interrogative clause modality compared with statement clause modality. Imperf. = imperfective; perf. = perfective; spec. = speculation; supp. = supposition.

There are four interrogative forms in Kotiria. The imperfective and perfective forms *-hari* and *-ri* are used in questions referring to realis situations. They code an aspectual distinction and can be compared to the visual evidential category of statements, the default category of firsthand external evidence. The sequence of morphemes *-ka-ri* is used in questions involving supposition. Such questions can be compared to the assertion evidential category. Finally, the sequence of morphemes *-bo-ri* is used in questions indicating speculation or other more irrealis-like situations.

We should not be surprised to find interrogative forms expressing semantic differences corresponding to distinctions along the realis (evidential)–to–irrealis continuum in languages with grammaticalized evidentials. Floyd (1999:86–87) claims, for example, that the grounding notion behind evidential categories—the different kinds of relationships between the speaker and the content of the statement—can easily be extended to the addressee: a speaker can mark a question to indicate expectation as to the addressee's relationship to the proposition, in other words, to the addressee's knowledge and ability to answer.

9.4.1 Aspectual distinctions in questions

The Kotiria perfective and imperfective interrogatives are the default markers in most questions. They occur on both polar (yes-no) questions, as in (52)–(53) and (56), and information questions, as in (54)–(55) and (57)–(60). Questions marked by these suffixes express not only a request for information, but the speaker's expectation that the addressee has access to the information and can, in fact, provide it.

Like visual evidentials, these interrogative forms include aspectual information—imperfective *-hari* and perfective *-ri*. As *-ri* is the only morpheme common to all Kotiria interrogative forms, its principal semantic function is analyzed as marking a sentence as an interrogative, with perfective aspect (relating to the time when the addressee is assumed to have had access to the information about the event) as its default value (52)–(55).

(52) *tina yoari a'rire*
 tí-~da   yoá-ri   a'rí+ré
 ANPH-PL do/make-INT DEM.PROX+OBJ
 'Did they make these (baskets)?' [Baskets]

(53) *mɨ'ɨ ñuerari yɨ makɨre*
 ~bɨ'ɨ   ~yɨ-éra-ri   yɨ=~bak+ ɨ+ré
 2SG see/look-NEG-INT 1SG.POSS=child+MASC+OBJ
 'Didn't you see my son?' [A6.56]

(54) *mɨ'ɨ do'se yoa nari mɨ'ɨ yahiripho'nare*
 ~bɨ'ɨ   do'sé yoá   ~dá-ri   ~bɨ'ɨ=yahíri~pho'da+re
 2SG   WH   do/make get-INT 2SG(POSS)=heart+OBJ
 'How did you take out your heart?' [A7.75]

(55) *do'se yoakɨ ã yoari mɨ'ɨ*
 do'sé yoá-kɨ   ~a=yoá-ri   ~bɨ'ɨ
 WH   do/make-(1/2)MASC so=do/make-INT 2SG
 'Why did you (masc.) do that?'

The imperfective *-hari*, used in questions related to states (56)–(57) or other imperfective situations, to information about which the addressee is presumed to have unbounded access, is the marked form (58)–(60). The initial *ha* of this interrogative form is clearly reminiscent of the first person imperfective visual evidential, suggesting a se-

Clause modality 305

mantic link to this category. Note that the negative questions (53) and (59) are formed with the negative morpheme *-era*, followed by one of the interrogative suffixes.

(56) *phɨ'ɨse da'reina hihari tina*
      *phɨ'ɨ-sé   da'ré-~ida   hí-**hárí**   tí-~da*
      basket-PL make-NOM.PL COP-INT.IMPERF ANPH-PL
      'Are they basket-makers?' [Baskets]

(57) *do'se yoa phɨ'ɨse kã noahari*
      *do'sé yoá   phɨ'ɨ-sé-~ká   ~dóá-**hárí***
      WH   do/make basket-PL-DIM be.good-INT.IMPERF
      'What are these little baskets (good) for?' (lit., 'How are these baskets useful?') [Baskets]

(58) *do'se yoa yo'gahari a'rirore*
      *do'sé yoá   yo'gá-**hari**   a'rí+ró+ré*
      WH   do/make fish-INT.IMPERF DEM.PROX+SG+OBJ
      'How do you fish for this one (a specific type of fish)?'

(59) *do'se yoaro a'riro yɨ'ɨre yɨ'tierahari*
      do'sé yoá+ro   a'rí+ró   yɨ'ɨ+ré
      WH   do/make+(3)SG DEM.PROX+SG 1SG+OBJ
      *yɨ'ti-**éra-hari***
      answer-NEG-INT.IMPERF
      'Why isn't he answering me?' [A7.94]

(60) *mɨ'ɨ do'se yoa wãhahari*
      *~bɨ'ɨ do'sé yoá   ~wahá-**hari***
      2SG   WH   do/make kill-INT.IMPERF
      'How do you kill (so many animals)?' [A7.157]

9.4.2 Questions involving supposition or speculation

Kotiria speakers confirm that questions marked by *-ri* or *-hari* indicate an expectation on the part of the speaker that the addressee knows the desired information. Such an expectation is clearly exemplified in the contexts in which some of the questions in examples above occurred: e.g., (10), where the man asks his sons where their mother is, and (39), where my friend asked the neighbor about his brother Eugenio.

Further evidence that question forms imply speaker expectations comes from comparisons of *-ri* and *-hari* with the remaining interrogative markers. If a speaker supposes, but is not completely sure, that the addressee had or could have direct knowledge of the required information, the default interrogative suffix *-ri* is preceded by *-ka* (61). Like the imperfective form analyzed above, an evidential category is probably the semantic source for this optional morpheme. The morpheme -*ka* in the interrogative is in all likelihood linked to the imperfective form of the assertion category, specifically, to its semantic function as a marker of reasoned suppositions.

(61) *mipʉre yabame're phichakare yoakari*
~*bi-pʉ+ré*   *yabá=~be're*   *phichá-ká+ré*
now-LOC+OBJ   WH=COM/INST   fire-CLS:round+OBJ
*yoá-**ka-ri***
do/make-SUPP-INT
'How (do you think/suppose) fire is made nowadays?' [LSK: Firewood]

If, on the other hand, the speaker cannot assess the extent of the addressee's knowledge or in some way doubts the addressee's ability to answer a question because the addressee may have no access to the necessary information, the interrogative suffix is preceded by the dubitative morpheme -*bo*, as in (62).

(62) *tiro wʉ'ʉpʉ wa'abori*
tí+ró   *wʉ'ʉ-pʉ*   *wa'á-**bo-ri***
ANPH+SG house-LOC go-DUB-INT
'Did he go home?' ('Do you know if he went home?')

These different interrogative constructions and the semantic nuances they display indicate that a continuum analysis of realis-irrealis distinctions in several categories of clause modality is clearly appropriate for Kotiria. The realis evidential categories for statements are paralleled by the -*ri*/-*hari* interrogative forms used in realis questions, -*ka-ri* occupies a middle ground in the continuum and indicates supposition, while -*bo-ri* is used for irrealis. Thus, by adopting a view of the realis-irrealis distinction that includes the possibility of extended semantics of certainty, in one's own statement or in one's addressee's knowledge, we can see clear areas of semantic parallelism between statements and questions. That fewer distinctions are coded in the interrogative category is also not unexpected. Aikhenvald notes that languages with evidentials often code fewer distinctions in questions and commands than in statements. Tariana, for example, also has five evidential categories in statements but only three in questions (Aikhenvald 2003b:294, 311).

The relationship between evidential and interrogative categories has been considered in a few other studies of Eastern Tukanoan languages. Malone (1988) views the difference between the interrogative forms -*ri* and -*gari*/-*yiri* in Tuyuka as coding not aspect (as is the case in Kotiria), but a basic firsthand-nonfirsthand (evidential) distinction: "'firsthand' indicates that the interrogator assumes that the interrogee saw or sees the action taking place. The interrogator uses the 'nonfirsthand' form if he has reason to assume that the interrogee does not see or did not see the action take place" (Malone 1988:122). Gomez-Imbert (1997a:298) offers a similar analysis for the paradigm of interrogative markers in Barasana, in which there are three basic final forms: -*ri*/-*ti*, corresponding to the direct perfective and imperfective visual category, and -*hari*, used in questions about nonvisual (direct), inference, and reported (indirect) information. Finally, according to Ramirez (1997a:143), the interrogative forms for Tukano are -*ti*, used for questions about visual present or recent-past information, and -*ri*, used for visual past and all other categories.

9.5 Directive modality

The final group of markers in the Kotiria clause modality paradigm, shown in the last row of table 9.1, are those used in utterances with directive modal functions such as imperatives, exhortatives, permissives, requests, and warnings. Such utterances form a distinct semantic subgroup in which the speaker imposes some sort of condition on the addressee (Bybee, Perkins, and Pagliuca 1994:179). As with other subcategories of modality in Kotiria, directive modality is coded by a variety of means, including bound morphology, discourse markers, multi-word constructions, and use of verbs with extended semantic functions.

9.5.1 Imperative: +*ga*

The most common of the morphological markers of oriented modality is the imperative suffix +*ga*. The negative imperative in line 2 of (65), like the negative interrogatives in (53) and (59), is formed with the morpheme -*era*.

(63) *mʉ'ʉ yahiripho'nare yʉ'ʉre waga*

yʉ'ʉ+ré   ~bʉ'ʉ=yahíri~pho'da+re   yʉ'ʉ+ré   wá+gá
1SG+OBJ   2SG(POSS)=heart+OBJ   1SG+OBJ   give+IMPER

'Give me your heart.' [A7.43]

(64) 1 *mʉ'ʉ a'ritʉ me're wa'ikinawãhaga*

  ~bʉ'ʉ   a'rí-tʉ́=~be're   wa'i-~kidá-~wáhá+gá
  2SG   DEM.PROX-stick=COM/INST animal-PL-kill+IMPER

  'Go hunt with this stick.'

2 *yabaina mɨ'ɨ wãhaduainare wãhaga*
   *yabá-~ídá   ~bɨ'ɨ   ~wahá-dua-~ida+re   ~wahá+**ga***
   WH-NOM.PL 2SG   kill-DESID-NOM.PL+OBJ   kill+IMPER

   'Go kill (hunt) whatever you want.' (lit., 'the ones you want to kill') [A7.135–36]

(65) a. *kɨaga ãgare tiro bahkaro mahsawãhariro hira*
    *kɨá+**ga***   *~agá+ré   tí+ró   baká+ró*
    be.afraid+IMPER   snake+OBJ   ANPH+SG   bite+SG

    ~basá-~wáhá+rí+ró   hí+ra
    people-kill+NOM+SG   COP+VIS.IMPERF.2/3

    'Be wary of (poisonous) snakes, their bite is deadly.' [LSK: Snakes]

  b. *su'aropɨre wa'eraatiga*
    su'á+ro-pɨ+re   *wa'(a)-éra-ati+**ga***
    go.into.woods+SG-LOC+OBJ   go-NEG-IMPERF+IMPER

    'Don't be going into the woods.' [LSK: Snakes]

Waltz (2007:432) lists several additional imperative forms: "polite" *-risa*, "third person" *-haro*, "indifferent" *-wa'noharo*, "demonstrative" *-hɨ*, and "emphatic" *-~do'bɨ*. Besides the general imperative *+ga*, the only occurrence of any of these other forms in my data so far is given in (66) (where the emphatic form occurs unglottalized). However, the unusual combination of [+nasal] and [−nasal] syllables that Waltz attributes to the emphatic form suggests that it is morphologically complex, requiring further analysis.

(66) *ne noare ya'ukɨ ninobɨ, nia*
   ~dé   ~doá+re   ya'ú-kɨ   *~dí-~dobɨ*
   NEG   WH+OBJ   tell-(1/2)MASC   be.PROG-IMP.EMPH

   ~dí+a
   say+ASSERT.PERF

   '"Tell no one," he said.' [A7.152]

9.5.2 Permissive: -~ba

The permissive morpheme *-~ba* is used in utterances that respectfully request or elicit approval for the speaker's own actions (see §9.5.5 below for other kinds of request constructions), as we see in (67)–(68) (from a conversation). The speaker in (67) wanted to take a look at a basket that another woman was examining at the time. The utterance in (68) occurred as the speaker got up to take a large bottle of pop inside the house to keep it cool. The same morpheme *-~ba* also occurs as a marker of politeness or respect in formalized greetings such as *himahari mɨ'ɨ?* 'How are you?' and *sãtamahari mɨhsa!* 'Welcome!' (lit., 'Would you like to come in?').

(67)   *ñɨ sima yɨ'ɨ*
      ~yú   sí-~ba   yɨ'ɨ
      see/look DEM.DIST-PERMIS 1SG
      'May I look at (that one)?' / 'Let me look at that one.' [Baskets]

(68)   *a'rire nasã'ama*
      a'rí-ré   ~dá-~sa'a-~ba
      DEM.PROX-OBJ carry-MOV.inside-PERMIS
      'I'm taking this inside (OK?).' [Baskets]

9.5.3 Admonitive *-ri* and adversative *-kɨrɨ*

The admonitive *-ri* and the adversative *-kɨrɨ* are the two remaining suffixes that I have so far identified as belonging in the directive clause modality category. The admonitive is used in utterances that convey the negative consequences that will result from an unheeded warning. Such statements display a certain degree of semantic overlap with irrealis in that they make predictions regarding as-yet unrealized situations (69)–(70).

(69)   1   *sa nimaa wa'awa'a hi'na*
        sá   ~dí-~ba+a   wa'á-wa'a   ~hí'da
        EXRT say-FRUS+ASSERT.PERF go-go   EXRT
        'She urged (in vain), "Let's get out of here!"

      2   *ñaina hira*
        ~yá-~ida   hí+ra
        be.bad-NOM.PL COP+VIS.IMPERF.2/3
        '"These are evil beings."'

      3   *mɨ'ɨre chɨri nia*
        ~bɨ'ú+ré   chú-ri   ~dí+a
        2SG+OBJ eat-ADMON say+ASSERT.PERF
        '"Otherwise they'll eat you," she said.' [A5.28–30]

(70)   *mɨ'ɨre bakari*
      ~bɨ'ú+ré   baká-rí
      2SG+OBJ bite-ADMON
      '(Stay away from that dog) or else it will bite you.'

The adversative *-kɨrɨ* is a semantic cousin to the admonitive, but it is used to refer to events in the realm of realis. Utterances with this marker indicate the negative results or effects that the action of the verb actually had on the participant(s). The sentence in (70) comes at the conclusion of a story about the family dog being killed by a jaguar (text 2 in appendix 1). The speaker tells us that after the dog was killed by a jaguar, the family remained without a dog for a long time. The use of the adversative shows both the speaker's sadness over the loss of the dog and his assessment that being dogless is bad for a family, since the primary function of dogs is to aid in hunting. In (72), from a conversation, the young woman speaker was talking about having gone to a festival at which there was panflute dancing (which the Kotiria love) but where she did not get to dance.

(71) ã yoana sã dierome'reraina thuahãkurɨ yoaripa
~a=yoá-~da ~sá dié+ró=~be'r(e)-éra-~ida
so/then=do/make-(1/2)PL 1PL.EXC dog+SG=COM/INST-NEG-NOM.PL
thuá-~ha-**kurɨ** yoá+rí-pá
return-TERM-ADVERS be.long+NOM-CLS:time
'Then we (sadly) remained dogless for a long time.' [A2.12]

(72) ne bahseraphutiakurɨ yɨ'ɨ
~dé bas(a)-éra-phuti-a-**kurɨ** yɨ'ɨ
NEG sing/dance-NEG-blow-AFFEC-ADVERS 1SG
'I didn't dance (panflute dances) even a little.' [Baskets]

9.5.4 Exhortatives: (~sa . . .) ~(hi')da

Exhortatives are formed in two ways in Kotiria. The first is the multiword expression (~)sa . . . ~hi'da (see §5.3.5 and §11.2.3 for other uses of ~hi'da). The first element is the first person exclusive pronoun ~sa, which occurs sentence-initially and, for many speakers, with loss of nasality; see (73)–(74). The second element, ~hi'da, occurs sentence-finally (73), though it can also be shortened to -~da; when shortened, it becomes a bound morpheme on the verb as evidenced by the fact that it loses its inherent tonal melody and acquires the final tone of the verb root through spreading (74). The multiword expression has close cognates in other Eastern Tukanoan languages, e.g., Wa'ikhana ɨsa . . . -~ɨda. The second exhortative construction is a reduction of the full form: only the sentence-final and fully pronounced ~hi'da is used (75)–(76). Whether or not ~hi'da occurs in conjunction with the initial ~sa, and independent of its full (phonologically independent) or reduced (phonologically bound) form, ~hi'da in the exhortative construction regularly occurs after an otherwise uninflected verb. This is evidence that as a clause modality marker, ~hi'da is mutually exclusive with other markers in the paradigm and occupies the same slot. The one notable difference between ~hi'da and other clause modality markers is its ability to occur as an independent phonological word.

(73) *sa nimaa wa'awa'a hi'na*
sá   *~dí-~ba+a*   *wa'á-wa'a*   *~hí'da*
EXRT   say-FRUS+ASSERT.PERF   go-go   EXRT
'She urged (in vain), "Let's get out of here (escape) . . ."' (= (69), line 1) [A5.28]

(74) *sã ku'sina*
~sá   *ku'sí-~da*
EXRT   bathe-EXRT
'Let's go bathe/swim.'

(75) *kotiria yame're bu'e hi'na*
kó-ti+ri+a   *yá=~be're*   *bu'é*   *~hí'da*
water-VBZ+NOM+PL   POSS=COM/INST   study/learn   EXRT
'Let's study in (with our own) Kotiria (language).' [LSK: title]

(76) *numia ña'ana wa'a hi'na timahkapɨ nia kha'maduruku yoaa*
~dubí+a   *~ya'á-~da*   *wa'á*   *~hí'da*   *ti=~baká-pɨ*
woman+PL   catch-(1/2)PL   go   EXRT   ANPH=village-LOC
~dí+a   *~kha'bá-dú-rúkú+á*   *yoá+a*
say+ASSERT.PERF   do.RECIP-speak-stand+(3)PL   do/make+ASSERT.PERF
'"Let's go get women from that village," (the men) said among themselves.' [Ancestors]

9.5.5 Reporting requests, demands, and warnings

Kotiria employs several independent verbs of speech to report requests, demands, and warnings. The verbs *du'ti* 'tell', and *~sidi* 'ask for', refer to 'requests' or 'demands' (77)–(81). The verb *ya'u* 'tell' can also indicate 'warning' (82).

Such semantic extensions are sometimes established by combinations of morphemes and sometimes by contextual information. In the line preceding (77), for instance, a woman expressed a desire to eat a particular kind of fruit. The frustrative morpheme *-~ba* in the nominalization *du'ti-~ba+ri* indicates that her 'telling' was in fact the expression of an unfulfilled request or wish. In (78)–(809), contextual information provides the basis for the appropriate semantic interpretations. In (78), the culturally established relationship of authority between a father and a son (the speaker) yields a 'request'- or 'demand'-type reading rather than a more neutral interpretation of mere 'telling'. In (79), on the other hand, a father is telling his sons about a dangerous situation; contextually, this type of telling is interpreted as 'warning'.

As for (80), since it is a well known fact that curupiras are powerful and dangerous beings, when one such being 'asks for' the man's heart, the request is naturally interpreted more weightily as a 'demand' of the most threatening type! In (81), on the other hand, the lexicalized ~*sidítu* 'ask, interrogate', implies a more forceful demand for information, while the same root marked by the frustrative -~*ba* in (82) yields the notion of 'begging'.

(77) *to a'rire du'timari nihachʉ*
    to=a'rí+ré   ***du'tí-~bá+rí***   *~dí-~ha-chʉ*
    DEF=DEM.PROX+OBJ tell/request-FRUS+NOM   say-TERM-SW.REF
    'Just after (the woman) said that (made her request/wish) . . .' [A5.5]

(78) *marire sõ'oi sĩ'a phitibohka du'tire*
    ~barí+ré   *~so'ó+i*   *~si'á phití-boka*   ***du'tí+ré***
    1PL.INC+OBJ DEIC.DIST+LOC torch COLL-meet   request+VIS.PERF.2/3
    '(Our father) told/asked us to meet him over there with torches.' [A4.24]

(79) *ã yo bo'rero to pho'nare ya'ua hi'na*
    ~a=yó bo'ré+ro   *to=~pho'dá+re*   ***ya'ú+a***
    so=do be.light+SG 3SG.POSS=children+OBJ tell/warn+ASSERT.PERF
    ~hí'da
    EMPH
    'So, in the morning (the father) warned his sons . . .' [A6.66]

(80) *to yahiripho'nare sinia tirore*
    to=yahiri~pho'da+re   ***~sidítu+a***   *tí+ró+ré*
    3SG.POSS=heart+OBJ   ask+ASSERT.PERF   ANPH+SG+OBJ
    '(The curupira) asked him (the man) for his heart.' [A7.45]

(81) *mʉmʉ mahasũ tirore sinitua*
    ~bʉbʉ́ ~bahá-~sʉ́   *tí+ró+ré*   ***~sidítu+a***
    run   go.uphill-arrive ANPH+SG+OBJ   ask+ASSERT.PERF
    'He (the snake father) ran up to him (the man and) asked (demanded to know): . . .' [A6.56]

(82) *tinare sinitumakã sãre waaga*
    tí-~da+re   ***~sidítu-~ba-~ka***   *~sá+ré*   *wá+gá*
    ANPH-PL+OBJ   ask-FRUS-EMPH   1PL.EXC+OBJ   give+IMPER
    '(The woman-stealers) begged them for (to give them) the women . . .' [Ancestors]

10 Clause structure

This chapter describes the syntax of the Kotiria clause—in particular, the arguments taken by different categories of verbs and the prototypical grammatical and semantic roles associated with those arguments, as well as types of adjuncts. (Complement clauses and other multiple-verb constructions are treated in chapter 11.) The identification of subjects is accomplished by a mixture of head-marking and dependent-marking strategies; the latter are discussed in §10.1. The basic types of intransitive and transitive verbs and the semantic roles associated with their core arguments are examined in §§10.2–10.3. Section 10.3 also discusses the semantics of differential object marking, and presents a cross-linguistic overview of the object-marking morpheme +*re* and a hypothesis about the development of +*re* as a multifunctional 'objective' case marker. Ditransitive verbs, the semantic roles associated with their arguments, and the means used to code beneficiary and recipient objects are discussed in §10.4. The occurrence of oblique (locative and directional) arguments with stative and motion verbs and in constructions with verbs meaning 'take' and 'bring' is the topic of §10.5, while valence-changing verb serialization is discussed in §10.6. Locative, temporal, comitative and instrument adjuncts are described in §10.7.

Table 10.1 gives an overview of the arguments and adjuncts that occur in simple clauses in Kotiria. Part A of the table shows the grammatical and semantic roles of the arguments (obligatory participants) prototypically associated with each type of verb as well as the main coding means used to identify arguments; part B of the table shows adjuncts. In Kotiria, eight semantic roles—agent, patient, experiencer, beneficiary, comitative, instrument, locative (goal and source), and temporal—are mapped onto a smaller number of grammatical roles: subject (S) and object(s) (O);[1] oblique arguments; and locative, temporal, comitative, and instrumental adjuncts. The main coding means are agreement suffixes on verbs, for subjects, and case suffixes on nouns for all other arguments and adjuncts; word order plays a minor role.

---

[1] The abbreviation S includes both subjects of intransitive verbs and subjects of transitive verbs. Given its nominative-accusative alignment, Kotiria marks all subject arguments the same way.

TABLE 10.1. ARGUMENTS AND ADJUNCTS

A. ARGUMENTS

VERB TYPE:	SEMANTIC ROLE OF ARGUMENT:			
intransitive				
stative	patient			
nonstative				
active/motion	agent			
perception/m.p.	exp.			
transitive				
active	agent	patient		
perception/m.p.	exp.	patient		
complex	agent	patient	rec./ben.	loc.-goal
nonprototypical				
trans. stative	patient			loc.-ref.
trans. motion	agent			loc.-goal
GRAMMATICAL ROLE OF ARGUMENT:	subject	object$_1$	object$_2$	oblique
CODING OF ARGUMENT:	agreement	(+re)	+re	-pɨ+re

B. ADJUNCTS

SEMANTIC ROLE:	locative	temporal	comitative/instrument
CODING:	-pɨ / +i	(-pɨ)+re	=~be're

NOTE: Ben. = beneficiary; exp. = experiencer; loc. = locational; m.p. = mental process; rec. = recipient; ref. = referential.

10.1 Subject agreement

While subject nominals take regular lexical morphemes coding information such as number and class—e.g., ~*dubi+a* (woman+PL, animate) 'women' and ~*badu+ro* (husband-SG, animate) 'husband'—it can be seen from table 10.1 that they bear no overt morphology marking their semantic roles. This is our first indication that Kotiria verbal syntax orients primarily to the grammatical rather than to the semantic roles of arguments (see, however §8.5.2 and §11.5 for discussions of the semantic roles of the subject in perfective constructions with *wa'a* and *yoa*).

The table also shows that subject nominals also bear no morphology marking their grammatical role. Yet we can confidently identify subjects by examining other marking strategies in the language. Kotiria is generally a dependent-marking language; however, at the clause level, there is a mixed pattern combining head-marking for subjects (subject nominals induce cross-referencing morphology on verbs) with dependent-marking for other nominal arguments, which take case-marking morphology (see §§10.3–10.4). The distinctive morphology that appears on constituents such as adverbial clauses and verbal complements (see §10.1.2, as well as chapter 11) can be thought of as dependent-marking of those constituents as well. In other words, subjects can be identified, first of all, because they are generally the only unmarked nominal arguments in clauses, in contrast to other (case-marked) arguments (but see §10.3.1), and secondly, because they induce agreement morphology in verbal words or on dependent constituents.

The remainder of this section presents Kotiria subject agreement in detail. Realis finite verbs are treated in §10.1.1, while irrealis and nominalized verbs are treated in §10.1.2.

10.1.1 Subject agreement morphology on realis finite verbs

Agreement morphology cross-referencing the subject nominal on finite and nonfinite verbal words within the clause occurs in two different paradigms. The first of these paradigms occurs exclusively in the visual category of the clause-modality evidential suffixes used on finite verbs in realis statements (see §9.2.2). We recall that unlike most other Eastern Tukanoan languages, which code a third person vs. nonthird person distinction in the paradigm for this evidential category, Kotiria codes a first person vs. nonfirst person distinction (with number neutralized) that is combined with a distinction between imperfective and perfective aspect. The four suffixes coding subject agreement (as well as aspect) are, for first person, imperfective *-ha* (1) and perfective *+i* (2), and for second or third person, imperfective *+ra* (3) and perfective *+re* (4). Note that the same agreement suffixes are used with intransitive verbs, as in (1), and transitive verbs, as in (2)–(4). The subject and the agreement morpheme are both shown in bold type.

(1)   *yʉ'ʉ Mo mahkariropʉ hiha*
       yʉ'ʉ ~bó ~baká+ri+ro-pʉ   **hí-ha**
       1SG   Mõ   village+NOM+SG-LOC   COP-VIS.IMPERF.1
       'I am from Mõ.' [A1.2]

(2)   *to wa'ikiro wãhariroditare sã nathuai wʉ'ʉpʉre*
       to=wa'í-kíró   ~wahá+ri+ro-dita+re   ~***sá***
       DEF=animal+SG   kill+NOM+SG-SOL+OBJ   1PL.EXC

~dá-thúá+í   wʉ'ʉ́-pʉ́+ré
get-return+VIS.PERF.1 house-LOC+OBJ

'We took home only the dead animal (that the dog had hunted).' [A2.13]

(3)   numia, tina chʉare yoara

~dubí+a   tí-~da   chʉ́+a+re   yoá+ra
woman+PL ANPH-PL eat+PL+OBJ do/make+VIS.IMPERF.2/3

'(Kotiria) women make the food.' [A1.7]

(4)   mʉ'ʉ sãre ma'ñore

~bʉ'ʉ́ ~sá+re   ~ba'yó+re
2SG   1PL.EXC+OBJ lie+VIS.PERF.2/3

'You lied to us.' [A4.52]

10.1.2 Subject agreement morphology in other constructions

The second paradigm of subject agreement morphology occurs in two types of constructions: the finite verbal words in irrealis statements (see §9.3) and in nonfinite nominalizations. Table 10.2 (repeated from table 9.3) gives the paradigm for these two types of constructions. Note that, unlike the paradigm for the visual evidential category, the paradigm of subject agreement morphemes codes a distinction between third person vs. nonthird person (a pattern which, for the most part, parallels that of other Eastern Tukanoan languages); gender is marked in the singular nonthird person forms. Person referents in parentheses are added to the glosses of these agreement markers (e.g., "(1/2)FEM" or "(3)PL") as a reminder of their specific referential function in these constructions.

TABLE 10.2. SUBJECT AGREEMENT SUFFIXES FOR IRREALIS AND NOMINALIZED VERBS

	SINGULAR	PLURAL
FIRST/SECOND PERSON	-ko (fem.) -kʉ / +i (masc.)	-~da
THIRD PERSON	+ro	+a

The first-or-second-person singular subject agreement markers shown in table 10.2 are used in the nominalizations in (5)–(8) below. Example (5) is from a conversation that took place among several women. In this example, there is no overt second person subject (indicated by Ø in the example). Such omission is possible, for both subjects and objects, as long as contextual information makes reference clear (other examples with a null subject are (6), (9), (10), and (11), while (14) is an example with a null object). We can deduce that the subject referent is both second person and feminine from other morphological markers: the verb-final suffix +*ra* indicates a nonfirst person subject referent, and the morpheme *-ko* nominalizing *wese-wa'a* 'when you go to the garden' indicates a nonthird person singular feminine subject referent.

(5) *wehsewa'ako pihsaria hira*
 *Ø   wesé-wa'a-**ko**   pisá-ríá   hí+**ra***
 garden-go-(1/2)FEM   be.on-CLS:round   COP+VIS.IMPERF.2/3
 'It's a hat for when you go to the garden.' (lit., 'a garden-going hat', for a woman) [Baskets]

Note that there are two forms used for first-or-second-person masculine singular in table 10.2: *-kʉ* and *+i*. As observed in §9.3, I view both as derived from a single older morpheme *-kʉ*, a cognate form in Wa'ikhana and a number of other Eastern Tukanoan languages. In Kotiria, the full form has been retained as a relic in certain constructions alongside a more recent reduced form *+i*, which reflects two related phonological shifts evident elsewhere the language: the fronting of [ʉ] to [i] (see Waltz 2002:180), and the gradual loss of left-edge phonological material (such as morpheme-initial consonants) due to grammaticalization. Both processes are also reflected in the Kotiria nominalizer suffix *-iro*, cognate of Wa'ikhana *-kʉdo*.

Both *+i* and *-kʉ* are used on verbs in irrealis constructions and in nominalizations, as we see in (6) and (7). As in (5), (6) has no overt subject nominal, but we know that the subject referent is masculine by the two occurrences of the morpheme *-kʉ*, first as the nominalizer of the adverbial clause *~so'o waro+i hi-kʉ* 'when I'm right there', and then as the agreement marker in the verbal word in the predictive (irrealis) construction *pisʉ-kʉ-ka* 'I'll call'.

(6) *sõ'o waroi hikʉ pihsʉkʉka na'inokai*
 *Ø   ~so'ó   wáró+í   hí-**kʉ***   *pisú-**kú**-ká*
 DEIC.DIST   EMPH+LOC   COP-(1/2)MASC   call-(1/2)MASC-PREDICT
 ~da'i-~doka+i
 be.dark-COMPL+LOC
 'When I'm right over there, I'll call in the dark.' [A4.12]

In (7), the first person subject agreement suffix *+i* is used both to nominalize the complement to the verb *wa'a* and within the irrealis verb.

(7) *yʉ'ʉ mihchare wa'ikinawãhai wa'aika*
 *yʉ'**ʉ***   *~bichá+ré*   *wa'i-~kídá-~wáhá+**í***   *wa'á+**i**-ka*
 1SG   today+OBJ   animal-PL-kill+(1/2)MASC   go+(1/2)MASC-PREDICT
 'Today I'm going hunting.' [A7.4]

The suffix +*i* is also used in two nominalizations in the complex verbal construction in (8). It nominalizes ~*waha-~kha'ba+i* 'avenge', the complement verb in the purposive construction ~*waha-~kha'ba+i ta+i* 'come to avenge'; this in turn is the nominalized complement in a progressive construction with the finite auxiliary verb ~*di*, which is suffixed with the first person form of the visual evidential, -*ha*.

(8)   *yʉ'ʉ tirore wãha kha'mai tai niha*
       ***yʉ'ʉ**   tí+ró+ré   ~wahá=~kha'ba+i   tá+í*
       1SG   ANPH+SG+OBJ   kill=want+(1/2)MASC   come+(1/2)MASC
       ~*di-**ha***
       be.PROG-VIS.IMPERF.1
       'I'm coming here to avenge him (my dead son).' [A6.61]

Though both the suffixes +*i* and -*kʉ* are productively employed in nominalizations, there is some evidence to suggest a developing structural complementary distribution: beyond factors such as the personal preferences of specific speakers, the data reveal a tendency for -*kʉ* to be used as the nominalizer of adverbial clauses, particularly, though not exclusively (as we see in (6)) those that have second person referents, and for +*i* to be used as the nominalizer of nonfinite verbs in complement constructions, particularly (again, not exclusively) those with first person referents such as in the progressive in (8) (for more on these constructions, see §11.3).

The sentences in (9)–(11) also have no overt subjects, but we know, for example, that the null subject in (9) must be third person singular because of the nominalizer +*ro*. This suffix is used to nominalize the verb *wa'i-~kida-~waha+ro* 'hunting' (lit., 'animal-killing'; the patient noun is incorporated); this in turn is a constituent of the nominalized dependent clause *wa'i-~kida-~waha+ro wa'a+ro* 'when he went hunting'. We do not know, however, whether the referent is feminine or masculine, as gender is neutralized in the third person forms of this paradigm. Such information must be gleaned from context in the absence of full nouns or pronouns with feminine-marking morphemes.

(9)   *wa'ikinawãharo wa'aro, tʉre nawa'aka'a, wa'ikina phayʉ wãhaatia*
       *Ø   wa'i-~kidá-~wáhá+**ró**   wa'á+**ro**   tʉ́+re   ~dá-wa'a-ka'a*
             animal-PL-kill+(3)SG   go+(3)SG   stick+OBJ   get-go-do.moving
       wa'i-~kidá phayʉ́   ~wahá-ati+a
       animal-PL   many/a.lot   kill-IMPERF+ASSERT.PERF
       'When he went hunting, he took the stick along (and) would always kill lots of animals.' [A7.155]

Markers of agreement with plural subjects are shown in (10) and (11); the subjects are also null in these examples. Agreement with the nonthird person plural is coded by -~da in the nominalization of ~dubi+a ~ya'a 'women-catching/kidnapping' in (10), while in (11), +a marks agreement with a third person plural subject in the nominalization of ya'u in the purposive construction ya'u+a wa'a '(they) went to tell'.

(10) numia ña'ana wa'a hi'na ti mahkapɨ
 Ø ~dubí+a ~ya'á-~da wa'á ~hí'da ti=~baká-pɨ
 woman+PL catch-(1/2)PL go EMPH ANPH=village-LOC
 'Let's go get women from that village.' (lit., 'let's go bride-napping') [Ancestors]

(11) ti phɨkɨrore ya'ua wa'aa
 Ø ti=phɨk+ɨ́+ró+ré ya'ú+a wa'á+a
 3PL.POSS=parent+MASC+SG+OBJ tell+(3)PL go+ASSERT.PERF
 'They went to tell their father.' [A4.47]

Thus, while there is no nominal case marking of subject in Kotiria, morphology coding agreement with the subject nominal occurs in the verbal paradigm of the visual evidential category (by far the most commonly used inflectional category in everyday speech) as well as in irrealis constructions and nominalizations (which are also extremely common) and has two important syntactic functions. First, it creates a referential link to a subject nominal (overt or implied), and second, it is the most common means by which dependent constituents (nonfinite verbs and dependent clauses) are marked.

10.1.3 Adverbial clauses without subject agreement

There are two additional morphemes that function as subordinators but that do not mark person and number of the subject. Examples (12) and (13) show that an adverbial clause whose subject is different from the subject of the main, finite clause occurs with the switch-reference marker -chɨ. The treatment of adverbial clauses whose subjects are the same as or different from that of the main clause can be seen in the three sequential sentences in (13). In sentence 1, the adverbial and main clauses share the same first person plural subject and the initial subordinate clause is accordingly nominalized by -~da, the first person plural agreement marker. In sentences 2 and 3, however, the first person plural subjects of the initial adverbial clauses (as well as the final subordinate clause in sentence 3) are different from the third person subjects of the main clauses, and each subordinate clause is marked by -chɨ.

(12) to phichachʉta, phirorowʉ'rʉ tirore chowerʉkaa
to=phichá-**chʉ**=ta ~phiró+ró-wʉ́'rʉ́ tí+ró+ré
DEF=shoot-SW.REF=REF snake+SG-AUG ANPH+SG+OBJ
chówe-rʉka+a
vomit-begin+ASSERT.PERF

'When (the man) shot (it), the big snake began to vomit him (the dog) up.' [A6.36]

(13) 1 mari kherokã wa'aduana, wa'aka wʉria me're
~barí khé+ro-~ka wa'á-dua-~**da** wa'á-ka
1PL.INC be.fast+SG-DIM go-DESID-(1/2)PL go-ASSERT.IMPERF
wʉ́-ria=~be're
fly-CLS:round.elongated=COM/INST

'When we want to go (somewhere) quickly, we go by plane.'

2 mari khõaãwa'achʉ khuãyʉ'dʉra
~barí ~khóá-wá'á-**chʉ́** khuá-yʉ'dʉ+ra
1PL.INC throw-go-SW.REF be.dangerous-INTENS+VIS.IMPERF.2/3

'When we take off, it's very dangerous.'

3 to wãhkunoka wa'aka'achʉ, mari khapari bʉhkʉawa'ara, mari kʉachʉ
to=~wakú-~dóká wa'á-ka'a-**chʉ**
DEF=be.aware-COMPL go-do.moving-SW.REF
~barí=khapá+rí bʉkʉ́+a=wa'a+ra
1PL.INC.POSS=eye+PL grow+AFFEC=go+VIS.IMPERF.2/3
~barí kʉá-**chʉ**
1PL.INC be.afraid-SW.REF

'When we realize it's going up, our eyes grow big, because we're afraid.' [A12.3–5]

Another type of adverbial clause, denoting concomitant processes, is marked by the generic classifier -re.

(14) wa'mamahare, boraa ti kohpapʉ
~wa'bá-~báhá-**ré** borá+a
wrap.around-MOV.up/down-CLS:generic fall+ASSERT.PERF
ti=kopá-pʉ́
ANPH=hole-LOC

'Wrapping around him (a dog), (the snake) retreated down into a hole.' [A6.22]

Clause structure 321

10.2 Intransitives

Intransitive verbs require a single nominal argument with the grammatical role of subject. The semantic role associated with this single argument depends on the semantic class of the verb. Subjects of stative verbs prototypically have the semantic role of patient; in other words, a stative subject such as the first person singular pronoun *yɨ'ɨ* in (15) is a representative of, or participant in, the state expressed by the verb. Subjects of intransitive active or motion verbs prototypically have the semantic role of agent; in other words, subjects such as *~dubia* 'women' in (16), and *to ~badɨro* 'her husband' in (17) are the instigators or performers of the actions expressed by the verbs. Subjects of verbs of mental processes or verbs of perception, such as the first person plural exclusive pronoun *~sa* in (18), are experiencers, conscious participants in, but not initiators of, the actions expressed by this class of verbs. (The definitions here follow Givón [2001, vol. 1:107–50].)

(15) *yɨ'ɨ hiha koiro*
yɨ'ɨ-khɨ́ yɨ'ɨ hí-ha   kó-iro
1SG-ADD 1SG COP-VIS.IMPERF.1 relative-NOM.SG
'I am your/a relative.' [A7.39]

(16) *numia da'raa wa'ara wehsepɨre*
~dubí+a   da'rá+a   wa'á+ra   wesé-pɨ+re
woman+PL work+(3)PL go+VIS.IMPERF.2/3 garden-LOC+OBJ
'(In the morning, after they finish eating breakfast), women go to work in the garden.' [A1.9]

(17) *to manɨno pase'epɨ wa'aa*
to=~badɨ́+ro   pá=se'e-pɨ   wa'á+a
3SG.POSS=husband+SG ALT=CONTR-LOC go+ASSERT.PERF
'Her husband went off someplace.' [A5.5]

(18) *sã̄ yoaropɨ, yɨ'ɨ phɨkɨ me're thɨ'oi*
~sá   yoá+ro-pɨ   yɨ=phɨk+ɨ́=~be're
1PL.EXC be.far+SG-LOC 1SG=parent+MASC=COM/INST
thɨ'ó+i
hear+VIS.PERF.1
'We, from far away, (I) with my father, heard (the sounds).' [A2.9]

10.3 Transitives

Transitive verbs are defined as verbs that require two nominal arguments—one with the grammatical role of subject and the other with the grammatical role of object. A prototypical transitive verb expresses an action, and the subject argument of such an active transitive verb has the semantic role of agent—the instigator or performer of the action—as in (19) and (20), with the active verbs *hoa* 'write' and *~waha* 'kill'.

(19) *a'ri thure hoaha sã kotiria*
 [*a'rí-thú+ré*]ₒ   [*hoá-ha*]ᵥ   [*~sá*
 DEM.PROX-CLS:stacked+OBJ   write-VIS.IMPERF.1   1PL.EXC
 kó-ti+ri+a]ₛ
 water-VBZ+NOM+PL
 'We Kotiria are writing this book.' [A8.8]

(20) *tiro tiaro kayare wãhaa*
 [*tí+ró*]ₛ   [*tía+ro*   *ká-ya+re*]ₒ   [*~wahá+a*]ᵥ
 ANPH+SG   three+SG   black.monkey-PL+OBJ   kill+ASSERT.PERF
 'He killed three monkeys.' [A7.10]

As with the intransitive subject nominals in (15)–(18), transitive subject nominals have no case-marking morphology. Comparing the third person pronominal subjects in the transitive sentence (20) and the intransitive sentence (21) (both *ti+ro*), we also see that Kotiria does not mark subjects of transitive and intransitive clauses differently—evidence that Kotiria is typologically nominative-accusative. Moreover, as is seen in section 10.1, Kotiria subject agreement marking on the verb also treats subjects of transitive and intransitive clauses identically, further evidence of nominative-accusative alignment.

(21) *tiro topʉ pihsaga*
 [*tí+ró*]ₛ   *tó-pʉ*   [*pisá+á*]ᵥ
 ANPH+SG   REM-LOC   be.on+ASSERT.PERF
 'He (a boy) just stayed up there (on top of the roof of the house).' [A5.31]

The other nominal in a prototypical transitive clause, the object, usually has the semantic role of patient. With active transitive verbs such as those in (19)–(20) above, the object is a patient, a participant affected or changed by the action expressed by the verb—the 'book' in (19) and the 'monkeys' in (20). The patient object of verbs of sensory perception and verbs of mental processes (whose subjects are experiencers) are prototypically participants in the event but are unaffected by, or undergo no change as a result of, the action expressed by the verb. Examples (22)–(24) have transitive verbs with objects of this type. Example (22) has the perception verb *~yʉ* 'see' and the unaffected patient object *ti+ro+re* 'him'; (23) and (24) have verbs of mental processes, *~kha'i* 'love' and *chʉ-dua-~ba* 'wish to eat', whose unaffected patient objects are, respectively, *ti phᵻk+o+ro+re* 'their mother' and *waso+re* 'siringa fruit'.

(22) *ñᵻa tirore. phiriro khõaa*
 [Ø]ₛ [~yᵻ́+á]ᵥ   [tí+ró+ré]ₒ
       see/look+ASSERT.PERF   ANPH+SG+OBJ
 phí+ri+ro   ~khoá+a
 be.big+NOM+SG be.lying+ASSERT.PERF
 'He saw him. The big guy was lying there.' [A7.101]

(23) *ti phᵻkorore khã'i nᵻnᵻatiga te topᵻ*
 [Ø]ₛ [ti=phᵻk+ó+ró+ré]ₒ   [~kha'í]ᵥ
       3PL.POSS=parent+FEM+SG+OBJ   love
 [~dᵻdᵻ́-átí+á]ᵥ   té   tó-pᵻ
 follow-IMPERF+ASSERT.PERF all.the.way REM-LOC
 'They loved their mother (and) followed after (her) all the way there (to the place the devil had taken her).' [A4.45]

(24) *yᵻ'ᵻ wahsore chᵻduamaka*
 [yᵻ'ᵻ́]ₛ [wasó+ré]ₒ   [chᵻ́-dua-~ba-ka]ᵥ
 1SG   siringa.fruit+OBJ eat-DESID-FRUS-ASSERT.IMPERF
 'I wish I had some siringa fruit to eat.' [A5.4]

Looking at each of the object constituents in the transitive clauses above, we see that object nominals can be animate—'monkeys' (20), 'him, the big guy' (22), and 'their mother' (23)—or inanimate—'this book' (19) and 'siringa fruit' (24). They can be single lexical nouns (24), pronouns (22), or noun phrases, as in (19), (20), and (23). We should also note the tendency for objects to occur immediately before the verb (in all but (22)), and observe that all of the object arguments are morphologically marked by the suffix *+re*. Thus, we see that, as with S, it is the object's grammatical rather than semantic role that is morphologically marked in Kotiria. We also see that mixed means are used for argument coding in Kotiria: subject arguments are coded by agreement while object arguments take case-marking morphology.

10.3.1 Objects with and without *+re*

Examples (25)–(27) show that, although there is a tendency for object nouns to be marked by *+re*, in fact not all of them are.

(25) *mipᵻre yᵻ'ᵻ chᵻa bohkatu'sᵻha. thuai niha*
 ~bí-pᵻ́+ré   [yᵻ'ᵻ́]ₛ [chᵻ́a]ₒ [boká-tu'sᵻ-ha]ᵥ
 now-LOC+OBJ 1SG   food   find-finish-VIS.IMPERF.1

thuá+i ~*dí-ha*
   return+(1/2)MASC be.PROG-VIS.IMPERF.1
   'Now I've found food (and/so) I'm going home.' [A7.11]

(26)   *khɨbokɨri yoa*
   [∅]ₛ [*khɨbó-kɨ+rí*]ₒ   [*yoá*]ᵥ
         soaked.manioc-CLS:tree/shaft+PL do/make
   'We make soft manioc flatbread . . .' [Manioc]

(27)   *bɨhsarida yoaitai niha*
   [∅]ₛ [*bɨsá+ri-da*]ₒ
         adorn+NOM-CLS:threadlike
   [*yoá+i-ta+i*]ᵥ   ~*dí-ha*
   do/make+(1/2)MASC-INTENT+(1/2)MASC be.PROG-VIS.IMPERF.1
   'I'll be making (I'm going to make) a necklace.' [A7.114]

If some objects are coded by +*re* while others clearly are not, it would be reasonable to ask whether there are other means of coding objects besides morphological marking. The sentences in (28) can help us address this question. Sentence (28a) has prototypical subject-object-verb word order (see §10.4.3 below) with an unmarked object *chɨa* 'food', while in (28b) the object noun follows the verb and takes the suffix +*re*.

(28)   a. *hiphitiro chɨa natara*
       [*hí-phiti+ro*]ₛ [*chɨa*]ₒ [~*dá-ta+ra*]ᵥ
       COP-COLL+SG   food   get-come+VIS.IMPERF.2/3
       'Everyone brings a lot of food.'

   b. *tikoro, to namono, chɨduaatiga wahsore*
       [*tí-kó+ró*   *to=~dabó+ro*]ₛ
       ANPH-FEM+SG 3SG.POSS=wife+SG
       [*chɨ-dua-ati+a*]ᵥ   [*wasó+ré*]ₒ
       eat-DESID-IMPERF+ASSERT.PERF siringa.fruit+OBJ
       'The woman, his wife, wanted to eat (had a craving for) siringa fruit.' [A5.3]

These sentences suggest that word order may play at least a secondary role in the coding of object arguments—specifically, that a nominal constituent occupying the immediately preverbal position in a syntactically transitive clause (one requiring two arguments) is interpreted as the object argument even if it is not morphologically marked with the objective case suffix +*re*, as in (25)–(27) and (28a). (In the remainder of this discussion, "preverbal" is used as convenient shorthand for "immediately preverbal.") Such an interpretation is reinforced by the fact that objects occurring in any position other than preverbal are invariably marked with +*re*; this is seen for postverbal objects in (28b) and in (29)–(31), and for a sentence-initial object, preceding the subject, in (32).

(29) *wã'karukusu̵mu̵a, nia tirore*
 [Ø]ₛ [~*wa'ká-ruku-~su̵-~bu̵+a*]ᵥ ~*dí+a*
  wake.up-stand-arrive-run+AFFEC say+ASSERT.PERF
 [*tí+ró+ré*]ₒ
  ANPH+SG+OBJ
 'Waking and rising up quickly, (the curupira) said to him (the man) . . .' [A7.126]

(30) *wĩhsoa chu̵ka bu̵htiaditare*
 [~*wisó+á*]ₛ [*chú-ka*]ᵥ [*butí+a-dita+re*]ₒ
  squirrel+PL eat-ASSERT.IMPERF be.hard+PL-SOL+OBJ
 'Squirrels eat hard things only.' [LSK: Squirrels]

(31) *ñu̵a tirore. phiriro khõaa*
 [Ø]ₛ [~*yu̵+á*]ᵥ   [*tí+ró+ré*]ₒ
  see/look+ASSERT.PERF ANPH+SG+OBJ
 phí+ri+ro ~*khoá+a*
 be.big+NOM+SG be.lying+ASSERT.PERF
 'He saw him. The big guy was lying there.' (= (22)) [A7.101]

(32) *yu̵ me'remakinare yu̵'u̵ ñu̵tini wa'atii*²
 [*yu̵=~be'ré-~baka-~ida+re*]ₒ   [*yu̵'u̵*]ₛ
  1SG.POSS=COM/INST-village-NOM.PL+OBJ 1SG
 [~*yu̵-~tídí+i*   *wa'á-ati+i*]ᵥ
  see-visit+(1/2)MASC go-IMPERF+VIS.PERF.1
 'I used to go (travel) in order to see (visit) my friends.' [A3.3]

While likely significant on some level, however, word order alone cannot explain the coding of objects. Indeed, were word order the main coding means for objects, we would expect to find that nouns occupying the preverbal object slot were generally unmarked. However, most object nouns in this position are case-marked. In "The Curupira Story," for instance (text 7 in appendix 1), of the sixty-eight clauses with overt object nominals, in fifty-one the object nominal both occurs in preverbal position and is case-marked by +*re*. In eight instances, object nominals follow the verb and, as expected, all of these occur with +*re*. In only nine of the sixty-eight clauses does the object occur

---

² In this example, ~*yu̵-~tidi+i wa'a-ati+i* is a complex predicate that means something like '(I) used to go visiting'; ~*yu̵-tidi+i* is a nominalized complement and *wa'a-ati+i* is the finite verbal word.

immediately preceding the verb and without *+re*. This distribution suggests that while coding by word order may aid identification of the object argument, the primary coding means is morphological case suffixation.

10.3.2 More on the semantics of *+re*

To clarify just what the effect of marking by *+re* is, we need to expand on the observations in §10.3.1. First, we have seen that any object nominal that does not occur immediately before the verb must be marked by *+re*. This is the case no matter whether the object is referential or definite as in (29), (31)–(32), (34)–(35), and (37), nonreferential or indefinite, as in (28a), (30), (33), and (36), animate as in (29), (31) and (32), or inanimate, as in (28b), (30), and (33)–(37) below.

(33) *si'niare tina si'ni bahsa karisure phuti yoara*

    ~si'día+re   *ti-~da*   *~si'dí basá*   ***karísu+re***
    caxiri.beer+OBJ ANPH-PL drink sing/dance pan.flute+OBJ

    phutí   *yoá+ra*
    blow/play do/make+VIS.IMPERF.2/3

    'They drink drinks (caxiri beer and other fermented liquids), dance (and) play the flute.' [A3.15]

(34) *yʉ'ʉ boerakʉrʉ tire*

    yʉ'ʉ *bo-éra-kʉrʉ*   ***tí+re***
    1SG forget-NEG-ADVERS ANPH+OBJ

    'I've forgotten them (traditional dances and music), unfortunately.' [A3.20]

(35) *wa'a nʉa ti khumuwʉ'rʉpʉre*

    wa'á *~yʉ́+á*   ***ti=~khubú-wʉ'rʉ-pʉ+re***
    go see/look+ASSERT.PERF ANPH=log-AUG-LOC+OBJ

    'They went (and) looked at the big log.' [A4.59]

(36) *tikoro, to namono, chʉduaatiga wahsore*

    tí-kó+ró   *to=~dabó+ro*   *chú-dua-ati+a*
    ANPH-FEM+SG 3SG.POSS=wife+SG eat-DESID-IMPERF+ASSERT.PERF

    wasó+ré
    siringa.fruit+OBJ

    'The woman, his wife, wanted to eat (had a craving for) siringa fruit.' (= (28b)) [A5.3]

(37) *ã yoana, sã kotiria ne bosi sã yahoare durukuare*

    ~a=yoá-~da *~sá* *kó-ti+ri+a*   *~dé bó-sí*
    so=do-(1/2)PL 1PL.EXC water-VBZ+NOM+PL NEG forget-NEG.IRR

~sa=yá-hoa+re   dú-ruku+a+re
1PL.EXC.POSS=POSS-write+OBJ talk-stand+PL+OBJ

'This way, we Kotiria won't forget how to write and speak.' (lit., 'our writing and our language') [A8.3]

Marking of objects in preverbal position by +re, however, is not obligatory. Moreover, animacy cannot be identified as the factor that controls whether +re appears. The animate objects in (19) and (24) and the inanimate objects in (20) and (23) are marked, while the objects in (38)–(40), the first animate and the latter two inanimate, are not.

(38) *to yairo chɨto phanore tiro bohso wãha yoare*

    *tó   yaí+ró   chɨ   to=~phadó+re   tí+ró   **bosó***

    DEF jaguar+SG eat REM=do/be.before+OBJ ANPH+SG agouti

    ~wahá   yoá+re
    kill   do/make+VIS.PERF.2/3

    'Before the jaguar ate (him), (the dog had) hunted down an agouti.' [A2.7]

(39) *tirore topɨ khiti ya'uga*

    *tí+ró+ré   tó-pɨ   **khití**   ya'ú+a*
    ANPH+SG+OBJ REM-LOC story tell+ASSERT.PERF

    'There they told him the story.' [A4.50]

(40) *mipɨre yɨ'ɨ chɨa bohkatu'sɨha. thuai niha, nia*

    *~bí-pɨ́+ré   yɨ'ɨ   **chɨ́a**   boká-tu'sɨ-ha*
    now-LOC+OBJ 1SG food find-finish-VIS.IMPERF.1

    thuá+i   ~dí-ha   ~dí+a
    return+(1/2)MASC be.PROG-VIS.IMPERF.1 say+ASSERT.PERF

    '"I've found food now. I'm going home," he said/thought.' [A7.12]

What then is the semantic distinction between marked and unmarked objects in preverbal position? It appears to be that objects with +re (whether animate or inanimate) are more referential or specific than those without +re, the latter being more generic or unspecific. Referential or specific objects (marked with +re) include definite nouns, such as the brothers and mother in (41), the monkeys in (42), the blowgun and darts in (43) and the traditional dances and flute-playing in (44).

(41) *thɨ'o to koyare wã'ko, ti phɨkorore wã'koa*

    *thɨ'ó   **to=kó-ya+re**   ~wa'kó*
    hear 3SG.POSS=relative-PL+OBJ wake

ti=phuk+ó+ró+ré ~wa'kó+a
3PL.POSS=parent+FEM+SG+OBJ wake+ASSERT.PERF

'He heard (it), woke his brothers and woke their mother.' [A4.21]

(42) *yɨ'ɨ õse wa'ati, ni, a'rina kayare wãhai, nia*

yɨ'ɨ ~ó-sé wa'á-ati ~dí
1SG DEIC.PROX-be.like go-IMPERF say

a'rí-~dá ká-ya+re ~wahá+i
DEM.PROX-PL black.monkey-PL+OBJ kill+VIS.PERF.1

~dí+a
say+ASSERT.PERF

'"This is what happened," he said, "I killed these monkeys," he said.' [A7.108]

(43) *ã ni tu'sɨ tiro hi'na, to puhkare wɨa wakasare wɨamɨ wa'awa'aa mahkarokapɨ*

~a=~dí tu'sú tí+ró ~hí'da ***to=púka+re*** wɨá
so=say finish ANPH+SG EMPH 3SG.POSS=blowgun+OBJ carry

waká-sa+re wɨá-~bɨ wa'á-wa'a+a
poison.darts-carrier+OBJ carry-run go-go+ASSERT.PERF

~baká-róká-pɨ
origin-DIST-LOC

'As soon as he spoke, he got his blowgun, grabbed a basket of darts (and) went off into the forest.' [A7.8]

(44) *yɨ'ɨse'e phayɨwarore ti bahsaba'rore, karisu phutiabarore mahsierai*

*yɨ'ɨ-se'e phayɨ-wáró+ré **ti=basá=ba'ro+re***
1SG-CONTR many/a.lot-EMPH+OBJ ANPH=sing/dance=kind+OBJ

karísu phutí+a=ba'ro+re ~basi-éra+i
flute blow/play+PL=kind+OBJ know-NEG+VIS.PERF.1

'(Unlike the others) I hardly knew any of those kinds of dances and flute-playing.' (lit., 'I did not know many of those . . .') [A3.19]

However, *+re* marking also extends to referential objects that are indefinite. As was the case with definite nominals marked with *+re*, indefinite referential objects may be inanimate, such as the trees, manioc and sugarcane in (45)–(46), or animate, such as the people and animals in (47) and evil beings in (48).

(45) *tina wehsepɨre sũ, yɨkɨrire khãra*

*tí-~da wesé-pɨ+re ~sú **yɨkú+ri+re***
ANPH-PL garden-LOC+OBJ arrive tree+PL+OBJ

~khá+ra
chop/cut+VIS.IMPERF.2/3

'When they (the men) arrive at the garden, they chop down trees.' [A1.16]

(46) ã tina dᵾhkᵾre toa khanᵾre toara

~a=tí-~da **dᵾkᵾ́+ré** tóá ~khadᵾ́+ré
so=ANPH-PL manioc+OBJ plant sugarcane+OBJ
tóá+rá
plant+VIS.IMPERF.2/3

'They plant manioc and sugar cane.' [A1.10]

(47) tiro ba'ro mahsare wa'ikinare wa'asᵾ̃ wimika

tí+ró=ba'ro ~**basá+ré** **wa'í~kídá+ré** wa'á-~sᵾ
ANPH+SG=kind people+OBJ animal-PL+OBJ go-arrive
~wibí-ka
suck-ASSERT.IMPERF

'This kind (of insect) lands on people (and) animals (and) sucks (their blood).' [A9.2]

(48) painare khã, painare khã, painare khã, painare khã, painare khã, wãhaga

pá-~ida+re ~khá **pá-~ida+re** ~khá ~wahá+a
ALT-NOM.PL+OBJ hit ALT-NOM.PL+OBJ hit kill+ASSERT.PERF

'Other (evil beings) they hit, hit one, hit another [repeated five times], and killed.' [A4.64]

Thus, in Kotiria, +re marking of preverbal objects indicates not only a syntactic relation but also a semantic property of referentiality. This is not typologically uncommon; indeed, Hopper and Thompson (1980) find that special marking of objects is particularly likely to occur on definite or referential objects, while indefinite or nonreferential objects are relatively likely to be unmarked. Among the Eastern Tukanoan languages, Gomez-Imbert finds that for object marking in Tatuyo (1982:63–65) and Barasana (1997a:10; 2003a:182) the crucial opposition is definite vs. indefinite.

In Kotiria, the semantics of nonreferential objects without +re is very similar to that of incorporated objects (see §3.3.2 and §7.6), but the two constructions are still distinguishable according to phonological and, to a certain extent, semantic criteria. Fully incorporated objects become part of the same phonological word as the verb stem (the noun, being the initial root, is the phonological head and its tonal melody spreads to the rest of the word), while unincorporated objects without +re remain phonologically independent. Semantically, processes expressed by noun-incorporated predicates, such as food gathering (25), flatbread preparation (26), necklace making (27), reproducing (49), and hunting (50), also seem to be a bit more commonplace than situations involving unincorporated objects without +*re*, but the distinction is probably best viewed as gradation along a continuum. Mithun, in fact, discusses the possibility of juxtaposed noun-plus-verb constructions in which the constituents retain phonological independence as one type of incorporation (1984:849). Moreover, certain analyses of Eastern Tukanoan languages refer to all unmarked generic nouns in preverbal position as incorporated (Barnes 1999:220; Morse and Maxwell 1999:70–71). Unfortunately, these studies do not mention the phonological properties of such combinations and we thus do not know if the two phonological patterns observed here for Kotiria reflect a general pattern for the family.

(49) *yʉhkʉkʉ kohpapʉ diekũ pho'natira tiro*
yʉkú-kʉ   kopá-pʉ́   **dié-~ku**   ~pho'dá-ti+ra
tree-CLS:tree hole-LOC   egg-lay   offspring-VBZ+VIS.IMPERF.2/3
tí+ró
ANPH+SG

'(A toucan) reproduces by laying eggs (egg-laying) in a hollow tree.' [LSK: Toucans]

(50) *tʉ me're mʉ'ʉ wa'ikinawãha sihtotaga*
tʉ́=~be're   ~bʉ'ʉ́   wa'í-~kídá-~wáhá
stick=COM/INST   2SG   animal-PL-kill
sitó-ta+ga
MOV.circular-come+IMPER

'With this stick, you go around hunting (animal-killing).' [A7.131]

What the Kotiria patterns for use or omission of +*re* marking on preverbal object nominals indicate is a semantic continuum, one extreme of which is constituted by object nouns that are phonologically independent, referential (and often definite), and overtly case-marked. The other extreme is constituted by unmarked, phonologically dependent, indefinite and nonreferential incorporated objects.

The continuum implies that the more referential and definite the object noun is, the more likely it is to be marked by +*re*. Marking at the extremes of the continuum is fairly predictable and transparent. Pronominal objects, for example, can be considered inherently referential and, as we would expect, are always marked by +*re* when they occur as grammatical objects; incorporated nouns are always indefinite and nonreferential and are, unsurprisingly, never marked by +*re*.

Marking patterns in the middle region of the continuum, on the other hand, are less predictable, and it is within this middle region that we observe the more interesting, varied marking reflecting less easily interpretable combinations of definiteness and referentiality. We have seen, for example, that +re generally occurs on referential object nominals (which can be definite or indefinite, animate or inanimate). Non-referential objects in preverbal position, on the other hand, can conceivably be indicated by word order alone, and we would predict these not to require +re, as is the case for 'food' in (28a), repeated below as the first sentence of (51). Example (52), however, shows that even nonreferential objects can be marked by +re in preverbal position.

(51) 1 hiphitiro chɨa natara
         hí-phiti+ro   **chúa** ~dá-ta+ra
         COP-COLL+SG food   get-come+VIS.IMPERF.2/3
         'Everyone brings a lot of food.'

      2 tina nasã chɨare chɨ yoara
         tí-~da   ~dá-~sá   **chúa+re** chú yoá+ra
         ANPH-PL get-MOV.inside food+OBJ   eat do/make+VIS.IMPERF.2/3
         'They take the food inside and eat.' [A3.12–13]

(52) topɨ sũ, wa'ikinare mahkasitotaa
      tó-pɨ   ~sũ   **wa'í-~kídá+ré**
      REM-LOC arrive animal-PL+OBJ
      ~baká-sito-ta+a
      look/search.for-MOV.circular-come+ASSERT.PERF
      'Arriving there, he went around in search of animals.' [A7.9]

What further semantic properties might explain such variation? Ramirez's analysis of +re in Tukano sheds some light on this issue. He views +re as (potentially) a marker of "all non-subject complement constituents," but states that its actual usage is linked to the noun's position on a "scale of individuation." Nouns higher on the scale, those that can take some form of individualizing morphology—proper nouns, pronouns, animate humans, animate nonhumans, and inanimate countable nouns—are marked with +re, while generic or mass nouns are not (Ramirez 1997a:224). This analysis of +re in combination with an analysis of referentiality helps explain variation in the transitional area of the continuum in Kotiria. Though both 'food' in the first sentence of (51) and 'animals' in (52) are indefinite, 'animal' is classed among the categories of 'individualizable' nouns that are more likely to take +re than mass nouns such as 'food'. Still, the scale of individuation alone cannot explain the difference in marking in the two lines in (51), where we see that even a mass noun such as *chua* 'food' can be marked with *+re* if it is definite (or occurs in noncanonical position, as seen in (28b) at the beginning of this section). Overall, we can see that object coding is one of the most complex features of verbal syntax in Kotiria, requiring the speaker to attend constantly to both intrinsic properties of the lexical class of the noun (degrees of individuation, distinctions of animacy, and count vs. mass subclasses) and evaluation of discourse-level distinctions of referentiality.

The variation observed in Kotiria object marking constitutes a system of "differential object marking" (DOM), a term first proposed by Bossong (1991) to describe languages in which some direct objects receive overt marking while others do not, or, less commonly, languages in which distinct direct object markers are used for different categories of nouns. The criteria for differential marking of objects noted in Kotiria conform to the three prototypical parameters in DOM systems cross-linguistically—those identified by Bossong as relating to "constituence," where "independent" object nouns are marked and nouns "integrated" or "connected" to the verbal predicate are unmarked; to "reference," where marking is determined by interrelated notions of "individuality" and "discourse-related definiteness"; and to "inherence," where differential object marking is sensitive to a noun's inherent semantic features, such as [±human], [±animate], and [±discrete] (Bossong 1991:158–59). The [±human], [±animate], and [±discrete] features are often grouped together under the term "animacy hierarchy" and are identified as one of the parameters of "prominence" that typically trigger the development of DOM systems (de Swart 2007:135–95).

Using Bossong's framework, we can analyze the Kotiria DOM system as orienting overall to a hierarchy of "reference" (above all, referentiality) with distinctions of "inherence" (animacy) as a crucial secondary parameter. Such semantic organization implies that disambiguation of potential referents is not at the core of the system, in contrast to many languages, including some Nadahup languages spoken in the same region (discussed further in Stenzel 2008b). Except for the Kotiria-Wa'ikhana subbranch, head marking in Eastern Tukanoan languages generally codes very specific information about subjects, including information about gender and number (even for third person referents), so DOM plays virtually no role in the identification of nominal participants through disambiguation. Moreover, the role of word order in Kotiria object marking suggests the diachronic scenario for the development of DOM outlined below, in which the suffix *+re* was originally and primarily a grammatical case marker, only later developing the extended discourse-level nuances and functions attested synchronically.

As is shown in preceding sections, in Kotiria, the morpheme +*re* essentially marks a nominal argument as a grammatical object (for its use with locatives and temporal adjuncts, see §10.5 and §10.7). Indeed, case marking is the primary function of +*re* in all Eastern Tukanoan languages, as we see in table 10.3, which summarizes information on word order and object argument marking throughout the family.[3] Although sources vary as to the amount of information they provide on these topics, the table also shows that two of the tendencies found in Kotiria—the possibility of unmarked objects directly before verbs and obligatory object marking by +*re* when the object is not preverbal—recur elsewhere in the family. Moreover, for Kotiria, Wa'ikhana, Tukano, Kubeo and Barasano, +*re* is identified not only as the marker of patient (direct) objects, but also as the marker on all recipient or beneficiary arguments in ditransitive constructions (§10.4).

The "Basic order" column shows that all Eastern Tukanoan languages either require object-verb (OV) order, or at least allow object-verb order as an option, while there is quite a bit of variation in the position of the subject (S) argument. In the case of Kotiria, although Waltz and Waltz (2000) indicate that subject-object-verb order is basic, I have observed a link between discourse-level information and the positioning of the subject argument. New-information subjects (very frequently full NPs), which introduce or reintroduce referents into discourse, tend to occur before the verb (or before the object-verb nucleus of a transitive clause). Subjects presenting old information (very frequently pronominals) tend to occur after the verb. In narratives and conversations, null subjects are also extremely common, as was observed earlier in this chapter. Subject order variation of this type also appears to be the pattern in Wa'ikhana and Yuruti. It is not clear whether other cases of variation between subject-object-verb order and object-verb-subject order in Eastern Tukanoan languages reflect the same pragmatic criteria.

---

[3] Sources drawn on are: for Wa'ikhana, my own fieldwork; for Kubeo, Morse and Maxwell 1999; for Desano, Miller 1999; for Barasano, Jones and Jones 1991 and Gomez-Imbert 1997a; for Tatuyo, Gomez-Imbert 1982; for Tukano, Sorensen 1969 and Ramirez 1997a; for Retuarã, Strom 1992. The grammatical sketches published in *Lenguas indígenas de Colombia, una visión descriptiva* (González de Pérez and Rodriguez de Montes 2000) were also consulted—by Gomez-Imbert and Hugh-Jones (Tatuyo, Bará, Karapana, Barasana, and Makuna), Ferguson et al. (Kubeo); González de Pérez (Pisamira), Criswell and Brandrup (Siriano), Welch and West (Tukano), Barnes and Malone (Tuyuka), Waltz and Waltz (Kotiria), and Kinch and Kinch (Yuruti).

TABLE 10.3. WORD ORDER AND ARGUMENT CODING IN EASTERN TUKANOAN LANGUAGES

LANGUAGE	BASIC ORDER	ALTERNATE ORDER(S)	MARKING OF DIRECT OBJECT(S)
Kotiria	OV	S with new referent: clause-initial; S with known referent: clause-final	Ø/+*re* before V, +*re* elsewhere
Wa'ikhana	OV	S with new referent: clause-initial; S with known referent: clause-final	Ø/ +*d/re* before V, +*d/re* elsewhere
Tukano	SOV		Ø/+*re* before V, +*re* elsewhere
Bara	SOV	OVS (possible)	+*re*
Karapana	OVS	SOV	+*re* and object prefixes on V
Desano	SOV		+*re*
Siriano	SOV		+*re*
Tatuyo	OVS	SOV	+*re* and object prefixes on V
Tuyuka	SOV		+*re*
Kubeo	OVS	VSO	Ø/+*re* before V, +*re* elsewhere
Pisamira			+*re*
Yuruti	OV	S with new referent: clause-initial; S with known referent: clause-final	+*re*
Barasano	OVS (strict)		Ø before V, +*re* elsewhere
Makuna	SVO/OVS		+*re*
Retuarã	SOV	OSV (when S is prefix on V) OVS (in negative utterances only)	+*re* only on human arguments (S or O)

The common object-verb order of Eastern Tukanoan languages suggests that diachronically, word order may have been the more important means of identifying the object argument and that objects were fairly rigidly placed before verbs in all transitive clauses. If word order was thus used to code objects, +*re* might originally have been used only in more marked constructions involving recipient and beneficiary objects. As is shown in §10.4, recipients and beneficiaries are normally animate, individuated, and referential; increasing association of the suffix +*re* with these properties then allowed the suffix to spread to patient objects that shared them. From the information in table 10.3, however, it appears that in a number of Eastern Tukanoan languages (though not in Kotiria, Wa'ikhana, Tukano, Kubeo, Karapana, and Barasano), +*re* eventually became the obligatory marker on all objects, not just individuated or referential ones. As a result of greater use of morphological marking, word order flexibility increased, and use of object-verb order for coding grammatical relations declined, though it was by no means eliminated as a marking means. The decrease in the obligatoriness of object-verb order and the increase in overt morphological marking of both patient objects and inherently referential or specific beneficiary and recipient objects meant that the unmarked object in the object-verb nucleus was reinterpreted as coding nonreferentiality, permitting the synchronic instances of both marked and unmarked preverbal objects that were analyzed earlier in this section.

Despite the fact that +*re* clearly functions as a grammatical case marker in Eastern Tukanoan languages, straightforward analyses of this suffix are difficult to make due to the fact that we find +*re* morphemes used not only on object arguments but also on locatives and some temporal adjuncts (see §10.5 and §10.7; for Tukanoan languages in general, see Barnes 1999, Gomez-Imbert 2011). Finding a single, all-encompassing label for a morpheme with such an array of uses is admittedly tricky, and terms such as "specificity marker" (Barnes 1999:220) or "referential marker" (Waltz and Waltz 1997:32; Ramirez 1997a:223–25) have been employed. These terms, however, bleach +*re* of what I believe to be its essential function, that of a grammatical marker of case, albeit one whose use is differentiated according to intersecting semantic and pragmatic criteria. Thus, in this analysis, +*re* as a syntactic marker is glossed as "OBJ" ('objective' case marker) regardless of whether the constituent that it marks is an argument (object or oblique) or a temporal adjunct.[4]

---

[4] There are yet two additional suffixes with the shape -*re* in other paradigms: a noun classifier -*re*, used on generic or abstract nouns such as *a'ri-re* (DEM:PROX-CLS:generic) 'this thing', and a +*re* evidential in the visual category (VIS.PERF.2/3) within the paradigm of verb-final clause modality suffixes.

10.4 Ditransitives

Ditransitive verbs are defined here as verbs that require three arguments: a subject and two objects. Prototypical ditransitive verbs are those such as the Kotiria verb *wa* [wáa] 'give', or verbs morphologically coded as beneficiary. Such verbs have agentive subjects and two obligatory objects, one with the semantic role of patient and the other with the semantic role of recipient or beneficiary. In Kotiria, receiver or beneficiary arguments of ditransitive verbs are invariably case-marked by *+re*.

Prototypical ditransitive verbs are exemplified in (53)–(55). These code events in which an agentive subject moves or manipulates a patient object (O(pat)) (typically inanimate) to or for a second, recipient or beneficiary, object (O(rec), O(ben)) (typically animate, definite, and referential). In (53) and (54), there is actual physical movement of the patients *yahiri~pho'da* 'heart' and *ho* 'bananas', while in (55), the movement of the patient *khiti* 'story' is metaphorical. The sentence in (56) is an example of the recasting of a simple transitive verb (here *do'a* 'cook') as a ditransitive by the addition of the valency-changing dependent root *-bosa*, indicating that the action of the verb is done specifically for the benefit of a third party (see also §10.6).

(53) *mɨ'ɨ yahiripho'nare yɨ'ɨre waga*
  [~bɨ'ɨ=yahiri~pho'da+re]$_{O(pat)}$ [yɨ'ɨ+ré]$_{O(rec)}$ [wá+gá]$_V$
  2SG(POSS)=heart+OBJ 1SG+OBJ give+IMPER
  '(Relative), give me your heart.' [A7.43]

(54) *mihchare tikoro hore mahkɨnakãre ware*
  ~bichá+ré [tí-kó+ró]$_S$ [hó+ré]$_{O(pat)}$ [~bak+ɨ-~dá-ká+ré]$_{O(rec)}$
  today+OBJ ANPH-FEM+SG banana+OBJ child+MASC-DIM-PL+OBJ
  [wá+ré]$_V$
  give+VIS.PERF.2/3
  'Today she gave the little boys bananas.'

(55) *tirore topɨ khiti ya'ua*
  [∅]$_S$ [tí+ró+ré]$_{O(rec)}$ tó-pɨ [khití]$_{O(pat)}$ [ya'ɨ+a]$_V$
     ANPH+SG+OBJ REM-LOC story tell+ASSERT.PERF
  'There they told him the story.' [A4.50] (=(39))

(56) *yɨ'ɨ wa'ire do'abosaita mɨ'ɨre*
  [yɨ'ɨ]$_S$ [wa'í+ré]$_{O(pat)}$ [do'á-bósá+í-tá]$_V$
  1SG fish+OBJ cook-BEN+(1/2)MASC-INTENT

[~bɨ 'ɨ+ré]ₒ₍ben₎
2SG+OBJ

'I'm going to cook the fish for you.'

These examples show that the linear positioning of recipient and beneficiary objects is more flexible than that of patient objects. In (53)–(54), the recipient object occurs between the patient object and the verb; in (55), the recipient object occurs before the patient object and the verb; and in (56), the beneficiary object occurs after the verb. Such flexibility may be due to the fact that recipient and beneficiary objects cannot occur without the case marker +re, and thus do not rely in any way on word order as a means of indicating their grammatical status. The requirement that +re be used on recipient or beneficiary objects is most likely linked to the fact that such arguments are prototypically animate and inherently referential; as such, they must be morphologically marked by +re, as shown in §10.3.2.

10.5 Verbs with locative arguments

So far in this chapter, we have examined the prototypical argument structures of intransitive, transitive, and ditransitive verbs. In this section we look at verbs that take locative goal arguments marked with -pɨ+re.

10.5.1 Stative verbs with locative arguments

In Kotiria, nominals marked with the locative suffix -pɨ plus the object suffix +re can occur as oblique arguments in clauses with otherwise intransitive stative and motion verbs. In such cases, their semantic role is either goal or a highly unusual or particularly relevant location.

Recall that stative verbs, particularly the copula *hi* and positional predicates (§7.1.4), regularly occur with locative adjuncts marked by the suffixes -pɨ or +i (see also §10.7) to indicate spatial relations. To use Levinson's (2003) terms for constituents in such relations, we can say that in Kotiria, the nominal marked only by -pɨ/+i represents the "ground"—the referential location for the "figure," the entity whose location or position is being identified—in the "basic locative construction" in the language (see also Stenzel forthcoming). Locatives marked only by -pɨ/+i thus occur in all descriptions of spatial scenes, such as (57) and (58), that express a "spatial coincidence of figure and ground" (Levinson and Wilkins 2006:3).

(57) tiro topɨ pihsaga
  tí+ró   tó-**pɨ**   pisá+á
  ANPH+SG REM-LOC   be.on+ASSERT.PERF
  'He (a disobedient boy) just stayed up there (on the roof).' [A5.31]

(58) tiro diapɨ hika
  tí+ró   diá-**pɨ́**   hí-ka
  ANPH+SG river-LOC COP-ASSERT.IMPERF
  '(A bass) lives in the river.'[5]

While sentences such as these, with stative verbs and locative adjuncts marked by *-pɨ/+i*, are extremely common, sentences with stative verbs and locative arguments, marked by both *-pɨ* and *+re*, are not. Such locative arguments indicate an important "spatial *reference point* vis-a-vis which the subject is located" (Givón 2001, vol. 1:137; emphasis in the original), a particularly special or relevant location. I take constructions with oblique locatives, given the unusual coding with *-pɨ+re*, to be highly marked and used for specific pragmatic functions. The semantics of these rare cases can involve notions of unexpectedness, distal deixis or previous discourse or cultural reference, as we see in (59)–(61).

Example (59) is from a story in which some evil beings go to a house intending to eat the residents. One of the beings is hidden inside a large basket full of fruit. Although the finite verb in the sentence is a positional stative verb (§7.1.4) *~khoa* 'be lying down', the locative *phu'icha* 'inside surface or space' is marked not just with *-pɨ* but with *-pɨ+re*. The locative indicates that the creature's state of lying down took place 'inside' or 'within the basket', and it is likely that the more marked means of coding (with *-pɨ+re* rather than just *-pɨ*) is employed to emphasize how unusual and unexpected the situation is: baskets of fruit do not usually have evil creatures curled up inside them! Indeed, cross-linguistically it is often the case that the means used to indicate transitivity at the sentence level are employed as a device to foreground important information at the discourse level (Hopper and Thompson 1980:294).

(59) tipɨ phu'ichapɨre kɨiro mahsɨnose hiriro boraro ti(na) nirirore kɨ̃iro khõaga
  tí-pɨ   phu'icha-**pɨ+re**   ~kɨ́-író
  ANPH-CLS:basket   inside-LOC+OBJ   one/a-NOM.SG
  ~basɨ́+ró-sé   hí+ri+ro   borá+ro   tí-(~da)
  man+SG-be.like   COP+NOM+SG   curupira+SG   ANPH-PL

---

[5] From the short text that appears as example (118) in chapter 4.

~dɨ+ri+ro+re   ~kʉ-iró   ~khoá+a
say+NOM+SG+OBJ one/a-NOM.SG lie/be.lying+ASSERT.PERF
'A humanlike being they call a curupira was lying inside that basket.'
[A5.8]

In Kotiria, locatives derived from stative verbs such as the copula can also be marked with *-pʉ+re*, as in (60). In this example the locative gives important spatial reference information and establishes the context within which the main action of the clause occurs. The example is from the beginning of a story describing a typical festival in a Kotiria community. The speaker was my Kotiria consultant, who was living in the U.S. at the time. The main action of the clause, 'going to visit friends in other villages', takes place within the marked location *yʉ'ʉ hi+ro-pʉ+re* 'my being-place'—understood as 'in the place where I lived', the very special (and at the time still quite unknown to me) setting for the action, distant both in time and space from the speaker at the moment of speech.

(60) yʉ soanʉmarire, yʉ'ʉ hiropʉre, yʉ me'remahkainare yʉ'ʉ ñʉtinii wa'atii

yʉ=soá-~dʉba+ri+re   yʉ'ʉ=hí+ro-**pʉ+re**
1SG.POSS=rest-day+PL+OBJ   1SG(POSS)=COP+SG-LOC+OBJ

yʉ=~be'ré-~baka-~ida+re   yʉ'ʉ ~yʉ-~tídí+i
1SG.POSS=COM/INST-village-NOM.PL+OBJ 1SG   see-visit+(1/2)MASC

wa'á-ati+i
go-IMPERF+VIS.PERF.1

'On my resting days, where I lived, I used to go visit my friends.'
[A3.2–3]

Example (61) comes from a short written text about jaguars. The writer begins by establishing the fact that jaguars are wild, jungle-dwelling animals, and then goes on to talk about their habits. The writer's use of *to-pʉ+re ~duku-pʉ* 'out there in the jungle' as the referential locative in the nominalized relative clause describing jaguars' prey emphasizes that this specific location is the contextual backdrop against which all actions of jaguars are to be understood.

(61) topʉre nʉhkʉpʉ hiro wa'ikinare chʉra tiro yairo

tó-**pʉ+re**   ~dukú-pú   hí+ro
REM-LOC+OBJ   jungle-LOC   COP+SG

wa'í-~kídá+ré chú+ra   tí+ró   yaí+ró
animal-PL+OBJ eat+VIS.IMPERF.2/3 ANPH+SG jaguar+SG

'The jaguar eats animals living there in the jungle.' [A10.3]

10.5.2 Motion verbs with locative arguments

Like stative verbs, Kotiria motion verbs are prototypically intransitive and clauses with motion verbs do not necessarily require a locative argument. Sometimes, in fact, the lexical properties of the verbs themselves (see §7.3) or discourse context makes the referent location clear and no overt locative expression occurs at all in the sentence, as in (62)–(63).

(62)   ãta tina moño thuawa'awa'aa
~a=tá   tí-~da   ~boyó   thuá-wa'a-wa'a+a
so=REF   ANPH-PL   fail   return-go-go+ASSERT.PERF

'So they (the bride-nappers) failed (to get any women) and went all the way back (home, to their village).' [Ancestors]

(63)   pate karaka duripa yɨ'ɨ thuakɨka
pá-te   káráká   dú+ri-pa   yɨ'ɨ
ALT- CLS:time   rooster   speak+NOM- CLS:time   1SG
thuá-kɨ-ka
return-(1/2)MASC-PREDICT

'I'll probably come back (home) at the first crow of the cock.' [A4.11]

In most sentences with motion verbs, however, overt locative referents are present, and we find that these can be marked by just the suffix *-pɨ*, or by the combination *-pɨ+re*. In contrast to the situation with stative verbs, the two patterns of locative marking in sentences with motion verbs occur equally frequently in narratives and often occur with exactly the same verb roots. These observations, taken together with what we have learned about *+re* marking in general, suggest that it is not the case that certain verbs require locatives with one type of marking rather than the other, but that the use of *+re* on locatives probably involves pragmatic considerations similar to those identified in relation to its use with stative verbs and also in relation to differential *+re* marking on objects of transitive verbs.

Indeed, when we look at the discourse contexts in which sentences with motion verbs and locatives marked only by *-pɨ* and sentences with motion verbs and locatives marked by *-pɨ+re* occur, some tendencies begin to become clear. Comparing the locatives marked just by *-pɨ* in (64)–(66) with the *-pɨ+re* locatives in (67)–(68), we can once again recognize the notion of referentiality at work. Locatives with *-pɨ* only, such as the completely nonreferential 'someplace' and 'somewhere' of (64) and (66) and the generic reference to the 'forest' and 'there' in (65), are much less referential in their given contexts than the indication of 'that place' (the specific lakeside scenario of the man's encounter with the magical snake-being) in (67) or the deictic 'here' (the man's own house) in (68), both marked by -pɨ+re.

(64) to a'rire du'timari nihachɨ, to manɨno pase'epɨ wa'aa
to=a'rí+ré   du'tí-~bá+rí   ~dí-~ha-chɨ
DEF=DEM.PROX+OBJ   tell/request-FRUS+NOM say-TERM-SW.REF
to=~badú+ro   **pá=se'e-pɨ**   wa'á+a
3SG.POSS=husband+SG ALT=CONTR-LOC   go+ASSERT.PERF
'Just after she said that, her husband went off **someplace**.' [A5.5]

(65) 1 ã ni tu'sɨ tiro hi'na, to puhkare wɨa wahkasare wɨamɨ wa'awa'aa mahkarokapɨ
~a=~dí tu'sú   tí+ró   ~hí'da to=púka+re
so=say finish   ANPH+SG   EMPH   3SG.POSS=blowgun+OBJ
wɨá   waká-sa+re   wɨá-~bɨ   wa'á-wa'a+a
carry poison.darts-carrier+OBJ carry-run go-go+ASSERT.PERF
~baká-róká-pú
origin-DIST-LOC
'As soon as he spoke, he got his blowgun, grabbed a basket of darts (and) went off **into the forest**.'

2 topɨ sɨ, wa'ikinare mahkasihtotaa
tó-pɨ   ~sú   wa'í-~kídá+ré
REM-LOC   arrive animal-PL+OBJ
~baká-sito-ta+a
look/search.for-MOV.circular-come+ASSERT.PERF
'Arriving **there**, he went around in search of animals.' [A7.8–9]

(66) pase'epɨ wa'aa. tinisihtotaa
pá-se'e-pɨ   wa'á+a
ALT-CONTR-LOC   go+ASSERT.PERF
~tidí-sító-tá+á
walk-MOV.circular-come+ASSERT.PERF
'He went off **somewhere**. He wandered around and around.' [A7.15]

(67) ne topɨre tipɨre tinieraha ninokaa
~dé **tó-pɨ+re**   **tí-pɨ+re**   ~tidi-éra-ha
NEG REM-LOC+OBJ   ANPH-LOC+OBJ   wander-NEG-VIS.IMPERF.1
~dí-~doka+a
say-COMPL+ASSERT.PERF
'"I never go hunting there **in that place**," he insisted.' [A6.60]

(68) ā̃yo õpɨre yɨ'ɨ kho'awi'ikɨka
      ~a=yó ~ó-pɨ́+ré   yɨ'ɨ́ kho'á-wi'i-kɨ-ka
      so=do DEIC.PROX-LOC+OBJ 1SG   return-arrive-(1/2)MASC-PREDICT
      'That's how I'll get back **here**.' [A4.14]

The notion that greater discourse referentiality is indicated by -pɨ+re is well exemplified in (69), where the speaker's first mention of the 'clearing' occurs with only -pɨ, while the second mention (accompanied by hand gestures indicating a referential size and shape for the lake) occurs with -pɨ+re.

(69) ã̄ ta yoa ñamichapɨ hi'na, kɨ̃ ku'tukã̄pɨ, õpari ku'tukã̄pɨre phi'asɨ̃a
      ~a=tá yoá   ~yabícha-pɨ ~hí'da ~kɨ́   **ku'tɨ́-~ka-pɨ**
      so=REF do/make night-LOC   EMPH   one/a clearing-DIM-LOC

      ~ó-pá+rí   **ku'tɨ́-~ka-pɨ+re**
      DEIC.PROX-ALT+NOM   clearing-DIM-LOC+OBJ

      phi'a-~sɨ+a
      MOV.out.into-arrive+ASSERT.PERF

      'As night was falling, he went out into **a little clearing, a little clearing** like this.' [A7.18]

When motion verbs occur with locative arguments marked by -pɨ+re instead of just by -pɨ, the combination can be understood to express referential "events of spatial motion," with the oblique argument constituting "a spatial reference point vis-a-vis which the subject moves" (Givón 2001, vol. 1:137). Further examination of motion verbs that occur with locatives marked by -pɨ+re reveals that in most cases, the motion verbs are telic and the locative represents a specific or referential goal that figures prominently in the discourse.

Given this notion of referentiality, it is not surprising that the relational motion verbs ~sɨ [sɨ̃ɨ̃] 'arrive (there)' and wi'i 'arrive (here)' occur a bit more frequently with goal arguments marked with -pɨ+re than do other motion verbs. This is perhaps due to the fact that these roots are commonly used to indicate arrival at a new referential scene for a series of events in the discourse, as is the case in (70). Both roots are also used to indicate the action of 'arriving' at or near a specific animate entity rather than a spatial location. In such cases, the entity goal is more commonly marked only by +re, as in (71)–(72), rather than by -pɨ+re, as in (73). I speculate that in the case of entity goals, speakers are more highly attuned to the features of referentiality and animacy (associated with +re) than to identification of the entity as a referential location, though, as (73) shows, such identification is also possible.

(70) tina wehsepure sũ, yuhkurire khãra
    tí-~da **wesé-pu+re** ~sú yukú+ri+re
    ANPH-PL garden-LOC+OBJ arrive tree+PL+OBJ
    ~khá+ra
    chop/cut+VIS.IMPERF.2/3
    'When they (the men) arrive **at the garden**, they chop down trees.'
    (=(45) [A1.16]

(71) sũ tirore phichaba'a yoaa
    ~sú **tí+ró+ré** phichá-bá'á yoá+a
    arrive ANPH+SG+OBJ shoot-do/be.after do/make+ASSERT.PERF
    'He arrived (went over) **to it** (the snake and) shot (it).' [A6.34]

(72) sũnoka to mahkunokãre sõ'opu tiro pahpero minichakãre buepero nia
    ~sú-~doka+a **to=~bak+ú+ro-~ka+re**
    arrive-COMPL+ASSERT.PERF 3SG.POSS=child+MASC+SG-DIM+OBJ
    ~so'ó-pú tí+ró papé+ró ~bidícha-~ka+re
    DEIC.DIST-LOC ANPH+SG play+(3)SG bird-DIM+OBJ
    bué-pe+ro ~dí+a
    hunt.with.arrows-FAV+(3)SG be.PROG+ASSERT.PERF
    'She went over **to her son**, who was (on top of the house) playing at hunting birds.' [A5.26-27]

(73) tiro ti phukoropure wi'i sũ'aa
    tí+ró **ti=phuk+ó+ró-pú+ré** wi'í
    ANPH+SG 3PL.POSS=parent+FEM+SG-LOC+OBJ arrive
    ~su'á+a
    stick.onto+ASSERT.PERF
    'He came up to (and) stuck **onto their mother**.' [A4.31]

10.5.3 Another verb with object and oblique arguments

A final verb that can take a locative goal argument marked by *-pu+re* is *~da* [nãã́] 'get', which is often serialized with motion verbs to indicate actions of 'taking' and 'bringing' (§7.5.1). In Kotiria, *~da* is the only verb I have found to appear in this type of construction, in which an agentive subject moves a patient object to a specific locative goal marked with *-pu+re*, as we see in (74)–(75).

(74) tiro nara tire tiphĩre wehsepure
    tí+ro ~da+ra tí+re tí-~phí+ré
    ANPH+SG get+VIS.IMPERF.2/3 ANPH+OBJ ANPH-CLS:bladelike+OBJ
    wesé-pu+re
    garden-LOC+OBJ
    'He always takes the machete **to the garden**.'

(75) to wa'ikiro wãhariroditare sã nathuai wɨ'ɨpɨre
      to=wa'í-kíró   ~wahá+ri+ro-dita+re   ~sá
      DEF=animal+SG   kill+NOM+SG-SOL+OBJ   1PL.EXC
      ~dá-thúá+i   **wɨ'ɨ-pú+ré**
      get-return+VIS.PERF.1 house-LOC+OBJ
      'We took **home** only the dead animal.' (= (2)) [A2.13]

We can see in (9) and (28) above that the verb *~da* 'get' does not necessarily require a locative argument. However, when a clause with this verb does include a locative constituent (always marked with the locative morpheme *-pɨ*), it obligatorily takes the object suffix *+re* as well, as seen in (74)–(75) and in (76) below. We should also note that while receiver or benefactive objects can occur in a variety of positions (§10.4), goal arguments marked with *-pɨ+re* tend to occur after the verb.

(76) familiare wehsewa'ainare no'oi wa'ainare yahka, nawa'aka'aa te mahkarokapɨre
      família+re   wesé-wa'a-~ida+re   ~do'ó+i
      family[B]+OBJ   garden-go-NOM.PL+OBJ   WH+LOC
      wa'á-~ida+re   yakáv ~dá-wa'a-ka'a+av   té
      go-NOM.PL+OBJ   steal get-go-do.moving+ASSERT.PERF   all.the.way
      ~baká-róká-pú+ré
      origin-DIST-LOC+OBJ
      'They would steal (kidnap) families going to their gardens (or) people going anywhere (and) carry them off **into the jungle**.' [A4.4]

10.6 Valency-changing roots

There are at least two Kotiria verb roots that cause a change in the valency of an associated verb. The first is the root *~kha'ba* 'do reciprocally', 'do with each other', or 'do among themselves'. It can occur as a phonologically independent root (77)–(78) or as the initial root in a serialization (79). This root reduces the valency of an otherwise transitive verb to which it is associated, e.g., *do'ka* 'crash, hit' (77), *du-ruku* 'speak continuously, converse' (78) or *boka* 'meet' (79), because it eliminates the need for a marked object.

(77) kha'ma do'kaphitibohkaa noaro ti wɨ'dɨapo'kawaroi hi'na
      ~kha'bá   do'ká-phiti-boka+a   ~dóá+ró
      do.RECIP   crash-COLL-meet+ASSERT.PERF   be.good+SG

Clause structure 345

ti=wʉ'dʉapo'ka-waro+i   ~hi'da
3PL.POSS=forehead-EMPH+LOC   EMPH

'(The two men) crashed into each other, right here with their foreheads.' [Ancestors]

(78) *numia ña'ana wa'a hi'na ti mahkapʉ nia kha'ma durukua yoaa*

~dubí+a   ~ya'á-~da   wa'á   ~hí'da   ti=~baká-pʉ
woman+PL   catch-NOM   go   EMPH   ANPH=village-LOC

~dí+a   ~**kha'bá-dú-rúkú+á**   yoá+a
say+ASSERT.PERF   do.RECIP-speak-stand+(3)PL   do/make+ASSERT.PERF

'"Let's go get women from that village," they said among themselves.' [Ancestors]

(79) *mipʉkãre yoasinira. ã yoa tina kha'maphitibohka*

~bí-pʉ́-~ká+ré   yoá-~sidi+ra
now-LOC-DIM+OBJ   do/make-do.yet/still+VIS.IMPERF.2/3

~a=yoá   tí-~da   ~**kha'bá-phítí-bóká**
so=do/make   ANPH-PL   do.RECIP-COLL-meet

'Nowadays, they still do that: they get together (for festivals).' [A3.8–9]

The second such verb is *-bosa*, which always occurs as a dependent noninitial verb in a serialization, and shows that the action of the verb is being done for someone's benefit. Serializations with this benefactive verb increase the valency of the independent verb from one to two object arguments, each marked with *+re*, as we see in (80)–(81).

(80) *sikoro phʉ'ʉrore tirore yoabosaroka*

[*sí-kó+ró*]ₛ   [*phʉ'ʉ́+ro+re*]O[pat]   [*tí+ró+ré*]O[ben]
DEM.DIST-FEM+SG   basket+SG+OBJ   ANPH+SG+OBJ

[*yoá-bosa+ro-ka*]ᵥ
do/make-BEN+SG-PREDICT

'She (that woman) is going to make a basket for him.'

(81) *yʉ'ʉ wa'ire do'abosaita mʉ'ʉre*

[*yʉ'ʉ́*]ₛ   [*wa'í+ré*]O[pat]   [*do'á-bósá+í-tá*]ᵥ
1SG   fish+OBJ   cook-BEN+(1/2)MASC-INTENT

[*~bʉ'ʉ́+ré*]O[ben]
2SG+OBJ

'I'm going to cook the fish for you.' (= (56))

10.7 Adjuncts

For convenience, the lower portion of table 10.1 is reproduced below as table 10.4. It shows the four semantic roles coded by adjuncts in

Kotiria: locative, temporal, comitative, and instrument. Coding means for these adjuncts overlap: locatives are marked by *-pʉ* and temporals are marked by *(-pʉ)+re*. Both comitatives and instruments are coded by *=~be're*.

TABLE 10.4. MARKING OF ADJUNCTS

SEMANTIC ROLE:	locative	temporal	comitative/instrument
CODING:	*-pʉ /+i*	*(-pʉ)+re*	*=~be're*

10.7.1 Locative

In §10.5, we saw that nouns coded as locatives can, in certain contexts of discourse relevance, also be marked by *+re* as oblique arguments of stative or motion verbs, or in 'take'-type constructions with the verb *~da*. When so marked, they either have the semantic role of goal locative or indicate highly referential or unusual locations. In most cases, though, locatives are not coded as arguments but as simple adjuncts, providing additional information about the circumstances surrounding the state or event expressed by the verb. As adjuncts, locatives are marked just by *-pʉ* or by *+i* (§5.2.1).

By far the most common of the two suffixes is *-pʉ*, which has cognates of the form *-pʉ* or *-pi* in Wa'ikhana, Tukano, Bará, Karapana, Tatuyo, Tuyuka, Tatuyo, Yuruti and Pisamira. Its equivalent in Barasana and Makuna is *-hʉ*,[6] and cognate forms are found in Kubeo *-pi* and Retuarã *-i*, though additional locative morphemes occur in these two languages. In the Desano-Siriano subgroup of the family the locatives are, respectively, *-ge* and *-pʉroge* (Stenzel 2008*b*).

The Kotiria locative *+i* occurs much less frequently than *-pʉ*, and specifically indicates locative referents that are visually accessible, such as the potential sleeping spot in (82), comparatively closer to the speaker or contextual referent, for example, the man's side in (83), or already known, such as the as meeting place in (84). In the question-and-answer sequence in (85), from a narrative text, the use of *+i* in both the man's question (line 1) and his sons' answer (line 2) indicates proximity as well as known information, since the exchange takes place as they are all standing right next to the log into which the sons saw an evil being take their mother.

(82) *ti ku'tupʉ phi'asʉ̃, õita yʉ'ʉ khãriita, nia*
 ti=ku'tú-pʉ   phi'á-~sʉ   ~ó+í=ta   yʉ'ʉ́
 ANPH=clearing-LOC MOV.out.into-arrive DEIC.PROX+LOC=REF 1SG

---

[6] In these two languages, spoken in the Piraparaná region, [p] underwent general debuccalization to [h] (Gomez-Imbert 2011).

Clause structure 347

~kharí+i-ta ~dí+a
sleep-+(1/2)MASC-INTENT say+ASSERT.PERF
'Emerging into the clearing, he said/thought, "I'll sleep **here**."'
[A7.19]

(83) sũa to ka'ai bꭒenete khꭒanaka, bꭒeayꭒhkꭒri khꭒariro
~sꭒ+a **to=ka'á+i** bꭒé~dete
arrive+ASSERT.PERF 3SG.POSS=side+LOC bow.and.arrow

khꭒá-~daka bꭒé+a-yꭒkꭒ+ri khꭒá+ri+ro
hold/have-do/be.together arrow+PL-tree+PL hold/have+NOM+SG

'(The father snake) arrived at **(the man's) side** clutching a bow and arrows.' [A6.55]

(84) marire sõ'oi sĩ'a phitibohka du'tire
~barí+ré **~so'ó+i** ~si'á phití-boka du'tí+ré
1PL.INC+OBJ DEIC.DIST+LOC torch COLL-meet request+VIS.PERF.2/3

'"(Our father) asked us to meet him **there** with torches."' [A4.23]

(85) 1 no'oi hiri, nia
~do'ó+i hí-ri ~dí+a
WH+LOC COP-INT say+ASSERT.PERF
'"**Where** is she?" he said/asked.'

2 õi hire, nia
~ó+i hí+re ~dí+a
DEIC.PROX+LOC COP+VIS.PERF.2/3 say+ASSERT.PERF
'"**Here** she is," they said/answered.' [A4.57–58]

The suffix *-pꭒ*, though, is undoubtedly the default locative marker in Kotiria. It is used to indicate general, unknown, not visually accessible, or comparatively more distant locative referents. Just a few examples of the many locatives marked by *-pꭒ* are given in (86)–(90).

(86) tina hira diapꭒ mahkarokapꭒ mahkaina
tí-~da hí+ra **diá-pꭒ** **~baká-roka-pꭒ**
ANPH-PL COP+VIS.IMPERF.2/3 river-LOC origin-DIST-LOC

~baká-~ida
origin-NOM.PL

'They (turtles) live **in the river** or **in the jungle** (are jungle-dwellers).' [LSK: Turtles]

(87) diero parisabapꭒ khõara
dié+ró **parí-saba-pꭒ** ~khoá+ra
dog+SG lake-mud-LOC be.lying+VIS.IMPERF.2/3
'The dog is lying **in the mud puddle**.'

(88) *tiro tinika yɨhkɨri bu'ipɨ*
 *tí+ró   ~tidí-ká   **yɨkɨ́+ri bu'í-pɨ***
 ANPH+SG walk-ASSERT.IMPERF tree+PL top-LOC
 'It (a squirrel) moves around **in the treetops**.' [LSK: Squirrels]

(89) *diero mɨhsɨre wãhara kohpapɨ*
 *dié+ró   ~busɨ́+re   ~wahá+ra   **kopá-pɨ́***
 dog+SG anteater+OBJ kill+VIS.IMPERF.2/3 hole-LOC
 'Dogs kill anteaters **in their holes**.' [LSK: Anteaters]

(90) *tina tiroa wã'aka yɨhkɨdɨphŭripɨ*
 tí-~da   tíró+á   ~wa'á-ká
 ANPH-PL wasp+PL be.leaning-ASSERT.IMPERF
 yɨkɨ́-dɨ-~phɨ+ri-pɨ
 tree-CLS:cylindrical-leaf+PL-LOC
 'Wasps hang (in nests) **from the tree branches**.' [LSK: Wasps]

10.7.2 Temporal expressions and adjuncts

Temporal expressions have adverbial functions and tend to occur at the beginning of sentences. Temporal reference can be established by noun-verb compounds, as in (91) (where the compound occurs within an adverbial clause with the switch-reference marker), phrases such as the frequently occurring nominalizations for 'later' (from the verbal root *ba'a* 'do/be after'), 'morning' (from the verbal root *bo're* 'be light') and 'olden days' (from the verbal root *~phado* 'do/be before') in (92)–(94), or inherently temporal nouns (95)–(96).

(91) *tina khãria ñamichawa'achɨ, ti sa'sero, ti phɨkoro khãri, tiro ti phɨkuro topɨ wa'a to koya me're*
 *tí-~da   ~kharí+a   ~**yabícha-wa'a-chɨ**   ti=sa'sé+ró*
 ANPH-PL sleep+(3)PL night-go-SW.REF ANPH=be.alone+SG
 ti=phɨk+ó+ró   ~kharí tí+ró
 3PL.POSS=parent+FEM+SG sleep ANPH+SG
 ti=phɨk+ɨ́+ró   tó-pɨ   wa'á
 3PL.POSS=parent+MASC+SG REM-LOC go
 to=kó-ya=~be're
 3SG.POSS=relative-PL=COM/INST
 'Going to sleep **when night came**, alone with their mother, their father went off with his relatives . . .' [A4.15]

(92) *ba'aro hi'na ñamidahchomahka'i waroi, yoaropɨ kŭiro taro koataa sõ'oba'ropɨ*
 ba'á+ro   *~hí'da   ~yabí-dáchó-~báká+í   wáro+i*
 do/be.after+SG EMPH night-middle-origin-LOC EMPH+LOC

yoá+ró-pɨ ~kɨ́-író tá+ro
be.far+SG-LOC one/a-NOM.SG come+(3)SG
koá-ta+a ~so'ó-bá'á+ró-pɨ
NONVIS-come+ASSERT.PERF DEIC.DIST-do/be.after+SG-LOC
'**Later**, right in the middle of the night, in the distance (he heard) someone approaching.' [A7.27]

(93) ã yo bo'rero to pho'nare ya'ua hi'na
~a=yó **bo'ré+ro** to=~pho'dá+re ya'ú+a
so=do be.light+SG 3SG.POSS=children+OBJ tell/warn+ASSERT.PERF
~hí'da
EMPH
'So, **in the morning** he warned his sons: . . .' [A6.66]

(94) phanopɨre hiatiga mahsayahkaina
~phadó-pɨ+re hí-ati+a
do/be.before-LOC+OBJ COP-IMPERF+ASSERT.PERF
~basá-yáká-~ídá
people-steal-NOM:PL
'**In the olden days** there were people-stealers.' [A4.1]

(95) agã khõ'oyoa tiro hi'na, ti nɨmaita hi'na yariawa'aa hi'na tiro
~agá ~kho'ó yoá tí+ró ~hí'da
poisonous.snake bite do/make ANPH+SG EMPH
ti=~dúbá+í=ta ~hí'da yarí+á=wa'a+a ~hí'da
ANPH=day+LOC=REF EMPH die+AFFEC=go+ASSERT.PERF EMPH
tí+ró
ANPH+SG
'The snake bit him (and) **that very day** he just died.' [A7.164]

(96) ã ta yoa ñamichapɨ hi'na, kɨ̃ ku'tukãpɨ, õpari ku'tukãpɨre phi'asɨa
~a=tá yoá **~yabícha-pɨ** ~hí'da ~kɨ́ ku'tú-~ka-pɨ
so=REF do/make night-LOC EMPH one/a clearing-DIM-LOC
~ó-pá+rí ku'tú-~ka-pɨ+re
DEIC.PROX-ALT+NOM clearing-DIM-LOC+OBJ
phí'a-~sɨ+a
MOV.out.into-arrive+ASSERT.PERF
'As **night** was falling, he went out into a little clearing, a little clearing like this.' (=(69)) [A7.18]

Temporal expressions indicating sequential actions, such as 'as soon as X', 'just as X', and 'after X', are formed with the verb *tu'sɨ* 'finish', which also codes recently completed actions when it occurs as the noninitial root in a serialization (see §7.5.3). In expressions denoting sequential actions, however, *tu'sʉ* occurs as a phonologically independent root. The verb preceding *tu'sʉ* is uninflected; in this construction, *tu'sʉ* itself occurs without any additional morphology if the subjects performing the sequential actions are clearly the same, as in (97)–(98). When the subjects are different, *tu'sʉ* takes appropriate nominalizing morphology. In the sequential sentences in (99), the subject of sentence 1 and of the initial adverbial clause of sentence 2 is understood to be third person plural (the man and his sons); thus, in order to make it clear that the subject of the main clause in sentence 2 is different (the man alone), *tu'sʉ* takes the third person singular nominalizing suffix +*ro*. (In sentence 2 of (99), as well, no overt verb occurs before *tu'sʉ*, but it can be deduced from line 1 that the understood verb is *thua* 'return'.)

(97) *ã ni tu'sʉ tiro hi'na, to puhkare wʉa wakasare wʉamʉ wa'awa'aa mahkarokapʉ*

~*a=~dí tu'sú tí+ró ~hí'da to=púka+re wʉá*
so=say finish ANPH+SG EMPH 3SG.POSS=blowgun+OBJ carry

waká-sa+re wʉá-~bʉ wa'á-wa'a+a
poison.darts-carrier+OBJ carry-run go-go+ASSERT.PERF

~*baká-róká-pʉ́*
origin-DIST-LOC

'**As soon as he spoke,** he got his blowgun, grabbed a basket of darts (and) went off into the forest.' [A7.8]

(98) *chʉ tu'sʉ, nia: koiro mʉ'ʉ yahiripho'na noaphitiaro koaka, nia*

chú tu'sú ~*dí+a kó-iro* ~*bʉ'ʉ=yahíri~pho'da*
eat finish say+ASSERT.PERF relative-NOM.SG 2SG(POSS)=heart

~*dóá-phití+á+ró koá-ka* ~*dí+a*
be.good-COLL+AFFEC+SG taste-ASSERT.IMPERF say+ASSERT.PERF

'**When (the curupira) was done eating,** he said: "Relative, your heart tastes really good," he said.' [A7.61]

(99) 1 *thuaa pohtota te wʉ'ʉpʉ*

thuá+a potó=ta té wʉ'ʉ́-pʉ́
return+ASSERT.PERF direction=REF all.the.way house-LOC

'(The man and his sons) went straight back home.'

2 *tu'sʉro ka'a tiro nia: pairoba'aro mari wãhai ni*

tu'sʉ́+ro *ka'á tí+ró* ~*dí+a*
finish+SG near ANPH+SG say+ASSERT.PERF

pá-iro=ba'ro ~barí ~wahá+i ~dí
ALT+SG=kind 1PL.INC kill+VIS.PERF.1 say

'**Just as** (they were arriving home) he said: "We've killed another kind of (a magic) snake," he said.' [A6.50–51]

Spatial and temporal adjuncts are coded in very similar ways in Kotiria. For instance, spatial nominal locatives are marked by *-pɨ* and so are some nominals with temporal reference. We find, for instance, parallel coding of the locative *te wɨ'ɨ-pɨ* 'straight (all the way) back home' in (100) and the temporal *te pa-~dɨba-pɨ* 'until the next day/morning' in (101).

(100) *thuaa pohtota te wɨ'ɨpɨ*

    thuá+a   *potó=ta*   *té*   *wɨ'ɨ-pɨ*
    return+ASSERT.PERF direction=REF all.the.way house-LOC

    'He (and his sons) went straight **back home**.' [A6.50]

(101) *chɨ tu'sɨ, tina khãria wa'ara te panɨmapɨ tina hira*

    chɨ́ tu'sɨ́   *tí-~da*   *~kharí+a=wa'a+ra*   *té*
    eat finish ANPH-PL sleep+AFFEC= go+VIS.IMPERF.2/3 until

    pá-~dɨba-pɨ *tí-~da*   *hí+ra*
    ALT-day-LOC ANPH-PL COP+VIS.IMPERF.2/3

    'When they're done eating, they go to sleep **until the next day**.' [A1.23]

Just as some locative expressions are coded as oblique arguments by the objective case marker *+re,* some temporal adjuncts formed from derived nouns (102)–(103) or inherently temporal nouns, such as *~bicha* 'today', *~bi* 'now', *dacho* 'day', and *~yabi* 'night', are marked with *+re* and sometimes with the locatives *-pɨ/+i* as well (which, as is seen in (100)–(101) above, can indicate either spatial or temporal location). Examples (102)–(105) show that adjuncts indicating relatively unbounded spans of time, whether distant or current, are marked by both the locative *-pɨ* and the temporal *+re*.

(102) *phanopɨre hiatiga mahsayahkaina*

    ~phadó-pɨ+re   *hí-ati+a*
    do/be.before-LOC+OBJ COP-IMPERF+ASSERT.PERF

    ~basá-yáká-~ídá
    people-steal-NOM.PL

    '**In the olden days** there were people-stealers.' [A4.1]

(103) *wa'maropɨre, ñarana yare, bu'ena ñaro yɨ'dɨa thɨ'othui sã*

    ~wa'bá+ro-pɨ+re   *~yará-~da*   *yá-re*
    be.young+SG-LOC+OBJ white.people-PL POSS-CLS:generic

bu'é-~da ~yá+ro yɨ'dɨ́-a thɨ'ó-thɨ+i
study/learn-(1/2)PL be.bad+SG INTENS-AFFEC hear-think+VIS.PERF.1
~sá
1PL.EXC

'**When we were young**, it was really hard for us to understand school in the white people's language.' [A8.5]

(104) ã yoai, yɨ'ɨ õpɨre ta, mipɨre õpɨ yɨ'ɨ hiha
~a=yoá+i   yɨ'ɨ ~ó-pɨ́+ré   tá
so/then=do/make+(1/2)MASC 1SG DEIC.PROX-LOC+OBJ come
~bí-pɨ́+ré   ~ó-pɨ́   yɨ'ɨ hí-ha
now-LOC+OBJ DEIC.PROX-LOC 1SG COP-VIS.IMPERF.1

'Then I came here (the United States), and **now** here I am.' [A1.3]

(105) mipɨkã́re yoasinira
~bí-pɨ́-~ká+ré   yoá-~sidi+ra
now-LOC-DIM+OBJ do/make-do.yet/still+VIS.IMPERF.2/3

'**Nowadays**, they still do that.' [A3.8]

In contrast, (106)–(108) show that adjuncts indicating temporally bounded or singular temporal referents are marked only by +re.

(106) yɨ'ɨ mihchare wa'ikinawahai wa'aika
yɨ'ɨ   **~bichá+ré** wa'í-~kidá-~wáhá+í   wa'á+i-ka
1SG today+OBJ animal-PL-kill+(1/2)MASC go+(1/2)MASC-PREDICT

'"**Today** I'm going hunting."' [A7.4]

(107) dahchore tinika tiro mahkachɨro
dachó+ré ~tidí-ká   tí-ró
day+OBJ   wander- ASSERT.IMPERF ANPH+SG
~baká-chɨ+ro
look.for-eat+SG

'**During the day**, (the anteater) goes around looking for food.' [LSK: Anteaters]

(108) ne mihchakã́kãre wa'eraatiga khuarire tiro nia
~dé **~bichá-~ká-~ká+ré** wa'(a)-éra-ati+ga
NEG today-DIM-DIM+OBJ go-NEG-IMPERF+IMPER
khuá+ri+re
be.dangerous+NOM+OBJ

'Don't be going near that dangerous one **right now**.' [A6.69]

Considering the multiple uses of the suffix +re, it is not at all surprising that we come across sentences such as (109), in which every nominal constituent present (here, a temporal expression, a locative, and an object) has the suffix *+re*.

(109) *tu'sᵾ, ti ñamire hi'na khã'aropᵾre tirore ya'ua*
 tu'sᵾ   ti=~yabɨ+re   ~hí'da   ~kha'á+ro-pᵾ+re   tí+ró+ré
 finish ANPH=night+OBJ EMPH dream+SG-LOC+OBJ ANPH+SG+OBJ
 ya'ú+a
 warn+ASSERT.PERF
 'When he was done, that very night he was warned in a dream.'
 [A6.54]

10.7.3 Comitative

In addition to adjuncts with locative and temporal semantic roles, Kotiria marks a noun (usually animate) in a comitative role, 'with X', by the morpheme *=~be're* (see also §5.2.3). Both nouns in the comitative relationship can be mentioned in the sentence; thus in (110) both the subject *ti+ro* 'he' and the comitative noun *to ko-ya* 'his relatives' (with *=~be're*) are present. However, we have seen that sentences often have null subjects if reference is clear; thus, it is possible for the comitative noun alone to be overtly present in the sentence, as in (111) and (112). In (111) the referent of the noun marked as comitative is included within the reference of the plural subject (although the subject itself is null, note the third person plural agreement marker *+a* on the verb); we understand that 'they'—the man and the curupira—began to have a conversation. Similarly, in (112), the referent of the comitative-marked noun 'my father' is included within the group referred to by the plural pronoun *~sa*—'we, including my father'.

(110) *tiro soro kha'aro nia to koyame're sõ'o*
 tí+ró   *só+ro*   *~kha'á+ro*   *~dí+a*
 ANPH+SG be.different+SG dream+(3)SG be.PROG+ASSERT.PERF
 to=kó-ya=~be're   *~so'ó*
 3SG.POSS=relative-PL=COM/INST DEIC.DIST
 '**He** was off in that other place dreaming (drunk) **with his relatives**.'
 [A4.48]

(111) *ãta yoa tirome're durukua yoaa*
 Ø   *~a=tá   yoá*   **tí+ró=~be're**   *dú-rúkú+á*
 so=REF do/make ANPH+SG=COM/INST speak-stand+(3)PL
 yoá+a
 do/make+ASSERT.PERF
 'So, **(the man)** started a conversation **with him** (the curupira).'
 [A7.41]

(112)   sã yoaropɨ yɨphɨkume're thɨ'oi

   ~sá   yoá+ro-pɨ   yɨ=phɨk+ɨ́=~be're
   1PL.EXC   be.far+SG-LOC   1SG=parent+MASC=COM/INST
   thɨ'ó+i
   hear+VIS.PERF.1
   'We, from far away, (I) **with my father**, heard (the sounds).' [A2.9]

10.7.4 Instrumental

Nouns with an instrument role are also marked by the morpheme =~be're. Instrument nouns are those used by agents to perform or accomplish the action expressed by the verb 'do X with (by means of) Y', or 'use Y to X'. Prototypically, instruments are inanimate: *tɨ* 'stick' (113), *~phicho+ro* 'tail' (114), *wɨ-ria* 'planes' (lit., 'flying things') (115), *kotiria ya* 'Kotiria language' (116), and *a'ri-~phi* 'this knife' (117).

(113)   tɨ me're mɨ'ɨ wa'ikinawãha sihtotaga

   tɨ́=~be're   ~bɨ'ɨ   wa'í-~kídá-~wáhá   sitó-ta+ga
   stick=COM/INST   2SG   animal-PL-kill   MOV.circular-come+IMPER
   '**With this stick,** you go around hunting (animal-killing).' (=(50)) [A7.131]

(114)   emo to phichõnome're wa'maduhi sɨ̃ chuka

   ~ebó   **to=~phichó+ro=~be're**   ~wa'bá-dúhí-~sɨ
   howler.monkey   3SG.POSS=tail+SG=COM/INST   wrap-sit-arrive
   chɨ́-ká
   eat-ASSERT.IMPERF
   'A howler monkeys **uses its tail** to wrap (around a branch while it) eats.' [LSK: Tails]

(115)   mari kherokã wa'aduana wa'aka wɨriame're

   ~barí   khé+ro-~ka   wa'á-dua-~da   wa'á-ka
   1PL.INC   be.fast+SG-DIM   go-DESID-(1/2)PL   go-ASSERT.IMPERF
   wɨ́-ria=~be're
   fly-CLS:round.elongated=COM/INST
   'When we want to go (somewhere) quickly, we go **by plane**.' [A12.3]

(116)   kotiria yame're bu'e hi'na

   Ø   kó-ti+ri+a   yá=~be're   bu'é   ~hí'da
       water-VBZ+NOM+PL   POSS=COM/INST   study/learn   EXRT
   'Let's study **in Kotiria** (using our own Kotiria language).' [LSK: title]

(117) *a'riphĩ me're narokha'mare*
Ø ***a'rí-~phĩ=~be're***
   DEM.PROX-CLS:bladelike=COM/INST
   ~dá+ro=~kha'ba+re
   get+(3)SG=want/need+VIS.PERF.2/3
   '(You) have to take it (your heart) out **with this knife**.' [A7.76]

The fact that the comitative and instrument roles are coded by the same morpheme is certainly a reflection of their closely linked semantics. In (118), for example, *die-ro=~be're* 'with dogs' could have two possible interpretations. If we interpret the relationship between people and dogs as comitative, we understand the sentence to mean that if you go hunting 'accompanied by dogs', you are more likely to find wild turtles. However, we could also interpret 'the dogs' in this case as a rare instance of an animate coded as an instrument: you will find wild turtles if you hunt 'using dogs' (this was, in fact, the interpretation suggested by the speaker).

(118) *mahkaroka mahkainare dierome're bohkaro kha'mara*
Ø *~baká-roka ~baká-~ida+re* ***dié+ró=~be're***
   origin-DIST origin-NOM.PL+OBJ dog+SG=COM/INST
   boká+ro=~kha'ba+ra
   find+(3)SG=want/need+VIS.IMPERF.2/3
   'People have to find (hunt) the wild ones (turtles) **with dogs**.' [LSK: Turtles]

10.7.5 The status of *=~be're*

The morpheme *=~be're*, productively used as a marker of nouns with comitative or instrument roles, also has an extended function. It is used in the derivation of adverbials of manner from nominalized verbs, such as *toa+ro=~be're wa'a* (be.fast+SG=COM/INST go), literally 'go with haste' (discussed further in §11.2.2).

Unlike *+re*, which clearly displays suffixlike features (it is monomoraic and has no underlying specification for any suprasegmental phonological features), the morpheme *=~be're* has the shape and nearly all the specifications characterizing lexical roots. Even when it functions as a grammatical marker, it is bimoraic, glottalized, and [+nasal], though it does display phonological reduction and consistently occurs with low tone. Because of these phonological characteristics, *=~be're* is analyzed as a cliticized root (in §3.6), and indeed, it occurs as the independent root in the derived nominal word for 'friend' in (60), *~be're-~baka-iro* (literally, 'a fellow villager').

Kotiria =~*be're* has close cognates in other Eastern Tukanoan languages. The Tatuyo counterpart ~*beda* functions not only as an associative-instrumental, but also a pluralizer of certain nouns (Gomez-Imbert 1982:66–67). The associative-instrumental morpheme in Barasana, ~*raka*, parallels Kotiria =~*be're* and is analyzed as an independent clitic with underlying specifications for nasality and low tone (Gomez-Imbert 1997a:178–79). The Desano cognate is ~*beda* (Miller 1999:62), and -*ke* functions as the marker of instruments and accompaniment in Kubeo (Morse and Maxwell 1999:119). The status of the morpheme is not addressed for either language. Ramirez (1997a:249–50) views the cognate morpheme in Tukano, *me'ra*, as a dependent noun meaning 'with', used as marker of instruments, modes of transport, etc. He ascribes to it the same instrumental, comitative, and adverbial-type functions found for Kotiria =~*be're*.

11 Complex sentences

This chapter discusses additional features of Kotiria clause structure beyond arguments and basic adjuncts. Section 11.1 considers the order of constituents in the clause; in the basic template, arguments, modifiers, and all verbal complements precede the verb. Modification, including adverbial nominalizations indicating distinctions of manner and quality, the independent emphasis modifier ~hi'da, and a construction indicating similarity are discussed in §11.2. Besides serialized verb constructions, which were analyzed in chapter 7, Kotiria has additional types of multiple-verb constructions; verbs that require nominalized verbal complements are discussed in §11.3 and constructions with speech verbs and fully inflected verbal complements in §11.4. The perfective and causative functions of sequencing constructions with the verb *yoa* are outlined in §11.5, while §11.6 shows that chained clauses can be represented by a simple series of independent verb stems, the final one taking finite inflection. The properties of multiple-verb constructions—serialized verb constructions, complement constructions, and verb sequencing—are summarized and compared in §11.7.

11.1 Order of constituents in clauses

In chapter 10, we saw that there is a good deal of word order flexibility in Kotiria. The flexible order of object arguments was discussed in §10.3.1, and in table 10.3, we saw that in Kotiria and a number of other Eastern Tukanoan languages subject argument positioning depends, to a large extent, on discourse-level considerations. Despite this flexibility, some general tendencies are nevertheless clear. First, the most common final element in a Kotiria clause is a finite verb or a sequence of verbs, the last one of which is in finite form. Subject (S) and object (O) arguments, along with adverbial modifiers, tend to precede the verbal component. Temporal adverbial constructions tend to occur sentence-initially, preceding subject and object arguments (see §10.7.2), while most other types of adverbial elements tend to occur directly preceding the verb. The only constituents that consistently tend to occur postverbally are locative adjuncts or oblique arguments, though any constituent, including subjects and objects, can occur postverbally for pragmatic purposes. The structure in (1) represents the most common order of constituents based on these overall tendencies ("nonfin. verb" indicates a verb that has nominalized or other nonfinite inflection, or is uninflected).

(1) ADVERB   S   O   ADVERB   NONFIN. VERB   FINITE VERB   LOCATIVE
     [temporal]   [manner,
                          quality,
                          emphatic,
                          etc.]

11.2 Preverbal modification

Adverbial information is expressed by a variety of means in Kotiria, which, as we saw in chapter 3, has no lexical class of adverbs per se. A number of adverbial lexical elements are derived from nouns or are nominalizations of stative verb roots. Such nominalizations occur immediately before the verb and function as lexical verbal modifiers whose semantic uses tend to be complementary to those of the serial verb constructions discussed in §7.5.1. Serialized verbs with adverbial interpretations primarily code spatial manner information, whereas lexical adverbials express other manner distinctions as well as temporal, qualitative, instrumental, and emphatic qualities.

11.2.1 Adverbials: quality and evaluation

Lexical adverbials indicating quality or evaluation generally occur immediately preceding the verb. They are derived from stative verbs such as ~doa 'be good' (2)–(3) and ~ya [ɲãá] 'be bad' (4) by means of the nominalizer +ro; as we saw in §4.5.1, +ro can be used to derive abstract nominals from verbs.

(2) to di'i noaro koaka

    to=di'i   **~dóá+ró**   koá-ka
    3SG.POSS=meat be.good+SG taste-ASSERT.IMPERF

    'Its (a cow's) meat tastes good.' [LSK: Cows]

(3) ã yoana noaro wahkũmahsi duhimahsiha

    ~a=yoá-~da   **~dóá+ró**   ~wakú-~bási
    so=do/make-(1/2)PL be.good+SG be.aware-know

    duhí-~basi-ha
    sit-know-VIS.IMPERF.1

    'So (in an airplane), we should pay close attention (and) sit still.'
    [A12.6]

(4) ñaro wihkĩrika tina wimia
    ~yá+ro   ~wikí-ri-ka   tí-~da   ~wibí+a
    be.bad+SG itch-ADMON-ASSERT.IMPERF ANPH-PL suck+(3)PL
    '(Beware!) it itches badly when they (horseflies) bite.' (lit., 'their sucking itches badly') [A9.4]

A real-life example of these adverbs can be seen in the form in figure 11.1, which the Kotiria themselves designed for a linguistic census.[1] Each participant in the census was to list the languages he or she was familiar with in the left-hand column and then evaluate his or her ability to speak that language *noano* 'very well (i.e., fluently)', *phiro* 'fairly well' (from the stative verb *phi* 'be large') or *ñano* 'badly, not well'.

wamã [name]: bʉhkʉaro [age]: mahkã [village]:			
yʉ'ʉ durukua [languages I speak]	do'se duruhari? [how do I speak?]		
	noano [very well]	phiro [fairly well]	ñano [badly]
kotiria [Kotiria]	✓		
dahsea [Tukano]	✓		
português [Portuguese]	✓		
buisemakã [Kubeo]		✓	
espanhol [Spanish]			✓
[etc.]			
phukʉro durukua [father's language]: phukoro durukua [mother's language]: mahkã mahkaina durukua [language of the community in which I live]:			

Figure 11.1. A sample form from a Kotiria linguistic census.

11.2.2 Adverbials: manner

Like the derived adverbs of quality, adverbials indicating the manner in which an action took place also tend to occur immediately preceding

---

[1] This form shows evidence of ongoing work on practical orthography issues, e.g., whether or not to write preaspiration in words such as *dahsea* 'Tukano' or *mahka* 'village' and how to mark nasalization in words such as *wamã*.

the verb and are derived from stative verbs by means of the nominalizer +*ro* (5)–(6). These same examples also contain the diminutive suffix -~*ka*, which, as we saw in §5.1.2, can be used to augment a described quality. In (7)–(9), the nominalized verb is additionally marked by the comitative-instrumental morpheme =~*be're*, yielding an adverb that can be read literally as 'with X' (compare (5) and (8), both formed from the same verb root), while in (10), both -~*ka* and =~*be're* occur, but there is no overt nominalizer. In contrast to adverbials nominalized only by +*ro*, adverbials with =~*bere* often occur postverbally, as in (7), (8), and (10).

(5) *kherokã chɨa*
   khé+ro-~ka   *chɨ́+á*
   be.fast+SG-DIM eat+ASSERT.PERF
   'He gobbled it up (ate very quickly).' [A7.67]

(6) *ã mɨ'ɨ phirokã yoaka mɨ'ɨ nia*
   ~*á* ~*bɨ'ɨ* **phí+ró-~ká** *yoá-ka*   ~*bɨ'ɨ*
   so   2SG   be.slow+SG-DIM do/make-ASSERT.IMPERF 2SG
   ~*dí+a*
   say+ASSERT.PERF
   '"You're doing it too slowly," (the man) said.' [A7.81]

(7) *kherokã yoarokã naka'aro kha'mare tuaro me're*
   khé+ro-~ka   *yoá+ro-~ka*
   be.fast+SG-DIM be.far+SG-DIM
   ~*dá-ka'a+ro*=~*kha'ba+re*
   get-do.moving+(3)SG=want/need+VIS.PERF.2/3
   tuá+ro=~be're
   be.strong+SG=COM/INST
   'It (the knife) has to go in quickly, hard (with force).' [A7.83]

(8) *ni thuata ma'a kherokã me're*
   ~*dí thuá=ta*   ~*ba'á* **khé+ro-~ka=~be're**
   say return=REF path   be.fast+SG-DIM=COM/INST
   '(He) said/thought, "(I'll) hurry back quickly (with haste)."' [A7.13]

(9) *ã yoa ñɨna, yɨ phukɨ toaro me're wa'a ñɨro wa'are dierore*
   ~*a=yoá*   ~*yɨ́-~dá*   *yɨ=phuk+ɨ́*
   so/then=do/make see/realize-(1/2)PL 1SG.POSS=parent+MASC
   toá+ro=~be're   *wa'á* ~*yɨ́+ró*   *wa'á+re*
   be.fast+SG=COM/INST   go   see/look+(3)SG go+VIS.PERF.2/3

      dié+ró+ré
      dog+SG+OBJ

      'When we realized (what had happened), my father quickly (with haste) went to look for the dog.' [A2.10]

(10)   *kasɨa hikoerakã me're*
      kasɨ+a   *híkó(á)-éra-~ka=~be're*
      revive+ASSERT.PERF like-NEG-DIM=COM/INST

      '(The men) woke up embarrassed (with dislike or shame).' [Ancestors]

11.2.3 Adverbials: *~hi'da* 'emphatic'

One of the most frequently occurring morphemes in Kotiria is *~hi'da*. Although it has the bimoraic shape and the tone, glottalization, and nasality specifications characteristic of roots, and is always phonologically independent, *~hi'da* is never inflected. Furthermore, it behaves more independently than most roots do, cooccurring with a number of different clausal constituents. Waltz and Waltz analyze *~hi'da* as a marker of "finality" or of the "culminating point in an episode" (1997: 43; my translation). While this is certainly one of its functions, *~hi'da* codes several other emphasis-related functions as well, with variations depending on its position in a clause and the constituent it modifies. For these reasons, it is analyzed here as an independent adverbial discourse marker.

As Waltz and Waltz point out, one of the uses of *~hi'da* is to indicate finality or the end point in an episode. When employed in this function, *~hi'da* occurs postverbally.

(11)   *tiro tinare ko'taga hi'na*
      tí+ró   *tí-~da+re*   *ko'tá+a*   ***~hí'da***
      ANPH+SG ANPH-PL+OBJ wait+ASSERT.PERF EMPH

      '. . . (the evil being) was lying in wait for them.' [A4.28]

(12)   *ti batopɨ tikoro wihataga hi'na*
      ti=bató-pɨ   *tí-kó+ró*   *wihá-ta+a*
      ANPH=be.last-LOC ANPH-FEM+SG MOV.outward-come+ASSERT.PERF
      ~hí'da
      EMPH

      'Right at the end, the woman finally came out.' [A4.65]

However, the most frequent use of *~hi'da* is as an adverbial emphasizing the immediacy of an action. When employed in this function, *~hi'da* occurs somewhere before the verb (in most cases, before any objects, and sometimes before the subject as well, as in (14) and

(15)) and yields the interpretation that the action was done 'immediately', 'right then', or 'right away'.

(13) ã ni tu'sɨ tiro hi'na, to puhkare wɨa wahkasare wɨamɨ wa'awa'aa mahkarokapɨ

~a=~dí tu'sɨ́ tí+ró ~**hí'da** to=púka+re wɨá
so=say finish ANPH+SG EMPH 3SG.POSS=blowgun+OBJ carry

waká-sa+re wɨá-~bɨ wa'á-wa'a+a
poison.darts-carrier+OBJ carry-run go-go+ASSERT.PERF

~baká-róká-pɨ́
origin-DIST-LOC

'As soon as (the man) spoke, he got his blowgun, grabbed a basket of darts (and) went off into the forest.' [A7.8]

(14) ã yo hi'na, tiro topɨre wihsiawa'aa to ma'are

~a=yó ~**hí'da** tí+ró tó-pɨ+re
so=do EMPH ANPH+SG REM-LOC+OBJ

wisí+a-wa'a+a to=~ba'á+re
be.lost+AFFEC-go+ASSERT.PERF 3SG.POSS=path+OBJ

'Right then, (the man) got lost from his path.' [A7.14]

(15) bo'reka'achɨ ñɨ hi'na tiro wihaa

bo'ré-ka'a-chɨ ~yɨ́ ~**hí'da** tí+ró
be.light-do.moving-SW.REF realize EMPH ANPH+SG

wihá+a
MOV.outward+ASSERT.PERF

'When he realized it was morning, (the man) went out (of his shelter).' [A7.100]

(16) tiphĩre tiro hi'na ña'a to yahiripho'nare phirokã beñɨa

tí-~phi+re tí+ró ~**hí'da** ~ya'á
ANPH-CLS:bladelike+OBJ ANPH+SG EMPH grab

to=yahíri~pho'da+re phí+ró-~ká bé-~yɨ+a
3SG.POSS=heart+OBJ be.slow+SG-DIM inject/insert-try+ASSERT.PERF

'(The curupira) immediately grabbed the knife (and) tried rather slowly to cut out its (own) heart.' [A7.77]

In (17), we can see that, as with the case marker +re, there is no restriction on multiple occurrences of ~hi'da within a single sentence. In line 1, ~hi'da emphasizes the preceding noun, a function discussed in §5.3.6, whereas in lines 2 and 3, it is an adverbial emphasizing the immediacy of the actions 'getting his knife' and 'cutting out the monkey's heart'.

(17) 1 *ba'aro mahsɨno hi'na . . .*
    *ba'á+ro   ~basɨ́+ro   ~**hí'da***
    do/be.after+SG man+SG   EMPH
    'The (same) guy . . .'

   2 *topɨrota hi'na to yɨ'soriphĭkãre na . . .*
    *tó-pɨ+ro=ta   ~**hí'da**   to= yɨ'só+ri-~phi-~ka+re*
    DEF-LOC+SG=REF EMPH   3SG.POSS=cut+NOM-CLS:bladelike-DIM+OBJ
    ~dá
    get
    'immediately got his knife . . .'

   3 *hi'na tiro ka yahiripho'nare wayerɨkaa*
    *~**hí'da** tí+ró   ká   yahíri~pho'da+re*
    EMPH   ANPH+SG black.monkey heart+OBJ
    wayé-rɨká+á
    cut.open-begin+ASSERT.PERF
    '(and) right away started to cut out one of the monkeys' hearts.'
    [A7.54]

11.2.4 Adverbials: similarity, comparison, and contrast

The adverbial expression indicating similarity ('do/be like X') can occur before or after the verb. In this construction, the verb *yoa* 'do, make' is nominalized by the morpheme *+ro* and followed by the morpheme *-se* 'be like', while the standard of comparison is represented by a noun that precedes *yoa* and has no case marking. The morpheme *-se* also occurs in demonstrative or deictic expressions, *a'rí+á-sé* in (21) and *~o-se* in (22)–(24), to call attention to a particular verbal action or notion.

(18) *phirota sañoa mahsɨno yoarose phinonowɨ'rɨ*
    *phí+ró=ta   ~sayó+a   ~**basɨ́+ro***
    be.big+SG=REF scream+ASSERT.PERF person+SG
    yoá+ro-se   *~phidó+ró-wɨ́'rɨ́*
    do/make+SG-be.like snake+SG-AUG
    'The snake screamed loudly **like a person**.' [A6.38]

(19) *chĭpe yoarose, chĭpe yoarose, wĩhtariro hia tiro to pakɨpɨ*
    *~**chĭpe yoá+ro-se**   ~**chĭpe yoá+ro-se***
    sap do/make+SG-be.like sap do/make+SG-be.like
    ~wita+ri+ro   hí+a   tí+ró   to=páku-pɨ
    be.sticky+NOM+SG COP+ASSERT.PERF ANPH+SG 3SG.POSS=body-LOC
    '**Like sap, like sap,** he was sticky all over his body.' [A4.43]

(20) *topɨ dohparoa yoarose nure sãga tina pe'ri*

tó-pɨ   **dopá+ró+á**   **yoá+ró-sé**   *~dú-re*
REM-LOC   bee+SG+PL   do/make+SG-be.like   buzz-CLS:generic

~sá+a   *tí-~da*   *pé'ri*
be.inside+ASSERT.PERF   ANPH-PL   all

'There inside all of them (evil beings) were buzzing **like bees**.' [A4.60]

(21) *a'riase sĩomɨ wihatanokaa*

a'rí+á-sé   *~sió-~bɨ*
DEM.PROX+PL-be.like   slide-run

wihá-ta-~doka+a
MOV.outward-come-COMPL+ASSERT.PERF

'It (the snake) came sliding out (of its hiding place) **like this**.' [A6.37]

(22) *tɨre ña'a õse khãka'a yoaa*

tú+re   *~ya'á*   *~ó-sé*   *~khá-ka'a*
stick+OBJ   grab   DEIC.PROX-be.like   chop-do.moving

yoá+a
do/make+ASSERT.PERF

'He took the stick (and) shook it **like this** (chopping/hitting motion).' [A7.144]

(23) *õse wa'aatiga phanopɨre*

~ó-sé   *wa'á-ati+a*   *~phadó-pɨ+re*
DEIC.PROX-be.like   go-IMPERF+ASSERT.PERF   do/be.before-LOC+OBJ

'**This** is how things used to be long ago.' [A5.43]

(24) 1 *kũta hia kũiro mɨno to namonore õse nia:*

~kú=ta   *hí+a*   *~kú-író*   *~bú+ro*   *to=~dabó+ro+re*
one/a=REF   COP+PL   one/a-NOM.SG   man+SG   3SG.POSS=wife+SG+OBJ

~ó-sé   *~dí+a*
DEIC.PROX-be.like   say+ASSERT.PERF

'Once a man said **(like) this** to his wife:'

2 *yɨ'ɨ mihchare wa'ikinawahai wa'aika*

yɨ'ɨ   *~bichá+ré*   *wa'í-~kídá-~wáhá+í*
1SG   today+OBJ   animal-PL-kill+(1/2)MASC

wa'á+i-ka
go+(1/2)MASC-PREDICT

'"Today I'm going hunting."' [A7.3–4]

I have only two examples in my data in which one entity of a set is identified as having the highest degree of a given quality (a superlative-like notion). In (25) the augmentative suffix *-wɨ'rɨ* is used, while in (26), the suffix *-kure* (tentatively glossed as "comparative") occurs. I do not yet know which type of expression may be more common nor can I speculate on the possible differences between them; these questions remain for future research.

(25) *kʉ̃iro diero, phirirowʉ'rʉ hirirowʉ'rʉ buhtiawa'aa*
~*kú-iró*   *dié+ró*   *phí+ri+ro-**wʉ'rʉ***   *hí+ri+ro-**wʉ'rʉ***
one/a-NOM:SG dog+SG be.big+NOM+SG-AUG COP+NOM+SG-AUG
butí+a=wa'a+a
disappear+AFFEC=go+ASSERT.PERF
'One dog, the biggest of all, disappeared.' [A6.7]

(26) *kʉ̃iro to mahkʉro buhkʉrokurero thʉ'oga*
~*kú-iró*   *to=~bak+ʉ́+ró*   *buk+ʉ́+ro-**kure**+ro*
one-NOM:SG 3SG.POSS=child+MASC+SG elder+MASC+SG-COMP+SG
thʉ'ó+a
hear+ASSERT.PERF
'One of his sons, the oldest, heard it.' [A4.20]

Semantically related to similarity and comparison is the notion of contrast—that in a given situation, something or someone is expressly different in some (probably unexpected) way. Such notions appear to be expressed in Kotiria by use of the rootlike morpheme *wi'o*, as in (27)–(28). Like the comparative constructions in (25)–(26), full understanding of this root (including evaluation of its status as a noun or verb root) requires further investigation.

(27) *wi'omeheta yariaropʉ nia*
***wi'ó**-~behe=ta*   *yarí+á+ro-pʉ*
CONTR-NEG.INTENS=REF die+AFFEC+(3)SG-EMPATH
~*dí+a*
be.PROG+ASSERT.PERF
'But (poor thing, she) was already (at the point of) death/dying.' [A4.66]

(28) *phanopʉ mahkadʉ ti ñohsadi'odʉ hiati hire, wi'o*
~*phadó-pʉ*   ~*baká-dʉ*
do/be.before-LOC origin-CLS:cylindrical.straight
ti=~yosá-di'o-dʉ   *hí-ati*
ANPH=force.into-particles-CLS:cylindrical.straight COP-IMPERF
hí+re   ***wi'ó***
COP+VIS.PERF.2/3 CONTR
'It was an old-fashioned one, the kind you used to shove the ammunition into, right?' [A6.31]

11.2.5 Adverbials: interrogative

In §6.5 we saw that Kotiria has several nominal interrogatives used to form questions of the types 'which X?', 'what kind of X?', 'how much/many X?', 'who?', 'from/to where?', 'what X?', and 'whose X?'. In addition to these nominal forms, there are three adverbial question constructions composed with the morpheme *do'se*.

In a statement, *do'se* modifies processes or states to give the meaning 'how X', as in (29), where the speaker is explaining how something looks. This morpheme consistently occurs in questions about the manner in which the activity or state expressed by the verb is realized: 'how does/did/can one X (activity)?', 'how is X (state) realized?'. Examples (30)–(32) specifically question the manner in which processes occur—the best way to catch a particular species of fish (30), how to remove one's own heart (31), and what to do in a particular situation (32). The manner of realization of a state is questioned in (33), and in (34), *do'se* is used to question the content of the complement of a speech verb: 'what (lit., 'how') was said?'.

(29) *do'se bahuina hira tina*
 do'sé bahú-~ida   *hí+ra*   *tí-~da*
 WH   appear-NOM.PL   COP+VIS.IMPERF.2/3   ANPH-PL
 'This is how they (different types of fish) look: . . .' [LSK: Fish]

(30) *do'se yoa yo'gahari a'rirore*
 do'sé yoá   ***yo'gá-hari***   *a'rí+ró+ré*
 WH   do/make   fish-INT.IMPERF   DEM.PROX+SG+OBJ
 'How do you fish for this one (a type of fish)?'

(31) *mɨ'ɨ do'se yoa nari mɨ'ɨ yahiripho'nare*
 ~bɨ'ɨ ***do'sé yoá***   *~dá-ri*   *~bɨ'ɨ=yahíri~pho'da+re*
 2SG   WH   do/make   get-INT   2SG(POSS)=heart+OBJ
 'How did you take out your heart?' [A7.75]

(32) *do'se yoamahsi mari a'ria ñarire*
 do'sé yoá-~basi   *~barí*   *a'rí+á*   *~yá+ri+re*
 WH   do/make-know   1PL.INC   DEM.PROX+PL   be.bad+NOM+OBJ
 'What can we do about these evil ones?' [A4.61]

(33) *do'se yoa phɨ'ɨsekã noahari*
 do'sé yoá   *phɨ'ɨ-sé-~ká*   *~dóá-hári*
 WH   do/make   basket-PL-DIM   be.good-INT.IMPERF
 'What are these little baskets (good) for?' (lit., 'How are these baskets good/useful?') [Baskets]

(34) *do'se ni durukuri tikoro*
　　do'sé ~dí dú-ruku-ri   tí-kó+ró
　　WH   say speak-stand-INT ANPH-FEM+SG
　　'What did she say?'

Interrogative *do'se* is also used in questions about 'when' something occurred. Such questions are formed with a nominalized dependent clause composed of *do'se* and the copula with the switch-reference marker *-chɨ* (§10.1.3): *do'se hichɨ*, literally 'when was it that X?'

(35) *do'se hichɨ mɨ'ɨ wi'iri*
　　do'sé hí-chɨ   ~bɨ'ɨ wi'í-ri
　　WH   COP-SW.REF 2SG   arrive-INT
　　'When did you arrive?'

(36) *do'se hichɨ mɨ'ɨre ya'uri*
　　do'sé hí-chɨ   ~bɨ'ɨ+ré   ya'ú-rí
　　WH   COP-SW.REF 2SG+OBJ tell-INT
　　'When did they tell you (something)?'

Finally, *do'se* is also used in 'why' questions. These are formed with a dependent clause composed of *do'se* and the verb *yoa* 'do', nominalized by subject agreement markers: *-kɨ* 'first or second person masculine' in (37); *-da* 'first or second person plural' in (38); and *+ro* 'third person singular' in (39).

(37) *do'se yoakɨ ã yoari mɨ'ɨ*
　　do'sé yoá-kɨ   ~a=yoá-ri   ~bɨ'ɨ
　　WH   do/make-(1/2)MASC so=do/make-INT 2SG
　　'Why did you (masc.) do that?'

(38) *do'se yoana nihari mɨhsa*
　　do'sé yoá-~da   ~dí-hari   ~bɨsá
　　WH   do/make-(1/2)PL be.PROG-INT.IMPERF 2PL
　　'Why are you (plural) doing that?'

(39) *do'se yoaro a'riro yɨ'ɨre yɨ'tierahari*
　　do'sé yoá+ro   a'rí+ró   yɨ'ɨ+ré
　　WH   do/make+(3)SG DEM.PROX+SG 1SG+OBJ
　　yɨ'ti-éra-hari
　　answer-NEG-INT.IMPERF
　　'Why isn't he answering me?' [A7.94]

11.3 Verbs with clausal complements

There are a number of constructions in Kotiria in which verbs occur with clausal complements. Two of these are the nonvisual and inference evidential constructions formed with the verbs *koa* and *hi* (§§9.2.3–9.2.4). We now turn to other constructions with verbs requiring clausal complementation, most often in the form of nominalizations. Among these are a modal construction indicating necessity, recommendation, or obligation, a purposive construction, and a frequently occurring construction that codes progressive aspect. Finally, we examine quoted speech constructions, in which the verb of speech takes a full, finite clausal complement.

11.3.1 Modal with ~*kha'ba*

In §7.5.4, we saw that certain types of agent-oriented modality—specifically, ability, possibility, and desire—are coded in Kotiria by serialized verb constructions with the verbal roots ~*basi* 'know' and the desiderative -*dua*. To indicate the deontic notions of strong recommendation, obligation, or necessity, a different kind of construction is used, involving the root ~*kha'ba*. When it occurs as an independent root, ~*kha'ba* simply means 'want' (40).

(40) mari mahsa no'o kha'mana po'ka me're moreka phiaa si'niduara
~*barí*   ~*basá*   ~*do'ó*   ~**kha'bá**-~*da*   *po'ká*=~*be're*
1PL.INC people   WH   want-(1/2)PL   manioc.flour=COM/INST
~*boré-ka*   *phiá+a*   ~*si'dí-dua+ra*
mix-ASSERT.IMPERF be.sour+PL   drink-DESID+VIS.IMPERF.2/3
'When people want to, (we) mix (lime juice) with manioc flour to make a tangy drink.' [LSK: Limes]

The deontic construction with ~*kha'ba*, however, follows the general pattern of Kotiria complement constructions in that the complement clause is nominalized and precedes the main verb. However, the construction with ~*kha'ba* has two notable distinctive features. First, we can see in (41)–(43) that the nominalized complement always has third person marking (+*ro*), perhaps to be understood as impersonal;[2] ~*kha'ba* itself likewise always has third person subject marking. The sentences in example (41) occur at the point in a narrative when the man has tricked a curupira into cutting out its own heart and is giving it instructions as to how to go about it. Examples (42) and (43) are, respectively, from explanations about the best way to hunt

---

[2] Example (43) suggests that even when the subject of the clause is clearly not third person, the complement of ~*kha'ba* still takes third person marking (*wa'a+ro*), overriding other agreement marking requirements.

turtles and the best way to make woven sieves. These examples also show that, whereas in most complement constructions the nominalized complement and the finite verb are separate phonological words, ~kha'ba in this construction is undergoing cliticization and consistently occurs with low tone. In this respect it is similar to the perfective construction with wa'a, discussed in §8.5.2.

(41) a. *a'riphĩ me're nano kha'mare*
a'rí-~phí=~be're
DEM.PROX-CLS:bladelike=COM/INST
~dá+ro=~**kha'ba**+re
get+(3)SG=want/need+VIS.PERF.2/3
'(One) has to take (one's heart) out with this knife.' [A7.76]

b. *kherokã yoarokã naka'aro kha'mare*
khé+ro-~ka   yoá+ro-~ka
be.fast+SG-DIM be.far+SG-DIM
~dá-ka'a+ro=~**kha'ba**+re
get-do.moving+(3)SG=want/need+VIS.PERF.2/3
'It (the knife) has to go in quickly, hard.' (=(7)) [A7.83]

(42) *mahkaroka mahkainare dierome're bohkaro kha'mara*
~baká-roka ~baká-~ida+re   dié+ró=~be're
origin-DIST origin-NOM.PL+OBJ dog+SG=COM/INST
boká+ro=~**kha'ba**+ra
find+(3)SG=want/need+VIS.IMPERF.2/3
'People have to find (hunt) the wild ones (turtles) with dogs.' [LSK: Turtles]

(43) *tiare su'anatana, nɨhkɨpɨ nana wa'aro kha'mara*
tí-ka+re   su'á-~dá=ta-~da
ANAF-CLS:round +OBJ weave-(1/2)PL=REF-(1/2)PL
~dɨkɨ́-pɨ́ ~dá-~da   wa'á+ro =~**kha'ba**+ra
jungle-LOC get-(1/2)PL go+(3)SG=want/need+VIS.IMPERF.2/3
'To weave (sieves), we have to go get (arumã fiber) in the jungle.'[3]

11.3.2 Progressive with ~di

Actions and certain types of mental states that are in progress at a contextually established time are coded in Kotiria by a complement construction with the auxiliary verb ~di [nĩĩ]. In other Eastern Tukanoan languages, this verb is given various glosses—as 'do' by Miller (1999) and Kaye (1970) for Desano, as 'be' by Ramirez (1997a) and

---

[3] From a text about sieves and other woven artifacts written by a student in 2009 for the Kotiria practical grammar (not included in appendix 1).

Sorensen (1969) for Tukano, and simply as 'AUX' by Waltz and Waltz for Kotiria (1997:47). As it is used exclusively in this progressive construction, and as a number of Eastern Tukanoan languages have cognate forms ~(a)di with the gloss 'be', ~di is glossed here as 'be.PROG'.

The reference time for the progressive construction is quite often the moment of speech, as in (44)–(47), though (48)–(49) demonstrate that this is not always the case. As with other complement constructions, the constituent preceding ~di is a verb nominalized by subject agreement morphology, and both ~di and the nominalized complement verb agree with the subject of the construction, as shown by (44), (46) and (47).

(44) yʉ'ʉ tirore wãha kha'mai tai niha
yʉ'ʉ tí+ró+ré   ~wahá=~kha'ba+i tá+í
1SG ANPH+SG+OBJ kill=want+(1/2)MASC come+(1/2)MASC
~dí-ha
be.PROG-VIS.IMPERF.1
'I'm **coming here** to avenge him.' [A6.61]

(45) yʉ'ʉre a'riro chʉduaro nika
yʉ'ʉ+ré a'rí+ró   **chʉ-dua+ro**   **~dí-ka**
1SG+OBJ DEM.PROX+SG eat-DESID+(3)SG be.PROG-ASSERT.IMPERF
'This thing (the curupira) wants (is wanting) to eat me.' [A7.53]

(46) mipʉre yʉ'ʉ chʉa bohkatu'sʉha thuai niha
~bí-pʉ́+ré   yʉ'ʉ chʉa   boká-tu'sʉ-ha
now-LOC+OBJ 1SG food find-finish-VIS.IMPERF.1
thuá+i   **~dí-ha**
return+(1/2)MASC be.PROG-VIS.IMPERF.1
'Now I've found food (and/so) I'm **going home**.' [A7.12]

(47) numia ña'aina taa nia koatara
~dubí+a ~ya'á-~ida   **tá+á**   **~dí+a**
woman+PL catch-NOM.PL come+(3)PL be.PROG+(3)PL
koá-ta+ra
NONVIS-come+VIS.IMPERF.2/3
'Women-kidnappers **are coming**.' (the speaker hears them) [Ancestors]

(48) sʉ̃noka, to mahkʉrokãre sõ'opʉ tiro pahpero minichakãre bʉepero nia
~sʉ́-~doka+a   to=~bak+ʉ́+ró-~ká+ré
arrive-COMPL+ASSERT.PERF 3SG.POSS=child+MASC+SG-DIM+OBJ
~so'ó-pʉ́   tí+ró   papé+ró   ~bidícha-~ka+re
DEIC.DIST-LOC ANPH+SG play+(3)SG bird-DIM+OBJ

bué-pe+ro ~*dí+a*
hunt.with.arrows-FAV+(3)SG be.PROG+ASSERT.PERF

'She went over to her son, who was (on top of the house) playing at **hunting** birds.' [A5.26–27]

(49) *ã yo tirore wãhatu'sʉ chʉropʉ nia*
~*a=yó tí+ró+ré* ~*wahá-tu'sʉ chú+ro-pʉ*
so=do ANPH+SG+OBJ kill-finish eat+(3)SG-EMPATH
~*dí+a*
be.PROG+ASSERT.PERF

'He (the snake) had just killed the poor dog (and) was already **eating** it.' [A6.23]

11.3.3 Purposive with *wa'a* and *ta*

Kotiria 'go' and 'come' verbs, among their many uses, also occur with clausal complements to indicate purpose or intention—to 'come to (do) X' as in (44) above, or 'go to (do) X' as in (50)–(52). Complement verbs are nominalized by subject agreement morphology, following the general pattern for complement clauses.

(50) *numiaña'ana wa'ahi'na timahkapʉ*
~*dubí+a-~ya'a-~da* *wa'á* ~*hí'da ti=~baká-pʉ*
woman+PL-catch-(1/2)PL go EXRT ANPH=village-LOC

'Let's **go get women** from that village.' (i.e., 'let's go "bride-napping"') [Ancestors]

(51) *yʉ me'remahkinare yʉ'ʉ ñʉtini wa'atii*
yʉ=~be'ré-~baka-~ida+re *yʉ'ʉ* ~*yú-~tídí+í*
1SG.POSS=COM/INST-village-NOM.PL+OBJ 1SG see-visit+(1/2)MASC
wa'á-ati+i
go-IMPERF+VIS.PERF.1

'I used to **go (travel) in order to see (visit)** my friends.' [A3.3]

(52) *ti phʉkʉrore ya'ua wa'aga*
ti=phʉk+ú+ró+ré *ya'ú+a* *wa'á+a*
3PL.POSS=parent+MASC+SG+OBJ tell+(3)PL go+ASSERT.PERF

'They **went to tell** their father.' [A4.47]

11.4 Quoted speech constructions

Unlike the constructions discussed in §11.3, in which a finite verb takes a nonfinite, nominalized verbal complement, the all-purpose speech verb ~*di* [nĩĩ]—employed indifferently in the senses 'say', 'ask', and 'answer' throughout most quoted dialogues—takes a full finite clause complement. In other words, utterances with quoted speech and the speech verb ~*di* contain two inflected verbs—a finite one within the quoted speech complement, and the speech verb itself. The speech verb ~*di* usually follows the quoted speech complement. In (53)–(54), all three instances of ~*di* are marked as finite by +*a*, the evidential marker (perfective assertion) used in narratives. However, any kind of finite verb construction can occur within the quoted speech complement of ~*di*, as can be seen in the variety of finite constructions in the examples below. In (53), the verb *wa* in the complement clause is marked as finite by the imperative suffix +*ga*. The complement clause in sentence 1 of (54) is a question and the verb *hi* is marked as finite by the interrogative suffix -*ri*, while the complement clause in sentence 2 is the answer to the question, a statement in which the verb *hi* is marked as finite by the evidential suffix +*re*.

(53) *mɨ'ɨ yahiripho'nare yɨ'ɨre waga nia*
 ~*bɨ'ɨ=yahíri~pho'da*+*re yɨ'ɨ*+*ré wá*+*gá   ~dí*+*a*
 2SG(POSS)= heart+OBJ   1SG+OBJ give+IMPER say+ASSERT.PERF
 '"Give me your heart," he (the curupira) said.' [A7.51]

(54) 1 *no'oi hiri nia*
  ~*do'ó*+*í hí-ri   ~dí*+*a*
  WH+LOC COP-INT say+ASSERT.PERF
  '"Where is (she)?" he said/asked.'

 2 *õi hire nia*
  ~*ó*+*í   hí*+*re   ~dí*+*a*
  DEIC.PROX+LOC COP+VIS.PERF.2/3 say+ASSERT.PERF
  '"Here (she) is," they said/answered.' [A4.57–58]

Certain other verbs represent specific speech acts: ~*sidi(tu)* 'ask, demand' and *yɨ'ti* 'answer', and these verbs can occur, albeit rarely, in quoted speech constructions. However, when they do, they do not occur by themselves, but must be accompanied by the all-purpose ~*di*, as in (55)–(57) below; it is ~*di* that actually takes the quoted speech complement.

(55) *ã tia ni yɨ'tia tirose'e*
 ~*a=tía   ~dí yɨ'tí*+*a   tí*+*ró-sé'é*
 that's.right say answer+ASSERT.PERF ANPH+SG-CONTR
 '"Right," the other one (the curupira) responded.' [A7.49]

(56) 1 *toa nichɨpɨ hi'na, do'se a'riro mahsɨro tikari chẽ'eni yɨ'tia*
  toá   ~di-chɨ-pɨ   ~hi'da do'sé a'rí+*ró*
  do.again say-SW.REF-LOC EMPH   WH   DEM.PROX+SG

Complex sentences

~basɨ+ro   tí-ka-ri   ~che'é-~dí   yɨ'tí+a
being+SG   ANPH-SUPP-INT   doubt-say   answer+ASSERT.PERF

'When (the curupira) said that, (the man) wondered: "What kind of being can this be?"'

2   yɨ'tiro tirore nia
    yɨ'tí+ro   tí+ró+ré   ~dí+a
    answer+SG   ANPH+SG+OBJ   say+ASSERT.PERF

    'Answering, (the man) said to him (the curupira):'

3   yɨ'ɨkhɨ hiha koiro, nia
    yɨ'ɨ-khɨ   hí-ha   kó-iro   ~dí+a
    1SG-ADD   COP-VIS.IMPERF.1   relative-NOM.SG   say+ASSERT.PERF

    '"I too am your/a relative," (the man) said.' [A7.37–39]

(57)   1   ba'arokãta tirore siniata toa
           ba'á+ro-~ka=ta   tí+ró+ré   ~sidí+a=ta
           do/be.after+SG-DIM=REF   ANPH+SG+OBJ   ask.for+ASSERT.PERF=REF
           toá
           do.again

           'Soon after, (the curupira) asked him (the man) again:'

       2   mɨ'ɨ yahiripho'nare yɨ'ɨre waga, nia
           ~bɨ'ɨ=yahíri~pho'da+re   yɨ'ɨ+ré   wá+gá
           2SG(POSS)= heart+OBJ   1SG+OBJ   give+IMPER
           ~dí+a
           say+ASSERT.PERF

           '"Give me your heart," he said.' (=(49)) [A7.50–51]

11.5   Perfective and causative constructions with *yoa*

Besides occurring in the adverbial constructions described in §11.2.4 and §11.2.5 above, the verb *yoa* is used as a kind of auxiliary in a perfective construction parallel to the construction with =*wa'a* discussed in §8.5.2. There are, however, two interesting differences between these perfective constructions. First, the grammatical subjects of constructions with =*wa'a* have the semantic role of affected patients (the construction specifically indicating a completed change of state), while the subjects in constructions with *yoa* are agentive. Comparing (58) with (59) we see that while all the clauses refer to perfective actions, the subject of the clause with =*wa'a* in (58) is an experiencer, but the subjects in the lines in (59) with *yoa* are agents. Thus, perfective constructions with =*wa'a* and *yoa* occur in semantic complementary distribution. The second difference between these constructions is phonological. In §8.5.2, it is pointed out that =*wa'a* in the perfective construction is undergoing a process of cliticization; it consistently occurs with a low tone and does not form a separate phonological word, whereas all the verbal constituents in constructions with *yoa* retain phonological independence.

(58) *wa'a sɨhka khãriawa'aa*
      wa'á súka   ~kharí+a=wa'a+a
      go   lie.down sleep+AFFEC=go+ASSERT.PERF
      '... he lay down (and) **went to sleep**.' [A7.98]

(59) 1 *to yawɨ'ɨpɨ thuasɨ̃, tirore khatama'are to namonore wa yoaa*
      to=yá-wɨ'ɨ-pɨ   *thuá-~sɨ*   *tí+ró+ré*
      3SG.POSS=POSS-house-LOC return-arrive ANPH+SG+OBJ
      khatá~bá'á+ré   to=~dabó+ro+re   wá
      jacu.bird+OBJ 3SG.POSS=wife+SG+OBJ give
      yoá+a
      do/make+ASSERT.PERF
      '(He) **returned** to his house (and) **gave** the jacú bird to his wife.'

   2 *tirore tikoro sɨ'o chɨada're chɨ yoaa tirore*
      tí+ró+ré   *tí-kó+ró*   *sɨ'ó*   ***chúa-da're chú***
      ANPH+SG+OBJ ANPH-FEM+SG do.together food-prepare eat
      yoá+a   *tí+ró+ré*
      do/make+ASSERT.PERF ANPH+SG+OBJ
      'She **cooked** it (and) **ate** it together with him.' [A7.149–50]

As there are no conjunctions in Kotiria, each clause in a series of chained clauses is represented by an uninflected verbal word, which may be a single root, e.g., *wa* in sentence 1 and *chɨ* in sentence 2 of (59) and in (60) below, two or more serialized roots, e.g., *thua-~sɨ* in sentence 1 of (59), or a verb with an incorporated noun, e.g., *chɨada're* in sentence 2 of (59). In this construction, *yoa* maintains its phonological independence as the last verb in the series, its use underscoring the perfectivity of the sequence. In short, *yoa* occurs as an auxiliary verb in utterances expressing two or more perfective actions performed by the same agentive subject, as is evident in (60)–(61). In such utterances, the order of the sequenced verbs (with the exception of the final inflected verb *yoa*, of course) is iconic, and each uninflected verb in the sequence is realized as an independent phonological word. Here we have a clear example of phonological and semantic independence reflecting and reinforcing each other; at the same time, syntactic unity implying that the same subject is the performer of each of the sequential acts is guaranteed by the the fact that inflection occurs only once,

Complex sentences 375

on the auxiliary verb *yoa* (but see more on chained clauses in §11.6 below).

(60) *tirore nathuaa. tirore do'a chɨ yoara mahsa*
 tí+ró+ré ~*dá-thua+a* *tí+ró+ré*
 ANPH+SG+OBJ get-return+ASSERT.PERF ANPH+SG+OBJ
 do'á chú yoá+ra ~*basá*
 cook eat do/make+VIS.IMPERF.2/3 people
 'People take (dead anteaters they've hunted) home. They/we **cook** (and) **eat** them.' [LSK: Anteaters]

(61) *wɨha soa wihpe yoara*
 wɨhá sóá wipé yoá+ra
 peel grate sieve do/make+VIS.IMPERF.2/3
 '(Women) **peel, grate,** (and) **sieve** (the manioc).' [A1.12]

An interesting related semantic extension of this same construction with *yoa* is to code causation. Sentence 2 of (62) is an example of direct causation, while indirect causation is indicated by *yoa* in dependent clauses that introduce or indicate the consequence or result of a previously completed verbal action. In sentence 3 of (63), for example, the expected result of the elaboration of a storybook in the Kotiria language is that children will remember their own language and writing system, while in (64), a man's spectacular success at hunting using a secret magical stick (sentence 1) leads to his being questioned by suspicious relatives (sentence 2). Such discourse-linking clauses can be glossed as 'so', 'consequently', 'for this reason', or (the gloss most frequently suggested by Kotiria speakers) 'that's why'. The extension of *yoa* to causative situations is not at all surprising when we recall that 'how' and 'why' questions also contain the verb *yoa* (see §11.2.5 and the question in sentence 2 of (64)).

(62) 1 *mɨ'ɨ yahiripho'nare yɨ'ɨre waga nia*
 ~*bɨ'ɨ=yahíri~pho'da+re yɨ'ɨ+ré wá+gá* ~*dí+a*
 2SG(POSS)= heart+OBJ 1SG+OBJ give+IMPER say+ASSERT.PERF
 '"Give me your heart," (the curupira) said.'

 2 *tirose'e mahsɨnose'e kɨa yoaa*
 tí+ró-sé'é ~*basɨ+ro-se'e* ***kɨá***
 ANPH+SG-CONTR man+SG-CONTR be.afraid
 yoá+a
 do/make+ASSERT.PERF
 'That made the man afraid.' [A7.51–52]

(63) 1 *a'rithu hira wa'ikina khiti yaya'urithu*
a'rí-thú   hí+ra   wa'í-~kídá khití
DEM.PROX-CLS:stacked COP+VIS.IMPERF.2/3 animal-PL story
yá-ya'u+ri-thu
POSS-tell+NOM-CLS:stacked
'This is our own (Kotiria) animal storybook.'

2 *sã pho'na bu'eti hira*
~sa=~pho'dá   bu'é-ti   hí+ra
1PL.EXC.POSS=children   study/learn-VBZ COP+VIS.IMPERF.2/3
'It is for our children to study.'

3 *ã yoana, sã kotiria ne bosi sã yahoare durukuare*
~a=yoá-~da   ~sá   kó-ti+ri+a   ~dé bó-sí
so=do-(1/2)PL 1PL.EXC   water-VBZ+NOM+PL NEG forget-NEG. IRR
~sa=yá-hoa+re   dú-ruku+a+re
1PL.EXC.POSS=POSS-write+OBJ   talk-stand+PL+OBJ
'This way, we Kotiria won't forget how to write (and) speak.' (lit.,
   '... our writing and our language') [A8.1–3]

(64) 1 *wa'ikinawãharo wa'aro, tɨre nawa'aka'a, wa'ikina phayɨ wãhaatia*
wa'í-~kídá-~wáhá+ró wa'á+ro   tɨ+re   ~dá-wa'a-ka'a
animal-PL-kill+(3)SG go+(3)SG stick+OBJ   get-go-do.moving
wa'í-~kídá phayɨ ~wahá-ati+a
animal-PL   many   kill-IMPERF+ASSERT.PERF
'When (the man) went hunting, he took the stick along (and) would always kill lots of animals.'

2 *ã ta yoa to koyase'e tirore sinituaatimaa: mɨ'ɨ do'se yoa wãhahari*
~á=ta yoá to=kó-ya-se'e   tí+ró+ré
so=REF do   3SG.POSS=relative-PL-CONTR   ANPH+SG+OBJ
~sidítu+a-ati-~ba+a
ask+PL-IMPERF-FRUS+ASSERT.PERF
~bɨ'ɨ   do'sé   yoá   ~wahá-hari
2SG   WH   do/make   kill-INT.IMPERF
'His relatives, though, were always demanding (unsuccessfully) to know: "How do you kill (so many animals)?"' [A7.155–56]

11.6 Other clauses with sequences of verbs

The previous section examined a construction with the auxiliary verb *yoa* that indicates a series of sequential actions performed by a single, agentive subject. Parallel to the construction with the auxiliary verb *wa'a* (§8.5.2), indicating a perfective change to a new state with an experiencer subject, the construction with *yoa* emphasizes the perfective nature of each action in the sequence that is closed by the *yoa* auxiliary.

Sentences containing similar sequences of verbs, but without the auxiliary *yoa*, occur very frequently in the language—indeed, much more frequently overall than sentences with the *yoa* construction. Just a few examples of such sentences from this chapter are (13), (16), (17), (49), as well as (65)–(72) below. These sentences, which may contain sequences of two or more than two verbs (e.g., (13)), are similar to the *yoa* construction in that all verbal words in the sequence (which may be simple or complex lexical stems) are phonologically independent, and all but the final verbal word are uninflected (though they may be nominalized, as in (71)–(72)). Moreover, much like the *yoa* construction, we find many cases of sequenced verbs that represent a series of perfective actions performed by agentive subjects; however, in contrast to the *yoa* construction, we also see instances of imperatives (71) and progressive actions (72).

The many similarities between chained clauses in sentences with and without *yoa,* taken together with their relative frequencies, suggest that the *yoa* construction is more semantically marked, and that in general, sequences of chained clauses do not require use of the *yoa* auxiliary. Further analysis is needed to determine whether the *yoa* construction has additional semantic characteristics or pragmatic conditioning, or whether it perhaps reflects an older syntactic construction that is gradually falling into disuse.

(65) *tiro ti phɨkoropɨre wi'i sɨ̃'aga*
 tí+ró   ti=phɨk+ó+ró-pɨ́+ré   wi'í
 ANPH+SG 3PL.POSS=parent+FEM+SG-LOC+OBJ arrive
 ~sɨ'á+a
 stick.onto+ASSERT.PERF
 'He **came up** to (and) **stuck onto** their mother.' [A4.31]

(66) *mahata tirokãre wi'i, chɨa*
 ~bahá-ta   tí+ró-~ká+ré   wi'í   chɨ́+a
 go.uphill-come ANPH+SG-DIM+OBJ arrive eat+ASSERT.PERF
 'When they got there, they **went up** to the boy (and) **ate** him.' [A5.40]

(67) *ã yoana noaro wahkɨ̃mahsi duhimahsiha*
 ~a=yoá-~da   ~dóá+ró   ~wakɨ́-~bási̋
 so=do/make-(1/2)PL be.good+SG be.aware-know

duhí-~basi-ha
sit-know-VIS.IMPERF.1

'So (in an airplane), we should **pay close attention** (and) **sit still**.'
(=(3)) [A12.6]

(68) *thɨbaamɨ wihawa'aa diapɨ kotĩaropɨ*

    thú-báá-~bú   wihá-wa'a+a   diá-pɨ
    push-swim-run MOV.outward-go+ASSERT.PERF river-LOC

    kó-~tia+ro-pɨ
    water-current+SG-LOC

    'She **pushed off** (and) **quickly swam out** into the river current.' [A5.35]

(69) *kɨ̃ nɨma ba'aro wi'i ñɨga*

    ~kɨ̃   ~dɨbá ba'á+ro   wi'í   ~yɨ́+á
    one/a day do/be.after+SG arrive see/look+ASSERT.PERF

    'The next day, (the mother) **went home** (and) **saw** (the skin of her dead son).' [A5.41]

(70) *ãta yoa, kɨ̃iro dierokã paritarore, paritarore hiritarore, mɨmɨbu'asɨ̃ thutia*

    ~a=tá yoá ~kú-író   dié+ró-~ká parí-taro+re
    so=REF do/make one/a-NOM.SG dog+SG-DIM form-CLS:lake+OBJ

    parí-taro+re   hí+ri-taro+re
    form-CLS:lake+OBJ COP+NOM-CLS:lake+OBJ

    ~bubú-bu'a-~sɨ   thutí+a
    run-MOV.downward-arrive bark+ASSERT.PERF

    'Meanwhile, one little dog **ran down** to a lake, a lake like this, (and) **barked**.' [A6.13]

(71) *yɨ'ɨre sĩ'ariphĩ sĩ'a, phiti bohkana wa'aga yɨ'ɨre*

    yɨ'ɨ́+ré ~si'á+ri-~phi   ~si'á phití-boka-~da
    1SG+OBJ ignite+NOM-CLS:bladelike ignite COLL-meet-(1/2)PL

    wa'á+ga   yɨ'ɨ́+ré
    go+IMPER 1SG+OBJ

    '"You **light** a torch for me (and) **go meet** me."' [A4.13]

(72) *ã yo tirore wãhatu'sɨ chɨropɨ nia*

    ~a=yó tí+ró+ré   ~wahá-tu'sɨ chú+ro-pɨ
    so=do ANPH+SG+OBJ kill-finish eat+(3)SG-EMPATH

    ~dí+a
    be.PROG+ASSERT.PERF

    'He (the snake) **had just killed** the poor dog (and) **was already eating** it.' (=(45)) [A6.23]

11.7 A summary comparison of multiple-verb constructions

Table 11.1 summarizes the general properties of the different types of multiple-verb constructions in Kotiria: serialized verb constructions (as discussed in §7.5); verbs that take verbal complements, which are in most cases nonfinite nominalized verbs (§11.3); speech verbs and their complements (§11.4) and sequences of independent verbs in chained clauses (§§11.5–11.6).

TABLE 11.1. PROPERTIES OF MULTIPLE-VERB CONSTRUCTIONS

CONSTRUCTION	PHONOLOGY	SEMANTICS	SYNTAX
serialization	• realized as a single PW	• a single, semantically detailed event	• have no markers of subordination • share core arguments • only the final root has inflectional markers
nominalized complement	• the main verb and the complement are realized as separate PWs	• a single conceptual event	• subordinate complements are nominalized by subject-agreement morphology • only the final verb is inflected
verb sequence	• each stem is realized as a separate PW	• a series of separate, sequential events	• share the same subject • only the final root (which may be an auxiliary verb) has inflectional markers
speech-verb complement	• each verb is a separate PW	• different events	• do not share arguments • both the verb in the complement clause and the final speech verb are fully inflected

NOTE: PW = phonological word.

Appendix 1: Texts

Oral narratives

The seven oral narratives included in this appendix were all collected during the first years of my work on Kotiria and constitute an integral element of my analysis of the language. The narratives were told by my consultants Mateus Cabral (texts 1–3), his older brother Ricardo Cabral (texts 6 and 7), and another older gentleman originally from a neighboring village, Agostinho Ferraz (texts 4 and 5). The first three narratives were recorded in the United States, where my work with Mateus Cabral began. The others were recorded in São Gabriel da Cachoeira: Ricardo's texts at the home of his sister, Emilia, and Agostinho's texts at his own home. With the exception of Mateus's narratives, there were always other family members present for the story-telling and the choice of narrative was always left completely up to the speaker. The initial transcription and analysis of each narrative was done together with the original speakers (and often with input from other family members); the title for each narrative was provided by the narrator.

Mateus (who spent a good part of his life as a youngster in boarding school and did not have the opportunity to learn many traditional stories from his elders) chose to relate personal experiences and facts about life among the Kotiria, while both Ricardo and Agostinho chose to tell the kinds of traditional stories passed down from generation to generation. Although I did not realize it at first, this was fortunate for my analysis, since different kinds of linguistic structures appear in each genre and contrasts quickly became apparent.

The narratives included in this appendix represent only a fraction of the oral literature recorded and analyzed since my work with the Kotiria began (as of 2011, the Kotiria archive of oral literature and examples other of natural speech genres contains over sixty annotated recordings).[1] But I will always consider these particular stories to be special. Not only were they offered by speakers who are very dear to me, but they represent my port of entry into the Kotiria language and culture. Far beyond the rich linguistic information contained in each

---

[1] These recordings have been deposited both at the Endangered Language Archive at the School of Oriental and African Studies, University of London, and at the Archive of the Indigenous Languages Documentation Project, FUNAI, in Rio de Janeiro; they will be available for consultation from 2012 on.

narrative (many aspects of which still remain to be explored), each story also provides a wealth of cultural information and knowledge, a window through which we catch fascinating glimpses of the life and thinking of the Kotiria people.[2]

1. The Kotiria Study Book

This is the first of three short personal narratives told by Mateus Cabral, a speaker in his early thirties with whom I worked when he was living in the U.S. I find the title Mateus gave to the narrative uncannily appropriate because it reflects the fact that Mateus knew I was initiating my study of the language with this narrative; indeed, it was my first real contact with the language in more natural, narrative form. Thus, this short narrative, "The Kotiria Study Book," was in a very real sense the seed of the much expanded Kotiria Study Book that is this grammar. The narrative is a short description of the daily routines of men and women in a Kotiria community. We learn that Kotiria women are responsible for planting and tending the gardens, where, among other things, they grow manioc and pineapples. It is also the women's job to process the manioc, which involves soaking, peeling, grating, extracting its poisonous liquid, toasting it into coarse flour, or baking the meal into flatbread. Kotiria men also help with the process by clearing ground and preparing the gardens for planting, but their main responsibility is fishing.

1.1   *kotiria bu'erithu*

    kó-ti+ri+a   bu'é+ri-thu
    water-VBZ+NOM+PL   study/learn+NOM-CLS:stacked
    'The Kotiria study book'

1.2   *yɨ'ɨ Mo mahkariropɨ hiha.*

    yɨ'ɨ   ~bó   ~baká+ri+ro-pɨ   hí-ha
    1SG   Mõ   village+NOM+SG-LOC   COP-VIS.IMPERF.1
    'I am from Mõ.'[3]

1.3   *ã yoai, yɨ'ɨ õpɨre ta, mipɨre õpɨ yɨ'ɨ hiha.*

    ~a=yoá+i   yɨ'ɨ   ~ó-pɨ+ré   tá
    so/then=do/make+(1/2)MASC 1SG   DEIC.PROX-LOC+OBJ come

    ~bí-pɨ+ré   ~ó-pɨ   yɨ'ɨ   hí-ha
    now-LOC+OBJ   DEIC.PROX-LOC   1SG   COP-VIS.IMPERF.1
    'Then I came here (the United States), (and) now here I am.'

---

[2] For information on the orthography used in the first lines of texts, see §2.10.

[3] *Mõ* is short for the village whose full Kotiria name is *Moa Phoaye* or *Koama Phoaye*, and whose Portuguese name is Carurú Cachoeira.

1.4 *yɨ'ɨ topɨre a'rikorore kristinare ya'uika yɨ'ɨse'e.*
yɨ'ɨ tó-pɨ+re a'rí-kó+ró+ré
1SG REM-LOC+OBJ DEM.PROX-FEM+SG+OBJ
kristína+re ya'ú+i-ka yɨ'ú-se'e
Kristine+OBJ tell+(1/2)MASC-PREDICT 1SG-CONTR
'I'm going to tell this woman Kristine (how it is) there.'

1.5 *mari hiropɨre.*
~bari=hí+ro-pɨ+re
1PL.INC.POSS=COP+SG-LOC+OBJ
'Our way of being/living there.'

1.6 *ã yoai tikorore ya'uika yɨ'ɨse'e.*
~a=yoá+i tí-kó+ró+ré
so/then=do/make+(1/2)MASC ANPH-FEM+SG+OBJ
ya'ú+i-ka yɨ'ú-se'e
tell+(1/2)MASC-PREDICT 1SG-CONTR
'So, I'm going to tell her.'

1.7 *numia, tina chɨare yoara.*
~dubí+a tí-~da chú+a+re yoá+ra
woman+PL ANPH-PL eat+PL+OBJ do/make+VIS.IMPERF.2/3
'(Kotiria) women, they make the food.'

1.8 *ã yoa, tina mɨase'e yo'gaa wa'ara.*
~a=yóá tí-~da ~bú+a-se'e yo'gá+a
so/then=do/make ANPH-PL man+PL-CONTR fish+(3)PL
wa'á+ra
go+VIS.IMPERF.2/3
'(Kotiria) men, they go fishing.'

1.9 *tina bo'reka'arore biato chɨ tu'sɨ numia da'raa wa'ara wehsepɨre.*
tí-~da bo'ré-ka'a+ro+re biátó chú tu'sú
ANPH-PL be.light-do.moving+SG+OBJ pepper/fish.stew eat finish
~dubí+a da'rá+a wa'á+ra wesé-pɨ+re
woman+PL work+(3)PL go+VIS.IMPERF.2/3 garden-LOC+OBJ
'In the morning, after they finish eating breakfast, women go to work in the garden.'

1.10 *ã tina dɨhkɨre toa khanɨre toara.*
~a=tí-~da dukú+ré tóá ~khadú+ré
so=ANPH-PL manioc+OBJ plant sugarcane+OBJ

tóá+rá
plant+VIS.IMPERF.2/3
'They plant manioc (and) sugar cane.'

1.11 *sãre, phayɨ tina da'rara wehsepɨre.*
~saré   phayɨ   tí-~da   da'rá+ra
pineapple many/a.lot ANPH-PL work+VIS.IMPERF.2/3
wesé-pɨ+re
garden-LOC+OBJ
'(And) pineapple . . . they work a lot in the garden.'

1.12 *ã yoa tina thuatapɨ khɨre nathuata, wɨha soa wihpe yoara.*
~a=yoá   tí-~da   thuá-ta-pɨ   khɨ́+re
so=do/make ANPH-PL return-come-LOC manioc+OBJ
~dá-thúá-tá   wɨhá   sóá   wipé yoá+ra
get-return-come peel grate sieve do/make+VIS.IMPERF.2/3
'Then they go back home, taking manioc with them, (and they) peel, grate, (and) sieve it.'

1.13 *ti me're ti wiperiba'ro, tina tɨhpu sɨ'a, sɨ'a tu'sɨ tina nahokhɨrire yoara.*
tí=~be're   ti=wipé+ri=ba'ro   tí-~da   tɨ́pu sɨ'á
ANPH=COM/INST ANPH=sieve+NOM=kind ANPH-PL dry sift
sɨ'á tu'sɨ́ tí-~da   ~dahó-khɨ́+rí+ré
sift finish ANPH-PL flatbread-manioc+PL+OBJ
yoá+ra
do/make+VIS.IMPERF.2/3
'They dry (and) sift the stuff that's left after sieving, (and) after sifting it, they make flatbread.'

1.14 *ã yoa ti(na) tu'sɨchɨta, mɨase'e wi'i tina yo'ga sɨina tina natara wa'ire.*
~a=yoa   tí(-~da)   tu'sɨ́-chɨ=ta   ~bɨ́+a-se'e
so/then=do/make ANPH(-PL) finish-SW.REF=REF man+PL-CONTR
wi'í   tí-~da   yo'gá ~sɨ́-~ida   tí-~da
return ANPH-PL fish arrive-NOM.PL ANPH-PL
~dá-ta+ra   wa'í+re
get-come+VIS.IMPERF.2/3 fish+OBJ
'Just when (the women are) finishing, the men return home, bringing fish from their fishing.'

1.15 *mɨase'e tina bo'reka'arore, biato chɨ tu'sɨ tinakhɨ wehsepɨre wa'ara.*

~bɨ+a-se'e   tí-~da   bo'ré-ka'a+ro+re
man+PL-CONTR ANPH-PL be.light-do.moving+SG+OBJ
biátó   chɨ   tu'sɨ   tí-~da-khɨ
pepper/fish.stew eat   finish   ANPH-PL-ADD
wesé-pɨ+re   wa'á+ra
garden-LOC+OBJ go+VIS.IMPERF.2/3

'The men, after eating breakfast, they also go (there) to the garden.'

1.16 *tina wehsepɨre sɨ, yɨkɨrire khãra.*

tí-~da   wesé-pɨ+re   ~sɨ   yɨkɨ+ri+re
ANPH-PL garden-LOC+OBJ arrive tree+PL+OBJ
~khá+ra
chop/cut+VIS.IMPERF.2/3

'When they arrive at the garden, they chop down trees.'

1.17 *tina tha khã yoá+ra wehserire.*

tí-~da   thá   ~khá   yoá+ra   wesé+ri+re
ANPH-PL grass chop/cut do/make+VIS.IMPERF.2/3 garden+PL+OBJ

'(And) they cut down the grass in the gardens.'

1.18 *ti khãriba'aro, tina yoadora hɨ̃ hɨ̃are khãtaboro tina wehsepɨ.*

ti=~khá+ri-ba'a+ro   tí-~da   yoádo+ra
ANPH=chop/cut+NOM-do/be.after+SG ANPH-PL help+VIS.IMPERF.2/3
~hɨ̃   ~hɨ̃+a+re   ~khá-tá-bóró   tí-~da   wesé-pɨ
burn burn+PL+OBJ chop/cut-come-separate ANPH-PL garden-LOC

'After chopping down (the trees), they help burn (and) chop up the charred (trees) in the garden.'

1.19 *da'ratu'sɨ tina thuataa.*

da'rá-tu'sɨ   tí-~da   thuá-ta+a
work-finish ANPH-PL return-come+ASSERT.PERF

'As soon as they're done working, they return home.'

1.20 *wi'i, tina yo'gaa wa'ara.*

wi'í   tí-~da   yo'gá+a   wa'á+ra
arrive ANPH-PL fish+(3)PL go+VIS.IMPERF.2/3

'When they get home, they go fishing.'

1.21 *yo'gawa'a, no'opena ti wa'i wãhainare nata tina wara numiare.*

yo'gá-wa'a   ~do'ó-pé-~dá   ti=wa'i   ~wahá-~ida+re
fish-go   WH-CQUANT-PL 3PL.POSS=fish kill-NOM.PL+OBJ

~dá-ta   tí-~da   wá+ra   ~dubí+a+re
get-come   ANPH-PL   give+VIS.IMPERF.2/3 woman+PL+OBJ

'They go fishing, and whatever their catch (is), they bring (it) back (and) give (it) to the women.'

1.22 numiase'e ña'a wa'ire do'a, ti tu'sʉriba'aro tina chʉ yoara.

~dubí+a-se'e   ~ya'á   wa'í+ré   do'á
woman+PL-CONTR   get.with.hand   fish+OBJ   cook

ti=tu'sʉ́+ri-ba'a+ro   tí-~da   chʉ́
ANPH=finish+NOM-do/be.after+SG   ANPH-PL   eat

yoá+ra
do/make+VIS.IMPERF.2/3

'The women take the fish and cook (it, and) afterwards, they eat.'

1.23 chʉ tu'sʉ, tina khãria wa'ara te panʉmapʉ tina hira.

chʉ́ tu'sʉ́   tí-~da   ~kharí+a=wa'a+ra
eat finish ANPH-PL   sleep+AFFEC= go+VIS.IMPERF.2/3

té   pá-~dʉba-pʉ   tí-~da   hí+ra
until   ALT-day-LOC   ANPH-PL   COP+VIS.IMPERF.2/3

'When they're done eating, they go to sleep until the next day.'

2. The Hunting Dog Story

This story recounts an experience from Mateus's childhood. One day when he was a young boy, Mateus and his father were going off to work (in the family's garden plot) accompanied by their dog. The dog killed a small agouti and then ran off into the forest in search of other animals. Suddenly, Mateus and his father heard the sound of the dog being attacked by a jaguar.[4] His father went running in the direction of the sound, but the jaguar had already carried off the dog to eat it. Mateus and his father returned home only with the animal the dog had killed. Saddened by the loss of this beloved hunting dog, the family remained dogless for quite some time.

2.1 diero wa'ikina nʉnʉiro khiti

dié+ró   wa'í-~kídá   ~dʉdú-iro   khití
dog+SG   animal-PL   follow/chase-NOM.SG   story

'The hunting dog story'

2.2 yʉ'ʉ yairo yare ya'uika.

yʉ'ʉ́   yaí+ró   yá+ré   ya'ú+i-ka
1SG   jaguar+SG   POSS+OBJ   tell+(1/2)MASC-PREDICT

'I'm going to tell a jaguar story.'

---

[4] "Dog," Mateus once told me, "is Jaguar's favorite snack."

2.3   yairo dierore to chʉri khitire ya'uika yʉ'ʉ.
      yaí+ró   dié+ró+ré   to=chʉ+ri   khití+re
      jaguar+SG   dog+SG+OBJ   3SG.POSS-eat+NOM   story+OBJ
      ya'ʉ́+i-ka   yʉ'ʉ́
      tell+(1/2)MASC-PREDICT   1SG
      'I'm going to tell a jaguar-eating-the-dog story.'

2.4   ã yoana sãse'e bo'reka'arore sã da'rana wa'achʉ,
      ~a=yoá-~dá   ~sá-se'e
      so/then=do/make-(1/2)PL   1PL.EXC-CONTR
      bo'ré-ka'a+ro+re   ~sa=da'rá-~da   wa'á-chʉ
      be.light-do.moving+SG+OBJ   1PL.EXC.POSS=work-(1/2)PL go-SW.REF
      'So, (once) while we were going to our work in the morning . . .'

2.5   yʉ phʉkʉ me're wa'ai da'rana wa'ana,
      yʉ=phʉk+ʉ́=~be're   wa'á+i   da'rá-~da
      1SG=parent+MASC=COM/INST   go+VIS.PERF.1   work-(1/2)PL
      wa'á-~da
      go-(1/2)PL
      '(I) with my father going to work . . .'

2.6   ã yoa dierose'e wa'ikirore nʉnʉro nire.
      ~a=yoá   dié+ró-sé'é   wa'í-kíró+ré   ~dʉdʉ́+ro
      so/then=do/make   dog+SG-CONTR   animal+SG+OBJ   chase+(3)SG
      ~dí+re
      be.PROG+VIS.PERF.2/3
      'then (our) dog was chasing after an animal.'

2.7   to yairo chʉto phanore tiro bohso wãha yoare.
      tó   yaí+ró   chʉ   to=~phadó+re   tí+ró   bosó
      DEF   jaguar+SG   eat   REM=do/be.before+OBJ   ANPH+SG   agouti
      ~wahá   yoá+re
      kill   do/make+VIS.PERF.2/3
      'Before the jaguar ate (him), (the dog had) hunted down an agouti.'

2.8   ã yoa tu'sʉ, pairore nʉnʉ wãharo, toi yairose'e tirore nʉnʉti ña'aro
      koatare.
      ~a=yoá   tu'sʉ́   pá-iro+re   ~dʉdʉ́   ~wahá+ro
      so=do   finish   ALT-NOM.SG+OBJ   follow/chase   kill+(3)SG
      to+i   yaí+ró-sé'é   tí+ró+ré   ~dʉdʉ́-ati
      REM+LOC   jaguar+SG-CONTR   ANPH+SG+OBJ   follow/chase-IMPERF

~ya'á+ro koá-ta+re
catch+(3)SG NONVIS-come+VIS.PERF.2/3
'Afterwards, while (the dog was) chasing after another animal out there, a jaguar caught him.'

2.9 *sã yoaropɨ, yɨ phɨkɨ me're thɨ'oi.*
~sá yoá+ro-pɨ yɨ=phɨk+ɨ́=~be're
1PL.EXC be.far+SG-LOC 1SG=parent+MASC=COM/INST
thɨ'ó+i
hear+VIS.PERF.1
'We, from far away, (I) with my father, heard (the sounds).'

2.10 *ã yoa ñɨna, yɨ phɨkɨ toaro me're wa'a ñɨro wa'are dierore.*
~a=yoá ~yɨ́-~dá yɨ=phɨk+ɨ́
so/then=do/make see/realize-(1/2)PL 1SG.POSS=parent+MASC
toá+ro=~be're wa'á ~yɨ+ró wa'á+re
be.fast+SG=COM/INST go see/look+(3)SG go+VIS.PERF.2/3
dié+ró+ré
dog+SG+OBJ
'When we realized (what had happened), my father quickly went to look for the dog.'

2.11 *ã yoa yairose'e tirore nawa'aka'a wa'are chɨro wa'aro.*
~a =yoá yaí+ró-sé'é tí+ró+ré
so/then=do/make jaguar+SG-CONTR ANPH+SG+OBJ
~dá-wa'a-ka'a wa'á+re chɨ́+ro wa'á+ro
get-go-do.moving go+VIS.PERF.2/3 eat+(3)SG go+(3)SG
'But the jaguar (killed and) took (the dog) away to eat it.'

2.12 *ã yoana sã diero me'reraina thuahãkɨrɨ yoaripa.*
~a=yoá-~da ~sá dié+ró=~be'r(e)-éra-~ida
so/then=do/make-(1/2)PL 1PL.EXC dog+SG=COM/INST-NEG-NOM.PL
thuá-~ha-kɨrɨ yoá+rí-pá
return-TERM-ADVERS be.long+NOM-CLS:time
'Then we sadly remained dogless for a long time.'

2.13 *to wa'ikiro wãhariroditare sã nathuai wɨ'ɨpɨre.*
to=wa'í-kíró ~wahá+ri-ro-dita+re ~sá
DEF=animal+SG kill+NOM+SG-SOL+OBJ 1PL.EXC
~dá-thúá+i wɨ'ɨ́-pɨ́+ré
get-return+VIS.PERF.1 house-LOC+OBJ
'We took home only the dead animal (that the dog had hunted).'

3. The Celebration Day Story

In this text, Mateus describes what happens at typical gatherings for festivals in his village. First, friends from the neighboring villages of *Mahaphoa* 'Arara Cachoeira' and *Khanako* 'Ilha de Inambú' (both close by, slightly downriver) arrive and gather in the chapel. After prayers, people take the food they have brought into the longhouse and all join in a communal meal. After the meal, people sit around and talk and later, there is music and dancing, accompanied by a traditional drink, caxiri beer, made from fermented manioc liquid. Men play pan flutes and other instruments and the dancing, drinking, and conversation go on throughout the night.[5] Mateus tells us that he will never forget those festivals, and laments that his going away to boarding school as a child prevented him from learning how to play the flute and dance the traditional dances. "If I ever went back," he says, "I would also learn."

3.1   *soadahchori khiti*

     soá-dacho+ri   khití
     rest-day+NOM story

     'The celebration day story'

3.2   *yʉ soanʉmarire yʉ'ʉ hiropʉre,*

     yʉ=soá-~dʉba+ri+re   yʉ'ʉ=hí+ro-pʉ+re
     1SG.POSS=rest-day+PL+OBJ 1SG(POSS)=COP+SG-LOC+OBJ

     'On my special (resting) days, where I lived . . .'

3.3   *yʉ me'remahkinare yʉ'ʉ ñʉtinii wa'atii.*

     yʉ=~be'ré-~baka-~ida+re   yʉ'ʉ ~yʉ-~tídí+i
     1SG.POSS=COM/INST-village-NOM.PL+OBJ 1SG   see-visit+(1/2)MASC

     wa'á-ati+i
     go-IMPERF+VIS.PERF.1

     'I used to go (travel) in order to see (visit) my friends.'

---

[5] I have witnessed a number of such festivals, and the events proceed exactly as Mateus recalls and are quite interesting. The Kotiria are extremely proud of their traditional dances and songs, which are accompanied by pan pipes and other types of flutes, as well as some rhythmic instruments. Most traditional dances comprise several parts, some of which are performed while it is still light and others only after dark. There is always a main group of male dancers who wear traditional feathered headdresses and other types of adornments, and both men and women paint themselves using traditional red and black paints. Women join the dances at appointed times, and one woman accompanies the male dancers, encouraging them with her call. In between parts of the traditional dances, there are other dances to pan pipes, and all (even visiting linguists) are enthusiastically encouraged to participate.

3.4 yɨ me'remahkinase'e ñahpibapɨ hira.
yɨ=~be'ré-~baka-~ida-se'e ~yapíba-pɨ
1SG.POSS=COM/INST-village-NOM.PL-CONTR Ñapima-LOC
hí+ra
COP+VIS.IMPERF.2/3
'(Some of) my friends live in Ñapima (Jutica, upriver).'

3.5 pabɨ'se dohkare hira mahaphoa mahkaina khanako mahkaina.
pá-bɨ'se doká-ré hí+ra
ALT-side below-CLS:generic COP+VIS.IMPERF.2/3
~baháphóá ~baká-~ídá ~khádákó ~baká-~ídá
Mahaphoa village-NOM.PL Khanako village-NOM.PL
'The downriver ones (friends) are Mahaphoa (Arara Cachoeira) (and) Khanako (Ilha de Inambú) villagers.'

3.6 tinare ñɨi wa'atii yɨ'ɨ ya mahkapɨ hii.
tí-~da+re ~yɨ́+í wa'á-ati+i
ANPH-PL+OBJ visit+(1/2)MASC go-IMPERF+VIS.PERF.1
yɨ=yá-~báká-pɨ hí+i
1SG.POSS=POSS-village-LOC COP+(1/2)MASC
'They are the ones I used to go see when I lived in my village.'

3.7 topɨre tina ti phiri bahsadahchorire yoaa.
tó-pɨ+re tí-~da ti=phí+ri
REM-LOC+OBJ ANPH-PL 3PL.POSS=be.big+NOM
basá-dacho+ri+re yoá+a
sing/dance-day+PL+OBJ do/make+ASSERT.PERF
'There (wherever) they had their big ceremonies.' (basá-dacho 'ceremony', lit., 'dancing day')

3.8 mipɨkãre yoasinira.
~bí-pɨ́-~ká+ré yoá-~sidi+ra
now-LOC-DIM+OBJ do/make-do.yet/still+VIS.IMPERF.2/3
'Nowadays, they still do that.'

3.9 ã yoa tina kha'maphitibohka chɨ ñobo'e wa'a yoara.
~a=yoá tí-~da ~kha'bá-phítí-bóká chɨ ~yó-bo'e wa'á
so=do/make ANPH-PL do.RECIP-COLL-meet eat show-pray go
yoá+ra
do+VIS.IMPERF.2/3
'They get together to eat (and) pray.'

3.10 *ti ñobo'e wa'a, wihatu'sʉ tina chʉara.*
 ti=~yó-bo'e   wa'á wihá-tu'sʉ   tí-~da
 3PL.POSS=show-pray go   MOV.outward-finish   ANPH-PL
 chʉ́+ra
 eat+VIS.IMPERF.2/3
 'After their prayers when they all go out (of the chapel), they eat.'

3.11 *phayʉ mahsa kha'machʉ ti phiri wʉ'ʉpʉ.*
 phayʉ́ ~basá   ~kha'bá-chʉ   ti=phí+ri-wʉ'ú-pʉ
 many   people do.RECIP-eat   ANPH=be.big+NOM-house-LOC
 'People eat together in the longhouse.'

3.12 *hiphitiro chʉa natara.*
 hí-phiti+ro   chʉa ~dá-ta+ra
 COP-COLL+SG   food get-come+VIS.IMPERF.2/3
 'Everyone brings a lot of food.'

3.13 *tina nasã chʉare chʉ yoara.*
 tí-~da   ~dá-~sá   chʉa+re   chʉ́ yoá+ra
 ANPH-PL   get-MOV.inside   food+OBJ   eat do/make+VIS.IMPERF.2/3
 'They take the food inside (and) eat.'

3.14 *chʉ tu'sʉ tina duhisʉ̃ durukuduhi,*
 chʉ́ tu'sʉ́   tí-~da   duhí-~sʉ   dú-rúkú-dúhi
 eat finish ANPH-PL   sit-arrive   speak-stand-sit
 'As soon as they're done eating, they sit around conversing . . .'

3.15 *si'niare tina si'ni bahsa karisure phuti yoara.*
 ~si'día+re   tí-~da   ~si'dí basá   karísu+re
 caxiri.beer+OBJ   ANPH-PL   drink   sing/dance   pan.flute+OBJ
 phutí   yoá+ra
 blow/play   do/make+VIS.IMPERF.2/3
 'They drink drinks (caxiri beer and other fermented liquids), dance (and) play the flute.'

3.16 *tire yʉ'ʉ mipʉre ne boerasinika.*
 tí+re   yʉ'ʉ́   ~bí-pʉ́+ré   ~dé
 ANPH+OBJ   1SG   now-LOC+OBJ   NEG
 bo-éra-~sidi-ka
 forget-NEG-do.yet/still-ASSERT.IMPERF
 'That I have never forgotten.'

3.17 *tire, yʉ'ʉ patere wãhkuatii.*
  tí+re yʉ'ʉ pá-te+re ~wakú-átí+í
  ANPH+OBJ 1SG ALT-CLS:time+OBJ remember-IMPERF+VIS.PERF.1
  'That, I remember (think about) sometimes.'

3.18 *yʉ'ʉse'e bu'ewa'a yoatii hi'na.*
  yʉ'ʉ-se'e bu'é-wa'a yoá-ati+i ~hí'da
  1SG-CONTR study/learn-go do/make-IMPERF+VIS.PERF.1 EMPH
  '(But) I was always going away to study.'

3.19 *yʉ'ʉse'e phayʉwarore ti bahsaba'rore, karisu phutiaba'rore mahsierai.*
  yʉ'ʉ-se'e phayú-wáró+ré ti=basá=ba'ro+re
  1SG-CONTR many/a.lot-EMPH+OBJ ANPH=sing/dance=kind+OBJ
  karísu phutí+a=ba'ro+re ~basi-éra+i
  flute blow/play+PL=kind+OBJ know-NEG+VIS.PERF.1
  '(Unlike the others) I didn't know hardly any of those kinds of dances (and) flute-playing.'

3.20 *yʉ'ʉ boerakʉrʉ tire.*
  yʉ'ʉ bo-éra-kʉrʉ tí+re
  1SG forget-NEG-ADVERS ANPH+OBJ
  'I've forgotten them (unfortunately).'

3.21 *yʉ me'remahkinase'e tina yoaripa hia.*
  yʉ=~be'ré-~baka-~ida-se'e tí-~da
  1SG.POSS=COM/INST-village-NOM.PL-CONTR ANPH-PL
  yoá+rí-pá hí+a
  be.long+NOM- CLS:time COP+ASSERT.PERF
  'But my friends have stayed there all this long time.'

3.22 *tina karisu phutimahsi,*
  tí-~da karísu phutí-~basi
  ANPH-PL flute blow/play-know
  'They can (know how to) play the flute . . .'

3.23 *tina bʉhkʉna bahsakãre bahsamahsi yoara.*
  tí-~da bʉk+ʉ́-~da basá-~ka+re basá-~basi
  ANPH-PL elder+MASC-PL sing/dance-DIM+OBJ sing/dance-know
  yoá+ra
  do/make+VIS.IMPERF.2/3
  '(and) dance traditional (ancestor) dances.'

3.24   *pate ni yɨ'ɨ thuakɨ, yɨ'ɨkhɨ yɨ'ɨ bu'eboka.*

pá-te   ~dí   yɨ'ɨ   thuá-kɨ   yɨ'ɨ-khɨ   yɨ'ɨ
ALT-CLS:time   say   1SG   return-(1/2)MASC   1SG-ADD   1SG

bu'é-bo-ka
study/learn-DUB-ASSERT.IMPERF

'If I ever went back, I would also learn.'

4. In the Olden Days There Were People-Stealers

This is one of two texts told by Agostinho Ferraz, a man in his fifties originally from the village of Arara Cachoeira and currently living with his family in São Gabriel. This narrative is an example of a more traditional genre of stories that describe norms of appropriate behavior and warn listeners of the negative consequences that can come about when people are careless. He begins by telling us that there used to be a kind of evil being that would steal people and take them away into the forest to eat them. Once, a man decided to visit some relatives in a nearby village and told his sons that he would probably be returning around the time of the first crow of the cock. Because it would still be dark at that time, he instructs his sons to listen for his call and then meet him on the path with torches. He then goes off to the village, where he spends the night drinking and dancing, completely unconcerned about his family. In the meantime, at the appointed hour, the sons hear a call and, presuming it to be their father, go to meet him with torches. Their mother, following them along the trail, is overtaken by an evil being with a sticky body, who embraces and glues her onto him, carrying her off into the forest. The boys follow them until the being enters the great hollow log where it lives. The boys then run off to find their father and tell him what happened. When he hears the news, he goes raging to the log, which is buzzing with the sound of the many evil creatures living inside. He searches for his wife to no avail and they realize she is still inside. So the man and his sons decide to make a fire to force the beings out. As each one comes out, they strike and kill it. Finally, the sticky being comes out with the woman still attached, but her flesh has melted and she is dying. "That is how people used to lose their families," Agostinho concludes. People should be careful of what they say because evil beings can eavesdrop on people's plans and come at the appointed time to trick them.

4.1   *phanopɨre hiatiga mahsayahkaina.*

~phadó-pɨ+re   hí-ati+a
do/be.before-LOC+OBJ   COP-IMPERF+ASSERT.PERF

   ~basá-yáká-~ídá
   people-steal-NOM.PL
   'In the olden days there were people-stealers'

4.2 *kũiro hiatiga phanopʉ, diamini to phanopʉ.*
   ~kʉ́-író hí-ati+a   ~phadó-pʉ
   one/a-NOM.SG COP-IMPERF+ASSERT.PERF do/be.before-LOC
   diá-~bídí to=~phadó-pʉ
   river-high.water DEF=do/be.before-LOC
   'There was once a man, long ago (before) the flood.'[6]

4.3 *phanopʉ tipapʉre phayʉ yahkaina hiatiga.*[7]
   ~phadó-pʉ   tí-pá-pʉ́+ré   phayʉ́ yaká-~ídá
   do/be.before-LOC ANPH-CLS:time-LOC+OBJ many steal-NOM.PL
   hí-ati+a
   COP-IMPERF+ASSERT.PERF
   'In those olden times, there were many people-stealers.'

4.4 *familiare wehsewa'ainare no'oi wa'ainare yahka, nawa'aka'aa te mahkarokapʉre.*
   familia+re wesé-wa'a-~ida+re ~do'ó+i wa'á-~ida+re
   family[B][8]+OBJ garden-go-NOM.PL+OBJ WH+LOC go-NOM.PL+OBJ
   yaká ~dá-wa'a-ka'a+a   té
   steal get-go-do.moving+ASSERT.PERF all.the.way
   ~baká-róká-pʉ́+ré
   origin-DIST-LOC+OBJ
   'They would steal (kidnap) families going to their gardens (or) people going anywhere (and) carry them off into the jungle.'

4.5 *wãha, wãhaina khõarokaa.*
   ~wahá ~wahá-~ida ~khoá-roka+a
   kill kill-NOM.PL lie-DIST+ASSERT.PERF
   'The murders killed (them and left them) lying off somewhere.'

4.6 *chʉa. chʉnokaa.*
   chʉ́+a   chʉ́-~doka+a
   eat+ASSERT.PERF eat-COMPL+ASSERT.PERF
   '(Or) they ate (them); ate (them) all up.'

---

[6] An example of a Biblical reference that has made its way into a traditional story.

[7] For this speaker, pronunciation of the perfective assertion suffix varies between +*a* and +*ga*. He is the only speaker I worked with who presented this variation, which has been preserved in the first lines of examples. The morphemically analyzed line, however, reflects the common underlying form +*a*.

[8] The notation "[B]" indicates a word borrowed from Portuguese.

4.7   ne mahsi to mahsieratiga.
      ~dé   ~basi to=~basi-era-ati+a
      NEG   know   3SG.POSS=know-NEG-IMPERF+ASSERT.PERF
      'We never knew what had happened to them.'

4.8   kɨta kɨ familia pasitiopɨ pa tokoyaka'apɨtini na'iro wa'aga
      ~kɨ́=ta   ~kɨ́   familia   pá-sitio-pɨ   pá
      one=REF   one   family[B] ALT-village[B]-LOC ALT
      to=kó-ya-ka'a-pɨ   ~tidí   ~da'í+ro   wa'á+a
      3SG.POSS=relative-PL-near-LOC visit   be.dark+SG go+ASSERT.PERF
      'Once a family went to visit their close relatives' village in the late afternoon.'

4.9   tiro to pho'na me're khɨariro to pho'nare ya'uga, to namonore hiphitina ya'ua:
      tí+ró   to=~pho'dá=~be're   khɨá+ri+ro
      ANPH+SG   3SG.POSS=children=COM/INST have-NOM+SG
      to=~pho'dá+re   ya'ɨ́+a   to=~dabó+ro+re
      3SG.POSS=children+OBJ tell+ASSERT.PERF 3SG.POSS=wife+SG+OBJ
      hí-phiti-~da   ya'ɨ́+a
      COP-COLL-PL   tell+ASSERT.PERF
      'The man, who had a family, told his children, his wife, (and) everyone:'

4.10 yɨ'ɨ sõ'opɨ tinikɨ wa'aha koyaka'apɨ.
      yɨ'ɨ́   ~so'ó-pɨ́   ~tidí-kɨ   wa'á-ha
      1SG   DEIC.DIST-LOC visit-(1/2)MASC   go-VIS.IMPERF.1
      kó-ya-ka'a-pɨ
      relative-PL-near-LOC
      '"I'm going to visit (our) relatives' (village)."'

4.11 pate karaka duripa yɨ'ɨ thuakɨka.
      pá-te   káráká   dú+ri-pa   yɨ'ɨ́
      ALT-CLS:time   rooster speak+NOM-CLS:time   1SG
      thuá-kɨ-ka
      return-(1/2)MASC-PREDICT
      '"I'll probably come back at the first crow of the cock."'[9]

4.12 sõ'o waroi hikɨ, pihsukɨka na'inokai.
      ~so'ó   wáró+í   hí-kɨ   pisú-kɨ́-ká
      DEIC.DIST   EMPH+LOC   COP-(1/2)MASC   call-(1/2)MASC-PREDICT

---

[9] According to the Kotiria daily time system, around three in the morning.

~da'í-~doka+i
be.dark-COMPL+LOC
"'When I'm right over there, I'll call in the dark.'"

4.13 yʉ'ʉre sĩ'ariphĩ sĩ'a, phiti bohkana wa'aga yʉ'ʉre.
yʉ'ʉ́+ré   ~si'á+ri-~phi   ~si'á   phití-boka-~da
1SG+OBJ ignite+NOM-CLS:bladelike ignite COLL-meet-(1/2)PL
wa'á+ga   yʉ'ʉ́+ré
go+IMPER   1SG+OBJ
"'You light a torch for me, (and) go meet me.'"

4.14 ãyo õpʉre yʉ'ʉ kho'awi'ikʉka, nia.
~a=yó ~ó-pʉ́+ré   yʉ'ʉ́ kho'á-wi'i-kʉ-ka
so=do DEIC.PROX-LOC+OBJ 1SG   return-arrive-(1/2)MASC-PREDICT
~dí+a
say+ASSERT.PERF
'"That's how I'll get back here," he said.'

4.15 tina khãria ñamichawa'achʉ, ti sa'sero, ti phʉkoro khãri, tiro ti phʉkʉro topʉ wa'a to koya me're.
tí-~da   ~kharí+a   ~yabícha-wa'a-chʉ   ti=sa'sé+ró
ANPH-PL sleep+(3)PL night-go-SW.REF   ANPH=be.alone+SG
ti=phʉk+ó+ró   ~kharí tí+ró
3PL.POSS=parent+FEM+SG sleep   ANPH+SG
ti=phʉk+ʉ́+ró   tó-pʉ   wa'á
3PL.POSS=parent+MASC+SG REM-LOC go
to=kó-ya=~be're
3SG.POSS=relative-PL=COM/INST
'Going to sleep when night came, alone with their mother, their father went off with his relatives . . .'

4.16 si'nia bohkasũ, si'nikhã'aa.
~si'día   boká-~sʉ   ~si'dí-~kha'a+a
caxiri.beer find-arrive drink-dream+ASSERT.PERF
'He found caxiri beer there (and) got drunk.'

4.17 ne ahikʉ nieraa topʉ.
~dé   ahí-kʉ   ~di-éra+a   tó-pʉ
NEG be.concerned-(1/2)MASC be.PROG-NEG+ASSERT.PERF REM-LOC
'He was there, concerned about nothing/no one.'

4.18 *bo'retoaa topʉ.*
  bo'ré-toa+a   tó-pʉ
  be.light-be.fast+ASSERT.PERF REM-LOC
  '(He was) there at dawn.' (*bo'retoa* 'to become morning')

4.19 *to khĩ'ori ora karaka duripa, topʉ pihsutaa ñami kʉ̃ta karaka duripa.*
  tó   ~khi'ó+ri   óra   káráká dú+ri-pa
  DEF   be.arranged+NOM hour[B] rooster speak+NOM- CLS:time
  tó-pʉ   pisú-ta+a   ~yabí ~kʉ́=ta   káráká
  REM-LOC call-come+ASSERT.PERF   night one=REF rooster
  dú+ri-pa
  speak+NOM-CLS:time
  'At the appointed cock-crowing hour, (from) that place came a call, at the first nighttime crowing hour.'

4.20 *kʉ̃iro to mahkʉro bʉhkʉrokurero thʉ'oga.*
  ~kʉ́-iró   to=~bak+ʉ́+ró   bʉk+ʉ́+ro-kure+ro
  one-NOM.SG   3SG.POSS=child+MASC+SG elder+MASC+SG-COMP+SG
  thʉ'ó+a
  hear+ASSERT.PERF
  'One of his sons, the oldest, heard it.'

4.21 *thʉ'o to koyare wã'ko, ti phʉkorore wã'koa.*
  thʉ'ó to=kó-ya+re   ~wa'kó
  hear   3SG.POSS=relative-PL+OBJ wake
  ti=phʉk+ó+ró+ré   ~wa'kó+a
  3PL.POSS=parent+FEM+SG+OBJ   wake+ASSERT.PERF
  'He heard (it), woke his brothers (and) woke their mother.'

4.22 *mari phʉkʉ tatu'sʉro koataka.*
  ~bari=phʉk+ʉ́   tá-tú'sʉ+ró
  1PL.INC.POSS=parent+MASC come-finish+(3)SG
  koá-ta-ka
  NONVIS-come-ASSERT.IMPERF
  '"Our father's just come (to the meeting place)."'

4.23 *marire sõ'oi sĩ'a phitibohka du'tire.*
  ~barí+ré   ~so'ó+i   ~si'á phiti-boka   du'tí+ré
  1PL.INC+OBJ   DEIC.DIST+LOC   torch   COLL-meet   request+VIS.PERF.2/3
  '"He asked us to meet him there with torches."'

4.24 sã sĩ'a phitibohkana, ni.

~sa=~si'á   phití-boka-~da   ~dí
1PL.EXC.POSS=torch COLL-meet-EXRT say

'"Let's go meet him with our torches," he said.'

4.25 naboroa ti sĩ'ari khɨarire.

~dá-boro+a   ti=~si'á+rí   khɨá+ri+re
get-lower+ASSERT.PERF   ANPH=torch+PL   hold/have+NOM+OBJ

'They took down (from a suspended storage platform) the torches they had.'

4.26 naboro phichaka'apɨ sĩ'aa.

~dá-boro   phichá-ká'á-pɨ   ~si'á+a
get-lower firewood-side-LOC   ignite-ASSERT.IMPERF

'Got them down (and) lit (the ends).'

4.27 pairo ãta, pairo, wa'aga.

pá-iro   ~á=ta   pá-iro   wa'á+a
ALT-NOM.SG   so/then=REF   ALT-NOM.SG   go+ASSERT.PERF

'(They lit) another (and) another and left.'

4.28 ti phɨkoro ti ba'aro ti ma'aro wa'a, ti yoaroi tiro tinare ko'taga hi'na.

ti=phɨk+ó+ró   ti=ba'a+ro   ti=~ba'a+ro
3PL.POSS=parent+FEM+SG   ANPH=do/be.after+SG   ANPH=path+SG

wa'á   ti=yoá+ró+í   tí+ró   tí-~da+re
go   ANPH=be.far+SG+LOC   ANPH+SG   ANPH-PL+OBJ

ko'tá+a   ~hí'da
wait+ASSERT.PERF   EMPH

'Their mother was going after them on the path, and at the place (they had agreed on), he (an evil spirit) was lying in wait for them.'

4.29 ñariro hia.

~yá+ri+ro   hí+a
be.bad+NOM+SG   COP+ASSERT.PERF

'It was an evil being.'

4.30 tiro wãhtiro sɨ̃'ariro hia.

tí+ró   ~watí+ró   ~sɨ'á+ri+ro   hí+a
ANPH+SG   devil+SG   be.sticky+NOM+SG   COP+ASSERT.PERF

'That devil was all sticky.'

4.31 tiro ti phɨkoropɨre wi'i sɨ̃'aga.

tí+ró   ti=phɨk+ó+ró-pɨ+ré   wi'í
ANPH+SG   3PL.POSS=parent+FEM+SG-LOC+OBJ   arrive

~sɨ'á+a
stick.onto+ASSERT.PERF
'He came up to (and) stuck onto their mother.'

4.32 *tikorore kɨ̃ sɨ̃'suroseta yoamɨa.*
tí-kó+ró+ré   ~kɨ́   su'sɨ́+ro-se=ta
ANPH-FEM+SG+OBJ one/a embrace+SG-be.like=REF
yoá-~bɨ+a
do/make-run+ASSERT.PERF
'Quickly, as if he were embracing her.'

4.33 *tikorore sɨ̃'aawa'aga.*
tí-kó+ró+ré   ~sɨ'á=wa'a+a
ANPH-FEM+SG+OBJ stick.on=go+ASSERT.PERF
'He stuck onto her.'

4.34 *hierara. a'riro ñariro hira.*
hi-éra+ra   a'rí+ró   ~yá+ri+ro
COP-NEG+VIS.IMPERF.2/3 DEM.PROX+SG be.bad+NOM+SG
hí+ra
COP+VIS.IMPERF.2/3
'"It's not (our father). It's an evil being."'

4.35 *ne mari phɨkɨ hierara. a'riro wãhtiro hiri hira.*
~dé ~bari=phɨk+ɨ́   hi-éra+ra
NEG 1PL.INC.POSS=parent+MASC COP-NEG+VIS.IMPERF.2/3
a'rí+ró   ~watí+ró hí+ri   hí+ra
DEM.PROX+SG devil+SG COP+NOM(INFER) COP+VIS.IMPERF.2/3
'"It's not our father. This is (it must be) a devil."'

4.36 *tina wa'aga te mahkarokapɨ.*
tí-~da   wa'á+a   té   ~baká-róká-pɨ́
ANPH-PL go+ASSERT.PERF all.the.way origin-DIST-LOC
'They went deep into the forest.'

4.37 *khumu phiri khumu hia.*
~khubú phí+ri   ~khubú hí+a
log   be.big+NOM log   COP+ASSERT.PERF
'There was a great fallen log there.'

4.38 *õ wɨ'ɨ yoarose phiri khumu, ti khumupɨ, tina phosaatiga.*
~ó   wɨ'ɨ́   yoá+ro-se   phí+ri   ~khubú
DEIC.PROX house be.long+SG-be.like be.big+NOM log

ti=~khubú-pɨ   tí-~da   phosá-ati+a
ANPH=log-LOC   ANPH-PL   fill-IMPERF+ASSERT.PERF

'It was like a longhouse, the log, (and) they filled it (they were all living inside it).'

4.39 phayɨ wãhtia no'opuro topɨre hia ti wɨ'ɨpɨ.
      phayɨ́   ~watí+á   ~do'ó-púró   tó-pɨ+re   hí+a
      many   devil+PL   WH-MQUANT   REM-LOC+OBJ   COP+ASSERT.PERF
      ti=wɨ'ɨ́-pɨ́
      ANPH=house-LOC

      'There were all kinds of evil beings in that house.'

4.40 ti khumu phɨ'ichapɨ tina hiatiga.
      ti=~khubú   phɨ'ichá-pɨ   tí-~da   hí-ati+a
      ANPH=log   inside-LOC   ANPH-PL   COP-IMPERF+ASSERT.PERF

      'They were all there inside the log.'

4.41 tina nɨnɨatiga: kũiro wa'mɨatariro, do'kai, pairo, tiaro to pho'na hia.
      tí-~da   ~dɨdɨ́-ati+a   ~kɨ́-író
      ANPH-PL   follow/chase-IMPERF+ASSERT.PERF   one-NOM.SG
      ~wa'búátá+rí+ró   do'kái   pá-iro   tiá+ró
      adolescent.boy+NOM+SG   young.boy   ALT-NOM.SG   three+SG
      to=~pho'dá   hí+a
      3SG.POSS=children   COP+ASSERT.PERF

      'They chased (after their mother): one adolescent, a younger boy (and) another one; her three sons.'

4.42 ti phɨkoro tiro wãhtiro me're sɨ̃'awa'a wa'aa.
      ti=phɨk+ó+ró   tí+ró   ~watí+ró=~be're
      3PL.POSS=parent+FEM+SG   ANPH+SG   devil+SG=COM/INST
      ~sɨ'á-wa'a   wa'á+a
      stick.onto-go   go+ASSERT.PERF

      'Their mother had become stuck onto that devil.'

4.43 chĩpe yoarose, chĩpe yoarose, wĩhtariro hia tiro to pahkɨpɨ.
      ~chípe yoá+ro-se   ~chípe yoá+ro-se
      sap   do/make+SG-be.like   sap   do/make+SG-be.like
      ~wita+ri+ro   hí+a   tí+ró
      be.sticky+NOM+SG   COP+ASSERT.PERF   ANPH+SG
      to=páku-pɨ
      3SG.POSS=body-LOC

      'Like sap, like sap, he was sticky all over his body.'

4.44 ã yo wãhanoka nia tikoro
~a=yó   ~wahá-~doka   ~dí+a   tí-kó+ró
so=do/make kill-COMPL   be.PROG+ASSERT.PERF   ANPH-FEM+SG
'That's why she was dying.'

4.45 ti phɨkorore khã'i nɨnɨatiga te topɨ.
ti=phɨk+ó+ró+ré   ~kha'í   ~dɨdɨ́-áti+á
3PL.POSS=parent+FEM+SG+OBJ   love   follow-IMPERF+ASSERT.PERF
té   tó-pɨ
all.the.way   REM-LOC
'They loved their mother (and) followed after (her) all the way there (to the place the devil had taken her).'

4.46 to sãchɨpɨ ñɨ nɨnɨati, thuataa.
to=~sá-chu-pɨ   ~yɨ́   ~dɨdɨ́-ati
3SG.POSS=MOV.inside-SW.REF-LOC   see/look follow/chase-IMPERF
thuá-ta+a
return-come+ASSERT.PERF
'When they saw him going in (to the hole), they chased after, but then left.'

4.47 ti phɨkɨrore ya'ua wa'aga.
ti=phɨk+ɨ́+ró+ré   ya'ɨ́+a   wa'á+a
3PL.POSS=parent+MASC+SG+OBJ   tell+(3)PL go+ASSERT.PERF
'They went to tell their father.'

4.48 tiro soro khã'aro, nia, to koya me're sõ'o.
tí+ró   só+ro   ~kha'á+ro   ~dí+a
ANPH+SG   be.different+SG dream+(3)SG   be.PROG+ASSERT.PERF
to=kó-ya=~be're   ~so'ó
3SG.POSS=relative-PL=COM/INST DEIC.DIST
'He was off in that other place dreaming (drunk) with his relatives.'

4.49 bo're to wa'aa khã'ara. bo're to ~si'di ~kha'aro ~di'a tiro.
bo'ré   to=wa'á+a   ~kha'á+ra
be.light 3SG.POSS=go+(3)SG   dream+VIS.IMPERF.2/3
bo'ré   to=~si'dí-~kha'a+ro   ~dí+a
be.light 3SG.POSS=drink-dream+(3)SG   be.PROG+ASSERT.PERF
tí+ró
ANPH+SG
'He had been drunk all night (and) he was still drunk in the morning.'

4.50 *tirore topɨ khiti ya'uga.*
 tí+ró+ré   tó-pɨ   khití   ya'ú+a
 ANPH+SG+OBJ REM-LOC   story tell+ASSERT.PERF
 'There they told him the story.'

4.51 *mamaere yoatapɨ wãhtiro sɨ̃'awa'a nawa'are.*
 mamáé+ré   yoá-tá-pɨ   ~watí+ró ~sɨ'á-wa'a
 mother[B]+OBJ be.far=REF-LOC devil+SG be.sticky-go
 ~dá-wa'a+re
 get-go+VIS.PERF.2/3
 '"A devil stuck on mom (and) took (her) away."'

4.52 *mɨ'ɨ sãre ma'ñore.*
 ~bɨ'ɨ   ~sá+re   ~ba'yó+re
 2SG   1PL.EXC+OBJ lie+VIS.PERF.2/3
 '"You lied to us (about when you were coming back)."'

4.53 *mɨ'ɨ ã nierabori hira sãre, ni.*
 ~bɨ'ɨ   ~a=~di-éra-bo+ri   hí+ra
 2SG   so=say-NEG-DUB+NOM(INFER) COP+VIS.IMPERF.2/3
 ~sá+re   ~dí
 1PL.EXC+OBJ say
 '"You didn't call us (but something else did)," they said.'

4.54 *tire thɨ'o, tiro suataa te ti ka'apɨ.*
 tí+ré   thɨ'ó tí+ró   suá-ta+a   té
 ANPH+OBJ hear   ANPH+SG be.angry-come+ASSERT.PERF all.the.way
 ti=ka'á-pɨ
 ANPH=near-LOC
 'When he (the father) heard that, he raged off until he was there by (the log).'

4.55 *wi'i tiro mahkamaa to namono.*
 wi'í   tí+ró   ~baká-~ba+a
 arrive ANPH+SG look/search.for-FRUS+ASSERT.PERF
 to=~dabó+ró
 3SG.POSS=wife+SG
 'When he got there, he looked in vain for his wife.'

4.56 *ne maniaa to namono.*
 ~dé   ~badía+a   to=~dabó+ro
 NEG not.exist+ASSERT.PERF 3SG.POSS=wife+SG
 'His wife wasn't there.'

4.57 *no'oi hiri, nia.*
~do'ó+i hí-ri ~dí+a
WH+LOC COP-INT say+ASSERT.PERF
'"Where is she?" he said/asked.'

4.58 *õi hire, nia.*
~ó+i hí+re ~dí+a
DEIC.PROX-LOC COP+VIS.PERF.2/3 say+ASSERT.PERF
'"Here she is," they said/answered.'

4.59 *wa'a ñua ti khumuwu'rupure.*
wa'á ~yú+á ti=~khubú-wu'ru-pu+re
go see/look+ASSERT.PERF ANPH=log-AUG-LOC+OBJ
'They went (and) looked at the big log.'

4.60 *topu dohparoa yoarose nure sãga tina pe'ri.*
tó-pu dopá+ró+á yoá+ró-sé ~dú-re
REM-LOC bee+SG+PL do/make+SG-be.like buzz-CLS:generic
~sá+a ti-~da pé'ri
be.inside+ASSERT.PERF ANPH-PL all
'There inside all of them were buzzing like bees.'

4.61 *ã yochu ñu, tida do'se yoamahsi mari, a'ria ñarire, ni.*
~a=yó-chu ~yú ti-~da do'sé yoá-~basi
so=do-SW.REF see/look ANPH-PL WH do/make-know
~barí a'rí+á ~yá+ri+re ~dí
1PL.INC DEM.PROX+PL be.bad+NOM+OBJ say
'When they saw that, they said, "What can we do about these evil ones?" they said.'

4.62 *phichaka wĩha, tu duhseroi phichaka wĩha, noaro wa'ba yoa fogo yoaa.*
phichá-ká ~wihá tú dusé+ró+i
firewood-CLS:round set.afire stick mouth+SG-LOC
phichá-ká ~wihá ~dóá+ró wa'bá yoá fogo
firewood-CLS:round set.afire be.good+SG fan do/make fire[B]
yoá+a
do/make+ASSERT.PERF
'They made a fire with sticks at the mouth of the log, a good fire (and) fanned it well.'

4.63 *tinare wĩha phayu huga tipare tina wãhtia.*
ti-~da+re ~wihá phayú ~hú+a
ANPH-PL+OBJ set.afire many burn+ASSERT.PERF

tí-pá+ré   ti-~da   ~watí+á
ANPH-CLS:time+OBJ ANPH-PL devil+PL
'They set fire to them (and) burned many of those devils that day.'

4.64 *painare khã, painare khã, painare khã, painare khã, painare khã, wãhaga.*

pá-~ida+re   ~khá pá-~ida+re   ~khá ...
ALT-NOM.PL+OBJ hit   ALT-NOM.PL+OBJ hit

~wahá+a
kill+ASSERT.PERF

'Others they hit, hit one, hit another [repeated five times], (and) killed.'

4.65 *ti bahtopɨ tikoro wihataga hi'na.*

ti=bató-pɨ   tí-kó+ró   wihá-ta+a
ANPH=be.last-LOC ANPH-FEM+SG MOV.outward-come+ASSERT.PERF

~hí'da
EMPH

'Right at the end, the woman finally came out.'

4.66 *wi'omeheta yariaropɨ nia.*

wi'ó-~behe=ta   yarí+á+ro-pɨ
CONTR-NEG.INTENS=REF die+AFFEC+(3)SG-EMPATH

~dí+a
be.PROG+ASSERT.PERF

'But poor thing, she was already (at the point of) death/dying.'

4.67 *to di'i sɨ'awa'a wa'aga, to kɨhtiropɨ, to pahkɨpɨ.*

to=di'i   ~sɨ'á-wa'a   wa'á+a
3SG.POSS=flesh stick.on-go go+ASSERT.PERF

to=kɨtí+ro-pɨ   to=pakɨ-pɨ
3SG.POSS=chest+SG-LOC 3SG.POSS=body-LOC

'Her flesh had become stuck, onto his (the devil's) chest, onto his body.'

4.68 *ã wa'a to familiare perdeatiga.*

~a=wa'á   to=família+re   perdé-ati+a
so=go   3SG.POSS=family[B]+OBJ lose[B]-IMPERF+ASSERT.PERF

'That's how people used to lose their families.'

4.69 *ñamire pihsuga nichɨ, ti orare wãhtiro pihsutaga.*

~yabí+ré   pisú+gá   ~dí-chɨ   ti=ora+re   ~watí+ró
night+OBJ call+IMPER say-SW.REF ANPH=hour[B]+OBJ devil+SG

pisú-ta+a
call-come+ASSERT.PERF

'If you told (someone) to call at night, a devil called (instead) at that hour.'

4.70   *ã hiatiga diamini to phanopɨre.*

~a=hí-ati+a   diá-~bídí
so=COP-IMPERF+ASSERT.PERF   river-high.water

to=~phadó-pɨ+re
DEF=do/be.before-LOC+OBJ

'That's how it used to be long ago, before the flood.'

5. The Curupira Who Went to the Man's House Wanting to Eat Him

The second story by Agostinho Ferraz tells of a woman who mentions to her husband one morning that she wishes she had a particular kind of fruit to eat. Her husband goes off for the day, leaving the woman and her children at home. Late in the afternoon, a strange family comes to the door carrying a large basket filled with exactly the fruit the woman had been craving. They come in, offering her their gift. However, there is an evil being, a curupira,[10] crouching inside the basket, hidden under a layer of fruit. When the woman reaches into the basket to examine the fruit, her hand grazes the top of the being's head; it is startled and jumps. The woman feels the movement and realizes that something is amiss, so she makes up a story that she needs to fetch water to wash the fruit, gathers her two small children, and makes for the river. On her way out, she grabs a large basin to use as raft for the children. A short distance from the house, she remembers her third child, a young boy who is up on the roof playing at shooting birds with his bow and arrow. She signals to him to join their escape, but he refuses to come down. She warns him that the "visitors" are evil beings who will eat him, but he ignores her. So she has no choice but to leave him behind and hurry to the river, where she puts her little ones into the basin and swims out into the current to escape. Just as she is swimming away, the evil beings run down to the shore, congratulating her on her cleverness. "We would have eaten you," they say. Then they head back to the house to consume the boy who remained behind. The

---

[10] The term "curupira" is borrowed from Língua Geral (Nheengatú) and is used throughout Amazonia. Curupiras are malicious, jungle-dwelling creatures who can take on humanlike form and humanlike characteristics, and who are usually out to do people harm. If people can recognize them in time, however, they can sometimes be tricked into harming themselves or fooled long enough to allow humans to escape.

next morning the woman returns to search for her son, but finds only his empty skin draped over the windowsill.

5.1 *boraro sãwi'ia to yawɨ'ɨpɨ tirore chɨduaro*
    borá+ro   ~sá-wi'i+a
    curupira+SG MOV.inside-arrive+ASSERT.PERF
    to=yá-wɨ'ɨ-pɨ   tí+ró+ré   chú-dua+ro
    3SG.POSS=POSS-house-LOC ANPH+SG+OBJ eat-DESID+(3)SG
    'The curupira who went to the man's house wanting to eat him'

5.2 *kũiro hiatiga to pho'na, namono, hiphitiro.*
    ~kú-író   hí-ati+a   to=~pho'dá   ~dabó+ro
    one/a-NOM.SG COP-IMPERF+ASSERT.PERF 3SG.POSS=children wife+SG
    hí-phiti+ro
    COP-COLL+SG
    'Once there was a man (with) children, a wife, everything.'

5.3 *tikoro, to namono, chɨduaatiga wahsore.*
    tí-kó+ró   to=~dabó+ro   chú-dua-ati+a
    ANPH-FEM+SG 3SG.POSS=wife+SG eat-DESID-IMPERF+ASSERT.PERF
    wasó+ré
    siringa.fruit+OBJ
    'The woman, his wife, wanted to eat (had a craving for) siringa fruit.'

5.4 *yɨ'ɨ wahsore chɨduamaka nia.*
    yɨ'ú   wasó+ré   chú-dua-~ba-ka
    1SG   siringa.fruit+OBJ eat-DESID-FRUS-ASSERT.IMPERF
    ~dí+a
    say+ASSERT.PERF
    '"I wish I had some siringa fruit to eat," she said (to herself).'

5.5 *to a'rire du'timari nihachɨ, to manɨno pase'epɨ wa'aa.*
    to=a'rí+ré   du'tí-~bá+ri   ~dí-~ha-chɨ
    DEF=DEM.PROX+OBJ tell/request-FRUS+NOM   say-TERM-SW.REF
    to=~badú+ro   pá=se'e-pɨ   wa'á+a
    3SG.POSS=husband+SG ALT=CONTR-LOC go+ASSERT.PERF
    'Just after she said that, her husband went off someplace.'

5.6 *às quatro horas da tarde ñamicha, kũ familiase hina wi'iga phɨ'ɨro me're, wahso phɨ'ɨro kũpɨ.*
    às quatro horas da tarde ~yabicha,   ~kú   familia-se
    at four in the afternoon[B] afternoon one/a family[B]-be.like
    hí-~ida   wi'í+á   phɨ'ú+ro=~be're   wasó
    COP-NOM.PL arrive+ASSERT.PERF basket+SG=COM/INST siringa.fruit

       phʉ'ʉ́+ro   ~kʉ́-pʉ
       basket+SG one-CLS:basket

       'At four in the afternoon, a family of beings arrived with a basket, a basket of siringa fruit.'

5.7   *bu'i dahpu so'toi wahso makã du'uphayo.*

       bu'í   dapú so'tó+i   wasó   ~bá-~ká   du'ú-pháyó
       surface head top+LOC   siringa be.small-DIM put-spread.out

       'They had put just a little bit of siringa fruit covering the top of (one being's) head.'

5.8   *tipʉ phu'ichapʉre kʉiro mahsʉnose hiriro boraro ti(na) nirirore kʉ̃iro khõaga.*

       tí-pʉ   phu'ícha-pʉ+re ~kʉ́-író   ~basʉ́+ró-sé
       ANPH-CLS:basket inside-LOC+OBJ one/a-NOM.SG man+SG-be.like

       hí+ri+ro   borá+ro   tí-(~da)   ~dí+ri+ro+re
       COP+NOM+SG   curupira+SG ANPH-PL   say+NOM+SG+OBJ

       ~kʉ́-író   ~khoá+a
       one/a-NOM.SG lie/be.lying+ASSERT.PERF

       'A humanlike being they call a curupira was lying inside that basket.'

5.9   *sãwi'i tikorore hi'na, to mahkʉno kʉ̃iro mʉno, kʉ̃koro numinokã, pairo mʉaropʉ wʉ'ʉpʉ pihsaga.*

       ~sá-wi'i   tí-kó+ró+ré   ~hí'da
       MOV.inside-arrive ANPH-FEM+SG+OBJ EMPH

       to =~bak+ʉ́+ró   ~kʉ́-író ~bʉ́+ro   ~kʉ́-kó+ró
       3SG.POSS=child+MASC+SG one+SG   man+SG   one/a-FEM+SG

       ~dubí+ro-~ka   pá-iro   ~bʉá+ró-pʉ́   wʉ'ʉ́-pʉ́
       female+SG-DIM ALT+SG be.high+SG-LOC house-LOC

       pisá+á
       be.on+ASSERT.PERF

       'They came right up to the woman, her little baby boy and little girl (while) another boy was up on top of the roof.'

5.10   *mʉ'ʉ chʉduare natai.*

       ~bʉ'ʉ=chú-dua+re   ~dá-ta+i
       2SG(POSS)=eat-DESID+OBJ get-come+VIS.PERF.1

       '"We brought what you wanted to eat."'

5.11   *a'ri hira nia.*

       a'rí   hí+ra   ~dí+a
       DEM.PROX COP+VIS.IMPERF.2/3 say+ASSERT.PERF

       '"Here it is," (they) said.'

5.12 *hai. noana nia tikoro.*
      hái   ~dóádá   ~dí+a   tí-kó+ró
      yes   thank.you   say+ASSERT.PERF   ANPH-FEM+SG
      '"Yes, thank you," said the woman.'

5.13 *wahche yoa, tire ña'a du'uda'po, noaka hire nia.*
      waché   yoá   tí+re   ~ya'á   du'ú-da'po
      be.happy do/make   ANPH+OBJ   get.with.hand   put-foot
      ~dóá-~ka   hí+re   ~dí+a
      be.beautiful-DIM   COP+VIS.PERF.2/3   say+ASSERT.PERF
      'Happy, she took it (the basket and) put it down (at her feet); "(These) are beautiful," (she) said.'

5.14 *õse more, mahkamɨ sãma'no to dahpu so'to,*
      ~ó-sé   ~boré   ~baká-~bɨ   ~sá-~ba'do
      DEIC.PROX-be.like   mix   search-run   be.inside-MOV.into
      to=dapú   so'tó
      3SG.POSS=head   top
      'As if she were mixing like this, she reached (into the basket and) grazed) the top (of the curupira's) head . . .'

5.15 *õba'aroi tirore fantasma duraphayoga.*
      ~ó-ba'a+ro+i   tí+ró+ré   fantasma
      DEIC.PROX-do/be.after+SG+LOC   ANPH+SG+OBJ   ghost[B]
      durá-phayo+a
      put.over-spread.out+ASSERT.PERF
      'They had spread (a layer of fruit) over the curupira (inside).'

5.16 *topɨ wãhkuro to duraphayochɨ, tiro kɨamɨa.*
      tó-pɨ   ~wakú+ro   to=durá-phayo-chɨ
      REM-LOC   be.aware+SG   3SG.POSS-put.over-spread.out-SW.REF
      tí+ró   kɨá-~bɨ+a
      ANPH+SG   be.surprised-run+ASSERT.PERF
      'When he felt her reaching into (the layer of fruit), he started.'

5.17 *tikorokhɨ thɨ'omahsimɨa.*
      tí-kó+ró-khɨ   thɨ'ó-~basi-~bɨ+a
      ANPH-FEM+SG-ADD   feel-know-run+ASSERT.PERF
      'She too could feel it right away.'

5.18 *hierara a'rina.*
      hi-éra+ra   a'rí-~idá
      COP-NEG+VIS.IMPERF.2/3   DEM.PROX-NOM.PL
      '"These aren't (people)."'

5.19 *ñaina hira nia.*
~yá-~ida   hí+ra   ~dí+a
be.bad-NOM.PL COP+VIS.IMPERF.2/3 say+ASSERT.PERF
'"They're evil beings," (she) said (to herself).'

5.20 *to mahkʉnokãre nawʉarʉkaga.*
to=~bak+ʉ́+ró-~ká+ré   ~dá-wʉ́á-rʉ́ká+á
3SG.POSS=child+MASC+SG-DIM+OBJ get-carry-begin+ASSERT.PERF
'She picked up (grabbed) her little boy.'

5.21 *pakorokãre tuinakaa.*
pá-ko+ro-~ka+re   tuí-~daka+a
ALT-FEM+SG-DIM+OBJ put.in.front-do/be.together+ASSERT.PERF
'She clasped her (other) little girl to the front (of her body).'

5.22 *pihtamapʉ bu'awa'aga.*
pitá-~ba-pʉ   bu'á-wa'a+a
port-river-LOC go.downhill-go+ASSERT.PERF
'(They) headed down to the river port.'

5.23 *panela phiri panela nanaka wa'awa'aga.*
panela phí+ri   panela ~dá-~daka wa'á-wa'a+a
pot[B] be.big+NOM pot[B] get-do.together go-go+ASSERT.PERF
'Escaping, she grabbed a big pot.'

5.24 *ko'taga. a'rire yʉ'ʉ po'asãati ko nasiniko wa'aha.*
ko'tá+ga   a'rí+ré   yʉ'ʉ́ po'á-~sa-ati   kó
wait+IMPER DEM+OBJ 1SG clean-MOV.inside-IMPERF water
~dá-~sídí-kó   wa'á-ha
get-do.then/now-(1/2)FEM go-VIS.IMPERF.1
'"Wait. I'm going to get some water to wash these (the siringa fruit)."'

5.25 *to ba'aro wihawa'aa.*
to=ba'á+ro   wihá-wa'a+a
REM=do/be.after+SG MOV.outward-go+ASSERT.PERF
'Afterwards, she left.'

5.26 *ma'aro wa'a sõ'oba'aro sʉnoka, to mahkʉrokãre sõ'opʉ.*
~ba'á+ró wa'á ~so'ó-bá'á+ró   ~sʉ́-~doka+a
path+SG go DEIC.DIST-do/be.after arrive-COMPL+ASSERT.PERF
to=~bak+ʉ́+ró-~ká+ré   ~so'ó-pʉ́
3SG.POSS=child+MASC+SG-DIM+OBJ DEIC.DIST-LOC
'Then, just outside (on the path), she went over to her son.'

5.27 *tiro pahpero minichakãre bɨepero nia. bɨaphimaa.*
   tí+ró   papé+ró   ~bidícha-~ka+re   bɨé-pe+ro
   ANPH+SG   play+(3)SG   bird-DIM+OBJ   hunt.with.arrows-FAV+(3)SG
   ~dí+a
   be.PROG+ASSERT.PERF
   bɨáphi-~ba+a
   motion-FRUS+ASSERT.PERF
   'He was (on top of the house) playing at hunting birds. She motioned (to him, to no avail).'

5.28 *sa nimaa wa'awa'a hi'na.*
   sá   ~dí-~ba+a   wa'á-wa'a   ~hí'da
   EXRT   say-FRUS+ASSERT.PERF   go-go   EXRT
   'She urged (in vain) "Let's get out of here!"'

5.29 *ñaina hira.*
   ~yá-~ida   hí+ra
   be.bad-NOM.PL   COP+VIS.IMPERF.2/3
   '"These are evil beings."'

5.30 *mɨ'ɨre chɨri nia.*
   ~bɨ'ɨ́+ré   chú-ri   ~dí+a
   2SG+OBJ   eat-ADMON   say+ASSERT.PERF
   '"Otherwise they'll eat you," she said.'

5.31 *tiro topɨ pihsaga.*
   tí+ró   tó-pɨ   pisá+á
   ANPH+SG   REM-LOC   be.on+ASSERT.PERF
   'He just stayed up there.'

5.32 *soro pahpekɨ niha nia.*
   sóró   papé-kɨ́   ~dí-ha   ~dí+a
   not.now play-(1/2)MASC   be.PROG-VIS.IMPERF.1   say+ASSERT.PERF
   '"Not now. I'm playing," he said.'

5.33 *bu'aa.*
   bu'á+á
   go.downhill+ASSERT.PERF
   'She went down (to the river port).'

5.34 *bu'asɨ̃ tinakãre topɨ pohsaa.*
   bu'á-~sɨ́   tí-~da-~ka+re   tó-pɨ   posá+a
   go.downhill-arrive ANPH-PL-DIM+OBJ   REM-LOC   fill+ASSERT.PERF
   'When she got down (to the port), she put the little ones in (the basin).'

5.35 *thɨbaamɨ wihawa'aa diapɨ kotĩaropɨ.*

thɨ́-báá-~bɨ́   wihá-wa'a+a   diá-pɨ
push-swim-run MOV.outward-go+ASSERT.PERF river-LOC

kó-~tia+ro-pɨ
water-current+SG-LOC

'She pushed off (and) quickly swam out into the river current.'

5.36 *yoerachɨ, ta tina mɨmɨmɨ sɨ̃tu'sɨa.*

yo(a)-éra-chɨ   tá   tí-~da   ~bɨbɨ́-~bɨ
be.long-NEG-SW.REF come ANPH-PL run-run

~sɨ́-tu'sɨ+a
arrive-finish+ASSERT.PERF

'Not long after (she escaped), they (the evil beings) came racing down (to the port).'

5.37 *wãhkumahsiko mɨ'ɨ ñakã du'tira.*

~wakɨ́-~basi-ko   ~bɨ'ɨ́ ~yá-~ka   du'tí+ra
be.aware-know-FEM 2SG   be.bad-DIM escape+VIS.IMPERF.2/3

'"You escaped, evil clever woman."'

5.38 *mɨ'ɨre chɨnokaboka nia.*

~bɨ'ɨ́+ré   chɨ́-~doka-bo-ka   ~dí+a
2SG+OBJ eat-COMPL-DUB-ASSERT.IMPERF say+ASSERT.PERF

'"(We) would have eaten you up" (they) said.'

5.39 *mahare.*

~bahá+ré
go.uphill+VIS.PERF.2/3

'They went back up (to the house).'

5.40 *mahata tirokãre wi'i, chɨa.*

~bahá-ta   tí+ró-~ká+ré   wi'í   chɨ́+a
go.uphill-come ANPH+SG-DIM+OBJ arrive eat+ASSERT.PERF

'When they got there, they went up to the boy (and) ate him.'

5.41 *kɨ̃ nɨma ba'aro wi'i ñɨga.*

~kɨ̃   ~dɨ́bá ba'á+ro   wi'í   ~yɨ́+á
one/a day   do/be.after+SG arrive see/look+ASSERT.PERF

'The next day, (the mother) went home (and) saw (him).'

5.42 *to ka'sarore õba'aroi pihsarukuga.*

to=ka'sá+ro+re   ~ó-bá'á+ró+í
3SG.POSS=skin+SG+OBJ DEIC.PROX-do/be.after+SG-LOC

pisá-rúkú+á
be.on-stand+ASSERT.PERF
'His skin was there draped (over the windowsill).'

5.43 õse wa'aatiga phanopɨre.

~ó-sé   wa'á-ati+a   ~phadó-pɨ+re
DEIC.PROX-be.like   go-IMPERF+ASSERT.PERF   do/be.before-LOC+OBJ

'This is how things used to be long ago.'

6. A Hunter and His Dogs

Evil beings and dogs also figure in two of the texts provided by Ricardo Cabral, the eldest of Mateus's brothers, a man in his fifties born and raised in Carurú but currently living in São Gabriel. Ricardo's first text (told to a roomful of women) is the tale of a man who goes hunting with his sons. They take along several dogs that go running off in search of animals. One small dog disappears and the man goes to look for it, but does not find it. While the man is off searching, the dog comes to a lake across which a log has fallen. It begins to bark and run across the log. The man hears the dog barking and goes to find it, but when he arrives, he sees that the dog is being swallowed by a large snake that had been hiding in a hole by the log. He calls to his sons and they come running. He then takes his old-fashioned shotgun and shoots the snake, which comes sliding out of the hole. It vomits up the dog and emits a humanlike scream. As the scream dies away, from far away across the lake, it is answered by another, also humanlike, call. The man then realizes that he has shot not a regular snake but some kind of magical evil snake-being. He shoots the snake again to make sure it is dead, chops it up, and flings the pieces out into the forest. He buries the dog and heads home, where he smokes, blessing himself with the protective smoke. That night, the man is visited in a dream by the dead snake's father, who comes, with bow and arrow in hand, to ask the man if he knows about his son's whereabouts. "My son was killed when he was hunting," he says. "I come to avenge him." The man denies knowing anything about it and claims that he never goes hunting in that place. The snake father leaves, but the man wakes up fearful. In the morning, he blesses himself and his children again. He warns them to stay away from that place, where evil beings dwell.

6.1 wa'ikina ko'tariro to dieya me're

wa'í-~kídá   ko'tá+ri+ro   to=dié-yá=~be're
animal-PL   wait+NOM+SG   3SG.POSS=dog-PL=COM/INST

'A hunter and his dogs'

6.2 yɨ'ɨ mihchakãkãre a'ri numiakinare kũro khitikã ya'uperɨkasinitai niha.

yɨ'ɨ   ~bichá-~ká-~ká+ré   a'rí   ~dubí+a-~kida+re   ~kɨ+ró
1SG   today-DIM-DIM+OBJ   DEM.PROX   woman+PL-PL+OBJ   one/a+SG

khití-~ka   ya'ɨ-pe-rɨka-~sidi-ta+i
story-DIM   tell-FAV-begin-do.then/now-INTENT+(1/2)MASC

~dí-ha
be.PROG-VIS.IMPERF.1

'I'm happy to be telling these women a little story right now.'

6.3 kũta hia, kũiro mɨno to pho'na me're wa'ikina ko'taro wa'aa mahkarokapɨ.

~kɨ=ta   hí+a   ~kɨ-író   ~bɨ+ro
one/a=REF   COP+SG   one/a-NOM.SG   man+SG

to=~pho'dá=~be're   wa'í-~kídá   ko'tá+ro
3SG.POSS=children=COM/INST   animal-PL   wait+(3)SG

wa'á+a   ~baká-róká-pɨ
go+ASSERT.PERF   origin-DIST-LOC

'Once, a man went hunting with his children in the forest.'

6.4 yoaro ko'tawa'aka'a yoachɨ, to dieya wa'ikiro bokaa nɨnɨwa'aka'a tina.

yoá+ró   ko'tá-wa'a-ka'a   yoá-chɨ
be.far+SG   wait-go-do.moving   do/make-SW.REF

to= dié-yá   wa'í-kíró   boká+a
3SG.POSS=dog-PL   animal+SG   find+ASSERT.PERF

~dɨdɨ-wa'a-ka'a   ti-~da
follow/chase-go-do.moving   ANPH-PL

'As they went farther away, his dogs found an animal (and) went chasing after it.'

6.5 yoaro ñɨsemahari, sihtotaa ti(na).

yoá+ró   ~yɨ-sé-~báhá+rí
be.far+SG   see/look-be.like-MOV.up/down+NOM

sitó-ta+a   ti(-~da)
MOV.circular-come+ASSERT.PERF   ANPH-PL

'Over there, they (the dogs) looked around like this.'

6.6 yoaripa nɨnɨsihtotaa.

yoá+rí-pá   ~dɨdɨ-sito-ta+a
be.long+NOM-CLS:time   chase-MOV.circular-come+ASSERT.PERF

'They chased around for a long time.'

6.7   *kɨ̃iro diero, phirirowɨ'rɨ hirirowɨ'rɨ buhtiawa'aa.*

       ~kú-iró   dié+ró   phí+ri+ro-wɨ'rɨ   hí+ri+ro-wɨ'rɨ
       one/a-NOM.SG   dog+SG   be.big+NOM+SG-AUG   COP+NOM+SG-AUG
       butí+a=wa'a+a
       disappear+AFFEC=go+ASSERT.PERF

       'One dog, the biggest of all, disappeared.'

6.8   *kɨ̃irokã marirokãdita hia nɨnɨsihtota.*

       ~kú-iró-~ká   ~bá+rí+ró-~ká-dítá   hí+a
       one/a-NOM.SG-DIM   be.small+NOM+SG-DIM-SOL   COP+ASSERT.PERF
       ~dɨdú-sito-ta
       chase-MOV.circular-come

       '(And) there was a little one chasing around alone (by itself).'

6.9   *tiro wa'ikirore bohãa, tirokhɨ hi'na.*

       tí+ró   wa'i-kíró+ré   bó-~ha+a
       ANPH+SG   animal+SG+OBJ   lose-be.unexpected+ASSERT.PERF
       tí+ró-khɨ́   ~hí'da
       ANPH+SG-ADD   EMPH

       'He (the little dog) lost the animal he was hunting (and) he too suddenly got lost.'

6.10   *ã̰yo õita wa'are ni, tiro to pho'na me're mahkasihtotaa.*

       ~a=yo   ~ó+i=ta   wa'á+re   ~dí
       so=do   DEIC.PROX+LOC=REF   go+VIS.PERF.2/3   say
       tí+ró   to=~pho'dá=~be're
       ANPH+SG   3SG.POSS=children=COM/INST
       ~baká-sito-ta+a
       look/search.for-MOV.circular-come+ASSERT.PERF

       '"He went over here," the father said, and he and his children went (and) looked around.'

6.11   *tiro bɨhkɨro ne maniaa. ne bohkeraa.*

       tí+ró   bɨk+ɨ́+ro   ~dé   ~badía+a
       ANPH+SG   elder+MASC+SG   NEG   not.exist+ASSERT.PERF
       ~dé   bok(a)-éra+a
       NEG   find-NEG+ASSERT.PERF

       'The old man (was too late and) there was nothing, (he) didn't find anything.'

6.12   *ne maniaa tina paina dieyakã.*

       ~dé   ~badía+a   tí-~da   pá-~ida   dié-yá-~ká
       NEG   not.exist+ASSERT.PERF   ANPH-PL   ALT-NOM.PL   dog-PL-DIM

       'There were no little dogs there.'

6.13 ãta yoa, kũiro dierokã paritarore, paritarore hiritarore, mumubu'asũ thutia.

~a=tá   yoá   ~kú-író   dié+ró-~ká   parí-taro+re
so=REF do/make one/a-NOM.SG dog+SG-DIM form-CLS:lake+OBJ

parí-taro+re   hí+ri-taro+re
form-CLS:lake+OBJ   COP+NOM-CLS:lake+OBJ

~bubú-bu'a-~su   thutí+a
run-MOV.downward-arrive   bark+ASSERT.PERF

'Meanwhile, one little dog ran down to a lake, a lake like this, (and) barked.'

6.14 cho! õita hinokaboka ni, tiro buhkuro ni.

chó   ~ó+í=ta   hí-~doka-bo-ka   ~dí
oh   DEIC.PROX-LOC=REF COP-COMPL-DUB- ASSERT.IMPERF say

tí+ró   buk+ú+ro   ~dí
ANPH+SG elder+MASC+SG say

'"Oh! Maybe he's here," he said, the old man said.'

6.15 ñubu'aa. ñubohkaa.

~yú-bú'á+á   ~yú-bóká+á
see/look-MOV.downward+ASSERT.PERF see/look-find+ASSERT.PERF

'He looked down. He spotted it.'

6.16 topu phinonowu'ru tiro dierokãre ña'akhoãa.

tó-pu   ~phidó+ró-wú'rú   tí+ró   dié+ró-~ká+ré
REM-LOC snake+SG-AUG   ANPH+SG dog+SG-DIM+OBJ

~ya'á-~khoa+a
catch-lie+ASSERT.PERF

'There, a big snake was wrapped around the little dog.'

6.17 dierore chuburoropu nia.

dié+ró+ré   chú-búró+ró-pú   ~dí+a
dog+SG+OBJ eat-go.down+(3)SG-EMPATH   be.PROG+ASSERT.PERF

'It was already swallowing down the poor dog.'

6.18 õ to dahpudita bahua chuburochu.

~ó   to=dapú-dita   bahú+a
DEIC.PROX 3SG.POSS=head-SOL be.visible+ASSERT.PERF

chú-búró-chú
eat-go.down-SW.REF

'Only the (dog's) head was still showing as it (the snake) swallowed.'

6.19 õ paritaroi õse hirikhũmukã, õ parikhũmukã himʉpaa.
~ó   parí-taro+i   ~ó-sé
DEIC.PROX   form-CLS:lake+LOC   DEIC.PROX-be.like
hí+ri-~khubu-~ka   ~ó   parí-~kubu-~ka
COP+NOM-tree.trunk-DIM   DEIC.PROX   form-tree.trunk-DIM
hí-~bʉpa+a
COP-be.across+ASSERT.PERF
'Here at the lake, there was a log like this, a little tree fallen across.'

6.20 topʉ phinono ñakã ko'tapihsaa.
tó-pʉ   ~phidó+ró   ~yá-~ka   ko'tá-pisa+a
REM-LOC   snake+SG   be.bad-DIM   wait-be.on.top+ASSERT.PERF
'There the evil snake was waiting (lying) on top.'

6.21 dierose'e mʉmʉphã'arirore ñaro tirore bahkañaa.
dié+ró-sé'é   ~bʉbú-~pha'a+ri+ro+re
dog+SG-CONTR   run-MOV.across+NOM+SG+OBJ
~yá+ro   tí+ró+ré   baká-~yá+á
be.bad+SG   ANPH+SG+OBJ   bite-be.bad+ASSERT.PERF
'The evil snake bit him, the dog that was running across.'

6.22 wa'mamahare, boraa ti kohpapʉ.
~wa'bá-~báhá-ré   borá+a
wrap.around-MOV.up/down-CLS:generic   fall+ASSERT.PERF
ti=kopá-pʉ́
ANPH=hole-LOC
'Wrapping around him, (the snake) retreated down into the hole.'

6.23 ã yo tirore wãhatu'sʉ chʉropʉ nia.
~a=yó   tí+ró+ré   ~wahá-tu'sʉ   chʉ́+ro-pʉ
so=do   ANPH+SG+OBJ   kill-finish   eat+(3)SG-EMPATH
~dí+a
be.PROG+ASSERT.PERF
'He (the snake) had just killed the poor dog (and) was already eating it.'

6.24 ã yo tiro hi'na bʉhkʉro mʉmʉ busũ ñʉ õpʉ hira yʉ pho'na.
~a=yó   tí+ró   ~hí'da   bʉk+ʉ́+ró   ~bʉbú bú-~sʉ
so=do   ANPH+SG   EMPH   elder+MASC+SG   run   shore-arrive
~yʉ́
see/look

~ó-pɨ hí+ra yɨ=~pho'dá
DEIC.PROX-LOC COP+VIS.IMPERF.2/3 1SG.POSS=children

'Then the same old man ran to the shore, looked, (and said), "Here he is, my sons."'

6.25 yoatapɨ wãhanokari hira mari dierore.

yoá=ta-pɨ ~wahá-~doka+ri hí+ra
do=REF-LOC kill-COMPL+NOM(INFER) COP+VIS.IMPERF.2/3

~bari=dié+ró+ré
1PL.INC.POSS=dog+SG+OBJ

'"Our dog has just been killed."'

6.26 phinonowɨ'rɨ hira nia.

~phidó+ró-wɨ'rɨ hí+ra ~dí+a
snake+SG-AUG COP+VIS.IMPERF.2/3 say+ASSERT.PERF

'"(By) a big snake," he said.'

6.27 ã nichɨ, tina mɨrɨkawa'aka'a sɨ̃ ñɨa.

~a=~dí-chɨ ti-~da ~bɨ-rɨka-wa'a-ka'a ~sɨ̃
so=say-SW.REF ANPH-PL run-begin-go-do.moving arrive

~yɨ+á
see/look+ASSERT.PERF

'When he said that, they (the sons) went off running over there (and) looked.'

6.28 yoatapɨ chɨbɨroropɨ nia.

yoá-ta-pɨ chɨ-bɨro+ro-pɨ ~dí+a
do/make=REF-LOC eat-go.down+SG-LOC be.PROG+ASSERT.PERF

'(The snake) was already swallowing down (the dog).'

6.29 to dahpudita bahua.

to=dapú-dita bahú+a
3SG.POSS=head-SOL be.visible+ASSERT.PERF

'Only the (dog's) head was still out.'

6.30 ã yo tiro phichakɨ khɨaa.

~a=yó tí+ró phichá-kɨ khɨá+a
so=do ANPH+SG shoot-CLS:tree hold/have+ASSERT.PERF

'So, he (the old man) had/was holding a shotgun.'

6.31 phanopɨ mahkadɨ ti ñohsadi'odɨ hiati hire, wi'o.

~phadó-pɨ ~baká-dɨ
do/be.before-LOC origin-CLS:cylindrical.straight

ti=~yosá-di'o-dɨ hí-ati
ANPH=force.into-particles-CLS:cylindrical.straight COP-IMPERF

hí+re   wi'ó
COP+VIS.PERF.2/3 CONTR

'It was an old-fashioned one, the kind you used to shove the ammunition into, right?'

6.32 *phichayahpari ñohsadi'o phichayɨhkɨre.*
phichá-yápá+rí   ~yosá-di'o   phichá-yɨkɨ-ré
shoot-seed+PL   force.into-particles shoot-tree-CLS:generic

'A shotgun [lit., 'shooting tree'] with pellets [lit., 'shooting seeds'] packed in.'

6.33 *tɨba'ro titereba'ro me're,*
tɨ́=ba'ro   tí-té+ré=ba'ro=~be're
stick=kind ANPH-CLS:time+OBJ=kind=COM/INST

'With that kind (of shotgun), that old kind . . .'

6.34 *sɨ̃ tirore phichaba'a yoaa.*
~sɨ́   tí+ró+ré   phichá-bá'á   yoá+a
arrive   ANPH+SG+OBJ   shoot-do/be.after   do/make+ASSERT.PERF

'He went right over to it (the snake and) shot (it).'

6.35 *to dahpuwaroi phichawa'arokaa.*
to=dapɨ́-waro+i   phichá-wá'á-róká+á
3SG.POSS=head-EMPH+LOC   shoot-go-DIST+ASSERT.PERF

'Its head exploded.'

6.36 *to phichachɨta, phinonowɨ'rɨ tirore chowerɨkaa.*
to=phichá-chɨ́=ta   ~phiró+ró-wɨ́'rɨ́   tí+ró+ré
DEF=shoot-SW.REF=REF   snake+SG-AUG   ANPH+SG+OBJ

chówe-rɨka+a
vomit-begin+ASSERT.PERF

'When he shot (it), the big snake began to vomit him (the dog) up.'

6.37 *a'riase sĩomɨ wihatanokaa, phiridawɨ'rɨta.*
a'rí+á-sé   ~sió-~bɨ́
DEM.PROX+PL-be.like slide-run

wihá-ta-~doka+a
MOV.outward-come-COMPL+ASSERT.PERF

phí+ri-da-wɨ'rɨ=ta
be.big+NOM-CLS:ropelike-AUG=REF

'It came sliding out like this, a long ropelike thing.'

6.38 *õparithu khõasɨ phirota sañoa mahsɨno yoarose phinonowɨ'rɨ.*
~ó-pá+rí-thú   ~khoá-~sɨ   phí+ró=ta
DEIC.PROX-ALT+NOM-CLS:stacked   lie-arrive be.big+SG=REF

~sayó+a ~basú+ro yoá+ro-se
scream+ASSERT.PERF person+SG do/make+SG-be.like

~phidó+ró-wɨ'rɨ
snake+SG-AUG

'Lying in a big pile like this, the big snake screamed loudly like a person.'

6.39 to saño dɨ'tamaniaboraachɨ, pɨ diabu'ipɨ pairo sañoro koataa.

to=~sayó   dɨ'tá-~badia-bora+a-chɨ
3SG.POSS=yell/scream make.noise-not.exist-fall+PL-SW.REF

pɨ   diá-bu'i-pɨ   pá-iro   ~sayó+ró
LOC river-top-LOC ALT-NOM.SG   yell/scream+SG

koá-ta+a
NONVIS-come+ASSERT.PERF

'Just as his scream died away, from far away upriver, another one screamed (they heard it).'

6.40 yɨ'tiro koataa.

yɨ'tí+ró   koá-ta+a
answer+SG   NONVIS-come+ASSERT.PERF

'(It was) an answer (they heard it).'

6.41 mahsɨno pihsuro yoarose, pa hierara tiro.

~basú+ro   pisú+ró yoá+ro-se   pá
person+SG call+SG do/make+SG-be.like   ALT

hi-éra+ra   tí+ró
COP-NEG+VIS.IMPERF.2/3 ANPH+SG

'A human-like scream, but he (the screamer) wasn't (human).'

6.42 tiro bɨhkɨro yairobɨhkɨri hia, wi'owĩhĩi yoariroba'ro.

tí+ró   bɨk+ɨ+ro   yaí+ro-bɨk+ɨ+ri
ANPH+SG   elder+MASC+SG   shaman+SG-elder+MASC+NOM(INFER)

hí+a
COP+ASSERT.PERF

~wi'ó-~wíhí   yoá+ri+ro=ba'ro
hallucinatory.powder-sniff do/make+NOM+SG=kind

'The father was (apparently) kind of a shaman, the kind who uses (hallucinatory) powder. (So he was able to recognize that the being wasn't human.)'

6.43 pa hierara.

pá   hi-éra+ra
ALT COP-NEG+VIS.IMPERF.2/3

'"It's not (a regular snake)!"'

6.44 *a'riro pairoba'ro hira nia.*

a'rí+ró   pá-iro=ba'ro   hí+ra   ~dí+a
DEM.PROX+SG ALT+SG=kind COP+VIS.IMPERF.2/3 say+ASSERT.PERF

'"This is some different kind of being," he said.'

6.45 *ñairo pairoba'ro hira a'riro.*

~yá-iro   pá-iro=ba'ro   hí+ra   a'rí+ró
be.bad+SG ALT+SG=kind COP+VIS.IMPERF.2/3 DEM.PROX+SG

'"This is some other evil kind."'

6.46 *to hiriro a'riro soro hira ni, tirore topɨrota phichanamoatoa.*

tó   hí+ri+ro   a'rí+ró   só+ró   hí+ra
REM COP+NOM+SG DEM.PROX+SG different+SG COP+VIS.IMPERF.2/3

~dí   tí+ró+ré   tó-pɨ+ró=ta
say ANPH+SG+OBJ DEF-LOC+SG=REF

phichá-~dábó+á-tóá
shoot-repeat+AFFEC-do.again

'"And over there is another different one," he said, (and) he shot it (the snake) again.'

6.47 *wãhanokaa.*

~wahá-~doka+a
kill-COMPL+ASSERT.PERF

'He killed it.'

6.48 *dɨ'teta khõarokaa.*

dɨ'té-ta   ~khóá-róká+á
chop-separate throw-DIST+ASSERT.PERF

'He cut it into pieces (and) threw them apart.'

6.49 *tiro dierore wahawa'aka'a sõ'oba'aropɨ ñarikohpa sa'a, yakhõ'anokaa.*

tí+ró   dié+ró+ré   wahá-wa'a-ka'a
ANPH+SG dog+SG+OBJ pull-go-do.moving

~so'ó-bá'á+ró-pɨ   ~yá+ri-kopa   sa'á
DEIC.DIST-be.after+SG-LOC be.bad+NOM-hole dig

yá-~kho'a-~doka+a
bury-lie-COMPL+ASSERT.PERF

'He dragged the dog a little way away, dug a rough hole (and) buried (it).'

6.50   *thuaa pohtota te wɨ'ɨpɨ.*
       thuá+a   potó=ta   té   wɨ'ɨ-pɨ
       return+ASSERT.PERF   direction=REF   all.the.way house-LOC
       'He (and his sons) went straight back home.'

6.51   *tu'sɨro ka'a tiro nia: pairoba'aro mari wãhai ni.*
       tu'sɨ+ro   ka'á   tí+ró   ~dí+a
       finish+SG   near   ANPH+SG   say+ASSERT.PERF
       pá-iro=ba'ro   ~barí   ~wahá+i   ~di
       ALT+SG=kind   1PL.INC   kill+VIS.PERF.1   say
       'Just as they arrived he said: "We've killed another kind of (a magic) snake," he said.'

6.52   *korida'rea, mɨ'noro phidɨ, õpadɨwɨ'rɨ yoaa.*
       kó+rí-dá'ré+á   ~bɨ'dó+ro
       bless+NOM-prepare+ASSERT.PERF   tobacco+SG
       phí-dɨ
       big-CLS:cylindrical.straight
       ~ó-pá-dɨ-wɨ'rɨ   yoá+a
       DEIC.PROX-ALT-CLS:cylindrical.straight-AUG   do/make+ASSERT.PERF
       'For protection, he rolled a big cigar, made one this big.'

6.53   *bahsakoriti hu yoaa, phutiphayo, to pho'nakhɨre phutiphayo.*
       basá-kó+rí-tí   hú   yoá+a
       sing/dance-bless+NOM-VBZ   smoke   do/make+ASSERT.PERF
       phutí-pháyó   to=~pho'dá-khɨ+re   phutí-pháyó
       blow-spread.out   3SG.POSS=children-ADD+OBJ   blow/play-spread.out
       'He blessed himself, blowing smoke (on himself) and on his sons too.'

6.54   *tu'sɨ, ti ñamire hi'na khã'aropɨre tirore ya'ua.*
       tu'sɨ   ti=~yabí+re   ~hi'da   ~kha'á+ro-pɨ+re   tí+ró+ré
       finish   ANPH=night+OBJ   EMPH   dream+SG-LOC+OBJ   ANPH+SG+OBJ
       ya'ú+a
       warn+ASSERT.PERF
       'When he was done, that very night he was warned in a dream.'

6.55   *sũa to ka'ai bɨenete khɨanaka, bɨeayɨhkɨri khɨariro.*
       ~sɨ+a   to=ka'á+i   bɨé~dete
       arrive+ASSERT.PERF   3SG.POSS=side+LOC   bow.and.arrow
       khɨá-~daka   bɨé+a-yɨkɨ+ri   khɨá+ri+ro
       hold/have-do/be.together   arrow+PL-tree+PL   hold/have+NOM+SG
       '(The father snake) arrived at his side clutching a bow and arrows.'

6.56 *mɨmɨ mahasũ tirore sinitua: mɨ'ɨ ñɨerari yɨ mahkɨre?*

~bubɨ́ ~bahá-~sɨ́ tí+ró+ré ~sidítu+a
run go.uphill-arrive ANPH+SG+OBJ ask+ASSERT.PERF

~bɨ'ɨ́ ~yɨ-éra-ri yɨ=~bak+ɨ́+ré
2SG see/look-NEG-INT 1SG.POSS=child+MASC+OBJ

'He ran up to him (the man) (and) asked (demanded to know): "Didn't you see my son?"'

6.57 *wãharokari hire wa'ikinawãharo wa'arirore, pɨwa'ikinawãharo wa'arirore.*

~wahá-roka+ri hí+re wa'í-~kídá-~wáhá+ró
kill-DIST+NOM(INFER) COP+VIS.PERF.2/3 animal-PL-kill+(3)SG

wa'á+ri+ro-re
go+NOM+SG-CLS:generic

pɨ́ wa'í-~kídá-~wáhá+ró wa'á+ri+ro-re
LOC animal-PL-kill+(3)SG go+NOM+SG-CLS:generic

'"(It seems) he was killed when he was off hunting, when far away hunting animals."'

6.58 *yɨ mahkɨre wãharokari hire nia.*

yɨ=~bak+ɨ́+ré ~wahá-roka+ri hí+re
1SG.POSS=child+MASC+OBJ kill-DIST+NOM(INFER) COP+VIS.PERF.2/3

~dí+a
say+ASSERT.PERF

'"My son's been killed," he said.'

6.59 *ñɨera ti mahsieraka yɨ'ɨ nia tirose'e.*

~yɨ-éra ti-(ro) ~basi-éra-ka yɨ'ɨ́
see-NEG ANPH-(SG) know-NEG-ASSERT.IMPERF 1SG

~dí+a tí+ró-sé'é
say+ASSERT.PERF ANPH+SG-CONTR

'"I didn't see (anything/anyone), I know nothing (about it)," the man said.'

6.60 *ne topɨre tipɨre tinieraha ninokaa.*

~dé tó-pɨ+re tí-pɨ+re ~tidi-éra-ha
NEG REM-LOC+OBJ ANPH-LOC+OBJ wander-NEG-VIS.IMPERF.1

~dí-~doka+a
say-COMPL+ASSERT.PERF

'"I never go hunting there in that place," he insisted.'

6.61 *ã yoakɨ yɨ'ɨ tirore wãha kha'mai tai niha, nia tiro.*

~a=yoá-kɨ yɨ'ɨ́ tí+ró+ré ~wahá=~kha'ba+i
so/then=do-(1/2)MASC 1SG ANPH+SG+OBJ kill=want+(1/2)MASC

tá+i   ~dí-ha   ~dí+a   tí+ró
come+(1/2)MASC be.PROG-VIS.IMPERF.1 say+ASSERT.PERF ANPH+SG

'"So, I'm coming here to avenge him," he (the father snake) said.'
('avenge': lit., 'kill' + 'want, need')

6.62 *ni ba'aro hi'na, õpɨ wa'ari hire.*

  ~di ba'á+ro ~hí'da ~ó-pɨ wa'á+ri
  say do/be.after+SG EMPH DEIC.PROX-LOC go+NOM(INFER)

  hí+re
  COP+VIS.PERF.2/3

  'Afterward he said, "He (apparently) went this way."'

6.63 *tiro ñɨi wa'aha ni, mɨyɨ'dɨwa'aa.*

  tí+ró ~yɨ+í   wa'á-ha   ~dí
  ANPH+SG see/look+(1/2)MASC go-VIS.IMPERF.1 say

  ~bɨ-yɨ'dɨ-wa'a+a
  run-INTENS-go+ASSERT.PERF

  '"I'm going to look for him," (the father snake) said (and he) ran off.'

6.64 *tiro bɨhkɨro topɨrota hi'na khaniwã'kaa.*

  tí+ró bɨk+ɨ+ro tó-pɨ+ro=ta ~hí'da
  ANPH+SG elder+MASC+SG DEF-LOC+SG=REF EMPH

  ~khadí-~wa'ka+a
  sleep-wake.up+ASSERT.PERF

  'The old man immediately woke up.'

6.65 *bahsarɨkata namo thɨ'othɨyohsaa.*

  basá-rɨka=ta ~dabó thɨ'ó-thu-yosa+a
  bless-begin=REF repeat hear-think-be.hanging+ASSERT.PERF

  'He blessed himself again (and) hung (lying in his hammock) contemplating.'

6.66 *ãyo bo'rero to pho'nare ya'ua hi'na:*

  ~a=yó bo'ré+ro to=~pho'dá+re ya'ú+a
  so=do be.light+SG 3SG.POSS=children+OBJ tell/warn+ASSERT.PERF

  ~hí'da
  EMPH

  'So, in the morning he warned his sons:'

6.67 *ahiriro hiri hire.*

  ahí+ri+ro   hí+ri   hí+re
  be.concerned+NOM+SG COP+NOM(INFER) COP+VIS.PERF.2/3

  '"(It seems) there's a dangerous (worrisome) being in that place."'

6.68 wãkumahsiga tore.
~wakú-~bási+gá   tó-re
be.aware-know+IMPER REM-CLS:generic
'"Be careful there."'

6.69 ne mihchakãkãre wa'eraatiga khuarire tiro nia.
~dé ~bichá-~ká-~ká+ré wa'(a)-éra-ati+ga
NEG today-DIM-DIM+OBJ go-NEG-IMPERF+IMPER
khuá+ri+re   tí+ró   ~dí+a
be.dangerous+NOM+OBJ ANPH+SG   say+ASSERT.PERF
'"Don't be going near that dangerous one right now," he said.'

6.70 a'ri khiti õita phitira.
a'rí   khití ~ó+í=ta   phití+ra
DEM.PROX   story DEIC.PROX-LOC=REF   end+VIS.IMPERF.2/3
'Here's where this story ends.'

7. The Curupira Story

The final oral narrative in this small collection was also told by Ricardo Cabral. It tells of a man who goes hunting in the forest, kills three monkeys, and then becomes lost on his way home. As night falls, he comes to a clearing and decides to build himself a shelter. He gathers some leaves, builds a small hut, and lies down to sleep. In the middle of the night, he hears someone—or something—approaching. As the man hears the unknown visitor moving closer, he becomes frightened. The visitor stops just outside the shelter and greets the man. When he does not answer, the visitor again greets him; the man finally responds and they talk a little. At the end of the conversation, the visitor asks the man to give him his heart. The man is taken aback and realizes that the visitor is some kind of evil creature who wants to eat him. Thinking quickly, he grabs his knife and cuts out the heart of one of the dead monkeys. He sticks it on the tip of his knife and offers it out through an opening in the wall of the shelter to the creature, who gobbles it up. Twice more the creature asks for additional pieces of the man's heart to eat, until the man has given it all three monkey hearts. Then the man turns the table and asks the creature to offer up his own heart. The creature agrees, but says he does not know how to take it out. The man gives him the knife and instructs him to push hard, all at once. The creature, tricked into stabbing itself, falls over. The man calls to it but there is no answer. Concluding that the strange visitor must be dead, the man goes back to sleep. In the early morning light, the man leaves the shelter and sees that indeed, the visitor was a great hairy creature known as a curupira. He gathers his weapons and monkeys and heads home.

Four years later, the man decides to return to the clearing to look for the creature's remains. He wants to make a necklace out of the creature's beautiful, shiny teeth, but when he arrives at the spot, he finds no trace of the being, which has apparently decomposed. But when he takes his knife and digs into the ground at the spot where the creature died, he releases the spirit of the creature, which rises up and stands before him. Grateful to be awakened after a long "sleep," the creature offers the man a magic stick to hunt with. All the man has to do, it says, is point the stick at an animal and the animal will fall over dead. However, the curupira warns, the man must not tell anyone about it; it must remain a secret or the man will die. The man takes the stick and heads back home, rather skeptical until he comes across a jacú bird. He waves the stick at the bird and it promptly dies. The man then realizes that the stick is indeed truly magical. He uses the stick to hunt from then on, but never tells anyone how he has become such a successful hunter. People ask him how he manages to kill so many animals, but he never reveals his secret—until one day when he becomes completely drunk and spills the beans about the magic stick. The very next day, he is bitten by a poisonous snake and dies, his spirit going off to join that of the curupira.

7.1 *boraro khiti*
     borá+ro   khiti
     Curupira+SG story
     'The curupira story'

7.2 *yɨ'ɨ õi kɨ khiti ya'usinitai niha.*
     yɨ'ɨ   ~ó+i   ~kɨ   khiti ya'ú-~sidi=ta+i
     1SG   DEIC.PROX+LOC one/a story tell-do.then/now=REF+(1/2)MASC
     ~dí-ha
     be.PROG-VIS.IMPERF.1
     'I'm going to tell a little story now.'

7.3 *kɨta hia kɨiro muno to namonore õse nia:*
     ~kɨ=ta   hí+a   ~kɨ-iró   ~bɨ+ro   to=~dabó+ro+re
     one/a=REF COP+PL one/a-NOM.SG man+SG 3SG.POSS=wife+SG+OBJ
     ~ó-sé   ~dí+a
     DEIC.PROX-be.like say+ASSERT.PERF
     'Once a man said this to his wife:'

7.4 *yʉ'ʉ mihchare wa'ikinawãhai wa'aika.*
    yʉ'ʉ   ~bichá+ré   wa'i-~kídá-~wáhá+í   wa'á+i-ka
    1SG   today+OBJ   animal-PL-kill+(1/2)MASC   go+(1/2)MASC-PREDICT
    '"Today I'm going hunting."'

7.5 *marire chʉa maniara, nia.*
    ~barí+ré   chʉa   ~badía+ra   ~dí+a
    1PL.INC+OBJ   food   not.exist+VIS.IMPERF.2/3   say+ASSERT.PERF
    '"There isn't any food for us," he said.'

7.6 *ã nichʉ, thʉ'oro to namono:*
    ~a=~dí-chʉ   thʉ'ó+ro   to=~dabó+ro
    so=say-SW.REF   hear+(3)SG   3SG.POSS=wife+SG
    'Saying that, he heard (from) his wife:'

7.7 *hai, wa'aga, nia tirore.*
    hái   wa'á+ga   ~dí+a   tí+ró+ré
    okay   go+IMPER   say+ASSERT.PERF   ANPH+SG+OBJ
    '"All right. Go," (she) said to him.'

7.8 *ã ni tu'sʉ tiro hi'na, to puhkare wʉa wahkasare wʉamʉ wa'awa'aa mahkarokapʉ.*
    ~a=~dí   tu'sʉ   tí+ró   ~hí'da   to=púka+re   wʉá
    so=say   finish   ANPH+SG   EMPH   3SG.POSS=blowgun+OBJ   carry
    waká-sa+re   wʉá-~bʉ   wa'á-wa'a+a
    poison.darts-carrier+OBJ   carry-run   go-go+ASSERT.PERF
    ~baká-róká-pʉ
    origin-DIST-LOC
    'As soon as he spoke, he got his blowgun, grabbed a basket of darts (and) went off into the forest.'

7.9 *topʉ sũ, wa'ikinare mahkasihtotaa.*
    tó-pʉ   ~sʉ́   wa'i-~kídá+ré
    REM-LOC   arrive   animal-PL+OBJ
    ~baká-sito-ta+a
    look/search.for-MOV.circular-come+ASSERT.PERF
    'Arriving there, he went around in search of animals.'

7.10 *bohkaa. tiro tiaro kayare wãhaa.*
    boká+a
    find+ASSERT.PERF
    tí+ró   tiá+ró   ká-ya+re   ~wahá+a
    ANPH+SG   three+SG   black.monkey-PL+OBJ   kill+ASSERT.PERF
    'He found (some). He killed three monkeys.'

7.11 *tinare wãha tiro wahcheawa'aa.*
 tí-~da+re   ~wahá   tí+ró   waché+a=wa'a+a
 ANPH-PL+OBJ kill   ANPH+SG be.happy+AFFEC=go+ASSERT.PERF
 'He killed them (and) he became happy.'

7.12 *mipɨre yɨ'ɨ chɨa bohkatu'sɨha. thuai niha, nia.*
 ~bí-pɨ́+ré   yɨ'ɨ́   chɨ́a   boká-tu'sɨ-ha
 now-LOC+OBJ 1SG food   find-finish-VIS.IMPERF.1
 thuá+i   ~dí-ha   ~dí+a
 return+(1/2)MASC be.PROG-VIS.IMPERF.1 say+ASSERT.PERF
 '"I've found food now. I'm going home," he said/thought.'

7.13 *ni thuata ma'a kherokã me're.*
 ~dí thuá=ta   ~ba'á khé+ro-~ka=~be're
 say return=REF path be.fast+SG-DIM=COM/INST
 '(He) said/thought, "(I'll) hurry back quickly."'

7.14 *ã yo hi'na, tiro topɨre wihsiawa'aa to ma'are.*
 ~a=yó ~hí'da tí+ró   tó-pɨ+re
 so=do EMPH   ANPH+SG   REM-LOC+OBJ
 wisí+a=wa'a+a   to=~ba'á+re
 be.lost+AFFEC=go+ASSERT.PERF 3SG.POSS=path+OBJ
 'Right then, he got lost from his path.'

7.15 *pase'epɨ wa'aa. tinisihtotaa.*
 pá-se'e-pɨ   wa'á+a
 ALT-CONTR-LOC go+ASSERT.PERF
 ~tidí-sító-tá+á
 walk-MOV.circular-come+ASSERT.PERF
 'He went off somewhere. He wandered around and around.'

7.16 *to wa'ari ma'are, ma'are ne bohkeraa.*
 to=wa'á+ri   ~ba'á+re ~ba'á+re ~dé
 3SG.POSS=go+NOM   path+OBJ   path+OBJ   NEG
 bok(a)-éra+a
 find-NEG+ASSERT.PERF
 'His way (home), he couldn't find his way.'

7.17 *te namicha na'itõa duhkuseawa'a pase'epɨ ne to mahsierapɨ.*
 té   ~yabicha ~da'í-~tóá   dukú-se+a=wa'a
 until   night   be.dark-be.fast stand-be.like+AFFEC=go

pá-se'e-pɨ   ~dé tó   ~basi-éra-pɨ
ALT-CONTR-LOC NEG REM know-NEG-LOC

'(He wandered) until it quickly got dark out there in that unknown place.'

7.18 *ã ta yoa ñamichapɨ hi'na, kɨ̃ ku'tukãpɨ, õpari ku'tukãpɨre phi'asɨ̃a.*

~a=tá   yoá   ~yabícha-pɨ   ~hí'da ~kɨ́   ku'tú-~ka-pɨ
so=REF do/make night-LOC   EMPH   one/a clearing-DIM-LOC

~ó-pá+rí   ku'tú-~ka-pɨ+re
DEIC.PROX-ALT+NOM clearing-DIM-LOC+OBJ

phí'a-~sɨ+a
MOV.out.into-arrive+ASSERT.PERF

'As night was falling, he went out into a little clearing, a little clearing like this.'

7.19 *ti ku'tupɨ phi'asɨ̃, õita yɨ'ɨ khãriita, nia.*

ti=ku'tú-pɨ   phi'á-~sɨ   ~ó+í=ta   yɨ'ɨ
ANPH=clearing-LOC MOV.out.into-arrive DEIC.PROX+LOC=REF 1SG

~kharí+i-ta   ~dí+a
sleep-+(1/2)MASC-INTENT say+ASSERT.PERF

'Emerging into the clearing, he said/thought, "I'll sleep here."'

7.20 *ã nirota hi'na, ñɨmɨ phɨ̃rire mahkasihtotaa.*

~a=~dí+ro=ta   ~hí'da ~yɨbɨ́   ~phɨ́+rí+ré
so=say+SG=REF   EMPH   bacaba leaf+PL+OBJ

~baká-sito-ta+a
look/search.for-MOV.circular-come+ASSERT.PERF

'That said, he went around looking for bacaba (fruit) leaves.'

7.21 *to'i dɨ'tesihtotaa. nataa.*

tó+í   dɨ'té-sító-tá+á
REM+LOC chop-MOV.circular-come+ASSERT.PERF

~dá-ta+a
get-come+ASSERT.PERF

'He went around cutting them. He brought them back.'

7.22 *õpari wɨ'ɨkã yoaa.*

~ó-pá+rí   wɨ'ɨ́-~ká   yoá+a
DEIC.PROX-ALT+NOM house-DIM do/make+ASSERT.PERF

'He made a little house, this big.'

7.23　õpari wʉ'ʉkã.

　　　~ó-pá+rí　　　　　　wʉ'ʉ́-~ká
　　　DEIC.PROX-ALT+NOM　house-DIM

　　　'A little house like this.'

7.24　tu'sʉ noano ti phũri me'reta, noano phitia.

　　　tu'sʉ́　~dóá+ró　ti=~phú+rí=~be're=ta　　　~dóá+ró
　　　finish　be.good+SG　ANPH=leaf+PL=COM/INST=REF　be.good+SG

　　　phití+a
　　　complete+ASSERT.PERF

　　　'He finished (making) a nice (shelter) with those leaves, completed it well.'

7.25　nuhusũawa'aa.

　　　~duhú-~sʉ+a=wa'a+a
　　　accommodate.oneself-arrive+AFFEC=go+ASSERT.PERF

　　　'(He) went in to make himself comfortable.'

7.26　tokakai tiro khãrikhõaa.

　　　tó-kaka+i　　　tí+ró　　　~khari-~khoa+a
　　　DEF-EMPH+LOC　ANPH+SG　sleep-be.lying+ASSERT.PERF

　　　'There he lay down and went to sleep.'

7.27　ba'aro hi'na ñamidahchomahka'i waroi, yoaropʉ kũiro taro koataa sõ'oba'ropʉ.

　　　ba'á+ro　　　　~hí'da　~yabí-dáchó-~báká+í　　wáró+í
　　　do/be.after+SG　EMPH　night-middle-origin-LOC　EMPH+LOC

　　　yoá+ró-pú　　~kú-iró　　　　tá+ro
　　　be.far+SG-LOC　one/a-NOM.SG　come+(3)SG

　　　koá-ta+a　　　　　　　　~so'ó-bá'á+ró-pú
　　　NONVIS-come+ASSERT.PERF　DEIC.DIST-do/be.after+SG-LOC

　　　'Later, right in the middle of the night, in the distance (he heard) someone approaching.'

7.28　yabariro hikari hi'na ni tiro.

　　　yabá+rí+ró　hí-ka-ri　　　　~hí'da　~dí　tí+ró
　　　WH+NOM+SG　COP-SUPP-INT　EMPH　say　ANPH+SG

　　　'"Who (in the world!) could that be?" he said/thought.'

7.29　kʉa masʉro, to kapoto'i thuaro koataa.

　　　kʉá　　　~basú+ro　　to=~ká-poto+i　　　　　　thuá+ro
　　　be.afraid　person+SG　3SG.POSS=EMPH-direction+LOC　return+(3)SG

koá-ta+a
NONVIS-come+ASSERT.PERF
'Frightened, (the man heard) it (the curupira) coming in his direction.'

7.30 te õba'aro'i wi'itarokaro koataa.
té   ~ó-bá'á+ró+i   wi'í-tá-róká+ró
all.the.way DEIC.PROX-do/be.after-LOC arrive-come-DIST+(3)SG
koá-ta+a
NONVIS-come+ASSERT.PERF
'(The man heard) him (the curupira) approaching from afar.'

7.31 tiro kʉayʉ'dʉawa'aa.
tí+ró   kʉá-yʉ'dʉ+a=wa'a+a
ANPH+SG be.afraid-INTENS+AFFEC=go+ASSERT.PERF
'He became very frightened.'

7.32 ba'aro thuaro koatata te toka'ai wi'ita'arukusʉ̃a.
ba'á+ro   thuá+ro   koá-ta=ta   té
do/be.after+SG return+(3)SG NONVIS-come=REF all.the.way
to=ka'á+i   wi'í-tá-rúkú-~sʉ́+á
3SG.POSS=next.to+LOC arrive-come-stand-arrive+ASSERT.PERF
'Then he (the man) heard him (the curupira) coming all the way up close.'

7.33 toi tirore sinitua.
tó+i   tí+ró+ré   ~sidítu +a
DEF-LOC ANPH+SG+OBJ ask+ASSERT.PERF
'There, (the curupira) asked him:'

7.34 ne koiro, nia tiro.
~dé   kó-iro   ~dí+a   tí+ró
hello relative-NOM.SG say+ASSERT.PERF ANPH+SG
'"How's it going, relative?" he said.'

7.35 yʉ'tieraa tirose'e koiro.
yʉ'ti-éra+a   tí+ró-sé'é   kó-iro
answer-NEG+ASSERT.PERF ANPH+SG-CONTR relative-NOM.SG
'But he (the man; lit., 'the other relative') didn't answer.'

7.36 ba'aro toa ne koiro, nia tirore.
ba'á+ro   toá   ~dé   kó-iro
do/be.after+SG do.again hello relative-NOM.SG

~dí+a   tí+ró+ré
say+ASSERT.PERF   ANPH+SG+OBJ

'Afterward, (the curupira asked) him again: "How's it going, relative?"'

7.37 *toa nichupɨ hi'na, do'se a'riro mahsɨro tikari chẽ'eni yɨ'tia.*

toá   ~dí-chu-pɨ   ~hí'da do'sé a'rí+ró   ~basú+ro
do.again say-SW.REF-LOC   EMPH   WH   DEM.PROX+SG being+SG

tí-ka-ri   ~che'é-~dí   yɨ'tí+a
ANPH-SUPP-INT   doubt-say   answer+ASSERT.PERF

'When (the curupira) said that, (the man) wondered: "What kind of being can this be?"'

7.38 *yɨ'tiro tirore nia:*

yɨ'tí+ro   tí+ró+ré   ~dí+a
answer+SG   ANPH+SG+OBJ   say+ASSERT.PERF

'Answering, (the man) said to him (the curupira):'

7.39 *yɨ'ukhɨ hiha koiro, nia.*

yɨ'ú-khú   hí-ha   kó-iro   ~dí+a
1SG-ADD   COP-VIS.IMPERF.1   relative-NOM.SG   say+ASSERT.PERF

'"I too am your/a relative," (the man) said.'

7.40 *ã tia, nia.*

~a=tía   ~dí+a
that's.right   say+ASSERT.PERF

'"That's right," (the curupira) said.'

7.41 *ãta yoa, tiro me're durukua yoaa.*

~a=tá   yoá   tí+ró=~be're   dú-rúkú+á
so=REF   do/make   ANPH+SG=COM/INST   speak-stand+(3)PL

yoá+a
do/make+ASSERT.PERF

'So, (the man) started a conversation with him (the curupira).'

7.42 *duruku tu'sɨ, tirore nia:*

dú-rúkú   tu'sɨ   tí+ró+ré   ~dí+a
speak-stand   finish   ANPH+SG+OBJ   say+ASSERT.PERF

'When it was over, (the curupira) said to him (the man):'

7.43 *koiro yɨ'ɨre, mɨ'ɨ yahiripho'nare yɨ'ɨre waga.*

kó-iro   yɨ'ú+ré   ~bɨ'ɨ=yahíri~pho'da+re   yɨ'ú+ré
relative-NOM.SG   1SG+OBJ   2SG(POSS)=heart+OBJ   1SG+OBJ

wá+gá
give+IMPER
'"To me, relative, give me your heart."'

7.44 *yʉ'ʉ chʉduaka, nia.*
  yʉ'ʉ chú-dua-ka   ~dí+a
  1SG eat-DESID-ASSERT.IMPERF say+ASSERT.PERF
  '"I want to eat it," (the curupira) said.'

7.45 *to yahiripho'nare sinia tirore.*
  to=yahíri~pho'da+re ~sidí+a   tí+ró+ré
  3SG.POSS=heart+OBJ ask.for+ASSERT.PERF ANPH+SG+OBJ
  '(The curupira) asked him (the man) for his heart!'

7.46 *to ã nichʉ, tiro mahsʉnose'e tirore nia.*
  to=~á=~dí-chʉ tí+ró ~basú+ro-se'e tí+ró+ré
  DEF=so=say-SW.REF ANPH+SG man+SG-CONTR ANPH+SG+OBJ
  ~dí+a
  say+ASSERT.PERF
  'When (the curupira) said that, the man responded:'

7.47 *cho'o, yʉ'ʉ yahiripho'nare wamahsieraka nia.*
  cho'ó yʉ'ʉ=yahíri~pho'da+re wa-~basi-éra-ka
  how's.that? 1SG(POSS)=heart+OBJ give-know-NEG-ASSERT.IMPERF
  ~dí+a
  say+ASSERT.PERF
  '"How's that? I can't give you my heart," he said.'

7.48 *na to mahsieraka, nia.*
  ~dá tó ~basi-éra-ka   ~dí+a
  get DEF know-NEG-ASSERT.IMPERF say+ASSERT.PERF
  '"I don't know how to (I can't) take it out," he said.'

7.49 *ã tia ni yʉ'tia tirose'e.*
  ~a=tía ~dí yʉ'tí+a   tí+ró-sé'é
  that's.right say answer+ASSERT.PERF ANPH+SG-CONTR
  '"Right," the other one (the curupira) responded.'

7.50 *ba'arokãta tirore siniata toa.*
  ba'á+ro-~ka=ta   tí+ró+ré   ~sidí+a=ta
  do/be.after+SG-DIM=REF ANPH+SG+OBJ ask.for+ASSERT.PERF=REF
  toá
  do.again
  'Soon after, (the curupira) asked him (the man) again:'

7.51 *mɨ'ɨ yahiripho'nare yɨ'ɨre waga, nia.*

~*bɨ'ɨ=yahíri~pho'da+re   yɨ'ɨ́+ré   wá+gá   ~dí+a*
2SG(POSS)= heart+OBJ   1SG+OBJ   give+IMPER   say+ASSERT.PERF

'"Give me your heart," he said.'

7.52 *tirose'e mahsɨnose'e kɨa yoaa.*

tí+ró-sé'é   ~basɨ́+ro-se'e   kɨá   yoá+a
ANPH+SG-CONTR   man+SG-CONTR   be.afraid   do/make+ASSERT.PERF

'That made the man afraid.'

7.53 *yɨ'ɨre a'riro chɨduaro nika nithɨ'othua*

yɨ'ɨ́+ré   a'rí+ró   chɨ́-dua+ro   ~dí-ka
1SG+OBJ   DEM.PROX+SG   eat-DESID+(3)SG   be.PROG-ASSERT.IMPERF

~*dí-thɨ'o-thɨ+a*
say-hear-think+ASSERT.PERF

'"This thing wants to eat me," he said to himself.'

7.54 *ba'aro mahsɨno hi'na topɨrota hi'na to yɨ'soriphĩkãre na hi'na tiro ka yahiripho'nare wayerɨkaa.*

ba'á+ro   ~basɨ́+ro   ~hí'da   tó-pɨ+ro=ta   ~hí'da
do/be.after+SG   man+SG   EMPH   DEF-LOC+SG=REF   EMPH

to=yɨ'só+ri-~phi-~ka+re   ~dá   ~hí'da   tí+ró
3SG.POSS=cut+NOM-CLS:bladelike-DIM+OBJ   get   EMPH   ANPH+SG

ká   yahíri~pho'da+re   wayé-rɨ́ká+á
black.monkey   heart+OBJ   cut.open-begin+ASSERT.PERF

'The (same) guy immediately took out his knife (and) started to cut out one of the monkeys' hearts.'

7.55 *yɨ'sota yoa, ti phĩ yɨ'soriphĩkãpɨ be phu'a phari, kohpakã yoa ñuiwĩoa.*

yɨ'só-ta   yoá   tí-~phí
cut-separate   do/make   ANPH-CLS:bladelike

yɨ'só+ri-~phi-~ka-pɨ   bé   phu'á   phárí
cut+NOM-CLS:bladelike-DIM-LOC   insert   stab   opening

kopá-~ká yoá   ~yuí-~wio+a
hole-DIM do/make   offer-go.out+ASSERT.PERF

'After cutting it out, he stuck the heart on (the tip of) the knife, made a little hole (in the wall and) held it out.'

7.56 *to ñuiwĩochɨ, tiro boraro, boraro hia tiro ...*

to=~yuí-~wio-chɨ   tí+ró   borá+ro
DEF=offer-go.out-SW.REF   ANPH+SG   curupira+SG

borá+ro   hí+a   tí+ró
curupira+SG   COP+ASSERT.PERF   ANPH+SG
'Offering it out, the one who was a curupira . . .'

7.57 n**ʉ**hk**ʉ**wãhtiro hia . . .
~d**ʉ**kú-~watí+ró hí+a
forest-devil+SG   COP+ASSERT.PERF
'(He) was a forest devil . . .'

7.58 tiro boraro to yahiripho'nakãre ña'ar**ʉ**kaa
tí+ró   borá+ro   to=yahíri~pho'da-~ka+re
ANPH+SG   curupira+SG   3SG.POSS=heart-DIM+OBJ
~ya'á-rʉ́ká+á
grab-begin+ASSERT.PERF
'The curupira grabbed at his little heart.'

7.59 ch**ʉ**roka'aro koataa.
chʉ́+ro-ka'a+ro   koá-ta+a
eat+SG-do.immediately+(3)SG   NONVIS-come+ASSERT.PERF
'(The man could hear) the curupira eating it right away.'

7.60 kherokã me're ch**ʉ**pha'yoroka'aro koataa.
khé+ro-~ka=~be're   chʉ́-pha'yo+ro-ka'a+ro
be.fast+SG-DIM=COM/INST   eat-COMPL+SG-do.immediately+(3)SG
koá-ta+a
NONVIS-come+ASSERT.PERF
'(He heard) the curupira gobble it up completely.'

7.61 ch**ʉ** tu's**ʉ**, nia: koiro m**ʉ**'**ʉ** yahiripho'na noaphitiaro koaka, nia.
chʉ́ tu'sʉ́   ~dí+a   kó-iro   ~bʉ'ʉ=yahíri~pho'da
eat   finish   say+ASSERT.PERF   relative-NOM.SG   2SG(POSS)=heart
~dóá-phítí+á+ró   koá-ka   ~dí+a
be.good-COLL+AFFEC+SG   taste-ASSERT.IMPERF   say+ASSERT.PERF
'When (the curupira) was done eating, he said: "Relative, your heart tastes really good," he said.'

7.62 y**ʉ**'**ʉ**re wanamoata payahiripho'nare, nia.
yʉ'ʉ́+ré   wá-~dábó+gá=ta   pá-yahiri~pho'da+re
1SG+OBJ   give-repeat+IMPER=REF   ALT-heart+OBJ
~dí+a
say+ASSERT.PERF
'"Give me another heart," (he) said.'

7.63 hai, niata.
 hái ~dí+a=ta
 okay say+ASSERT.PERF=REF
 '"Okay," (the man) said.'

7.64 yɨ'soriphĩ na pairo ka yahiripho'nare ta wayerɨkaa. nawĩoa.
 yɨ'só+ri-~phi ~dá pá-iro ká yahíri~pho'da+re=ta
 cut+NOM-CLS:bladelike get ALT-NOM.SG monkey heart+OBJ=REF
 wayé-rɨká+á
 cut.open-begin+ASSERT.PERF
 ~dá-~wio+a
 get-MOV.outward+ASSERT.PERF
 'He took his knife (and) cut the heart of another monkey. He took it out.'

7.65 yɨ'soriphĩkã so'towai sĩ'ophĩrãpo ñuiwĩoa.
 yɨ'só+ri-~phi-~ka so'tó-wa+i ~si'ó-~phi-~rapo
 cut+NOM-CLS:bladelike-DIM end-go+LOC pierce-CLS:bladelike-put.on
 ~yui-~wio+a
 offer-MOV.outward+ASSERT.PERF
 'He stuck it on the end of his knife (and) offered it out (of the hole).'

7.66 tirose'e ña'arokaa chɨba'aropha'yoa.
 tí+ró-sé'é ~ya'á-roka+a
 ANPH+SG-CONTR grab-DIST+ASSERT.PERF
 chɨ́-ba'a+ro-pha'yo+a
 eat-do/be.after+SG-COMPL+ASSERT.PERF
 'He (the curupira) grabbed (it) off (and) ate it up.'

7.67 kherokã chɨa.
 khé+ro-~ka chɨ́+a
 be.fast+SG-DIM eat+ASSERT.PERF
 'He gobbled it up.'

7.68 chɨ tu'sɨ ba'arokãta toa tirore sinituata.
 chɨ́ tu'sɨ́ ba'á+ro-~ka=ta toá tí+ró+ré
 eat finish do/be.after+SG-DIM=REF do.again ANPH+SG+OBJ
 ~sidítu+a=ta
 ask+ASSERT.PERF=REF
 'Just after he was done eating, he asked right away again:'

7.69 mɨ'ɨ yahiripho'nare waga toa, nia.
   ~bɨ'ɨ=yahíri~pho'da+re   wá+gá   toá   ~dí+a
   2SG(POSS)=heart+OBJ   give+IMPER   do.again   say+ASSERT.PERF
   '"Give me more of your heart," he (the curupira) said.'

7.70 hai, nia tirokɨ.
   hái   ~dí+a   tí+ró-kɨ́
   okay   say+ASSERT.PERF   ANPH+SG-MASC
   '"Okay," said the man.'

7.71 pairo yahiripho'nare ka yahiripho'nareta wayena, wayena tirore wawĩoa.
   pá-iro   yahíri~pho'da+re   ká   yahíri~pho'da+re=ta
   ALT-NOM.SG   heart+OBJ   monkey   heart+OBJ=REF
   wayé-~da   wayé-~da   tí+ró+ré
   cut.open-get   cut.open-get   ANPH+SG+OBJ
   wá-~wio+a
   give-MOV.outward+ASSERT.PERF
   '(He got) another monkey heart, cut it out, cut it out (and) stuck it out to him (the curupira).'

7.72 ba'aro mahsɨnose'e hi'na tirore nia.
   ba'á+ro   ~basɨ́+ro-se'e   ~hí'da   tí+ró+ré
   do/be.after+SG   man+SG-CONTR   EMPH   ANPH+SG+OBJ
   ~dí+a
   say+ASSERT.PERF
   'Afterwards, the man himself said to him (the curupira):'

7.73 mɨ'ɨkhɨ yɨ'ɨre mɨ'ɨ yahiripho'nare waga koiro, nia.
   ~bɨ'ɨ́-khɨ   yɨ'ɨ́+ré   ~bɨ'ɨ=yahíri~pho'da+re   wá+gá
   2SG-ADD   1SG+OBJ   2SG(POSS)=heart+OBJ   give+IMPER
   kó-iro   ~dí+a
   relative-NOM.SG   say+ASSERT.PERF
   '"Now you too give me your heart, relative," he said.'

7.74 to ã nichɨ, thɨ'oro tiro boraro ñakã yɨ'tia.
   to=~á=~dí-chɨ   thɨ'ó+ro   tí+ró   borá+ro   ~yá-~ka
   DEF=so=say-SW.REF   hear+SG   ANPH+SG   curupira+SG   be.bad-DIM
   yɨ'tí+a
   answer+ASSERT.PERF
   'Hearing what (the man) said, the evil curupira responded:'

7.75 mɨ'ɨ do'se yoa nari mɨ'ɨ yahiripho'nare, nia,
~bɨ'ɨ́   do'sé yoá   ~dá-ri   ~bɨ'ɨ=yahíri~pho'da+re
2SG   WH   do/make   get-INT   2SG(POSS)=heart+OBJ
~dí+a
say+ASSERT.PERF
"How did you take out your heart?" he said.'

7.76 a'riphĩ me're narokha'mare, ni, yɨ'soriphĩre ñui wĩoa tirore.
a'rí-~phí=~be're
DEM.PROX-CLS:bladelike=COM/INST
~dá+ro=~kha'ba+re   ~dí yɨ'só+ri-~phi+re
get+(3)SG=want/need+VIS.PERF.2/3   say cut+NOM-CLS:bladelike+OBJ
~yuí-~wio+a   tí+ró+ré
offer-MOV.outward+ASSERT.PERF   ANPH+SG+OBJ
"'(You) have to take it out with this knife," he (the man) said (and) offered it out to him (the curupira)."

7.77 tiphĩre tiro hi'na ña'a to yahiripho'nare phirokã beñɨa.
tí-~phi+re   tí+ró   ~hí'da   ~ya'á
ANPH-CLS:bladelike+OBJ   ANPH+SG   EMPH   grab
to=yahíri~pho'da+re   phí+ró-~ká   bé-~yɨ+a
3SG.POSS=heart+OBJ   be.slow+SG-DIM   inject/insert-try+ASSERT.PERF
'He (the curupira) immediately grabbed the knife (and) slowly tried to cut out his heart.'

7.78 phũriyɨ'dɨaka.
~phurí-yɨ'dɨ+a-ka
hurt-INTENS+AFFEC-ASSERT.IMPERF
'It hurt a lot.'

7.79 to phũrichɨ, thɨ'othu hi'na nia boraro mahsɨnore.
to=~phurí-chɨ   thɨ'ó-thu   ~hí'da   ~dí+a   borá+ro
DEF=hurt-SW.REF   hear-think   EMPH   say+ASSERT.PERF   curupira+SG
~basɨ́+ro+re
man+SG+OBJ
'When it hurt, the curupira then said to the man:'

7.80 phũriyɨ'dɨaka. thɨ'oro do'se yoa mɨ'ɨ nari, nia.
~phurí-yɨ'dɨ+a-ka
hurt-INTENS+AFFEC-ASSERT.IMPERF
thɨ'ó+ro   do'sé yoá   ~bɨ'ɨ́ ~dá-ri   ~dí+a
hear+(3)SG   WH   do/make   2SG   get-INT   say+ASSERT.PERF
"'It hurts a lot. How did you take it out?" he said.'

7.81 ã mʉ'ʉ phirokã yoaka mʉ'ʉ nia.
   ~á   ~bʉ'ʉ́ phí+ró-~ká   yoá-ka   ~bʉ'ʉ́
   so   2SG   be.slow+SG-DIM   do/make-ASSERT.IMPERF 2SG
   ~dí+a
   say+ASSERT.PERF
   '"You're doing it too slowly," (the man) said.'

7.82 phirokã mʉ'ʉ beñʉka mʉ'ʉ, nia.
   phí+ró-~ká   ~bʉ'ʉ́ bé-~yʉ-ka   ~bʉ'ʉ́
   be.slow+SG-DIM   2SG   inject/insert-try-ASSERT.IMPERF 2SG
   ~dí+a
   say+ASSERT.PERF
   '"You're trying to cut too slowly," (the man) said.'

7.83 kherokã yoarokã naka'aro kha'mare tuaro me're nia.
   khé+ro-~ka   yoá+ro-~ka
   be.fast+SG-DIM   be.far+SG-DIM
   ~dá-ka'a+ro=~kha'ba+re
   get-do.moving+(3)SG=want/need+VIS.PERF.2/3
   tuá+ro=~be're   ~dí+a
   be.strong+SG=COM/INST   say+ASSERT.PERF
   '"It has to go in quickly, hard," (the man) said.'

7.84 to ã nichʉ thʉ'oro hi'na, tiro boraro ñakã tiphĩ yʉ'soriphĩre ña'a
   hi'na, wa'kʉenoka ñosaphu'anoka sãnokaa.
   to=~á=~dí-chʉ   thʉ'ó+ro   ~hí'da tí+ró   borá+ro
   DEF=so=say-SW.REF   hear+(3)SG   EMPH   ANPH+SG   curupira+SG
   ~yá-~ka   tí-~phí   yʉ'só+ri-~phi+re
   be.bad-DIM   ANPH-CLS:bladelike   cut+NOM-CLS:bladelike+OBJ
   ~ya'á   ~hí'da wa'kʉé-~doka   ~yosá-phu'a-~doka
   grab   EMPH   do.unexpectedly-COMPL   force.into-stab-COMPL
   ~sá-~doka+a
   MOV.inside-COMPL+ASSERT.PERF
   'Hearing/understanding what (the man) said, the evil curupira took the little knife (and) suddenly stabbed it in, driving it in all the way.'

7.85 ñohsaphu'aroka sãnokaa.
   ~yosá-phu'a-roka   ~sá-~doka+a
   force.into-stab-DIST   MOV.inside-COMPL+ASSERT.PERF
   '(The curupira) stabbed himself.'

7.86 *borasʉka'a wa'aro koataa.*
borá-~sʉ-ka'a   wa'á+ro   koá-ta+a
fall-arrive-do.moving go+(3)SG NONVIS-come+ASSERT.PERF
'(The man heard) He fell right down.'

7.87 *phũ! do'kaka'asʉ̃'awa'aa.*
~phu do'ká-ka'a-~sʉ+a=wa'a+a
phum crash-do.moving-arrive+AFFEC=go+ASSERT.PERF
'Phum! He fell flat on the ground.'

7.88 *toita yariawa'aa.*
tó+i=ta   yarí+á=wa'a+a
REM+LOC=REF die+AFFEC=go+ASSERT.PERF
'He died right there.'

7.89 *tiro mahsʉnose'e sinitua.*
tí+ró   ~basʉ́+ro-se'e   ~sidítu+a
ANPH+SG man+SG-CONTR ask+ASSERT.PERF
'The man asked:'

7.90 *ne koiro, nia.*
~dé   kó-iro   ~dí+a
hello relative-NOM.SG say+ASSERT.PERF
'"How's it going, relative?" he said.'

7.91 *yʉ'ʉre khero mʉ'ʉ yahiripho'nare yʉ'ʉre waga nimaa.*
yʉ'ʉ́+ré khé+ro   ~bʉ'ʉ=yahíri~pho'da+re yʉ'ʉ́+ré   wá+gá
1SG+OBJ be.fast+SG 2SG(POSS)=heart+OBJ   1SG+OBJ   give+IMPER
~dí-~ba+a
say-FRUS+ASSERT.PERF
'"Give me your heart right now," he demanded (to no avail).'

7.92 *dʉ'tamaniaa.*
dʉ'tá-~badia+a
make.noise-not.exist+ASSERT.PERF
'There was no sound (from the curupira).'

7.93 *yaria wa'ari hia topʉrota.*
yarí+á   wa'á+ri   hí+a   tó-pʉ+ro=ta
die+AFFEC go+NOM(INFER) COP+ASSERT.PERF REM-LOC+SG=REF
'He had (apparently) died right there.'

7.94 *do'se yoaro a'riro yʉ'ʉre yʉ'tierahari ni tiro mahsʉnose'e hi'na.*
do'sé   yoá+ro   a'rí+ró   yʉ'ʉ́+ré
WH   do/make+(3)SG DEM.PROX+SG 1SG+OBJ

yu'ti-éra-hari   ~dí tí+ró   ~basú+ro-se'e ~hí'da
answer-NEG-INT.IMPERF say ANPH+SG man+SG-CONTR EMPH
'"Why isn't he answering me?" the man then wondered.'

7.95 *õpari kohpaka phorerokã wĩoñurokaa.*
    ~ó-pá+rí   kopá-ká   phoré+ró-~ká
    DEIC.PROX-ALT+NOM hole-CLS:round make.hole+SG-DIM
    ~wió-~yu-roka+a
    MOV.outward-look-DIST+ASSERT.PERF
    'He made a little hole like this (and) peered out.'

7.96 *phirirota khõaro khõa yaria wa'ari hia.*
    phí+ri+ro=ta   ~khoá+ro ~khoa yarí+á wa'á+ri
    be.big+NOM+SG=REF be.lying+SG be.lying die+AFFEC go-NOM(INFER)
    hí+a
    COP+ASSERT.PERF
    'The big guy was lying there, (apparently) lying there dead.'

7.97 *yu'soriphĩ to yahiripho'naputa duhkua.*
    yu'só+ri-~phi   to=yahíri~pho'da-pu=ta
    cut+NOM-CLS:bladelike 3SG.POSS=heart-LOC=REF
    dukú+a
    stand+ASSERT.PERF
    'The knife was sticking (lit., 'standing') right in his heart.'

7.98 *ã yoachu ñu, yariawa'aro hi'na ti ñaka, ni wa'a suhka khãriawa'aa.*
    ~a=yoá-chu   ~yú
    so=do/make-SW.REF realize
    yarí+á=wa'a+ro ~hí'da ti=~yá-~ka ~dí
    die+AFFEC=go+(3)SG EMPH ANPH=be.bad-DIM say
    wa'á suka ~kharí+a=wa'a+a
    go lie.down sleep+AFFEC=go+ASSERT.PERF
    'When he realized (the curupira was dead), he said/thought "That evil guy is really dead,' (and) he went, lay down, (and) went to sleep.'

7.99 *to ã yoachuta, bo'reka'awa'aa.*
    to=~á   yoá-chu=ta   bo'ré-ka'a-wa'a+a
    REM= so do/make-SW.REF=REF be.light-do.moving-go+ASSERT.PERF
    'While he slept, dawn came.'

7.100 *bo'reka'achu ñu hi'na tiro wihaa.*
    bo'ré-ka'a-chu   ~yú ~hí'da tí+ró
    be.light-do.moving-SW.REF realize EMPH ANPH+SG

wihá+a
MOV.outward+ASSERT.PERF
'When he realized it was morning, he went out.'

7.101 *ñua tirore. phiriro khõaa.*

~yɨ+á   tí+ró+ré   phí+ri+ro
see/look+ASSERT.PERF ANPH+SG+OBJ be.big+NOM+SG

~khoá+a
be.lying+ASSERT.PERF

'He saw him (the curupira). The big guy was lying there.'

7.102 *borarowɨ'rɨ hia tiro.*

borá+ro-wɨ'rɨ   hí+a   tí+ró
curupira+SG-AUG COP+ASSERT.PERF ANPH+SG

'It was a huge curupira.'

7.103 *phoari ñatirirowɨ'rɨ hia tiro.*

phoá+rí ~yá-ti+ri+ro-wɨ'rɨ   hí+a
hair+PL be.bad-ATTRIB+NOM+SG-AUG COP+ASSERT.PERF

tí+ró
ANPH+SG

'He was a large horribly hairy being.'

7.104 *topɨre tiro wiha wa'aa.*

tó-pɨ+re   tí+ró   wihá   wa'á+a
REM-LOC+OBJ ANPH+SG MOV.outward go+ASSERT.PERF

'He (the man) went out (and) left that place.'

7.105 *to kayare naka'aa, to yɨ'soriphĩre thɨawera thuaa te to yawɨ'ɨpɨ.*

to=ká-ya+re   ~da-ka'a+a
3SG.POSS=black.monkey-PL+OBJ get-do.moving+ASSERT.PERF

to=yɨ'so+ri-~phí+re   ~thɨá-wera
3SG.POSS=cut+NOM-CLS:bladelike+OBJ pull.out-remove

thuá+a   té   to=yá-wɨ'ɨ-pɨ
return+ASSERT.PERF all.the.way 3SG.POSS=POSS-house-LOC

'He grabbed the monkeys, yanked out his knife, (and) went all the way back home.'

7.106 *sɨnokaa tiro.*

~sú-~doka+a   tí+ró
arrive-COMPL+ASSERT.PERF ANPH+SG

'He got back (home).'

7.107 *topɨ sɨ to namonore ya'ua:*
    tó-pɨ   *~sɨ́*   *to=~dabó+ro+re*   *ya'ú+a*
    REM-LOC arrive 3SG.POSS=wife+SG+OBJ tell+ASSERT.PERF
    'Arriving there, he told his wife:'

7.108 *yɨ'ɨ õse wa'ati, ni, a'rina kayare wãhai, nia.*
    yɨ'ɨ   *~ó-sé*   *wa'á-ati*   *~dí*
    1SG DEIC.PROX-be.like go-IMPERF say
    a'rí-~dá   *ká-ya+re*   *~wahá+i*
    DEM.PROX-PL black.monkey-PL+OBJ kill+VIS.PERF.1
    ~dí+a
    say+ASSERT.PERF
    '"This is what happened," he said, "I killed these monkeys," he said.'
    (lit., '"Here's how it went," he said . . .')

7.109 *hai ni. tikoro wahche tinare hi'na.*
    hái   *~dí*   *tí-kó+ró*   *waché*   *tí-~da+re*   *~hí'da*
    okay say ANPH-FEM+SG be.happy ANPH-PL+OBJ EMPH
    '"Good," she said (and) was happy with the monkeys.'

7.110 *cha da're tirore sɨ'ochɨ yoaa.*
    chá   *da'ré*   *tí+ró+ré*   *sɨ'ó-chɨ*
    prepared.food prepare ANPH+SG+OBJ do.together-eat
    yoá+a
    do/make+ASSERT.PERF
    'She prepared him a meal (and) they ate together.'

7.111 *ba'aro hi'na yoaa, phititia khɨ'mari yɨ'dɨri.*
    ba'á+ro   *~hí'da*   *yoá+a*
    do/be.after+SG EMPH do/make+ASSERT.PERF
    phitítia-~khɨ'ba+ri   *yɨ'dɨ+ri*
    four-year+PL time.pass+NOM
    'A long time passed, a period of four years.'

7.112 *tirota, yɨ'ɨ boraro yɨ'ɨ wãhakɨrirore ñɨsibɨ nia.*
    tí+ró=ta   *yɨ'ɨ́*   *borá+ro*   *yɨ'ɨ́*   *~wahá-kɨ+ri+ro+re*
    ANPH+SG=REF 1SG curupira+SG 1SG kill-MASC+NOM+SG+OBJ
    ~yɨ-síbɨ́   *~dí+a*
    see/look-intend say+ASSERT.PERF
    'The same guy (said) "I'm going there to see that curupira that I killed," he said.'

7.113 *to pirire natai niha.*
    to=pí+ri+re   *~dá-ta+i*   *~dí-ha*
    3SG.POSS=tooth+PL+OBJ get-come+(1/2)MASC be.PROG-VIS.IMPERF.1
    "'I'm bringing back his teeth.'"

7.114 *bʉhsarida yoaitai niha.*
    busá+ri-da   *yoá+i-ta+i*
    adorn+NOM-CLS:threadlike do/make+(1/2)MASC-INTENT+(1/2)MASC
    ~dí-ha
    be.PROG-VIS.IMPERF.1
    "'I'm going to make (I'll be making) a necklace.'"

7.115 *tina noaro sihpa hiso'a, ni.*
    tí-~da   *~dóá+ró*   *sípa*   *hí-so'a*   *~dí*
    ANPH-PL be.beautiful+SG be.shiny COP-appear.to.be say
    '"Those beautiful (teeth) seemed to be very shiny," he said.'

7.116 *wa'aa te topʉ.*
    wa'á+a   *té*   *tó-pʉ*
    go+ASSERT.PERF all.the.way REM-LOC
    'He went back there.'

7.117 *topʉ sʉ̃ ñʉ mahkamaa.*
    tó-pʉ   *~sʉ́*   *~yʉ́*   *~baká-~ba+a*
    REM-LOC arrive see/look look/search.for-FRUS+ASSERT.PERF
    'He got there (and) looked, searching to no avail.'

7.118 *ne maniaa.*
    ~dé   *~badía+a*
    NEG not.exist+ASSERT.PERF
    'There was nothing.'

7.119 *bayʉ'dʉkã wa'ari hia.*
    bá-yʉ'dʉ-~ka   *wa'á+ri*   *hí+a*
    decompose-INTENS-DIM go+NOM(INFER) COP+ASSERT.PERF
    'It (the curupira's body) had (apparently) decomposed completely.'

7.120 *ne bahueraa.*
    ~dé   *bahu-éra+a*
    NEG be.visible-NEG+ASSERT.PERF
    'There was no trace of it.'

7.121 *bayʉ'dʉkã buhtiari hia.*
    bá-yʉ'dʉ-~ka   *butí+a+ri*
    decompose-INTENS-DIM disappear+AFFEC+NOM(INFER)

hí+a
COP+ASSERT.PERF
'Completely rotted, it had (apparently) disappeared.'

7.122 *ã yoachɨ ñɨ, hi'na tiro to yoariphĩre na hi'na,*
~*a=yoá-chɨ* ~*yɨ* ~*hí'da tí+ró*
so=do-SW.REF see EMPH ANPH+SG
to=yoá+rí-~phí+ré ~*dá* ~*hí'da*
3SG.POSS=be.long+NOM-CLS:bladelike+OBJ get EMPH
'Realizing that, he immediately took out his machete . . .'

7.123 *õita tiñakã khõamare, ni.*
~*ó+í=ta* *tí-~yá-~ká* ~*khoá-~ba+re*
DEIC.PROX-LOC=REF ANPH-be.bad-DIM be.lying-FRUS+VIS.PERF.2/3
~*dí*
say
'"Right here where that evil thing used to be lying," he said . . .'

7.124 *dɨ'teka yoa ya'papɨre hi'na.*
dɨ'té-ka *yoá* *ya'pá-pɨ+ré* ~*hí'da*
chop-PREDICT do/make ground-LOC+OBJ EMPH
'"I'm going to dig up this very ground."'

7.125 *to õse dɨ'terokãchɨ, toita tiro borarowɨ'rɨ wã'karuku sɨ bahuanokaa.*
to=~ó-sé *dɨ'té+ro-~ka-chɨ* *tó+i=ta*
DEF=DEIC.PROX-be.like chop+SG-DIM-SW.REF REM+LOC=REF
tí+ró *borá+ro-wɨ'rɨ* ~*wa'ká-ruku-~sɨ*
ANPH+SG curupira+SG-AUG wake.up-stand-arrive
bahú+a-~doka+a
be.visible+AFFEC-COMPL+ASSERT.PERF
'When he sliced into the ground like this, the big curupira revived (and) appeared whole before him.'

7.126 *wã'karukusɨ̃mɨa, nia tirore:*
~*wa'ká-ruku-~sɨ-~bɨ+a* ~*dí+a* *tí+ró+ré*
wake.up-stand-arrive-run+AFFEC say+ASSERT.PERF ANPH+SG+OBJ
'(The curupira) waking and rising up quickly, said to him (the man):'

7.127 *noana, mɨ'ɨ yɨ'ɨre wã'kora, nia.*
~*dóádá* ~*bɨ'ɨ* *yɨ'ɨ+ré* ~*wa'kó+ra*
thank.you 2SG 1SG+OBJ wake.up+VIS.IMPERF.2/3
~*dí+a*
say+ASSERT.PERF
'"Thank you, you woke me up," (the curupira) said.'

7.128 *yɨ'ɨ khãriyɨ'dɨa wa'ari hika, nia.*
      yɨ'ɨ   *~kharí-yɨ'dɨ+a*   *wa'á+ri*   *hí-ka*
      1SG   sleep-INTENS+AFFEC   go+NOM(INFER)   COP-ASSERT.IMPERF
      ~dí+a
      say+ASSERT.PERF
      '"I've been asleep a long time!" (the curupira) said.'

7.129 *mɨ'ɨ hikɨ yɨ'ɨre wã'kora, nia . . .*
      ~bɨ'ɨ   *hí-kɨ*   *yɨ'ɨ+ré*   *~wa'kó+ra*
      2SG   COP-(1/2)MASC   1SG+OBJ   wake+VIS.IMPERF.2/3
      ~dí+a
      say+ASSERT.PERF
      '"You're the one who woke me up," he said.'

7.130 *mipɨre ã hikɨ mɨ'ɨre yɨ'ɨ mɨ'ɨ wa'ikina wãhasihtotatɨ kɨ̃dɨ yɨhkɨkɨsika õpadɨ hidɨ mɨ'ɨre waita, nia.*
      ~bí-pɨ́+ré   *~a=hí-kɨ*   *~bɨ'ɨ́+ré* *yɨ'ɨ́* *~bɨ'ɨ́*
      now-LOC+OBJ so=COP-(1/2)MASC 2SG+OBJ 1SG 2SG(POSS)
      wa'í-~kídá *~wahá-sito-ta-tɨ*   *~kɨ́-dɨ*
      animal-PL   kill-MOV.circular-come-stick one-CLS:cylindrical.straight
      yɨkɨ́-kɨ-sika   *~ó-pá-dɨ́*
      tree-CLS:tree-piece   DEIC.PROX-ALT-CLS:cylindrical.straight
      hí-dɨ   *~bɨ'ɨ́+ré* *wá+i-ta*
      COP-CLS:cylindrical.straight 2SG+OBJ give+(1/2)MASC-INTENT
      ~dí+a
      say+ASSERT.PERF
      '"Now, for this reason, I'm going to give you a hunting stick, one this big," he said.'

7.131 *tɨ me're mɨ'ɨ wa'ikinawãha sihtotaga, nia.*
      tɨ́=~be're   *~bɨ'ɨ́*   *wa'í-~kídá-~wáhá*
      stick=COM/INST 2SG   animal-PL-kill
      sitó-ta+ga   *~dí+a*
      MOV.circular-come+IMPER say+ASSERT.PERF
      '"With this stick, you go around hunting," he (the curupira) said.'

7.132 *hai, nia.*
      hái   *~dí+a*
      okay say+ASSERT.PERF
      '"Okay," (the man) said.'

7.133 *ã nirota tiro boraro ñakã hi'na tɨ yɨhkɨkɨkãre bahua me'rea.*
      ~a=~dí+ro=ta   *tí+ró*   *borá+ro*   *~yá-~ka*   *~hí'da*
      so=say+SG=REF ANPH+SG curupira+SG be.bad-DIM EMPH

        tú   yukú-ku-~ka+re   bahú+a=~be're+a
        stick tree-CLS:tree-DIM+OBJ appear+AFFEC=COM/INST+ASSERT.PERF
        'Saying that, the evil curupira then made a little stick appear (with him).'

7.134 *tirore waa.*

        tí+ró+ré   wá+a
        ANPH+SG+OBJ give+ASSERT.PERF
        '(The curupira) gave (it) to him (the man).'

7.135 *mʉ'ʉ a'ritʉ me're wa'ikinawãhaga.*

        ~bʉ'ʉ a'rí-tʉ́=~be're   wa'í-~kídá-~wáhá+gá
        2SG   DEM.PROX-stick=COM/INST animal-PL-kill+IMPER
        '"Go hunt with this stick."'

7.136 *yabaina mʉ'ʉ wãhaduainare wãhaga, nia.*

        yabá-~ídá   ~bʉ'ʉ ~wahá-dua-~ida+re   ~wahá+ga
        WH-NOM.PL   2SG   kill-DESID-NOM.PL+OBJ kill+IMPER
        ~dí+a
        say+ASSERT.PERF
        '"Go kill (hunt) whatever you want," he said.'

7.137 *hai, nia tirokhʉ.*

        hái   ~dí+a   tí+ró-khʉ
        okay say+ASSERT.PERF ANPH+SG-ADD
        '"It's okay," (the curupira) also said.'

7.138 *ã ni tirore tʉre waa.*

        ~a=~dí tí+ró+ré   tú+re   wá+a
        so=say ANPH+SG+OBJ stick+OBJ give+ASSERT.PERF
        'Saying that, (the curupira) gave him (the man) the stick.'

7.139 *hai, ni tiro.*

        hái   ~dí tí+ró
        okay say ANPH+SG
        '"Okay," he (the man) said.'

7.140 *tʉre ña'anahkaa. thuawa'aa.*

        tú+re   ~ya'á-~daka+a   thuá-wa'a+a
        stick+OBJ grab-do.together+ASSERT.PERF return-go+ASSERT.PERF
        'He took the stick with him. (He) went back home.'

7.141 *tiro borarokhɨ wa'awa'aa.*
    tí+ró   borá+ro-khɨ   wa'á-wa'a+a
    ANPH+SG curupira+SG-ADD go-go+ASSERT.PERF
    'The curupira also went away.'

7.142 *thuwa'a to'i kɨ̃iro khatama'a bohkasɨ̃a toi.*
    thuá-wa'a   tó+i   ~kú-író   khatá~bá'á
    return-go   REM+LOC one/a-NOM.SG jacú.bird
    boká-~sɨ+a   tó+i
    find-arrive+ASSERT.PERF REM+LOC
    '(The man) going back, came upon a jacú bird.'

7.143 *tirore ñɨ, photokatihari, ni.*
    tí+ró+ré   ~yɨ́   photó-~ka-ti-hari   ~dí
    ANPH+SG+OBJ look truth-DIM-VBZ-INT.IMPERF say
    'Looking at it (the jacú), he said/thought, "Could it be really true?"'

7.144 *tɨre ña'a õse khãka'a yoaa.*
    tɨ́+re   ~ya'á   ~ó-sé   ~khá-ka'a
    stick+OBJ grab DEIC.PROX-be.like chop-do.moving
    yoá+a
    do/make+ASSERT.PERF
    'He took the stick (and) shook it like this (chopping/hitting motion).'

7.145 *thõ'ose tɨre khãka'a yoachɨta, tiro boradihiawa'aa.*
    ~tho'ó-sé   tɨ́+re   ~khá-ka'a   yoá-chɨ=ta
    shake-be.like stick+OBJ chop-do.moving do/make-SW.REF=REF
    tí+ró   borá-diha+a=wa'a+a
    ANPH+SG fall-MOV.down+AFFEC=go+ASSERT.PERF
    'As soon as he shook the stick like this, it (the jacú bird) fell over.'

7.146 *pa! photokãtiri hira, ni.*
    pa   photó-~ka-ti+ri   hí+ra   ~dí
    wow! truth-DIM-VBZ+NOM(INFER) COP+VIS.IMPERF.2/3 say
    '"Wow. It (apparently) is really true," he said.'

7.147 *tirore nanakaa. tiro thuaa.*
    tí+ró+ré   ~dá-~daka+a
    ANPH+SG+OBJ get-do/be.together+ASSERT.PERF
    tí+ró   thuá+a
    ANPH+SG return+ASSERT.PERF
    '(The man) took it (the bird) with him. He went back home.'

7.148 *te to yawɨ'ɨpɨ sɨ̃a.*
 té   to=yá-wɨ'ɨ-pɨ   ~sɨ́+a
 all.the.way 3SG.POSS=POSS-house-LOC arrive+ASSERT.PERF
 'He went all the way back to his house.'

7.149 *to yawɨ'ɨpɨ thuasɨ̃, tirore khata~ba'are to namonore wa yoaa.*
 to=yá-wɨ'ɨ-pɨ   thuá-~sɨ   tí+ró+ré
 3SG.POSS=POSS-house-LOC return-arrive ANPH+SG+OBJ
 khatá~bá'á+ré   to=~dabó+ro+re   wá   yoá+a
 jacú.bird+OBJ 3SG.POSS=wife+SG+OBJ give do/make+ASSERT.PERF
 '(He) returned to his house (and) gave the jacú bird to his wife.'

7.150 *tirore tikoro sɨ'o chɨada're chɨ yoaa tirore.*
 tí+ró+ré   tí-kó+ró   sɨ'ó   chɨa-da're chɨ́
 ANPH+SG+OBJ ANPH-FEM+SG do.together food-prepare eat
 yoá+a   tí+ró+ré
 do/make+ASSERT.PERF ANPH+SG+OBJ
 'She cooked it (and) ate it together with him.'

7.151 *ã yo tiro borarose'e tɨkãre waro nia.*
 ~a=yó   tí+ró   borá+ro-se'e   tɨ́-~ka+re
 so=do/make ANPH+SG curupira+SG-CONTR stick-DIM+OBJ
 wá+ro   ~dí+a
 give+(3)SG say+ASSERT.PERF
 'So, when the curupira gave him (the man) the stick, he said:'

7.152 *ne noare ya'ukɨ ninobɨ, nia.*
 ~dé   ~doá+re   ya'ú-kɨ   ~dí-~dobɨ
 NEG WH+OBJ tell-(1/2)MASC be.PROG-IMP.EMPH
 ~dí+a
 say+ASSERT.PERF
 '"Tell no one," he said.'

7.153 *mɨ'ɨ ya'ukɨ yariawa'akɨka, nia tirore.*
 ~bɨ'ɨ   ya'ú-kɨ   yarí+á=wa'a-kɨ-ka
 2SG tell-(1/2)MASC die+AFFEC=go-(1/2)MASC-PREDICT
 ~dí+a   tí+ró+ré
 say+ASSERT.PERF ANPH+SG+OBJ
 '"If you tell, you'll die," he told him (the man).'

7.154 *ã nire niro, tɨre nɨo khɨatia tiro.*
 ~a=~dí-re   ~dí+ro   tɨ́+re   ~dɨó
 so=say-CLS:generic say+SG stick+OBJ hide

       khɨá-ti+a   *tí+ró*
       hold/have-go.behind+ASSERT.PERF   ANPH+SG

       'Because the curupira warned him, he (the man) hid the stick away.'

7.155 *wa'ikinawãharo wa'aro, tɨre nawa'aka'a, wa'ikina phayɨ wãhaatia.*

       wa'i-~kídá-~wáhá+ró   *wa'á+ro*   *tɨ+re*   *~dá-wa'a-ka'a*
       animal-PL-kill+(3)SG go+(3)SG stick+OBJ get-go-do.moving

       wa'i-~kídá *phayɨ́* *~wahá-ati+a*
       animal-PL   many   kill-IMPERF+ASSERT.PERF

       'When he went hunting, he took the stick along (and) would always kill lots of animals.'

7.156 *ã ta yoa to koyase'e tirore sinituaatimaa:*

       ~á=ta *yoá* *to=kó-ya-se'e*   *tí+ró+ré*
       so=REF do 3SG.POSS=relative-PL-CONTR ANPH+SG+OBJ

       ~sidítu+a-ati-~ba+a
       ask+PL-IMPERF-FRUS+ASSERT.PERF

       'His relatives, though, were always demanding to know (unsuccessfully):'

7.157 *mɨ'ɨ do'se yoa wãhahari?*

       ~bɨ'ɨ *do'sé* *yoá*   *~wahá-hari*
       2SG   WH   do/make kill-INT.IMPERF

       '"How do you kill (hunt so many animals)?"'

7.158 *topeina pe'ri wãheratii, nia.*

       tó-pe-~ida   *pé'ri*   *~wah(a)-éra-ati+i*
       DEF-CQUANT-NOM.PL many kill-NEG-IMPERF+VIS.PERF.1

       ~dí+a
       say+ASSERT.PERF

       '"We don't kill that many," they said.'

7.159 *to ã nichɨ thɨ'o tirose'e ya'ueraatia.*

       to=á   *~dí-chɨ*   *thɨ'ó* *tí+ró-sé'é*
       DEF=so say-SW.REF hear   ANPH+SG-CONTR

       ya'u-éra-ati+a
       tell-NEG-IMPERF+ASSERT.PERF

       'Even when he heard them say that, he didn't tell.'

7.160 *ãta yoa kɨta hi'na tiro phayuru si'nikhã'ayɨ'dɨawa'aa.*

       ~á=ta *yoá* *~kɨ=ta*   *~hí'da* *tí+ró*   *phayúrú*
       so=REF do   one=REF EMPH   ANPH+SG caxiri.beer

~si'dí-~kha'a-yɨ'dɨ+a=wa'a+a
drink-dream-INTENS+AFFEC=go+ASSERT.PERF

'Then, one day he got really drunk on caxiri beer.'

7.161 khã'ayɨ'dɨamaro, tinare tiro ya'unokaa.

~kha'á-yɨ'dɨ+a-~ba+ro   tí-~da+re   tí+ró
dream-INTENS+AFFEC-FRUS+(3)SG ANPH-PL+OBJ ANPH+SG

ya'ú-~doka+a
tell-COMPL+ASSERT.PERF

'Getting really drunk, he told them everything.'

7.162 yɨ'ɨ ã yoa wa'ikinawãhaha, ni ya'ua.

yɨ'ɨ   ~a=yoá wa'í-~kídá-~wáhá-há   ~dí ya'ú+a
1SG   so=do   animal-PL-kill-VIS.IMPERF.1 say tell+ASSERT.PERF

'"That's how I hunt all those animals," he confessed.'

7.163 ã ni tu'sɨ hi'na, panɨma, tiro hi'na õ ba'arokãi wɨ'ɨdu'tuka'ai sã'ama'nota ãga khõ'oawa'aa.

~a=~dí tu'sɨ ~hí'da pá-~dɨba tí+ró   ~hí'da
so=say finish EMPH   ALT-day ANPH+SG EMPH

~ó   ba'á+ro-~ka+i   wɨ'ɨ-du'tu-ka'a+i
DEIC.PROX do/be.after+SG-DIM+LOC house-around-side+LOC

~sá-~ba'do=ta   ~agá
MOV.inside-penetrate=REF   poisonous.snake

~kho'ó+a=wa'a+a
bite+AFFEC=go+ASSERT.PERF

'No sooner had he said that, the very next day, he was just going a little way into (the brush) around his house (and) he was bitten by a poisonous snake.'

7.164 agã khõ'o yoa tiro hi'na, ti nɨmaita hi'na yariawa'aa hi'na tiro.

~agá   ~kho'ó yoá   tí+ró   ~hí'da
poisonous.snake bite   do/make ANPH+SG EMPH

ti=~dɨbá+í=ta   ~hí'da yarí+á=wa'a+a   ~hí'da
ANPH=day+LOC=REF   EMPH   die+AFFEC=go+ASSERT.PERF EMPH

tí+ró
ANPH+SG

'The snake bit him (and) that very day he just died.'

7.165 kotimaa, kotirose'e, ne tirore thɨoeraa.

kó-ti-~ba+a   kó-ti+ro-se'e
medicine-VBZ-FRUS+ASSERT.PERF medicine-VBZ+SG-CONTR

~dé tí+ró+ré   thʉo-éra+a
NEG ANPH+SG+OBJ   be.successful-NEG+ASSERT.PERF

'He took medicine, however it (the medicine-taking) didn't cure him.'

7.166 *tiro yariawa'a, to yahiripho'na hi'na tiro boraro ka'apʉ wa'awa'aa.*
tí+ró   yari+á=wa'a   to=yahíri~pho'da   ~hí'da   tí+ró
ANPH+SG   die+AFFEC=go 3SG.POSS=heart   EMPH   ANPH+SG

borá+ro   ka'á-pʉ   wa'á-wa'a+a
curupira+SG   near-LOC   go-go+ASSERT.PERF

'After he died, his heart (spirit) went off to be with the curupira.'

7.167 *ðĩ phitira a'ri khiti.*
~ó+í   phití+ra   a'rí   khiti
DEIC.PROX-LOC   end+VIS.IMPERF.2/3   DEM.PROX   story

'Here ends this story.'

Written texts from *Let's Study in Kotiria*

The five short written texts below are all from the book *Let's Study in Kotiria: Kotiria Animal Stories*. The book is comprised of texts written during the first two Kotiria language workshops;[11] the original idea was that it would be a resource for teachers working on Kotiria literacy with young school children. The animal theme and the title of the book were chosen during the first workshop, and most of the stories are indeed about animals (the theme very generally including four-legged creatures, monkeys, insects, birds, and fish). However, during the second workshop, when we analyzed the different syllables represented in the animal names in the texts they had already written (the names being the intended focus words for literacy work), we realized that for a few important syllables (such as *wʉ*), we had no corresponding texts. The next problem was that they could not think of animal names that contained the particular missing syllables, so it was decided that a few more short stories whose focus words had the appropriate syllables would be added to the collection, even if they were on topics other than animals. This explains why we find stories such as text 12 (about airplanes, the initial syllable of the Kotiria word being *wʉ*) in the Kotiria "animal" storybook.

---

[11] Most of the texts were written by individual participants, whose names appear after the titles of their stories. The introductory text was written collectively by a group of teachers from the Kotiria school. The first lines of all texts in the collection were later revised to reflect decisions made regarding orthographic representation (see §2.10).

8. Introduction to *Let's Study in Kotiria: Kotiria Animal Stories* (written collectively)

8.1 *a'rithu hira wa'ikina khiti yaya'urithu.*
    a'rí-thú   *hí+ra*   *wa'i-~kídá khiti*
    DEM.PROX-CLS:stacked COP+VIS.IMPERF.2/3 animal-PL story
    yá-ya'u+ri-thu
    POSS-tell+NOM-CLS:stacked
    'This is our own (Kotiria) animal storybook.'

8.2 *sã pho'na bu'eti hira.*
    ~sa=~pho'dá   *bu'é-ti*   *hí+ra*
    1PL.EXC.POSS=children study/learn-VBZ COP+VIS.IMPERF.2/3
    'It is for our children to study.'

8.3 *ã yoana, sã kotiria ne bosi sã yahoare durukuare.*
    ~a=yoá-~da   *~sá*   *kó-ti+ri+a*   *~dé bó-sí*
    so=do-(1/2)PL 1PL.EXC water-VBZ+NOM+PL NEG forget-NEG.IRR
    ~sa=yá-hoa+re   *dú-ruku+a+re*
    1PL.EXC.POSS=POSS-write+OBJ talk-stand+PL+OBJ
    'This way, we Kotiria won't forget how to write (and) speak.' (lit., 'our writing and our language')

8.4 *a'ripa mahkaina, ba'aro mahkaina, hipitina.*
    a'rí-pá   *~baká-~ida*   *ba'á+ro*   *~baká-~ida*
    DEM.PROX-CLS:time origin-NOM.PL do/be.after+SG origin-NOM.PL
    hí-phiti-~da
    COP-COLL-PL
    'For those here now, and for those who come later, for everybody.'

8.5 *wa'maropure, ñarana yare, bu'ena ñaro yu'dua thu'othui sã.*
    ~wa'bá+ro-pu+re   *~yará-~da*   *yá-re*
    be.young+SG-LOC+OBJ white.people-PL POSS-CLS:generic
    bu'é-~da   *~yá+ro*   *yu'dú-a*   *thu'ó-thu+i*
    study/learn-(1/2)PL be.bad+SG INTENS-AFFEC hear-think+VIS.PERF.1
    ~sá
    1PL.EXC
    'When we were young, it was really hard for us to understand school in the white people's language.'

8.6 *mipure sã yakotiria yare bu'ena phiro wahcheha.*
    ~bí-pú+ré   *~sa=yá-ko-ti+ri+a*   *yá-re*
    now-LOC+OBJ 1PL.EXC.POSS=POSS-water-VBZ+NOM+PL POSS-CLS:generic

bu'é-~da   phi+ro   waché-ha
study-(1/2)PL be.big+SG be.happy-VIS.IMPERF.1

'Now we're very happy to have our own Kotiria learning (writing system or school).'

8.7 *yoaripa sã thʉ'oturi ba'aro a'rire sʉ̃ha.*
yóá+rí-pá   ~sá   thʉ'ó-tu+ri   ba'á+ro
be.long+NOM-CLS:time 1PL.EXC hear-think+NOM do/be.after+SG
a'rí+ré   ~sʉ́-ha
DEM.PROX+OBJ arrive-VIS.IMPERF.1

'What we've been thinking about for a long time has arrived.'

8.8 *ã yoana, a'ri thure hoaha sã kotiria.*
~a=yoá-~da   a'rí-thú+ré   hoá-ha   ~sá
so=do-(1/2)PL DEM.PROX-CLS:stacked+OBJ write-VIS.IMPERF.1 1PL.EXC
kó-ti+ri+a
water-VBZ+NOM+PL

'That's why we Kotiria are writing this book.'

8.9 *setembro 2002 khʉ'ma hichʉ, yoarithu hira.*
setembro 2002   ~khʉ'bá hí-chʉ   yoá+ri-thʉ
September[B] 2002 year   COP-SW.REF do/make+NOM-CLS:stacked
hí+ra
COP+VIS.IMPERF.2/3

'It's September of the year 2002, and we're making this book.'

8.10 *wa'ikina khiti kotiria ya me're.*
wa'í-~kídá   khití   kó-ti+ri+a   yá=~be're
animal-PL story   water-VBZ+NOM+PL POSS=COM/INST

'Animal stories in our own Kotiria (language).'

9. *Nunana* 'Horsefly'
(written by João Paulo Almeida)

9.1 *a'riro wamatira nunana.*
a'rí+ró   ~wabá-tí+rá   ~dudá-~da
DEM.PROX+SG name-VBZ+VIS.IMPERF.2/3 horsefly-PL

'This is called a horsefly (biting fly).'

9.2 *tiro ba'ro mahsare wa'ikinare wa'asʉ̃ wimika.*
tí+ró=ba'ro   ~basá+ré   wa'í-~kídá+ré   wa'á-~sʉ
ANPH+SG=kind people+OBJ animal-PL+OBJ go-arrive

~wibí-ka
suck-ASSERT.IMPERF

'This kind (of insect) lands on people (and) animals (and) sucks (their blood).'

9.3 tina ba'ro buhuina dainakã hika.
tí-~da=ba'ro   buhú-~ida   dá-~ídá-~ká
ANPH-PL=kind be.large-NOM.PL be.small-NOM.PL-DIM
hí-ka
COP-ASSERT.IMPERF

'There are large and small ones.'

9.4 ñaro wihkĩrika tina wimia.
~yá+ro   ~wikí-ri-ka   tí-~da   ~wibí+a
be.bad+SG itch-ADMON-ASSERT.IMPERF ANPH-PL suck+(3)PL

'It itches badly when they bite.'

10. *Yairo* 'Jaguar'
(written by Armando Filho Paiva)

10.1 yairo khiti hira.
yaí+ró   khití hí+ra
jaguar+SG story COP+VIS.IMPERF.2/3

'This is a jaguar story.'

10.2 a'riro yairo hira nuhkupu.
a'rí+ró   yaí+ró   hí+ra   ~dukú-pú
DEM.PROX+SG jaguar+SG COP+VIS.IMPERF.2/3 jungle-LOC

'This is a wild jaguar.' (lit., 'from the jungle')

10.3 topure nuhkupu hiro wa'ikinare chura tiro yairo.
tó-pu+re   ~dukú-pú   hí+ro
REM-LOC+OBJ jungle-LOC COP+SG
wa'í-~kídá+ré   chú+ra   tí+ró   yaí+ró
animal-PL+OBJ eat+VIS.IMPERF.2/3 ANPH+SG jaguar+SG

'The jaguar eats animals living there in the jungle.'

10.4 tu'su dieyare chura tiro mahsa yainare.
tu'sú dié-yá+ré   chú+ra   tí+ró   ~basá
also dog-PL+OBJ eat+VIS.IMPERF.2/3 ANPH+SG people
yá-~ida+re
POSS-NOM.PL+OBJ

'They also eat dogs that belong to people.'

10.5 *topɨrota hira yairo khiti.*

    tó-pɨ+ro=ta   *hí+ra*   *yaí+ró*   *khití*
    DEF-LOC+SG=REF   COP+VIS.IMPERF.2/3   jaguar+SG   story

    'That's all there is to the jaguar story.'

11. *Wachɨphamo* 'Giant Armadillo'
(written by Elizabete Teixeira)

11.1 *a'riro hira wahchɨphamo.*

    a'rí+ró   *hí+ra*   *wachú-~phábó*
    DEM.PROX+SG   COP+VIS.IMPERF.2/3   bull-armadillo

    'This is a giant armadillo.'

11.2 *õpeina hira tina ba'ro.*

    ~ó-pé-~ídá   *hí+ra*   *tí-~da=ba'ro*
    DEIC.PL-CQUANT-NOM.PL   COP+VIS.IMPERF.2/3   ANPH-PL=kind

    'There are many types of these (armadillos).'

11.3 *wahchɨphamo, phamo dahsaka.*

    wachú-~phábó   *~phabó*   *dásá-ka*
    bull-armadillo   armadillo   be.smaller-ASSERT.IMPERF

    'Giant armadillos and smaller ones.'

11.4 *tina ba'ro chɨra buhtua mahchɨ khãsipoka phũri.*

    tí-~da=ba'ro   *chú+ra*   *butúá*   *~bachú*
    ANPH-PL=kind   eat+VIS.IMPERF.2/3   termites   leafcutter.ants

    ~khasí-poka   *~phú+rí*
    roach-CLS:elongated   leaf+PL

    'This kind (of animal) eats termites, leafcutter ants, roaches, and leaves.'

11.5 *phamo mahsa ti chɨriro hira.*

    ~phabó   *~basá*   *ti=chú+ri+ro*   *hí+ra*
    armadillo   people   3PL.POSS=eat+NOM+SG   COP+VIS.IMPERF.2/3

    'Armadillos are food for people (lit., 'ones that people eat').'

11.6 *tirore diero bohkamahsira yɨhkɨkohpapɨ, kohpapɨ.*

    tí+ró+ré   *dié+ró*   *boká-~basi+ra*   *yɨkú-kopa-pɨ*
    ANPH+SG+OBJ   dog+SG   find-know+VIS.IMPERF.2/3   tree-hole-LOC

    kopá-pɨ
    hole-LOC

    'Dogs can find them in holes in trees (or) holes (in the ground).'

11.7 ã yoana sã nɨnɨwa'aka'a wãhamahsiha.
 ~a=yoá-~da ~sá ~dɨdɨ́-wa'a-ka'a
 so=do/make-PL 1PL.EXC follow/chase-go-do.moving
 ~wahá-~basi-ha
 kill-know-VIS.IMPERF.1
 'That's how we go after them (and) are able to kill them.'

11.8 tina ba'ro phayɨ pho'natira.
 tí-~da=ba'ro phayɨ́ ~pho'dá-ti+ra
 ANPH-PL=kind many/a.lot offspring-VBZ+VIS.IMPERF.2/3
 'These have a lot of offspring.'

11.9 phɨaria ña'aina waro hira to pho'na.
 phɨá+ri+a ~ya'á-~ida wáró hí+ra
 two+NOM+PL get.with.hand-NOM.PL EMPH COP+VIS.IMPERF.2/3
 to=~pho'dá
 3SG.POSS=offspring
 '(Perhaps) even a dozen [lit., 'two more than the hands'].'

11.10 wĩainakã hia pũ mahsaka.
 ~wiá-~ida-~ka hí+a ~pú ~basá-ka
 be.young-NOM.PL-DIM COP+PL suckle grow-ASSERT.IMPERF
 'When they're very young, they suckle (and) grow.'

12. Wɨria 'Airplanes'
(written by Franssinete Ferraz)

12.1 no'opari mɨhsa wɨriapɨ wa'anɨhari?
 ~do'ó-pá+rí ~busá wɨ́-ria-pɨ
 WH-CLS:time+PL 2PL fly-CLS:round.elongated-LOC
 wa'á-~dɨha-ri
 go-try-INT
 'How many times have you flown in an airplane?'

12.2 a'ria wɨria wɨka minichakã yoarose.
 a'rí+á wɨ́-ria wɨ́-ka
 DEM.PROX+PL fly-CLS:round.elongated fly-ASSERT.IMPERF
 ~bidícha-~ka yoá+ro-se
 bird-DIM do/make+SG-be.like
 'These planes fly like birds.'

12.3 mari kherokã wa'aduana, wa'aka wɨria me're.
 ~barí khé+ro-~ka wa'á-dua-~da wa'á-ka
 1PL.INC be.fast+SG-DIM go-DESID-(1/2)PL go-ASSERT.IMPERF

wɨ-ria=~be're
fly-CLS:round.elongated=COM/INST
'When we want to go (somewhere) quickly, we go by plane.'

12.4 *mari khõaãwa'achɨ, khuãyɨ'dɨra.*
~barí ~khóá-wá'á-chɨ khuá-yɨ'dɨ+ra
1PL.INC throw-go-SW.REF be.dangerous-INTENS+VIS.IMPERF.2/3
'When we take off, it's very dangerous.'

12.5 *to wahkɨnoka wa'aka'achɨ, mari khapari bɨhkɨawa'ara, mari kɨachɨ.*
to=~wakú-~dóká wa'á-ka'a-chɨ ~barí=khapá+rí
DEF=be.aware-COMPL go-do.moving-SW.REF 1PL.INC.POSS=eye+PL
bɨkú+a=wa'a+ra ~barí kɨá-chɨ
grow+AFFEC=go+VIS.IMPERF.2/3 1PL.INC be.afraid-SW.REF
'When we realize it's going up, our eyes grow big, because we're afraid.'

12.6 *ã yoana noaro wahkɨmahsi duhimahsiha.*
~a=yoá-~da ~dóá+ró ~wakú-~básí
so=do/make-(1/2)PL be.good+SG be.aware-know
duhí-~basi-ha
sit-know-VIS.IMPERF.1
'So, we should pay close attention (and) sit still.'

Appendix 2: Vocabulary

The Kotiria-English and English-Kotiria vocabulary lists in this appendix are based on the words in the examples and texts in this grammar. They include noun, verb, and particle roots (including roots that only occur as noninitial serialized elements), as well as noun classifiers, pronominal forms, and some common expressions. Morphemes that occur in noninitial position only, or that have alternate semantics in this position, are indicated by a preceding dash. A list of grammatical markers with their properties and functions follows the vocabulary list. The following abbreviations for parts of speech are used:

n	noun
cls	noun classifier
vi	intransitive verb
vt	transitive verb
exp	expression
pro	pronoun (personal or possessive)
part	particle root

Morphemes are given in their underlying forms in the following alphabetical order.

a ~a b ~b[m] ch[tʃ] ~ch d ~d[n] e ~e h ~h k ~k kh ~kh o ~o p ~p ph ~ph r ~r[r̃] s ~s t ~t th ~th u ~u ʉ ~ʉ w ~w y ~y[ɲ]

(Notice that this means that all [+nasal] roots that begin with a given segment follow all [−nasal] roots that begin with the same segment; thus, ~da follows duti and du'tu.) Glottalization (marked by ') is ignored in alphabetization. Tonal melodies are indicated for root morphemes (L = low tone, H = high tone); morphemes with clitic status are indicated as L, and morphemes that occur exclusively in noninitial position and are thus always subject to tonal spread from the initial root are listed without a tone melody. Tones in parentheses are revealed only when CV roots undergo lengthening in their citation forms.

Kotiria-English

-a, -ka (cls) classifier for round objects (§4.3.3)
ahi_{LHL} (vt) (be) concerned, worry

$a'ri_{LH}$ (part) this (proximal demonstrative, §4.5.2, §6.2)
$\sim a_L =$ (exp) so, then
$\sim aga_{LH}$ (n) snake (poisonous)
ba_{HL} (vi) decompose
$ba_{(L)H}$ (vi) swim
$ba'a_{LH}$ (n) bass
$ba'a_{LH}$ (vi) (be) close by (in space); after (in time)
$bahu_{LHL}$ (vi) (be) visible, appear
$baka_{LH}$ (vt) bite
$ba'o_{LH}$ (n) sister (younger)
$basa_{LHL}$ (vi) sing, dance
$bato_{LHL}$ (vi) (be) last (spatial reference)
$ba'ʉ_{LH}$ (n) brother (younger)
be_H (vt) inject, plant
bia_{LH} (n) pepper
$bi'a_{LHL}$ (vt) close
$biato_{LH}$ (n) pepper and fish stew
$bi'i_{LH}$ (n) rat
$bi'sa_{LHL}$ (vi) (be) narrow
$bo_{(L)H}$ (vt) forget, lose
$-bo'e$ (vi) pray
$boka_{LH}$ (n) ant
$boka_{LHL}$ (vt) meet, find
$bora_{LHL}$ (n) curupira (humanlike evil being)
$bora_{LHL}$ (vi) fall
$bo're_{LHL}$ (vi) (be) light
$boro_{LHL}$ (vi) lower
$-boro$ (vt) separate
$-bosa$ (vt) benefactive (§10.6)
$boso_{LH}$ (n) agouti
$buʉ_H$ (n) agouti
$bu'a_{LH}$ (vi) (go) downhill, (go) downriver
$-bu'a$ (vi) move downward (serialized motion verb, §7.5.1)
$bu'e_{LHL}$ (vi) study, learn
$bu'i_{LHL}$ (n) top (horizontal surface) of, over (spatial reference)
$buti_{LHL}$ (vi) disappear
$butua_{LH}$ (n) termites
$bʉ_H$ (n) edge of, shore
$bʉaphi_{LHL}$ (vi) motion/signal with one's hand
$bʉe_{LHL}$ (n) arrow
$bʉe_{LHL}$ (vt) hunt with arrows
$bʉe\sim dete_{LHL}$ (n) bow and arrows
$buhawiti_{LH}$ (vi) (be) sad
$buhʉ_{LHL}$ (vi) (be) large
$buhʉ_{LHL}$ (vi) laugh
$bukʉ_{LHL}$ (n) elder, ancestor
$bukʉ_{LHL}$ (vi) grow, open

Vocabulary 459

-buro (vi) move downward (serialized motion verb, §7.5.1)
*busa*_{LHL} (vt) adorn, decorate
*bu'se*_{LH} (n) side
*buso*_{LHL} (n) canoe
*buti*_{LHL} (vi) (be) hard (physical property)
*bu'u*_{LH} (n) piranha
~*ba(a)*_H (n) stream
~*ba(a)*_{(L)H} (vi) (be) small
~*ba'a*_{LH} (n) path
~*bachu*_{LHL} (n) leafcutter ant
~*badia*_{LHL} (vi) not exist (§7.1.2)
-~*ba'do* (vt) penetrate; move into (serialized motion verb, §7.5.1)
~*badu*_{LHL} (n) husband
~*baha*_{LH} (n) macaw
~*baha*_{LH} (vi) (go) uphill
-~*baha* (vi) move up and down (serialized motion verb, §7.5.1)
~*bahaphoa*_{LH} (n) Mahaphoa (placename; "Arara Cachoeira" in Portuguese)
~*baka*_{LHL} (n) village, origin
~*baka*_{LHL} (vt) look for
~*bakaroka*_{LHL} (n) jungle
~*bako*_{LH} (n) daughter
~*bako*_{LHL} (n) pakú fish
~*baku*_{LH} (n) son
~*bari*_L= (pro) our (first person plural inclusive possessive pronoun, §6.4.1)
~*bari*_{LH} (pro) we (first person plural inclusive pronoun, §4.7.1, §6.4.1)
~*basa*_{LH} (n) people, beings
~*basa*_{LHL} (vi) grow, mature
~*basi*_{LHL} (vt) know
-~*basi* (vt) can (ability, possibility), should (serialized verb of deontic modality, §7.5.4)
~*basu*_{LHL} (n) man, person, being
~*ba'yo*_{LHL} (vi) lie (tell a lie)
~*bede*_{LHL} (n) ingá fruit
~*bi*_H (n) honey
~*bi*_{(L)H} (n) now
~*bia*_{HL} (n) sardine
~*bicha*_{LH} (n) today
-~*bidi* (n) high water
~*bidicha*_{LHL} (n) bird
~*bie*_{LHL} (n) giant anteater
~*bisi*_{LH} (n) fiber, vine
~*bo*_H (n) Mõ (placename; "Carurú Cachoeira" in Portuguese)
~*boa*_H (n) salt; salt plant
~*boko*_{HL} (n) catfish
~*bore*_{LHL} (vt) mix
~*boyo*_{LHL} (vi) fail
~*bu*_H (vt) carry on one's back by means of headstrap

~bʉ_HL (n) man (male)
~bʉ_L= (pro) your (second person singular possessive pronoun, §6.4.1; cf. ~bʉ'ʉ_LH)
-~bʉ (vi) do quickly (serialized verb, §7.5.1; cf. ~bʉbʉ_LHL)
~bʉa_LH (n) roof, sky
~bʉa_LH (vi) (be) high
~bʉbʉ_LHL (vi) run (cf. -~bʉ)
~bʉ'do_LHL (n) tobacco
~bʉpa (vi) (be) across
~bʉsa_L= (pro) your (second person plural possessive pronoun, §6.4.1)
~bʉsa_LH (pro) you (second person plural pronoun, §4.7.1, §6.4.1)
~bʉsʉ_LH (n) lesser anteater
~bʉ'ʉ_LH (pro) you (second person singular pronoun, §4.7.1, §6.4.1)
cha_H (n) prepared food, meal
cho'o_LH (exp) what?, how's that? (interjection)
chowe_HL (vi) vomit
chʉ_HL (vt) eat
chʉa_HL (n) food
~che'e_LH (n) doubt
~chipe_HL (n) sap
da_H (vi) (be) small
-da (cls) classifier for ropelike or threadlike objects (§4.3.3)
dacho_LH (n) day
dacho_LH (n) maggot
-dacho (n) middle of, half of
da'po_LH (n) foot, paw
dapu_LHL (n) head
da'ra_LHL (vi) work
da're_LHL (vt) prepare, perform
dasa_LH (n) toucan
dasa_H (vi) (be) smaller
di(i)_H (n) blood
dia_LH (n) river
dicha_LH (n) fruit
die_LH (n) dog
die_LHL (n) egg
diha_LHL (vi) fall
-diha (vi) move downward (serialized motion verb, §7.5.1)
di'i_LH (n) flesh, meat, clay
-di'o (n) particles
dise_LH, dʉse_LH (n) mouth, opening (e.g., of a log)
disi_LH (n) disi fish
doa_LHL (vt) envy
do'a_LH (n) illness
do'a_LH (vt) cook
doka_LH (n) under, below
doka_LHL (vt, vi) throw (cf. -roka)

Vocabulary 461

do'ka~LHL~ (vt) crash into
do'kai~LHL~ (n) young boy
dopa~LH~ (n) bee
do'se~LH~ (n) how, what, when, why (interrogative adverb, §11.2.5)
du~HL~ (vi) speak, talk
-dua desiderative (§7.5.4)
duhi~LHL~ (vi) sit, be sitting (be in a seated position; assume a seated position)
duku~LHL~ (vi) stand (be in a standing position; assume a standing position) (cf. *-ruku*)
dura~LHL~ (vt) put over, cover
duti~LHL~ (n) illness
du'ti~LHL~ (vi) escape
du'ti~LH~ (vt) request
-du'tu (n) around
du'u~LH~ (vt) put or place in specific position
-dʉ (cls) classifier for cylindrical objects (§4.3.3)
dʉka~LH~ (vt) begin (cf. *-rʉka*)
dʉkʉ~LH~ (n) manioc plant
dʉse~LH~, *dise*~LH~ (n) mouth, opening (e.g., of a log)
dʉ'ta~LHL~ (vi) make noise
dʉ'te~H~ (vt) tie up
dʉ'te~LHL~ (vt) chop, cut
~*da(a)*~(L)HL~ (vt) get
~*da'a*~LH~ (n) buriti fruit
~*da'ba*~LH~ (vt) turn over
~*dabo*~LHL~ (n) wife
~*dabo*~LHL~ (vi) repeat (repetitive aspect §7.5.3)
~*da'bo*~LH~ (n) rope
~*da'bo*~LH~ (n) flute (type of)
~*daho*~LH~ (n) flatbread
~*da'i*~LH~ (vi) (be) dark
~*daka*~LH~ (n) miriti fruit
-~*daka* (vi) (do) together (serialized verb, §7.5.3)
~*de*~H~ (exp) negative nominal (§4.6)
~*de*~H~ (exp) hello, how's it going?
~*di*~H~ (n) which (interrogative modifier, §6.5.2)
~*di*~HL~ (vi) progressive auxiliary (§11.3.2)
~*di*~HL~ (vi) say, warn, wonder
~*doa*~H~ (vi) (be) good, (be) beautiful
~*doa*~LHL~ (n) who (interrogative nominal or possessive modifier, §§6.5.1–6.5.2)
~*doada*~H~ (exp) thanks!, congratulations!
-~*doka* (vi) do completely (aspectual serialized verb, §7.5.3)
~*do'o*~LH~ (n) where (interrogative nominal, §6.5.1)
~*do'o-pe*~LH~ (n) how many (inanimate)? (interrogative modifier, §6.5.2)
~*do'o-pe-~da*~LH~ (n) how many (animate)? (interrogative modifier, §6.5.2)
~*do'o-puro*~LH~ (n) how much (mass)? (interrogative modifier, §6.5.2)

~du_H (vi) buzz (noise)
~$dubi_{LHL}$ (n) woman, female
~$duda_{LHL}$ (n) horsefly
~$duhu_{LH}$ (vi) accommodate oneself
~$dɨba_H$ (n) day
~$dɨdɨ_{LHL}$ (vt) follow, chase
-~$dɨha$ (vi) try
~$dɨko_{LH}$ (n) island
~$dɨkɨ_{LH}$ (n) jungle
~$dɨo_{LHL}$ (vi) hide
~$dɨtɨ_{LH}$ (n) scale (of a fish)
~ebo_{LH} (n) red howler monkey
go_{HL} (vi) be skillful (as a fisherman)
hai_H (exp) yes, okay, good!
hi_{HL} (vi) be, exist (copula, §7.1.1)
$hikoa_H$ (vt) like
$hiphiti(\sim da)_{HL}$ (n) everybody
$hiphiti(ro)_{HL}$ (n) everything
ho_H (n) banana
ho_H (n) drawing, letter (of the alphabet)
hoa_H (vi) write
hu_H (n) smoke
~$hi'da_{HL}$ (part) emphatic particle (§5.3.5, §11.2.3)
~hu_{HL} (n) worm
~$hɨ_{HL}$ (vt) burn
~$iriboa_{LHL}$ (n) lime (from Portuguese *limão*)
ka_{HL} (n) black monkey
-ka, -a (cls) classifier for round objects (§4.3.3)
$ka'a_{LH}$ (n) side, near, next to (spatial reference)
-$ka'a$ (vi) (do) immediately (temporal reference) (§7.5.1)
-$ka'a$ (vi) do while moving (serialized motion verb, §7.5.1)
-$kapa$ (n) shoot, seedling
$karaka_H$ (n) rooster, chicken
$karisu_{LHL}$ (n) pan-flute
$ka'sa_{LH}$ (n) skin
$kasɨ_{LHL}$ (vi) revive
$kaye_H$ (n) fishtrap (large, erected in the rapids)
ki_H (n) mandi fish
$ko_{(L)HL}$ (n) water, medicine
ko_{HL} (n) relative (fellow person of Kotiria ethnicity)
-ko (cls) classifier for liquids (§4.3.3)
koa_{LHL} (vi) taste, perceive, make noise; nonvisual evidence auxiliary (§9.2.3)
$kopa_{LH}$ (n) hole
$ko'ta_{LHL}$ (vi) wait
-$kuru$ (n) group (of people)
$ku'si_{LHL}$ (vi) bathe

ku'tu~LHL~ (n) clearing
-ku (cls) classifier for trees and shaftlike objects (§4.3.3)
kɨa~LHL~ (vi) (be) afraid, (be) surprised
kɨti~LHL~ (n) chest
~*ka*~H~ (n) a few, some
~*ke*~H~ (n) beak, nose
-~*ku* (vt) lay (an egg)
~*kɨ*~H~ (part) one; a
kha~H~ (n) hawk
khapa~LH~ (n) eye
khasi~LH~ (n) roach
khata~LH~ (n) flatbread oven
khata~ba'a~LH~ (n) jacú bird
kha'ti~LH~ (vi) live
khe~HL~ (vi) (be) fast
khiti~LHL~ (n) story
khoa~H~ (n) half, part
kho'a~LHL~ (vi) return
kho'a~LHL~ (vi) sweep
khu~(L)H~ (n) turtle
khua~LHL~ (vi) (be) dangerous
khɨ~(L)HL~ (n) manioc root
khɨa~LHL~ (vt) hold, have
khɨ'a~LH~ (n) lice
khɨbo~HL~ (n) soaked manioc
~*kha*~(L)HL~ (vt) chop, cut, hit
~*kha'a*~LHL~ (vi) dream
~*kha'ba*~LH~ (vi) (do) reciprocally, (do) collectively (§10.6)
~*kha'ba*~LHL~ (vt) want
~*kha'bo*~LH~ (n) ear
~*khadako*~H~ (n) Khanako (placename; "Ilha de Inambú" in Portuguese)
~*khadɨ*~LH~ (n) sugarcane
~*khadɨ*~LH~ (n) yesterday
~*kha'i*~LHL~ (vt) love
~*khari*~LHL~ (vi) sleep
~*khi'o*~LH~ (vi) (be) arranged, (be) agreed upon
~*khoa*~H~ (vi) take off (in an airplane)
~*khoa*~H~ (vt) throw
~*khoa*~LHL~ (vi) lie, be lying (be in a lying position; assume a lying position)
~*kho'a*~LHL~ (n) bone
~*khoba*~LHL~ (n) ax
~*khobada*~LHL~ (n) flies
~*kho'o*~LHL~ (vt) bite
~*khubu*~LHL~ (n) log, sitting object
~*khɨ'ba*~LHL~ (n) year
o~H~ (n) acari fish
~*o*~H~ (part) here (proximal deictic, §4.5.2)

~o_H (vi) hang by a thread or stem
~o-pa_H (exp) like this (indicating type or size, usually accompanied by deictic motion of the hands)
~o-se_H (exp) like (similarity; also used to introduce quoted speech)
pa_{HL} (part) other, another (alternate particle, §4.5.2)
-pa (cls) classifier for times (§4.3.3)
$pakɨ_{HL}$ (n) body
$pape_{LH}$ (vi) play
$pari_{LHL}$ (n) form, shape
$pari_{LHL}$ (n) lake
pa-se('e)$_{HL}$ (n) somewhere (§4.5.2)
pa-te$_{HL}$ (n) sometime(s), if (§4.5.2)
pe'ri$_{HL}$ (n) all, many
pi_{HL} (n) tooth
$piri_{HL}$ (n) teeth
$piri_H$ (n) three-sided basket
$pisa_{LH}$ (vi) (be) on top or on horizontal surface of
$pisu_{LH}$ (vt) call
$pita_{LHL}$ (n) port
po'a$_{LHL}$ (vt) clean or prepare (fruit)
po'ka$_{LHL}$ (n) manioc flour, manioc meal
po'sa$_{LHL}$ (n) direction of, front of
$poto_{LHL}$ (n) direction of, front of
$puka_{HL}$ (n) blowgun
-pɨ (cls) classifier for baskets (§4.3.3)
~pe_H (n) breast
~pu_H (vi) suckle
~$pɨ_H$ (n) freshwater crab
pha_H (n) stomach
$phari_{LH}$ (n) opening
$phayo_{LH}$ (vt) spread out (verb of placement, §7.3.4, §7.5.1)
-pha'yo (vt) (do) completely (§7.5.3)
$phayuru_{LH}$ (n) caxiri beer
$phayɨ_{LH}$ (n) many
phi_{HL} (vi) (be) big, (be) slow
$phia_{LHL}$ (vi) (be) sour
phi'a$_{HL}$ (vi) move out into open area (relational motion verb, §7.3.3)
$phicha_{LH}$ (n) wood
$phicha_{LH}$ (vt) shoot
$phiti_{LHL}$ (n) collective (§6.3.1, §7.1.1)
$phiti_{LHL}$ (vi) end, complete
$phiti_{LHL}$ (vt) accompany
$phititia_{LHL}$ (n) four
$phoa_{LH}$ (n) hair, feathers
$phoaye_{LH}$ (n) rapids, falls
-phoka (cls) plural classifier for rounded objects (§4.3.3)
$phore_{LH}$ (vt) hole (make a)

phosa~LHL~ (vi) filled with, containing
photo~LHL~ (n) truth
phu'a~LH~ (vt) stab
phu'icha~LHL~ (n) inside part or surface of, space within
phuti~LH~ (vt) blow, play (a flute), inflate
phu'ti~LH~ (n) grated manioc
phɨa~LHL~ (n) two
phɨko~LH~ (n) mother
phɨkɨ~LH~ (n) father
phɨto~LH~ (n) leader, supervisor
phɨ'ɨ~LH~ (n) basket
~*pha'a*~LHL~ (vi) move across (relational motion verb, §7.3.3, §7.5.1)
~*phabo*~LH~ (n) armadillo
~*phado*~LHL~ (vi) (do/be) before (§10.7.2)
-~*phare* (n) side
-~*phi* (cls) classifier for sharp or bladelike objects (§4.3.3)
~*phicho*~LH~ (n) tail
~*phido*~LHL~ (n) snake, anaconda
~*pho'da*~LHL~ (n) children, offspring
~*phu*~H~ (n) leaf
~*phube*~LHL~ (vi) (be) tired
~*phuri*~LHL~ (vi) hurt
~*phuria*~LHL~ (n) poison, pain
-*re* (cls) generic classifier (§4.3.3)
-*ria* (cls) classifier for round elongated objects (§4.3.3)
-~*rapo* (vt) put on (tip of something) (§7.3.4)
-*roka* (vt, vi) do/be at a distance (distal aspect, §7.5.2; cf. *doka*~LHL~)
-*ruku* (vi) continuous/durative aspect (§7.5.2; cf. *duku*~LHL~)
-*ruka* (vt) inceptive aspect (§7.5.2; cf. *dɨka*~LH~)
-*sa* (cls) classifier for carriers (§4.3.3)
sa~H~ ... ~*hi'da*~HL~, ~*sa*~H~ ... ~*hi'da*~HL~ (exp) let's (exhortative marker, §9.5.4)
sa'a~LH~ (vi) dig
saba~LH~ (n) mud
sase~LH~ (vi) (be) gluttonous
sa'se~LHL~ (vi) (be) alone
sa'wi~LH~ (n) bump (on one's body)
se~H~ (n) cucura fruit
-*se* (vi) (be) like
si~H~ (part) that (distal demonstrative, §4.5.2, §6.2)
si~HL~ (vi) (be) hot
si~HL~ (vt) heat up
-*sibɨ* (vt) intend to (§7.5.4)
-*sika* (n) piece of
sio~LH~ (vi) (be) sharp
sio~LH~ (vt) sharpen
sipa~HL~ (vi) (be) shiny
sito~LHL~ (vi) move in a circular path, go around (motion verb, §7.3.1)

situ~LH~ (n) clay pot
-*situ* (cls) classifier for pots (§4.3.3)
so~HL~ (vi) (be) different
soa~H~ (vt) grate, grind
soa~LHL~ (vi) rest
so'a~LH~ (n) sarapo (long-tailed) fish
-*so'a* (vi) appear (to be)
sopaka~LHL~ (n) outside, door
soro~H~ (exp) not now!
so'to~LHL~ (n) top, end
sua~LH~ (vt) pick (fruit)
sua~LHL~ (vi) (be) angry
su'a~LH~ (vt) weave
su'a~LHL~ (vi) go into the brush/woods
su'su~LHL~ (n) embrace
sʉ'a~LHL~, *sʉ'o*~LHL~ (vt) sift
sʉka~HL~ (vi) lie down
sʉ'o~LHL~ (vi) (do) together
sʉ'o~LHL~, *sʉ'a*~LHL~ (vt) sift
~*sa*~H~ (pro) we (our) (first person plural exclusive pronoun, §4.7.1, §6.4.1)
~*sa*~H~ ... ~*hi'da*~HL~, *sa*~H~ ... ~*hi'da*~HL~ ... (exp) 'let's' (exhortative marker, §9.5.4)
~*sa*~L~= (pro) our (first person plural exclusive possessive pronoun, §6.4.1)
~*sa*~(L)HL~ (vi) (be) inside
-~*sa*, -~*sa'a* (vi) move inside (serialized relational motion verb, §7.5.1)
~*sa'a*~LH~ (n) electric eel
~*sare*~LH~ (n) pineapple
~*sayo*~LHL~ (vi) yell, scream
~*si'a*~LHL~ (n) torch
~*si'a*~LHL~ (vt) ignite
~*sidi*~LHL~ (vt) ask for, request
~*si'di*~LHL~ (vt) drink
-~*sidi* (vi) still (do), then, now (serialized aspectual verb, §7.5.3)
~*si'dia*~LHL~ (n) fermented drinks (usually referring to different types of caxiri beer)
~*siditu*~LHL~ (vt) ask (a question)
~*sio*~LH~ (vi) slide
~*si'o*~LHL~ (vt) pierce
~*so'a*~LHL~ (vi) (be) red, ripen
~*so'o*~LH~ (part) there (distal deictic, §4.5.2)
~*sʉ*~(L)HL~ (vi) arrive (there)
-~*sʉ* (vi) completive aspect for motion verbs (serialized aspectual verb, §7.5.2)
~*sʉ'a*~LHL~ (vi) (be) sticky
~*sʉ'a*~LHL~ (vt) stick onto
~*sʉ'i*~LH~ (n) snail
ta~(L)H~, -*ta'a* (vi) come (also serialized, §7.5.1)

Vocabulary 467

-ta (vt) separate
-ta'a, ta₍L₎H (vi) come
-taro (cls) classifier for lakes (§4.3.3)
*tatia*LHL (n) room
*te*H (part) until (temporal reference), all the way to (spatial reference) (probably a borrowing of the Portuguese preposition *até*)
-te (cls) classifier for times (§4.3.3)
*ti*H(L) (part) that, the (anaphoric particle from which definite modifiers 'that X' or 'the X' as well as third person pronominal forms *tiro* 'he, it' and *tikoro* 'she' are formed, §§4.7.2–4.7.3, §6.2)
*ti*L= (pro) their (third person plural possessive pronoun, §6.4.1)
*tia*LH (n) three
*tipa*LHL (vi) (be) flat
*tiroa*H (n) wasps
*to*H(L) (part) there, the (remote deictic, §4.5.2; definite, §4.3.7)
*to*L= (pro) his, her (third person singular possessive pronoun, §6.4.1)
*toa*H (vt) plant
*toa*LH (vi) (do) again
*toa*LHL (vi) (be) fast
*tua*LHL (vi) (be) strong
*tui*LHL (vt) (put in) front
*tu'sʉ*LH (exp) also, additionally
*tu'sʉ*LH (vt) finish
-tu'sʉ (vt) just completed (serialized aspectual verb, §7.5.3)
*tʉ*HL (n) stick
*tʉpu*HL (vi) dry
*~ta*H (n) rock
*~tayo*LH (n) female cross-cousin (marriageable)
*~tayʉ*LH (n) male cross-cousin (marriageable)
-~tia (n) water current
*~tidi*LH (vi) walk, wander, visit
-~tidi (vi) do over and over (serialized motion verb, §7.5.1)
-~to (cls) classifier for stems (§4.3.3)
*tha*H (n) grass
-thu (cls) classifier for stacked objects (§4.3.3)
-thu (vi) think
*thua*LH (vi) (be) placed
*thua*LHL (vi) return
*thuti*LHL (vi) bark (dog)
*thʉ*H (vt) push
*thʉo*LH (vi) (be) successful
*thʉ'o*LHL (vt) hear, feel, understand
*~tho'o*LH (vt) shake
*~thʉa*LHL (vt) pull out
*~ʉri*LHL (vi) (be) smelly
*wa(a)*H (vt) give
*wa'a*LHL (vi) go (also serialized, §7.5.1)

-*wa'a* (vi) become, change of state (perfective marker, §8.5.2)
wa'ba~LH~ (n) fan
wache~LHL~ (vi) (be) happy
wacho~LHL~ (n) parrot
wachɨ~LH~ (n) tapir
wachɨ~LH~ (n) cow
waha~LHL~ (vt) pull, row
wa'i~LH~ (n) fish, animal
waka~LHL~ (n) poison darts
wa'kɨe~LHL~ (vi) (do) unexpectedly, (do) suddenly
(-)*waro*~H~ (n) right there; emphatic (§5.1.2)
waso~LH~ (n) siringa fruit
wato~LH~ (n) flooded forest
wato~LHL~ (n) middle
waye~LH~ (vt) cut open
wera (vt) remove
wese~LHL~ (n) garden
wi'bo~LH~ (vt) store
wiha~LHL~ (vi) move outward/outside (relational motion verb, §7.3.3)
wihi~LHL~ (vi) (go) outside
wi'i~LHL~ (vi) arrive (here)
-*wi'i* (vi) completive aspect for motion verbs (§7.5.2)
wi'o~LHL~ (exp) contrastive (§11.2.4)
wipe~LHL~ (vt) sieve
wisi~LHL~ (vi) (be) lost
wɨ(ɨ)~HL~ (vi) fly
wɨa~LH~ (vt) carry, pick up
wɨ'a~LH~ (vt) peel
wɨ'dɨapo'ka~LHL~ (n) forehead
wɨpo~LH~ (n) hairy caterpillar
wɨpɨ~LH~ (n) spider
wɨ'ɨ~LH~ (n) house
~*wa'a*~LH~ (vi) lean, be leaning (nonhorizonal attachment or support)
~*waba*~LH~ (n) name
~*wa'ba*~LH~ (vt) wrap around
~*wa'ba*~LHL~ (vi) (be) young, (be) new
~*wa'bi*~LH~ (n) older brother
~*wa'bio*~LH~ (n) older sister
~*wabo(ka)*~LHL~ (n) hand
~*wa'bɨ*~LH~ (vi) mature
~*wa'bɨa*~LH~ (n) adolescent boy
~*waha*~LHL~ (vt) kill
~*wa'ka*~LHL~ (vi) wake up
~*wa'ko*~LHL~ (vt) wake someone up
~*waku*~LH~ (vt) remember, (be) aware of, (be) careful of
~*wati*~LH~ (n) devil, evil being
~*wia*~LH~ (vi) (be) young

~wibi~{LHL}~ (vt) suck
~wiha~{LH}~ (vt) set afire
~wihi~{LH}~ (vt) sniff
~wiki~{LH}~ (vi) itch
~wio~{LHL}~ (vi) move out of enclosed space (relational motion verb, §7.3.3, §7.5.1)
~wi'o~{LH}~ (n) hallucinogenic powder
~wipi~{LH}~ (n) açaí fruit
~wiso~{LH}~ (n) squirrel
~wita~{LHL}~ (vi) (be) sticky
~wɨpo~{LHL}~ (vt) tie off; finish the edge of a basket or woven item
ya~{HL}~ (vt) bury
ya~{(L)HL}~ (n) possession
yaba~{LH}~ (n) what (interrogative nominal, §6.5.1)
yahiri~pho'da~{LHL}~ (n) heart, spirit
yai~{LH}~ (n) jaguar; shaman
yaka~{LHL}~ (vt) steal
yapa~{LH}~ (n) ground
yapa~{LHL}~ (n) seed, drop
yapi~{LH}~ (vi) (be) full of food, satisfied
ya'pi~{LH}~ (vi) (be) smooth
yari~{LH}~ (vi) die
ya'u~{LHL}~ (vt) tell, warn
yese~{LHL}~ (n) wild pig
yo(o)~{H}~ (n) corn
yoa~{LH}~ (vi) (be) long, (be) far
yoa~{LHL}~ (vt) do, make
yoado~{LHL}~ (n) help
yo'ga~{LHL}~ (vt) fish
yoha~{LHL}~ (vi) (go) upriver
yosa~{LH}~ (vi) hang, be hanging
yu'dɨ~{LHL}~ (vi) pass out
yɨ~{L}~= (pro) my (first person singular possessive pronoun, §6.4.1; cf. yɨ'ɨ~{LH}~)
-yɨ'dɨ (vi) intensifier (§8.3)
yɨkɨ~{LHL}~ (n) tree
yɨ'so~{LHL}~ (vt) cut
yɨ'ti~{LHL}~ (vi) answer
yɨ'ɨ~{LH}~ (pro) I (first person singular pronoun)
~ya~{HL}~ (vi) (be) bad, (be) ugly, (be) evil
~ya'a~{LHL}~ (vt) grab with one's hand, catch with a paw
~yaba~{LH}~ (n) deer
~ya'ba~{LH}~ (n) tongue
~yabi~{LH}~ (n) night
~yabicha~{LHL}~ (n) afternoon
~yabɨ~{LHL}~ (n) cará tuber
~yara~{LHL}~ (n) white people
~yo~{HL}~ (vt) show

-~yo (cls) classifier for palms (§4.3.3)
~yoka$_{LH}$ (n) manioc liquid
~yosa$_{LHL}$ (vt) force into
~yui$_{LHL}$ (vt) offer
~yɨ$_H$ (vt) see, look, visit, realize
~yɨ$_H$ (vt) try (§7.5.4)
~yɨbɨ$_{LH}$ (n) bacaba fruit
~yɨcho$_{LH}$ (n) grandmother
~yɨchɨ$_{LH}$ (n) grandfather
~yɨchɨ$_{LH}$ (n) leg

English-Kotiria

a ~kɨ$_H$
a few, some ~ka$_H$
açaí fruit ~wipi$_{LH}$
acari fish o$_H$
accommodate oneself ~duhu$_{LH}$
accompany phiti$_{LHL}$
across (be) ~bɨpa
across (move) (relational motion verb, §7.5.1) ~pha'a$_{LHL}$
additionally tu'sɨ$_{LH}$
adolescent boy ~wa'bɨa$_{LH}$
adorn bɨsa$_{LHL}$
afraid (be) kɨa$_{LHL}$
after (in time) ba'a$_{LH}$, -ba'a
afternoon ~yabicha$_{LHL}$
again (do) toa$_{LH}$
agouti boso$_{LH}$, bɨ$_H$
agreed upon (be) ~khi'o$_{LH}$
all pe'ri$_{HL}$
all the way to (spatial reference) te (probably from Portuguese até)
alone (be) sa'se$_{LHL}$
also tu'sɨ$_{LH}$
anaconda ~phido$_{LHL}$
ancestor bɨkɨ$_{LHL}$
angry (be) sua$_{LHL}$
animal wa'i$_{LH}$
another, other (alternate particle, §4.5.2) pa$_{HL}$
anaphoric pronoun or modifier (third person, §§4.7.2–4.7.3) ti$_{H(L)}$
answer yɨ'ti$_{LHL}$
ant boka$_{LH}$
anteater (giant) ~bie$_{LHL}$
anteater (lesser) ~bɨsɨ$_{LH}$
appear bahu$_{LHL}$
appear (seem) -so'a

Arara Cachoeira (placename, Mahaphoa) ~bahaphoa$_{LH}$
armadillo ~phabo$_{LH}$
around -du'tu
around (move) (verb of motion, §7.3.1) sito$_{LHL}$
arranged (be) ~khi'o$_{LH}$
arrive (here) wi'i$_{LHL}$
arrive (there) ~sʉ$_{(L)HL}$
arrow bʉe$_{LHL}$
ask (a question) ~siditu$_{LHL}$
ask for ~sidi$_{LHL}$
aware of (be) ~waku$_{LH}$
ax ~khoba$_{LHL}$
bacaba fruit ~yʉbʉ$_{LH}$
bad (be) ~ya$_{HL}$
banana ho$_H$
bark (dog) thuti$_{LHL}$
basket phʉ'ʉ$_{LH}$
bass ba'a$_{LH}$
bathe ku'si$_{LHL}$
be (copula, §7.1.1) hi$_{HL}$
be (progressive auxiliary, §11.3.2) ~di$_{HL}$
beak ~ke$_H$
beautiful (be) ~doa$_H$
become (perfective marker, §8.5.2) -wa'a
bee dopa$_{LH}$
before (do, be) ~phado$_{LHL}$
begin duka$_{LH}$
being ~basʉ$_{LHL}$
beings ~basa$_{LH}$
below doka$_{LH}$
benefactive (§10.6) -bosa
big (be) phi$_{HL}$
bird ~bidicha$_{LHL}$
bite ~kho'o$_{LHL}$, baka$_{LH}$
black monkey ka$_{HL}$
blood di(i)$_H$
blow phuti$_{LH}$
blowgun puka$_{HL}$
body pakʉ$_{HL}$
bone ~kho'a$_{LHL}$
bow and arrows bʉe~dete$_{LHL}$
boy (young) do'kai$_{LHL}$
breast ~pe$_H$
brother (older) ~wa'bi$_{LH}$
brother (younger) ba'ʉ$_{LH}$
bump (on one's body) sa'wi$_{LH}$
buriti fruit ~da'a$_{LH}$

burn ~hɨ$_{HL}$
bury ya$_{HL}$
buzz (noise) ~du$_H$
call pisu$_{LH}$
can (ability, possibility) (§7.5.4) -~basi
canoe bɨso$_{LHL}$
cará tuber ~yabɨ$_{LHL}$
careful of (be) ~waku$_{LH}$
carry wɨa$_{LH}$
carry on one's back by means of headstrap ~bɨ$_H$
Carurú Cachoeira (placename, Mõ) ~bo$_H$
catch with a paw ~ya'a$_{LHL}$
caterpillar (hairy) wɨpo$_{LH}$
catfish ~boko$_{HL}$
caxiri beer phayuru$_{LH}$
chase ~dɨdɨ$_{LHL}$
chest kɨti$_{LHL}$
chicken karaka$_H$
child: *see* daughter, son
children ~pho'da$_{LHL}$
chop dɨ'te$_{LHL}$, ~kha$_{(L)HL}$
circular path (move in a) (verb of motion, §7.3.1) sito$_{LHL}$
clay di'i$_{LH}$
clean or prepare (fruit) po'a$_{LHL}$
clearing ku'tu$_{LHL}$
classifier (§4.3.3) for baskets -pɨ
classifier (§4.3.3) for bladelike objects -~phi
classifier (§4.3.3) for carriers -sa
classifier (§4.3.3) for cylindrical objects -dɨ
classifier (§4.3.3) for disklike objects -tɨ
classifier (§4.3.3) for lakes -taro
classifier (§4.3.3) for liquids -ko
classifier (§4.3.3) for palms -~yo
classifier (§4.3.3) for pots -situ
classifier (§4.3.3) for plural round objects -phoka
classifier (§4.3.3) for ropelike or threadlike objects -da
classifier (§4.3.3) for round objects -ka, -a
classifier (§4.3.3) for round elongated objects -ria
classifier (§4.3.3) for stacked objects -thu
classifier (§4.3.3) for stems -~to
classifier (§4.3.3) for times -pa, -te
classifier (§4.3.3) for trees or shaftlike objects -kɨ
classifier (generic) (cf. §4.3.3) -re
close bi'a$_{LHL}$
close by (be, in space) ba'a$_{LH}$, -ba'a
collective (§6.3.1, §7.1.1) phiti$_{LHL}$
collectively (do) (§10.6) ~kha'ba$_{LH}$

Vocabulary

come $ta_{(L)H}$, $-ta'a$
complete $phiti_{LHL}$
completed (just completed) (§7.5.3) $-tu's\mopen{}ʉ$
completely (do) (completive aspect, §7.5.3) $-\sim doka$, $-pha'yo$
completive aspect for motion verbs (§7.5.2) $-\sim s\mopen{}ʉ$
completive aspect for motion verbs (§7.5.2) $-wi'i$
concerned (be) ahi_{LHL}
congratulations! (interjection) $\sim doada_H$
containing $phosa_{LHL}$
continuous/durative aspect (§7.5.2) $-ruku$
contrastive (§11.2.4) $wi'o_{LHL}$
cook $do'a_{LH}$
copula (§7.1.1) hi_{HL}
corn $yo(o)_H$
cover $dura_{LHL}$
cow $wach\mopen{}ʉ_{LH}$
crab (freshwater) $\sim p\mopen{}ʉ_H$
crash into $do'ka_{LHL}$
cross-cousin (female, marriageable) $\sim tayo_{LH}$
cross-cousin (male, marriageable) $\sim tay\mopen{}ʉ_{LH}$
cucura fruit se_H
current (in water) $-\sim tia$
curupira $bora_{LHL}$
cut $y\mopen{}ʉ'so_{LHL}$, $d\mopen{}ʉ'te_{LHL}$, $\sim kha_{(L)HL}$
cut open $waye_{LH}$
dance $basa_{LHL}$
dangerous (be) $khua_{LHL}$
dark (be) $\sim da'i_{LH}$
daughter $\sim bako_{LH}$
day $\sim d\mopen{}ʉba_H$, $dacho_{LH}$
decompose ba_{HL}
decorate $b\mopen{}ʉsa_{LHL}$
deer $\sim yaba_{LH}$
devil $\sim wati_{LH}$
die $yari_{LH}$
different (be) so_{HL}
dig $sa'a_{LH}$
direction of $po'sa_{LHL}$, $poto_{LHL}$
disappear $buti_{LHL}$
disi fish $disi_{LH}$
distal aspect (§7.5.2) $-roka$
distal deictic (§4.5.2) $\sim so'o_{LH}$
distal demonstrative (§4.5.2, §6.2) si_H
do yoa_{LHL}
dog die_{LH}
door $sopaka_{LHL}$
doubt $\sim che'e_{LH}$

down and up (move) (motion verb, §7.3.2, §7.5.1) -~baha
downhill (go), downriver (go) (directional motion verb, §7.3.2) bu'a$_{LH}$
downward (moving) (serialized motion verb, §7.5.1) -buro, -diha
drawing ho$_H$
dream ~kha'a$_{LHL}$
drink ~si'di$_{LHL}$
drinks (fermented, usually types of caxiri beer) ~si'dia$_{LHL}$
drop yapa$_{LHL}$
dry tupu$_{HL}$
durative/continuous aspect (§7.5.2) -ruku
ear ~kha'bo$_{LH}$
eat chu$_{HL}$
edge of bu$_H$
egg die$_{LHL}$
elder buku$_{LHL}$
electric eel ~sa'a$_{LH}$
embrace su'su$_{LHL}$
emphatic (§5.1.2) (-)waro$_H$
emphatic particle (§5.3.5, §11.2.3) ~hi'da$_{HL}$
end phiti$_{LHL}$, so'to$_{LHL}$
envy doa$_{LHL}$
escape du'ti$_{LHL}$
everybody hiphiti(~da)$_{HL}$
everything hiphiti(ro)$_{HL}$
evil (be) ~ya$_{HL}$
evil being ~wati$_{LH}$
exist hi$_{HL}$
exhortative marker (§9.5.4) sa$_H$ ... ~hi'da$_{HL}$, ~sa$_H$ ... ~hi'da$_{HL}$
eye khapa$_{LH}$
fail ~boyo$_{LHL}$
fall bora$_{LHL}$, diha$_{LHL}$
falls phoaye$_{LH}$
fan wa'ba$_{LH}$
far (be) yoa$_{LH}$
fast (be) khe$_{HL}$, toa$_{LHL}$
feathers phoa$_{LH}$
feel thu'o$_{LHL}$
female ~dubi$_{LHL}$
fermented drinks (usually caxiri beer) ~si'dia$_{LHL}$
fiber ~bisi$_{LH}$
filled with phosa$_{LHL}$
find boka$_{LHL}$
finish tu'su$_{LH}$
fish yo'ga$_{LHL}$, wa'i$_{LH}$
fishtrap (large, erected in the rapids) kaye$_H$
flat (be) tipa$_{LHL}$
flatbread ~daho$_{LH}$

Vocabulary

flatbread oven   *khata*$_{LH}$
flesh   *di'i*$_{LH}$
flies   ~*khobada*$_{LHL}$
flooded forest   *wato*$_{LH}$
flute (type of)   ~*da'bo*$_{LH}$
fly   *wɨ(ɨ)*$_{HL}$
follow   ~*dɨdɨ*$_{LHL}$
food   *chɨa*$_{HL}$
foot   *da'po*$_{LH}$
force into   ~*yosa*$_{LHL}$
forehead   *wɨ'dɨapo'ka*$_{LHL}$
forget   *bo*$_{(L)H}$
form   *pari*$_{LHL}$
four   *phititia*$_{LHL}$
front of   *po'sa*$_{LHL}$, *poto*$_{LHL}$
front (put in)   *tui*$_{LHL}$
fruit   *dicha*$_{LH}$
full of food   *yapi*$_{LH}$
garden   *wese*$_{LHL}$
get   ~*da(a)*$_{(L)HL}$
give   *wa(a)*$_{H}$
gluttonous (be)   *sase*$_{LH}$
go   *wa'a*$_{LHL}$
go into the brush/woods   *su'a*$_{LHL}$
good (be)   ~*doa*$_{H}$
good! (interjection)   *hai*$_{H}$
grab with one's hand   ~*ya'a*$_{LHL}$
grandfather   ~*yɨchɨ*$_{LH}$
grandmother   ~*yɨcho*$_{LH}$
grass   *tha*$_{H}$
grate   *soa*$_{H}$
grated manioc   *phu'ti*$_{LH}$
grind   *soa*$_{H}$
ground   *yapa*$_{LH}$
group (of people)   *-kuru*
grow   ~*basa*$_{LHL}$, *bɨkɨ*$_{LHL}$
hair   *phoa*$_{LH}$
half   *khoa*$_{H}$
half of   *-dacho*
hallucinogenic powder   ~*wi'o*$_{LH}$
hand   ~*wabo(ka)*$_{LHL}$
hang (be hanging)   *yosa*$_{LH}$
hang by a thread or stem   ~*o*$_{H}$
happy (be)   *wache*$_{LHL}$
hard (be) (physical property)   *bɨti*$_{LHL}$
have   *khɨa*$_{LHL}$
hawk   *kha*$_{H}$

head   *dapu*~LHL~
hear   *thɨ'o*~LHL~
heart   *yahiri~pho'da*~LHL~
heat up   *si*~HL~
hello, how's it going?   *~de*~H~
help   *yoado*~LHL~
her (possessive, §6.4.1)   *to*~L~
here (proximal deictic, §4.5.2)   *~o*~H~
hide   *~dɨo*~LHL~
high (be)   *~bɨa*~LH~
high water   *-~bidi*
his (§6.4.1)   *to*~L~
hit   *~kha*~(L)HL~
hold   *khɨa*~LHL~
hole   *kopa*~LH~
hole, make a   *phore*~LH~
honey   *~bi*~H~
horsefly   *~duda*~LHL~
hot (be)   *si*~HL~
house   *wɨ'ɨ*~LH~
how (question, §11.2.5)   *do'se*~LH~
how's that? (interjection)   *cho'o*~LH~
hunt with arrows   *bɨe*~LHL~
hurt   *~phuri*~LHL~
husband   *~badɨ*~LHL~
I (§4.7.1, §6.4.1)   *yɨ'ɨ*~LH~
if   *pa-te*~HL~
ignite   *~si'a*~LHL~
Ilha de Inambú (placename, Khanako)   *~khadako*~H~
illness   *do'a*~LH~, *duti*~LHL~
immediately (do)   *-~yo, -ka'a*
inceptive aspect (§7.5.2)   *-rɨka*
inflate   *phuti*~LHL~
ingá fruit   *~bede*~LHL~
inject   *be*~H~
inside (be)   *~sa*~(L)HL~
inside (move) (serialized motion verb, §7.5.1)   *-~sa, -~sa'a*
inside part or surface of   *phu'icha*~LHL~
intensifier (§8.3)   *-yɨ'dɨ*
intend to   *-sibɨ*
into (move) (serialized motion verb, §7.5.1)   *-~ba'do*
island   *~dɨko*~LH~
itch   *~wiki*~LH~
jacú bird   *khata~ba'a*~LH~
jaguar   *yai*~LH~
jungle   *~bakaroka*~LHL~, *~dɨkɨ*~LH~
just completed (§7.5.3)   *-tu'sɨ*

Khanako (placename, Ilha de Inambú) ~khadako$_H$
kill ~waha$_{LHL}$
know ~basi$_{LHL}$
lake pari$_{LHL}$
large (be) buhu$_{LHL}$
last (be) (spatial reference) bato$_{LHL}$
laugh buhu$_{LHL}$
lay (an egg) -~ku
leader phuto$_{LH}$
leaf ~phu$_H$
leafcutter ant ~bachu$_{LHL}$
lean (be leaning; nonhorizontal attachment or support) ~wa'a$_{LH}$
learn bu'e$_{LHL}$
leg ~yuchu$_{LH}$
let's (exhortative marker, §9.5.4) sa$_H$ . . . ~hi'da$_{HL}$, ~sa$_H$ . . . ~hi'da$_{HL}$
letter (of the alphabet) ho$_H$
lice khu'a$_{LH}$
lie (be lying, in recumbent position) ~khoa$_{LHL}$
lie down suka$_{HL}$
lie (tell a lie) ~ba'yo$_{LHL}$
light (be) bo're$_{LHL}$
like hikoa$_H$
like (be) -se
like this ~o-pa$_H$ (usually accompanied by hand gesture)
like (similarity) ~o-se$_H$
lime ~iriboa$_{LHL}$
live kha'ti$_{LH}$
log ~khubu$_{LHL}$
long (be) yoa$_{LH}$
look ~yu$_H$
look for ~baka$_{LHL}$
lose bo$_{(L)H}$
lost (be) wisi$_{LHL}$
love ~kha'i$_{LHL}$
lower boro$_{LHL}$
macaw ~baha$_{LH}$
Mahaphoa (placename, Arara Cachoeira) ~bahapoa$_{LH}$
make noise du'ta$_{LHL}$
make yoa$_{LHL}$
maggot dacho$_{LH}$
man (human being) ~basu$_{LHL}$
man (male) ~bu$_{HL}$
mandi fish ki$_H$
manioc flour/meal po'ka$_{LHL}$
manioc liquid ~yoka$_{LH}$
manioc plant duku$_{LH}$
manioc root khu$_{(L)HL}$

manioc (soaked) khɨbo$_{HL}$
many pe'ri$_{LH}$, phayɨ$_{LH}$
mature ~wa'bɨ$_{LH}$, ~basa$_{LHL}$
meal cha$_H$
meat di'i$_{LH}$
medicine ko$_{(L)HL}$
meet boka$_{LHL}$
middle wato$_{LHL}$
middle of -dacho
miriti fruit ~daka$_{LH}$
mix ~bore$_{LHL}$
Mõ (placename, Carurú Cachoeira) ~bo$_H$
motion/signal with one's hand bɨaphi$_{LHL}$
mouth dɨse$_{LH}$, dise$_{LH}$
move across (relational motion verb, §7.5.1) ~pha'a$_{LHL}$
move in a circular path, around (verb of motion, §7.3.1) sito$_{LHL}$
move inside (serialized motion verb, §7.5.1) -~sa, -~sa'a
move into (serialized motion verb, §7.5.1) -~ba'do
move out into open area (relational motion verb, §7.3.3) phi'a$_{HL}$
move out of enclosed space (relational motion verb, §7.3.3, §7.5.1) ~wio$_{LHL}$
move outward/outside (relational motion verb, §7.3.3) wiha$_{LHL}$
move up and down (motion verb, §7.3.2, §7.5.1) -~baha
moving (do while m.) (serialized motion verb, §7.5.1) -ka'a
moving downward (serialized motion verb, §7.5.1) -bɨro, -diha$_{LHL}$
mud saba$_{LH}$
my (§6.4.1) yɨ$_L$=
name ~waba$_{LH}$
narrow (be) bi'sa$_{LHL}$
near ka'a$_{LH}$
negative nominal (nothing, no one, none, never) (§4.6) ~de$_H$
never (negative nominal, §4.6) ~de$_H$
new (be) ~wa'ba$_{LHL}$
next to (spatial reference) ka'a$_{LH}$
night ~yabi$_{LH}$
no one (negative nominal, §4.6) ~de$_H$
noise: make noise koa$_{LHL}$
none (negative nominal, §4.6) ~de$_H$
nonvisual evidence auxiliary (§9.2.3) koa$_{LHL}$
nose ~ke$_H$
not exist ~badia$_{LHL}$
not now! (interjection) soro$_H$
nothing (negative nominal, §4.6) ~de$_H$
now ~bi$_{(L)H}$
now (do) (§7.5.3) -~sidi
offer ~yui$_{LHL}$
offspring ~pho'da$_{LHL}$
okay hai$_H$

Vocabulary

on (be) top or on horizontal surface of $pisa_{LH}$
one $\sim k\mathit{u}_H$
open $buku_{LHL}$
opening $phari_{LH}$
opening (e.g., of a log) $duse_{LH}$, $dise_{LH}$
origin $\sim baka_{LHL}$
other, another (alternate particle, §4.5.2) pa_{HL}
our (exclusive) (§6.4.1) $\sim sa_L$
our (inclusive) (§6.4.1) $\sim bari_L$
out into open area (move) (relational motion verb, §7.3.3) $phi'a_{HL}$
out of enclosed space (move) (relational motion verb, §7.3.3, §7.5.1) $\sim wio_{LHL}$
outside $sopaka_{LHL}$
outside (go) $wihi_{LHL}$
outward/outside (move) (relational motion verb, §7.3.3) $wiha_{LHL}$
over (spatial reference) $bu'i_{LHL}$
over and over (do) (§7.5.1) $-\sim tidi$
pain $\sim phuria_{LHL}$
pakú fish $\sim bako_{LHL}$
pan-flute $karisu_{LHL}$
parent: *see* father, mother
parrot $wacho_{LHL}$
part $khoa_H$
particles $-di'o$
pass out $yu'du_{LHL}$
path $\sim ba'a_{LH}$
paw $da'po_{LH}$
peel $wu'a_{LH}$
penetrate $-\sim ba'do$
people $\sim basa_{LH}$
pepper bia_{LH}
pepper and fish stew $biato_{LH}$
perceive koa_{LHL}
perfective marker (§8.5.2) $-wa'a$
perform $da're_{LHL}$
person $\sim basu_{LHL}$
pick (fruit) sua_{LH}
pick up wua_{LH}
piece of $-sika$
pierce $\sim si'o_{LHL}$
pig (wild) $yese_{LHL}$
pineapple $\sim sare_{LH}$
piranha $bu'u_{LH}$
placed (be) $thua_{LH}$
plant (verb) toa_H, be_H
play $pape_{LH}$
play (a flute) $phuti_{LH}$
poison $\sim phuria_{LHL}$

poison darts $waka_{LHL}$
port $pita_{LHL}$
possession $ya_{(L)HL}$
pot (clay) $situ_{LH}$
pray $-bo'e$
prepare $da're_{LHL}$
prepared food cha_H
progressive auxiliary (§11.3.2) $\sim di_{HL}$
proximal deictic (§4.5.2) $\sim o_H$
proximal demonstrative (§4.5.2, §6.2) $a'ri_{LH}$
pull $waha_{LHL}$
pull out $\sim thua_{LHL}$
push thu_H
put on (tip of something) (§7.3.4) $-\sim rapo$
put over $dura_{LHL}$
put/place in specific position $du'u_{LH}$
quickly (do) (§7.5.1) $-\sim bu$
quoted speech introducer $\sim o\text{-}se_H$
rapids $phoaye_{LH}$
rat $bi'i_{LH}$
realize $\sim yu_H$
reciprocally (do) $\sim kha'ba_{LH}$
red (be) $\sim so'a_{LHL}$
red howler monkey $\sim ebo_{LH}$
relative (fellow person of Kotiria ethnicity) ko_{HL}
remote deictic (§4.5.2) to_{HL}
remember $\sim waku_{LH}$
remove $wera$
repeat (repetitive aspect, §7.5.3) $\sim dabo_{LHL}$
request $du'ti_{LH}$, $\sim sidi_{LHL}$
rest soa_{LHL}
return $kho'a_{LHL}$, $thua_{LHL}$
revive $kasu_{LHL}$
right there $waro_{HL}$
ripen $\sim so'a_{LHL}$
river dia_{LH}
roach $khasi_{LH}$
rock $\sim ta_H$
roof $\sim bua_{LH}$
room $tatia_{LHL}$
rooster $karaka_H$
rope $\sim da'bo_{LH}$
row $waha_{LHL}$
run $\sim bubu_{LHL}$
sad (be) $buhawiti_{LH}$
salt, salt plant $\sim boa_H$
sap $\sim chipe_{HL}$

Vocabulary

sarapo (long-tailed) fish $so'a_{LH}$
sardine $\sim bia_{HL}$
satisfied (full of food) (be) $yapi_{LH}$
say $\sim di_{HL}$
scale (of a fish) $\sim dutu_{LH}$
scream $\sim sayo_{LHL}$
see $\sim yu_{H}$
seed $yapa_{LHL}$
seedling $-kapa$
separate $-boro, -ta$
set afire $\sim wiha_{LH}$
shake $\sim tho'o_{LH}$
shaman yai_{LH}
shape $pari_{LHL}$
sharp (be) sio_{LH}
sharpen sio_{LH}
shiny (be) $sipa_{HL}$
shoot $phicha_{LH}$
shoot (seedling) $-kapa$
shore bu_{H}
should (§7.5.4) $-\sim basi$
show $\sim yo_{HL}$
side $bu'se_{LH}, ka'a_{LH}, -\sim phare$
sieve $wipe_{LHL}$
sift $su'o_{LHL}, su'a_{LHL}$
signal/motion with one's hand $buaphi_{LHL}$
sing $basa_{LHL}$
siringa fruit $waso_{LH}$
sister (older) $\sim wa'bio_{LH}$
sister (younger) $ba'o_{LH}$
sit, sitting (be) $duhi_{LHL}$
sitting object $\sim khubu_{LHL}$
skillful (be) (as a fisherman) go_{HL}
skin $ka'sa_{LH}$
sky $\sim bua_{LH}$
sleep $\sim khari_{LHL}$
slide $\sim sio_{LH}$
slow (be) phi_{HL}
small (be) $\sim ba(a)_{LH}, da_{H}$
smaller (be) $dasa_{H}$
smelly (be) $\sim uri_{LHL}$
smoke hu_{H}
smooth (be) $ya'pi_{LH}$
snail $\sim su'i_{LH}$
snake $\sim phido_{LHL}$
snake (poisonous) $\sim aga_{LH}$
sniff $\sim wihi_{LH}$

so ~a_L=
soaked manioc *khɨbo*$_{HL}$
some ~*ka*$_H$
sometime(s) *pa-te*$_{HL}$
somewhere *pa-se('e)*$_{HL}$
son ~*bakɨ*$_{LH}$
sour (be) *phia*$_{LHL}$
space within *phu'icha*$_{LHL}$
speak *du*$_{HL}$
spider *wɨpɨ*$_{LH}$
spread out *-phayo*
squirrel ~*wiso*$_{LH}$
stab *phu'a*$_{LH}$
stand *duku*$_{LHL}$
steal *yaka*$_{LHL}$
stick *tɨ*$_{HL}$
stick onto ~*sɨ'a*$_{LHL}$
sticky (be) ~*sɨ'a*$_{LHL}$, ~*wita*$_{LHL}$
still (do) (§7.5.3) -~*sidi*
stomach *pha*$_H$
store *wi'bo*$_{LH}$
story *khiti*$_{LHL}$
stream ~*ba(a)*$_H$
strong (be) *tua*$_{LHL}$
study *bu'e*$_{LHL}$
successful (be) *thɨo*$_{LH}$
suck ~*wibi*$_{LHL}$
suckle ~*pu*$_H$
suddenly (do) *wa'kɨe*$_{LHL}$
sugarcane ~*khadɨ*$_{LH}$
supervisor *phɨto*$_{LH}$
surprised (be) *kɨa*$_{LHL}$
sweep *kho'a*$_{LHL}$
swim *ba*$_{(L)H}$
tail ~*phicho*$_{LH}$
take off (in an airplane) ~*khoa*$_H$
talk *du*$_{HL}$
tapir *wachɨ*$_{LH}$
taste *koa*$_{LHL}$
teeth *piri*$_{HL}$
tell *ya'u*$_{LHL}$
termite *butua*$_{LH}$
thanks! ~*doada*$_H$
that (distal demonstrative, §4.5.2, §6.2) *si*$_H$
that (anaphoric pronoun or modifier, §§4.7.2–4.7.3, §6.2) *ti*$_{H(L)}$
the (anaphoric pronoun or modifier, §§4.7.2–4.7.3, §6.2) *ti*$_{H(L)}$
the (remote deictic, definite §4.5.2) *to*$_{HL}$

Vocabulary 483

their (possessive pronoun, §6.4.1) $ti_L=$
then $\sim a_L=$
then (do) (§7.5.3)   -$\sim sidi$
there (distal deictic, §4.5.2) $\sim so\,'o_{LH}$
there (remote deictic, §4.5.2) to_{HL}
think $-thu$
this (proximal demonstrative, §4.5.2, §6.2) $a\,'ri_{LH}$
three tia_{LH}
three-sided basket $piri_H$
throw $\sim khoa_H$, $doka_{LHL}$
tie off (finish the edge of a basket or woven item) $\sim wupo_{LHL}$
tie up (finish a woven edge) $du\,'te_{LH}$
tired (be) $\sim phube_{LHL}$
tobacco $\sim bu\,'do_{LHL}$
today $\sim bicha_{LH}$
together (do)   -$\sim daka$, $su\,'o_{LHL}$
tongue $\sim ya\,'ba_{LH}$
tooth pi_{HL}
top $so\,'to_{LHL}$
top (horizontal surface) of $bu\,'i_{LHL}$
torch $\sim si\,'a_{LHL}$
toucan $dasa_{LH}$
tree $yuku_{LHL}$
truth $photo_{LHL}$
try   -$\sim duha$, $\sim yu_H$
turn over $\sim da\,'ba_{LH}$
turtle $khu_{(L)H}$
two $phua_{LHL}$
ugly (be) $\sim ya_{HL}$
under $doka_{LH}$
understand $thu\,'o_{LHL}$
unexpectedly (do) $wa\,'kue_{LHL}$
until (temporal reference) te (probably from Portuguese *até*)
up and down (move) (motion verb, §7.3.2, §7.5.1)   -$\sim baha$
uphill (go) $\sim baha_{LH}$
upriver (go) (directional motion verb, §7.3.2) $yoha_{LHL}$
village $\sim baka_{LHL}$
vine $\sim bisi_{LH}$
visible (be) $bahu_{LHL}$
visit $\sim yu_H$, $\sim tidi_{LH}$
vomit $chowe_{HL}$
wait $ko\,'ta_{LHL}$
wake someone up $\sim wa\,'ko_{LHL}$
wake up $\sim wa\,'ka_{LHL}$
walk $\sim tidi_{LH}$
wander $\sim tidi_{LH}$
want $\sim kha\,'ba_{LHL}$

warn ~di_{HL}, ya'u_{LHL}
wasps tiroa$_H$
water ko$_{(L)HL}$
we (exclusive, §4.7.1, §6.4.1) ~sa$_H$
we (inclusive, §4.7.1, §6.4.1) ~bari$_{LH}$
weave su'a$_{LH}$
what (question, §6.5.1, §11.2.5) yaba$_{LH}$, do'se$_{LH}$
what? (interjection) cho'o$_{LH}$
where (question, §6.5.1) ~do'o$_{LH}$
which (question, §6.5.2) ~di$_H$
white people ~yara$_{LHL}$
who, whose (question, §§6.5.1–6.5.2) ~doa$_{LHL}$
why (question, §11.2.5) do'se$_{LH}$
wife ~dabo$_{LHL}$
woman ~dubi$_{LHL}$
wonder ~di$_{HL}$
wood phicha$_{LH}$
work da'ra$_{LHL}$
worm ~hu$_{HL}$
worry ahi$_{LHL}$
wrap around ~wa'ba$_{LH}$
write hoa$_H$
year ~khɨ'ba$_{LHL}$
yell ~sayo$_{LHL}$
yes hai$_H$
yesterday ~khadɨ$_{LH}$
you (pl.) (§4.7.1, §6.4.1) ~bɨsa$_{LH}$
you (sg.) (§4.7.1, §6.4.1) ~bɨ'ɨ$_{LH}$
young (be) ~wia$_{LH}$, ~wa'ba$_{LHL}$
young boy do'kai$_{LHL}$
your (pl.) (§6.4.1) ~bɨsa$_L$=
your (sg.) (§6.4.1) ~bɨ$_L$=

Grammatical suffixes and enclitics

Nonroot grammatical morphemes—suffixes and enclitics—that occur in nominal and verbal words are listed below. Suffixes and enclitics that occur in nominal words include derivational suffixes as well as suffixes and enclitics that code lexical, syntactic, and discourse-level information; these are discussed for the most part in chapters 4 and 5 and are shown in positions 1 through 7 of figure 5.1. Suffixes and enclitics that occur in verbal words include the derivational suffix *-ti*, discussed in chapter 3, as well as suffixes and other nonroot morphemes shown in positions 4 through 6 in figure 8.1 and generally discussed in chapters 8 and 9. Proclitics (for the most part pronouns,

Vocabulary

which can also occur as independent morphemes) and roots that undergo cliticization in certain constructions are listed in the main vocabulary.

Suffixes marked with + rather than - are [Ø nasal]; = marks enclitics (always with L tone).

+*a* plural (animate) (§4.2.2); mass noun derivation (§4.3.1); third person plural subject agreement in irrealis constructions and nominalized complements (§10.1.2)
+*a* assertion evidential (perfective) (§9.2.5)
+*a* affectedness (§8.5.3)
-*ati* imperfective aspect (§8.5.1)
=*ba'ro* type, kind (§3.6)
-*bo* dubitative (§8.4.1)
-*bo-ri* speculative interrogative (§9.4.2)
-~*ba* permissive (and marker of politeness) (§9.5.2)
-~*ba* frustrative (§8.4.2)
-~*behe* negative assessment (§8.4.4)
=~*be're*$_L$ comitative-instrumental case (§5.2.3, §§10.7.3–10.7.5); manner adverbial derivation (§11.2.2)
-*chʉ* switch reference (§10.1.2)
-*dita* solitary (§5.1.2)
-~*da* plural (animate, human) (§4.2.1); first or second person plural subject agreement in irrealis constructions and nominalized complements (§10.1.2)
~*do'bʉ* emphatic imperative (§9.5.1)
-*era*$_{HL}$ negative (§8.2)
+*ga* imperative (§9.5.1)
-*ha* visual evidential (imperfective first person) (§9.2.2)
-*hari* interrogative (imperfective) (§9.4.1)
-~*ha* terminative (§8.4.4)
+*i* locative (§5.2.1)
+*i* visual evidential (perfective first person) (§9.2.2)
-*iro* nominalizer (singular animate) (§4.5.1)
-~*ida* nominalizer (plural animate) (§4.5.1)
-*ka* assertion evidential (imperfective) (§9.2.5)
-*ka* predictive (§9.3.1)
-*ka-ri* interrogative (supposition) (§9.4.2)
-*kiro* individualizer, singular (animates, relic form) (§4.2.2, §4.2.3)
-*(k)o* feminine (§4.2.1); first or second person singular feminine subject agreement in irrealis constructions and nominalized complements (§10.1.2)
-*koro* feminine, singular (animates, relic form) (§4.2.2)
-*kure* comparative (§11.2.4)
-*(k)ʉ, -i* masculine (§4.2.1); first or second person singular masculine subject agreement in irrealis constructions and nominalized complements (§10.1.2)
-*kʉrʉ* adversative (§9.5.3)
-~*ka* diminutive, emphasis (§5.1.1, §11.2.2)
-~*kida* plural (relic form for some animates) (§4.2.2)

-*khʉ* additive (§5.2.1)
=~*kha'ba* need, have to, must (deontic modality auxiliary, §11.3.1)
-*pe* countable quantity (§6.5.2)
-*pe* favoritive (§8.4.3)
-*puro* uncountable quantity (§6.5.2)
-*pʉ* empathetic (§8.4.4)
-*pʉ* locative (§5.2.1, §10.5, §10.7.1)
+*ra* visual evidential (imperfective second or third person) (§9.2.2)
+*re* visual evidential (perfective second or third person) (§9.2.2)
+*re* objective case (§5.2.2, §§10.3–10.3.5, §10.7.2); generic reference classifier (§4.7.3)
-*ri* admonitive (§9.5.3)
-*ri* interrogative (perfective) (§9.4.1)
+*ri* nominalizer (§4.5.1)
+*ri* plural (inanimate) (§4.3)
+*ro* singular (animate) (§4.2; §4.5.1); partitive derivatives of mass nouns (§§4.3.1–4.3.2); adverbials of quality and evaluation (§11.2.1); third person singular subject agreement in irrealis constructions and nominalized complements (§10.1.2)
-*se(ri)* plural (used for a few inanimates) (§4.3.2)
-*se* be like (similarity) (§11.2.4)
-*se'e* contrastive subject (§5.3.2)
-*si* negative irrealis (§9.3.2)
=*ta*$_L$ referential (§5.3.1)
-*ta* intention (§9.3.1)
-*ti* verbalizer (have attribute) (§3.3.2)
-*wʉ'rʉ* augmentative (§5.1.1)
-*ya* plural (used for a small subset of animates) (§4.2.2)
-*yu'ka* quotative evidential (§9.2.1)
-*yu'ti* diffuse hearsay evidential (§9.2.1)

References

Aikhenvald, Alexandra Y.
1999   Areal Diffusion and Language Contact in the Içana-Vaupés Basin, North West Amazonia. *In* The Amazonian Languages, edited by R. M. W. Dixon and Alexandra Y. Aikhenvald, 385–415. Cambridge: Cambridge University Press.
2000   Classifiers: A Typology of Noun Categorization Devices. Oxford: Oxford University Press.
2002a   Language Contact in Amazonia. Oxford: Oxford University Press.
2002b   Typological Parameters for the Study of Clitics, with Special Reference to Tariana. *In* Word: A Cross-Linguistic Typology, edited by R. M. W. Dixon and Alexandra Y. Aikhenvald, 42–48. Cambridge: Cambridge University Press.
2003a   Evidentiality in Typological Perspective. *In* Studies in Evidentiality, edited by Alexandra Y. Aikhenvald and R. M. W. Dixon, 1–31. Amsterdam and Philadelphia: John Benjamins.
2003b   A Grammar of Tariana, from Northwest Amazonia. Cambridge: Cambridge University Press.
2004   Evidentiality. Oxford: Oxford University Press.
2006   Serial Verb Constructions in Typological Perspective. *In* Serial Verb Constructions: A Cross-Linguistic Typology, edited by Alexandra Y. Aikhenvald and R. M. W. Dixon, 1–68. Oxford: Oxford University Press.

Aikhenvald, Alexandra Y., and Robert M. W. Dixon
1998   Evidentials and Areal Typology: A Case Study from Amazonia. Language Sciences 20(3):241–57.

Allan, Keith
1977   Classifiers. Language 53:285–311.

Amorim, Antonio Brandão de
1987   Lendas em nheengatu e em português. Manaus: Fundo Editorial, Associação Comercial do Amazonas. (Originally published in 1928.)

Anderson, Lloyd B.
1986   Evidentials, Paths of Change, and Mental Maps: Typologically Regular Asymmetries. *In* Evidentiality: The Linguistic Coding of Epistemology, edited by Wallace Chafe and Johanna Nichols, 273–312. Norwood, N.J.: Ablex.

Andrello, Geraldo
2006   Cidade do índio: Transformações e cotidiano em Iauaretê. São Paulo: Editora UNESP and Instituto Socioambiental; Rio de Janeiro: Núcleo de Transformações Indígenas.

Andrello, Geraldo, Dominique Buchillet, and Marta Azevedo
2002   Levantamento sócio-econômico, demográfico e sanitário de Iauaretê/Centro. São Paulo: Instituto Socioambiental.

Ardila, Olga
2000   Reseña bibliográfica del piratapuyo. *In* Lenguas indígenas de Colombia: Una visión descriptiva, edited by María Stella González de Pérez and María Luisa Rodríguez de Montes, 493–94. Bogotá: Instituto Caro y Cuervo.

Ärhem, Kaj
1981   Makuna Social Organization. Stockholm: Almqvist & Wiksell International.

Azevedo, Marta Maria
2005   Povos indígenas no alto rio Negro: Um estudo de caso de nupcialidade. *In* Demografia dos povos indígenas no Brasil, edited by Heloísa Pagliaro, Marta Maria Azevedo, and RicardoVentura Santos, 33–58. Rio de Janeiro: Fiocruz; Campinas: Associação Brasileira de Estudos Populacionais.

Barnes, Janet
1984   Evidentials in the Tuyuca Verb. International Journal of American Linguistics 50(3):255–71.
1990   Classifers in Tuyuca. *In* Amazonian Linguistics: Studies in Lowland South American Languages, edited by Doris L. Payne, 273–92. Austin: University of Texas Press.
1996   Autosegments with Three-Way Lexical Contrasts in Tuyuca. International Journal of American Linguistics 62(1):31–58.
1999   Tucano. *In* The Amazonian Languages, edited by R. M. W. Dixon and Alexandra Y. Aikhenvald, 207–226. Cambridge: Cambridge University Press.
2006   Tucanoan Languages. *In* Encyclopedia of Language and Linguistics. Vol. 13, edited by Keith Brown, 130–42. 2nd ed. Boston: Elsevier.

Barnes, Janet, and Terrell Malone
2000   El tuyuca. *In* Lenguas indígenas de Colombia: Una visión descriptiva, edited by María Stella González de Pérez and María Luisa Rodríguez de Montes, 437–50. Bogotá: Instituto Caro y Cuervo.

Bossong, George
1991   Differential object marking in romance and beyond. In New Analses in Romance Linguistics. Edited by Douglas A. Kibbee and Dieter Wanner, 143-170. Amsterdam/Philadelphia, Benjamins

Brüzzi, Antonio Alves da Silva
1977   A civilização indígena do Uaupés. Rome: Libreria Ateneo Salesiano.

Buchillet, Dominique
1983   Maladie et mémoire des origines chez les Desana du Uaupés. Ph.D. diss., University of Paris X.

Bybee, Joan
1985   Morphology: A Study of the Relation between Meaning and Form. Typological Studies in Language 9. Amsterdam: John Benjamins.

1998	Irrealis as a Grammatical Category. Anthropological Linguistics 40(7):257–71.

Bybee, Joan, Revere Perkins, and William Pagliuca
    1994   The Evolution of Grammar: Tense, Aspect, and Modality in the Languages of the World. Chicago: University of Chicago Press.

Cabalzar, Aloisio
    2000   Descendência e aliança no espaço tuyuka: A noção de nexo regional no noroeste amazônico. Revista de Antropologia 43(1):61–88.

Cabalzar, Aloisio, and Ricardo, Carlos Alberto
    2006   Povos indígenas do rio Negro: Uma introdução à diversidade socioambiental do noroeste da Amazônia brasileira; Mapa-livro. São Paulo: Instituto Socioambiental; São Gabriel da Cachoeira: Federação das Organizações Indígenas do Rio Negro.

Chafe, Wallace, and Johanna Nichols (eds.)
    1986   Evidentiality: The Linguistic Coding of Epistemology. Advances in Discourse Processes 20. Norwood, N.J.: Ablex.

Chernela, Janet M.
    1983   Hierarchy and Economy of the Uanano (Kotiria) Speaking Peoples of the Middle Uaupes Basin. Ph.D. diss., Columbia University.
    1989   Marriage, Language, and History Among Eastern Tukanoan Speaking Peoples of the Northwest Amazon. Latin American Anthropology Review 1(2):36–41.
    1993   The Wanano Indians of the Brazilian Amazon: A Sense of Space. Austin: University of Texas Press.

Clements, George N., and Elizabeth V. Hume
    1996   The Internal Organization of Speech Sounds. *In* Handbook of Phonological Theory, edited by John A. Goldsmith, 245–306. Cambridge: Blackwell.

Craig, Colette
    1992   Classifiers in a Functional Perspective. *In* Layered Structure and Reference in a Functional Perspective: Papers from the Functional Grammar Conference in Copenhagen, 1990, edited by Michael D. Fortescue, Peter Harder, and Lars Kristoffersen, 277–301. Amsterdam: John Benjamins.

Criswell, Linda, and Beverly Brandrup
    2000   Un bosquejo fonológico y gramatical del siriano. *In* Lenguas indígenas de Colombia: Una visión descriptiva, edited by María Stella González de Pérez and María Luisa Rodríguez de Montes, 395–415. Bogotá: Instituto Caro y Cuervo.

de Haan, Ferdinand
    1999   Evidentiality and Epistemic Modality: Setting Boundaries. Southwest Journal of Linguistics 18(1):83–101.
    2001a   The Cognitive Basis of Visual Evidentials. *In* Conceptual and Discourse Factors in Linguistic Structure, edited by Alan J.

Cienki, Barbara J. Luka, and Michael B. Smith, 91–106. Stanford: CSLI Publications.
2001b The Place of Inference within the Evidential System. International Journal of American Linguistics 67(2):193–219.

DeLancey, Scott
1997 Mirativity: The Grammatical Marking of Unexpected Information. Linguistic Typology 1:33–52.

Derbyshire, Desmond C., and Doris L. Payne
1990 Noun Classification Systems of Amazonian Languages. *In* Amazonian Linguistics: Studies in Lowland South American Languages, edited by Doris L. Payne, 243–71. Austin: University of Texas Press.

Dixon, R. M. W.
1986 Noun Classes and Noun Classification in Typological Perspective. *In* Noun Classes and Categorization: Proceedings of a Symposium on Categorization and Noun Classification, Eugene, Oregon, October 1983, edited by Colette Grinevald Craig, 105–12. Amsterdam and Philadelphia: John Benjamins.

Dixon, R. M. W., and Alexandra Y. Aikhenvald
1999 The Amazonian Languages. Cambridge: Cambridge University Press.
2002 Word: A Cross-Linguistic Typology. Cambridge: Cambridge University Press.

Durie, Mark
1997 Grammatical Structures in Verb Serialization. *In* Complex Predicates, edited by Alex Alsina, Joan Bresnan, and Peter Sells, 289–354. CSLI Lecture Notes 64. Stanford: CSLI.

Epps, Patience
2005 Areal Diffusion and the Development of Evidentiality: Evidence from Hup. Studies in Language. 29(3):617–49.
2007 The Vaupés Melting Pot: Tukanoan Influence on Hup. *In* Grammars in Contact: A Cross-Linguistic Typology, edited by Alexandra Y. Aikhenvald and R. M. W. Dixon, 267–89. Explorations in Linguistic Typology 4. Oxford: Oxford University Press.
2008 A Grammar of Hup. Mouton Grammar Library 43. Berlin: Mouton de Gruyter.

Ewen, Colin J., and Harry van der Hulst
2001 The Phonological Structure of Words: An Introduction. Cambridge: Cambridge University Press.

Federação das Organizações Indígenas do Rio Negro and Instituto Socioambiental
2005 Levantamento socioeconômico, demográfico e sanitário da cidade de São Gabriel da Cachoeira. São Gabriel da Cachoeira: Federação das Organizações Indígenas do Rio Negro and Instituto Socioambiental.

Ferguson, Judith, Cari Hollinger, Linda Criswell, and Nancy L. Morse
2000   El cubeo. *In* Lenguas indígenas de Colombia: Una visión descriptiva, edited by María Stella González de Pérez and María Luisa Rodríguez de Montes, 357–70. Bogotá: Instituto Caro y Cuervo.

Floyd, Rick
1999   The Structure of Evidential Categories in Wanka Quechua. Dallas: Summer Institute of Linguistics; [Arlington]: University of Texas at Arlington.

Foley, William A., and Mike Olson
1985   Clausehood and Verb Serialization. *In* Grammar inside and outside the Clause: Some Approaches to Theory from the Field, edited by Johanna Nichols and Anthony C. Woodbury, 17–60. Cambridge: Cambridge University Press.

Frajzyngier, Zygmunt
1985   Truth and the Indicative Sentence. Studies in Language 9(2):243–54.

Franchetto, Bruna
2005   Línguas em perigo e línguas como patrimônio imaterial: Duas idéias em discussão. Revista do Patrimônio Histórico e Artístico Nacional 32:182–205.

Franchetto, Bruna, and Elsa Gomez-Imbert
2003   Review of *The Amazonian Languages,* edited by R. M. W. Dixon and Alexandra Y. Aikhenvald. International Journal of American Linguistics 69(2):232–41.

Giacone, Antônio
1967   Pequena Gramática e Dicionário da Língua Kótiria ou Uanano. Belém: Imprensa Universitária.

Givón, Talmy
1981   On the Development of the Numeral 'One' as an Indefinite Marker. Folia Linguistica Historica 2(1):35–53.
1982   Evidentiality and Epistemic Space. Studies in Language 6(1):23–49.
2001   Syntax: An Introduction. 2 vols. Amsterdam and Philadelphia: John Benjamins.

Goldman, Irving
1963   The Cubeo: Indians of the Northwest Amazon. Urbana: University of Illinois Press.

Goldsmith, John A.
1999   An Overview of Autosegmental Phonology. *In* Phonological Theory: The Essential Readings, edited by John A. Goldsmith, 137–61. Oxford: Blackwell.

Gomez-Imbert, Elsa
1982   De la forme et du sens dans la classification nominale en tatuyo (langue Tukano Orientale d'Amazonie Colombienne). Doctorat de Troisième Cycle, Université de Paris–Sorbonne.

1986	Conocimiento y verdad en tatuyo. Antropología 2:117–25. Bogotá: Universidad de los Andes.
1988	Construcción verbal en barasana y tatuyo. Amerindia 13:97–108.
1991	Force des langues vernaculaires en situation d'exogamie linguistique: Le cas du Vaupés colombien, Nord-ouest amazonien. Cahiers des Sciences Humaines 27(3–4):535–59.
1996	When Animals Become "Rounded" and "Feminine": Conceptual Categories and Linguistic Classification in a Multilingual Setting. *In* Rethinking Linguistic Relativity, edited by John J. Gumperz and Stephen C. Levinson, 438–69. Cambridge: Cambridge University Press.
1997a	Morphologie et phonologie barasana: Approche non-linéaire. Ph.D. diss., Université de Paris VIII.
1997b	Structure prosodique et processus segmentaux en barasana (langue Tukano orientale d'Amazonie colombienne). Cahiers de Grammaire 22:97–125.
1998	Nasalité en barasana. *In* Langues et Grammaire: Phonologie II & III, communications presentées aux Colloques Langues et Grammaire, 1995, 1997, edited by Patrick Sauzet, 43–60. Paris: Département des Sciences du Langage, Université de Paris.
1999a	Les catégories de base de la conjugaison dans deux langues Tukano orientales. MS.
1999b	Variations tonales sur fond d'exogamie linguistique. Phonologie: théorie et variation, edited by Jacques Durand, 67–94. Cahiers de Grammaire 24. [Toulouse]: Equipe de recherche en syntaxe et sémantique, Université de Toulouse-Le Mirail.
2001	More on the Tone versus Pitch-Accent Typology: Evidence from Barasana and Other Eastern Tukanoan Languages. *In* Proceedings of the Symposium "Cross-Linguistic Studies of Tonal Phenomena: Tonogenesis, Typology, and Related Topics," December 12–14, 2000, Tokinagawa City Hall, Tokyo, edited by Shigeki Kaji, 369–412. Tokyo: Institute for the Study of Languages and Cultures of Asia and Africa, Tokyo University of Foreign Studies, Tokyo University of Foreign Studies.
2003a	Une langue du Nord-oueste amazonien: le barasana. *In* Méso-Amérique, Caraïbes, Amazonie. Vol. 2, edited by Jon Landaburu and Francisco Queixalos, 171–83. Faits de Langue 21. Fontenay-aux-Roses: Ophrys.
2003b	Voir et entendre comme sources de connaissance grammaticalmente explicites. *In* Langues et cognition, edited by Claude Vandeloise, 117–33. Paris: Hermès Science.
2005	Fonologia de dos idiomas tukano del Piraparaná: barasana y tatuyo. Amerindia 29–30:43–80.
2007a	Construcciones seriales en tatuyo y barasana (familia tukano): Hacia una tipología de la serialización verbal. *In* Lenguas indígenas de América del Sur: Estudios descriptivo-tipológicos y sus contribuciones para la lingüística teórica, edited by Andrés

	Romero-Figueroa, Anna Fernández Garay, and Angel Corbera, 172–89. Caracas: Universidad Católica Andrés Bello.
2007b	La vue ou l'ouïe: La modalité cognitive des langues tukano orientales. *In* L'énonciation médiatisée: Illustrations amérindiennes et caucasiennes. Vol. 2: Le traitement épistémologique de l'information, 65–85, edited by Zlatka Guentchéva and Jon Landaburu. Louvain: Peeters.
2007c	Tukanoan Nominal Classification: The Tatuyo System. *In* Language Endangerment and Endangered Languages: Linguistic and Anthropological Studies with Special Emphasis on the Languages and Cultures of the Andean-Amazonian Border Area, edited by Leo Wetzels, 401–28. Indigenous Languages of Latin America 5. Leiden: CNWS Publications.
2011	La famille tukano. *In* Dictionnaire des langues, edited by Emilio Bonvini, Joëlle Busuttil, and Alain Peyraube, 1454–60. Paris: Presses Universitaires de France.

Gomez-Imbert, Elsa, and Stephen Hugh-Jones
    2000   Introducción al estudio de las lenguas del Piraparaná (Vaupés). *In* Lenguas indígenas de Colombia: Una visión descriptiva, edited by María Stella González de Pérez and María Luisa Rodríguez de Montes, 321–56. Bogotá: Instituto Caro y Cuervo.

Gomez-Imbert, Elsa, and Michael Kenstowicz
    2000   Barasana Tone and Accent. International Journal of American Linguistics 66(4):419–63.

González de Pérez, Maria Stella
    2000   Bases para el estudio de la lengua pisamira. *In* Lenguas indígenas de Colombia: Una visión descriptiva, edited by María Stella González de Pérez and María Luisa Rodríguez de Montes, 373–91. Bogotá: Instituto Caro y Cuervo.

González de Pérez, Maria Stella, and Maria Luisa Rodríguez de Montes (eds.)
    2000   Lenguas indígenas de Colombia: Una visión descriptiva. Bogotá: Instituto Caro y Cuervo.

Hopper, Paul J., and Sandra A. Thompson
    1980   Transitivity in Grammar and Discourse. Language 56(2):251–99.

Hugh-Jones, Christine
    1979   From the Milk River: Spatial and Temporal Processes in Northwest Amazonia. Cambridge: Cambridge University Press.

Hugh-Jones, Stephen
    1979   The Palm and the Pleiades: Initiation and Cosmology in Northwest Amazonia. Cambridge: Cambridge University Press.

Hyman, Larry M.
    1978   Tone and/or Accent. *In* Elements of Tone, Stress, and Intonation, edited by Donna Jo Napoli, 1–20. Washington D.C.: Georgetown University.

Jackson, Jean E.
    1983   The Fish People: Linguistic Exogamy and Tukanoan Identity in Northwest Amazonia. Cambridge: Cambridge University Press.

Jones, Wendel, and Paula Jones
1991   Barasano Syntax. Dallas: Summer Institute of Linguistics.
Kaye, Jonathan D.
1970   The Desano Verb: Problems in Semantics, Syntax and Phonology. Ph.D. diss., Columbia University.
1971   Nasal Harmony in Desano. Linguistic Inquiry 2:37–56.
Kenstowicz, Michael
1994   Phonology in Generative Grammar. Cambridge, Mass.: Blackwell.
Kinch, Pamela G., and Rodney A. Kinch
2000   El yurutí. In Lenguas indígenas de Colombia: Una visión descriptiva, edited by María Stella González de Pérez and María Luisa Rodríguez de Montes, 469–87. Bogotá: Instituto Caro y Cuervo.
Klumpp, James, and Delores Klumpp
1973   Sistema fonológico del piratapuyo. In Sistemas fonológicos de idiomas colombianos. Vol. 2, 107–20. Lomalinda, Colombia: Editorial Townsend.
Koch-Grünberg, Theodor
1913–16 Die Betoya-Sprache Nordwestbrasiliens und der angrenzenden Gebiete. Anthropos 10–11: 421–49.
1995   Dos años entre los indios: Viajes por el noroeste brasileño 1903–1905. 2 vols. Vol. 1 translated by Adolf Watzke and Rosario Camacho Koppel; vol. 2 translated by María Mercedes Ortiz Rodríguez and Luis Carlos Francisco Castillo Serrano. Bogotá: Editorial Universidad Nacional. (German original published in 1909–10).
Ladefoged, Peter, and Ian Maddieson
1996   The Sounds of the World's Languages. Oxford: Blackwell.
Lasmar, Cristiane
2005   De volta ao Lago de Leite: Gênero e transformação no alto rio Negro. São Paulo: Editora UNESP and Instituto Socioambiental; Rio de Janeiro: Núcleo de Transformações Indígenas.
Leite, Yonne, and Bruna Franchetto
2006   500 anos de línguas indígenas no Brasil. In Quinhentos anos de história lingüística do Brasil, edited by Suzana Alice Cardoso, Jacyra Mota, and Rosa Virgínia Mattos e Silva, 15–61. Salvador: Fundo de Cultura da Bahia, Governo da Bahia, Secretaria da Fazenda, Secretaria da Cultura e Turismo.
Levinson, Stephen C.
2003   Space in Language and Cognition: Explorations in Cognitive Diversity. Language, Culture and Cognition 5. Cambridge: Cambridge University Press.
Levinson, Stephen C., and David P. Wilkins
2006   Grammars of Space: Explorations in Cognitive Diversity. Cambridge: Cambridge University Press.

Lewis, M. Paul (ed.)
2009　　Ethnologue: Languages of the World. 16th ed. Dallas: SIL International. Online version: http://www.ethnologue.com.

Licht, Daniel A., and Andrés Reinoso
2006　　El Amazonas colombiano: Pluralidad étnica y lingüística. *In* Lenguas y tradiciones orales de la Amazonía: ¿Diversidad en peligro?, 123–80. Havana: Oficina Regional de Cultura para América Latina y el Caribe de la UNESCO; Fondo Editorial Casa de las Américas.

Longacre, Robert E.
1983　　Switch Reference Systems from Two Distinct Linguistic Areas: Wojokeso (Papua New Guinea) and Guanano (Northern South America). *In* Switch-Reference and Universal Grammar, edited by J. Haiman and P. Munro, 185–207. Amsterdam and Philadelphia: John Benjamins.

Malone, Terrell
1987　　Proto-Tucanoan and Tucanoan Genetic Relationships. MS, Instituto Lingüístico de Verano, Colombia.
1988　　The Origin and Development of Tuyuca Evidentials. International Journal of American Linguistics 54(2):119–40.

Matthews, Peter
1997　　The Concise Oxford Dictionary of Linguistics. Oxford: Oxford University Press.

Michael, Lev David
2008　　Nanti Evidential Practice: Language, Knowledge, and Social Action in an Amazonian Society. Ph.D diss., University of Texas.

Miller, Marion
1999　　Desano Grammar. Dallas: Summer Institute of Linguistics; [Arlington]: University of Texas at Arlington.

Mithun, Marianne
1984　　The Evolution of Noun Incorporation. Language 60(4):847–94.
1986　　Evidential Diachrony in Northern Iroquoian. *In* Evidentiality: The Linguistic Coding of Epistemology, edited by Wallace Chafe and Johanna Nichols, 89–112. Norwood, N.J.: Ablex.
1999　　The Languages of Native North America. Cambridge: Cambridge University Press.

Mondragón, Maria Cortez
2006　　Perú: Reflexiones em torno a las lenguas em peligro y sus tradiciones orales em la Amazonía. *In* Lenguas y tradiciones orales de la Amazonia: ¿Diversidad en peligro?, 253–80. Havana: Oficina Regional de Cultura para América Latina y el Caribe de la UNESCO; Fondo Editorial Casa de las Américas.

Moore, Denny
2006　　Brazil: Language Situation. *In* Encyclopedia of Language and Linguistics. Vol. 2, edited by Keith Brown, 117–28. 2nd ed. Boston: Elsevier.

Morse, Nancy L., and Michael B. Maxwell
1999   Cubeo Grammar. Dallas: Summer Institute of Linguistics; [Arlington]: University of Texas at Arlington.

Muniz, Abrão Alves
2001   Wakoenai yako: Terra das línguas. Manaus: Secretaria de Estado da Educação e Qualidade do Ensino, Governo do Estado do Amazonas.

Neves, Eduardo
1998   Paths in Dark Waters: Archaeology as Indigenous History in the Upper Rio Negro Basin, Northwest Amazon. Ph.D. diss., Indiana University.

Palmer, Frank. R.
1986   Mood and Modality. Cambridge: Cambridge University Press.

Prince, Alan S.
1999   Relating to the Grid. *In* Phonological Theory: The Essential Readings, edited by John A. Goldsmith, 403–14. Oxford: Blackwell.

Ramirez, Henri
1997a   A fala tukano dos ye'pâ-masa. Vol. 1: Gramática. Manaus: Centro "Iauareté" de Documentação Etnográfica e Missionária.
1997b   A fala tukano dos ye'pâ-masa. Vol. 2: Dicionário. Manaus: Centro "Iauareté" de Documentação Etnográfica e Missionária.

Reichel-Dolmatoff, Gerardo
1971   Amazonian Cosmos: The Sexual and Religious Symbolism of the Tukano Indians. Chicago: University of Chicago Press.

Ribeiro, Berta G.
1995   Os índios das águas pretas: Modo de produção e equipamento produtivo. São Paulo: Editora da Universidade de São Paulo and Companhia das Letras.

Ricardo, Carlos Alberto, and Fany Ricardo
2006   Povos indígenas no Brasil 2001/2005. São Paulo: Instituto Socioambiental.

Rodrigues, Aryon Dall'Igna
2005   Sobre as línguas indígenas e sua pesquisa no Brasil. Ciência e Cultura 57(2):35–38.

Sorensen, Arthur P., Jr.
1967   Multilingualism in the Northwest Amazon. American Anthropologist 69:670–84.
1969   Morphology of Tucano. Ph.D. diss., Columbia University.

Stenzel, Kristine
2005   Multilingualism: Northwest Amazonia Revisited. Paper presented at the Second Congress on Indigenous Languages of Latin America, Austin, Texas, 27–29 October. Memorias del Congreso de Idiomas Indígenas de Latinoamérica II. http://www.ailla.utexas.org/site/cilla2_toc_sp.html.
2006   Lenguas y tradiciones orales en la Amazonia brasileña. *In* Lenguas y tradiciones orales de la Amazonia: ¿Diversidad en peligro? 71–121. Havana: Oficina Regional de Cultura para

América Latina y el Caribe de la UNESCO; Fondo Editorial Casa de las Américas.
2007a   Glottalization and Other Suprasegmental Features in Wanano. International Journal of American Linguistics 73(3):331–66.
2007b   The Semantics of Serial Verb Constructions in Two Eastern Tukanoan languages: Kotiria (Wanano) and Waikhana (Piratapuyo). *In* Proceedings of SULA 4: Semantics of Under-Represented Languages in the Americas, edited by Amy Rose Deal, 275–90. University of Massachusetts Occasional Papers 35. Amherst: Graduate Linguistics Student Association, University of Massachusetts at Amherst.
2008a   Evidentials and Clause Modality in Wanano. Studies in Language 32(2):404–44.
2008b. Kotiria "Differential Object Marking" in Cross-Linguistic Perspective. Amerindia 32:153–81.
forthcoming   Butterflies 'Leaning' on the Doorframe: Expressions of Location and Position in Kotiria and Wa'ikhana. *In* Expresión de nociones espaciales en lenguas amazónicas, edited by Elsa Gomez-Imbert and Ana María Ospina Bozzi. Bogotá: Universidad Nacional de Colombia.

Stenzel, Kristine, and Elsa Gomez-Imbert
   2009   Contato lingüístico e mudança lingüística no noroeste amazônico: o caso do Kotiria (Wanano). Revista da ABRALIN 8:71–100.

Strom, Clay
   1992. Retuarã Syntax. Studies in the Languages of Colombia 3. Dallas: Summer Institute of Linguistics; [Arlington]: University of Texas at Arlington.

Valencia López, Simón
   1994   ~Pamiene toivaiyede mahikaitukubo: Cartilla para aprender a escribir ~pamie (kubeo). [Mitú] : Centro Experimental Piloto del Vaupés.

UNESCO
   2006   Lenguas y tradiciones orales de la Amazonia: ¿Diversidad en peligro? Havana: Oficina Regional de Cultura para América Latina y el Caribe de la UNESCO; Fondo Editorial Casa de las Américas.

Wallace, Alfred Russel
   1969   A Narrative of Travels on the Amazon and Rio Negro. New York: Haskell House. (Originally published in 1870.)

Waltz, Carolyn
   1982   Algunas observaciones sobre el dialogo guanano. Bogotá: Instituto Lingüístico de Verano.

Waltz, Nathan E.
   1976a Hablemos el guanano: Una gramatica pedagogica del guanano. Bogotá: Instituto Lingüístico de Verano.
   1976b Discourse functions of Guanano sentence and paragraph. *In* Discourse Grammar: Studies in Indigenous Languages of Colombia, Panama, and Ecuador, Vol. 1, edited by Robert

            Longacre and Francis Woods, 21–145. Norman: Summer Institute of Linguistics.
2002   Innovations in Wanano (Eastern Tucanoan) When Compared to Piratapuyo. International Journal of American Linguistics 68(2):157–215.
2007   Diccionario bilingüe, wanano o guanano–español. Bogotá: Editora Buena Semilla.

Waltz, Nathan E., and Carolyn Waltz
1967   Guanano Phonemics. In Phonemic Systems of Colombian Languages, 25–36. Norman: Summer Institute of Linguistics.
1997   El agua, la roca y el humo: Estudios sobre la cultura wanana del Vaupés. Bogotá: Instituto Lingüístico de Verano.
2000   El wanano. In Lenguas indígenas de Colombia: Una visión descriptiva, edited by María Stella González de Pérez and María Luisa Rodríguez de Montes, 453–67. Bogotá: Instituto Caro y Cuervo.

Waltz, Nathan E., Carolyn Waltz, and Pedro Melo (translators)
1982   Cohamacu yare yahuri tju: El Nuevo Testamento en guanano. [New York]: Sociedad Bíblica de Nueva York Internacional.

Waltz, Nathan E., and Alva Wheeler
1972   Proto Tucanoan. In Comparative Studies in Amerindian Languages, edited by Esther Matteson, 119–49. Janua Linguarum Series Practica 127. The Hague: Mouton.

Welch, Betty, and Birdie West
2000   El Tucano. In Lenguas indígenas de Colombia: Una visión descriptiva, edited by María Stella González de Pérez and María Luisa Rodríguez de Montes, 419–36. Bogotá: Instituto Caro y Cuervo.

West, Birdie
1980   Gramática popular del tucano. Bogotá: Instituto Lingüístico de Verano.

Wheeler, Alva
1992   Comparaciones lingüísticas en el grupo tucano occidental. In Estudios comparativos: Proto tucano, edited by Stephen H. Levinsohn, 17–53. Bogotá: Editorial Alberto Lleras Camargo.

Willett, Thomas
1988   A Cross-Linguistic Survey of the Grammaticalization of Evidentiality. Studies in Language 12(1):51–97.

Wright, Robin M.
2005   História indigena e do indigenismo no alto rio Negro. Campinas: Mercado de Letras; São Paulo: Instituto Socioambiental.

Index

abbreviations, xix–xxi, 457
activity verbs, 206–9, 281
additive, 152, 156–57, 172
adjectival words, 87–88, 194–95, 206, 250–51
adjuncts, 314, 345–56
admonitives, 269, 309, 311–12
adverbial clauses, 148, 315, 318, 319–20
adverbials, 87, 88–89, 222, 225–26, 250, 348, 358–67
adversatives, 269, 309–10
affectedness, 46, 263–64
affricates, 32–34, 44
agent-oriented modality. *See* deontic modality
Aikhenvald, Alexandra Y., 121, 298, 306
"Airplanes" (text), 455–56
allophones, 34–36, 38n12, 43–44; orthographic representation, 73. *See also* nasal allophones
Almeida, João Paulo, 452–53
"Amazônia Legal." *See* Brazilian Amazonia
anaphoric constructions, 143–49, 177, 183
anaphoric particles, 81, 98, 142, 143, 175
animacy, 128–29; and differential object marking, 326–32
Animal Stories. See Let's Study in Kotiria: Kotiria Animal Stories
animates, 99, 101–13, 125–26, 129–30, 342; augmentatives, 155; compounds, 150; derived from verbs, 130–33, 135–36; diminutives, 154; interrogatives and, 192; numbering, 177–79, 182; pronominal, 143–45, 149
Arapaso language, 3n10
Arapaso people, 15
Arawak language group, 10, 11, 17, 93, 100. *See also* Baniwa language; Tariana language
Arawak people, 11–12. *See also* Baniwa people; Tariana people
argument coding, 158–59, 161, 314, 315, 323, 324, 326, 333–37
arguments, locative. *See* locative arguments
assertion, 285–93, 295, 297–98
assertion evidential, imperfective, 269, 285–90
assertion evidential, perfective, 46, 269, 272–74, 285–86
augmentatives, 152, 153, 154–56, 172

Baniwa language, 27–28, 28n6, 100
Baniwa people, 10, 11, 12, 20, 24
Bará language, 3, 4, 5, 7; animate-inanimate distinction, 107; clause structure, 334; locatives, 346; phonology, 24n4, 25, 31, 32, 33, 62; word order and argument coding, 334
Barasana language, 3, 5, 6, 7; animate-inanimate distinction, 99, 107; augmentatives, 155; =~be're counterpart, 356; clause structure, 333, 334; copulas, 199n2; epistemic coding, 295–96n11; evidentials, 276, 283; interrogatives, 307; locatives, 346; phonology, 25, 41n15, 49, 62; possessives, 185; pronouns, 143; verbs, 221, 249; word order and argument coding, 334
Barnes, Janet: classification of Tukanoan languages, 4, 5; on hierarchy of categories in Tuyuka, 293–94; on pitch accent, 49; on tense in Tuyuka, 276; on voiceless fricatives, 32
body part nouns, 114, 116, 117, 118, 130, 189
borrowing, lexical, 17, 62, 108n5, 182
Bossong, Georg, 320
Brazilian Amazonia, 1–3
Bybee, Joan, 167

Cabral, Mateus, 380, 381–92
Cabral, Ricardo, 380, 411–50
Capuchins, 13

Cararú Cachoeira, 10–11, 12, 14, 282, 381n3
Carib people, 13
causative constructions, 375–76
"The Celebration Day Story" (text), 388–92
Christian missionaries, 8, 13–14
classifiers, inanimates with, 119–28
classifiers, shape. *See* shape classifiers
clausal nominalization, 284–85, 316–19
clause modality, 245, 256, 257, 268–312. *See also* directive modality; evidentials; interrogatives; irrealis statements; realis statements
clauses, adverbial. *See* adverbial clauses
clause structure, 313–79
clitics and cliticization, 74, 80, 81, 92, 93–95, 105, 148, 163; in verbs, 261, 262, 374. *See also* enclitics; proclitics
coding, discourse-level. *See* discourse-level coding
coding, grammatical. *See* grammatical coding
cognates, Eastern Tukanoan, 30, 33, 142–44, 153, 199, 263, 356, 370; locative, 316; nonexistence verbs, 202; Wa'ikhana, 28, 29–30, 33, 42, 61, 199, 229, 310, 317
cognition verbs, 216–17, 219–20
collective animates, 112–13
Colombia, 3, 4, 6, 7, 8, 10–11
comitative/instrumental role, 92, 163–64, 172, 313–14, 346, 353–55; in adverbials, 360; in other Tukanoan languages, 356
common languages. *See* lingua francas
comparison adverbials, 363–65
completive aspect, 237
compound nouns. *See* noun compounds
conjunctions, absence of, 374
consonants, 22, 23–36, 346n6. *See also* obstruents; plosives; postaspiration; preaspiration; unaspirated consonants
contrastive subject, 152, 165–67, 172
convergence of languages. *See* language convergence
copulas, 53, 199–202, 248, 261, 262, 281, 289, 337; in inference construction, 261, 284–85; noun complements of, 86–87
counting. *See* numbers
count nouns, 114, 116–19
Cubeo language. *See* Kubeo language
Cubeo people. *See* Kubeo people
curupiras, 108n5, 110, 404n10
"The Curupira Story" (text), 423–50

"The Curupira Who Went to the Man's House Wanting to Eat Him" (text), 404–11

dances, 388n5
debuccalization, 26, 27, 346n6
definiteness, 84, 144–47, 149, 177, 326, 330–31, 332, 336
deixis, 136, 142, 145, 147, 175, 338; in evidentials, 293–95; in verbs, 231
demands, 311–12
demonstratives, 81, 90, 136–37, 175
deontic modality, 238–41, 268, 368–69
Derbyshire, Desmond C., 99
derived nouns, 86–88, 105, 115, 121, 130–40, 199, 351. *See also* nominalized verbs
derived verbs, 83–85, 185, 242–43
Desano language, 3–4, 5, 7; animate-inanimate distinction, 99, 107; augmentatives, 155; =~*be're* counterpart, 356; clause structure, 334; evidentials, 291; locatives, 346; nonexistence verbs, 202; possessives, 185; phonology, 24n4, 25, 26, 27, 31, 33, 60, 61; progressive aspect, 369; pronouns, 143; spoken by Kotiria, 12; suffix +*a*, 263; syllable structure, 62; verbs, 221; word order and argument coding, 334
Desano people, 4
desiderative, 238, 239–40, 368
determiners, 175–77
~*di*, 369–71, 371–73
dialects, 3n10, 4
differential object marking (DOM), 332; by +*re* marker, 323–31
diminutives, 152, 153–55, 172, 360
directional verbs, 213
directive modality, 245, 268, 269, 307–12
directives, 268, 269, 307–12
direct object marking, 332, 333, 334
discourse-level coding, 164–69
drinking, 259n2, 388
dubitatives, 82, 241, 245, 252, 288, 296, 306
Dutch explorers and settlers, 13

Eastern Tukanoan cognates. *See* cognates, Eastern Tukanoan
Eastern Tukanoan languages, 3–5. *See also* Bará language; Barasana language; Desano language; Karapana language;

Index

Kubeo language; Makuna language; Pisamira language; Siriano language; Taiwano language; Tanimuka (Retuarã) language; Tatuyo language; Tukano language; Tuyuka language; Wa'ikhana (Piratapuyo) language; Yuruti language

Ecuador, 3
Eduuria. *See* Taiwano language
emigration, 4, 18–19
empathetic markers, 245, 255
emphatics, 152, 157–58, 167, 172, 361–63
enclitics, 76, 91, 92, 93, 94, 95–96, 164; list of, 484–86
English-Kotiria vocabulary list, 470–84
epenthesis, glottal, 63, 64
evaluatives, 152, 153–56
evidentials, 268–98, 299; assertion, 46, 285–93, 294, 295, 298; epistemic values of, 295–97; hearsay (secondhand), 271, 273n5, 276, 294, 297; inference, 284–85; nonvisual, 282–84; visual, 46, 274–81
exhortatives, 269, 310–11
existence verbs, 199–202
explorers and settlers, European, 13–14

favoratives, 253–54
feminine and masculine. *See* gender
Ferraz, Agostinho, 380, 392–411
Ferraz, Franssinete, 455–56
festivals, 38n5
fricatives, 33, 34, 44. *See also* affricates; glottal fricatives
frustratives, 252–53, 311, 312

geminate consonants, 25–26, 27
geminate vowels, 25, 63
gender, 99, 100, 101, 102–7, 129–30, 152, 172, 271; of nonhuman animate nouns, 108, 109, 110; in pronouns, 143; in subject agreement morphology, 316–17, 318
generic reference classifier, 81, 88, 136, 161–63, 243, 320, 323–35, 336; with ditransitives, 336–37; phonology, 45, 170, 172; with *pʉ*, 340–44; in temporal expressions, 351–52; with verbs with locative arguments, 337–43; with verbs with valency-changing roots, 345
genitive markers, 173, 184, 185–86
Giacone, Antônio, 8

"Giant Armadillo" (text), 454–55
Givón, Talmy, 256, 292, 293, 294, 297, 338, 342
glottal fricatives, 29, 71, 270n1
glottalization, 38, 39, 60, 66, 67–69; in evidentials, 299n13; orthographic representation, 72, 270n1, 457; tone and, 63, 64; in verbs, 250, 265. *See also* epenthesis, glottal; suprasegmental glottalization
Gomez-Imbert, Elsa, 41n15, 49, 62, 100, 107–8, 124n9, 222, 293; on epistemic coding, 295–96n11; on interrogatives, 307
grammatical coding, 158–64
grammaticalization, 91–92, 100, 103, 103n4, 107, 112, 128–30, 134, 171, 187, 223, 229, 240, 244–46, 262, 264–66, 317
grammatical morphemes, list of. *See* nonroot grammatical morphemes, list of
grammatical roles, 86, 144, 158, 165, 168, 313, 314, 321
grammatical words, 93–96

hearsay, 269, 272, 273, 274, 276, 291, 292, 293–94, 297
"Horsefly" (text), 452–53
"A Hunter and His Dogs" (text), 411–23
"The Hunting Dog Story" (text), 385–87
Hup language, 10n14, 150, 283
Hup people, 10

imperatives, 46, 269, 307–8, 372
imperfective aspect, 245, 255–58, 275–80, 281, 282–83, 286, 289, 290–91, 315; of interrogatives, 304
inanimates, 99, 113–28, 129–30; anaphoric forms, 145–49; augmentives, 156; compounds, 150; derived from verbs, 133–36; diminutives, 153–54; interrogatives and, 192; numbering, 177–82
indefiniteness, 183, 200, 201, 326, 328, 329, 330–31
individualizer, 112–13, 152, 168
inference, 284–85
inherently collective animates. *See* collective animates
Inkacha language, 11
Instituto Socioambiental (ISA), 2n4, 19, 20

instrument nouns, 354–55
intensifiers, 245, 250–51
intention, statements of, 30, 269, 299, 301
internalized evidence, 285–93, 294, 295, 298. *See also* evidentials, assertion
interrogatives, 245, 268, 269, 303–7; adverbial, 366–67; nominal, 191–94, 196; verbal, 268, 269, 303–7
"In the Olden Days There Were People-Stealers" (text), 392–404
intransitives, 321
irrealis, negative. *See* negative irrealis
irrealis constructions, 317
irrealis interrogatives, 303, 306
irrealis statements, 268, 269, 288, 293, 298–303

"Jaguar" (text), 453–54
Jesuits, 13

Kakua language, 10n14
Kakua people, 10
Karapana language, 3, 5, 7; clause structure, 334; locatives, 346; phonology, 24n4, 25, 33, 62; word order and argument coding, 334
Kenstowicz, Michael, 38
kinship terms, 15, 103–7
Koch-Grünberg, Theodor, 14
Koreguaje language, 3, 5, 63n25
"Kotiria" (term), 1n1
Kotiria Animal Stories. See *Let's Study in Kotiria: Kotiria Animal Stories*
Kotiria-English vocabulary list, 457–70
Kotiria people, 6, 8–21, 380–81
"The Kotiria Study Book" (text), 381–85
Kubeo language, 3, 4, 5, 7; animate-inanimate distinction, 99–100, 107; =~be're counterpart, 356; classifiers, 125; clause structure, 333, 334; locatives, 346; phonology, 33, 62; possessives, 185; pronouns, 143; spoken by Kotiria, 359; verbs, 198n1, 273; word order and argument coding, 334
Kubeo people, 6, 11, 12

language convergence, 17–18
language loss and maintenance, 2–3, 18–21
language research. *See* research on Tukanoan languages
languages, Arawak. *See* Arawak language group
languages, European. *See* Portuguese language; Spanish language
languages, Mayan. *See* Mayan languages
languages, Tukanoan. *See* Tukanoan language family
language shift, 4, 13, 15, 18–19
laryngealization, 22, 26–27, 43–45, 62, 63–64, 66, 67, 69
Let's Study in Kotiria: Kotiria Animal Stories, 20, 21, 450–56
lexemes, trisyllabic. *See* trisyllabic lexemes
lingua francas, 17, 18
Língua Geral (Nheengatú), 10n15, 108n5, 404n10
locative arguments, 337–38, 340–43, 344
locative possession, 188–89
locatives, 158, 159–62, 337, 346–48, 353

Makuna language, 3, 3–4n10, 5, 7; clause structure, 334; locatives, 346; phonology, 24n4, 25, 33, 62; pronouns, 143; word order and argument coding, 334
Makuna people, 6, 15–16n22
Malone, Terrell, 31, 63n25, 65n27, 272n4, 306–7
maps, 9–10
marriage practices, 12, 15–18; evident in nouns, 104
masculine and feminine. *See* gender
mass nouns, 114–16
Matapí, 10, 14
Maxwell, Michael B., 99, 198n1, 273n5
Mayan languages, 65n27
mental process verbs. *See* cognition verbs
Michael, Lev David, 297n12
migration, 4, 7, 11, 18–19
Miller, Marion, 221, 263
mirativity, 291, 298
Miriti(tapuya), 3–4n4
missionaries, Christian. *See* Christian missionaries
modality, 251–55. *See also* clause modality; deontic modality; directive modality
modifiers, 156–58, 173, 175–77; interrogative, 193–94; multiple, 195–96. *See also* adjectival words; adverbials; evaluatives; locatives; possessives; shape classifiers

Index 503

monomorphemic words, 77–78
moras: in prosodic structure, 23n1, 39–42, 92; tone, 50, 51, 55–59
morphology: nominal, 152–72; verbal, 198–312
Morse, Nancy L., 99, 198n1, 273n5
motion verbs, 209–16, 222, 223–29, 232–33, 257–58, 266, 340–43
motion verbs, cislocative *ta*, 56, 209–10, 223–24, 245; in nonvisual construction, 282–83; in purposive construction, 371
motion verbs, translocative *wa'a*, 34, 82, 209–10, 223–24, 245; to express perfective aspect, 258–63; in purposive construction, 371
multilingualism, 16–17

Nadahup language family, 10, 17n25, 332
nasal allophones, 38n12, 43–44
nasalization, 17, 22, 23n1, 36, 38n12, 169–71; in classifier compounds, 128; orthographic representation, 72–73; in possessives, 186; in verbs, 246, 248, 265. *See also* suprasegmental nasalization
negation, 245, 246–49, 264, 269, 301–3
negative irrealis, 269, 301–3
negative nouns, 140–42
negative verbs, 141, 246–50, 307, 308
Nheengatú. *See* Língua Geral (Nheengatú)
nominalization, clausal. *See* clausal nominalization
nominalized verbs, 46, 82–85, 152, 172, 199, 242–43, 244, 261, 283, 368–71, 379; classifiers and, 121; derivation of adverbials from, 355, 360; negation of, 246; subject agreement suffixes for, 300, 316
nonexistence verbs, 202–3
nonhuman animates, 102, 107–13, 331
nonroot grammatical morphemes, list of, 484–86
noun compounds, 128, 150–51
noun incorporation, 84–85, 242–43, 244
noun phrases (NPS), 78, 80, 81, 85, 144, 166, 173–97, 333
nouns, 86–87, 92, 94, 152–72; augmentatives, 153, 154–56; classification, 98–101, 128–30; diminutives, 153–55; in expression of adverbial notions, 88–89; negative, 140–42; with objective case marker +*re*, 323–44; roots, 78–79, 121, 140. *See also* animates; clausal nominalization; clause structure; count nouns; derived nouns; inanimates; instrument nouns; mass nouns; nominalized verbs; pronouns
Nukak language, 10n14
Nukak people, 10
number marking, 113, 114, 115
numbers, 177–85. *See also* quantity questioning

objective case marker, 46, 81, 88, 152, 161–63, 172, 242, 313, 323–35; with ditransitives, 336–37; phonology, 45–46, 170, 172; with *pu*, 340–44; in temporal expressions, 351–52; with verbs with locative arguments, 337–43; with verbs with valency-changing roots, 345
object marking, 163, 170, 323–44
obstruents, 22, 23
Ønasal morphemes, list of, 46
Orejón language, 3, 5, 63n25, 65n27
origin stories, 12
orthography, 20, 34–35, 36, 72–75, 96–97
out-migration. *See* emigration

paired consonants. *See* geminate consonants
paired vowels. *See* geminate vowels
Paiva, Armando Filho, 453–54
particle roots, 25, 36n10, 79–81, 86, 90, 92, 93, 94, 96; in nominal morphology, 152; nouns/pronouns derived from, 136, 143, 168
particles, anaphoric. *See* anaphoric particles
patrilineage, 15
patrilocality. *See* virilocal residence
Payne, Doris L., 99
perception verbs. *See* sensory perception verbs
perfective aspect, 258–63, 276, 277, 280, 282, 283, 285, 315; of interrogatives, 304
perfective constructions, 373–75
permissives, 245, 269, 308–9
Peru, 3
phonemes, 22–38, 43
phonological words, 45–48, 52, 57, 93–94, 95–96, 99
phonology, 22–75

phratic terms. *See* kinship terms
Piratapuyo. *See* Wa'ikhana (Piratapuyo) language
Pisamira language, 3, 4, 7; animate-inanimate distinction, 107; clause structure, 334; locatives, 346; phonology, 24n4, 31, 33, 62; word order and argument coding, 334
pitch variation. *See* suprasegmental tone
placement verbs, 215–16, 228
plosives, 24–30, 33, 38, 71, 103, 126
pluralization, 113–19, 152, 172, 173, 177–83; of animates, 46, 101–2, 105–13, of inanimates, 113–18; markers in derivation, 130–32; pronominal, 142–43
plural subjects, 142–44, 186, 283, 316, 319–21, 350, 353; comitative and, 367; imperfective and, 257
Pokanga, 3n10
polysemy, 130, 132
Portuguese explorers and settlers, 13
Portuguese language, 10n15, 17, 19, 34n9, 96, 182, 359
position verbs, 204–6, 228, 257–58
possessives, 173, 185–91, 194, 195–97, 203–4
postaspiration, 24, 27, 28, 180–81; orthographic representation, 73
preaspiration, 24–25, 27, 28, 103; glottalization and, 67–69; orthographic representation, 72
predictive statements, 269, 299–301
prefixes, 93
proclitics, 91, 92, 93, 94, 95, 96, 484–85; possessive, 173, 186, 189, 196; *ti* as, 146
progressive aspect, 57, 369–71, 377
pronouns, 93, 136, 142–49, 166, 175, 330; possessives and, 185, 186–87, 195–97
purposive constructions, 371

qualifiers. *See* modifiers
quantifiers, 177–85
quantity questioning, 193–94
questioning. *See* interrogatives
quoted speech constructions, 371–73

Ramirez, Henri, 100, 221, 263, 276, 294, 307; language classification by, 3n10, 4, 5; on phonology, 30, 40n13, 49, 61–62, 66
realis interrogatives, 303, 306

realis statements, 268, 269, 288, 293, 299; negation, 301
reasoned suppositions, 287, 288, 305–6
reciprocal, 344–45, 368–69
referential clitic, 93, 94, 152, 164–65, 168, 169, 172
relational motion verbs, 214–15
requests, 311–12
research on Tukanoan languages, 6–8; +*a*, 263; clause structure, 329, 330; epistemic values, 295, 297; evidentials, 270–71, 272, 274, 283, 292–94; internal classifications, 5; interrogatives, 306–7; noun classification, 98–101; temporal distinctions, 276; word order and argument coding, 334–35
residence, virilocal. *See* virilocal residence
respect, suffixes indicating, 105, 109n6, 308–9
Retuarã. *See* Tanimuka (Retuarã) language
rhyme, 39
Rio Negro, 13, 14, 110
roles, grammatical. *See* grammatical roles
roles, semantic. *See* semantic roles

Salesians, 14
São Gabriel da Cachoeira, 11, 13, 14, 16n23, 18, 380
schools, 14, 19–20
secondhand evidentials. *See* evidentials: hearsay (secondhand)
Secoya language, 3, 5
semantic roles, 313–14; agentive, 322, 373; beneficiary, 333, 335–36; experiencer, 260, 321–22, 373, 377; instrumental, 346, 354–55; patient, 321, 322, 336, 373; recipient, 336; temporal, 346, 348–53. *See also* comitative/instrumental role; locatives
semantics, verbal, 198–243
sensory perception verbs, 216–19, 261, 322
sentences, 81–82, 268, 269, 357–79
sequential actions, 349–50
serialized verb constructions (svcs), 221–41
settlers and explorers, European. *See* explorers and settlers, European
shape classifiers, 119, 120, 121–26, 130, 178
singular suffix, 46, 52, 79, 152, 172; on animates, 101–5, 107–9, 113; on body part nouns, 118; in derivations, 130–33;

Index

partitive function of, 114–15
Siona language, 3, 5; phonology, 24n4, 33, 60, 61, 63n25
Siriano language, 3, 5, 7; animate-inanimate distinction, 107; clause structure, 334; locatives, 346; mass-count distinction, 113; phonology, 25, 26, 31, 33, 60, 62, 63n25, 66n28; pronouns, 143; word order and argument coding, 334
solitary, 152, 156, 157, 172
Sorensen, Arthur P., Jr., 4, 5, 6, 263
Spanish language, 10n14, 17, 34n9, 96, 182, 359
speculative questions, 305–6
speech verbs, 371–73, 379
stative verbs, 198–206
stop consonants. *See* plosives
subject agreement, 314–20
subjects, plural. *See* plural subjects
suffixes, list of, 484–86
suppositions, reasoned. *See* reasoned suppositions
suprasegmental glottalization, 22, 38, 59–69, 70, 76, 78, 90
suprasegmental nasalization, 42–48, 52, 65, 76, 78, 90
suprasegmental tone, 48–59, 76, 78, 90
switch-reference marking, 165, 319, 348, 367
syllables, 38–42; erosion of, 28–29. *See also* moras; trisyllabic lexemes

Taiwano language, 3, 4, 5, 25, 33; word order and argument coding, 334
Tanimuka (Retuarã) language, 3, 3–4n10, 5; clause structure, 334; locatives, 346; phonology, 25, 33, 36, 60; word order and argument coding, 334
Tariana language, 11, 12–13, 17n25, 27–28, 292–93, 306
Tariana people, 10, 11, 12, 13, 15, 20
Tatuyo language, 3, 4, 5, 7; augmentatives, 155; =~*be're* counterpart, 356; clause structure, 334; epistemic coding, 295–96n11; evidentials, 283, 292–93; locatives, 346; numbers, 181n3; phonology, 24n4, 25, 28, 32, 62, 63; possessives, 185; verbs, 221; word order and argument coding, 334
Teixeira, Elizabete, 454–55
temporality, 275–80, 348–53

tense of verbs. *See* verbs: tense
terminative markers, 254
three-syllable lexemes. *See* trisyllabic lexemes
tone, 17, 22, 48–49, 169–71, 457; of =~*be're*, 163; of classifiers, 127, 128; in exhortatives, 310; glottal stops and, 63; in grammatical coding, 163; in possessives, 186; in verbs, 206n6, 242, 244, 246, 248, 249–50, 261, 265, 374. *See also* suprasegmental tone
transitives, 321–35
trisyllabic lexemes, 61–62
truth values, 295–97
"Tukano" and "Tukanoan" (terms), 1n2
Tukanoan language family, 1n2, 3–8. *See also* Eastern Tukanoan languages; Western Tukanoan languages
Tukanoan language research. *See* research on Tukanoan languages
Tukano language, 1n2, 3, 4, 5, 7, 15; +*a* in, 263; animate-inanimate distinction, 100, 107; augmentatives, 155; =~*be're* counterpart, 356; clause structure, 333, 334; cognates, 28, 29–30, 61, 356; interrogatives, 307; as lingua franca, 17, 18; locatives, 346; mass-count distinction, 113; nonexistence verbs, 202; nouns, 116, 331; phonology, 24n4, 25, 26, 27, 28, 29–30, 33, 62; phonology (glottalization), 60, 61–62, 63n25; possessives, 185; progressive aspect, 369; pronouns, 143, 144; +*re*, 331; spoken by Kotiria, 12, 359; verbs, 198n1, 221, 246, 276; word order and language coding, 334
Tukano people, 20
Tuyuka language, 3, 4, 7, 12; animate-inanimate distinction, 99, 107; clause structure, 334; evidentials, 293–94; interrogatives, 306–7; locatives, 346; phonology, 24n4, 25, 26, 27, 31, 33, 62, 63n25, 66; pronouns, 143; verbs, 202, 276; word order and argument coding, 334
Tuyuka people, 6, 20

unaspirated consonants, 24, 28, 29, 67

Vaupés (Uaupés) region, 4, 6, 11, 213, 274;

Vaupés (Uaupés) region (*cont.*)
  map of, 9; social system, 12, 15–18. *See also* Eastern Tukanoan languages
Vaupés (Uaupés) River, 8–10, 11, 12, 13, 14, 110, 213
verb phrases, 78
verbs, 78–79, 81–85, 92, 94, 198–243; aspectual functions, 229–38, 241, 267; with clausal complements, 368–71; clause modality, 245, 268–312; ditransitive, 336–57; in expression of adjectival and adverbial notions, 88, 89; imperative, 307–8; imperfective aspect, 255–58, 275–80, 281, 282–83, 286, 289, 290–91, 315; with locative arguments, 337–44; modal functions, 238–41, 251–55, 267; nonroot stem morphemes, 244–67; nonstative, 204, 206–20, 258, 260; order of morphemes, 264–67; perfective aspect, 258–63, 276, 277, 280, 283, 285, 315; permissive, 308–9; person, 270–71, 274, 294, 300, 301, 310, 315–21, 368; sequenced, 374–75, 376–78, 379; serialized constructions, 221–41, 379; stative, 198–206, 241, 258, 260, 337–39; tense, 270, 271, 272, 275–78, 280, 299; transitive, 321–35; with valency-changing roots, 344–45. *See also* activity verbs; cognition verbs; derived verbs; directional verbs; existence verbs; motion verbs; negative verbs; nominalized verbs; nonexistence verbs; placement verbs; position verbs; realis statements; sensory perception verbs; speech verbs
virilocal residence, 16, 18
visual evidentials, 46, 269, 274; aspect coding in, 275–80; epistemic values of, 295–97; in hierarchy, 294; semantic extensions, 281; use in inferential construction, 285; use in nonvisual construction, 282
vocabulary lists, 457–84
vowels, 36–38, 69–71, 229, 248–49; geminate, 25, 63

Wa'ikhana (Piratapuyo) language, 3, 5, 6, 7, 20; clause structure, 333, 334; cognates, 28, 29–30, 33, 42, 61, 199, 229, 310, 317; exhortatives, 310; gender markers, 109; locatives, 346; phonology, 24n4, 25, 26, 27, 29–30, 31, 33, 62; phonology (glottalization), 60, 61, 62; phonology (vowels), 37; possessives, 185; pronouns, 143–44; subject agreement, 317; verbs, 229, 249, 300; word order and argument coding, 334
Wa'ikhana people, 1n1, 4
Waimahã, 3n10, 5. *See also* Bará language
Wallace, Alfred, 14
Waltz, Carolyn, 8, 37, 49, 101, 263, 272, 299, 361
Waltz, Nathan, 6, 8, 63; as coauthor with Carolyn Waltz, 6, 8, 37, 49, 101, 263, 272, 299, 361; as coauthor with Wheeler, 3n10, 5, 38, 60, 61; on evidentials, 299n13; on phonology, 27, 33–34, 37, 38, 40n14, 49, 60, 61, 63
"Wanano" (term), 1n1
warnings. *See* admonitives
Western Tukanoan languages, 3, 5, 63n25. *See also* Orejón language; Siona language
Wheeler, Alva, 3n10, 5, 60, 61
word order, 82, 173, 313, 324, 325–26, 331, 332–35, 337, 357–58; Eastern Tukanoan languages compared, 334; of sequenced verbs, 374
words, 40, 73, 74, 76–97; monomoraic roots as, 57, 58–59; prosodic minimality, 41, 76. *See also* adjectival words; borrowing, lexical; grammatical words; monomorphemic words; nouns; phonological words; verbs; vocabulary lists
writing systems. *See* orthography

Yucatec Mayan language, 65n27
Yuhup language, 10n14
Yuhup people, 10
Yuruti language, 3, 7; animate-inanimate distinction, 107; clause structure, 333, 334; cognates, 28, 143, 346; locatives, 346; phonology, 24n4, 26, 28, 31, 33, 62; pronouns, 143; word order and argument coding, 334

In *Studies in the Native Languages of the Americas*

The Miami-Illinois Language
By David J. Costa

Caddo Verb Morphology
By Lynnette R. Melnar

A Grammar of Crow (Apsáalooke Aliláau)
By Randolph Graczyk

Topic and Discourse Structure in West Greenlandic Agreement Constructions
By Anna Berge

A Reference Grammar of Kotiria (Wanano)
By Kristine Stenzel

To order or obtain more information on these or other University of Nebraska Press titles, visit www.nebraskapress.unl.edu

www.ingramcontent.com/pod-product-compliance
Lightning Source LLC
Chambersburg PA
CBHW021812300426
44114CB00009BA/143